REMOVING THE CONDEMNATION

A COMMENTARY ON THE BOOK OF MORMON

Denver C. Snuffer, Jr.

Published in the United States by Mill Creek Press.
Mill Creek Press is a registered trademark of Mill Creek Press, LLC.
www.millcreekpress.com

ISBN-10: 0-615-43886-3
ISBN-13: 978-0-615-43886-3

Printed in the United States of America on acid-free paper.

First Edition

Cover design by Mill Creek Press.

Contents

PREFACE

This book is a reproduction of a blog I wrote during the year 2010. It was a stream-of-consciousness series of daily posts. This is that portion of the blog which dealt with the Book of Mormon. Other comments with varying issues are still on the Internet for anyone to read, if they choose. But the discussion of Book of Mormon doctrines and teachings are worth preserving as a separate book.

I've made no attempt to change, edit, clarify or add to the blog materials in this publication. There could be many clarifications, but I've resisted the temptation to do so. Since it was created as a spontaneous bit of daily writing, I think it best preserved in that format. This is a raw product, containing spontaneous thought.

I appreciate the effort of Jennifer Orten, who took the material from the blog and saved us a great deal of time by reducing it to a format which allowed for publication. I also appreciate the work of my wife, Stephanie, who did all the mechanical work of posting onto the blog. I would write the posts, then email them to her. She would take the email and publish them in the blog, adding hot-links to scripture citations and other references. This enabled readers to click on the citation and go directly to the scripture. Those scripture links have been turned into footnotes in this publication, so readers have the scripture available to them in this book and without the need to carry them along while reading.

I appreciate Mill Creek Press, also, which has continued to allow my uncensored writing to go to publication without editorial corruption by inserting a committee's thinking for my own. Though I may offend readers, they receive my unfiltered thinking and not a toned-down version of my thoughts. I do not think I could tolerate writing if I had to satisfy the whims and cowardice of an editorial board. It seems to me that if editors had something to say, they ought to write their own books rather than to reform the thoughts of others. Mill Creek Press has that rare form of masculine courage so lacking in the world today. My relationship with them is something which I value precisely because of the freedom they afford me to write authentically, and not artificially, about the most important subjects we can contemplate.

I also want to thank the readers whose reactions vary from enthusiastic appreciation to outright hostility. As Latter-day Saints, we live in a religious environment in which most thinking and writing comes from controlled, careful sources. In our own culture we are as "politically correct" as the larger American culture. This means that in all likelihood most of what we produce will fall into disuse, because over time inauthentic writing never survives. I have never intended to be a commercially successful writer; merely a truthful one. I would rather edify than entertain.

If there is any good in this book, the credit belongs to the Lord. I only take credit for the errors, which I presume are many.

Denver C. Snuffer, Jr., Sandy, Utah

Alma 13

It may as well be a dream. It involves our collective slumber. We get pictures in our head when we are taught some truth and presume that the picture is accurate. Then after we have repeated the "truth" often enough, we go on to believe the picture must be all-inclusive.

Once we've arrived at that point, the truth no longer matters. Our minds are made up. We've decided the answers, and no further evidence will be considered.

This certainty is reinforced when more people reach the same conclusion because they share the same picture in their head. You get together with others and testify that you are all in possession of the truth; not only **the** truth, but **ALL** of the truth. Before long every one of the group can pass a lie-detector test about the truth as they explain it.

As a result, this herd is incapable of ever seeing the picture differently. They cannot open their minds to the idea that their picture is skewed or off. It is most certainly incomplete. It is, in fact, so far short of the whole story that when any part of the remaining, missing information is shown to them they are certain it is a lie.

It is painful to part with our suppositions and the traditions we hold dear. It is painful to admit there may be much more of the picture we have not yet considered, much less seen. It causes anxiety and fear. So much fear in fact, that when it comes to "eternal truth," people literally put their lives in jeopardy if they denounce the falsehoods of the herd and proclaim the truth to those whose peace of mind and self-identity is tied to the incomplete and misleading picture they believe holds all truth.

Latter-day Saints are not immune from this process. We have wanted a complete, well defined statement of our faith since the time of Joseph Smith. We crave an "orthodox" faith so we, like the Historic Christians, can proclaim what is true and right and what is error and heresy. It gives us security. It is false security, purchased at the price of closed minds. It gives us hope. It is false hope, based on the foolishness of the deluded.

As we water down even further the true principles of what our faith contains by requiring Relief Society and High Priests to labor over a

Gospel Essentials Manual as the sole fodder for our spiritual fare, we strain every particle of solid food out of the diet. The remaining gruel is so thin, lacking in substance, that we become universally malnourished. Yet in that emaciated state, as our bellies distend from the bloating of starvation, we all proclaim how well fed we are. Our bellies are swollen! We have enough of the word of God! We need no more of the word of God! All is well! Better than well, we prosper in the land of promise!

When you surrender your superstitions and arrogance and read the scriptures for the first time with an open mind, they will astonish you. They will condemn you. They will demand you repent, open your heart, and receive more. They will offer you the bread of life, a living fountain of revelation from which, if you draw, you will find not only sustenance, but also the capacity to recognize that there are those who are starving.

We still weep for Zion; for Zion has fled.

Try reading Alma Chapter 13 and take **LITERALLY** every word there. Don't bring any pictures in your head and read them into the text. Forget every popular and correlated notion ever spoken about the priesthood for a moment and just look at the words. You will be shocked. If you can bring yourself to do that, then read the Book of Mormon again. It was written for our day, testifying **against** us. A former group of inhabitants who failed and were destroyed wrote their best advice and sent it to us. We are the ones being warned. We are in a great deal of peril. Our church, if the Book of Mormon is true, is filled with corruption and priestcraft.

Or, on the other hand, just chant that "you know (*insert the subject of choice here*) is true" and throw about the "name of Jesus Christ" as you do. It is a tried and true mantra, which when repeated often enough, can dull the senses and reinstate the slumber we are so often wrapped. So relax. Hum to yourself a hymn and you will soon be back asleep.

A few days ago I directed you to Alma 13. I suggested that it be read without preconceptions and you let the words just acquire whatever meaning they appear to have in the chapter itself. Some of you have begun that process and have raised questions. I thought I might revisit the chapter to open up a few ideas for those who haven't begun the exercise. Here's the first verse:

Alma 13:1

> **"And again, my brethren, I would cite your minds forward to the time when the Lord God gave these commandments unto his children; and I would that ye should remember that the Lord God ordained priests, after his holy order, which was after the order of his Son, to teach these things unto the people."**

Why "cite your minds forward?" Especially since it was talking in the past tense? Why is this idiom in the verse? How would Joseph Smith know about this kind of word usage? (Perhaps this is an indication the text is translated from another language rather than being composed in English.)

Why "the Lord God ordained priests?" Were they ordained by God indeed? Was there another man involved in conferring that authority? Did it necessarily come from God alone? What priesthood is it that is referred to?

What is "after his holy order?" Is this Aaronic? Is this Melchizedek? Or is this something different? There are three orders of priesthood, the third being "Patriarchal" as explained in *Beloved Enos*. Which one is this verse referring to of the three?

What form of priesthood is "after his holy order, which was after the order of his Son?" Are all three? Or is there one that is distinguished by being uniquely after the order of His Son?

What "things" are these people to "teach…unto the people?" Is there something associated with what is contained in the chapter that alone is the province of those possessing the "holy order" to teach? If so, why is that?

What is going on here? Is this deeper doctrine than we normally encounter? If so, why has it eluded our attention? If our preconceptions have blinded us to this material, then why would we want to ever read scripture through the blinding lens of the notions we have inherited? Is this part of the wicked "traditions of our fathers" that the Book of Mormon warn us against?

Oh ye Gentiles…

Now I'm missing the weekly Book of Mormon class I taught for so many years. There I could go ahead and discuss all the answers. My home was too small for the crowds and I wasn't going to export it to a less sacred place where the Spirit would not permit me to teach. Well, the questions are better than merely giving answers, as I have said before. If you can learn to ask good questions, then you can go to the Lord and get the answers. Who knows where that dialogue will lead you.

Alma 13:2

> **"And those priests were ordained after the order of his Son, in a manner that thereby the people might know in what manner to look forward to his Son for redemption."**

Now this is important stuff here. We are really being told something quite amazing. Look at these words!

To be "ordained after the order of his Son" it must be done "in a manner that thereby the people might know in what manner to look forward to his Son for redemption." Did you get that?

Think about these words carefully.

The "manner" must be in a way which will let people know or understand how to "look forward to His Son for redemption."

So, let's clear away the institutional garbage that surrounds our thinking.

- Christ WAS NOT ordained by being sustained by a congregation.

- Christ WAS NOT ordained by having hands laid upon Him by another man.

- Christ DID NOT carry a credential with Him or a certificate of priestly authority.

- Christ WAS NOT part of the established priestly hierarchy.

We have no record of His ordination at all. We only have established, priestly class officials asking Christ about where He got His authority from. And we have Christ simply refusing to answer their question.

Christ showed that He in fact held priestly authority by His demonstration of power. More importantly, He taught profound truths with such passing simplicity and convincing prose that His message necessarily came from a higher source. In word and deed He put on display His power and authority.

But what is the verse in Alma speaking about? How does one become "ordained" in such a manner that people learning of it will then know how to look forward (or back) to the Savior and understand His redeeming power?

Do they put on display, by the words and precepts they speak, the profound simplicity and convincing prose of the angels themselves? Are they able to show their ordination by speaking words of eternal life, as He did?

How does this "ordination" acquire or show redeeming power?

How can obtaining authority by ordination to this priesthood be something which will let people know their Lord better?

What is really going on for those who hold actual priestly authority, being ordained in the required manner? Do they acquire more than administrative authority from an institution? Do they receive power from on high? Can you get it anywhere other than from on high? Is this why the power of the priesthood is inseparably connected with the powers of heaven? What have we Saints been doing? Practicing? Holding ourselves forth to possess?

Where can we get this ordination after the order of the Son of God?

Forget what you've been taught. Read the Book of Mormon and remove the condemnation under which this people labor. Really study its words. They are alien to your prejudices and presumptions. But they ARE in fact the words of life. You really can get closer to God by abiding its precepts than through any other book! Amazingly, this is one of the very precepts which necessarily forces you to draw closer to God!

What a marvelous work and a wonder! Will the wonder never cease? (Only if you reject it.) It is a font of living water which constantly renews and floods forth more and new information endlessly, until at last we are also caught up in the visions of eternity and know our Lord. Then we needn't ask another to know the Lord, for all shall know Him.

I labor to help you know Him; to bring you to Him. The primary means to accomplish that remains the Book of Mormon. But only if you actually let it speak to you and reveal its many hidden secrets.

Alma 13: 3

> **"And this is the manner after which they were ordained—being called and prepared from the foundation of the world according to the foreknowledge of God, on account of their exceeding faith and good works; in the first place being left to choose good or evil; therefore they having chosen good, and exercising exceedingly great faith, are called with a holy calling, yea, with that holy calling which was prepared with, and according to, a preparatory redemption for such."**

It is too much! Too great of words for men to possess! Consider what they refer us to.

Called and prepared FIRST! From the foundation of the world!

So here priesthood has its beginning before this world even was organized. There is a necessary link between those hallowed days and power here. No person has authority here unless it was first obtained there.

How was it obtained first—before the foundation of the world?

It was because of the foreknowledge of God. And what was God's foreknowledge based upon? Their "exceeding faith and good works!"

How can a person have "faith" when they stand in the presence of God? Do they now have knowledge? This was before the mortal estate, right? If so, then how can there be faith? What good works were involved?

Then, too, the "faith" and the "good works" were done as a result of the person having been "left to choose between good and evil." Now this is surprising! You mean that before Adam partook of the fruit of the tree of knowledge of good and evil (i.e., before the foundation of the world) that some people had already obtained a knowledge of good and evil, been tempted, exhibited good works and acquired faith? How so? When and where did they do that? What does that tell us about them? Is this why Joseph said there were "sons of God who exalted themselves to be gods before the world was made?" (*TPJS* p. 375.) When and where and how did they do this? And was this required for any person to be able to claim they now have priestly authority here? Or is it only those who have the "holy order after the Son of God?" Is there something about these men's "holy calling" that distinguishes them from others here? If so, what is it? Who are these men? Are they always going to be from unlikely sources and places, so that people can know how to recognize the Lord?

Then, too, we have them in a class of people who had been through a "preparatory redemption" already. What does that mean? What does it imply? How did they qualify? How long have these souls been working on the process of redemption and thereby qualify through their faith and good works to hold authority in this estate? Who are they?

Oh, now my head is spinning. Can this doctrine really be true? Why do we know so little about it? Why did Joseph talk about it, but we have simply nothing to add? Indeed, we deny it exists… why is that?

This is certainly an interesting chapter. Fearsome and interesting. What a threatening, terrible, majestic, holy and challenging book this Book of Mormon turns out to be after all.

Alma 13: 4

> **"And thus they have been called to this holy calling on account of their faith, while others would reject the Spirit of God on account of the hardness of their hearts and blindness of their minds, while, if it had not been for this they might have had as great privilege as their brethren."**

The result of what went on before is the reason for the ordination or calling. That is, "thus they have been called." Meaning that all of what went into the earlier experiences i.e., being left to choose between good and evil, and having chosen good, having "faith" and good works, is the reason for their ordination. These souls are not novices. They are not getting authority here for the first time. They come with power from beyond this earth, bringing it with them to this earth. They qualified before and elsewhere.

All of this is "on account of their faith." All things are obtained through faith. That is explained in the Sixth Lecture, quoted here. Faith is a principle of power. It is capable of making things happen. There must be a connection between faith and power; between faith and priesthood.

Others reject the Spirit of God and, therefore, do not have this power. These others may claim to have authority, but they do not really receive power from the Spirit of God. They are animated by a different source.

What, then, causes someone who has a little authority "as they suppose" (they don't really have it, you see), to attempt to use that pretense to control and dominate others? The answer is contained in revelations already in print. It is their pride, their insecurities, the need to control, to be praised and celebrated, the need to gratify their vain ambition. These are character flaws. They cover up these flaws by claiming to have priestly authority from God.[1]

They are the world's Pharaohs, not the world's Abrahams. Their hearts are hard, their minds blind.

They do not hear the Spirit of God, and therefore none of the powers of heaven are with them.

This was/is their choice. They could have had the same privilege. But, alas, they prefer instead their own aggrandizement. They prefer monuments built with their names engraven on them. There is no message of truth and hope coming from them. Their words (the only things which really endure), will fall to the ground unfulfilled. They will not be remembered. They will return without a saved soul.

What stunning doctrines we have stumbled upon here! I'm getting worried about things as I look about. This Book of Mormon is alarming…

Alma 13: 5-6

> **"Or in fine, in the first place they were on the same standing with their brethren; thus this holy calling being prepared from the foundation of the world for such as would not harden their hearts, being in and through the atonement of the Only Begotten Son, who was prepared— And thus being called by this holy calling, and ordained unto the high priesthood of the holy order of God, to teach his commandments unto the children of men, that they also might enter into his rest—"**

[1] D&C 121: 33-44: "Behold, there are many called, but few are chosen. And why are they not chosen? Because their hearts are set so much upon the things of this world, and aspire to the honors of men, that they do not learn this one lesson—That the rights of the priesthood are inseparably connected with the powers of heaven, and that the powers of heaven cannot be controlled nor handled only upon the principles of righteousness. That they may be conferred upon us, it is true; but when we undertake to cover our sins, or to gratify our pride, our vain ambition, or to exercise control or dominion or compulsion upon the souls of the children of men, in any degree of unrighteousness, behold, the heavens withdraw themselves; the Spirit of the Lord is grieved; and when it is withdrawn, Amen to the priesthood or the authority of that man. Behold, ere he is aware, he is left unto himself, to kick against the pricks, to persecute the saints, and to fight against God. We have learned by sad experience that it is the nature and disposition of almost all men, as soon as they get a little authority, as they suppose, they will immediately begin to exercise unrighteous dominion. Hence many are called, but few are chosen. No power or influence can or ought to be maintained by virtue of the priesthood, only by persuasion, by long-suffering, by gentleness and meekness, and by love unfeigned; By kindness, and pure knowledge, which shall greatly enlarge the soul without hypocrisy, and without guile—Reproving betimes with sharpness, when moved upon by the Holy Ghost; and then showing forth afterwards an increase of love toward him whom thou hast reproved, lest he esteem thee to be his enemy; That he may know that thy faithfulness is stronger than the cords of death."

So there wasn't some great advantage for these people who hold actual priestly authority. We learn that "in the first place they were on the same standing with their brethren." Where was that "first place?" Is it also "from the foundation of the world" referred to earlier?

What does it mean that they were "on the same standing with their brethren" while in that first place?

What was it about these who receive authority that qualified them to receive the "holy calling" from the foundation of the world? What does it mean that they "would not harden their hearts" in the first place? If they didn't do it then, will they do it now?

Is foreknowledge about these individual's qualifications based on prior performance? Can you determine that since they did not harden their hearts in the first place, they will not begin to harden their hearts now?

What about the "atonement of the Only Begotten Son, who was prepared" made them qualified? Did they accept Him there? Did they soften their hearts there toward Him? Are they capable of having redeeming faith in Him here because they first acquired it there?

Is all this necessary to have preceded ordination here? If it was not acquired there, can an ordination here have any effect?

What, then, do those who qualify do? What does it mean "to teach his commandments unto the children of men?"

Is there something different between teaching commandments on the one hand, and "that they [who are taught] also might enter into his rest" on the other hand? Are the two linked together? Is it necessary to both "teach his commandments unto the children of men, that they also might enter into his rest" to show such priestly authority? That is, can anyone, regardless of their true ordination to authority teach commandments? But does it take something more, some higher ordination in order to bring those taught "to enter into His rest?" If so, what is the difference? How can you recognize such teachings if they are ever put on display?

Did Joseph Smith exhibit such powerful teachings?

Did Enoch?

Did Melchizedek? Abraham? Elijah? Elisha? Nephi? The Brother of Jared? Enos? Others?

Do we see that today? If so, where? Does anyone have the audacity to presume they can bring another soul back to the Lord's rest? Maybe Joseph Smith's comment on this point is appropriate: ""The things of God are of deep import and time and experience and careful and ponderous and solemn thoughts can only find them out. Thy mind O man if thou wilt lead a soul into salvation must search into and contemplate the darkest abyss and the broad expanse of eternity, thou must commune with God." (DHC Vol. 3, p. 295.) I'd like to meet such a man. They seem to be rather infrequent residents of this fallen world...

Alma 13: 7

"This high priesthood being after the order of his Son, which order was from the foundation of the world; or in other words, being without beginning of days or end of years, being prepared from eternity to all eternity, according to his foreknowledge of all things—"

Now we encounter comments that everyone seems to use about this priesthood. It is "without beginning of days or end of years." It is "from the foundation of the world."

It is "prepared from eternity to eternity."

When did eternity end and mortality begin?

When does mortality end and eternity begin again?

What does the phrase "from eternity to eternity" really refer to?

Do we pass "from eternity" then back "to eternity" as part of this mortal experience?

What went on before, back in the first "eternity?" We read elsewhere of this peaceful existence during "millennial" conditions, which end with rebellion, disputes and a war. Was Satan loosed in an earlier eternity after some season of peace to stir the hearts of men to anger one with another? (See Rev. 20: 7-9.) Was he cast out to hell, or the Telestial Kingdom, where we presently reside? What went on? How often would the Lord have gathered us as a hen gathers her chicks, but we would not be gathered? (I suppose His asking and the lack of an answer implies a great number.)

What is it about what went on before, in the earlier "eternity," that allows God to possess His perfect "foreknowledge of all things" now?

What is this strange doctrine and the implications which flow from them? Was Joseph Smith trying to tell us this in the later Nauvoo talks? (Maybe we should read them again…)

How is one to take it all in? How is the priesthood tied to this prior eternity? Why do we get side-tracked into the subject of "from eternity to eternity" when we learn about this endless priesthood which is without beginning of days or end of years?

What is really going on? How can we learn of the truth? Is there no prophet who can declare it to us?

The suspense is killing me. I'm hoping to get answers. I'm hoping you want them too. I'm confident if you ask the Lord, He will answer you. He intends to pour out knowledge upon the heads of the Saints. If we will stop making others accountable for what we learn, and go to Him to receive what He offers, by the power of the Holy Ghost you may know the truth of all things. I read that somewhere… But the words are mine, now.

Alma 13: 8

"Now they were ordained after this manner—being called with a holy calling, and ordained with a holy ordinance, and taking

upon them the high priesthood of the holy order, which calling, and ordinance, and high priesthood, is without beginning or end —"

The manner of such person's ordination is described but—

What does it mean to be "called with a holy calling?" Is there something about the nature of this "calling" that is different from an interview and being "found worthy of advancement in the priesthood" as we commonly see? What is a "holy calling" anyway? Why does this kind of priestly calling get described exclusively as "holy" by its nature? Is there some contact with God required (who is the source of all holiness) as part of this "holy calling?"

Then we have the description of their ordination. What does it mean to be "ordained with a holy ordinance?" Does our practice of laying on hands, conferring the Aaronic Priesthood and ordaining to the office of Priest answer to this description? What is the "holy ordinance" that is done to confer this priesthood?

Can we automatically rule out the entirety of Aaronic and most of the Melchizedek priesthood offices when we see the words: "taking upon them the high priesthood of the holy order?" Is there some office we are aware of which is appropriately described as "taking upon them the high priesthood of the holy order?" Think about that for a moment.

If this is a "holy calling" and it results in the person receiving it "taking upon them the high priesthood of the holy order" isn't this something perhaps quite different from what we do to disseminate the priesthood? And if all the Aaronic Priesthood and most of the Melchizedek Priesthood offices are not what we would appropriately call "the high priesthood of the holy order" then are we talking about either of these two commonly held priesthoods anyway?

Then we have the interesting addition that the "calling, and ordinance, and high priesthood, is without beginning or end" for those involved. That is, without reference to mortality. It was held before coming here, it will endure after leaving here. It is "endless" in the sense it comes "from eternity to eternity" as set out in the preceding verse.

This is potentially quite different from the manner in which we practice priestly ordinations in the church today. I suppose that some will want to confine all this description to our practices. They are free to see it in that way if they choose. I'm just asking if it is more likely that the words have a different meaning than we have associated with them before. If that is possible, then perhaps we ought to be asking the Lord to inform us more about the matter, rather than presuming we already possess what is being described here.

It may just be that our hopes for some great, eternal reward hinge upon getting to the bottom of this matter. It may just be that God's control over and involvement with the "holy calling" and "holy ordinance" of having the "high priesthood after the Son of God" is immediate and direct. It may be that this "holy ordinance" will only come from that God who employs no servant at the gate, but is Himself the gatekeeper.[2] Wouldn't that be wonderful. Think about it—no flawed process. No fooled bishop or stake president letting someone obtain an office for which they are completely unsuited. It sort of makes sense.

Alma 13: 9

> **"Thus they become high priests forever, after the order of the Son, the Only Begotten of the Father, who is without beginning of days or end of years, who is full of grace, equity, and truth. And thus it is. Amen."**

Several things about this formulation are interesting. Most interesting is the closing declaration, **"And thus it is. Amen."** It is iconic. It is as if the statement were an authorized, serious message, intended to be accompanied by the requisite formalities to let the reader know that this is serious stuff. This is "most holy." This is not just a passing description. It holds terrible, eternal significance. So the material that preceded it holds important keys to understanding. Important warnings and knowledge. Perhaps, as a result of the concluding punctuation, we should be very, very careful about the words that preceded it. [This is why I'm conducting this exercise.]

Now look at the beginning—

"Thus they become..." These individuals have become something. The "high priests" about whom this material has been written have been in the process of becoming something holy from before the foundation of the world. This is pre-earth or pre-mortal existence stuff. The history, or background leading up to finding a holy high priest in mortality is eons in the making. It goes back to before this world had been reorganized.

"...high priests forever..." This priestly authority and holy order is not mortal. It is without beginning in this mortal phase of existence.

Now comes the formula of the authority: "after the order of the Son, the Only Begotten of the Father, who is without beginning of days or end of years, who is full of grace, equity, and truth." Look at it in pieces.

- After the order of the Son

- After the order of the Only Begotten of the Father

- After the order of Him who is without beginning of days or end of years

- After the order of Him who is full of grace

- After the order of Him who is full of equity

[2] 2 Ne. 9: 41: "O then, my beloved brethren, come unto the Lord, the Holy One. Remember that his paths are righteous. Behold, the way for man is narrow, but it lieth in a straight course before him, and the keeper of the gate is the Holy One of Israel; and he employeth no servant there; and there is none other way save it be by the gate; for he cannot be deceived, for the Lord God is his name."

- After the order of Him who is full of truth.

What does it mean to be "begotten" of the Father?[3]
What does it mean to be a "son" of the Father?[4]
What does it mean to be full of "grace?"[5]
What does it mean to be full of "equity?"[6]
What does it mean to be full of "truth?"[7]

This is interesting. What are we to make of such "holy" men who are "high priests after the order of the Son of God?"

Do you think **we** make a man such a thing by sustaining him in Ward, Stake and General Conferences? Can **we** make one of them at all?

If we never realize who they are, does that mean they don't exist? Does it mean they weren't ordained before the foundation of the world?

If they come, minister in obscurity, never hold high office and never have a single building at BYU, BYU Hawaii or BYU Idaho named after them, are they any less?

Does our recognition of them make them any more?

---

[3] Ps. 2: 7: "I will declare the decree: the Lord hath said unto me, Thou art my Son; this day have I begotten thee."

[4] 1 John 3: 1-3: "Behold, what manner of love the Father hath bestowed upon us, that we should be called the sons of God: therefore the world knoweth us not, because it knew him not. Beloved, now are we the sons of God, and it doth not yet appear what we shall be: but we know that, when he shall appear, we shall be like him; for we shall see him as he is. And every man that hath this hope in him purifieth himself, even as he is pure."

[5] D&C 93: 11-20: "And I, John, bear record that I beheld his glory, as the glory of the Only Begotten of the Father, full of grace and truth, even the Spirit of truth, which came and dwelt in the flesh, and dwelt among us. And I, John, saw that he received not of the fulness at the first, but received grace for grace; And he received not of the fulness at first, but continued from grace to grace, until he received a fulness; And thus he was called the Son of God, because he received not of the fulness at the first. And I, John, bear record, and lo, the heavens were opened, and the Holy Ghost descended upon him in the form of a dove, and sat upon him, and there came a voice out of heaven saying: This is my beloved Son. And I, John, bear record that he received a fulness of the glory of the Father; And he received all power, both in heaven and on earth, and the glory of the Father was with him, for he dwelt in him. And it shall come to pass, that if you are faithful you shall receive the fulness of the record of John. I give unto you these sayings that you may understand and know how to worship, and know what you worship, that you may come unto the Father in my name, and in due time receive of his fulness. For if you keep my commandments you shall receive of his fulness, and be glorified in me as I am in the Father; therefore, I say unto you, you shall receive grace for grace."

[6] Prov. 2: 9: "Then shalt thou understand righteousness, and judgment, and equity; yea, every good path."

[7] D&C 93: 24: "And truth is knowledge of things as they are, and as they were, and as they are to come;"

Are they here to be recognized? Are they here just to teach so that others may be brought back to God by learning His commandments and enter into His rest?

This is quite different than what I've been told in Gospel Doctrine class. It is beginning to look and feel a lot like what Joseph Smith was saying right at the end in the Nauvoo period. I wonder why we neglect this today?

Alma 13: 10

> **"Now, as I said concerning the holy order, or this high priesthood, there were many who were ordained and became high priests of God; and it was on account of their exceeding faith and repentance, and their righteousness before God, they choosing to repent and work righteousness rather than to perish;"**

Immediately following the formula, the explanation continues that "many" were able to become ordained as such "high priests of God." But the way they did this was through several specific actions.

They had "exceeding faith." What do you suppose "exceeding faith" means? Why not "faith?" What is the difference between "faith" and "exceeding faith?"

They went through "repentance." So we know they made the same kinds of mortal mistakes as we do. They experience the bitter and then are able to prefer the sweet. They knew what it was like to feel the bitterness of hell, because they felt the sting of sin. So they repented. These great souls are NOT perfect, after all! They "repented" because they didn't do it right the first time. What a refreshing idea. They weren't fake. They didn't feign virtue. They had failing. They were filled with life, made errors, and needed to repent. They were not immune to the circumstances of this fallen world.

More importantly, do the terms "exceeding faith" and "repentance" go together? That is, do you necessarily have to possess "exceeding faith" in order to become one who fully "repents?" If so, why? How is it done? This may be an important clue to the process of "keeping the second estate" and "proving" that you are ready to move on. Perhaps it is in this manner that some will then have "glory added upon their heads forever," (Abr. 3:) and in another cycle of existence and eternal progression then also join in the ranks of those belonging to the "holy order after the Son of God."

These called persons are, despite everything, "righteous before God." God measures differently than do we. Being "righteous before God" may not mean the same thing we think "righteous" means. We want outward signs, symbols, dress, grooming and conformity. God looks at the intent of the heart.

Interestingly, they "choose to repent and work righteousness rather than to perish." What do you suppose that means? First, they "repent," then they "work righteousness." Because of this, they do not "perish." So do these things all go together? Can a person "repent" but then not "work righteousness?" Does a person have to "repent" and "work righteousness" in order to not "perish?"

Alma 13: 11

> **"Therefore they were called after this holy order, and were sanctified, and their garments were washed white through the blood of the Lamb."**

If you understand these phrases, this verse clarifies the matter.

Being called into this holy order requires a person to be more than a church member, or a follower, or a believer. They need to be "sanctified."

"Their garments were washed white through the blood of the Lamb." No small feat!

To have white garments is to have the blood and sins of your generation removed from you. To be purified. To be sanctified by the Lamb—removing from you, and taking upon Himself the responsibility to answer for whatever failings you have.

This is not ritual purity. This is purity in fact.

The person described by this phrase is qualified to stand in the presence of God without sin. Clean of all blood and sin—righteous forever. He is Christ's, and Christ is the Father's, and all that each of them will be is the same; for we shall see Him as He is, because we will be like Him. To be like Him is to be sanctified.

I can use the words, but I am powerless beyond that. This is more than you think it is. Words are inadequate to explain it. Eye hath not seen, nor ear heard, nor has it entered **into the heart of man** what great things the Lord has in mind by inheriting these promises. Indeed, to receive an understanding is **to cease to be a man and become something else altogether**. A stranger and sojourner here, but a resident with God in another condition altogether. It is written by the Lord concerning them: "These are they who are come unto Mount Zion, and unto the city of the living God, the heavenly place, the holiest of all. These are they who have come to an innumerable company of angels, to the general assembly and church of Enoch, and of the Firstborn. These are they whose names are written in heaven, where God and Christ are the judge of all. These are they who are just men made perfect through Jesus the mediator of the new covenant, who wrought out this perfect atonement through the shedding of his own blood." (D&C 76: 66-69.)

Such persons are still in this world, but they are also associated with innumerable others who are not present here. Although mortals associate with each other, these individuals obtain a higher order. They connect with a higher plane, because a more sure word has been spoken to them. As a result they belong to an order of holy priesthood. That priesthood is an order without beginning of days or end of years, from eternity to eternity. This new, higher order, when it occurs can be the spark through which heaven itself can return to the earth.

To others looking in from outside, these are words without meaning, or definition. To those who hold this priestly position, these words are a perfect fit. The gulf between the two positions is so great that even a common vocabulary won't make meanings connect.

We proclaim we "have the truth" but we do not preach it. We claim to have authority, but we have no power to redeem and exalt. We pretend it is unlawful to preach mysteries, yet Alma is preaching the deepest doctrines to the non-converted. If we preach the truth, it will attract those whose lives are empty. Why would they join us if what we offer is as trite and superficial as the false religions they already believe?

Is there no need to cry repentance to this generation with power and authority? With the tongue of an angel? To cry out as the Book of Mormon declares the message to the non-believing and skeptical?

It does raise some troubling concerns as we claim to be the "true church" but do not act the part as shown in these scriptures. How are we justified in masking the fullness, hiding the mysteries, putting away deep doctrine that will save, and still proclaim that we are the "only true and living church upon the earth?" Does "living" require us to create sons and daughters of God who are "come to an innumerable company of angels, to the general assembly and church of Enoch, and of the Firstborn?" If so, why do we hear so little about it in our day?

I suppose our audacity springs from our history? If we have lost something vital that conflicts with our current understanding of the history that GUARANTEES us that we are perfect, and that we cannot be misled, then we wouldn't want to acknowledge that. Thank goodness for these guarantees. It does let us relax a bit, doesn't it? Broad and wide are the guarantees we have inherited. We don't need to worry about that narrow and strait fringe who rummage about in the mysteries.

Alma 13: 12

> **"Now they, after being sanctified by the Holy Ghost, having their garments made white, being pure and spotless before God, could not look upon sin save it were with abhorrence; and there were many, exceedingly great many, who were made pure and entered into the rest of the Lord their God."**

If the earlier verse were not clear enough, the point is reiterated again here. These people are "sanctified by the Holy Ghost" as a result of "having their garments made white." They are "pure and spotless before God!"

This is the reason they can enter His presence. He has accepted them because just like Him, they are without sin. They were not perfected by their own acts. The earlier reference to their repentance makes that clear.

They become pure and spotless before God because they have done what was asked of them to become clean. They have repented.

Now, measure the effects of their repentance. It has been so complete, so heartfelt, and deeply prized that they "could not look upon sin save it were with abhorrence." It is this notion that underlies the mistaken idea that once someone's calling and election has been made sure they are required to suffer for their own sins, because they have knowledge they are redeemed. This is a twisted view, designed by the adversary to discourage those who might otherwise seek and find.

It is not that the atonement ceases to operate for the redeemed. The atonement continues to cover the on-going sins of these redeemed souls which arise from their foolishness, mistakes, errors of comprehension, and the things they don't understand yet. Christ does not require them to do what they don't know is a requirement yet. As the gentle and kind Lord, He will forgive all they do that is wrong, while He reveals through greater light and knowledge a higher path. As He unfolds to their understanding more light, they can measure their conduct according to that greater light.

As they gain greater truth and light they see things how they really are. Right and wrong are seen differently. What once was "right" is now wrong as greater light and truth is received. What was once "wrong" is now seen clearly, without all the errors of understanding held before.

The spotlessness is because their heart is right. They WANT to please their Lord. They WANT to be like Him. Sin is not tempting because it is contrary to Him whom they love.

The abhorrence they feel at sin is not within them. It is not the temptations they struggle against. That is not the meaning at all. It is what they see all about them. The lost souls are the object of their compassion and care. They WANT to have others redeemed and saved from this lost and fallen world. The fruit they tasted is something they desire to share. They WANT many, an exceeding many, to share with them in the hope that can be won by repentance.

They would shout *"flee from Babylon"* if they thought it would do any good. But shouting does no good among a darkened and benighted people. They may speak the words of an angel to others, but it is up to others to decide whether they will listen. It will be a still, small, quiet pleading they make to others. Within their entreaties will be found the Master's words.

Many may claim to speak in His name, but only these few have the ability to speak with His approval. These are holy men, possessing words of eternal life. In them will be found truths that come from eternity and that will save to all eternity.

Only a few will listen. That won't detract from the power of the message delivered by those who are after the holy order of the Son of God, for their words can save any who will listen.

What an interesting chapter we have found here. And we are only a dozen verses into it! We should press on.

Alma 13: 13

> **"And now, my brethren, I would that ye should humble yourselves before God, and bring forth fruit meet for repentance, that ye may also enter into that rest."**

Think about what you're reading here. Alma is essentially declaring himself as one of those possessing this priesthood because he is inviting others to enter into the rest which these people enjoy. That is, "come, join in the rest of the Lord."

Alma has just revealed something profound about himself. It is subtle, but nonetheless true. In meekness he has proffered an invitation. He has not set himself up to be admired. He does not consider himself better. He has delivered the invitation to those to whom he is ministering, just as you would expect someone possessing this great, holy calling to do.

All the more remarkable is that he extends this invitation to an unredeemed, critical, reproachful audience of unconverted. He does not shield them from these great mysteries.

He does not flinch or hold back because it would be to "cast pearls before swine." He knows where the line is drawn, for in the preceding chapter they have explained to an audience that there are mysteries withheld from the public.[8] There are things kept from public knowledge and obtained only by heed and diligence. The line involves sacred ordinances, NOT higher knowledge. You give that and you make converts. You withhold it and you blend into the morass of churches who teach merely a form of godliness without any power to save.[9]

It was the same during Christ's ministry. The line is drawn as sacred events turn to ordinances. They are withheld. NOT the teaching of deep doctrine.

So when we refuse to discuss "mysteries" and limit our correlated curriculum to an approved list of 52 subjects, recycling them endlessly,

---

[8] Alma 12: 9-11: "And now Alma began to expound these things unto him, saying: It is given unto many to know the mysteries of God; nevertheless they are laid under a strict command that they shall not impart only according to the portion of his word which he doth grant unto the children of men, according to the heed and diligence which they give unto him. And therefore, he that will harden his heart, the same receiveth the lesser portion of the word; and he that will not harden his heart, to him is given the greater portion of the word, until it is given unto him to know the mysteries of God until he know them in full. And they that will harden their hearts, to them is given the lesser portion of the word until they know nothing concerning his mysteries; and then they are taken captive by the devil, and led by his will down to destruction. Now this is what is meant by the chains of hell."

[9] JS-H 1: 19: "I was answered that I must join none of them, for they were all wrong; and the Personage who addressed me said that all their creeds were an abomination in his sight; that those professors were all corrupt; that: 'they draw near to me with their lips, but their hearts are far from me, they teach for doctrines the commandments of men, having a form of godliness, but they deny the power thereof'."

we are not in conformity with the pattern shown in the Book of Mormon. The "most correct book" condemns us. But, then again, so does the word of the Lord precisely because we are not following the Book of Mormon.[10]

The highest form of acceptance and redemption is to have your calling and election made sure; to be washed and cleansed from sin every whit. Alma is preaching this to unconverted, investigating, potential converts. Today we won't even permit the subject to be raised in adult Sunday School, Priesthood, or Relief Society meetings because it is considered to be "too sensitive" for the members to consider. Have we, the Gentiles, rejected "the fullness of the Gospel?"[11] Not as long as any of us (like salt or leaven) keep these doctrines alive.

If you want to know about this fullness and how to obtain it, then read the books I have written. That is what they are about. Alma was right! His message was true!

Let all come and partake. Everyone is invited. No institutional control should be used to prevent your search into this matter. It is right in the Book of Mormon. Though the institution may be condemned for neglecting it, you don't need to be.

So, let's turn to the next verse and see what wonders continue to unfold before our eyes…

Alma 13: 14

> **"Yea, humble yourselves even as the people in the days of Melchizedek, who was also a high priest after this same order which I have spoken, who also took upon him the high priesthood forever."**

We have named a portion of the priesthood after Melchizedek. (It is not, however, the form which Melchizedek held. That is another topic I am not going to address here now. This area is complete mush in the minds of Latter-day Saint writers and commentaries. I can't straighten that out on this blog. I might take it up in a book and go through it methodically there.)

---

[10] D&C 84: 55-57: "Which vanity and unbelief have brought the whole church under condemnation. And this condemnation resteth upon the children of Zion, even all. And they shall remain under this condemnation until they repent and remember the new covenant, even the Book of Mormon and the former commandments which I have given them, not only to say, but to do according to that which I have written—"

[11] 3 Ne. 16: 10: "And thus commandeth the Father that I should say unto you: At that day when the Gentiles shall sin against my gospel, and shall reject the fulness of my gospel, and shall be lifted up in the pride of their hearts above all nations, and above all the people of the whole earth, and shall be filled with all manner of lyings, and of deceits, and of mischiefs, and all manner of hypocrisy, and murders, and priestcrafts, and whoredoms, and of secret abominations; and if they shall do all those things, and shall reject the fulness of my gospel, behold, saith the Father, I will bring the fulness of my gospel from among them."

What is important is that the great events of Melchizedek's time began when people humbled themselves and accepted the teachings of this "high priesthood" holder and were, thereby, saved. Not only saved but also led into a fellowship which eventually turned into a City of Peace, or City of Salem, or Jerusalem, which was taken into heaven.

This prototype was so influential in the thinking of all who followed, that the high priesthood was named after Melchizedek. Even though he held Patriarchal Priesthood with its associated sealing power, he was the one after whom Melchizedek Priesthood was named in the form it was later transmitted which lacked sealing authority. (Again, another topic.)

What is important in this verse is the connection between the existence of the one holding this authority (Melchizedek), and a humble people who would accept and follow those teachings. The result of the combination of the two was that God came and dwelt among them.

This is a pattern that followed the previous pattern with Enoch. This was the pattern Joseph wanted to return through his teaching and ministry. Joseph wasn't able to accomplish it. We now hope to see it someday occur in the unfolding history of The Church of Jesus Christ of Latter-day Saints. The most recent book on this subject, now on sale at Deseret Book (unfortunately a red-flag for me) urges the idea that the only Zion we should expect to see will come when the church president allows or directs it to happen.

This verse suggests what is needed is 1) humble people willing to accept teaching from a high priest after the ancient order and 2) a person having that authority who will teach.

What does this do to our current accepted model?

If Zion is to return, how will it return? Will it mirror what the Book of Mormon is teaching here?

Is the church president the one who will bring this gathering to pass?

Is the church president teaching doctrine about the fullness which will bring others into the rest of the Lord?

Has the church president brought a company into the Lord's presence? Attempted to do so? Taught or written about how that will happen? (If so, can someone point that out to me so I can read the talk, get the book or watch the video.)

How can I know I would actually have followed Melchizedek and become a part of his city by what I do today? (I'd like to be among them, you see.)

Alma 13: 15

> **"And it was this same Melchizedek to whom Abraham paid tithes; yea, even our father Abraham paid tithes of one-tenth part of all he possessed."**

Abraham, father of the righteous, paid tithe to this Melchizedek. Not the reverse.

I've already commented that I believe Melchizedek (whose name means "king and priest") was in fact Shem. I believe those who disagree (McConkie and Joseph Fielding Smith) base their conclusion on the words of D&C 84: 14 which reads: "Which Abraham received the priesthood from Melchizedek, who received it through the lineage of his fathers, even till Noah;". I believe the lineage referred to there is from the fathers who preceded Noah. But Noah was Shem/Melchizedek's father.

Abraham received the priesthood which had been promised to him by God, from Melchizedek. He (Abraham) already had the records of the fathers.[12] He already had the promise of priestly authority.[13] So the question should be asked as to why Abraham would need to be ordained by Melchizedek when the Lord was speaking directly to him and could have taken care of that directly. It is an important question. It is necessary to understand why the question should be asked and also what the answer is.

First, why would Abraham, who was directly in contact with God, be sent to another to receive the priesthood? What sense does it make the Lord would make him wait and send him to another? Particularly when Abraham had understanding that stretched into heavens and also possessed the records of the fathers, back to Adam. Why do that?

You should struggle with this question yourself. I feel like I'm robbing you by answering. Nevertheless, Abraham needed to be endowed and Melchizedek was set up to provide to Abraham the endowment. Therefore to receive the ordinance (Abraham was raised by apostates who had not provided that for him), he was sent to Melchizedek from whom he received necessary ordinances. As long as the ordinances needed to be performed and there was an officiator there to accomplish it, the Lord sent Abraham to Melchizedek.

---

[12] Abr. 1: 31: "But the records of the fathers, even the patriarchs, concerning the right of Priesthood, the Lord my God preserved in mine own hands; therefore a knowledge of the beginning of the creation, and also of the planets, and of the stars, as they were made known unto the fathers, have I kept even unto this day, and I shall endeavor to write some of these things upon this record, for the benefit of my posterity that shall come after me."

[13] Abr. 2: 6-9: "But I, Abraham, and Lot, my brother's son, prayed unto the Lord, and the Lord appeared unto me, and said unto me: Arise, and take Lot with thee; for I have purposed to take thee away out of Haran, and to make of thee a minister to bear my name in a strange land which I will give unto thy seed after thee for an everlasting possession, when they hearken to my voice. For I am the Lord thy God; I dwell in heaven; the earth is my footstool; I stretch my hand over the sea, and it obeys my voice; I cause the wind and the fire to be my chariot; I say to the mountains—Depart hence—and behold, they are taken away by a whirlwind, in an instant, suddenly. My name is Jehovah, and I know the end from the beginning; therefore my hand shall be over thee. And I will make of thee a great nation, and I will bless thee above measure, and make thy name great among all nations, and thou shalt be a blessing unto thy seed after thee, that in their hands they shall bear this ministry and Priesthood unto all nations;"

Abraham also received the accouterments of kingship that descended from Adam. Melchizedek was the reigning high priest on the earth, Abraham was to replace him at his passing, and Melchizedek had awaited the promised successor's arrival for years. When at last Abraham arrived, Melchizedek was able to provide ordinances, answer questions, minister as was needed, then turn over the accouterments of kingship and withdraw from this earth. No sooner had Abraham been prepared than Melchizedek and his city also withdraw to join Enoch's people.

Second, why were tithes paid to a great high priest who would shortly be translated? What need was there for tithing?

The form the tithing took was not a check or bank draft. It was animals, food and usable material. What was provided would be used in sacrifices, feasts, celebrations and decoration of the temple maintained by Melchizedek. In short, Abraham provided material through his tithing that could be incorporated into the celebrations to which he was invited and from which he derived his own blessing and endowment. He gave, in turn he received.

Now, if you do not understand the concept of meekness and its importance for one who should hold this holy priesthood, then you do not understand either Melchizedek or Abraham. Each was a minister who served others. Each was a faithful guide because neither sought to be greater than another. They were great servants, who could be trusted with great authority because they did not seek their own will. They were interested in following the Lord's will. Even at the price of great inconvenience and sacrifice to them. They were willing to sacrifice all things, and were therefore called to the work.

Alma 13: 16

> **"Now these ordinances were given after this manner, that thereby the people might look forward on the Son of God, it being a type of his order, or it being his order, and this that they might look forward to him for a remission of their sins, that they might enter into the rest of the Lord."**

Notice the shifting back to "ordinances" from the discussion of priesthood. What ordinances? What manner?

Why would what happened with Melchizedek and Abraham be something pointing to the Son of God?

Why would such an ordination and ordinance always be something that would prepare people to understand and accept the Son of God?

How was it a "type" of the Son of God's order?

What is this referring to in plain language? Is it that the ordinances will reveal a pattern that will unmistakably point back to the ministry of Christ? How?

What is there in conferring priesthood and endowing with understanding that points to Christ? Was Christ endowed with knowledge? Power? Authority? From on-high? When? What account do we have of it? Was it at His baptism when the voice of God declared, "thou art my Son, this day have I begotten thee" (which wording was deliberately changed during the Fourth Century Christological debates to read instead: "this is my beloved Son, in whom I am well pleased")? How does this identify both the holder of this holy order of priesthood and confirm Christ's ministry as the Son of God?

More importantly, why are these things not being taught to us today? This is such basic and important doctrine that Alma is teaching it as introductory material to a potential group of converts. But as faithful members of the Church we aren't even familiar with them. What have we been doing with the Gospel we received?

Why was the "manner" something which would let those who learned about it know and identify the Lord?

Do we expect to follow Christ? If so, why aren't we anxious to learn about this holy order? Can we follow Him unless we do what is necessary to take upon us that same holy order? If so, then how are we to find it today? Who teaches about it?

It is interesting to read this chapter of Alma. It reinforces that the Book of Mormon is still being neglected. We cycle through it every four years. Perhaps we are still neglecting it's true message? I think this chapter gets lumped in with three others and covered in a 50 minute class every four years. Maybe that is what is meant by "neglect."

Alma 13: 17-18

> **"Now this Melchizedek was a king over the land of Salem; and his people had waxed strong in iniquity and abomination; yea, they had all gone astray; they were full of all manner of wickedness; But Melchizedek having exercised mighty faith, and received the office of the high priesthood according to the holy order of God, did preach repentance unto his people. And behold, they did repent; and Melchizedek did establish peace in the land in his days; therefore he was called the prince of peace, for he was the king of Salem; and he did reign under his father."**

He was a king over people who had "waxed strong" in both "iniquity" and also "abomination." Keep in mind that "waxing strong" means to be increasingly determined or committed. "Iniquity" is generally evil practice, but "abomination" involves the **religious justification** of wrongdoing. That is, something becomes "abominable" when it is motivated out of a false form of religious observance or is justified because of religious error.

The people to whom Melchizedek would minister were not simply in error, they were motivated by a false set of religious beliefs and errors. The result was that "they had all gone astray." They were "full of all manner of wickedness." This was a challenging audience for this man to minister to and try to convert to the truth.

Melchizedek began by "exercising mighty faith" in order to understand the truth and discern the difference between truth and error. Remember how difficult it is to be taught truth. It is more difficult to learn truth than it is to perform miracles.[14] Despite this, Melchizedek was able to set aside all he beheld and through faith acquire an understanding of the truth for himself. Conferred upon him as part of this education was the priestly authority with which to minister to others.

He "did preach repentance unto his people." This required him to expose the errors, show them they were involved in iniquity and to expose how their religious errors had made them abominable. This preaching is always most difficult because it confronts the audience with a challenge to their mistaken beliefs, and false religion. There is a risk of violence when this happens. People who entertain abominable religious practices are more often moved to violence than to repentance. The Lord was greeted with violence. So was Lehi, Isaiah, Nephi, Samuel the Lamanite, Abinadi, Peter, Paul, Stephen, James, Zacharias and too many others to mention. To their credit, and to Melchizedek's, the preaching resulted in repentance.

The serious errors, iniquity, and abominations of these people did not prevent Melchizedek from establishing a Zion. These people were able to acquire "peace in the land" because of their repentance. As used here, however, peace means more than the absence of violence, it means the presence of the Lord.

The statement that he established peace as the King of Salem (Shalom means peace) and "he did reign under his father" is a play on words. Which "father" is being identified in the statement. Was it Noah, or Gabriel? (A man who would also be translated and have a ministry as the Lord's herald before the birth of John the Baptist and Christ.) Or was the "father" Him would would declare that Melchizedek was "begotten" as a "son of God?" It likely meant both. But it is also likely written this way to let those who do not understand what is being said to read it in a way that conceals the dual meanings. The scriptures are filled with such dual meanings.

---

[14] 3 Ne. 17: 2-7: "I perceive that ye are weak, that ye cannot understand all my words which I am commanded of the Father to speak unto you at this time. Therefore, go ye unto your homes, and ponder upon the things which I have said, and ask of the Father, in my name, that ye may understand, and prepare your minds for the morrow, and I come unto you again. But now I go unto the Father, and also to show myself unto the lost tribes of Israel, for they are not lost unto the Father, for he knoweth whither he hath taken them. And it came to pass that when Jesus had thus spoken, he cast his eyes round about again on the multitude, and beheld they were in tears, and did look steadfastly upon him as if they would ask him to tarry a little longer with them. And he said unto them: Behold, my bowels are filled with compassion towards you. Have ye any that are sick among you? Bring them hither. Have ye any that are lame, or blind, or halt, or maimed, or leprous, or that are withered, or that are deaf, or that are afflicted in any manner? Bring them hither and I will heal them, for I have compassion upon you; my bowels are filled with mercy."

What is hopeful for us today, is that no matter how much "iniquity" and religious error we engage in that results in our "abominations" in our pride and foolishness, we still may be candidates to receive something similar to what befell the City of Salem. The first step is to acquire the presence of this priesthood through individual repentance.

We envy these ancients. But we do nothing to try and follow the pattern revealed to us in their course. The Book of Mormon is a course in ancient failure and ancient success. We just do not respect what we have in that volume.

Alma 13: 19-20

> **"Now, there were many before him, and also there were many afterwards, but none were greater; therefore, of him they have more particularly made mention. Now I need not rehearse the matter; what I have said may suffice. Behold, the scriptures are before you; if ye will wrest them it shall be to your own destruction."**

The "many before him, and also…many afterwards" in this sermon is not just a reference to believers, but to those who held this "holy order after the Son of God." It it a reference to those who were made clean and pure by their repentance. It is those who, having been called by the Lord, chosen to this holy order, having their calling and election secure, hold power as a result of this relationship with God.

But none of these, before or since, (at the time of the writing by Alma) who held authority were greater than Melchizedek. As a result, he merited particular mention to identify those who held the holy priesthood after the order of the Son of God. It was merited because his example and his ministry illustrated perfectly what the "holy order" was intended to accomplish. It is designed to save others.

It was not to exalt the man.

It was not to bring attention to the man. It was not to amass praise or a following.

It was not to make the man a ruler over others. It was not to gain control or domination.

It was not to subjugate or force compulsive obedience upon the souls of men.

It was to serve and exalt those to whom he ministered. His greatness was derived by the fruit of saved, exalted souls whom he saved. There is no record of a single sermon preached by Melchizedek. We have evidence of the following things he did with his authority and power:

- He received tithes from Abraham.[15]

---

[15] Alma 13: 15: "And it was this same Melchizedek to whom Abraham paid tithes; yea, even our father Abraham paid tithes of one-tenth part of all he possessed."

- He ordained Abraham.[16]
- He saved an entire population from iniquity and abominations, and converted them to the truth.[17]
- He made those he converted qualified to behold the Lord's presence.[18]
- He performed a form of ceremony with Abraham involving breaking bread and wine.[19]

He served. He blessed. He produced exalted souls. He was not great by what he received, but by what he did with what he received to bless and exalt others.

We would see this if we understood the scriptures. We would not be following a false tradition wherein men are famous, celebrity-like, fawned over, held up to acclaim and given the authority to exercise control over men. This is a false model that the Gentiles follow, and not the way in which true priesthood holders operate.[20] No one possessing power from heaven will do this.[21]

---

[16] D&C 84: 14: "Which Abraham received the priesthood from Melchizedek, who received it through the lineage of his fathers, even till Noah;"

[17] Alma 13: 18: "But Melchizedek having exercised mighty faith, and received the office of the high priesthood according to the holy order of God, did preach repentance unto his people. And behold, they did repent; and Melchizedek did establish peace in the land in his days; therefore he was called the prince of peace, for he was the king of Salem; and he did reign under his father."

[18] Alma 13: 11: "But Melchizedek having exercised mighty faith, and received the office of the high priesthood according to the holy order of God, did preach repentance unto his people. And behold, they did repent; and Melchizedek did establish peace in the land in his days; therefore he was called the prince of peace, for he was the king of Salem; and he did reign under his father."

[19] Gen. 14: 18-19: "And Melchizedek king of Salem brought forth bread and wine: and he was the priest of the most high God. And he blessed him, and said, Blessed be Abram of the most high God, possessor of heaven and earth:"

[20] Matt. 20: 25-28: "But Jesus called them unto him, and said, Ye know that the princes of the Gentiles exercise dominion over them, and they that are great exercise authority upon them. But it shall not be so among you: but whosoever will be great among you, let him be your minister; And whosoever will be chief among you, let him be your servant: Even as the Son of man came not to be ministered unto, but to minister, and to give his life a ransom for many."

[21] D&C 121: 36-37: "That the rights of the priesthood are inseparably connected with the powers of heaven, and that the powers of heaven cannot be controlled nor handled only upon the principles of righteousness. That they may be conferred upon us, it is true; but when we undertake to cover our sins, or to gratify our pride, our vain ambition, or to exercise control or dominion or compulsion upon the souls of the children of men, in any degree of unrighteousness, behold, the heavens withdraw themselves; the Spirit of the Lord is grieved; and when it is withdrawn, Amen to the priesthood or the authority of that man."

Now, if you make this mistake and follow in this false tradition, it will be to your own destruction. Alma has warned you.

What a marvelously relevant book this Book of Mormon is for our own day! It is almost as if they saw our time, knew what we would struggle with, and had teachings designed to let us see the error and repent. I truly believe that we can get closer to God by abiding the precepts of the Book of Mormon than we can from any other book! Joseph Smith was right.

Now we see this startling continuation in the next two verses.

Alma 13: 21-22

> **"And now it came to pass that when Alma had said these words unto them, he stretched forth his hand unto them and cried with a mighty voice, saying: Now is the time to repent, for the day of salvation draweth nigh; Yea, and the voice of the Lord, by the mouth of angels, doth declare it unto all nations; yea, doth declare it, that they may have glad tidings of great joy; yea, and he doth sound these glad tidings among all his people, yea, even to them that are scattered abroad upon the face of the earth; wherefore they have come unto us."**

Now we get to some things which the record does not fully disclose, but does allow those with eyes to see behold it. Be careful how you respond to this, because some correct answers are not going up if they cross a line. But think of the answers to these questions:

Why does he "stretch forth his hand?" What does that signify?

In what way would that become significant, even a sign that he is a true messenger?

Why does he now "cry with a mighty voice" to make the call?

What is a "mighty voice?" Is it distinguished by volume or is there something more and quite different about it? Importantly, it is not "loud" but instead "mighty." Is that significant? How? Why?

What does it mean that "*the Lord*, by the mouth of angels, doth declare it?" Who is really speaking? Who is He speaking through? What person is delivering the message? How is Alma identifying himself in this "mighty cry" he makes?

Who are these angels sent to all nations?

What is the difference in this statement by Alma and the others who can speak with tongue of angels?[22]

If one should possess such a right or commission, then whose words are they actually speaking?

Why do His sheep hear HIS voice? Even when spoken by another man or empowered priestly minister?

What does Alma actually say about his own authority as he delivers this warning? What can Alma lead you to inherit if you will heed his counsel and warning? How can we know he is a true messenger sent by the Lord?

If the Lord sends these messages and messengers to all His people, have they been sent to us? If so, where would we be able to find them and hear their message? How are we to know they are true ministers? Should I just trust that some institutional office and office holder is a guaranteed place in which to locate such a true minister? If it is always that convenient, why hasn't the Lord implemented that system before, instead of letting people have their free agency and permitting them to make mistakes? Why did the Lord allow Eli, Caiphus and Annas become High Priests? Why didn't He come up with this neat system before? [Clearly our system makes it so much easier. It throws God's fairness into question, since He made is so much harder for earlier Israelites to figure out where the truth was being proclaimed. I think the Lord must owe them an apology.]

Well, more can be said, but I leave it to you to reach your own conclusions about this startling comment coming from a true messenger. It makes one wonder why we've been missing it, as it has been before us for so many years.

"Why reveal a sacred sign?" First, "reveal" may not be the case because 1) it was not in connection with covenant-making, 2) it was accompanied with warning of judgment, not ceremonial in a Temple setting, 3) the audience may already know the meaning, in which case nothing is being "revealed", though they may be reminded, and if not,

---

[22] 2 Ne. 31: 13-14: "Wherefore, my beloved brethren, I know that if ye shall follow the Son, with full purpose of heart, acting no hypocrisy and no deception before God, but with real intent, repenting of your sins, witnessing unto the Father that ye are willing to take upon you the name of Christ, by baptism—yea, by following your Lord and your Savior down into the water, according to his word, behold, then shall ye receive the Holy Ghost; yea, then cometh the baptism of fire and of the Holy Ghost; and then can ye speak with the tongue of angels, and shout praises unto the Holy One of Israel. But, behold, my beloved brethren, thus came the voice of the Son unto me, saying: After ye have repented of your sins, and witnessed unto the Father that ye are willing to keep my commandments, by the baptism of water, and have received the baptism of fire and of the Holy Ghost, and can speak with a new tongue, yea, even with the tongue of angels, and after this should deny me, it would have been better for you that ye had not known me."

2 Ne. 32: 2: "Do ye not remember that I said unto you that after ye had received the Holy Ghost ye could speak with the tongue of angels? And now, how could ye speak with the tongue of angels save it were by the Holy Ghost?"

then 4) if the audience did not know the meaning then nothing is "revealed" to the audience who, in ignorance, will not associate keys or meaning to it.

Further, even you do not know the sign used unless it has been shown to you by revelation. You can know that a sign was used, but which is not stated.

Alma 13: 23

> **"And they are made known unto us in plain terms, that we may understand, that we cannot err; and this because of our being wanderers in a strange land; therefore, we are thus highly favored, for we have these glad tidings declared unto us in all parts of our vineyard."**

This doctrine contained in the scriptures was understood by this audience. The same audience who was full of iniquity and abominations because of their false religious traditions. It was in "plain terms" in the scriptures, if one doesn't "wrest" them to their destruction.

To "wrest" means to apply such twisted reasoning that the philosophies of men are mingled with scriptures so that the result is error.

The object of the scriptures is to make matters "plain" and prevent people from "erring" in their effort to follow God.

What is the difference between someone who with their scriptures before them, finds their message sufficiently "plain" and "understood" that they "cannot err," and someone who has the same set of scriptures and engages in "iniquity" and "abominations" because of their false religious ideas? How can someone who is religious be certain they are not among those who err, but is instead among those who find holiness and develop faith to repent?

How do we know which side of this line we are on?

Both sides are religious. Both sides have their traditions and teachings. Both sides are sincere and following what they believe to be true. However, one is engaged in "abominations" because of their false beliefs, and the other has entertained angels and received such cleansing that their garments are white before God. One side does not understand their awful state. But the other is certain of their promise of exaltation and purity before God.

So, how certain are you? Do you know you are pure before God? Holy? Having entered into His holy order after the order of the Son of God? Or do you entertain some doubt about whether the traditions which you value are actually based on the truth? Is it possible that you "err" or "wrest" the scriptures as part of your religious tradition?

According to Alma, all of this care by the Lord is because they are "wanderers in a strange land." Meaning that they are in this spot at this time because they have been taken from Jerusalem, the land of their forefathers, and placed in a new, promised land. They have been persecuted and evicted from land by their aggressive cousins. All of this to stir them up to repentance. It is God's care for them, God's careful tutelage of them, that leads them to receive this profound understanding. They are on God's errand, and therefore entitled to God's guidance. God is providing the "glad tidings" which will permit repentance to occur.

So, applying Alma's teaching to us, we should ask ourselves if we have repented? If we have received a message from angels declaring glad tidings? If we have received what we would recognize as a message from the Lord by someone declaring repentance? Or do we have a weak tradition which assures us that we are right, while letting us entertain abominable (false, religious-based) errors in our beliefs?

These are troubling questions. Worth careful, solemn and ponderous thought. Perhaps even prayerful thought where we ask the Lord if these things are not true. And if we ask with real intent, He may make the truth known to us. At least that is what He has said through past messengers. I see no reason why it would not work for us. It's at least worth a try, isn't it?

Powerful teachings from Alma. But then again, one should expect nothing less from a true messenger bearing a holy order of power and authority after the order of the Son of God. A weak and vacillating voice telling us all is well and we're going to be fine just seems wrong by comparison. At least I would think so.

Alma 13: 24

> **"For behold, angels are declaring it unto many at this time in our land; and this is for the purpose of preparing the hearts of the children of men to receive his word at the time of his coming in his glory."**

If "angels are declaring it unto many" at the time of Alma's remarks, why are they not declaring it unto many now? Are we any less important than they were? If we are as important, then why are we not hearing of this now?

What is the definition of "angels" who are doing this "declaring" to "many?" Was Alma included? If so, what is it that turns a man from a mortal to ministering angel? Can a mortal become a ministering angel? How would that occur? What would it require? Can we thereby entertain angels unawares?[23]

If an angel comes to visit with a man, gives him a message, and the man then declares it, are they both made "angels" by this message? Are "angels" always either deceased or unborn? If they are, then why did Joseph teach that "there are no angels who minister to this earth but

---

[23] Heb. 13: 2: "Be not forgetful to entertain strangers: for thereby some have entertained angels unawares."

those who do belong or have belonged to it?"[24] If angels "do belong" to the earth are they still mortal?

How would you recognize such a person? Would it be the same way the Lord was known before He showed Himself to the disciples on the Road to Emmaus?[25]

If it is the "hearts" which are to be prepared, then does this relate to the disciples "hearts burning within them" as the Lord spoke to them while in the way? Why do His sheep hear His voice? How do they hear his voice?

Why is preparing "the hearts" enough to prepare a people to "receive His word?" Is it more important to "receive His word" than to receive His person? Why would that be so?

Why are we unable to receive Him in His glory until after our hearts have first "received His word?"

It is more difficult to be taught than to have faith for miracles.[26] Even should you behold the Lord "in His glory" just as the Nephites, it would still be more difficult for you to have the faith to be taught by Him and accept what He has to teach than for Him to perform a miracle.

How alike all the generations of men are. How very relevant, therefore, these words remain for us!

Alma 13: 25

> **"And now we only wait to hear the joyful news declared unto us by the mouth of angels, of his coming; for the time cometh, we know not how soon. Would to God that it might be in my day; but let it be sooner or later, in it I will rejoice."**

---

[24] D&C 130: 5: "I answer, Yes. But there are no angels who minister to this earth but those who do belong or have belonged to it."

[25] Luke 24: 32: "And they said one to another, Did not our heart burn within us, while he talked with us by the way, and while he opened to us the scriptures?"

[26] 3 Ne. 17: 2-8: "I perceive that ye are weak, that ye cannot understand all my words which I am commanded of the Father to speak unto you at this time. Therefore, go ye unto your homes, and ponder upon the things which I have said, and ask of the Father, in my name, that ye may understand, and prepare your minds for the morrow, and I come unto you again. But now I go unto the Father, and also to show myself unto the lost tribes of Israel, for they are not lost unto the Father, for he knoweth whither he hath taken them. And it came to pass that when Jesus had thus spoken, he cast his eyes round about again on the multitude, and beheld they were in tears, and did look steadfastly upon him as if they would ask him to tarry a little longer with them. And he said unto them: Behold, my bowels are filled with compassion towards you. Have ye any that are sick among you? Bring them hither. Have ye any that are lame, or blind, or halt, or maimed, or leprous, or that are withered, or that are deaf, or that are afflicted in any manner? Bring them hither and I will heal them, for I have compassion upon you; my bowels are filled with mercy. For I perceive that ye desire that I should show unto you what I have done unto your brethren at Jerusalem, for I see that your faith is sufficient that I should heal you."

This comment is made in expectation that the Nephites will be told by heaven as soon as Christ is born. "...we only wait to hear the joyful news declared unto us by the mouth of angels..."

Angels declared it to the shepherds near Bethlehem.[27] Alma expected a similar announcement.

"We only wait to hear the joyful news." He EXPECTED the news to be shared. He knew they would have the announcement. He EXPECTED the angels to declare the arrival. He knew heaven would not leave these people without a herald of the news.

Imagine that. A prophet confident that the Lord will do nothing without first making known to the people His secrets![28] It is one thing to teach this concept. It is another to live it. Alma is living it. Therefore angels did come and did make things known to him.

What does it take to have faith like this?

If you do not possess this kind of faith, can you be saved? Moroni taught that the absence of such faith condemns the people who no longer have such things happening among them.[29]

Do we expect the Lord to tell US about things by the mouth of angels before they happen? Or do we expect the Lord will tell someone inside the bowels of an organization, and we will get some announcement through the prescribed channels, thereby relieving us from obtaining the ministry of angels? Then why is the visitation of angels an Aaronic (lowest) priesthood key?[30] This is the right of young

---

[27] Luke 2: 8-15: "And there were in the same country shepherds abiding in the field, keeping watch over their flock by night. And, lo, the angel of the Lord came upon them, and the glory of the Lord shone round about them: and they were sore afraid. And the angel said unto them, Fear not: for, behold, I bring you good tidings of great joy, which shall be to all people. For unto you is born this day in the city of David a Saviour, which is Christ the Lord. And this shall be a sign unto you; Ye shall find the babe wrapped in swaddling clothes, lying in a manger. And suddenly there was with the angel a multitude of the heavenly host praising God, and saying, Glory to God in the highest, and on earth peace, good will toward men. And it came to pass, as the angels were gone away from them into heaven, the shepherds said one to another, Let us now go even unto Bethlehem, and see this thing which is come to pass, which the Lord hath made known unto us."

[28] Amos 3:7: "Surely the Lord God will do nothing, but he revealeth his secret unto his servants the prophets."

[29] Moroni 7: 36-37: "Or have angels ceased to appear unto the children of men? Or has he withheld the power of the Holy Ghost from them? Or will he, so long as time shall last, or the earth shall stand, or there shall be one man upon the face thereof to be saved? Behold I say unto you, Nay; for it is by faith that miracles are wrought; and it is by faith that angels appear and minister unto men; wherefore, if these things have ceased wo be unto the children of men, for it is because of unbelief, and all is vain."

[30] D&C 84: 26: "And the lesser priesthood continued, which priesthood holdeth the key of the ministering of angels and the preparatory gospel;"

people beginning at age 12, mind you. Should we expect the angelic heralds to come to everyone, 12 year of age or older? Why or why not?

Alma knows it will happen. But he does not know when it will happen. He would like it to have been in his day. It was not. But whether it was to happen in his life or afterwards, he nonetheless had faith, knew angels, awaited the message, and rejoiced at the idea of His coming.

How meek! How faithful! No wonder such a man possessed and knew the details of this holy order from God. No wonder he could teach with authority about it. How great the lesson he has left for any who will take seriously the message he taught.

Faith of this sort should be the common heritage of the Lord's people. It was never intended that an elite, distant hierarchy would be put between God and His people. If you are His, then you should KNOW Him. If you do not know Him, then you are not His. Heed His voice when you hear it. No matter how surprising a place or person from which it may come. If it is His voice, then you have heard Him.

Alma 13: 26

> **"And it shall be made known unto just and holy men, by the mouth of angels, at the time of his coming, that the words of our fathers may be fulfilled, according to that which they have spoken concerning him, which was according to the spirit of prophecy which was in them."**

Here is a simple, but compound thought. Alma is saying this:

There were "fathers" who recorded words of prophecy.

The "fathers" had the "spirit of prophecy which was in them."

These words of the prophetic fathers promised that "the mouths of angels" will declare Christ's birth into the world.

The declaration of Christ's birth will come to "just and holy men" by these angels.

So, Alma is assured that the promises will be fulfilled. He knows this because the fathers who revealed the promises were trustworthy and had the spirit of prophecy.

Now comes the real question: What does it mean that "just and holy men" will be the ones to whom the angels will come and make the declaration?

Is this a description of those who hold the same priesthood as Melchizedek discussed by Alma? If so, then does access to that priestly order after the order of the Son of God put the possessors into contact with heavenly messengers? Can a person hold that authority and not receive messages from angels from time to time? Who is it among us who begins an address by referring to the angel who visited the them the preceding night?[31]

I have to assume that this is the kind of information that would be generally known among faithful followers of Christ's Gospel. After all, Alma is speaking to apostates, non-believers and critics who hold a false and abominable religion. One would expect that such things are not really so sacred that they can't be preached. Why would it be "off limits" to us and be something freely declared as part of a missionary effort in the Book of Mormon? So assuming it ought to be known, *if it is occurring*, is this among us? Where? Who has received these angelic messengers? Where are these "just and holy" men who entertain angelic ministers?

Or is it that we don't expect angels, so we don't entertain them? Perhaps they come and we don't notice them? Perhaps we are blind that we cannot see, deaf because we will not hear, and our minds are darkened because we will not abide the teachings of the Book of Mormon? What is going on with us, when we compare and measure ourselves against this message from Alma?

Should I be concerned?

Is all well?

Will we endure sound doctrine?[32]

Alma 13: 27

> **"And now, my brethren, I wish from the inmost part of my heart, yea, with great anxiety even unto pain, that ye would hearken unto my words, and cast off your sins, and not procrastinate the day of your repentance;"**

This is the reality of those who hold this holy order. They feel absolute charity toward others. It causes them "great anxiety even unto pain" to consider how others might be lost. This was exactly the same

---

[31] 2 Ne. 10: 3: "Wherefore, as I said unto you, it must needs be expedient that Christ—for in the last night the angel spake unto me that this should be his name—should come among the Jews, among those who are the more wicked part of the world; and they shall crucify him—for thus it behooveth our God, and there is none other nation on earth that would crucify their God."
3 Ne. 7: 15: "And it came to pass that Nephi—having been visited by angels and also the voice of the Lord, therefore having seen angels, and being eye-witness, and having had power given unto him that he might know concerning the ministry of Christ, and also being eye-witness to their quick return from righteousness unto their wickedness and abominations;"

[32] 2 Tim. 4: 3: "For the time will come when they will not endure sound doctrine; but after their own lusts shall they heap to themselves teachers, having itching ears;"

charity that motivated the born-again sons of Mosiah to perform their missionary labors at great personal peril.[33]

When you hear such a man after this order speaking in plain, even blunt words, it is not because they are unkind. It is not because they are uncharitable or brash. It is because they are filled with care, concern, and longing to share eternal life with those who would otherwise be lost.

Look at his words. What does it mean that Alma's motivation now comes from "the inmost part of my heart?" How is it possible that Alma can have such concern that it causes him "great anxiety even unto pain?" Why does he long so for others to "hearken unto his words?"

Is this motivation for Alma the same as he described Melchizedek having? Is the plea to "cast off your sins" the same plea which Melchizedek made to his people?

If this is the plea of both Melchizedek and Alma, and it is a burden which causes pain for fear that the mission would fail, where do we find such souls today crying repentance? Are they among us? Do we have ministers using the words of angels, declaring a message from heaven, who suffer anxiety and pain at the thought we will not repent?

Are you one of them? If you are not, then why procrastinate? Why not also join in the process? All that is required is repentance to make yourself clean, followed by keeping the word of God until you entertain angels, receive your assignment, and having been commissioned to then proclaim repentance to others.

Alma is inviting people to join the order after the Son of God, becoming thereby sons of God themselves. This is the great message of the Book of Mormon. I've discussed in six books the mysteries of godliness, using primarily the Book of Mormon as the scriptural source to explain these doctrines. It is the most correct book we have to set out these doctrines and inform us of the process. It is interesting how little of that message we've uncovered as yet.

Alma 13: 28

> **"But that ye would humble yourselves before the Lord, and call on his holy name, and watch and pray continually, that ye may not be tempted above that which ye can bear, and thus be led by the Holy Spirit, becoming humble, meek, submissive, patient, full of love and all long-suffering;"**

Alma's formula is quite direct and clear:

"Humble yourselves:" Without humility you are not teachable. Humility and the capacity to accept new truth are directly related. This is the character flaw that prevents the Lord from teaching the Nephites

---

[33] Mosiah 28: 3: "Now they were desirous that salvation should be declared to every creature, for they could not bear that any human soul should perish; yea, even the very thoughts that any soul should endure endless torment did cause them to quake and tremble."

when He appeared to them. They THOUGHT they already knew things. Therefore nothing that contradicted their false notions would be accepted. Christ advised the Nephites who saw Him descend from heaven to go prepare themselves for His teaching. "Therefore, go ye unto your homes, and ponder upon the things which I have said, and ask of the Father, in my name, that ye may understand, and prepare your minds for the morrow, and I come unto you again." (3 Ne. 17: 3.) This was the Lord telling these witnesses that they were not humble enough to be taught—even by Him! So the first requirement is no small matter. Are you really humble? Can you accept truth if it is taught to you? Even if it contradicts your traditions? Even if it alienates you from family, friends, comfortable social associations, your neighbors?[34] See, humbling yourself is not just some droop-faced, hang-dog expression to wear on your countenance. Rather it is opening your heart up to higher things.

"Call upon God:" Not just prayer. Call upon Him. To call is to invite Him to come. How do you call Him? By devoting yourself, in humility, to living every principle He has taught to you through His messengers and in His scriptures. It's not a laundry list of "to-do's." It is meekness and prayerful watching; humbling yourself and accepting what His spirit will advise you to do. When He testifies to you that you are hearing a true principle, accept it. No matter the effect it may have upon your life. Change your life, but never abandon His truths. Call, listen, and obey what you are told. Never close that line of communication. Don't trust a message which does not come from Him.

"Watch and pray:" Answers may come in many ways. Be watchful so you don't miss them when they are given to you. Pray that you might be seeking, preparing your mind to behold what He sends. Stay tuned, and stay attuned. Without such diligence you will miss His messages, that come sometimes frequently, but from unexpected sources.

"That ye may not be tempted above that which ye can bear:" Implicit in this is that you may be tempted beyond what you can bear. So how do you avoid falling? Does humility and calling upon God and watching and praying insure that you can avoid an excess of temptation? How would they all go together? In particular, how would being "humble" be a protection against this kind of temptation?

Alma connects all this together with the word: "thus." Meaning as a consequence of the foregoing. As a result of what he's just told you. As a product of this approach, you will then "be led by the Holy Spirit." You can't do what comes next without being so led. It isn't in you. Not without help from within through the Holy Spirit.

So, if you do all the above, and then acquire the Holy Spirit to be your guide, then it follows that you will "become humble, meek,

---

[34] Matt. 19: 29: "And every one that hath forsaken houses, or brethren, or sisters, or father, or mother, or wife, or children, or lands, for my name's sake, shall receive an hundredfold, and shall inherit everlasting life."

submissive, patient, full of love and all long-suffering." You won't be imitating humility, but you will be humble with the Holy Spirit's assistance. You won't feign meekness, but you will acquire the power to be meek (in the sense it is explained in *Beloved Enos*). You won't pretend to submission, patience, love and long suffering, but you will be these things as a result of the Spirit within you. This will be your character. Not as the world understands such things, but through the power of the Spirit to lay hold upon such things.

Formulas like this one are inspired statements, providing a road map to the Lord's methods of changing lives. Alma is making such a declaration and invitation in this sermon. It is amazing, really. How succinctly he cuts to the core of the matter.

Alma 13: 29

> **"Having faith on the Lord; having a hope that ye shall receive eternal life; having the love of God always in your hearts, that ye may be lifted up at the last day and enter into his rest."**

Here you have faith, hope and charity (or love). You only have a fraction of the understanding of what faith in the Lord means until you have done as Alma is explaining here. True "faith" which is a principle of power, is acquired by the method Alma is preaching.

Hope that one can receive eternal life is not the vague optimism that it might happen—it is a certitude. You have the promise. You know you will have eternal life. You haven't died and entered into the resurrected state yet. Between the time of the promise and the time you leave this sphere, you have hope. (The way it is used here is defined in *Eighteen Verses*.)

When God has promised you eternal life then you have "the love of God always in your heart." It is there through the indelible promise He has made. He has changed your status. He has declared through His own voice what great thing you have become. Therefore it is by knowledge alone that such love resides in the heart of man.

This life will end. But you will be raised up. You know when you are lifted up in the last day it will be the power of God that raises you. Such power as God employs to lift a man up confers upon such a person eternal life. The promise alone is a power, conferring the right to lay hold on eternal life when the moment comes. No power in earth or hell can rescind God's word.[35] It cannot be done. Therefore, you have knowledge that you will not only be raised from the dead, but "lifted up" as well. Powers, principalities, dominions, exaltations are all promised as yours.

---

[35] D&C 1: 38: "What I the Lord have spoken, I have spoken, and I excuse not myself; and though the heavens and the earth pass away, my word shall not pass away, but shall all be fulfilled, whether by mine own voice or by the voice of my servants, it is the same."

This is how you attain to "rest." It is the "rest of the Lord" as soon as the promise is made by Him. It is His rest when you inherit it in the last day. The words of the promise are enough to guarantee the inheritance. Therefore once the promise is made it is true enough that you have entered into the rest of the Lord. However, until you depart this life, you remain subject to the difficulties of mortality. Graduation is assured, but you must tarry for a little while here.

As one possessing this hope, being filled with faith, hope and charity, it becomes your responsibility to raise up others. Hence the ministry of Alma, and Alma's exposition on the ministry of Melchizedek. God does send true messengers. They can lead you in the way of life and salvation.

Alma 13: 30

> **"And may the Lord grant unto you repentance, that ye may not bring down his wrath upon you, that ye may not be bound down by the chains of hell, that ye may not suffer the second death."**

Alma's closing remark here is a prayer. He is asking that the Lord "grant unto you repentance." This is an interesting cause-and-effect way to state the proposition. We cause it by our desire and willingness to become humble and repent. The Lord causes it because without His atoning sacrifice it could not be done.

We receive the effect because we are cleansed by our acts, humility and willingness to accept what is offered. The Lord receives the effect because He has allowed us to join Him in being pure and holy. He acquires a brother (or, more correctly a son). But He has no jealousy, allowing His brothers/sons to sit upon His own throne.[36] He wants to have "all things in common" with us.

Alma's petition goes further to ask that the wrath of God not be poured out upon these people to whom he is preaching. There are, of course, two levels of wrath. One is temporal—here and now. The wicked are often punished here by letting them pursue their own evil course until it destroys them. Repentance in that sense relieves them of the physical, emotional, social, military, economic, and interpersonal disasters they bring upon themselves by their ruinous pursuit of destructive behavior.

The other is eternal—meaning coming after this life. That second "wrath" is a result of leaving this life with accountability for what happened here, and the lack of preparation for the moment when "judgment" is rendered. That "judgment" consists of you finally facing reality. When you are in His presence you can accurately measure the difference between what you are and what He wanted you to become—i.e., like Him. The gulf is so great that you would rather be in hell than

[36] Rev. 3: 21: "To him that overcometh will I grant to sit with me in my throne, even as I also overcame, and am set down with my Father in his throne."

in the presence of a just and holy being when you are stained with the blood and sins of your generation.[37]

I have been in the presence of President Ronald Reagan. I met with President Spencer W. Kimball at the law school at BYU when he would come to visit with his son, who was a criminal law professor there. I shook hands and spoke with Chief Justice Warren Burger for about a half hour in the law library at BYU. I have appeared at the US Supreme Court, the Utah Supreme Court, argued before Federal and State courts in Utah, Idaho, Arizona, Texas, California, Virginia, Washington DC, New York, Oregon, Nevada, Montana and New Mexico. I have seen Congress in session. Although a boy at the time, I was there when President Kennedy came to Berlin and spoke at Checkpoint Charlie, giving his *"Ich Bin Ein Berliner"* speech. I have seen many other men who have shaped history. But there simply is no comparison between these mere children, these insubstantial and powerless creatures, and the holiness, power, majesty and glory of the one True Man, clothed in light. You may see what the world reckons as a "great man" and think he was impressive. But you come from the presence of glory with only one conclusion: Surely man is nothing, which I had never before supposed.[38]

It is awful, fearful and dreadful to be in the presence of God. You realize the horror of your own darkness.[39] You cry out with the realization that you are unclean, living your life among the unclean, and

---

[37] Mormon 9: 4: "Behold, I say unto you that ye would be more miserable to dwell with a holy and just God, under a consciousness of your filthiness before him, than ye would to dwell with the damned souls in hell."

[38] Moses 1: 10: "And it came to pass that it was for the space of many hours before Moses did again receive his natural strength like unto man; and he said unto himself: Now, for this cause I know that man is nothing, which thing I never had supposed."

[39] Gen. 15: 7-18: "And he said unto him, I am the Lord that brought thee out of Ur of the Chaldees, to give thee this land to inherit it. And he said, Lord God, whereby shall I know that I shall inherit it? And he said unto him, Take me an heifer of three years old, and a she goat of three years old, and a ram of three years old, and a turtledove, and a young pigeon. And he took unto him all these, and divided them in the midst, and laid each piece one against another: but the birds divided he not. And when the fowls came down upon the carcases, Abram drove them away. And when the sun was going down, a deep sleep fell upon Abram; and, lo, an horror of great darkness fell upon him. And he said unto Abram, Know of a surety that thy seed shall be a stranger in a land that is not theirs, and shall serve them; and they shall afflict them four hundred years; And also that nation, whom they shall serve, will I judge: and afterward shall they come out with great substance. And thou shalt go to thy fathers in peace; thou shalt be buried in a good old age. But in the fourth generation they shall come hither again: for the iniquity of the Amorites is not yet full. And it came to pass, that, when the sun went down, and it was dark, behold a smoking furnace, and a burning lamp that passed between those pieces. In the same day the Lord made a covenant with Abram, saying, Unto thy seed have I given this land, from the river of Egypt unto the great river, the river Euphrates:"

you are not ready for His presence.[40] You are not prepared, and all your careful pretensions dissolve until you stand naked, revealed, hollow and unworthy to stand in His presence.

How, then, does a man stand in His presence? Through the merits and mercy and grace of this, our Lord.[41] If your mouth is unclean, He will use an ordinance to cleanse your lips.[42] If you are covered by the blood and sins of your generation, He will cleanse them.[43] If you cannot stand, He will raise you up with His own hand.[44] He is the God of mercy. Your discomfort is relieved by what He does, and this not of yourself, lest you should boast. There is nothing in you from which to

---

[40] Isa. 6: 5: "Then said I, Woe is me! for I am undone; because I am a man of unclean lips, and I dwell in the midst of a people of unclean lips: for mine eyes have seen the King, the Lord of hosts."

[41] 2 Ne. 2: 8: "Wherefore, how great the importance to make these things known unto the inhabitants of the earth, that they may know that there is no flesh that can dwell in the presence of God, save it be through the merits, and mercy, and grace of the Holy Messiah, who layeth down his life according to the flesh, and taketh it again by the power of the Spirit, that he may bring to pass the resurrection of the dead, being the first that should rise."

42 Isa. 6: 6-7: "Then flew one of the seraphims unto me, having a live coal in his hand, which he had taken with the tongs from off the altar: And he laid it upon my mouth, and said, Lo, this hath touched thy lips; and thine iniquity is taken away, and thy sin purged."

[43] John 13: 5-13: "After that he poureth water into a bason, and began to wash the disciples' feet, and to wipe them with the towel wherewith he was girded. Then cometh he to Simon Peter: and Peter saith unto him, Lord, dost thou wash my feet? Jesus answered and said unto him, What I do thou knowest not now; but thou shalt know hereafter. Peter saith unto him, Thou shalt never wash my feet. Jesus answered him, If I wash thee not, thou hast no part with me. Simon Peter saith unto him, Lord, not my feet only, but also my hands and my head. Jesus saith to him, He that is washed needeth not save to wash his feet, but is clean every whit: and ye are clean, but not all. For he knew who should betray him; therefore said he, Ye are not all clean. So after he had washed their feet, and had taken his garments, and was set down again, he said unto them, Know ye what I have done to you? Ye call me Master and Lord: and ye say well; for so I am."

[44] Dan. 10: 5-10: "Then I lifted up mine eyes, and looked, and behold a certain man clothed in linen, whose loins were girded with fine gold of Uphaz: His body also was like the beryl, and his face as the appearance of lightning, and his eyes as lamps of fire, and his arms and his feet like in colour to polished brass, and the voice of his words like the voice of a multitude. And I Daniel alone saw the vision: for the men that were with me saw not the vision; but a great quaking fell upon them, so that they fled to hide themselves. Therefore I was left alone, and saw this great vision, and there remained no strength in me: for my comeliness was turned in me into corruption, and I retained no strength. Yet heard I the voice of his words: and when I heard the voice of his words, then was I in a deep sleep on my face, and my face toward the ground. 10 And, behold, an hand touched me, which set me upon my knees and upon the palms of my hands."

boast other than the merit and mercy and love and sacrifice given to you by Him.

How can He love so? It defies explanation. Words fail. You can search your lifetime through every word you have ever seen or heard—nothing comes close to being able to describe it. It cannot be spoken… Too sacred for language to capture. Beyond our power. So, you are left saying only: "Come, see."

How, then, can a man come to the judgment and not feel the wrath which they might have overcome by His grace and mercy? Through the merits of Him bestowing upon a man the power to stand in His presence.

Alma's pain at the thought of these people perishing was real. He was powerless to bring them to Christ. That power consists only in the authorized and truthful declaration of an invitation to come to Him. But the choice remained in those who, having heard, must decide for themselves whether they will repent. They were free to choose iniquity and abominations. Alma was only able to invite.

The invitation, if rejected, will cause those who die to die yet again. The way is broad which leads to such eternal deaths.[45]

Alma 13: 31

> **"And Alma spake many more words unto the people, which are not written in this book."**

This is often the case. John's Gospel ended with this observation:

"And there are also many other things which Jesus did, the which, if they should be written every one, I suppose that even the world itself could not contain the books that should be written." (John 21: 25.) Records are incomplete. We do not have the full account of Christ's acts and words. We don't have Alma's either.

Mormon was the editor of this portion of the Book of Mormon. He was the one who determined to omit portions what Alma said to these people on this occasion. From what Mormon left for us to read, his intent is clear. He wanted us to understand the bigger picture of God's dealings with man, man's possession of priestly power, and the importance of repentance and defeating religious error. Mormon had seen us, and included specific warnings addressed to us, the Gentiles. He cautioned us about the Book of Mormon as follows:

"And then, O ye Gentiles, how can ye stand before the power of God, except ye shall repent and turn from your evil ways? Know ye not that ye are in the hands of God? Know ye not that he hath all power, and at his great command the earth shall be rolled together as a scroll? Therefore, repent ye, and humble yourselves before him, lest he shall

---

[45] D&C 132: 25: "Broad is the gate, and wide the way that leadeth to the deaths; and many there are that go in thereat, because they receive me not, neither do they abide in my law."

come out in justice against you—lest a remnant of the seed of Jacob shall go forth among you as a lion, and tear you in pieces, and there is none to deliver."[46]

Mormon knew the book would initially be in the hands of the Gentiles. So you can know we are identified as "Gentiles" in the Book of Mormon. Also, Joseph Smith declared in the dedicatory prayer for the Kirtland Temple that we are identified with the Gentiles.[47] Although Brigham Young and President Joseph Fielding Smith taught that Joseph was a "pure blooded Ephraimite." (Doctrines of Salvation, Vol 3: 253-54.)

The selected materials that Mormon gave to us were targeted to the purpose of the Book of Mormon. The title page (written by Moroni) tells us the purpose: "Written to the Lamanites, who are a remnant of the house of Israel; and also to Jew and Gentile—Written by way of commandment, and also by the spirit of prophecy and of revelation—Written and sealed up, and hid up unto the Lord, that they might not be destroyed—To come forth by the gift and power of God unto the interpretation thereof—Sealed by the hand of Moroni, and hid up unto the Lord, to come forth in due time by way of the Gentile."

Gentiles would receive, translate and disseminate the Book of Mormon. But the Gentiles are prophesied to fail in their faith. They are to become full of their own abominations. When they reject the fullness of the Gospel, then it will be taken from them and given back to the remnant.[48]

---

[46] Mormon 5: 22-24: "And then, O ye Gentiles, how can ye stand before the power of God, except ye shall repent and turn from your evil ways? Know ye not that ye are in the hands of God? Know ye not that he hath all power, and at his great command the earth shall be rolled together as a scroll? Therefore, repent ye, and humble yourselves before him, lest he shall come out in justice against you—lest a remnant of the seed of Jacob shall go forth among you as a lion, and tear you in pieces, and there is none to deliver."

[47] D&C 109: 59-60: "We ask thee to appoint unto Zion other stakes besides this one which thou hast appointed, that the gathering of thy people may roll on in great power and majesty, that thy work may be cut short in righteousness. Now these words, O Lord, we have spoken before thee, concerning the revelations and commandments which thou hast given unto us, who are identified with the Gentiles."

[48] 3 Ne. 16: 10-11: "And thus commandeth the Father that I should say unto you: At that day when the Gentiles shall sin against my gospel, and shall reject the fulness of my gospel, and shall be lifted up in the pride of their hearts above all nations, and above all the people of the whole earth, and shall be filled with all manner of lyings, and of deceits, and of mischiefs, and all manner of hypocrisy, and murders, and priestcrafts, and whoredoms, and of secret abominations; and if they shall do all those things, and shall reject the fulness of my gospel, behold, saith the Father, I will bring the fulness of my gospel from among them. And then will I remember my covenant which I have made unto my people, O house of Israel, and I will bring my gospel unto them."

Mormon is using the message from Alma to provide to the Gentiles (who will reject the invitation), an opportunity to understand the fullness which was offered to them. It was intended to remove from them the excuse that they were not given an opportunity and did not understand. Therefore, the Book of Mormon's primary purpose, to make the Gentiles aware and accountable for their failure, is accomplished by Mormon including this portion of Alma's teachings. The fact that other portions were left out mean that they would not have contributed to the task before Mormon.

A few of the Gentiles happily may be numbered with the remnant.[49] That is conditioned upon their repentance. The degree and completion of that repentance is shown by this portion of the sermon by Alma which Mormon preserved for us.

We are on notice. We are accountable for how we react to that notice. For the most part, the expectation is that we tell one another in reassuring words that "all is well." and that "Zion prospers," and to generally allow our souls to be cheated while we are led carefully down to hell.[50] Still, some few will follow Christ, despite the leaders' teachings that will cause them to err.[51]

The Book of Mormon is a record that will be used as evidence we have been warned. In plain language and with sufficient truth to hold us all accountable, this is the standard by which we are to find our way back to the Lord in this last dispensation before His return. We remain, of course, under condemnation because we are unwilling to do that.[52]

What a great and terrible book. What an alarming message. It is no wonder we neglect it so.

---

[49] 3 Ne. 16: 13: "But if the Gentiles will repent and return unto me, saith the Father, behold they shall be numbered among my people, O house of Israel."

[50] 2 Ne. 28: 21-25: "And others will he pacify, and lull them away into carnal security, that they will say: All is well in Zion; yea, Zion prospereth, all is well—and thus the devil cheateth their souls, and leadeth them away carefully down to hell. And behold, others he flattereth away, and telleth them there is no hell; and he saith unto them: I am no devil, for there is none—and thus he whispereth in their ears, until he grasps them with his awful chains, from whence there is no deliverance. Yea, they are grasped with death, and hell; and death, and hell, and the devil, and all that have been seized therewith must stand before the throne of God, and be judged according to their works, from whence they must go into the place prepared for them, even a lake of fire and brimstone, which is endless torment. Therefore, wo be unto him that is at ease in Zion! Wo be unto him that crieth: All is well!"

[51] 2 Ne. 28: 14: "They wear stiff necks and high heads; yea, and because of pride, and wickedness, and abominations, and whoredoms, they have all gone astray save it be a few, who are the humble followers of Christ; nevertheless, they are led, that in many instances they do err because they are taught by the precepts of men."

[52] D&C 84: 57: "And they shall remain under this condemnation until they repent and remember the new covenant, even the Book of Mormon and the former commandments which I have given them, not only to say, but to do according to that which I have written—"

3 NEPHI 16

3 Nephi 16: 7

> **"Behold, because of their belief in me, saith the Father, and because of the unbelief of you, O house of Israel, in the latter day shall the truth come unto the Gentiles, that the fulness of these things shall be made known unto them."**

This is a teaching from the first day of Christ's visit with the Nephites. It is a quote from Christ.

The time frame in which the Gentiles were to have "belief in [Christ,]" and merit a special blessing as a result, was the time immediately following the Judean ministry. The Gospel would be taken to the Gentiles and they would believe. The Jews were going to reject Him and oppose His faith, the Gentiles would welcome it and have belief.

Now the words Christ spoke and Nephi's record preserved were from "the Father." Christ's explanation of these prophecies originate with His Father.

Gentiles will believe. Moreover, the "house of Israel" will not believe in Him. The result of that acceptance and rejection is the juxtaposition of the roles of Gentiles and Israel.

Whereas, the Gospel came to the Jews first, and by the Jews it was transmitted to the Gentiles, later the opposite will occur. The pattern will reverse. It will go from the last back to the first. (It is an historic chiasm.)

Accordingly, the Gentiles will be the ones to whom the restoration of the "fullness" will come in the latter day. The reward for earlier faithfulness is later recognition and reward.

Now, it should take no amount of brilliant insight to realize that the restoration involved Joseph Smith. A man of English descent. May have some Israelite blood in him from the earlier Diaspora of the Lost Ten Tribes, but he is nevertheless the one through whom the restoration was brought. He is necessarily identified as a "Gentile" in this prophecy by Christ, given by the Father. If Joseph Smith is NOT a Gentile, then the whole promise of the Father and word of the Son is defeated. Therefore, you may know for a surety that the Gentiles are not those nasty non-members. It is US. WE are the Gentiles who receive the first offer in the last offering.

The "others" (nonLDS) are not necessarily a focus for the Book of Mormon prophecies. They inherit the blessing of being here, as Nephi foresaw. They are blessed to be on the land, but they are not given anything other than a conditional possession. They are those who get offered the restored Gospel when it returned, and if they accept it they become part of the prophetic subject. When, however, they reject the offered restoration, then they are background and will be swept away just as the Saints who reject the fullness of the Gospel will be swept away.

So it was that the Father determined and Christ taught that the Gentiles would be the ones to whom the Gospel message would first come in our day. Now we have it. (Or had it anyway.)

This movement from Israel to Gentile and from Gentile to Israel is evening the playing field. This is balancing out the record of history. It is not that one is more favored than another. Rather it is that each one will have a suitable turn and opportunity to receive what the Lord offers. In the end, no people will be able to say the opportunities were unfair, unequal, or more challenging for one than for another. [I leave it to you to determine why that is so when lives come and go across generations and one dispensation may include different people than another. It raises the question as to how certain we should be about some of our premises. That, however, is too far afield at the moment. And it may not matter anyway. Today is the day of salvation, not yesterday or tomorrow. So we should confine ourselves to solving the problem we face at the moment.]

The promise is that the "fullness of these things" will come to the Gentiles. What things? What does it mean that the "fullness" will be coming to the Gentiles? Have the Gentiles in fact received it?

If we received it, what have we done with it? Do we still have it? If not, how do I know that? What will happen if we have not retained that fullness?

Fortunately for us, Christ will answer all those questions as He moves along in the message He delivers here.

3 Nephi 16: 8

> **"But wo, saith the Father, unto the unbelieving of the Gentiles—for notwithstanding they have come forth upon the face of this land, and have scattered my people who are of the house of Israel; and my people who are of the house of Israel have been cast out from among them, and have been trodden under feet by them;"**

So now the time frame is the latter day when the Gentiles have been given this restoration of the fullness. This comment moves forward from the reasons of the restoration to the Gentiles (earlier faithfulness) to the time when the Gentiles have received the fullness.

To make the time frame abundantly clear to both the Nephites and to us, the Lord explains in passing that the Gentiles will come to "this land." The full description of them coming is set out in the earlier prophecy of Nephi as set out at length in 1 Nephi 13 & 14. But here Christ reminds the audience that when the Gentiles come, they will "scatter my people who are of the house of Israel."

Gentiles certainly did come. They did scatter the remnants who were on the American continent. Not only did they scatter them, but they also "cast out" and "trodden down" those populations who were here when the Gentiles arrived. Smallpox wiped out the Great Plains Indians. There were an estimated 20 million plus Plains Indians when Columbus arrived. Smallpox all but annihilated them. So few survived that by the time of the western push of the United States, it was believed the Great Plains had never been populated.

To say they were "trodden underfoot" is descriptive. The native populations were destroyed. They were conquered. They died. Their remains returned to the earth upon which the Gentiles trod.

You must keep this image in mind as you read about the future of the Gentiles being trodden underfoot. We will get to that later in this same prophecy by Christ.

"Wo" is pronounced upon those Gentiles who are 'unbelieving' toward the Gospel. This is confirmed again in Section 76, describing those who are Telestial. They are religious, and follow even true messengers. However, they follow, believe in, trust and hope for salvation from the messenger, but fail to have faith, believe in, trust and receive salvation through Christ. They even claim to follow Christ. But they fall short of having a saving testimony of Him. It warns: "And the glory of the telestial is one, even as the glory of the stars is one; for as one star differs from another star in glory, even so differs one from another in glory in the telestial world; For these are they who are of Paul, and of Apollos, and of Cephas. These are they who say they are some of one and some of another—some of Christ and some of John, and some of Moses, and some of Elias, and some of Esaias, and some of Isaiah, and some of Enoch; But received not the gospel, neither the testimony of Jesus, neither the prophets, neither the everlasting covenant."[53]

---

[53] D&C 76: 98-101: "And the glory of the telestial is one, even as the glory of the stars is one; for as one star differs from another star in glory, even so differs one from another in glory in the telestial world; For these are they who are of Paul, and of Apollos, and of Cephas. These are they who say they are some of one and some of another—some of Christ and some of John, and some of Moses, and some of Elias, and some of Esaias, and some of Isaiah, and some of Enoch; But received not the gospel, neither the testimony of Jesus, neither the prophets, neither the everlasting covenant."

There is a great gulf between those who claim they follow Christ and those who receive the "testimony of Jesus." There is a difference between claiming to follow a recognized authority such as Paul, Apollos, Cephas, Moses, Elias, Esaias, Isaiah, John or Enoch on the one hand and "receiving the prophets" on the other.

How easy it is to quote a dead prophet. How unlikely it always is to recognize a living one.

What is meant then by saying "they are of Christ" on the one hand, and saying, "receive not the Gospel, neither the testimony of Jesus?" on the other. How do you reconcile these two things? One damns to the Telestial Kingdom, the other exalts.

How perilous it is for the latter day Gentiles!

3 Nephi 16: 9

> **"And because of the mercies of the Father unto the Gentiles, and also the judgments of the Father upon my people who are of the house of Israel, verily, verily, I say unto you, that after all this, and I have caused my people who are of the house of Israel to be smitten, and to be afflicted, and to be slain, and to be cast out from among them, and to become hated by them, and to become a hiss and a byword among them—"**

Notice once again the Lord's motivation for speaking these words: The Father's "mercies" and the Father's "judgments" are what drives the coming events in history. The Father is in control and Christ does not question or gainsay the results. The Father's mercy is not questioned by Christ, nor is there any degree of shame shown for the terrible circumstances which follow from His "mercies." Nor does Christ hesitate to announce the Father's "judgments" despite the anxiety which some may feel at hearing the future.

Truth should be delivered in a forthright and plain manner, whether the result is fearful or vindicating; whether you take joy in the news or you cower at what is to come.

Notice, however, that when the Father's judgment has been given, then the Lord assumes personal responsibility for the punishment to be inflicted. He does not say it is the Father's punishment. It is His own. Christ will personally be the one who "caused my people who are of the house of Israel to be smitten." Christ will personally "afflict" and "slay" the people. The Father decides, Christ fulfills. He seeks no cover, looks to no-one else to be held to account, He does as His Father judges.

Why would Christ assume responsibility to "smite" to "afflict" and to "slay" when it is the Father's judgment?

What does this tell us about Christ's acceptance of the Father's decisions?

Is (or has) there been some good result from those whom Christ calls "my people" (i.e., His people) being smitten, afflicted, slain, and cast out by the Gentiles? If so, what good has come to the Lord's people?

How can these things that have lasted now for over two hundred years have been beneficial to the Lord's people? What can we learn about the Lord calling afflicted, smitten and outcast people as "His people" despite their centuries of subordination?

What does the Gentile "hatred" of the Lord's people do to diminish the Lord's plans for them? What does casting them out and making them a "hiss and a byword" by the Gentiles do to remove the Lord's promised blessing and covenant to "His people?"

What foolish pride allows Gentiles to measure the Lord's people as stricken, smitten of God and afflicted?[54]

Why would the Gentiles be put in this position? Why would Israel? What does it do to the Gentiles' ability to see through the deception of their time into truth which is timeless?[55]

How should the Gentiles view their momentary triumph and unchallenged possession of the land promised to others?

Why are those smitten and afflicted called by the Lord "my people" and the Gentiles referred to as "Gentiles?"

Is the irony of this beginning to dawn on you? Maybe you should re-read the title page of the Book of Mormon.[56]

3 Nephi 16: 10

> **"And thus commandeth the Father that I should say unto you: At that day when the Gentiles shall sin against my gospel, and shall reject the fulness of my gospel, and shall be lifted up in the pride of their hearts above all nations, and above all the people of the whole earth, and shall be filled with all manner of lyings,**

---

[54] Isa. 53: 4: "Surely he hath borne our griefs, and carried our sorrows: yet we did esteem him stricken, smitten of God, and afflicted."

[55] D&C 93: 24: "And truth is knowledge of things as they are, and as they were, and as they are to come;"

[56] Title Page of the Book of Mormon: "Wherefore, it is an abridgment of the record of the people of Nephi, and also of the Lamanites—Written to the Lamanites, who are a remnant of the house of Israel; and also to Jew and Gentile—Written by way of commandment, and also by the spirit of prophecy and of revelation—Written and sealed up, and hid up unto the Lord, that they might not be destroyed—To come forth by the gift and power of God unto the interpretation thereof—Sealed by the hand of Moroni, and hid up unto the Lord, to come forth in due time by way of the Gentile—The interpretation thereof by the gift of God. An abridgment taken from the Book of Ether also, which is a record of the people of Jared, who were scattered at the time the Lord confounded the language of the people, when they were building a tower to get to heaven—Which is to show unto the remnant of the House of Israel what great things the Lord hath done for their fathers; and that they may know the covenants of the Lord, that they are not cast off forever—And also to the convincing of the Jew and Gentile that Jesus is the Christ, the Eternal God, manifesting himself unto all nations—And now, if there are faults they are the mistakes of men; wherefore, condemn not the things of God, that ye may be found spotless at the judgment-seat of Christ."

> **and of deceits, and of mischiefs, and all manner of hypocrisy, and murders, and priestcrafts, and whoredoms, and of secret abominations; and if they shall do all those things, and shall reject the fulness of my gospel, behold, saith the Father, I will bring the fulness of my gospel from among them."**

These words come from the Father.

The Father has commanded Christ to speak them.

This material is important to understand.

"At the day when the Gentiles shall sin against the Gospel..." Not IF. Not SHOULD THEY HAPPEN TO DO SO. It is in the day WHEN the Gentiles SHALL sin against the Gospel.

The Father has already seen this happen.[57] He has told Christ to speak about it. But it is before the Father and therefore He can speak with knowledge of the coming rejection by the Gentiles.

What do the Gentiles do as they reject the Gospel? They *"shall be lifted up in the pride of their hearts above all nations... above all the people of the whole earth."* Read again the prior post. The Gentiles take their inheritance of the promised land as their birthright. They presume God's favor. They mistake their probation and testing as proof of having God's favor. They are on trial, and presume they aren't being tested.

What, then, do the Gentiles do with their highly favored status? The list is sobering:

- Lyings

- Deceits

- Mischiefs

- All manner of hypocrisy

- Murders

- Priestcrafts

- Whoredoms

- Secret combinations

Read the list and contemplate how much of this is among us. If we do not murder, do we delight in bloodshed? Are we warlike? Are there people whom we kill daily somewhere in the world to project our national will and great power?

Notice that hypocrisy leads to murder. Murder leads to priestcrafts. Priestcrafts lead to whoredoms. Are we seeing a progression here? By the time we have whoredoms, have we already passed through murders and priestcrafts?

---

[57] D&C 130: 7: "But they reside in the presence of God, on a globe like a sea of glass and fire, where all things for their glory are manifest, past, present, and future, and are continually before the Lord."

What are priestcrafts?[58] What does it mean to seek the welfare of Zion? Is "Zion" the same thing as the institutional church? What is the difference? Can a person seek the welfare of Zion without seeking to succeed inside the institutional church? What is the difference between seeking to be a "light unto the world," on the one hand, and seeking the welfare of Zion, on the other? Can one seek to be a light pointing to Zion, and never be a "light unto the world?" What is the world? What is Zion? How are they different? Can one who seeks the welfare of Zion ever get praise from the world? Can a person curry favor with the world while also seeking to benefit Zion?

If not hiring a whore, do we nonetheless watch with delight the portrayal of sexual license to entertain us, fill our thoughts, satisfy our lusts? Do you need to hire a prostitute to be practicing "whoredoms?" Utah is one of the largest consumers of pornography in the US. Hence, the continual return to this subject in General Conference.

When they do this, in turn the Gentiles will "reject the fullness of my Gospel." To reject the fullness is not to reject the Gospel itself. As we have seen, some fragment of the Gospel remains even when it has turned into "iniquity" and "abomination." Without some fractured segment of the Gospel to salve the conscious and let the people feel good about their sins, there couldn't be "abominations."

It is not the "Gospel" which is lost. Rather it is the "fullness of my Gospel" which is rejected and then taken away. It is first rejected, then it is forfeited. The Gentiles lose their entitlement to possess what they have rejected.

The Father has decreed it will happen. The Gentiles will change the ordinance and break the everlasting covenant.[59] What ordinance? What change? Has it happened? If not, what will be required to make a change and lose the "everlasting covenant" by the Gentiles? I hope to avoid that.

3 Nephi 16: 11

> **"And then will I remember my covenant which I have made unto my people, O house of Israel, and I will bring my gospel unto them."**

When the Gentiles have rejected the fullness of the Gospel, the Lord's memory will be stirred. He will "remember His covenant" again.

Notice the covenant He will remember is for "His people," whose interests and inheritance will now be vindicated. His words will be

---

[58] 2 Ne. 26: 29: "He commandeth that there shall be no priestcrafts; for, behold, priestcrafts are that men preach and set themselves up for a light unto the world, that they may get gain and praise of the world; but they seek not the welfare of Zion."

[59] Isa. 24: 5: "The earth also is defiled under the inhabitants thereof; because they have transgressed the laws, changed the ordinance, broken the everlasting covenant."

fulfilled. The Father's promises will all be realized. But "His people" are not the Gentiles. His people are the remnant to whom the Gospel will come as a matter of covenant and inheritance to reclaim a fallen people. This is the re-grafting of the natural branches referred to in Jacob 5: 67-75.[60] It is important to note that the Lord of the vineyard was directly involved with the few servants assigned to accomplish this final work of gathering together.[61]

This is to be done after the Gentiles (who are the European Latter-day Saints who descend from the bloodlines that overran and dispossessed the native people in North America), have rejected the fullness of the Gospel. Therefore, you should not expect that the institutional church, controlled as it is by those very same bloodlines, will be the means through which this final effort will be accomplished.

When the time comes, the Lord will "bring [His] gospel to them." How will He do this? What "laborers" should we expect to be sent?

---

[60] Jacob 5: 67-75: "And the branches of the natural tree will I graft in again into the natural tree; And the branches of the natural tree will I graft into the natural branches of the tree; and thus will I bring them together again, that they shall bring forth the natural fruit, and they shall be one. And the bad shall be cast away, yea, even out of all the land of my vineyard; for behold, only this once will I prune my vineyard. And it came to pass that the Lord of the vineyard sent his servant; and the servant went and did as the Lord had commanded him, and brought other servants; and they were few. And the Lord of the vineyard said unto them: Go to, and labor in the vineyard, with your might. For behold, this is the last time that I shall nourish my vineyard; for the end is nigh at hand, and the season speedily cometh; and if ye labor with your might with me ye shall have joy in the fruit which I shall lay up unto myself against the time which will soon come. And it came to pass that the servants did go and labor with their mights; and the Lord of the vineyard labored also with them; and they did obey the commandments of the Lord of the vineyard in all things. And there began to be the natural fruit again in the vineyard; and the natural branches began to grow and thrive exceedingly; and the wild branches began to be plucked off and to be cast away; and they did keep the root and the top thereof equal, according to the strength thereof. And thus they labored, with all diligence, according to the commandments of the Lord of the vineyard, even until the bad had been cast away out of the vineyard, and the Lord had preserved unto himself that the trees had become again the natural fruit; and they became like unto one body; and the fruits were equal; and the Lord of the vineyard had preserved unto himself the natural fruit, which was most precious unto him from the beginning. And it came to pass that when the Lord of the vineyard saw that his fruit was good, and that his vineyard was no more corrupt, he called up his servants, and said unto them: Behold, for this last time have we nourished my vineyard; and thou beholdest that I have done according to my will; and I have preserved the natural fruit, that it is good, even like as it was in the beginning. And blessed art thou; for because ye have been diligent in laboring with me in my vineyard, and have kept my commandments, and have brought unto me again the natural fruit, that my vineyard is no more corrupted, and the bad is cast away, behold ye shall have joy with me because of the fruit of my vineyard."

[61] Jacob 5: 72: "And it came to pass that the servants did go and labor with their mights; and the Lord of the vineyard labored also with them; and they did obey the commandments of the Lord of the vineyard in all things."

How, if the Gentiles have rejected the fullness of His Gospel, will the Gentiles be involved?

Can Gentiles who are lifted up in the pride of their hearts above all nations of the earth assist? If not, then what Gentiles can assist?

Isn't Ephraim to be involved? After all, they have the birthright. Are they not involved?

If they are, who will it be from among Ephraim?

How can the remnant to whom these blessings are promised, have still among them a few descendants of Ephraim? Why will Manassah, through the remnant, build the New Jerusalem, yet it will be Ephraim through whom the blessings are conferred upon the returning Lost Tribes?[62]

How can the New Jerusalem be the property of the remnant, but there be a group of Ephraimite who bestow crowns? What must these Ephraimite possess to be able to accomplish this task? How can they possess it and not be lifted up in pride above all other people of the whole earth? How can such power be put upon some group and they remain willing to ever bend the knee and confess before Him whose right it is to rule?

How can the Gentiles both reject the fullness of the Gospel, yet there be some who are of Ephraim who are able to bestow crowns?

What an interesting picture begins to emerge. Gentile rejection, but a tiny group of Ephraimite servants whose lives are lived so as to bestow blessings upon others.

The main body in the New Jerusalem coming from the remnant, who are to build the City of the New Jerusalem, yet within that City a functioning group of Ephraimites who will crown others with glory. All this preparatory to the Lord's return to a City set upon a hill which cannot be hid. To a location in the tops of the everlasting mountains, where all will gather from every nation.

Well, let's keep going to see how much we can figure out from the scriptures to correct our foolish traditions about these future roles and perhaps gain an even better idea of locations.

---

[62] D&C 133: 26-34: "And they who are in the north countries shall come in remembrance before the Lord; and their prophets shall hear his voice, and shall no longer stay themselves; and they shall smite the rocks, and the ice shall flow down at their presence. And an highway shall be cast up in the midst of the great deep. Their enemies shall become a prey unto them, And in the barren deserts there shall come forth pools of living water; and the parched ground shall no longer be a thirsty land. And they shall bring forth their rich treasures unto the children of Ephraim, my servants. And the boundaries of the everlasting hills shall tremble at their presence. And there shall they fall down and be crowned with glory, even in Zion, by the hands of the servants of the Lord, even the children of Ephraim. And they shall be filled with songs of everlasting joy. Behold, this is the blessing of the everlasting God upon the tribes of Israel, and the richer blessing upon the head of Ephraim and his fellows."

The relative size is referred to by the Lord in a number of places where He contrasts the "few there be who find it" with the "many who go in thereat." He also uses the parable of wise and foolish virgins. I take the meaning of "virgin" who are attired in wedding garments and have both oil and lamps to mean those who have: 1) been endowed; 2) been sealed; 3) come into possession of both oil and a lamp—meaning the Spirit has visited with them and they have shown its fruits at some point in their lives. From this group half will be unprepared at His coming and kept from the wedding feast.

There are others, and perhaps a post would be better than a comment. But the point is not to discourage anyone. It is to make us take a sober inventory of our lives and what we do with the Gospel we've been given. Are we taking it seriously enough? Do we do what we can to follow Him? Are we safely aboard, or yet in peril? If aboard, are we crying repentance and warning our neighbor? Do we really love Him? Do we love His children?

Whether the Church's leadership is or is not going to lead us there remains an open question. As with all things, they and we are free to choose. But their choice should not affect yours, or mine.

3 Nephi 16: 12

> **"And I will show unto thee, O house of Israel, that the Gentiles shall not have power over you; but I will remember my covenant unto you, O house of Israel, and ye shall come unto the knowledge of the fulness of my gospel."**

Gentiles shall NOT have power over Israel. Gentiles, filled with pride, claiming to hold the power of God, sitting in the Temple of God and acting as if they were God, will lose their grip.[63] They will be cast down like Lucifer, after claiming they would sit in the congregations of the north, like the Gods.[64]

---

[63] 2 Thes. 2: 2-4: "That ye be not soon shaken in mind, or be troubled, neither by spirit, nor by word, nor by letter as from us, as that the day of Christ is at hand. Let no man deceive you by any means: for that day shall not come, except there come a falling away first, and that man of sin be revealed, the son of perdition; Who opposeth and exalteth himself above all that is called God, or that is worshipped; so that he as God sitteth in the temple of God, shewing himself that he is God."

[64] Isa. 14: 13-15: "For thou hast said in thine heart, I will ascend into heaven, I will exalt my throne above the stars of God: I will sit also upon the mount of the congregation, in the sides of the north: I will ascend above the heights of the clouds; I will be like the most High. Yet thou shalt be brought down to hell, to the sides of the pit."

These Gentiles will not have "power" over the house of Israel, though they may claim to possess great authority.[65] What, then, is the difference between the Gentiles lacking "power," but holding authority?

How will the Lord remember the covenant?

What does it mean to come to "the knowledge" of something, rather than to start believing in something?

What does it mean to have the "fulness of [His] Gospel?"

What does "knowledge... of the fulness" imply about the degree to which it will be revealed as part of remembering the covenant?

Why is the Gentile rejection of the fullness tied to the house of Israel receiving the fullness?

Are the basic Gospel Principles the same as the fullness? If not, what is the difference? What do the Gentiles risk when they reject the fullness and focus instead upon the basic principles?

How perilous is it for the Gentiles to suppress the mysteries of godliness and retain only the most basic of doctrines as their focus?

Unto whom is the Lord to teach doctrine? Who is prepared to hear? Are they necessarily to be first weaned from milk and prepared to understand meat?[66] If that is so, then what do we need to do to wean ourselves off the milk and be prepared to receive weighter matters?

When will these things be? How will you know when the spirit begins to withdraw from the Gentiles and blessings begin to be poured out on others of the house of Israel?

3 Nephi 16: 13-14

> **"But if the Gentiles will repent and return unto me, saith the Father, behold they shall be numbered among my people, O house of Israel. And I will not suffer my people, who are of the house of Israel, to go through among them, and tread them down, saith the Father."**

Here Gentiles are given hope. Although as a group, they will fall away and reject the fullness, if there are any among them who "repent and return" they may still be numbered among those who are the Lord's

---

[65] D&C 121: 36-37: "That the rights of the priesthood are inseparably connected with the powers of heaven, and that the powers of heaven cannot be controlled nor handled only upon the principles of righteousness. That they may be conferred upon us, it is true; but when we undertake to cover our sins, or to gratify our pride, our vain ambition, or to exercise control or dominion or compulsion upon the souls of the children of men, in any degree of unrighteousness, behold, the heavens withdraw themselves; the Spirit of the Lord is grieved; and when it is withdrawn, Amen to the priesthood or the authority of that man."

[66] Isa. 28: 9-10: "Whom shall he teach knowledge? and whom shall he make to understand doctrine? them that are weaned from the milk, and drawn from the breasts. For precept must be upon precept, precept upon precept; line upon line, line upon line; here a little, and there a little"

people. Those whom He calls "my people." Those dear to Him by covenant and promise.

The few who do will be required to "repent and return." Why do they need to "repent?" Why do they need to "return?" What have they been doing that will require this "repentance" and "return?"

Does it mean they will not remain in the way, but will have been led out of it? Will they necessarily have to abandon the abominations, or false beliefs, which have become part of their religious traditions?

Where did these false religious ideas arise? If the Gentiles inherit the fullness of the Gospel, then reject the fullness, what did they first receive? What did they do with what they received?

How can some few still persist and be numbered among the house of Israel? What must those who "repent and return" accomplish? How will they be able to accomplish this?

Nephi had described these "few" earlier in a prophecy about our day in 2 Nephi 28: 14: "They wear stiff necks and high heads; yea, and because of pride, and wickedness, and abominations, and whoredoms, they have all gone astray save it be a few, who are the humble followers of Christ; nevertheless, they are led, that in many instances they do err because they are taught by the precepts of men."

What does it mean to have "all gone astray?" Does "all" truly mean "all?" How can a "few, who are the humble followers of Christ" exist? Do these "few" "nevertheless err?"

What causes the "few" to err? What does it mean that they are "led, that in many instances they do err?" What does it mean to be "taught by the precepts of men?" Wasn't that the very problem that provoked the Restoration in the first place? Weren't men teaching for doctrines the commandments of men? Did that produce only a form of godliness, which had no power?[67]

Those who "repent and return" will be spared from being trodden down and torn up. Others of the Gentiles, who do not "repent and return" are destined, like the original inhabitants of this land, to be trodden down and torn up. Their inheritance here is probationary. If they fail the probation, they will be swept away. The Gentiles will be gone, just as the earlier civilizations are gone. It will be the Father's doing.

3 Nephi 16: 15

"But if they will not turn unto me, and hearken unto my voice, I will suffer them, yea, I will suffer my people, O house of Israel,

---

[67] JS-H 1: 19: "I was answered that I must join none of them, for they were all wrong; and the Personage who addressed me said that all their creeds were an abomination in his sight; that those professors were all corrupt; that: 'they draw near to me with their lips, but their hearts are far from me, they teach for doctrines the commandments of men, having a form of godliness, but they deny the power thereof.'"

> **that they shall go through among them, and shall tread them down, and they shall be as salt that hath lost its savor, which is thenceforth good for nothing but to be cast out, and to be trodden under foot of my people, O house of Israel."**

The Gentiles, to whom the restoration of the Gospel came, will fail to repent and return to the Lord, and will doom themselves to destruction.

The land reverts back to those to whom it was originally promised. They, the rightful heirs, will "go through among them, and shall tread them down." What does it mean to be "tread down?"

When salt has lost its savor, it becomes useless. The preservative has become a contaminant. The corruption, the abominable religion, is worse than what they were before inheriting the fullness of the Gospel. They have sinned against a greater light. And in the process they have rejected the Greatest Light of all.

What did the Gentiles do to become salt without savor? Why are they good for nothing but to be cast out? Why is it appropriate that the Gentiles who previously cast out and trod down previous inheritors should now be trodden down? What did the earlier heirs do to merit destruction at the hands of the Gentiles? How does the cycle seem to repeat itself in the actions of both of these peoples?

Why do the trodden down peoples, who were the first heirs, remain the "Lord's people" even when they have been dispossessed of the land and destroyed by the Gentiles? Why are the first to become the last, and the last to become the first? Why do such cycles of history repeat themselves? Why is the Book of Mormon unable to help the Gentiles avoid this cycle of destruction? Was the Book of Mormon intended to help the Gentiles avoid their fate? What did the Gentiles do with the Book of Mormon instead of using it as a guide to avoid destruction?

These prophecies are spoken by Christ, but ordained by the Father. What does it tell us about the Father's involvement with this unfolding history? How does the "foot of my people" reflect symbolically upon the process of destruction? If the Gentiles have rejected the fullness of the Lord's Gospel, but the feet of those who cry peace are beautiful upon the mountains, why do the one people get trodden and the others tread upon them? Why are clean feet preserved and the filthy cast out and trodden down?

How serious a matter is this Gospel? How should we conduct ourselves toward the Gospel? What is the Gospel's fullness?

This becomes more than interesting; it is gripping.

3 Nephi 16: 16

> **"Verily, verily, I say unto you, thus hath the Father commanded me—that I should give unto this people this land for their inheritance."**

As a result of the their behavior, the Gentiles forfeit the land. The ones who inherit the land will be "this people" or the ones to whom Christ was speaking. The land will belong to the remnant—those who were standing before Christ at the time of this address.

Now, the actual inheritors will not be those people, but those who claim the right as descendants through their fathers. It will not, and cannot be the Gentiles. There were no European migrants in the audience when Christ spoke on this occasion.

We need to know who "this people" is to know who will inherit the land.

We also need to know what "this land" was to be able to know if the Gentiles who inherited the "land of liberty"[68] which would "never fall into captivity except for wickedness" was North America.[69] Hence the relevance of knowing the location of the Book of Mormon lands.

That is such a side-track that I hesitate to even revisit the subject. I will only add that there are arguments for both North American and Central America. I think the better argument is for North America.

The various possessors of the land all have the same condition: They either follow Christ as they occupy the ground or they are swept away and others who will follow Christ will supplant them.

---

[68] 2 Ne. 10: 11: "And this land shall be a land of liberty unto the Gentiles, and there shall be no kings upon the land, who shall raise up unto the Gentiles."

[69] 2 Ne. 1: 6-11: "Wherefore, I, Lehi, prophesy according to the workings of the Spirit which is in me, that there shall none come into this land save they shall be brought by the hand of the Lord. Wherefore, this land is consecrated unto him whom he shall bring. And if it so be that they shall serve him according to the commandments which he hath given, it shall be a land of liberty unto them; wherefore, they shall never be brought down into captivity; if so, it shall be because of iniquity; for if iniquity shall abound cursed shall be the land for their sakes, but unto the righteous it shall be blessed forever. And behold, it is wisdom that this land should be kept as yet from the knowledge of other nations; for behold, many nations would overrun the land, that there would be no place for an inheritance. Wherefore, I, Lehi, have obtained a promise, that inasmuch as those whom the Lord God shall bring out of the land of Jerusalem shall keep his commandments, they shall prosper upon the face of this land; and they shall be kept from all other nations, that they may possess this land unto themselves. And if it so be that they shall keep his commandments they shall be blessed upon the face of this land, and there shall be none to molest them, nor to take away the land of their inheritance; and they shall dwell safely forever. But behold, when the time cometh that they shall dwindle in unbelief, after they have received so great blessings from the hand of the Lord—having a knowledge of the creation of the earth, and all men, knowing the great and marvelous works of the Lord from the creation of the world; having power given them to do all things by faith; having all the commandments from the beginning, and having been brought by his infinite goodness into this precious land of promise—behold, I say, if the day shall come that they will reject the Holy One of Israel, the true Messiah, their Redeemer and their God, behold, the judgments of him that is just shall rest upon them. Yea, he will bring other nations unto them, and he will give unto them power, and he will take away from them the lands of their possessions, and he will cause them to be scattered and smitten."

This was established by covenant with Lehi generations before Christ visited with and taught Lehi's descendants. Lehi recorded the covenant:

> "Wherefore, I, Lehi, have obtained a promise, that inasmuch as those whom the Lord God shall bring out of the land of Jerusalem shall keep his commandments, they shall prosper upon the face of this land; and they shall be kept from all other nations, that they may possess this land unto themselves. And if it so be that they shall keep his commandments they shall be blessed upon the face of this land, and there shall be none to molest them, nor to take away the land of their inheritance; and they shall dwell safely forever. But behold, when the time cometh that they shall dwindle in unbelief, after they have received so great blessings from the hand of the Lord—having a knowledge of the creation of the earth, and all men, knowing the great and marvelous works of the Lord from the creation of the world; having power given them to do all things by faith; having all the commandments from the beginning, and having been brought by his infinite goodness into this precious land of promise—behold, I say, if the day shall come that they will reject the Holy One of Israel, the true Messiah, their Redeemer and their God, behold, the judgments of him that is just shall rest upon them. Yea, he will bring other nations unto them, and he will give unto them power, and he will take away from them the lands of their possessions, and he will cause them to be scattered and smitten." (2 Nephi 1: 9-11.)

Christ's words dovetail with the covenant made with Lehi. The same Lord announcing them both. That condition and lease of this land remains conditional. Keep the conditions and you may be preserved to inherit the land and be numbered with the house of Israel. Violate them and be swept away.

So we see that the times of the Gentiles, as they end, become quite perilous for the Gentiles upon the land. They will forfeit their hold, however improbable it may seem to them at the present. Christ's Father has declared it so. Who, then, can disannul?

The many confident assurances of God's favor we have do give us comfort, don't they? They are either true and right, and we have little to fear. Or they are among the abominations that allow foolish, vain and false notions lull us to sleep. The difference between those two propositions is quite alarming. I hate it when we have to make hard choices.

3 Nephi 16: 17-20

> **"And then the words of the prophet Isaiah shall be fulfilled, which say: Thy watchmen shall lift up the voice; with the voice together shall they sing, for they shall see eye to eye when the Lord shall bring again Zion. Break forth into joy, sing together, ye waste places of Jerusalem; for the Lord hath comforted his**

people, he hath redeemed Jerusalem. The Lord hath made bare his holy arm in the eyes of all the nations; and all the ends of the earth shall see the salvation of God."

Given the scholarly arguments over the meaning and application of Isaiah, here we encounter a profound insight from Christ. He attributes this quote from Isaiah to the coming events in the Americas. In this declaration by Christ we learn Isaiah was NOT speaking of the return to the Middle East for these events to unfold. Instead the "waste places of Jerusalem" are nowhere near Jerusalem. It is another place, far away, where the residue of Jerusalem's scattered people are wasted, then restored again. It is also plural. One is here, in the Americas, on an "isle of the sea."[70] Now we can know from Christ's own interpretation that Jerusalem's "waste places" are scattered throughout the world. This land is one of them.

Then we see something odd. After the removal of the Gentiles, there is joy, rejoicing, singing together, seeing eye to eye and a return to Zion. The emotional setting seems at odds with what we anticipate. Destroying Gentiles and having the trauma of those days would seem to produce mourning and lamentation. It does not. Instead it produces singing in joy.

To redeem Jerusalem is to re-establish the promised heirs upon their own land, and bring again Zion. Whatever bottle-neck of destruction needed to bring that triumph to pass will be worth it. So great will be the peace that follows that it will wipe away all tears. Truth, saving doctrine and being fed by Christ's own message will end all laments.[71]

How is the Lord's "holy arm" made bare? How will "the eyes of all nations" see it? What will the ends of the earth behold, as the salvation of God takes place? Why is it "all the ends of the earth" which will behold it?

What does it mean to "see eye to eye" when Zion is brought again?

Why is Zion to be "brought again" rather than re-built?

If the Lord is to comfort His people, what will that "comfort" include? Why has He consistently used the word "comfort" to describe His visit with people?

Why, when the waste places are redeemed, does it say "Jerusalem" will be redeemed? Is redeeming the "waste places" the same as

---

[70] 2 Ne. 10: 20: "And now, my beloved brethren, seeing that our merciful God has given us so great knowledge concerning these things, let us remember him, and lay aside our sins, and not hang down our heads, for we are not cast off; nevertheless, we have been driven out of the land of our inheritance; but we have been led to a better land, for the Lord has made the sea our path, and we are upon an isle of the sea."

[71] Rev. 7: 17: "For the Lamb which is in the midst of the throne shall feed them, and shall lead them unto living fountains of waters: and God shall wipe away all tears from their eyes."

redeeming "Jerusalem" itself? How does that affect the meaning of other scriptures?

Why are "singing together" and "seeing eye to eye" connected in the same thought?

What does it mean to "become one" as a people? Can we ever accomplish that by acquiring enough "sameness" or "uniformity" in conduct, thought and speech? Is it worth any effort at all to mimic one another? If we are to "become one" how should each of us proceed to accomplish that? How does Christ expect us to become "one?"[72]

Only the Lord can "bring it again." That is why He is said to "bring" it rather than for others to build it. All the labor may come from men, but it will the the Lord's command, Lord's direction, Lord's word which will cause it. Until He speaks it, it simply cannot come again. Hence the need for us to be able to speak with Him. He cannot bring it until a people exist who will listen to Him (or those who speak His words, no matter how unlikely the source they may seem to be). Oddly, until such spokesmen or spokeswomen should be listening to Him, and then He tells them to begin, and in turn a group should be here who would listen and hear Him in that call, there is simply no need to worry about Zion.

There are some great comments on the previous posts. I've not wanted to interrupt what I was doing to address them. Before moving on to another set of scriptures relating to those questions and comments, here are a few responses:

To whom has the Book of Mormon been written?

What possible good would it be for a message to be written for an audience who would never read the Book of Mormon?

If the term "Gentiles" is sometimes quite broad (and it is in some contexts), does the message get addressed to all of them? Is the message tailored to those who would read the book?

If the warnings are read to apply only to non-LDS occupants of the land, then what do the warnings accomplish? Do they make us proud? Do they make us feel better than "them," since only "they" are condemned and not us? What kind of a warning is it if the only ones being warned are those who will never read the book?

Does The Church of Jesus Christ of Latter-day Saints at least retain the power and authority to preach the Gospel and administer the rites of baptism, and laying on of hands for the gift of the Holy Ghost? When I prayed, as the missionaries were instructing me, I got an answer that led me to baptism. I believe that baptism to be authoritative and approved by the Lord. Does anyone think the church lacks the authority to baptize for the remission of sins? I do not. If, therefore, the church has that

---

72 1 John 3: 2: "Beloved, now are we the sons of God, and it doth not yet appear what we shall be: but we know that, when he shall appear, we shall be like him; for we shall see him as he is."

authority, does it not continue to occupy an important, even central role in the Lord's work?

If you teach someone, and they want to "convert" and be baptized, would you not baptize them into The Church of Jesus Christ of Latter-day Saints?

What is the mission field for The Church of Jesus Christ of Latter-day Saints? Who is not included?

If all the world is the mission field for the church, what, then, becomes the mission field for the Church of the Firstborn? [I do not hold that the Church of the Firstborn is a formal organization, existing here as a formal order. I believe its members associate with others who are not of this world, and consequently the Church of the Firstborn is never in competition with The Church of Jesus Christ of Latter-day Saints.]

Would members of the Church of the Firstborn not pay tithes to The Church of Jesus Christ of Latter-day Saints? Would they not attend its meetings? Would they not support its programs? Would they not use The Church of Jesus Christ of Latter-day Saints to assist them in raising their children? Would they not have their families baptized into The Church of Jesus Christ of Latter-day Saints? Even if they held authority given them directly from the Lord, would they not continue to be faithful members of The Church of Jesus Christ of Latter-day Saints? To uphold and respect the authorities who are given the duty to preside?

Until the Lord brings again Zion, where should we all join in fellowship?

Would members of the Church of the Firstborn ever envy those presiding in The Church of Jesus Christ of Latter-day Saints? Ever challenge their right to preside? Did Christ ever try and displace Caiaphus? Did He not admonish us to follow His example?

Does The Church of Jesus Christ of Latter-day Saints limit the amount of light you can acquire by your own heed and diligence?[73] Can any man prevent God from pouring out knowledge upon you if you will

---

[73] D&C 130: 18-19: "Whatever principle of intelligence we attain unto in this life, it will rise with us in the resurrection. And if a person gains more knowledge and intelligence in this life through his diligence and obedience than another, he will have so much the advantage in the world to come."

receive it in the proper way?[74] Can any soul approach the Lord, see His face, and know that He is?[75]

Of what relevance is it if other Saints give no heed or are not willing to receive knowledge from the Lord? Should we belittle them? If not, what then is our responsibility toward them?[76]

What does it mean to let a "light shine?"

Why, upon seeing that light, would someone "glorify **your** Father who is in heaven" rather than heap praise and attention upon you? What is it about the nature of the light which you are to shine that produces notice of the Father rather than notice of you?

David Christensen's definition of "whoredoms" was interesting. Whether you take the meaning in 1830, or you take our modern sexual meaning, would it change the result of any analysis? One fellow who worked at the Church Office Building told me that approximately 60% of active adult male members of the church regularly view pornography.

Kisi also raised a question regarding Ishmael's Ephraimite lineage. Orson Pratt, Franklin D. Richards and Erastus Snow all said Joseph Smith mentioned in passing that the lost 116 pages included a reference to Ishmael's lineage and he was from Ephraim. Does this change anything? If so, how? What other outcome might then be possible? Would this potentially even further limit the Gentile involvement?

On the subject of Joseph's statements contained in the Nauvoo era transcripts: These were the very materials from which Joseph's talks were reproduced. *The Documentary History of the Church*, by Joseph Smith, Jr., was compiled from these original materials. When *The Teachings of the Prophet Joseph Smith* was prepared, it was done using these materials. The paper I wrote included the original source materials, not the derivative compilations.

As to the importance and reliability of these materials, first, those involved were the leading church fathers at the time. Thomas Bullock was the official scribe for Joseph Smith during the Nauvoo talks. His versions were kept at Joseph's request and were official accounts. Second, the Joseph Smith Papers project now underway through the

---

[74] D&C 121: 32-33: "According to that which was ordained in the midst of the Council of the Eternal God of all other gods before this world was, that should be reserved unto the finishing and the end thereof, when every man shall enter into his eternal presence and into his immortal rest. How long can rolling waters remain impure? What power shall stay the heavens? As well might man stretch forth his puny arm to stop the Missouri river in its decreed course, or to turn it up stream, as to hinder the Almighty from pouring down knowledge from heaven upon the heads of the Latter-day Saints."

[75] D&C 93: 1: "VERILY, thus saith the Lord: It shall come to pass that every soul who forsaketh his sins and cometh unto me, and calleth on my name, and obeyeth my voice, and keepeth my commandments, shall see my face and know that I am;"

[76] 3 Ne. 12: 16: "Therefore let your light so shine before this people, that they may see your good works and glorify your Father who is in heaven."

Church Historian's Office is attempting to make more of these original source materials available to the Saints. If they are not important, then the Church would not be investing millions of man-hours and dollars to bring the sources into the hands of the Saints.

It is not wise to dismiss as "mud" the very kinds of materials that give the best source for Joseph's teachings. Indeed, D&C 130 is an amalgam of comments Joseph made in a talk given April 2, 1843 recorded by some of the very same scribes used in the paper I wrote. I'm just using original materials, rather than derivative, second hand interpretations made years later by others who were not present (or living) when the statements were made by Joseph.

1 NEPHI 13

The role of gentiles in the history of this land, promised to Lehi's descendants, is not just covered in the Lord's words. It is set out in some detail by Nephi. Therefore, we will look at some of Nephi's prophecy from 1 Nephi 13.

1 Nephi 13: 30

> **"Nevertheless, thou beholdest that the Gentiles who have gone forth out of captivity, and have been lifted up by the power of God above all other nations, upon the face of the land which is choice above all other lands, which is the land that the Lord God hath covenanted with thy father that his seed should have for the land of their inheritance; wherefore, thou seest that the Lord God will not suffer that the Gentiles will utterly destroy the mixture of thy seed, which are among thy brethren."**

This comes after an explanation of how the gentiles will flee oppression in another land (Europe), come here, and overtake this land. Nephi has been shown the establishment of a great church that alters the teachings to be given by Christ to the Jews. Then the prophecy continues with the above statement.

Flight from captivity has brought the Gentiles here. They came here (originally) for religious freedom. They wanted to follow their conscious when it came to matters of God and belief. This land was a land of religious freedom for these gentiles.

They then were "lifted up by the power of God above all other nations." This "lifting up" is not only to enjoy religious freedom to worship God. It also included the power to retain that freedom against any foreign threat to remove it. Therefore, ancillary to the religious freedom, the gentiles were necessarily given economic and military might with which to retain that freedom against "all other nations." But the "power of God" which "lifted [them] up" is conditioned upon them always serving the God of this land, who is Jesus Christ.[77] The power of God cannot be used to protect a wicked people.

The land is "choice above all other lands." Why is that so? What is it about the American continent which makes it more "choice" than any other location on earth?

Notice that here again Nephi is told that the land has been given to Lehi's descendants as "the land for their inheritance." Whatever dispossession the gentiles cause, these people have God's covenant to return the land to them. What does it mean to have this land promised by God through covenant to Lehi's descendants? Does that promise contain any condition? Will these people forfeit their right if they are wicked? If they will not forfeit the right, then what will happen to them if they cease to serve the God of this land?

Because of the covenant, the Lord will "not suffer that the Gentiles will utterly destroy" the covenant people? Note the "mixture of thy seed" mentioned to Nephi. Why is Nephi promised a "mixture of thy seed" will be preserved? Does gentile oppression remove the promises to Lehi and Nephi? If not, what then do the promises assure them?

Why does God make a covenant to a worthy prophet-patriarch and bind Himself to fulfill the promise even with a posterity which may not be similarly faithful? Has the Lord done this before with Abraham? With Isaac? With Jacob? With Noah? Even though we knew nothing of these covenants when the gentiles overran the land, are they nonetheless God's promise and something which He will fulfill? How certain should we be that the Lord will deliver this land back to those who descend from Lehi and Nephi?

Why can a righteous prophet-patriarch obtain such promises from the Lord? What reason is there for such covenants to be made? Can they still be made? How? What did Lehi and Nephi do to qualify to receive such a covenant? Was there any intermediary? Will the Lord employ a servant when making such a covenant?

Well, this is interesting stuff. Worth continuing to consider, I think.

1 Nephi 13: 31-32

> **"Neither will he suffer that the Gentiles shall destroy the seed of thy brethren. Neither will the Lord God suffer that the Gentiles shall forever remain in that awful state of blindness, which thou beholdest they are in, because of the plain and most precious parts of the gospel of the Lamb which have been kept back by that abominable church, whose formation thou hast seen."**

---

[77] Ether 2: 12: "Behold, this is a choice land, and whatsoever nation shall possess it shall be free from bondage, and from captivity, and from all other nations under heaven, if they will but serve the God of the land, who is Jesus Christ, who hath been manifested by the things which we have written."

The gentiles are limited in how far they may go. Although the covenant people will be smitten and afflicted, they will not be utterly destroyed. Diminished, broken to the dust, but not altogether lost. And, no matter what afflictions they may be called to endure, the Lord intends to give them this, their promised land.

A hopeful note sounds for the gentiles: The Lord will not let them "forever remain in that awful state of blindness" they are in when they arrive here. The Lord has commended the gentiles for coming to this land. They did so in response to the Spirit of God which "wrought" upon them.[78] The gentiles came out of captivity and humbled themselves before God.[79] The gentiles were given the "power of the Lord" because of their humility.[80] In the preceding verse, the power of God was how they were delivered from their captivity.[81] Despite all this, these gentiles are "in that awful state of blindness."

How can the gentiles be both blessed to inherit all the Lord's assistance and yet in an awful state of blindness?

What caused them to be blind?

If something is "plain" in the scriptures what must it include?

If something is "precious" in the scriptures what must it include?

If something both "plain" and "precious" has been removed, what has happened to the scriptures?

What does it mean to be blind? What does it mean to "stumble?"

What does it mean to cause plain and precious things "to be held back?"

Does any organization or group which "holds back" plain and precious things become part of that "abominable church?" Since "abominable" requires the use of religion to suppress truth or impose a false form of truth, can the definition of "abominable church" be limited to Historic Christianity? What about a modern church, even a restorationist church like the Community of Christ (formerly RLDS) which suppresses or abandons truth? If they "hold back" truth, do they join in the collective assembly of false religions called the "abominable church?" Even it they came through Joseph Smith and accept the Book of Mormon?

---

[78] 1 Ne. 13: 13: "And it came to pass that I beheld the Spirit of God, that it wrought upon other Gentiles; and they went forth out of captivity, upon the many waters."

[79] 1 Ne. 13: 16: "And it came to pass that I, Nephi, beheld that the Gentiles who had gone forth out of captivity did humble themselves before the Lord; and the power of the Lord was with them."

[80] Ibid.

[81] 1 Ne. 13: 30: "Nevertheless, thou beholdest that the Gentiles who have gone forth out of captivity, and have been lifted up by the power of God above all other nations, upon the face of the land which is choice above all other lands, which is the land that the Lord God hath covenanted with thy father that his seed should have for the land of their inheritance; wherefore, thou seest that the Lord God will not suffer that the Gentiles will utterly destroy the mixture of thy seed, which are among thy brethren."

What are the "plain and most precious" parts of the Gospel, anyway? Would it have anything to do with knowing Christ? Since this is life eternal, to "know" Him, would it be a simple and plain, but most precious teaching to urge people to part the veil of unbelief and behold their Lord?[82]

Where do we hear that message preached today? I think when I find such a message taught, I will give heed to it.

Nephi's vision of these events does inform us, does it not?

1 Nephi 13: 33-34

> **"Wherefore saith the Lamb of God: I will be merciful unto the Gentiles, unto the visiting of the remnant of the house of Israel in great judgment. And it came to pass that the angel of the Lord spake unto me, saying: Behold, saith the Lamb of God, after I have visited the remnant of the house of Israel—and this remnant of whom I speak is the seed of thy father—wherefore, after I have visited them in judgment, and smitten them by the hand of the Gentiles, and after the Gentiles do stumble exceedingly, because of the most plain and precious parts of the gospel of the Lamb which have been kept back by that abominable church, which is the mother of harlots, saith the Lamb—I will be merciful unto the Gentiles in that day, insomuch that I will bring forth unto them, in mine own power, much of my gospel, which shall be plain and precious, saith the Lamb."**

Here is meat indeed! What amazing truths unfold in this announcement!

Notice the definition of the "remnant" to whom the prophecies apply has now been given. The distinction between the "gentiles" and the "remnant" are apparent here. Notice that although the gentiles will receive "much of my gospel" they will still remain identified as "Gentiles." We may refer to the restored church as "latter-day Israel" or similar terms, but the Book of Mormon vocabulary applies the term "Gentiles" to us. This is akin to the "Samaritans" many of whose blood was as Jewish as those who were exiled to Babylon and returned. Even Christ didn't acknowledge they were Jewish.

Why is it that the gentiles receive "much of my gospel" rather than the "fullness of my Gospel?" As you consider that, remember Joseph used to lament about the Saints' unwillingness to be taught new truths. Here are two of his comments:

> "There has been a great difficulty in getting anything into the heads of this generation. It has been like splitting hemlock knots with a

[82] John 17: 3: "And this is life eternal, that they might know thee the only true God, and Jesus Christ, whom thou hast sent."

corn-dodger for a wedge, and a pumpkin for a beetle. Even the Saints are slow to understand." (DHC vol 6, p.184).

"Paul ascended into the third heavens and he could understand the three principle rounds of Jacob's ladder—the telestial, the terrestrial, and the celestial glories or kingdoms, when Paul saw and heard things which were not lawful to utter. I could explain a hundredfold more than I ever have of the glories of the kingdoms manifested to me in the vision were I permitted and were the people ready to receive them." (DHC vol 5, p. 402.)

Joseph administered a form of endowment ceremony in Nauvoo, but told Brigham Young that he would have to finish it. Joseph initiated a few in the manner he received, but was not content with the form of the endowment. Brigham Young reported that Joseph told him, **"Brother Brigham, this is not arranged right. But we have done the best we could under the circumstances in which we are placed, and I wish you to take this matter in hand and organize and systematize all these ceremonies."** (See Journal of L. John Nuttal, Vol. 1, pp. 18-19, quoted in Truman G. Madsen, Joseph Smith the Prophet, Salt Lake City: Bookcraft, 1999, p. 97.)

Joseph also initiated a practice of sealing others to him, as the Patriarchal head of a dispensation. The nature of Patriarchal authority Joseph administered is different from what we currently understand or teach. Today we "seal" families together in genealogical lines based upon birth or legal adoption. Our families are tied together in what we understand was the intended purpose of Elijah's prophecy about "turning hearts of the fathers to the children, and the children to the fathers" so that the earth would not be smitten with a curse at the Lord's return. But Joseph's practice was somewhat different.

Joseph, who received the revelations on this matter, attempted to set out the manner in which the "family" will be constituted in eternity. He used Christ's comment in Matt. 19: 29 to support the idea that those who are worthy will be placed in a family organization that would be completely restructured in the resurrection.[83] Orson Hyde later constructed a diagram of this teaching and published it in the Millennial Star Vol. 9 [15 January 1847] at pages 23-24. If you search for that online you can find it. You need both the diagram and the explanation to understand the teaching. It is also in *The Words of Joseph Smith,* page 297. Please find and read it. You need to understand that teaching, which came to Orson Hyde from Joseph Smith.

As a result of this teaching, beginning with Joseph Smith and continuing until Wilford Woodruff discontinued it, sealing for eternity was not done in family lines. It was done instead to bind those who had

[83] Matt. 19: 29: "And every one that hath forsaken houses, or brethren, or sisters, or father, or mother, or wife, or children, or lands, for my name's sake, shall receive an hundredfold, and shall inherit everlasting life."

received the Gospel to Joseph Smith, as the Patriarchal head of this dispensation. Joseph's teaching was followed by Brigham Young, who sealed himself to Joseph as his (Joseph's) son. John D. Lee, who was executed for the Mountain Meadows Massacre, was another sealed to Brigham Young as his son. Heber Grant's mother was sealed to Joseph Smith, although his father was Jedediah Grant. As a result he (President Grant) considered himself Joseph's son. That's a side issue.

Returning to the gentile inheritance of "much of my gospel" referred to above, does it suggest that the gentiles are not/never were given generally or as a group possession of "the fullness?" Is "much of my gospel" something worth considering? Can you be certain Joseph delivered all he could or would, were the Saints willing to receive it? If it was "much" rather than "the fullness" then how does that change things?

Assuming "much of my gospel" includes (as it tells us) those things which "shall be plain and precious" then do the gentiles have enough to allow them to receive an audience with Christ as the promised Second Comforter from John's Gospel?[84] If so, then will not Christ, along with the Holy Ghost, teach you all things needed, even if the gentiles are not in possession of the "fullness" of it all?[85]

This is important to understand. Nephi makes it clear how the gentiles can become adopted into the promised line and inherit a place among the chosen people who will be preserved, inherit this land, and be numbered among the house of Israel. While that jumps us ahead a bit, it is directly connected here. The first two verses of the next chapter state the following:

> "And it shall come to pass, that if the Gentiles shall hearken unto the Lamb of God in that day that he shall manifest himself unto them in word, and also in power, **in very deed**, unto the taking away of their stumbling blocks—And harden not their hearts against the Lamb of God, they shall be numbered among the seed of thy father; yea, they shall be numbered among the house of Israel; and they shall be a blessed people upon the promised land forever; they shall be no more brought down into captivity; and the house of Israel shall no more be confounded." (1 Ne. 14: 1-2)

If the gentiles will hearken to the Lamb, He will manifest Himself to them. What does that mean?

---

[84] John 14: 18, 23: "I will not leave you comfortless: I will come to you. ...Jesus answered and said unto him, If a man love me, he will keep my words: and my Father will love him, and we will come unto him, and make our abode with him."

[85] John 14: 26: "But the Comforter, which is the Holy Ghost, whom the Father will send in my name, he shall teach you all things, and bring all things to your remembrance, whatsoever I have said unto you."

What does it mean to manifest Himself to us "in word?" What does it mean to manifest Himself to us "in power?" What does it mean to manifest Himself to us "in very deed?"

How would Christ manifesting Himself to you in word, in power, and in deed "take away your stumbling block?"

These are the means promised by the Book of Mormon to deliver gentiles so that they may become "a blessed people upon the promised land forever" so as to never be brought down into captivity. But to know this would require you to come into possession of the fullness. Gentile possession of the fullness does not come from group-think, or group possession of some institutional magic. It comes by the same means as salvation has come to mankind from the beginning. The Catholics don't have it and can't give it to you. No institutional church has the means to deliver the gentiles. It will come, if it comes at all, from Christ and on the same conditions as saved Joseph Smith, Paul, Alma, Moroni, Peter, Moses, Enoch, Abraham and others.

Now there is a great deal to understand about how to move from having "much of the Gospel" to having a fullness of it. But it was always planned for that final step to be taken by you with the Lord. After all, He is the gatekeeper who employs no servant between you and Him.[86] This is why true servants will always point you to Him. False ones will claim they can save you, they have power to bring you to Him, they have been entrusted to open the door for you. The "gatekeeper" however does not need a doorman. Nor can He be fooled by men making pretensions to have authority while lacking any of His power. You must confront Him; or, to use His description, you must be comforted by Him.

If Joseph taught the organization of the Celestial Kingdom would involve reconstructed "family units" based upon the capacity of the individuals' involved, did he understand doctrine differently than we now do? Why were the original sealings performed to bind people to Joseph as the Patriarch? Why was that continued through Wilford Woodruff? Why was it discontinued? Although it was replaced with a method that provides us with sentimental associations, is there something about our understanding that is less complete, less accurate and less of how Christ intends to organize the eternal family?

It is clear from these verses in 1 Nephi 13 that the Lord intends to make redemption available to the gentiles, if they will receive it. But the primary means was never intended to be an institution. It was intended to be the Book of Mormon. The Book of Mormon speaks right over the heads of those who are trying to distract you from returning to Christ.

---

[86] 2 Ne. 9: 41: "O then, my beloved brethren, come unto the Lord, the Holy One. Remember that his paths are righteous. Behold, the way for man is narrow, but it lieth in a straight course before him, and the keeper of the gate is the Holy One of Israel; and he employeth no servant there; and there is none other way save it be by the gate; for he cannot be deceived, for the Lord God is his name."

You must either seek and find Him while here, or remain in this Telestial state worlds without end. His invitation is extended. He will open the gate.

Where will we find true doctrine taught? From what source does it come? Will He not, as He has promised, send true messengers to warn before He cuts off and divides asunder? If you do not understand this it is because you will not ask Him.

So, let us press on. I find this is more interesting a Gospel than I had at first imagined. Truly, such things do not enter into the heart of man. They must be revealed, or they stand unknown. Fortunately for us, the Lord has provided the Book of Mormon and sent Joseph Smith to establish a foundation from which we gentiles may derive hope.

1 Nephi 13: 35

> **"For, behold, saith the Lamb: I will manifest myself unto thy seed, that they shall write many things which I shall minister unto them, which shall be plain and precious; and after thy seed shall be destroyed, and dwindle in unbelief, and also the seed of thy brethren, behold, these things shall be hid up, to come forth unto the Gentiles, by the gift and power of the Lamb."**

It is the Lamb who makes this promise. He declares He will "manifest" Himself to Nephi's seed. Christ promises the same thing (to "manifest" Himself) to the gentiles in our day.[87] This original promise would be repeated by later Book of Mormon prophets.

The descendants of Nephi to whom the Lord would manifest Himself "shall write many things" which the Lord would minister. What does the qualification "many things" imply? Is "many" the same as "all things?"

The things to be written are what Christ "shall minister unto them." Is this limited to His ministry after His resurrection? Would it include all things which He "ministered" to them, even through prophetic ministers sent by Him?

Here again the words "plain and precious" are repeated. Why is this phrase used? What does it mean? Why was this what was removed by the "great and abominable church," but replaced through the things to be written by the Nephites? Is the fact Christ "ministered" to the Nephites, over a thousand-year dispensation, through many different ministers, in many different settings, alone evidence of something "plain and precious" to us? When Nephi would later write: "Wo be unto him that shall say: We have received the word of God, and we need no more of the word of God, for we have enough! For behold, thus saith the Lord God: I will give unto the children of men line upon line, precept upon

---

[87] 1 Ne. 14: 1: "And it shall come to pass, that if the Gentiles shall hearken unto the Lamb of God in that day that he shall manifest himself unto them in word, and also in power, in very deed, unto the taking away of their stumbling blocks—"

precept, here a little and there a little; and blessed are those who hearken unto my precepts, and lend an ear unto my counsel, for they shall learn wisdom; for unto him that receiveth I will give more; and from them that shall say, We have enough, from them shall be taken away even that which they have. Cursed is he that putteth his trust in man, or maketh flesh his arm, or shall hearken unto the precepts of men, save their precepts shall be given by the power of the Holy Ghost Wo be unto the Gentiles, saith the Lord God of Hosts! For notwithstanding I shall lengthen out mine arm unto them from day to day, they will deny me; nevertheless, I will be merciful unto them, saith the Lord God, if they will repent and come unto me; for mine arm is lengthened out all the day long, saith the Lord God of Hosts."[88]

Is not speaking to the Lord, and more importantly hearing from Him the most plain, the most precious of things? Would the Lord have ever promised to come, take up His abode[89] and sup with you[90] if He did not mean it? Does the Book of Mormon reiterate the promises given in the New Testament? Have they been restored to us by the Book of Mormon?

Here again we find the word "destroyed" used. "Destroyed" does not mean complete eradication. It means the loss of order, political independence and social coherence. Many will die, but they will not cease to exist.

What does "dwindle in unbelief" mean? Will anything be kept, although they should "dwindle?" Can a people "dwindle" and yet retain some truths?

It is not just the Nephite descendants who will "dwindle in unbelief," but "also the seed of thy brethren," the Lamanites. Whatever truths

---

[88] 2 Ne. 28: 29-32: "Wo be unto him that shall say: We have received the word of God, and we need no more of the word of God, for we have enough! For behold, thus saith the Lord God: I will give unto the children of men line upon line, precept upon precept, here a little and there a little; and blessed are those who hearken unto my precepts, and lend an ear unto my counsel, for they shall learn wisdom; for unto him that receiveth I will give more; and from them that shall say, We have enough, from them shall be taken away even that which they have. Cursed is he that putteth his trust in man, or maketh flesh his arm, or shall hearken unto the precepts of men, save their precepts shall be given by the power of the Holy Ghost. Wo be unto the Gentiles, saith the Lord God of Hosts! For notwithstanding I shall lengthen out mine arm unto them from day to day, they will deny me; nevertheless, I will be merciful unto them, saith the Lord God, if they will repent and come unto me; for mine arm is lengthened out all the day long, saith the Lord God of Hosts."

[89] John 14: 23: "Jesus answered and said unto him, If a man love me, he will keep my words: and my Father will love him, and we will come unto him, and make our abode with him."

[90] Rev. 3: 20-21: "Behold, I stand at the door, and knock: if any man hear my voice, and open the door, I will come in to him, and will sup with him, and he with me. To him that overcometh will I grant to sit with me in my throne, even as I also overcame, and am set down with my Father in his throne."

remain will not permit them to have on-going access to the Lord's presence. However, that does not mean they will not have Divine favor, does it? After all, the Lord gives to everyone precisely what will be best for them to know according to His wisdom.[91] Does dwindling mean that people are altogether lost to some portion of God's teachings and favor? How is it possible to determine if any people from any society are not being brought wisely along by the Lord?

The teachings that Christ will "minister" to the Nephites will be written, and then "these things shall be hid up, to come forth unto the Gentiles" at the appointed time. Why write them? Why preserve them? Why are the records of His acts important for others to learn about? Why would a record of His dealings need to eventually be brought to light? Will all His dealings eventually be brought to light?[92] If He, therefore, imparts His word to you, what becomes your responsibility?

What does the coming forth of the Nephite record "by the gift and power of the Lamb" mean? Will this same pattern repeat?[93] Will the "gift and power of the Lamb" be on display again? Will this "make bare His arm?" Will people finally consider things which they have previously ignored?[94] Can you and I consider them now?

1 Nephi 13: 36

> **"And in them shall be written my gospel, saith the Lamb, and my rock and my salvation."**

Christ's Gospel is in the Book of Mormon. I've written books explaining just how much of His Gospel is contained in the Book of Mormon. When writing *The Second Comforter* I found the Book of Mormon was the best source to explain the process. In the Preface to *Eighteen Verses* I wrote (and meant) the following: "I am convinced the

---

[91] Alma 29: 8: "For behold, the Lord doth grant unto all nations, of their own nation and tongue, to teach his word, yea, in wisdom, all that he seeth fit that they should have; therefore we see that the Lord doth counsel in wisdom, according to that which is just and true."

[92] 2 Ne. 29: 13: "And it shall come to pass that the Jews shall have the words of the Nephites, and the Nephites shall have the words of the Jews; and the Nephites and the Jews shall have the words of the lost tribes of Israel; and the lost tribes of Israel shall have the words of the Nephites and the Jews."
D&C 133: 30: "And they shall bring forth their rich treasures unto the children of Ephraim, my servants."

[93] D&C 133: 26: "And they who are in the north countries shall come in remembrance before the Lord; and their prophets shall hear his voice, and shall no longer stay themselves; and they shall smite the rocks, and the ice shall flow down at their presence."

[94] Isa. 52: 15: "So shall he sprinkle many nations; the kings shall shut their mouths at him: for that which had not been told them shall they see; and that which they had not heard shall they consider."

Book of Mormon is the preeminent sacred text for our times. All other volumes of scriptures are not just inferior to it, but vastly so." (Id. p. iii.)

The Book of Mormon contains Christ's Gospel. It also contains His "rock" and His "salvation." What is the "rock" contained within it?

John Hall thought the better translation of Christ's colloquy with Peter would have included the Lord identifying Peter not as a "rock" but as a "seer stone." And upon the stone or seership would the Lord build His church.

I've thought the Book of Mormon was more a Urim and Thummim than a book. It is a tremendous source of subject matter upon which to ponder, oftentimes drawing a veil at critical moments while inviting the reader to ponder, pray and ask to see more. Used in that fashion, the Book of Mormon can open the heavens and make any person a seer indeed.

The words of a prophet are best understood by a prophet. If you can come to understand the Book of Mormon's words, you can become a prophet. Or, more correctly, a seer before whom scenes of God's dealings with mankind, past, present and future, will be put on display. Mosiah 8: 17 reports: "But a seer can know of things which are past, and also of things which are to come, and by them shall all things be revealed, or, rather, shall secret things be made manifest, and hidden things shall come to light, and things which are not known shall be made known by them, and also things shall be made known by them which otherwise could not be known."

Another way to interpret the "rock" is found in *Eighteen Verses* where I discussed the meaning of 1 Ne. 1: 6.[95] The meaning of the "rock" before Lehi (who wrote in Egyptian and would therefore understand meanings) would mean Ma'-at. Facsimile 2. figure 4, for example, shows the image of the Horus Hawk atop a rock and on the heavenly boat.

Still another meaning is found in the Book of Moses where Christ uses the term as a proper noun, or name for Himself.[96] He is "the Rock of Heaven." In this instance the meaning of the above verse is that you can find the Lord within the Book of Mormon. (Remember that E.B. Grandin's print shop provided all punctuation and capitalizations to the first edition. It was actually John H. Gilbert who did the work, which he described in a written recollection of the events dated 8 September 1892. (John Gilbert's September 8, 1892 recollections). If this was a

---

[95] 1 Ne. 1: 6: "And it came to pass as he prayed unto the Lord, there came a pillar of fire and dwelt upon a rock before him; and he saw and heard much; and because of the things which he saw and heard he did quake and tremble exceedingly."

[96] Moses 7: 53: "And the Lord said: Blessed is he through whose seed Messiah shall come; for he saith—I am Messiah, the King of Zion, the Rock of Heaven, which is broad as eternity; whoso cometh in at the gate and climbeth up by me shall never fall; wherefore, blessed are they of whom I have spoken, for they shall come forth with songs of everlasting joy."

proper noun and Gilbert did not capitalize it, we still don't. But that would not mean the word "rock" ought not to be rendered instead "Rock" as a proper name for Christ.)

The "salvation" to be found in the Book of Mormon is the same as salvation to be found in all the Gospel. That is, by finding Christ. For life eternal consists in coming to know Christ, and in turn Christ introducing you to the Father.[97] It is this ***appearing*** which Joseph Smith referred to as literal, not figurative.[98]

The prophetic message of the Book of Mormon is deeper and more profound the closer you examine it. It begins to become quite unlikely Joseph Smith could have produced such wisdom unless it truly is an ancient document. Of course the critics labor to make it seem so, but they haven't seriously examined its contents to see what it says.

1 Nephi 13: 37

> **"And blessed are they who shall seek to bring forth my Zion at that day, for they shall have the gift and the power of the Holy Ghost; and if they endure unto the end they shall be lifted up at the last day, and shall be saved in the everlasting kingdom of the Lamb; and whoso shall publish peace, yea, tidings of great joy, how beautiful upon the mountains shall they be."**

Now we encounter words that require us to know meanings first. For the Lord's "Zion" to be brought forth, we need to know what "Zion" means. What is it? When the Lord calls it "my Zion" does it belong to Him. Will the Lord be the one who "brings again Zion" as stated earlier in the 3 Nephi materials of Christ's prophecy?[99] What are the role of people in "seeking to bring forth His Zion?"

Will they actually "bring again Zion" or is that the Lord's doing? Unless the Lord determines to "bring again Zion" will men be able to accomplish it? Even if they are quite sincere and determined? What, then, must precede Zion's return?

Even if they are not given the commission or command to participate in Zion's return, will they nevertheless be blessed if they seek to bring it again? Is the promised "gift and power of the Holy Ghost" promised to those who would seek to bring forth Zion? What does that mean? How could anyone accomplish that?

---

[97] John 17: 2-3: "As thou hast given him power over all flesh, that he should give eternal life to as many as thou hast given him. And this is life eternal, that they might know thee the only true God, and Jesus Christ, whom thou hast sent."

[98] D&C 130: 3: "John 14:23—The appearing of the Father and the Son, in that verse, is a personal appearance; and the idea that the Father and the Son dwell in a man's heart is an old sectarian notion, and is false."

[99] 3 Ne. 16: 18 (quoting Isa. 52: 8): "Thy watchmen shall lift up the voice; with the voice together shall they sing, for they shall see eye to eye when the Lord shall bring again Zion."

What does it mean to "publish peace?"

What does it mean to "publish tidings of great joy?"

How does the "publishing of peace" and "tidings of great joy" relate to having your feet become beautiful upon the mountains?

Why feet "upon the mountains?" What "mountains?" Are these literal, or figurative, or both? If the "mountains" are a symbol, what do they symbolize?

The feet of those who walk upon the mountains crying peace are beautiful[100] because they are clean from the blood and sins of their generation.

In the ancient ceremonies involving animal sacrifice, blood was shed upon the ground and the feet of those involved in the rites became bloody. The blood of the sacrifice upon the feet became a symbol of the sins for which the sacrifice was offered.

The feet of those who walk upon the mountains crying peace are cleansed from that blood. Christ's washing of His Apostles' feet was to symbolize this cleansing which He alone could provide. He employs no servant to provide such a cleansing.[101] These feet, washed by Him are, therefore, beautiful because they connote the sanctity of the one crying peace.

"Crying peace" because the only thing which stills the mind of man, and brings rest from the trouble of this world, is the atonement of Christ. That is why it is called "the rest of the Lord." When cleansed, it becomes the consuming desire of those who are clean to bring others to partake. Just like Lehi's dream, when those who had eaten of the fruit of the tree of life ate, they immediately invited others to come and join them.

"Upon the mountains" because the mountain is nature's symbol of the ascent to God. The climb represents repentance and purification of the soul. When a person stands upon the top of the mountain, she appears to be part of heaven itself and no longer earthbound. Her profile is with the sky, symbolizing the completion of the ascent back to God.

It is beautiful. All of it is beautiful. All of it is a reflection of the purity and intelligence of God, whose ways are higher than man's ways as the heavens are higher than the earth.[102]

---

[100] Isa. 52: 7: "How beautiful upon the mountains are the feet of him that bringeth good tidings, that publisheth peace; that bringeth good tidings of good, that publisheth salvation; that saith unto Zion, Thy God reigneth!"

[101] 2 Ne. 9: 41: "O then, my beloved brethren, come unto the Lord, the Holy One. Remember that his paths are righteous. Behold, the way for man is narrow, but it lieth in a straight course before him, and the keeper of the gate is the Holy One of Israel; and he employeth no servant there; and there is none other way save it be by the gate; for he cannot be deceived, for the Lord God is his name."

[102] Isa. 55: 8-9: "For my thoughts are not your thoughts, neither are your ways my ways, saith the Lord. For as the heavens are higher than the earth, so are my ways higher than your ways, and my thoughts than your thoughts."

Tuesday I went to the Salt Lake Temple early with a missionary who reported to the MTC on Wednesday. I teach him in priest quorum. I wanted to make sure before his departure that the "endowment" he received would include some details of what the Mountain of the Lord's House was intended to confer. Young men are still teachable. I'd really like to move to the Primary, however. Primary kids, despite their energy, have open hearts and they are willing to receive.

By the time we get LDS adults to teach there is just too much idolatry to deal with…

1 Nephi 13: 38

> **"And it came to pass that I beheld the remnant of the seed of my brethren, and also the book of the Lamb of God, which had proceeded forth from the mouth of the Jew, that it came forth from the Gentiles unto the remnant of the seed of my brethren."**

Roles and definitions continue to be established here. Nephi's seed has been "destroyed" and only a "mixture" of his blood remains at the time of these events. Nephi has taken to calling them "the seed of my brethren" rather than a "mixture" of his (Nephi's) seed.

The "book of the Lamb of God" is later identified as the record we know as the New Testament. Altered, limited, with plain and precious materials removed, nevertheless called the "book of the Lamb of God." Acceptance of this New Testament book, notwithstanding its limitations and omissions, is akin to Christ referring to the Temple of Herod as His "Father's house" despite the fact that it had been profaned.

Although Christ called Herod's Temple His Father's house, He did not commune with His Father there. Christ visited with angelic ministers on the Mount of Transfiguration[103], in the Garden of Gethsemane[104], in the wilderness[105], and alone while apart from others. But there is no record of Him entertaining angels while in Herod's Temple. Though the Temple had been profaned and was unworthy to receive such visitors, Christ still honored the site and referred to it in sacred terms. This is a great key to understanding Christ's language here.

The "book of the Lamb of God" is revered and held in extraordinary esteem, as is evidenced by the terminology used in this revelation to Nephi. Nevertheless the book is corrupted, changed, with many plain and precious things removed.

---

[103] Matt. 17: 1-3: "And after six days Jesus taketh Peter, James, and John his brother, and bringeth them up into an high mountain apart, And was transfigured before them: and his face did shine as the sun, and his raiment was white as the light. And, behold, there appeared unto them Moses and Elias talking with him."

[104] Luke 22: 43: "And there appeared an angel unto him from heaven, strengthening him."

[105] Matt. 4: 11: "Then the devil leaveth him, and, behold, angels came and ministered unto him."

Can the book that has come to the "seed of Nephi's brethren" be said to be less than a fullness? Can the book be called "the book of the Lamb of God?" If it can be called "the book of the Lamb of God" can it also be said to contain a fullness?

[Here's a modern detour in question-asking: Do you focus on the book's value and worth by calling it the "book of the Lamb of God" or do you focus on the book's failings by saying many plain and precious things have been removed? If you do the one are you "positive" and "hopeful" and "Christ-like?" And if you focus on the other are you "negative" and "judgmental" and "un-Christ-like?" Is Nephi being fair and accurate by including the book's limitations? Or is he just another crank, tearing down the good works and valuable intent of others? Should he repent of his negativity? Ought we be offended?

These kinds of questions are more a reflection of our own insecurities and foolishness than they are helpful to understanding Christ's "strange act" unfolding before our disbelieving eyes.[106]]

This "book of the Lamb of God" will originate from the Jews, be brought by gentiles, and provided to the "remnant" who are identified with the "seed of Nephi's brethren." Since we can recall the history of these events, and know it is talking of the New Testament, we can see the various identities. New Testament converts from Judaism to Christianity, including the Apostles, Seventy, and Paul, are called "Jews." The descendants of the Puritans, English Colonies, American States and United States who dispossessed the native peoples are all referred to as "gentiles" in the prophecy. (I'm ignoring Central and South American for the moment.) The natives will include among them some faction which is the "seed of my brethren" that is the "remnant" about whom these promises are being made.

The question remains as to the identity of the "remnant" about whom these prophecies are speaking.

I know side-issues are arising throughout this discussion. But I've been focusing only on the "remnant" for weeks now. I won't depart from that single subject, despite the temptations that arise from questions flooding in on tangents. Bear with me. We'll eventually get to other issues.

I've debated whether it is even possible to cover this subject on a blog. This is an experiment. I'm trying to cover a topic that should rightly be put into a book. Whether it will work or not is still an open question. I think it is helpful even if the ultimate objective can't be met. We'll press forward and see how it turns out.

---

[106] D&C 101: 93-93: "What I have said unto you must needs be, that all men may be left without excuse; That wise men and rulers may hear and know that which they have never considered; That I may proceed to bring to pass my act, my strange act, and perform my work, my strange work, that men may discern between the righteous and the wicked, saith your God."

1 Nephi 13: 39

> **"And after it had come forth unto them I beheld other books, which came forth by the power of the Lamb, from the Gentiles unto them, unto the convincing of the Gentiles and the remnant of the seed of my brethren, and also the Jews who were scattered upon all the face of the earth, that the records of the prophets and of the twelve apostles of the Lamb are true."**

We know the New Testament will come forth first and get into the hands of the "remnant" of the promised people. It will get into their hands BEFORE some other materials will also come forth.

When did that happen? Was it something that occurred before the publication of the Book of Mormon in 1830? Which native tribes received copies of the New Testament before the "other books" came forward? What are these "other books" referred to here? They "came forth by the power of the Lamb" but came "after" the New Testament was given to the "remnant." What books have come forth "by the power of the Lamb" to your knowledge? Apart from the Book of Mormon, Doctrine and Covenants, Book of Moses, Book of Abraham and Joseph Smith History and Matthew, what other books would qualify? Did all these come after the "remnant" had first received the New Testament "book of the Lamb of God?"

The effect of the "other books" will be to "convince" the gentiles as well as "the remnant of the seed of my brethren" of the truth of the New Testament and "records of the prophets." Have the gentiles become convinced? Have the "remnant" become convinced? Have the Jews who were scattered upon all the face of the earth become convinced? Are they convinced of the truth of "the records of the prophets" even if they are not yet convinced of the truth of the "twelve apostles of the Lamb?"

Is this a serial progression? That is, does it come and convince the gentiles first? Then, having convinced them, does it next convince the "remnant?" Then, after having convinced both the gentiles and the "remnant," does it in turn convince the scattered Jews? If serial, what stage of the unfolding of these events is happening now? What is needed before the phase would be completed and the next one begin?

What does it mean that "other books" will come forth? What kinds of "books" would they be? Who would have written them? Why would they come "by the power of the Lamb" only to meet the criteria? Is a good commentary written by CES among the promised "books" coming forward? What about the *Ensign*?

How would you be able to recognize a book coming "by the power of the Lamb" in fulfillment of this promise? Will these "books" be recognized as scripture? Do they include discoveries at Qumran and Nag Hammadi? Was Hugh Nibley working on such projects, and if so, was he among those in whom the "power of the Lamb" was working?

This verse has potential for broad application. It raises questions worth contemplating and may surprise you at some of the issues it requires us to confront. Such are the Lord's dealings with mankind in every generation. We are made prayerful because He gives us great subjects with which to grapple.

1 Nephi 13: 40-41

> **"And the angel spake unto me, saying: These last records, which thou hast seen among the Gentiles, shall establish the truth of the first, which are of the twelve apostles of the Lamb, and shall make known the plain and precious things which have been taken away from them; and shall make known to all kindreds, tongues, and people, that the Lamb of God is the Son of the Eternal Father, and the Savior of the world; and that all men must come unto him, or they cannot be saved. And they must come according to the words which shall be established by the mouth of the Lamb; and the words of the Lamb shall be made known in the records of thy seed, as well as in the records of the twelve apostles of the Lamb; wherefore they both shall be established in one; for there is one God and one Shepherd over all the earth."**

The "books" that the prior verse referred to are now called "records" by the angel. The "records" will be among and originate from the gentiles. The purpose of the "records" is to establish the truth of the original records of "the twelve apostles of the Lamb." The purpose of the whole is to confirm the reality of Christ in His mortal ministry. Christ, who came to earth, lived and died as a mortal, was the Savior of mankind. The New Testament record confirming His ministry, sacrifice and resurrection is true! Their testimonies of Christ are reliable. He is our Savior and our God!

The "plain and precious" things that got removed will be returned to us. I've spoken of that before and won't repeat it again here. But the "plain and precious" things will become known to "all kindreds, tongues and people" again.

I was thinking about what was required for Joseph Smith to be able to get a message out in his day. He needed a printing press, which he could not afford. He needed Martin Harris to give a $3,000 note backed by a mortgage on his home to motivate the printer to make the first printings of the Book of Mormon. He needed an army of disciples to distribute the material on foot or horseback. He needed an infrastructure that went well beyond his individual means. Today Joseph would need a keyboard and an internet connection. He could speak to more people in a few minutes, across a wider swath of the globe, as a single individual acting alone, than he was able to speak to through an army of followers who uprooted their lives to follow his teachings.

We continue to make great sacrifices in purse and time to send missionaries throughout the world even today. In truth, if Joseph Smith had access to the internet he could have restored more things to more people in less time than has been done from 1830 to the present. It makes you wonder—if the truth were not packaged, marketed, focus-grouped through approved language, and accompanied by supporting photos and digital graphics—if the truth were simply spoken plainly, would it have any effect? Does it need an infrastructure of trained professional marketing to accompany it? Does it need a slick website to attract His sheep? Is His voice enough?

What if someone were to declare "that all men must come unto the Lamb of God, who is the Son of the Eternal Father, and the Savior of the world, or they cannot be saved." What if they were to declare in sober words that the Lamb of God lives still! That He had appeared to and spoken with the one making the declaration. Would there yet be those who would hear and repent?

Would that message be drowned out by the chorus of foolish and vain things being spoken in the name of Jesus Christ by those who, despite having real intent and sincere desire, have not been given power to declare His words? Would such a message only be another bit of entertainment for the bored and curious to give but passing notice? Could the world be given such a message and warned, but fail to see what it is they are being offered for one last time before the harvest is to begin? If so, would we notice?

The verse raises interesting options for the Lord to fulfill His promises in ways which have only come into existence in the last few years. He certainly does have the ability to "hasten His work" when He chooses.[107]

Should someone choose to come, the verse reports: "they must come according to the words which shall be established by the mouth of the Lamb; and the words of the Lamb shall be made known in the records of thy seed, as well as in the records of the twelve apostles of the Lamb." What does that include? Authoritative baptism? Authoritative bestowal of the gift of the Holy Ghost? Prophecy? Revelation? The "rock" of seership we discussed a few days ago? How must they come? The Book of Mormon suggests it must be through the gate of revelation.[108] Without revelation you cannot obtain the testimony of Jesus; which is the spirit of prophecy.[109] Or, in other words, unless you find prophets who can bear testimony of Him, you have not yet found the means for salvation. This becomes quite interesting and important. Very frank about the conditions for salvation.

---

[107] D&C 88: 73: "Behold, I will hasten my work in its time."

[108] Moroni 10: 4-5: "And when ye shall receive these things, I would exhort you that ye would ask God, the Eternal Father, in the name of Christ, if these things are not true; and if ye shall ask with a sincere heart, with real intent, having faith in Christ, he will manifest the truth of it unto you, by the power of the Holy Ghost. And by the power of the Holy Ghost ye may know the truth of all things"

[109] Rev. 19: 10: "And I fell at his feet to worship him. And he said unto me, See thou do it not: I am thy fellowservant, and of thy brethren that have the testimony of Jesus: worship God: for the testimony of Jesus is the spirit of prophecy."

Then the promise is that all these witnesses, all these records, and all these disciples are to become "one." "[T]hey both (records) shall be established in one; for there is one God and one Shepherd over all the earth" who in turn makes people to be "one" as well. A great assembly, a general congregation and Church of the Firstborn.

How great a promise has been offered to those who will receive! What good, however, is it to offer a gift if the one to whom it is offered refuses to accept?[110]

1 Nephi 13: 42

> **"And the time cometh that he shall manifest himself unto all nations, both unto the Jews and also unto the Gentiles; and after he has manifested himself unto the Jews and also unto the Gentiles, then he shall manifest himself unto the Gentiles and also unto the Jews, and the last shall be first, and the first shall be last."**

Christ showed Himself to the Jews during His mortal ministry.

He showed Himself to the Nephites after His resurrection.

He visited others, who have also kept records of His appearances to them. The full extent of the records that have been kept has not become apparent to us yet. Nephi would report in the final summation of his lifelong ministry the following about the many records to come forth:

> "Wherefore, because that ye have a Bible ye need not suppose that it contains all my words; neither need ye suppose that I have not caused more to be written. For I command all men, both in the east and in the west, and in the north, and in the south, and in the islands of the sea, that they shall write the words which I speak unto them; for out of the books which shall be written I will judge the world, every man according to their works, according to that which is written. For behold, I shall speak unto the Jews and they shall write it; and I shall also speak unto the Nephites and they shall write it; and I shall also speak unto the other tribes of the house of Israel, which I have led away, and they shall write it; and I shall also speak unto all nations of the earth and they shall write it. And it shall come to pass that the Jews shall have the words of the Nephites, and the Nephites shall have the words of the Jews; and the Nephites and the Jews shall have the words of the lost tribes of Israel; and the lost tribes of Israel shall have the words of the Nephites and the Jews. And it shall come to pass that my people, which are of the house of Israel, shall be gathered home unto the lands of their possessions; and my word also shall be gathered in one. And I will show unto them that fight against my word and against my people, who are of

---

[110] D&C 88: 33: "For what doth it profit a man if a gift is bestowed upon him, and he receive not the gift? Behold, he rejoices not in that which is given unto him, neither rejoices in him who is the giver of the gift."

> the house of Israel, that I am God, and that I covenanted with Abraham that I would remember his seed forever." (2 Nephi 29: 10-14.)

The "lost tribes of Israel" are plural. However many the number may be, each kept records and they are to come into our possession at some point in fulfillment of this prophetic promise.

All of this was foreseen by Zenos even before Isaiah. Zenos tells us the lost tribes of Israel will be spread all about, into the "nethermost" parts of the earth:

> "And these will I place in the nethermost part of my vineyard, whithersoever I will, it mattereth not unto thee; and I do it that I may preserve unto myself the natural branches of the tree; and also, that I may lay up fruit thereof against the season, unto myself; for it grieveth me that I should lose this tree and the fruit thereof. And it came to pass that the Lord of the vineyard went his way, and hid the natural branches of the tame olive-tree in the nethermost parts of the vineyard, some in one and some in another, according to his will and pleasure." (Jacob 5: 13-14.)

Where is "nethermost?" How many were there?

When Christ informed the Nephites of His post-resurrection ministry, He informed them He would be visiting the various Israelite people: "But now I go unto the Father, and also to show myself unto the lost tribes of Israel, for they are not lost unto the Father, for he knoweth whither he hath taken them." (3 Nephi 17: 4.) He visited the Nephites. They were an organized body, led by prophets, expecting His birth and death. There were other organized believers who also looked for His coming. What their prophets told them, and how they understood His ministry will be in their records. What He taught them when He visited with them after His resurrection will also be in their records. It is likely to mirror the Nephite experience and record. However, it is undoubtedly true that we will again learn how involved a Redeemer He has been. Should we already realize that from what we've been given? We ought to welcome His direct ministry among us. Somehow we find His intimate involvement hard to comprehend. We think, if someone should acknowledge they have seen Him, that such a person is somehow special, different, or unique. It ought to be commonplace.

In the unfolding ministry of the Lord, the Jews were the first, but will be the last, to receive again His ministry. The gentiles have been given the Gospel. The remnant will be receiving it from them—soon.

1 NEPHI 14

1 Nephi 14: 1-2

> **"And it shall come to pass, that if the Gentiles shall hearken unto the Lamb of God in that day that he shall manifest himself unto them in word, and also in power, in very deed, unto the taking away of their stumbling blocks—And harden not their hearts against the Lamb of God, they shall be numbered among the seed of thy father; yea, they shall be numbered among the house of Israel; and they shall be a blessed people upon the promised land forever; they shall be no more brought down into captivity; and the house of Israel shall no more be confounded."**

I've referred to these verses before. When Elder Mark E. Peterson claimed the Lord would not visit with "gentiles" but only with the house of Israel, relying upon 3 Nephi 15: 23[111], it was my view that the 3 Nephi statement of Christ was as to His immediate post-resurrection appearances to the various scattered lost tribes. He had no commission from the Father to appear to the gentiles in that time frame. These verses are about a different, much later time. These are speaking of the time when the Book of Mormon (record of the Nephites) would come into the possession of the gentiles. The gentiles will, if they hearken to the "Lamb of God IN THAT DAY," have the Lamb manifest Himself to them. Today is THAT DAY. It is now when the gentiles are promised He will manifest Himself to us, in "word" and in "power" and "in very deed."

His assignment immediately post-resurrection was to visit with each of the still organized, prophet-led, but scattered children of Israel. They had been put into the "nethermost" parts of the earth. He went to and visited with each of them serially. He did not visit with gentiles during that ministry.

---

[111] 3 Ne. 15: 23: "And they understood me not that I said they shall hear my voice; and they understood me not that the Gentiles should not at any time hear my voice—that I should not manifest myself unto them save it were by the Holy Ghost."

But in the time following the publication of the Book of Mormon, and as part of removing the stumbling blocks of the gentiles, He is to visit the gentiles "in word" and "in power" and "in deed" so that it will "take away their stumbling blocks."

What does it mean to stumble? What is a "stumbling block?" What kinds of things would impede you from walking back to the presence of God? How will Christ's ministry in "word, power and deed" to gentiles remove these things?

It is AFTER the ministry of "word, power and deed" when the stumbling blocks are removed, that the gentiles are then "numbered among the seed of thy father." Note that they are not numbered among other branches of Israel. Note that they are not sealed to their fathers and made Ephraimites descended from other branches. They are to be "numbered among the seed of thy father" or counted as part of Lehi's seed. They are, in short, to be sealed to Lehi as their Patriarch and father. It is necessary to understand the doctrine discussed in this post.

This was always a part of the Gospel. Joseph Smith understood it and practiced it. Today we think it was an oddity that got corrected at the time of Wilford Woodruff. However, if you read the Book of Abraham you realize that the adoption of people into an inheritance was always the manner the Celestial Kingdom was to be organized here. Look at the Lord's discussion/explanation to Abraham:

> "My name is Jehovah, and I know the end from the beginning; therefore my hand shall be over thee. And I will make of thee a great nation, and I will bless thee above measure, and make thy name great among all nations, and **thou shalt be a blessing unto thy seed after thee**, that in their hands they shall bear this ministry and Priesthood unto all nations; And I will bless them through thy name; for **as many as receive this Gospel shall be called after thy name, and shall be accounted thy seed**, and shall rise up and bless thee, as their father; And I will bless them that bless thee, and curse them that curse thee; and in **thee (that is, in thy Priesthood) and in thy seed (that is, thy Priesthood)**, for I give unto thee a promise that this right shall continue in thee, and in thy seed after thee (that is to say, the literal seed, or the seed of the body) shall all the families of the earth be blessed, even with the blessings of the Gospel, which are the blessings of salvation, even of life eternal." (Abr. 2: 8-11)

Those who receive the same priesthood (Patriarchal) from the time of Abraham forward become his (Abraham's) seed. Therefore they become his (Abraham's) inheritance and posterity, sealed to him as a part of his family.

This was the priesthood that was bestowed upon Joseph Smith, as a result of which he received the promises of Abraham. While looking for references to Abraham throughout D&C 132 is interesting, I'll just take an excerpt. [PLEASE forget about plural wives while you read this. Think only about Patriarchal Priesthood and the authority which was with Abraham and renewed in Joseph. It is that issue that I want to focus, and not to become side-tracked on plural marriage. At some point I'll spend a few weeks on that side issue. NOT NOW.]

> "I am the Lord thy God, and will give unto thee the law of **my Holy Priesthood**, as was ordained by me and my Father before the world was. **Abraham received all things, whatsoever he received, by revelation and commandment, by my word, saith the Lord**, and hath entered into his exaltation and sitteth upon his throne. **Abraham received promises concerning his seed**, and of the fruit of his loins—from whose loins ye are, namely, my servant Joseph—which were to continue so long as they were in the world; and as touching Abraham and his seed, out of the world they should continue; both in the world and out of the world should they continue as innumerable as the stars; or, if ye were to count the sand upon the seashore ye could not number them. This promise is yours also, because ye are of Abraham, and **the promise was made unto Abraham; and by this law is the continuation of the works of my Father, wherein he glorifieth himself**. Go ye, therefore, and do the works of Abraham; enter ye into my law and ye shall be saved." (D&C 132: 28-32)

Exaltation came through this priesthood, which linked together the fathers and the children of promise. The priestly sealing together of Patriarchs into a family that will endure as the government in heaven was the object of the Gospel in every generation. We are returning, at the end, to what it was at the beginning. However, the way in which it was to occur was "by my word" and "by revelation and commandment" so that the person knows he is to have a part in the Father's kingdom. It was not to be merely a distant expectation, uncertain in origin and doubtful in authority. It was to be certain, not doubtful: "The more sure word of prophecy means a man's knowing that he is sealed up unto eternal life, by revelation and the spirit of prophecy, through the power of the Holy Priesthood."[112] It is directly connected with this Patriarchal Priesthood, the same authority which belonged to Abraham, the possession of which by any man makes him the seed of Abraham.

Returning to the subject of "remnant" and "gentiles," the Book of Mormon prophecies still do not refer to the latter-day gentiles as anything other than "gentiles" even when they are "numbered among the seed of Lehi." Gentiles retain in prophecy their identification with "gentiles" although they are adopted as Lehi's seed. Hence Joseph Smith's reference in the Kirtland Temple dedicatory prayer to the Latter-

[112] D&C 131: 5: "(May 17th, 1843.) The more sure word of prophecy means a man's knowing that he is sealed up unto eternal life, by revelation and the spirit of prophecy, through the power of the Holy Priesthood."

day Saints as "gentiles" by identity.[113] Whenever a gentile manages to acquire this adoption, they do not become identified as the "remnant" as a result. Instead, they become heirs to share in the promised blessings, but as "gentiles." They will get to assist the "remnant" but as "gentiles" not as the "remnant." Still, those who are adopted as Lehi's seed inherit with the "remnant" the Lord's promises. But they are nevertheless called in prophecy "gentiles" throughout.

The priesthood held by Melchizedek was Patriarchal. The "City" was a family, sealed to him. They came into the order through the authority given to him to seal on earth and in heaven.

We have two divisions of priesthood in the Church, one which we call Melchizedek and one which we call Aaronic. These are not the same as what Melchizedek held, because in the Melchizedek order sealing authority is not generally granted.

Moses had authority from Jethro, but also visited with the Lord face to face, at which time the Lord gave him a work to do. The work was greater than the authority given by Jethro, and of necessity included all keys to accomplish it (as I have explained earlier in a post about keys accompanying assignments).

Lehi was a descendant of Abraham, Isaac, Jacob and Joseph; as was Joseph Smith. There is no conflict with Joseph as Dispensation head being the Patriarch of all who came after him, and Lehi being the father of all gentiles who convert in this dispensation.

Go back and review the chart from Orson Hyde I referred to earlier and you will see that genealogical order does not control, but worthiness and capacity control. How the eternal family will be structured will be the result of what the Lord knows to be the right, joyful, best and holiest of family orders.

1 Nephi 14: 3-4

> **"And that great pit, which hath been digged for them by that great and abominable church, which was founded by the devil and his children, that he might lead away the souls of men down to hell—yea, that great pit which hath been digged for the destruction of men shall be filled by those who digged it, unto their utter destruction, saith the Lamb of God; not the destruction of the soul, save it be the casting of it into that hell which hath no end. For behold, this is according to the captivity of the devil, and also according to the justice of God, upon all those who will work wickedness and abomination before him."**

---

[113] D&C 109: 60: "Now these words, O Lord, we have spoken before thee, concerning the revelations and commandments which thou hast given unto us, who are identified with the Gentiles."

Now I wish Nephi would only prophecy smooth things to us.[114] But once again here we find him being negative. He needs to repent or he's going to lose readers.

The "great pit" is an interesting symbol. Remember when the brothers sought to kill Joseph? Before they sold him into slavery, they put him into a pit in which there was no water.[115] They stripped him of his sacred garment—not of "many colors" but of "sacred markings." Having stripped him of the garment that belonged to the heir, and assured him of his exaltation, they cast him into a pit without water. He descended, as the damned, into the waterless pit. This pit symbolizes the damned souls in spirit prison who, without deliverance from the waters of baptism, are left to suffer.[116] Joseph's pit without water is a reminder of how the ordinances that pass us through the water are the means of deliverance. (Hence the Red Sea and rebirth of Israel as they emerged from Egypt.) Christ also alluded to this in His parable of Lazarus, when the torment could only be cooled by covenantal water.[117]

Well the abominable church offers ordinances, but they leave people in a pit, without redemption and in need of authoritative washing to cleanse from sin. The devil and his children are the founders of this great and abominable order. They seek to cheat mankind of salvation. If they can cause even a little error that robs power from the ordinances performed, they can keep mankind captive. For death and hell will claim all those who have not been redeemed from the awful pit.

How unkind would it be to fail to warn people of this risk they face? How unkind would it be to allow them to proceed into the afterlife unprepared, uncleansed, and unredeemed? Which would be better, to stay silent while the idolatry of the Latter-day Saints robs them of redemption, or to speak up and warn? Men and institutions will never redeem a man. Idolizing an institution will damn every participant. Idolizing men will damn those false religionists. In the Latter-day Saint community we have two groups: Those who are humble and follow

---

[114] Isa. 30: 10: "Which say to the seers, See not; and to the prophets, Prophesy not unto us right things, speak unto us smooth things, prophesy deceits:"

[115] Gen. 37: 23-24: "And it came to pass, when Joseph was come unto his brethren, that they stript Joseph out of his coat, his coat of many colours that was on him; And they took him, and cast him into a pit: and the pit was empty, there was no water in it."

116 Zech. 9: 12: "Turn you to the strong hold, ye prisoners of hope: even to day do I declare that I will render double unto thee;"

117 Luke 16: 24: "And he cried and said, Father Abraham, have mercy on me, and send Lazarus, that he may dip the tip of his finger in water, and cool my tongue; for I am tormented in this flame."

Christ, but who are taught by the precepts of men and err.[118] And the rest are those who follow men and worship the institution and proclaim "All is well" with their faith. For the first group there is hope, so long as they are able to find the truth.[119] For the rest, they will become heirs of this prophecy of Nephi's, all the while assuring one another that the odds are they are going to be exalted.

The goal in every generation is to become Zion. To do that you must have a return of a Patriarchal head, as in Enoch's day or in Melchizedek's day, wherein they organized again after the pattern of heaven. A family. One. Where all things are in common because there is a loving environment where all are of equal worth. No one aspires to be a leader, but all become sons and daughters, brothers and sisters, husbands and wives where the care of all is as natural as family affection for one another.

The devil and his children seek to fragment, to divide, and to keep mankind from organizing into a family where the hearts of fathers are with the children and the hearts of children are toward their fathers. When you divide up into separate clans or divided families, while still paying tribute to the honored position of "family life" among the divided clans and families, you still have only a form of godliness without any power. This is the goal of the devil. It will prevent Zion from ever being brought again. It will leave people unorganized and unprepared to assume a place in the government of God, which is His eternal and singular extended family, where all are one.

The references to the "hell that hath no end" is that same play on words that is defined in D&C 19: 5-12.[120] It is a place of torment, where people suffer as in the Telestial Kingdom, or the world in which you

---

118 2 Ne. 28: 14: "They wear stiff necks and high heads; yea, and because of pride, and wickedness, and abominations, and whoredoms, they have all gone astray save it be a few, who are the humble followers of Christ; nevertheless, they are led, that in many instances they do err because they are taught by the precepts of men."

119 D&C 123: 12: "For there are many yet on the earth among all sects, parties, and denominations, who are blinded by the subtle craftiness of men, whereby they lie in wait to deceive, and who are only kept from the truth because they know not where to find it—"

120 D&C 19: 5-12: "Wherefore, I revoke not the judgments which I shall pass, but woes shall go forth, weeping, wailing and gnashing of teeth, yea, to those who are found on my left hand. Nevertheless, it is not written that there shall be no end to this torment, but it is written endless torment. Again, it is written eternal damnation; wherefore it is more express than other scriptures, that it might work upon the hearts of the children of men, altogether for my name's glory. Wherefore, I will explain unto you this mystery, for it is meet unto you to know even as mine apostles. I speak unto you that are chosen in this thing, even as one, that you may enter into my rest. For, behold, the mystery of godliness, how great is it! For, behold, I am endless, and the punishment which is given from my hand is endless punishment, for Endless is my name. Wherefore—Eternal punishment is God's punishment. Endless punishment is God's punishment."

presently reside (to paraphrase the Endowment). How long will people endure such an experience? Until they repent.[121] What if they do not repent? They will suffer, worlds without end.[122]

All of this according to "the justice of God."

Notice that people arrive here because of the "abominable church" that will always be ready to preach to you false, vain and foolish doctrines. They will offer anything to distract you and keep you from seeing the Lord "bring again Zion." They will use the words of Zion to preach a false faith. They are "abominable" because their false teachings are clothed in the vocabulary of truth.

At that day even the very elect will be the targets of deception. Those claiming falsely to be "prophets" will arise and lead away many. They will show great wonders, spacious and glorious buildings, feats of charity and good will. But the elect will not be deceived, though they may be troubled.[123] They will not be deceived because they treasure up His words. They know His voice, recognize when it speaks, and will use it to keep them from deception. They will have entertained angels, who will have gathered them, and will be waiting for His return.[124]

Now, indeed, is the great day of Satan's power; who rules from the rivers to the ends of the earth and there are none to molest him or make him afraid. We look for the day when, again, a voice will cry out in the wilderness saying to walk in the strait path of the Lord. It would be

---

[121] D&C 76: 99-101: "For these are they who are of Paul, and of Apollos, and of Cephas. These are they who say they are some of one and some of another—some of Christ and some of John, and some of Moses, and some of Elias, and some of Esaias, and some of Isaiah, and some of Enoch; But received not the gospel, neither the testimony of Jesus, neither the prophets, neither the everlasting covenant."

[122] D&C 76: 109-112: "But behold, and lo, we saw the glory and the inhabitants of the telestial world, that they were as innumerable as the stars in the firmament of heaven, or as the sand upon the seashore; And heard the voice of the Lord saying: These all shall bow the knee, and every tongue shall confess to him who sits upon the throne forever and ever; For they shall be judged according to their works, and every man shall receive according to his own works, his own dominion, in the mansions which are prepared; And they shall be servants of the Most High; but where God and Christ dwell they cannot come, worlds without end."

[123] JS-Matt. 1: 22-25: "For in those days there shall also arise false Christs, and false prophets, and shall show great signs and wonders, insomuch, that, if possible, they shall deceive the very elect, who are the elect according to the covenant. Behold, I speak these things unto you for the elect's sake; and you also shall hear of wars, and rumors of wars; see that ye be not troubled, for all I have told you must come to pass; but the end is not yet. Behold, I have told you before; Wherefore, if they shall say unto you: Behold, he is in the desert; go not forth: Behold, he is in the secret chambers; believe it not;"

[124] JS-Matt. 1: 37: "And whoso treasureth up my word, shall not be deceived, for the Son of Man shall come, and he shall send his angels before him with the great sound of a trumpet, and they shall gather together the remainder of his elect from the four winds, from one end of heaven to the other."

interesting if that should happen to see who would recognize it, and who would want to know instead "by what authority" such a voice cries out.

Well, there's more to the verse than this. Ask yourself:

- Why is it a "great pit which hath been digged for the destruction of men?"
- Who is it that "shall fill" it?
- What does "utter destruction" mean?
- What does the phrase "not the destruction of the soul, save it be the casting of it into that hell which hath no end" refer to?
- Why is this "according to the captivity of the devil?"
- Why is this "also according to the justice of God, upon all those who will work wickedness and abomination before him?"

It is an interesting insight into the patience of God, the eternal purposes of God, and the endless, even "worlds without end" which will be provided for all those who will not repent. What a vast, eternal work God has set about to accomplish! Imagine bringing to pass the immortality and eternal life of man! What an endless process such a work may entail! Why would anyone procrastinate the day of their repentance?

1 Nephi 14: 5

> **"And it came to pass that the angel spake unto me, Nephi, saying: Thou hast beheld that if the Gentiles repent it shall be well with them; and thou also knowest concerning the covenants of the Lord unto the house of Israel; and thou also hast heard that whoso repenteth not must perish."**

Again a reminder that Nephi's teachings come from an angel. He's not on his own errand in making these things known. I doubt a person of good faith and common sense would ever dare to make declarations as Nephi does unless he had received the message from such a source. Joseph put it this way: "None but fools will trifle with the souls of men. How vain and trifling have been our spirits, our conferences, our councils, our meetings, our private as well as public conversations—too low, too mean, too vulgar, too condescending for the dignified characters of the called and chosen of God, according to the purposes of His will, from before the foundation of the world!" (DHC Vol 3, pp. 295-96.) Nephi was no fool. He wanted us to understand these teachings came from a higher source, and not man's wisdom. Indeed, what man can open up the mysteries that have remained hidden? Either God makes them known or they remain a mystery!

I believe the wisest course would have been for all our teachers, from Joseph till today, to either declare what the Lord and His angels have made known to them or to remain silent. Had that been the practice our libraries would undoubtedly be sparse. But what few books that remained would be the "best books" worthy of study.[125] I understand that not all have faith. But teachers do a profound disservice whenever they pontificate about something they do not understand. No-one is an "authority" who has not received intelligence from the Lord or His angels. They are simply trying to be helpful, or seeking to magnify a calling, but they are not on His errand. Alas, the full extent of this problem cannot be known. All those who have spoken in His name, but without His instruction and direction, have indeed taken His name in vain. This will be a great burden for those who have chosen to use His name in violation of a fundamental commandment to the contrary.[126]

The happy news is that "if the Gentiles repent" is always a condition for moving forward. We can't get through carrying on our backs the false, vain and foolish traditions men have handed to us. We must lay them down. Unless we do so we wind up exactly at the point when this Dispensation began: suffering under doctrine which consists merely of the commandments of men, having a form of godliness without power.[127]

What must gentiles do to "repent?" All gentiles, including those who have accepted the Restoration and who claim to believe the Book of Mormon…What must they do? To answer that look again carefully at the Lord's condemnation of us:

> "And your minds in times past have been darkened because of unbelief, and because you have treated lightly the things you have received— Which vanity and unbelief have brought the whole church under condemnation. And this condemnation resteth upon the children of Zion, even all. And they shall remain under this condemnation until they repent and **remember the new covenant, even the Book of Mormon and the former commandments which I have given them, not only to say, but to do according to that which I have written**—That they may bring forth fruit meet for their Father's kingdom; otherwise there remaineth a scourge and judgment to be poured out upon the children of Zion." (D&C 84: 54-58.)

---

[125] D&C 88: 118: "And as all have not faith, seek ye diligently and teach one another words of wisdom; yea, seek ye out of the best books words of wisdom; seek learning, even by study and also by faith."

[126] Ex. 20: 7: "Thou shalt not take the name of the Lord thy God in vain; for the Lord will not hold him guiltless that taketh his name in vain."

[127] JS-H 1: 19: "I was answered that I must join none of them, for they were all wrong; and the Personage who addressed me said that all their creeds were an abomination in his sight; that those professors were all corrupt; that: 'they draw near to me with their lips, but their hearts are far from me, they teach for doctrines the commandments of men, having a form of godliness, but they deny the power thereof'."

Then Nephi's angel-minister reminds Nephi of two different thoughts: 1) There are covenants with the house of Israel. So they will be remembered. 2) Whoever repents will find things will be well. Nephi was told: "thou also knowest concerning the covenants of the Lord unto the house of Israel; and thou also hast heard that whoso repenteth not must perish." The result is that even though the gentiles are not given a covenant status, they are nonetheless included within the promise that it is well with whoever should repent. Accordingly, if they will repent, the gentiles will not perish but will have eternal life.

How beautiful upon the mountains are the feet of those who declare that God reigneth and will deliver His people. How merciful it is that the Lord God will accept all those as His people who will repent and come unto Him.

1 Nephi 14: 6

> **"Therefore, wo be unto the Gentiles if it so be that they harden their hearts against the Lamb of God."**

Interestingly, rather than shouting out in rejoicing that all who repent will escape punishment, the angel instead pronounces a "wo" upon the gentiles. It is almost as if the future of the gentile conduct inspires nothing but pessimism for the angel. It inspires another warning and condemnation for the gentiles who, having received the Book of Mormon and other sacred writings, are then fully responsible to repent.

Notice that the relationship is between the "Lamb of God" and the gentiles. It is not between the gentiles and "leaders" or "prophets" or "administrators" or "general authorities" or even messengers. It is between the gentiles and "the Lamb of God."

Why that specific a relationship? Why is it exclusively between the individual and Christ?

Read again the description of the Telestial folk who return "worlds without end" to their condemnation: "And the glory of the telestial is one, even as the glory of the stars is one; for as one star differs from another star in glory, even so differs one from another in glory in the telestial world; For these are they who are of Paul, and of Apollos, and of Cephas. These are they who say they are some of one and some of another—some of Christ and some of John, and some of Moses, and some of Elias, and some of Esaias, and some of Isaiah, and some of Enoch; But received not the gospel, neither the testimony of Jesus, neither the prophets, neither the everlasting covenant." (D&C 76: 98-101.)

From what you've now learned can you see how one might follow even a true messenger but fail to gain "the testimony of Jesus?"

Can you now understand why, although you have followed messengers, you may have not in fact received the "everlasting covenant?"

The Temple is a type and shadow. It is a symbol of the real thing, but it is not the real thing. The "everlasting covenant" is taught there. But to gain it you must receive it through "the testimony of Jesus." Is this "testimony of Jesus" yours? Or is it rather Jesus testifying to you? If it is He testifying to you, then what must His testimony be?

In light of that what does it mean then to "harden your hearts against the Lamb of God?" As you answer that, keep in mind His formula in D&C 93: 1: "Verily, thus saith the Lord: It shall come to pass that every soul who forsaketh his sins and cometh unto me, and calleth on my name, and obeyeth my voice, and keepeth my commandments, shall see my face and know that I am." Here Christ is but reiterating the message of the Book of Mormon.

Then how do you repent? I was asked about idolatry among the Saints. Anything that separates you from the Lamb of God is an idol. Cast it aside and come to Him. Why we have idols between us and the Lord is as different as one person is from another. Almost without exception, it comes as a result of a false tradition handed down. Your false traditions are based on your life's experiences while another's false traditions are based on theirs. No matter what they are or how they were acquired, whatever separates Christ from you must be set aside. Come to HIM. Not to me or any other. Only He can save you.

No wonder that after making great promises to the gentiles, *if they will but repent*, the angel cries out "wo be unto the Gentiles!" They won't receive: 1) the Gospel, neither 2) the testimony of Jesus, neither 3) the prophets sent to warn them and the message given to them, neither 4) the everlasting covenant offered to them.

Will you?

It's amazing the power (or influence) of one word: repent. There is quite a linguistic history of this one word. It comes from French *penitire* (to regret), from the Latin *poenitire* (make sorry), and *poene* (pain, punishment, penalty). Some say that it was used when translating to keep "the masses" in constant subjection to the (Catholic) Church. Back in the day, you could pull out your purse and "pay" for sins, or you could do penitence (self punishment) by whipping yourself or whatever. It's interesting how these "negative" Gentile definitions have worked their way into how view repentance today.

Contrast that with the word used in the Greek translation of the Bible: Metanoia (meta meaning change or turn, as in metamorphosis; and noia meaning mind or heart, as in paranoia). The Greek term for repentance, metanoia, denotes a change of mind, a reorientation, a fundamental transformation of outlook, of an individual's vision of the world and of her/himself, and a new way of loving others and the Universe. It involves, not mere regret of past evil but a recognition by a person of a darkened vision of her/his own condition, in which sin, by separating her/him from Deity, has reduced her/him to a divided, autonomous existence, depriving her/him of both her/his natural glory and freedom.

There is also an Aramaic version of repentance: *tubu*. It means return or come home.

1 Nephi 14: 7

> **"For the time cometh, saith the Lamb of God, that I will work a great and a marvelous work among the children of men; a work which shall be everlasting, either on the one hand or on the other —either to the convincing of them unto peace and life eternal, or unto the deliverance of them to the hardness of their hearts and the blindness of their minds unto their being brought down into captivity, and also into destruction, both temporally and spiritually, according to the captivity of the devil, of which I have spoken."**

There will be a time when the accounts will all be settled. Everything will become everlasting and people will either inherit eternal lives and move forward, or they will return to be destroyed both temporally and spiritually again. Joseph Smith commented in the King Follett Discourse about the process of gaining exaltation. He said, "you must begin with the first, and go on until you learn all the principles of exaltation. But it will be a great while after you have passed through the veil before you will have learned them. It is not all to be comprehended in this world; it will be a great work to learn our salvation and exaltation even beyond the grave."

Death and hell are the devil's domain. He's the god of that world, and since we have death and suffering here, he calls himself the god of this world. Those who come here are subject to his buffeting, and his will. They are tormented, tempted, troubled, and then they die. While captive here, they endure the insults of the flesh, and the difficulties of trying to find their way back to God.

Those who find Him, however, are able to receive "peace and life eternal" through a higher way. The devil is bound for them, and they are able to be "added upon" by the experiences and difficulties here.

All of this is called a "great and marvelous work" to occur "among the children of men." Note it isn't the "remnant" or the "gentiles" but "the children of men." Why so? Is everyone invited? Why, if everyone is invited, will it largely only affect the "remnant," and the "gentiles," and the "scattered Israel," and "Jews?" What about the "heathen," since they are also "the children of men?" Don't they also have part in the first resurrection?[128] Will even some of them be included among the "children of men" who behold this "great and marvelous work?"

Why is it "**everlasting**" whether it is for "peace and eternal life" or "captivity and destruction?" Isn't "*Everlasting*" another of God's names

[128] D&C 45: 54: "And then shall the heathen nations be redeemed, and they that knew no law shall have part in the first resurrection; and it shall be tolerable for them."

just like "*Eternal*" and "*Endless*?"[129] If so, then what does the "everlasting peace and eternal life," and "everlasting captivity and destruction" really involve? [You really need to read that paper I've been emailing out if you haven't read it already.]

Why does God want us to respond to His message and get out of this Telestial Kingdom into another, higher kingdom? Why does He want us to become like Him? How is this experience able to make us more like Him?

If one is involved in the "continuation of the lives"[130] is that distant and second-hand? Or does God (or the Gods) get involved directly with His/Their children?[131]

What causes "hardness of their hearts?" What causes "blindness of their eyes?" Why are those whose hearts are hard unable to receive Christ? Why are those who are blind unwilling to see Him?

This cycle of inviting people to come to the Lamb of God has been going on for some time now. When mankind generally rejected Him after the time of Noah, there was a chosen people who were given a sacred tradition. Ultimately they got proud, failed to recognize Him when He came, rejected His message, and killed Him. Gentiles converted and became the inheritors of His teachings. Then the gentiles began to persecute the previously chosen people for generations. In this verse the gentiles are remembered, sacred materials are entrusted to them with an obligation to spread that sacred material back to the earlier chosen people. However, for the gentiles to be able to accomplish this they need to hold onto the sacred materials and teachings. You simply can't spread abroad what you've failed to retain.

If the gentiles let the sacred materials and teachings fall into disuse, forfeit their priesthood by draining it of any power, and have nothing to offer the previously chosen people, then the gentiles will be cast off, trodden under foot and destroyed, as we have earlier seen.

This verse reminds us what is at stake: Eternity. Or at least God's judgment. It'll be embarrassing to return to Him unimproved and un-added upon. Particularly when His hand was stretched out to us all the

---

129 D&C 19: 10-12: "For, behold, the mystery of godliness, how great is it! For, behold, I am endless, and the punishment which is given from my hand is endless punishment, for Endless is my name. Wherefore—Eternal punishment is God's punishment. Endless punishment is God's punishment."

130 D&C 132: 22: "For strait is the gate, and narrow the way that leadeth unto the exaltation and continuation of the lives, and few there be that find it, because ye receive me not in the world neither do ye know me."

131 Abr. 3: 24-25: "And there stood one among them that was like unto God, and he said unto those who were with him: We will go down, for there is space there, and we will take of these materials, and we will make an earth whereon these may dwell; And we will prove them herewith, to see if they will do all things whatsoever the Lord their God shall command them;"

day long. Gentiles who do as they are asked are given all the blessings of the chosen people. Those who do not are rejected and destroyed.

As a friend and I discussed last week, Hindu's advise us to get off the wheel and return to God. They may be onto something with that thought. One eternal round, indeed…

1 Nephi 14: 8-9

> **"And it came to pass that when the angel had spoken these words, he said unto me: Rememberest thou the covenants of the Father unto the house of Israel? I said unto him, Yea. And it came to pass that he said unto me: Look, and behold that great and abominable church, which is the mother of abominations, whose founder is the devil."**

The dialogue between Nephi and the angel is interrupted. Nephi is brought into the dialogue as the angel interrupts and asks Nephi a question. You should ask yourself why an angel behaves in this manner? Why interrupt the teaching by asking Nephi questions?

And what a question it is: " Rememberest thou the covenants of the Father unto the house of Israel?" Once again, it is the "covenants of the Father" that is important and controls what is being taught and all history involved. It remains not only "in the beginning" but throughout "is the Word of God." Consider how broadly the "Word" of God may be applied:

- Christ is the "Word of God" because He lived and did all in conformity with the will of the Father.[132]
- All of creation came into being because of the Father's Word, or power.[133]
- Christ's spoken Word had such power as to astonish onlookers.[134]

---

[132] 3 Ne. 11: 11: "And behold, I am the light and the life of the world; and I have drunk out of that bitter cup which the Father hath given me, and have glorified the Father in taking upon me the sins of the world, in the which I have suffered the will of the Father in all things from the beginning."

[133] Mormon 9: 17: "Who shall say that it was not a miracle that by his word the heaven and the earth should be; and by the power of his word man was created of the dust of the earth; and by the power of his word have miracles been wrought?"

[134] Luke 4: 32, 36: "And they were astonished at his doctrine: for his word was with power. …And they were all amazed, and spake among themselves, saying, What a word is this! for with authority and power he commandeth the unclean spirits, and they come out."

- Nothing of power hereafter will exist unless obtained by the Father's Word.[135]
- Moses made water come forth from the rock by the Father's Word.[136]
- Joseph Smith was able to bring the Book of Mormon forth because of the Father's word.[137]
- His Word is "quick" and "powerful" and can cut like a two-edged sword.[138]
- It was by this Word of God that Enoch had power to hold at defiance the armies of nations.[139]

Without the "covenants of the Father" the best laid plans, the most noble aspirations, the desire to have Zion return, will all fail. It will return by a covenant or not at all. It will return in strict conformity with His covenant, His Word, and not according to the vain desires of men.

The angel is setting up a contrast for Nephi. First he asks if Nephi remembers the Father's covenants, to which Nephi responds that he does remember them. Now, often in the Book of Mormon the word "remember" is used to mean "keep." If that is the way it is used here, then Nephi is being asked if he keeps the covenants of the Father, so far as they apply to him. Using that meaning, the angel is inquiring about Nephi's worthiness to receive more. Or, in other words: "Do you follow the Father's commandments?" "Yes." "Then I will show you more." Reminding Nephi that the only reason he is beholding these things is

---

[135] D&C 132: 13: "And everything that is in the world, whether it be ordained of men, by thrones, or principalities, or powers, or things of name, whatsoever they may be, that are not by me or by my word, saith the Lord, shall be thrown down, and shall not remain after men are dead, neither in nor after the resurrection, saith the Lord your God."

[136] 1 Ne. 17: 29: "Yea, and ye also know that Moses, by his word according to the power of God which was in him, smote the rock, and there came forth water, that the children of Israel might quench their thirst."

[137] Mormon 8: 16: "And blessed be he that shall bring this thing to light; for it shall be brought out of darkness unto light, according to the word of God; yea, it shall be brought out of the earth, and it shall shine forth out of darkness, and come unto the knowledge of the people; and it shall be done by the power of God."

[138] D&C 11: 2: "Behold, I am God; give heed to my word, which is quick and powerful, sharper than a two-edged sword, to the dividing asunder of both joints and marrow; therefore give heed unto my word."

[139] Moses 7: 13: "And so great was the faith of Enoch that he led the people of God, and their enemies came to battle against them; and he spake the word of the Lord, and the earth trembled, and the mountains fled, even according to his command; and the rivers of water were turned out of their course; and the roar of the lions was heard out of the wilderness; and all nations feared greatly, so powerful was the word of Enoch, and so great was the power of the language which God had given him."

because of his obedience and sacrifice. Or, to put it more plainly, reminding US that this kind of information and learning from angelic ministers comes as a consequence of following everything taught to you before. You receive more because you follow what you already have.

Now, after the inquiry and answer, the contrast is shown—On the one hand: The Covenants of the Father. On the other hand: the Great and Abominable Church.

God's covenants are strict and apply in a very precise manner. The great whore uses religion to promise to all people everywhere their desires for being comforted in their sins. The great and abominable church does not want you to forsake your sins, but to retain them and expect God will forgive and overlook them. The great and abominable church wants you to believe that the way is broad and many will enter into exaltation. This whore teaches that no matter your conduct, the odds are you are going to be exalted. So eat, drink and be merry. If God is going to be upset He will merely beat you with a few stripes and promote you into the kingdom of God anyway.[140]

This contrast is drawn for Nephi because these are two extremes. Both of them are religious. One is founded on a true religion, the other is a false religion. One follows the Father's covenants and will result in God's promised results. The other follows the commandments of men who have mingled their own philosophies with scripture so that their doctrines are all corrupt. They share a vocabulary, but nothing else. For one, to "repent" is to return to God's presence, for the other "repent" is to satisfy institutional demands and surrender to control by others. The angel uses the contrast because this is where mankind finds themselves. We live between these two choices. Our eternal consequences hinge on how we choose. Among all sects there are good people who are blinded by the craftiness of deceitful men.[141] Even though they may be honorable, by surrendering to deceit they forfeit the crown.[142]

This contrast is shown to Nephi, and shared by him with us, because we are always facing the dilemma of choosing between those who will promise you everything and give you nothing, and those who warn you

---

140 2 Ne. 28: 8: "And there shall also be many which shall say: Eat, drink, and be merry; nevertheless, fear God—he will justify in committing a little sin; yea, lie a little, take the advantage of one because of his words, dig a pit for thy neighbor; there is no harm in this; and do all these things, for tomorrow we die; and if it so be that we are guilty, God will beat us with a few stripes, and at last we shall be saved in the kingdom of God."

141 D&C 123: 12: "For there are many yet on the earth among all sects, parties, and denominations, who are blinded by the subtle craftiness of men, whereby they lie in wait to deceive, and who are only kept from the truth because they know not where to find it—"

142 D&C 76: 74-76: "Who received not the testimony of Jesus in the flesh, but afterwards received it. These are they who are honorable men of the earth, who were blinded by the craftiness of men. These are they who receive of his glory, but not of his fulness."

to repent, as a result of which you may receive everything. Oddly, mankind seems to prefer the former.

1 Nephi 14: 10

> **"And he said unto me: Behold there are save two churches only; the one is the church of the Lamb of God, and the other is the church of the devil; wherefore, whoso belongeth not to the church of the Lamb of God belongeth to that great church, which is the mother of abominations; and she is the whore of all the earth."**

There are and always have been two churches only. One is true. Its members belong to the Lamb of God. The Lamb, and their Father.

Either you belong to the elect family of Christ, the Church of the Firstborn, or you don't. All other religions and philosophies are false. Read again the description of those who are saved. (See *What's in a name?*) There are only "two," and one of them is not the Catholic Church, nor the Presbyterian Church, nor the Lutheran Church, nor The Church of Jesus Christ of Latter-day Saints. However, the ordinances received through The Church of Jesus Christ of Latter-day Saints are expected for those who belong to "the church of the Lamb of God," but there is not a complete overlap of the "church of the Lamb of God" and The Church of Jesus Christ of Latter-day Saints.

Therefore, based on what Nephi says above, unless we are part of that body of believers whose Father is Christ, and who posses a covenant from Him that they will be His, we belong to the whore of all the earth, a church of abominations. Those who are believers are they who He has declared to His Father "...having been true and faithful in all things."

The other and all-inclusive great church is comprised of all philosophies, all belief systems, all unbelief systems, all rationalizations, all theories and vanities that distract people from repenting and following Christ. These vary from very good things that are uplifting, and possess even great portions of truth, to the degrading and perverse. This all-inclusive church is a "whore" because she is completely indiscriminate and open for all to have her acceptance and affection. She welcomes you. The only requirement being that you have false beliefs.

She will make you rich, or she will make you covet riches. If she gives them to you it is to corrupt you. If she withholds them from you, it is so you will lust and envy what you do not have.

Look at her list of trade goods, given in the description of her fall by John the Revelator:

> "And the merchants of the earth shall weep and mourn over her; for no man buyeth their merchandise any more: The merchandise of gold, and silver, and precious stones, and of pearls, and fine linen, and purple, and silk, and scarlet, and all thyine wood, and all manner vessels of ivory, and all manner vessels of most precious wood, and

of brass, and iron, and marble, And cinnamon, and odours, and ointments, and frankincense, and wine, and oil, and fine flour, and wheat, and beasts, and sheep, and horses, and chariots, and slaves, and souls of men." (Rev. 18: 11-13.)

The final two on the list are the reason for the other items. The earlier ones lead inevitably to slavery and loss of the souls of men. The devil, who founded her, is not interested in anything other than slavery and the loss of your soul.

The great illusion of a whore is to imagine she likes you. To imagine she cares for you. To imagine she desires what you desire and is cooperating with you because she finds you attractive, appealing, and that you fulfill her longing. It is a lie, an illusion and a fraud. Her bodily diseases are less virulent than her contamination of the soul. Empty, false, vain and foolish thoughts occupy the imagination of those who have intercourse with the great whore. She prefers the lie, relies on it. You would not be her customer if not for the lies.

What an amazing congruence of sexual images and religious failing have been given to us by Nephi and John the Revelator. How apt! How perfect! Imagining something that is degrading and debilitating to be sacred. It is a work of a god or a devil. And of course it is for us to decide between them.

The whore does have her allures, doesn't she? How many of us are in her embrace, speaking of love and Jesus and the joy of the Saints, while remaining wretched, poor, foolish and lost? She offers you vanity as a religion. "Vanity" because it is vain, or without any effect to save, i.e., without power. Only a form of godliness, nothing real.

Such powerful deception as is implied in these verses demands our attention. It ought to force us forward to seek and obtain a more sure word of prophecy, so we **know our God and covenant directly with Him**. It should make us refuse all the imitations, all the deceptions, all those who pretend to speak truth, and instead demand that true messengers be sent from whom we can be taught further light and knowledge.

There's the rub, isn't it? How to tell the one from the other? A concealed and veiled resurrected Christ laid aside all glory and walked with two of His disciples for approximately seven miles on the day of His resurrection. After His departure, the one asked the other: **"And they said one to another, Did not our heart burn within us, while he talked with us by the way, and while he opened to us the scriptures?"** (Luke 24: 32.) Undoubtedly the reason they already knew it was Him was because truth has power that vanity does not. Therefore, it appears that before our eyes are opened, we must determine truth first. I've written about this in the Appendix to *Eighteen Verses*.

Interesting cause and effect. Interesting the Lord would open the scriptures to touch their hearts. What a powerful pattern the Lord has given for those who follow Him.

1 Nephi 14: 11-12

> **"And it came to pass that I looked and beheld the whore of all the earth, and she sat upon many waters; and she had dominion over all the earth, among all nations, kindreds, tongues, and people. And it came to pass that I beheld the church of the Lamb of God, and its numbers were few, because of the wickedness and abominations of the whore who sat upon many waters; nevertheless, I beheld that the church of the Lamb, who were the saints of God, were also upon all the face of the earth; and their dominions upon the face of the earth were small, because of the wickedness of the great whore whom I saw."**

The whore has "dominion" over all. All nations. All kindreds. All tongues. All people. She has dominion over them all. What does "dominion" mean?

Notice the "church of the Lamb of God" are referred to as "the Saints of God."

The Saints on the other hand, were "few" in number by comparison with the great dominion of the whore.

The Saints numbers are few because of "the wickedness and abominations of the whore." How would the whore's wickedness and abominations cause the Saints to be "few" in number? What trouble must the Saints overcome because of the whore's widespread wickedness? What challenges must the Saints overcome because of the whore's universal abominations? How do they "overcome" these challenges?[143]

What does it mean the whore "sits upon many waters?"[144] Why are they likened to water?[145]

Note the Saints are also "upon all the face of the earth" but are not said to be "sitting upon many waters." They do have, however, "dominions" (in the plural). Why is the whore's dominion singular, while the Saint's plural? The whore's control is one, but the Saints are divided into sub-groups. Why? Will they be led by various prophets from various locations?[146]

---

143 D&C 76: 53: "And who overcome by faith, and are sealed by the Holy Spirit of promise, which the Father sheds forth upon all those who are just and true."

144 Rev. 17: 15: "And he saith unto me, The waters which thou sawest, where the whore sitteth, are peoples, and multitudes, and nations, and tongues."

145 Gen. 49: 4: "Unstable as water, thou shalt not excel; because thou wentest up to thy father's bed; then defiledst thou it: he went up to my couch."

146 D&C 133: 26: "And they who are in the north countries shall come in remembrance before the Lord; and their prophets shall hear his voice, and shall no longer stay themselves; and they shall smite the rocks, and the ice shall flow down at their presence."

This fragmentation of the Saints is set in a time frame of this prophecy and it will not last. However it will exist before the wrath poured out upon the whore begins.

Why is the whore much more successful than the church of the Lamb of God? Or, more importantly, is the number of those involved in these two different cultures any indication of their relative standing before the Lord? If not, then what matter? Is it the quantity of those who are following a particular creed or organization, or the quality of the knowledge some few possess of the Lord?

Will getting more people to join the Church change the outcome of this prophecy from Nephi?

What is important, then, for those who want to be on the right side of this divide? How do they become one of the "few" who are Saints belonging to the Lamb of God?

How should "success" be defined? By numbers, buildings, activity and wealth or possession of knowledge of Christ? If success has nothing to do with numbers, buildings, activity and wealth, why do we concern ourselves with them? If it has something to do with knowledge of Christ, why are so few able to declare they know Him? Who can state they have seen Him? Who can testify as a witness of Him? How successful have we been in distributing the knowledge of the Son of God?

Where should our efforts be focused? Is the Book of Mormon important in accomplishing what the Lord expects from His Saints?

What interesting information Nephi has given us in this verse. But it gets more interesting as it proceeds further…

1 Nephi 14: 13

> **"And it came to pass that I beheld that the great mother of abominations did gather together multitudes upon the face of all the earth, among all the nations of the Gentiles, to fight against the Lamb of God."**

Did you notice that? The whore is also a "mother?" Why is that? What do we learn from that bit of information? Just how loyal will the deceived be to the institution they regard as their great mother? It's no wonder they react with such hostility at the threat posed by the Lamb of God.

Now did you notice also that the fight is against "the Lamb of God" and not the "Saints?" They are opposed to Christ and are going to fight against Him.

This is akin to David's response to Goliath: "Thou comest to me with a sword, and with a spear, and with a shield: but **I come to thee in the name of the Lord of hosts, the God of the armies of Israel, whom thou hast defied. This day will the Lord deliver thee into mine hand**; and I will smite thee, and take thine head from thee; and I will give the carcasses of the host of the Philistines this day unto the fowls of the air, and to the wild beasts of the earth; that all the earth may know that there is a God in Israel. And all this assembly shall know that **the Lord saveth not with sword and spear: for the battle is the Lord's, and he will give you into our hands**." (1 Sam. 17: 45-47.) David knew the fight was between the Lord and Goliath, not between him and Goliath. Therefore the advantage was all the Lord's.

The coming fight will be between those who regard the worldly order as their mother, and the Lamb of God.

Did you notice also that the great mother whore includes "all the nations of the Gentiles?" Meaning that included among this great false order will be the United States, the greatest of the Gentile nations. We've been told in modern revelation that along with all other nations, the United States will be destroyed.[147] We disbelieve this and hope to save the nation. We want to follow the counsel of the Lord to make friends of the mammon of unrighteousness, that when we fail we may be received into everlasting habitations.[148] Your affiliations here will serve you here, but you will not be trusted with true riches.[149] The result is that we have no choice but to flee.

Well, the great whore wants to defeat the Lamb, but she cannot get access to Him. She must settle for destroying His teachings, His doctrines, His ordinances. She will target these truths because they link the Lord to some few who are here. She will at every turn deceive, mislead, corrupt and discourage. She understands that the fight is with the Lord, but to destroy Him she must destroy all that testifies truthfully of Him.

All that is corrupt and corrupted is welcomed by her. All that fails to redeem the souls of men and return them to the Lord's presence is welcomed here in her dominion. She will confer tax benefits, honors, protection and awards upon those who cannot teach the doctrines that save. Wealth will amass, privileges will be given, and the great whore's

---

[147] D&C 87: 6: "And thus, with the sword and by bloodshed the inhabitants of the earth shall mourn; and with famine, and plague, and earthquake, and the thunder of heaven, and the fierce and vivid lightning also, shall the inhabitants of the earth be made to feel the wrath, and indignation, and chastening hand of an Almighty God, until the consumption decreed hath made a full end of all nations;"

[148] Luke 16: 9: "And I say unto you, Make to yourselves friends of the mammon of unrighteousness; that, when ye fail, they may receive you into everlasting habitations."

[149] Luke 16: 11: "If therefore ye have not been faithful in the unrighteous mammon, who will commit to your trust the true riches?"

dominion will expand to include "all churches" in these last days.[150] Persecution is the heritage of the righteous because this world has no part in Christ.[151] When the righteous are no longer persecuted, and the honors and awards of men begin to be bestowed upon any religion, you may know they have made friends of the children of mammon.

She cannot destroy Him, so she will turn her anger upon those who preserve His doctrine, His teachings, His truths and destroy them that He may be cast out of this world. This is her plan.

But this battle is between principalities and dominions involving spiritual wickedness in high places, and not just flesh and blood.[152] Therefore we should fear not, because the battle is, always was, and always will be the Lord's.[153]

1 Nephi 14: 14

> **"And it came to pass that I, Nephi, beheld the power of the Lamb of God, that it descended upon the saints of the church of the Lamb, and upon the covenant people of the Lord, who were scattered upon all the face of the earth; and they were armed with righteousness and with the power of God in great glory."**

Once the whore sets about to destroy the Lamb of God, He does not remain in His pavilion away. He takes up the fight for His Saints.

What is the "power of the Lamb of God?"

Why does this "power" "descend" upon the Saints?

Why are there two groups identified, "the Saints of the Lamb of God," and also, "upon the covenant people of the Lord?" Are these the same or two different groups? If two, what is to happen in this descending of "power" upon these two?

---

[150] 2 Ne. 28: 12-14: "Because of pride, and because of false teachers, and false doctrine, their churches have become corrupted, and their churches are lifted up; because of pride they are puffed up. They rob the poor because of their fine sanctuaries; they rob the poor because of their fine clothing; and they persecute the meek and the poor in heart, because in their pride they are puffed up. They wear stiff necks and high heads; yea, and because of pride, and wickedness, and abominations, and whoredoms, they have all gone astray save it be a few, who are the humble followers of Christ; nevertheless, they are led, that in many instances they do err because they are taught by the precepts of men."

[151] John 14: 30: "Hereafter I will not talk much with you: for the prince of this world cometh, and hath nothing in me."

[152] Eph. 6: 12: "For we wrestle not against flesh and blood, but against principalities, against powers, against the rulers of the darkness of this world, against spiritual wickedness in high places."

[153] D&C 105: 14: "For behold, I do not require at their hands to fight the battles of Zion; for, as I said in a former commandment, even so will I fulfil—I will fight your battles."

Why are the "Saints" and the "covenant people" both "scattered upon all the face of the earth?" Why are they not gathered together in one place?

What does it mean to be "armed with righteousness?"

Why are "righteousness" and "the power of God" two different things?

Do the "covenant people" have to have "righteousness" to receive the "power of God?" Are they blessed for the covenant's sake? What about the others? Who are "righteous" and their protection? Are they protected for righteousness sake?

Assuming the "power of God" is given to protect these groups, do they need munitions? Do they need intercontinental firepower? Do they need to form an army for their own defense?

What is the "power of God in great glory?" Will the children of the great whore be able to behold this "power of God in great glory," or will it be hidden from them? If hidden, will they sense something? Will fear fall upon them that they flee from the presence of this glory? Wasn't that the case with Daniel's friends? (Daniel 10: 7.) Wasn't that the case with the companions of Saul? (JST Acts 9: 7 "And *they who were journeying* with him *saw indeed the light, and were afraid; but they heard not the voice of him who spake to him.*") Will Zion not be protected by this "power of God?"[154] If it is to be like the days of Noah[155], then won't there be someone who can speak the word of God and mountains flee, armies held at defiance, and rivers turned out of their course?[156]

Will the same things happen that happened at the time of the great flood? If so, how much relevance does the history from Enoch through Noah have to our day? Should we be familiar with that pattern to know how the pattern may repeat itself?

What can you do to be numbered with those who will be spared? Does the known history of the antediluvians tell you anything about how you need to prepare? Since Enoch had 365 years to develop a people who were worthy to be spared, how much greater a work will it be to prepare now that life spans are generally less than 90 years? How great a work lies before you?

---

[154] D&C 45: 70: "And it shall be said among the wicked: Let us not go up to battle against Zion, for the inhabitants of Zion are terrible; wherefore we cannot stand."

[155] Luke 17: 26-27: "And as it was in the days of Noe, so shall it be also in the days of the Son of man. They did eat, they drank, they married wives, they were given in marriage, until the day that Noe entered into the ark, and the flood came, and destroyed them all."

[156] Moses 7: 13: "And so great was the faith of Enoch that he led the people of God, and their enemies came to battle against them; and he spake the word of the Lord, and the earth trembled, and the mountains fled, even according to his command; and the rivers of water were turned out of their course; and the roar of the lions was heard out of the wilderness; and all nations feared greatly, so powerful was the word of Enoch, and so great was the power of the language which God had given him."

1 Nephi 14: 15-16

> **"And it came to pass that I beheld that the wrath of God was poured out upon that great and abominable church, insomuch that there were wars and rumors of wars among all the nations and kindreds of the earth. And as there began to be wars and rumors of wars among all the nations which belonged to the mother of abominations, the angel spake unto me, saying: Behold, the wrath of God is upon the mother of harlots; and behold, thou seest all these things—"**

God's wrath is "poured out" and takes a specific form: "wars and rumors of wars among all the nations and kindreds." People go to war. The "wicked kill the wicked."[157]

The wicked get to destroy one another, but they do not get to destroy the righteous.[158]

The destruction of God's judgment will be "among all the nations which belonged to the mother of abominations." But that was all nations, was it not? Therefore, what nation will not be at war in this coming day?

The angel makes a point of stating what Nephi is beholding: "Behold, the wrath of God is upon the mother of harlots." How is this God's wrath? The answer is that when God is angry, He withdraws His spirit.[159] And when He withdraws His spirit from one, He generally pours it out on another.[160] When His spirit withdraws, men are left to

---

[157] D&C 63: 33: "I have sworn in my wrath, and decreed wars upon the face of the earth, and the wicked shall slay the wicked, and fear shall come upon every man;"
Prov. 11: 5: "The righteousness of the perfect shall direct his way: but the wicked shall fall by his own wickedness."
Mormon 4: 5: "But, behold, the judgments of God will overtake the wicked; and it is by the wicked that the wicked are punished; for it is the wicked that stir up the hearts of the children of men unto bloodshed."

[158] 1 Ne. 22: 16: "For the time soon cometh that the fulness of the wrath of God shall be poured out upon all the children of men; for he will not suffer that the wicked shall destroy the righteous."

[159] Hel. 6: 35: "And thus we see that the Spirit of the Lord began to withdraw from the Nephites, because of the wickedness and the hardness of their hearts."
Hel. 13: 8: "Therefore, thus saith the Lord: Because of the hardness of the hearts of the people of the Nephites, except they repent I will take away my word from them, and I will withdraw my Spirit from them, and I will suffer them no longer, and I will turn the hearts of their brethren against them."

[160] Hel. 6: 34-36: "And thus we see that the Nephites did begin to dwindle in unbelief, and grow in wickedness and abominations, while the Lamanites began to grow exceedingly in the knowledge of their God; yea, they did begin to keep his statutes and commandments, and to walk in truth and uprightness before him. And thus we see that the Spirit of the Lord began to withdraw from the Nephites, because of the wickedness and the hardness of their hearts. And thus we see that the Lord began to pour out his Spirit upon the Lamanites, because of their easiness and willingness to believe in his words."

their natural, carnal state, filled with envy, jealousy, covetousness, ambition and greed. When the heavens become silent, the judgments of God follow.[161]

This is the means by which the tares ripen in iniquity, and the wheat ripens in righteousness. However, to preserve the spirit among those to be saved in the last days, it will be necessary for the same priesthood, the same calling, to be in possession of those to be preserved. Otherwise they can't ripen into wheat.[162] For the wheat are destined for Celestial

---

[161] Rev. 8: 1: "And when he had opened the seventh seal, there was silence in heaven about the space of half an hour."
D&C 88: 95: "And there shall be silence in heaven for the space of half an hour; and immediately after shall the curtain of heaven be unfolded, as a scroll is unfolded after it is rolled up, and the face of the Lord shall be unveiled;"

[162] D&C 86: 1-11: "Verily, thus saith the Lord unto you my servants, concerning the parable of the wheat and of the tares: Behold, verily I say, the field was the world, and the apostles were the sowers of the seed; And after they have fallen asleep the great persecutor of the church, the apostate, the whore, even Babylon, that maketh all nations to drink of her cup, in whose hearts the enemy, even Satan, sitteth to reign—behold he soweth the tares; wherefore, the tares choke the wheat and drive the church into the wilderness. But behold, in the last days, even now while the Lord is beginning to bring forth the word, and the blade is springing up and is yet tender —Behold, verily I say unto you, the angels are crying unto the Lord day and night, who are ready and waiting to be sent forth to reap down the fields; But the Lord saith unto them, pluck not up the tares while the blade is yet tender (for verily your faith is weak), lest you destroy the wheat also. Therefore, let the wheat and the tares grow together until the harvest is fully ripe; then ye shall first gather out the wheat from among the tares, and after the gathering of the wheat, behold and lo, the tares are bound in bundles, and the field remaineth to be burned. Therefore, thus saith the Lord unto you, with whom the priesthood hath continued through the lineage of your fathers—For ye are lawful heirs, according to the flesh, and have been hid from the world with Christ in God—Therefore your life and the priesthood have remained, and must needs remain through you and your lineage until the restoration of all things spoken by the mouths of all the holy prophets since the world began. Therefore, blessed are ye if ye continue in my goodness, a light unto the Gentiles, and through this priesthood, a savior unto my people Israel. The Lord hath said it. Amen."

Glory and eternal life.[163] This cannot be realized without a covenant[164] and the testimony of Jesus to them.[165]

How should we each proceed?

Can anyone make you "wheat" if you do not the things the Lord commands you to do?[166]

Can anyone give you "oil" for your lamp?

What is your responsibility to obtain these things?

When the time comes that all nations of the earth are at war with one another as the means for the Lord's wrath to be poured out upon the wicked, what is the role of the righteous? Will they join in the battle? Will they be spared?[167]

Why does the Lord not require the righteous to shed the blood of the wicked? Why would He use the wicked to destroy the wicked?

If His spirit withdraws from the world, but remains with His Saints, what peril is there if the Saints don't also withdraw from the world?

Will citizenship in both Babylon and Zion be possible? Will Zion need a bank?

---

[163] D&C 101: 65: "Therefore, I must gather together my people, according to the parable of the wheat and the tares, that the wheat may be secured in the garners to possess eternal life, and be crowned with celestial glory, when I shall come in the kingdom of my Father to reward every man according as his work shall be;"

[164] D&C 132: 20: "Then shall they be gods, because they have no end; therefore shall they be from everlasting to everlasting, because they continue; then shall they be above all, because all things are subject unto them. Then shall they be gods, because they have all power, and the angels are subject unto them."

[165] D&C 76: 51-57: "They are they who received the testimony of Jesus, and believed on his name and were baptized after the manner of his burial, being buried in the water in his name, and this according to the commandment which he has given—That by keeping the commandments they might be washed and cleansed from all their sins, and receive the Holy Spirit by the laying on of the hands of him who is ordained and sealed unto this power; And who overcome by faith, and are sealed by the Holy Spirit of promise, which the Father sheds forth upon all those who are just and true. They are they who are the church of the Firstborn. They are they into whose hands the Father has given all things—They are they who are priests and kings, who have received of his fulness, and of his glory; And are priests of the Most High, after the order of Melchizedek, which was after the order of Enoch, which was after the order of the Only Begotten Son."

[166] Luke 6: 46: "And why call ye me, Lord, Lord, and do not the things which I say?"

[167] D&C 45: 68-71: "And it shall come to pass among the wicked, that every man that will not take his sword against his neighbor must needs flee unto Zion for safety. And there shall be gathered unto it out of every nation under heaven; and it shall be the only people that shall not be at war one with another. And it shall be said among the wicked: Let us not go up to battle against Zion, for the inhabitants of Zion are terrible; wherefore we cannot stand. And it shall come to pass that the righteous shall be gathered out from among all nations, and shall come to Zion, singing with songs of everlasting joy."

1 Nephi 14: 17

> **"And when the day cometh that the wrath of God is poured out upon the mother of harlots, which is the great and abominable church of all the earth, whose founder is the devil, then, at that day, the work of the Father shall commence, in preparing the way for the fulfilling of his covenants, which he hath made to his people who are of the house of Israel."**

Now we get some indication of timing. A great deal has been described, but the timing of the events has been left out until now.

The "day cometh that the wrath of God is poured out upon the mother of harlots"—that is, when the great and abominable church is caught up in worldwide violence, every nation at war with its neighbor or within itself. It is when those events are underway "the work of the Father shall commence" to fulfill all the prior commitments and covenants.

First, the great whore will reel and stagger as a drunkard, drunk with her own blood.

Then the "work of the Father" will "commence." What does it mean to "commence?" Why choose such a desperate hour to begin?

Are there signs of this international and internal violence already afoot? Is the work of the Father now commenced?

The "commencement" of the work is "for the fulfilling of His covenants." What does it mean to "fulfill?" Will every whit of His covenants be all completed, all finished, all kept?[168]

Interestingly, the "fulfilling of His covenants which He hath made to His people who are of the house of Israel" is not divided into "remnant" and "gentile." At the time when His final work begins, all of "the house of Israel" will be remembered, in whatever scattered place they may be found. Why the change? Why no longer focus upon the "remnant" and "Jew" and "gentile" and "scattered house of Israel?" Why does He now call them all "his people?"

Do the fractures heal? Do the divided groups come together at last? Will the scattered, lost and forgotten remains of Israel be found throughout the world?[169] Will the results be a restoration of all Israel, no

---

[168] D&C 1: 38: "What I the Lord have spoken, I have spoken, and I excuse not myself; and though the heavens and the earth pass away, my word shall not pass away, but shall all be fulfilled, whether by mine own voice or by the voice of my servants, it is the same."

[169] Jacob 5: 67-68: "And the branches of the natural tree will I graft in again into the natural tree; And the branches of the natural tree will I graft into the natural branches of the tree; and thus will I bring them together again, that they shall bring forth the natural fruit, and they shall be one."

matter what group they may have been identified with previously?[170] Will these divided, but remembered people become one at last?[171]

How much purging will be needed to bring this to pass?[172]

If the work has begun, are there "servants" already here beginning to move the now wild branches back to their natural roots?[173] How does one respond and return to their natural roots? Who is the "tree of life?"

---

[170] Jacob 5: 72-73: "And it came to pass that the servants did go and labor with their mights; and the Lord of the vineyard labored also with them; and they did obey the commandments of the Lord of the vineyard in all things. And there began to be the natural fruit again in the vineyard; and the natural branches began to grow and thrive exceedingly; and the wild branches began to be plucked off and to be cast away; and they did keep the root and the top thereof equal, according to the strength thereof."

[171] Jacob 5: 74: "And thus they labored, with all diligence, according to the commandments of the Lord of the vineyard, even until the bad had been cast away out of the vineyard, and the Lord had preserved unto himself that the trees had become again the natural fruit; and they became like unto one body; and the fruits were equal; and the Lord of the vineyard had preserved unto himself the natural fruit, which was most precious unto him from the beginning."

[172] Jacob 5: 71: "And the Lord of the vineyard said unto them: Go to, and labor in the vineyard, with your might. For behold, this is the last time that I shall nourish my vineyard; for the end is nigh at hand, and the season speedily cometh; and if ye labor with your might with me ye shall have joy in the fruit which I shall lay up unto myself against the time which will soon come."
D&C 45: 68-71: "And it shall come to pass among the wicked, that every man that will not take his sword against his neighbor must needs flee unto Zion for safety. And there shall be gathered unto it out of every nation under heaven; and it shall be the only people that shall not be at war one with another. And it shall be said among the wicked: Let us not go up to battle against Zion, for the inhabitants of Zion are terrible; wherefore we cannot stand. And it shall come to pass that the righteous shall be gathered out from among all nations, and shall come to Zion, singing with songs of everlasting joy."
D&C 133: 9-12: "And behold, and lo, this shall be their cry, and the voice of the Lord unto all people: Go ye forth unto the land of Zion, that the borders of my people may be enlarged, and that her stakes may be strengthened, and that Zion may go forth unto the regions round about. Yea, let the cry go forth among all people: Awake and arise and go forth to meet the Bridegroom; behold and lo, the Bridegroom cometh; go ye out to meet him. Prepare yourselves for the great day of the Lord. Watch, therefore, for ye know neither the day nor the hour. Let them, therefore, who are among the Gentiles flee unto Zion."

[173] Jacob 5: 70: "And it came to pass that the Lord of the vineyard sent his servant; and the servant went and did as the Lord had commanded him, and brought other servants; and they were few."

How do we reattach ourselves to Him?[174] What of those who would have you attach yourselves to them, to become their disciples, to follow what they claim as their right to lead and control you?[175] How must they lead, if not by exercising control and dominion?[176]

[As long as we are in Section 121, there is an important but still unrecognized truth in that revelation. The caution in Section 121 about abuse is directed in whole at The Church of Jesus Christ of Latter-day Saints. Among other things, it is warning the LDS Church not to persecute the Lord's Saints, and thereby fight against God.[177] It has been traditionally interpreted by the LDS Church to the complete contrary. The LDS teaching turns the warning on its ear, and reads it to mean that you shouldn't fight against the LDS Church! The warning, however, is addressed to the Church and warning it to exercise caution, least they find themselves fighting against the Lord's Saints, and thereby in turn fighting against the Lord. Read it carefully. It is not a caution to you or me, but a caution to the LDS Church itself. It means that there may be Saints of God who are at times at odds with, or critical of the LDS Church. When that happens, the LDS Church is warned to refrain from persecuting them, or else they may find themselves fighting against God. It is an unnoticed warning because the traditional interpretation is used to give the LDS Church protection against criticism.]

Now we jump to late in His ministry where Christ is teaching the Nephites.

---

[174] John 15: 1-6: "I am the true vine, and my Father is the husbandman. Every branch in me that beareth not fruit he taketh away: and every branch that beareth fruit, he purgeth it, that it may bring forth more fruit. Now ye are clean through the word which I have spoken unto you. Abide in me, and I in you. As the branch cannot bear fruit of itself, except it abide in the vine; no more can ye, except ye abide in me. I am the vine, ye are the branches: He that abideth in me, and I in him, the same bringeth forth much fruit: for without me ye can do nothing. If a man abide not in me, he is cast forth as a branch, and is withered; and men gather them, and cast them into the fire, and they are burned."

[175] D&C 121: 36-37: "That the rights of the priesthood are inseparably connected with the powers of heaven, and that the powers of heaven cannot be controlled nor handled only upon the principles of righteousness. That they may be conferred upon us, it is true; but when we undertake to cover our sins, or to gratify our pride, our vain ambition, or to exercise control or dominion or compulsion upon the souls of the children of men, in any degree of unrighteousness, behold, the heavens withdraw themselves; the Spirit of the Lord is grieved; and when it is withdrawn, Amen to the priesthood or the authority of that man."

[176] D&C 121: 41-42: "No power or influence can or ought to be maintained by virtue of the priesthood, only by persuasion, by long-suffering, by gentleness and meekness, and by love unfeigned; By kindness, and pure knowledge, which shall greatly enlarge the soul without hypocrisy, and without guile—"

[177] D&C 121: 38: "Behold, ere he is aware, he is left unto himself, to kick against the pricks, to persecute the saints, and to fight against God."

3 Nephi 21

3 Nephi 21: 1

> **"And verily I say unto you, I give unto you a sign, that ye may know the time when these things shall be about to take place—that I shall gather in, from their long dispersion, my people, O house of Israel, and shall establish again among them my Zion;"**

Christ is telling the Nephites (and us) about timing. He will provide a "sign" to those who watch for such things. Contrary to what you've heard all your life about "signs," they are and always have been part of the true Gospel. They invariably follow faith, but do not and never have produced faith.[178] There are examples of signs throughout God's dealings with those who follow Him. (See, e.g., Helaman 14: 4; Ezek. 24: 24; Ex. 10: 2; Acts 2: 22, among many others.) **We** are supposed to see signs, that we may know God is dealing with **us**.[179]

Christ is giving a sign to us so we may understand when His Father's promises are being fulfilled.

The time when His Father's covenants are to be fulfilled will be the moment when Christ will "gather in, from their long dispersion, my people." Note it is "I" meaning Christ, who will do the gathering. Christ is the great husbandman of this, the Lord's vineyard. It is Christ who will personally do the gathering. How do you suppose Christ will "gather in" those whom He calls "His people?"

Notice how the gathered are referred to by Christ as "my people" and "house of Israel" and "my Zion." When the gathering is complete, the various groups are no longer separately identified. On the other side of this gathering they will be "one" people and a restored "house of Israel."

But note the sequence:

---

[178] D&C 63: 9-10: "But, behold, faith cometh not by signs, but signs follow those that believe. Yea, signs come by faith, not by the will of men, nor as they please, but by the will of God."

[179] D&C 68: 10-11: "And he that believeth shall be blest with signs following, even as it is written. And unto you it shall be given to know the signs of the times, and the signs of the coming of the Son of Man;"

First, gathering in from a long dispersion.

Second, they convert into "my people" or the "house of Israel."

Then they are "established" as "Zion."

Why does the Lord refer to it as "my Zion?" Can you have Zion without the Lord's presence? Can there be Zion without the Lord dwelling among them?[180] Notice in Enoch's City that it was the Lord who came and dwelt there, then later the Lord is the one who names or calls the people "Zion."

When the Lord calls it "my Zion" how literal is this? How directly will the Lord be involved?

If you want to have a place there, do your connections in a church, organization, fraternity, fellowship, quorum or brotherhood matter? If not, what association alone will allow you to participate? How important is the "testimony of Jesus?"

Read again the description of the group of Saints who are included with those who will comprise Zion. As you read, keep in mind all we have discussed up to this point as you recognize familiar words used below:

> 51 They are they who received the testimony of Jesus, and believed on his name and were baptized after the manner of his burial, being buried in the water in his name, and this according to the commandment which he has given—
>
> 52 That by keeping the commandments they might be washed and cleansed from all their sins, and receive the Holy Spirit by the laying on of the hands of him who is ordained and sealed unto this power;
>
> 53 And who overcame by faith, and are sealed by the Holy Spirit of promise, which the Father sheds forth upon all those who are just and true.
>
> 54 They are they who are the church of the Firstborn.
>
> 55 They are they into whose hands the Father has given all things—
>
> 56 They are they who are priests and kings, who have received of his fulness, and of his glory;
>
> 57 And are priests of the Most High, after the order of Melchizedek, which was after the order of Enoch, which was after the order of the Only Begotten Son.

---

[180] Moses 7: 16-18: "And from that time forth there were wars and bloodshed among them; but the Lord came and dwelt with his people, and they dwelt in righteousness. The fear of the Lord was upon all nations, so great was the glory of the Lord, which was upon his people. And the Lord blessed the land, and they were blessed upon the mountains, and upon the high places, and did flourish. And the Lord called his people Zion, because they were of one heart and one mind, and dwelt in righteousness; and there was no poor among them."

58 Wherefore, as it is written, they are gods, even the sons of God—

59 Wherefore, all things are theirs, whether life or death, or things present, or things to come, all are theirs and they are Christ's, and Christ is God's.

60 And they shall overcome all things.

61 Wherefore, let no man glory in man, but rather let him glory in God, who shall subdue all enemies under his feet.

62 These shall dwell in the presence of God and his Christ forever and ever." (D&C 76: 51-62.)

These, then are Zion. These are those who become "one" and are called by the Lord after they are gathered in the "house of Israel" and "my Zion."

3 Nephi 21: 2-3

"And behold, this is the thing which I will give unto you for a sign—for verily I say unto you that when these things which I declare unto you, and which I shall declare unto you hereafter of myself, and by the power of the Holy Ghost which shall be given unto you of the Father, shall be made known unto the Gentiles that they may know concerning this people who are a remnant of the house of Jacob, and concerning this my people who shall be scattered by them; Verily, verily, I say unto you, when these things shall be made known unto them of the Father, and shall come forth of the Father, from them unto you;"

The sign Christ is giving requires a specific knowledge of a sequence of events. These verses begin to detail how you will recognize the sign as the proper chronology unfolds.

First, Christ's words which were "declared unto you" (meaning the Nephites) will be "made known unto the gentiles." So, the Nephites must receive both what Christ *has* declared and *will* declare to them before His ministry was completed. Then these Nephites must record or preserve the words Christ declared. These words, recorded by the Nephites must in turn, become "known unto the gentiles." This initial part of Christ's sign is directly tied to the Book of Mormon. However, what does it mean that the words of Christ must be "made known unto the gentiles?" We have them, but do we know them in the sense that is being used here?

Second, the gentiles must come to a knowledge of "this people (Nephite audience) who are a remnant of the house of Jacob." The gentiles must understand or "know" that the promises made to the "remnant" exist. Has that happened? If not, why not? Is it happening at the moment as you become aware of this information that has been in the Book of Mormon since its publication in 1830? (No wonder the Lord's condemnation of the Latter-day Saints.)

Note the Lord calls the audience, and in turn their posterity, "this people who are a remnant of the house of Jacob… this my people." It is important to know that the Lord describes them with this identity as "my people" throughout His sermon and prophecy. This careful limitation of the reference to the Lord's "people" should not be applied broadly. It does not include gentiles. We should not change His meaning. He is speaking about a single identified group as "my people" and it is those before Him and their descendants.

Now, although it is a parenthetical thought, He adds a third event in the chronology. The third event is the scattering of the "Lord's people" who are the "remnant" by the gentiles. It will happen before the second listed event, but it is the third tier of the sign Christ is giving.

[By the way, this scrambled chronology is one of the things that evidences it is authentic and not a product of Joseph Smith's imagination. The time-line is always scrambled somewhat when the Lord or His true prophets speak. Information is not presented to their minds in a chronological manner, and therefore it is grouped by subject, not by time.[181] Isaiah, for example, was always grouping information according to subject, not chronology. Indeed, when looking back on a sweeping revelation, it is not possible to reconstruct a time line of events shown to a prophet in vision without some considerable effort. But this is merely an aside.]

The fourth portion of the sign is when the gentiles, who have the words, and appreciate or "know" them, bring them to the attention of the remnant. When those standing before Christ, through their descendants, come to receive these words of Christ from gentiles who know them to be true, then the fourth portion of the sign will have occurred.

Notice how Christ attributes the coming forth of the Book of Mormon to the gentiles as the work of "the Father." Christ was and is directly involved, He is the husbandman and the true vine. But He does not take credit as the Son. He says this coming forth will be "of the Father." All things are done by Christ according to the will of the Father, to whom He always gives the credit. There is a profound lesson in that for each of us. We are only accomplishing something good, enduring and valuable as we conform to the will of the Father and His Son. Whenever we are on our own errand, it is foolishness and vanity.

The "sign" given to us will continue in the Lord's statement which follows. So let's turn to more…

3 Nephi 21: 4

"For it is wisdom in the Father that they should be established in this land, and be set up as a free people by the power of the

---

[181] D&C 130: 7-8: "But they reside in the presence of God, on a globe like a sea of glass and fire, where all things for their glory are manifest, past, present, and future, and are continually before the Lord. The place where God resides is a great Urim and Thummim."

Father, that these things might come forth from them unto a remnant of your seed, that the covenant of the Father may be fulfilled which he hath covenanted with his people, O house of Israel;"

Christ attributes the wisdom of this plan to "the Father."

The gentiles will be set up "in this land." What land has become a land for free people "by the power of the Father?" The most common answer is the United States. That is the conclusion of Porter and Meldrum in their book *Prophecies and Promises—The Book of Mormon and the United State of America*.

The "wisdom of the Father" decrees that the gentiles will receive the record and the land where Christ visited the Nephites. Why is it wise for this to be the case?

From the gentiles, who inherit the record, the record will "come forth from them unto a remnant of your seed." The gentiles receive it first, then it will come from them to the "remnant." Who are the gentiles? Do the Latter-day Saints have the record? Even though they are in possession of the record, they are nonetheless called "gentiles"

Note that the "covenant of the Father" is the reason for these events to unfold. Why is the unfolding history of the remnant, gentiles and house of Israel to fulfill "the covenant of the Father?" What was/is Christ's role in the process? If Christ is directly involved, why is it nevertheless the "covenant of the Father?"

Christ refers to the objects of the covenant as "his people"—the Father's people. This is an important transition in the description. These people belong to the Father! Immortality and eternal life is a family affair. Christ's harvest of souls is for the glory of the Father. If there were any doubt of Christ's motivation and selfless service, His comments here remove that doubt.

From what source does the gentile freedom come?

If gentile freedom is based on the Father's power, how vulnerable is their hold on freedom if they rebel and reject the Father? How much credit can the gentiles take for establishing their land of freedom? To whom should gratitude flow for the gentile freedom?

The backdrop Christ gives to our history is wholly based on the Father's will, covenants and design for mankind. We tend to question how involved the Father and His Son are in the daily events of life. From Christ's statement here, how involved are they?

3 Nephi 21: 5-6

"Therefore, when these works and the works which shall be wrought among you hereafter shall come forth from the Gentiles, unto your seed which shall dwindle in unbelief because of iniquity; For thus it behooveth the Father that it should come forth from the Gentiles, that he may show forth his power unto the Gentiles, for this cause that the Gentiles, if they will not

harden their hearts, that they may repent and come unto me and be baptized in my name and know of the true points of my doctrine, that they may be numbered among my people, O house of Israel;"

Now keep in mind this is all within a "sign" Christ is telling to the Nephites. It is a "sign" of when the great latter-day work will begin to unfold.

What are "these works" referred to by Christ? Was it necessary for the "works which shall be wrought among you hereafter" to be included in the "works" the gentiles were to receive? Why? Why would the gentiles need to know of the great success and ultimate failure of Nephite faith? The greatest time in the Nephite history would be after Christ's visit, when they lived a united order. But the harrowing end described by Mormon and Moroni shows a depth of shocking evil. The violence, killing, cannibalism are disgusting to read and consider. Why did Christ want the "works which shall be wrought among you hereafter" to be included for the gentiles to have before them? What lessons would we not learn without these subsequent portions of the Nephite record?

Why do (from Christ's vantage point)/did (from our vantage point) the records need to come "from the gentiles?" And how did that "show forth [the Father's] power unto the gentiles?" What about the restoration was a visible display of the Father's power? Latter-day Saints have a "testimony" of the restoration, but gentiles seem unimpressed. The missionary effort among Americans today is nearly at a standstill. There are about as many people slipping into inactivity, or asking for their names to be removed as there are people volunteering to join at the present. So how is the restoration a display of "the Father's power" to the gentiles?

Does the Father use "small means" to display His power?[182] Is it possible for the Father to show forth His power and for people to miss it entirely? What kind of "power" is missed by those who reject it?

If they do not reject it, notice what the "Father's power" may lead the gentiles to receive:

- repentance

- baptism

- knowledge of the true points of Christ's doctrine

---

[182] 1 Ne. 16: 29: "And there was also written upon them a new writing, which was plain to be read, which did give us understanding concerning the ways of the Lord; and it was written and changed from time to time, according to the faith and diligence which we gave unto it. And thus we see that by small means the Lord can bring about great things."
Alma 37: 6: "Now ye may suppose that this is foolishness in me; but behold I say unto you, that by small and simple things are great things brought to pass; and small means in many instances doth confound the wise."

- being numbered among Christ's people, even Israel.

But if not, then they will be swept away by their own wickedness and violence.

Now it may not be appreciably "powerful" when the gentiles receive the Book of Mormon. But if they repent, and are baptized, and come to know the true points of His doctrine, how great a change will take place? How great a show of power is it when the only ones at peace are those who dwell in Zion?[183]

It is clear the Lord will only gather to Zion in the great day of calamity those who had previously seen in His "small means" the path to safety and redemption.

For the most part, the gentiles will be unimpressed with the Lord's stretched out arm. Gentiles will remain slow to respond, skeptical of the means, and dispute whether the Lord is really involved. Even those who claim to believe in His restored B ook of Mormon and covenant will take lightly what He offers them. Only a few will be willing to undertake a form of repentance. But to receive "knowledge of the true points of my doctrine" it will require something more than half-hearted conversion.

How do you suppose "knowledge of Christ's true points of doctrine" would change you?

Why do you think it will be necessary to "repent" before you receive "knowledge of the true points of His doctrine?"[184]

Why are both of these ("repentance" and "knowledge of true points of doctrine") required before you can be "numbered among Christ's people?"

Why do some of the gentiles need to become so numbered? How will we know when that sign has occurred? Has it already? If not, then the sign isn't before us yet—But if so, then the sign has begun. Are you among those who have repented, been baptized, know the true points of His doctrine, and become numbered with His people?

---

183 D&C 45: 68-71: "And it shall come to pass among the wicked, that every man that will not take his sword against his neighbor must needs flee unto Zion for safety. And there shall be gathered unto it out of every nation under heaven; and it shall be the only people that shall not be at war one with another. And it shall be said among the wicked: Let us not go up to battle against Zion, for the inhabitants of Zion are terrible; wherefore we cannot stand. And it shall come to pass that the righteous shall be gathered out from among all nations, and shall come to Zion, singing with songs of everlasting joy."

184 John 7: 17: "If any man will do his will, he shall know of the doctrine, whether it be of God, or whether I speak of myself."

3 Nephi 21: 7

"And when these things come to pass that thy seed shall begin to know these things—it shall be a sign unto them, that they may know that the work of the Father hath already commenced unto the fulfilling of the covenant which he hath made unto the people who are of the house of Israel."

Now the completion of the sign:

When all that has been described has happened, and the remnant will "begin to know these things," that beginning is the sign. Has it happened? Is it happening? Then who is the "remnant" that has or will "begin to know" about the Book of Mormon to fulfill the sign?

We've lost the history of Joseph Smith's efforts to locate the "remnant" of the Nephites. The first mission to locate them was called by revelation in the first 5 months after the church was organized.[185] Oliver was called and later that same month Peter Whitmer was also called.[186] This began an effort to locate the "remnant" that continued after the death of Joseph Smith. That will take some time to set out and cannot be dealt with in this post. We'll get to it.

When the remnant is at last identified, and have been given the Book of Mormon, and start to know about their history and the Lord's covenants with them, that will be the moment at which the "sign" given by Christ will have occurred.

It is when this happens that all of us will "know that the work of the Father hath already commenced." Or, in other words, the Father's hand is in motion to finish up what He promised to accomplish. What is it He intends to accomplish? What does it mean "fulfilling of the covenant?" What does the reference to "the people who are of the house of Israel" mean? How broadly will this final work of the Father spread? How many of those who are included in the covenant to Israel will become affected by the Father's work fulfilling the covenant?

---

185 D&C 28: 8-9: "And now, behold, I say unto you that you shall go unto the Lamanites and preach my gospel unto them; and inasmuch as they receive thy teachings thou shalt cause my church to be established among them; and thou shalt have revelations, but write them not by way of commandment. And now, behold, I say unto you that it is not revealed, and no man knoweth where the city Zion shall be built, but it shall be given hereafter. Behold, I say unto you that it shall be on the borders by the Lamanites."

186 D&C 30: 5-6: "Behold, I say unto you, Peter, that you shall take your journey with your brother Oliver; for the time has come that it is expedient in me that you shall open your mouth to declare my gospel; therefore, fear not, but give heed unto the words and advice of your brother, which he shall give you. And be you afflicted in all his afflictions, ever lifting up your heart unto me in prayer and faith, for his and your deliverance; for I have given unto him power to build up my church among the Lamanites;"

Assuming the work "commences" at that time, how long will it take for the work to be completed? Will it be a single generation?[187] How long is a "generation?"

Why is the fulfillment to result in "the house of Israel" being given their covenant again?

How can we participate?

Why would the "sign" be given? If it was given to inform us, how can we watch to behold the sign when it happens? Is there any indication that the sign is now unfolding?

If the organized church does not pay any attention to these things, and does not search for the remnant as Joseph did, will that change these promises? Will the covenant of the Father be forgotten by Him if the Saints themselves forget about it? What effect does our neglect have on the Father's covenants?

3 Nephi 21: 8-9

> **"And when that day shall come, it shall come to pass that kings shall shut their mouths; for that which had not been told them shall they see; and that which they had not heard shall they consider. For in that day, for my sake shall the Father work a work, which shall be a great and a marvelous work among them; and there shall be among them those who will not believe it, although a man shall declare it unto them."**

Christ is quoting from Isaiah and applying the words to a specific time frame. It is post-gentile receipt of the Book of Mormon, post-delivery of that book to the remnant, and post-opportunity for gentiles to repent and know of the true points of His doctrine. When that happens, the Lord will be freed up to fulfill the covenants of the Father.

When the Father's covenants are in being fulfilled, "kings shall shut their mouths." That is, the noble of this world will not know what to say. They will be at a loss of words because of the Father's acts.

Things that haven't been "told them" will take place, and they will not understand.

---

[187] JS-Matt. 1: 34-37: "Verily, I say unto you, this generation, in which these things shall be shown forth, shall not pass away until all I have told you shall be fulfilled. Although, the days will come, that heaven and earth shall pass away; yet my words shall not pass away, but all shall be fulfilled. And, as I said before, after the tribulation of those days, and the powers of the heavens shall be shaken, then shall appear the sign of the Son of Man in heaven, and then shall all the tribes of the earth mourn; and they shall see the Son of Man coming in the clouds of heaven, with power and great glory; And whoso treasureth up my word, shall not be deceived, for the Son of Man shall come, and he shall send his angels before him with the great sound of a trumpet, and they shall gather together the remainder of his elect from the four winds, from one end of heaven to the other."

Things that they never had taught to them will unfold, and they cannot comprehend, cannot get their hands around it all. It will dumbfound them.

Even when people who understand that the events are according to the Father's plan, and the Lord's covenant, they will not be able to believe it.

Too much! Too distressing! Too unexpected! Too great to take in! It will be confusion and distress, and the idea that God is behind it all will be unbelievable to them.[188]

Their plans for managing the world will be dashed and end. Their great investments will be lost. The control they imagined they had as "kings" will fade to dust.[189]

How can such splendor, such great and masterful arrangements, such glory in mankind become nothing? How can it all fall to the dust?[190]

It will be "great and marvelous" because it shows the Father's power and might. But it will be inconvenient and distressing, unbelievable and terrible.[191]

What is coming will leave proud men speechless and believing people vindicated. Everything will change.

Once again we see the tremendous relevance of Isaiah's words. You can search for language to capture our times and find no-one who has given phrases that capture this moment better than Isaiah. Even the Lord finds his words appropriate to quote as His own. Words of inspiration, given Isaiah by the Lord, become Isaiah's, then are taken by the Lord and used again as His. The symmetry of this chiasm is a reminder of how closely the Lord works with those He inspires. It is "His voice" even when the message comes from His servants. Who has ears to hear?

---

[188] Isa. 52: 15: "So shall he sprinkle many nations; the kings shall shut their mouths at him: for that which had not been told them shall they see; and that which they had not heard shall they consider."

[189] Hag. 2: 22: "And I will overthrow the throne of kingdoms, and I will destroy the strength of the kingdoms of the heathen; and I will overthrow the chariots, and those that ride in them; and the horses and their riders shall come down, every one by the sword of his brother."

[190] Rev. 14: 7-8: "Saying with a loud voice, Fear God, and give glory to him; for the hour of his judgment is come: and worship him that made heaven, and earth, and the sea, and the fountains of waters. And there followed another angel, saying, Babylon is fallen, is fallen, that great city, because she made all nations drink of the wine of the wrath of her fornication."

[191] Mal. 4: 1: "For, behold, the day cometh, that shall burn as an oven; and all the proud, yea, and all that do wickedly, shall be stubble: and the day that cometh shall burn them up, saith the Lord of hosts, that it shall leave them neither root nor branch."

3 Nephi 21: 10-11

> **"But behold, the life of my servant shall be in my hand; therefore they shall not hurt him, although he shall be marred because of them. Yet I will heal him, for I will show unto them that my wisdom is greater than the cunning of the devil. Therefore it shall come to pass that whosoever will not believe in my words, who am Jesus Christ, which the Father shall cause him to bring forth unto the Gentiles, and shall give unto him power that he shall bring them forth unto the Gentiles, (it shall be done even as Moses said) they shall be cut off from among my people who are of the covenant."**

This statement has caused endless conjecture. Who is the "servant?" Was this Joseph Smith? Wasn't it Joseph who was "given power to bring forth the words to the gentiles?" If Joseph was this "servant," then what does it mean he will be "marred," but the Lord will "heal him?" Is he coming back? Will Joseph be resurrected? Will he be born again?

Although Christ is speaking, this raises a matter worth addressing in connection with the statement. Therefore we'll take a bit of a detour and address it. First, the purpose of prophecy is not always to make a matter clear before it happens. Prophecy may not have a clear meaning before an event happens, but once it has happened it becomes apparent that the event was foretold. This keeps the prophecy from controlling the event, but allows those who have faith to see the Lord's hand in operation. Therefore, having some difficulty in attaching specific meaning to the prophecy is exactly in keeping with prophecy's traditional way of communicating an event.

Second, the words of prophecy are not always established in the same way. In fact, there are a variety of ways in which the language is fixed. Below are descriptions of the various ways the language of a prophecy comes about:

The Lord may give, announce or dictate the language and the prophet takes it down word for word. If this is the case, then the one who receives the language may not understand their meaning, even though they received the message. (In this case it is Christ who is speaking. We assume He would know fully the word's meaning. However, Christ has explained that His Father knows things that have been withheld from Him.[192] So, you cannot rule out that even in this case the language was given and the meaning withheld.)

Sometimes it is not the language or the words that are given to the prophet, but a vision is shown or opened and then the prophet is left to craft a description. In such cases the words are the prophet's, but the underlying meaning is the Lord's.

Sometimes a vision may be shown or opened, but when the prophet takes to write the description, the language is prescribed, or limited by

[192] Mark 13: 32: "But of that day and that hour knoweth no man, no, not the angels which are in heaven, neither the Son, but the Father."

inspiration. In this instance, the prophet's understanding may be greater than the words used, and the language will be designed to accomplish the Lord's purposes rather than to make what the prophet understands clear to the recipient.

With respect to when one or another form of language is in scripture, we may not always be able to tell. Section 76 is one example we know how the language came to us. There was a vision, opened to both Joseph Smith and Sydney Rigdon, and as the vision proceeded Joseph would dictate the words given to him by the Lord to describe what he and Sydney beheld. The words were the Lord's. The vision was greater or included more understanding for Joseph and Sydney than the words of the revelation. Hence Joseph's comment: *"I could explain a hundred fold more than I ever have of the glories of the kingdoms manifested to me in the vision, were I permitted, and were the people prepared to receive them."* (TPJS p. 304.)

It is not important to fully understand the statement of Christ in this prophecy until AFTER it is fulfilled. Before it is fulfilled the following questions are interesting to contemplate as you think about its meaning:

Is the "servant" who will be "marred" and then "healed" a single individual, or a people with whom the Lord is working? If a people rather than an individual, then who is this servant?

If the ones who will cause the servant to be "marred" are plural, who are they? Are they a group, or groups? If groups, which are they? What is their affiliation with the "great and abominable church?"

What does it mean that the "servant" will not be "hurt" but will be "marred?" How can one be "marred" without being "hurt?"

Is the "servant" in verse 10 the same as the "him" in verse 11? Have the subjects changed? That is, can verse 10 be speaking about a people, but verse 11 be addressing a person whose work it was (or is) to bring forth Christ's words? If an individual, is Joseph Smith the only one who can qualify? Can others also bring forth words of Christ to the gentiles, and the gentiles given an opportunity to accept or reject the words at their peril?

If they risk being cut off by rejecting the words, then can more than Joseph Smith be qualified to be "(even as Moses said) they shall be cut off from among my people who are of the covenant." That is, when the latter-day prophets are sounding alarms and warning, is the message from Christ—no matter who speaks it—something, if rejected, will cause people to be cut off from the covenant?

How does one cut themselves off from the covenant? If you will not listen to Christ's words, do you thereby cut yourself off by not listening? Would that be true if Joseph Smith is a prophet and you reject him? Would that be true if Brigham Young were a prophet and you rejected him? What about an angel sent to you? What about someone like Abinadi, or John the Baptist, or some other unexpected messenger? Would the same be true anytime someone decided to reject a message authorized or sent from the Lord?

Now go back and re-read verses 10 and 11 with these questions in mind and see if you get a different meaning from them.

3 Nephi 21: 12-14

> **"And my people who are a remnant of Jacob shall be among the Gentiles, yea, in the midst of them as a lion among the beasts of the forest, as a young lion among the flocks of sheep, who, if he go through both treadeth down and teareth in pieces, and none can deliver. Their hand shall be lifted up upon their adversaries, and all their enemies shall be cut off. Yea, wo be unto the Gentiles except they repent; for it shall come to pass in that day, saith the Father, that I will cut off thy horses out of the midst of thee, and I will destroy thy chariots;"**

Notice again the distinction between the gentiles and the remnant.

The "remnant" will behave in a way which will "tread down and tear in pieces" the gentiles. As they do this, "none can deliver" the gentiles.

Unlike the previous slaughter of the remnant by the gentiles, this time it is the gentiles who are slaughtered at the hands of the remnant. Those who are "enemies" to the remnant will all be "cut off." What does "cut off" mean?

The woes of that coming time can all be avoided by the gentiles—predicated upon their willingness to "repent." So we return again to the recurring question of what it means to "repent?" How can "repentance" be the only means by which the gentiles survive the slaughter? What is it about gentile repentance that spares them from the wrath that is to be otherwise poured out upon them?

What symbol comes to mind when you think of "horses?" What does cutting out the horses symbolize?

Does the symbol of the "horses" and the symbol of the "chariots" go together? That is, does cutting out the horses and destroying the chariots express a single thought? If it does, what do the horses and chariots symbolize? How vulnerable is the American military might to destruction? What effect would symbolically destroying the horses and chariots of the American population have?

If the United States is to be engulfed in domestic violence, will it continue to have foreign military influence? Economic influence? Social and cultural influence?

Assuming the gentile population is swept away, trodden under foot and torn in pieces, what culture and social influence will remain?

What symbol does the lion among the beasts of the forest suggest? The young lion among the sheep? What is the difference between the beasts of the forest and the sheep? If both beasts and sheep are gentiles, then are the beasts different than the sheep? What sort of person called a gentile "beast" will be swept away? What kind of person called a gentile "sheep" will be torn in pieces? Why would both gentile beasts and gentile sheep need to "repent?" Does repentance of a "beast" and repentance of "sheep" take the same form? Why would both need repentance when they are so remarkably different in symbol? Is it enough alone to be a gentile sheep?

What message is being sent by this warning?

3 Nephi 21: 15-18

> **"And I will cut off the cities of thy land, and throw down all thy strongholds; And I will cut off witchcrafts out of thy land, and thou shalt have no more soothsayers; Thy graven images I will also cut off, and thy standing images out of the midst of thee, and thou shalt no more worship the works of thy hands; And I will pluck up thy groves out of the midst of thee; so will I destroy thy cities."**

Cleaning up things so that the course of wickedness comes to an end involves some highly specific purging. However, the description is not given to us so we can know what will be coming as much as it is given to us to guide our own conduct and beliefs.

"Cities will be cut off" means what? "Strongholds thrown down" refers to what? Interesting things to contemplate to be sure. But much more relevant are the warnings in what follows:

"Cut off witchcrafts" is a warning to those who engage in certain practices. What should you do to avoid being cut off as a result of being involved in "witchcraft?" What does that mean? Are only wiccans being warned by this?

Who are the "soothsayers" who are to be terminated? What constitutes "soothsaying?" Look that word up. It appears in interesting contexts. The typical example involves predictions made using means other than true prophecy. But you should look at it and ask yourself how it would apply in modern applications: in business, government, economics, weather—especially long-term weather, politics, etc.

What are "graven images?" What are "standing images?" Why are the "standing images" said to be "in the midst of thee?"

What does it mean to "worship the works of thy hands?" How can a person worship their own works?

What are the "groves" that are to be plucked up? Why are the groves also "in the midst of thee?" The ancient usage of groves involved fertility rites, sacred sexual practices, or the worship of intercourse. What modern versions of this ancient form of fertility worship would be similar to the ancient behavior as to merit being called the same thing?

What does it mean to have our "cities destroyed?" Does this have anything to do with the other prophecy that the final victory of Israel will inhabit the desolate cities of the gentiles?[193]

---

[193] Isa. 54: 3: "For thou shalt break forth on the right hand and on the left; and thy seed shall inherit the Gentiles, and make the desolate cities to be inhabited."

Remember this is Christ speaking. This is the Redeemer, the merciful author of our salvation. Therefore, you must conclude that these direful predictions are actually based on the overall long-term best interest of those involved. They are better off, improved and advanced by these judgments. Imagine that. The wrath of God is best visited upon those who are destroyed, rather than leaving them to continue the course they are headed in. It is an interesting thing to contemplate.

3 Nephi 21: 19-20

> **"And it shall come to pass that all lyings, and deceivings, and envyings, and strifes, and priestcrafts, and whoredoms, shall be done away. For it shall come to pass, saith the Father, that at that day whosoever will not repent and come unto my Beloved Son, them will I cut off from among my people, O house of Israel;"**

Notice that the first four defects that are to end, include "lyings, and deceivings, and envyings, and strifes." These are somewhat different than the next two. These first four are character flaws that lead to the next two.

The character flaws should not be thought of as defects in our ability to do business or conduct commerce. These are flaws leading to the failures of our redemption. Therefore, think of them as flaws in our beliefs, leading us to have what the Book of Mormon terms unbelief.

What lying goes on among us leads to priestcraft? How is our lying keeping us from knowing the Lord? What is it about our peculiar form of false belief that leads us to believe in, and spread about lying as part of the fallen, false faith we entertain?

What deceivings are part of our culture of unbelief? How is it we can celebrate the great priesthood "authority" we possess while acknowledging that it lacks any "power?" Are we deceiving ourselves? Are we alienated from God while thinking ourselves His peculiar people?

What envy is there among us? Has envy become a tool for church governance? If so, how does it become a tool for church governance? Have we built it right into our system at present?

Are we filled with strife? Is strife among us suppressing healthy exchange of ideas by labeling such discussion as "contention?" Is strife different from contention? Is uniformity of ideas and suppression of dissent something that will remove strife? If not, then why not?

These character flaws in turn lead to "priestcrafts" where people seek approval of the world but not the best interest of Zion.[194] Do we want popularity from the "world?" What is the "world?" Why would someone practicing priestcraft seek in particular to have approval and lead the

---

[194] 2 Ne. 26: 29: "He commandeth that there shall be no priestcrafts; for, behold, priestcrafts are that men preach and set themselves up for a light unto the world, that they may get gain and praise of the world; but they seek not the welfare of Zion."

world? Why is the distinction made between the interests of Zion and the interests of the world? Is public relations always focused on approval from the world? If so, why are we seeking such approval? Does the world's opinion of us matter? Why? When have the followers of Jesus been popular? What have they suffered for His name?[195]

Then we see "whoredoms" which we have discussed earlier. David Christensen's comment on the meaning of false religion is worth returning to read again in this post.

Then Christ sounds the alarm, attributing it to the Father. Repent. Come unto Christ. Otherwise you will be cut off. What does it mean to come to Christ? Read the short statement in D&C 93: 1[196]. There is a succinct description of the process. You haven't come to Him until you have "seen His face and know that He is," or, in other words, until you hear from His own voice that He has atoned for your sins and He promises you a place in His kingdom.

All of these warnings are being given to orient you to what is important. The important thing is to come to Him. As Christ put it to Martha, "but one thing is needful."[197] Until we have come to Him, all our concerns about other matters must remain secondary. Of what good is it to know all mysteries, if we have not come to Him? This is why, in the middle of this warning of calamities to come, the Lord places this invitation to come to Him. He can help. He can restore and protect. But only if you are His.

3 Nephi 21: 21-22

> **"And I will execute vengeance and fury upon them, even as upon the heathen, such as they have not heard. But if they will repent and hearken unto my words, and harden not their hearts, I will**

---

[195] Heb. 11: 36-40: "And others had trial of cruel mockings and scourgings, yea, moreover of bonds and imprisonment: They were stoned, they were sawn asunder, were tempted, were slain with the sword: they wandered about in sheepskins and goatskins; being destitute, afflicted, tormented; (Of whom the world was not worthy:) they wandered in deserts, and in mountains, and in dens and caves of the earth. And these all, having obtained a good report through faith, received not the promise: God having provided some better thing for us, that they without us should not be made perfect."

[196] D&C 93: 1: "Verily, thus saith the Lord: It shall come to pass that every soul who forsaketh his sins and cometh unto me, and calleth on my name, and obeyeth my voice, and keepeth my commandments, shall see my face and know that I am;"

[197] Luke 10: 38-42: "Now it came to pass, as they went, that he entered into a certain village: and a certain woman named Martha received him into her house. And she had a sister called Mary, which also sat at Jesus' feet, and heard his word. But Martha was cumbered about much serving, and came to him, and said, Lord, dost thou not care that my sister hath left me to serve alone? bid her therefore that she help me. And Jesus answered and said unto her, Martha, Martha, thou art careful and troubled about many things: But one thing is needful: and Mary hath chosen that good part, which shall not be taken away from her."

establish my church among them, and they shall come in unto the covenant and be numbered among this the remnant of Jacob, unto whom I have given this land for their inheritance;"

Again the warning and the promise. Vengeance and fury are terrible words. It will be the responsibility of Christ to inflict it, and Christ says it will be His. "I will execute vengeance and fury" not "the Father." This is Christ's assignment—His cup.

His fury will be executed upon disbelieving gentiles, as well as the offending and violent heathen. When the spirit withdraws and they are left to themselves, it is only the limits of their cruel imagination that will compass the torture and evil they will visit upon one another. He will allow it by withdrawing the light of Christ, or His spirit. Without conscience, without remorse, without affection, filled with anger and hatred, it will be vengeance and fury.

This is juxtaposed with the reminder that "if they will repent and hearken unto my words, and harden not their hearts" He will be with them. If they will follow His path, His light and spirit will not forsake them. They will not descend into the same violent vengeance and fury. They will remain at peace. They will have hope in Him.

For those who will "repent," and "hearken unto His words," He will establish "my church" among them. Does this mean The Church of Jesus Christ of Latter-day Saints, or the church of the Firstborn?

When His church is joined it is through "the covenant." What "covenant" is that? Merely baptism, or something more?

When the "covenant" is given them, they become "numbered among this remnant of Jacob." Who is that remnant? When they become "numbered" among them, what significance does that hold? Does it imply a covenantal link which, like being sealed to someone, makes you part of that eternal family line (as discussed earlier)?

Why is it necessary to become first in the covenant and numbered with the remnant before they receive the blessings of being "given this land for their inheritance?" What does the promise of land have to do with entering into a covenant? Can it ever be the same as the covenant made with Abraham if it does not involve an inheritance of land? If, therefore, the covenant of land is part of that new and everlasting covenant which was begun through Joseph, is this a promise of reuniting the recipients with the "fullness of the Gospel" as opposed to receiving "much of the Gospel" discussed in earlier posts?

What is the Lord setting out in this declaration and prophecy? How do we become part of those promises? Is this something which an institution can do for you? Must you repent and come to Christ in order to become a part of it? If so, why not repent?

3 Nephi 21: 23-24

"And they shall assist my people, the remnant of Jacob, and also as many of the house of Israel as shall come, that they may build

> **a city, which shall be called the New Jerusalem. And then shall they assist my people that they may be gathered in, who are scattered upon all the face of the land, in unto the New Jerusalem."**

Who are those referred to as "my people?" "My people" are "the remnant of Jacob."

Who are those referred to as "they?" The "they" are gentiles who have repented, come to Christ, entered into a covenant with Him, received the fullness of His Gospel, become heirs, and received the promise of land, and a connection with the promises to the remnant.

So it will be these few, chosen, covenantal gentiles who will "ASSIST" the remnant.

- They won't lead them,
- preside over them
- control them
- subjugate them
- nor dominate them.

They will "assist" them. What does "assist" mean? Who is taking the lead if the gentiles are only to "assist" in the process?

What will the remnant do? What city is to be built? Why is it called the New Jerusalem?

Forget everything you think you know about where the New Jerusalem is to be built. Most of the myth and traditions about it are based on incomplete and inaccurate recreations of the events.

Joseph sent the first missionaries to the Lamanites to find the place. The entire block of Native Americans east of the Mississippi, from the Delaware to the Cherokee, had been relocated at the time of the 1834 revelations regarding the New Jerusalem. At that brief moment in time, all of them were located just over the boundary of western Missouri. The closest you could get to them was Independence, Missouri. Since it was the remnant who would build the New Jerusalem, the obligation was to find them, preach to them, and assist them in building. But the missionaries couldn't do that. When they tried, they were sent out of the Indian Territory on the threat of being imprisoned. So Independence was as close as they could get.

The Native Americans have relocated and relocated again. Now they are nowhere near Independence. When Joseph fled Nauvoo in late June, days before his death, he was leaving for the Rocky Mountains where he intended to locate the remnant. He returned, was killed, and never made it out here.

Brigham Young tried to locate the remnant. In fact, the St. George Temple was built as the next fully functioning Temple at the chosen location precisely because it was intended to be near the remnant. In the very first endowment session, the Hopi Chief and his wife went through, received their endowment, and were sealed the next day. They were invited to try and connect with the remnant and this tribe was suspected as the one the Saints were to locate.

We've lost that fervor. We've assumed Independence is the site. We think we're going to build it. We have no clue we are only to "assist" and not control.

All of this is worth some study. But you're going to have to search back into history and ignore all the recent re-done and re-worked histories that ignore this early material. It's too much to get into in this post, but maybe I'll take it up at some point.

3 Nephi 21: 25

> **"And then shall the power of heaven come down among them; and I also will be in the midst."**

What does the "power of heaven" include? (We've already looked at 1 Nephi 14: 14 which is speaking about this same event, you should read again that post.)

What is the difference between the "power of heaven" and the Lord's presence?

Why would the power of heaven come first, then the Lord?[198]

What would it require for you to be able to endure the presence of the Lord?[199]

If you are not prepared for His presence, what will your reaction be[200]?

Those who are directly in a covenant with Him, who have been promised forgiveness of their sins by Him, and who have sought and obtained His face, will be able to dwell in His presence. They will be prepared for His glory, have part in it, and thereby be protected when they are with Him.

If people have the "power of heaven" with them, do they need some other means to protect them as well? Why not?

---

[198] Moses 1: 11: "But now mine own eyes have beheld God; but not my natural, but my spiritual eyes, for my natural eyes could not have beheld; for I should have withered and died in his presence; but his glory was upon me; and I beheld his face, for I was transfigured before him."

[199] Moses 1: 2: "And he saw God face to face, and he talked with him, and the glory of God was upon Moses; therefore Moses could endure his presence."

[200] Mormon 9: 3-5: "Then will ye longer deny the Christ, or can ye behold the Lamb of God? Do ye suppose that ye shall dwell with him under a consciousness of your guilt? Do ye suppose that ye could be happy to dwell with that holy Being, when your souls are racked with a consciousness of guilt that ye have ever abused his laws? Behold, I say unto you that ye would be more miserable to dwell with a holy and just God, under a consciousness of your filthiness before him, than ye would to dwell with the damned souls in hell. For behold, when ye shall be brought to see your nakedness before God, and also the glory of God, and the holiness of Jesus Christ, it will kindle a flame of unquenchable fire upon you."

Haven't we already been promised this as early as 1833?[201] What happened that we did not obtain these things? Have our Temples been kept undefiled? If not, why? Have we permitted the unclean to enter? If so, why? Is the glory of the Lord in our Temples? Can we behold His presence there? If not, why not?

If the promise was made to us in 1833 and we haven't realized it from then till now, then are we to be numbered among those who will have the Lord "in their midst" as set out in this verse? What should we do to change that?

By and large, the church has failed to honor the Book of Mormon, keep its terms and become heirs of its promises. Our collective failure does not prevent individual success. Individuals may still realize the blessings offered. But each of us must meet the exact same conditions. Having met them, however, nothing can prevent you from obtaining the blessings.

The Lord has been willing to bring individuals back into His presence on the same conditions throughout all time. Read again *The Second Comforter* if you do not remember what those conditions are. He is as willing to make you a citizen of Zion, member of the church of the Firstborn, and part of the general assembly today[202] as in the future established Zion spoken of in the verses we have been reviewing. Many have done it in times past. Some have done it in our day. All are offered the same opportunity, but always on the same conditions.

The unchanging Gospel of Jesus Christ is always the same, and its blessings are always available.

3 Nephi 21: 26

> **"And then shall the work of the Father commence at that day, even when this gospel shall be preached among the remnant of this people. Verily I say unto you, at that day shall the work of**

---

[201] D&C 97: 15-19: "And inasmuch as my people build a house unto me in the name of the Lord, and do not suffer any unclean thing to come into it, that it be not defiled, my glory shall rest upon it; Yea, and my presence shall be there, for I will come into it, and all the pure in heart that shall come into it shall see God. But if it be defiled I will not come into it, and my glory shall not be there; for I will not come into unholy temples. And, now, behold, if Zion do these things she shall prosper, and spread herself and become very glorious, very great, and very terrible. And the nations of the earth shall honor her, and shall say: Surely Zion is the city of our God, and surely Zion cannot fall, neither be moved out of her place, for God is there, and the hand of the Lord is there;"

[202] D&C 76: 66-69: "These are they who are come unto Mount Zion, and unto the city of the living God, the heavenly place, the holiest of all. These are they who have come to an innumerable company of angels, to the general assembly and church of Enoch, and of the Firstborn. These are they whose names are written in heaven, where God and Christ are the judge of all. These are they who are just men made perfect through Jesus the mediator of the new covenant, who wrought out this perfect atonement through the shedding of his own blood."

the Father commence among all the dispersed of my people, yea, even the tribes which have been lost, which the Father hath led away out of Jerusalem."

Christ reiterates again the work of the Father is only at its "commencement" when the fullness of the gentiles is completed. The gentile day ends, the message goes to the remnant, and then will the work "commence at that day."

We think the work was underway when Joseph initiated it. In one respect it was. But Joseph never lived to locate the remnant, nor to deliver the Book of Mormon to them, nor to see them return to believe in and obtain a renewal of their covenant with Jesus Christ. It was one of his great priorities. But Joseph was killed before the work advanced to the point which is called the "commencement" by the Lord in this prophecy.

The work of the Father consists in fulfilling covenants. His great latter-day work of bringing the return of the Gospel to the remnant, who had the promise, used Joseph Smith and the gentiles to lay a foundation. The work of the covenant, however, will commence when the gentiles hand off the restored truths, the record of the fathers, and the reminder of what great things are promised, to the remnant.

The work of the Father, once it commences, is not limited to restoring the remnant to their former status. It reaches to all those who had been "led away out of Jerusalem." Therefore, all of those tribes who are "lost" to us, but are not lost to the Father, will be brought back and restored to the Lord.

This restoration of the lost tribes and return of the covenant is a subject Isaiah wrote and rejoiced about. I do not intend to take that detour in this post, but if you read Isaiah (particularly those portions quoted by Nephi), you will see how great a focus this final restoration has been.

We call our time the Dispensation of the Fullness of Time, because our time is leading to that return to fullness. However, in one sense Joseph Smith was much like the Protestant fathers who laid a groundwork for a greater, further return of light. They did not see the full return. We might.

From the time of Joseph Smith until now, however, we have neglected or forgotten a great deal of what Joseph was given. There are doctrines we circulate today that are incomplete or misleading. We have not been diligent, and as a result our conferences, meetings, associations and discussions continue to be too low, too vulgar, too condescending from what we were called to receive.

How few or many of us will be permitted to participate in the on going process of the Restoration remains to be seen. However, when the fullness returns, those who become the heirs will look back on the era of the Latter-day Saints with much the same reaction as we look back on the Jewish era in which Christ lived. They will be astonished at the great principles of truth we discarded, neglected or ignored. They will wonder in astonishment at our groveling to gain acceptance from a doomed and ignorant religious tradition calling itself "Christianity." They will find it utterly incomprehensible that we argued we should be regarded as one of them, rather than proclaiming their doctrines are the commandments of men, having a form of godliness but lacking any power. They will wonder why we would trade the power of God for acceptance and popularity; particularly when we were told that pandering for popularity is at the heart of priestcraft. Why, they will ask, did the Latter-day Saints invest tithing in opinion polling and focus group testing to insure the language and opinions of doomed Babylon were employed in declaring what little we kept of the restored Gospel? Our failure will be clear to them, although we find it quite opaque. We still think we're approved by the Lord, even though our condemnation is set out in scripture.

The work of the Father will commence in the future. What is underway at present cannot be what was intended to bring the return of the Lord's Zion because we have neglected the ordinances, forgotten the teachings, and drifted into a "feel good" sentimentality which suggests that all of us are likely to be exalted. Using a gambling term to capture the grave risks we take, Deseret Book proclaims: "Odds Are, You're Going To Be Exalted"—while they risk damning all those who are willing to gamble with them on such foolish, vain and untrue notions. Nephi condemned that foolish idea long ago in a book which, if we kept its principles, would have spared us from our current plight.[203]

3 Nephi 21: 27-28

> **"Yea, the work shall commence among all the dispersed of my people, with the Father to prepare the way whereby they may come unto me, that they may call on the Father in my name. Yea, and then shall the work commence, with the Father among all nations in preparing the way whereby his people may be gathered home to the land of their inheritance."**

When it begins in earnest and for the last time, it will be universal. There won't be an effort among one part of the vineyard which isn't mirrored by similar efforts in other parts of the vineyard. All the natural branches will be returned and reunited with the natural roots, as all are gathered again into one.

The Father will determine the timing. The Son will implement the plan. The process will require everyone, in every scattered part of the vineyard, to "come unto Christ." Unless they "come unto Christ," they will not be gathered and cannot be saved.

---

[203] 2 Ne. 28: 8: "And there shall also be many which shall say: Eat, drink, and be merry; nevertheless, fear God—he will justify in committing a little sin; yea, lie a little, take the advantage of one because of his words, dig a pit for thy neighbor; there is no harm in this; and do all these things, for tomorrow we die; and if it so be that we are guilty, God will beat us with a few stripes, and at last we shall be saved in the kingdom of God."

When they are brought again into their original state and begin to bear fruit, "they may call on the Father in [Christ's] name" with His approval and blessing. Without that, the "gathering home" cannot become a reality.

The Father's work will be "among all nations" because it will involve the judgment and destruction of all nations.[204]

This will "prepare the way." Why does the work need to happen "among all nations" for the way to be prepared?

What does it mean to now call all those who are to be included in this final gathering "his people" meaning the Father's people? Why would they end their long sojourn by becoming the "Father's people?" Christ has spoken of them being "His people" (meaning Christ's) but now the culmination will result in them becoming the "Father's people" as well.[205]

Notice that part of the final covenant being fulfilled involves re-gathering into the lands promised as their inheritance. This does not mean a single step. It means that the great work of the Father in destroying the nations, eliminating the wicked, and returning knowledge and a connection to Him through His Son, will prepare the way for the final step of gathering the chosen people into the lands of their inheritance.

There will be gatherings, and a great gathering, and at last a distribution of the survivors into their respective promised lands. Between the time of the great upheavals, and the time of the final distribution, there will be a season in which there will a great gathering in the "Mountains"[206] where it will be a fearsome, even terrible thing for the wicked to contemplate.[207] This will be in "the tops of the

---

[204] D&C 87: 6: "And thus, with the sword and by bloodshed the inhabitants of the earth shall mourn; and with famine, and plague, and earthquake, and the thunder of heaven, and the fierce and vivid lightning also, shall the inhabitants of the earth be made to feel the wrath, and indignation, and chastening hand of an Almighty God, until the consumption decreed hath made a full end of all nations;"

[205] D&C 76: 92-95: "And thus we saw the glory of the celestial, which excels in all things—where God, even the Father, reigns upon his throne forever and ever; Before whose throne all things bow in humble reverence, and give him glory forever and ever. They who dwell in his presence are the church of the Firstborn; and they see as they are seen, and know as they are known, having received of his fulness and of his grace; And he makes them equal in power, and in might, and in dominion."

[206] 2 Ne. 12:2: "And it shall come to pass in the last days, when the mountain of the Lord's house shall be established in the top of the mountains, and shall be exalted above the hills, and all nations shall flow unto it."

[207] D&C 45: 68-70: "And it shall come to pass among the wicked, that every man that will not take his sword against his neighbor must needs flee unto Zion for safety. And there shall be gathered unto it out of every nation under heaven; and it shall be the only people that shall not be at war one with another. And it shall be said among the wicked: Let us not go up to battle against Zion, for the inhabitants of Zion are terrible; wherefore we cannot stand."

mountains."[208] This will be where the New Jerusalem will exist. This will be before the final distribution into the various places of inheritance of the Lord's people.

[208] Micah 4: 1: "But in the last days it shall come to pass, that the mountain of the house of the Lord shall be established in the top of the mountains, and it shall be exalted above the hills; and people shall flow unto it."
2 Ne. 12: 2: ""And it shall come to pass in the last days, when the mountain of the Lord's house shall be established in the top of the mountains, and shall be exalted above the hills, and all nations shall flow unto it."
Isa. 2: 2: "And it shall come to pass in the last days, that the mountain of the Lord's house shall be established in the top of the mountains, and shall be exalted above the hills; and all nations shall flow unto it."

Before the return to the lands of inheritance, however, there will be terrible days, the likes of which have only been seen in the final pages of the Nephite record.[209]

The choice is between the Lord, His offered redemption and protection, and destruction. The gentiles are now offered a choice while

---

[209] Mormon 6: 6-22: "And it came to pass that when we had gathered in all our people in one to the land of Cumorah, behold I, Mormon, began to be old; and knowing it to be the last struggle of my people, and having been commanded of the Lord that I should not suffer the records which had been handed down by our fathers, which were sacred, to fall into the hands of the Lamanites, (for the Lamanites would destroy them) therefore I made this record out of the plates of Nephi, and hid up in the hill Cumorah all the records which had been entrusted to me by the hand of the Lord, save it were these few plates which I gave unto my son Moroni. And it came to pass that my people, with their wives and their children, did now behold the armies of the Lamanites marching towards them; and with that awful fear of death which fills the breasts of all the wicked, did they await to receive them. And it came to pass that they came to battle against us, and every soul was filled with terror because of the greatness of their numbers. And it came to pass that they did fall upon my people with the sword, and with the bow, and with the arrow, and with the ax, and with all manner of weapons of war. And it came to pass that my men were hewn down, yea, even my ten thousand who were with me, and I fell wounded in the midst; and they passed by me that they did not put an end to my life. And when they had gone through and hewn down all my people save it were twenty and four of us, (among whom was my son Moroni) and we having survived the dead of our people, did behold on the morrow, when the Lamanites had returned unto their camps, from the top of the hill Cumorah, the ten thousand of my people who were hewn down, being led in the front by me. And we also beheld the ten thousand of my people who were led by my son Moroni. And behold, the ten thousand of Gidgiddonah had fallen, and he also in the midst. And Lamah had fallen with his ten thousand; and Gilgal had fallen with his ten thousand; and Limhah had fallen with his ten thousand; and Jeneum had fallen with his ten thousand; and Cumenihah, and Moronihah, and Antionum, and Shiblom, and Shem, and Josh, had fallen with their ten thousand each. And it came to pass that there were ten more who did fall by the sword, with their ten thousand each; yea, even all my people, save it were those twenty and four who were with me, and also a few who had escaped into the south countries, and a few who had deserted over unto the Lamanites, had fallen; and their flesh, and bones, and blood lay upon the face of the earth, being left by the hands of those who slew them to molder upon the land, and to crumble and to return to their mother earth. And my soul was rent with anguish, because of the slain of my people, and I cried: O ye fair ones, how could ye have departed from the ways of the Lord! O ye fair ones, how could ye have rejected that Jesus, who stood with open arms to receive you! Behold, if ye had not done this, ye would not have fallen. But behold, ye are fallen, and I mourn your loss. O ye fair sons and daughters, ye fathers and mothers, ye husbands and wives, ye fair ones, how is it that ye could have fallen! But behold, ye are gone, and my sorrows cannot bring your return. And the day soon cometh that your mortal must put on immortality, and these bodies which are now moldering in corruption must soon become incorruptible bodies; and then ye must stand before the judgment-seat of Christ, to be judged according to your works; and if it so be that ye are righteous, then are ye blessed with your fathers who have gone before you. O that ye had repented before this great destruction had come upon you. But behold, ye are gone, and the Father, yea, the Eternal Father of heaven, knoweth your state; and he doeth with you according to his justice and mercy."

reenacting the same poor judgment that led to their own loss of opportunity. That needn't be true of individuals. It seems apparent that the prophetic message of the Book of Mormon foretells gentile arrogance and pride, collectively claiming they are on the road to Zion, while they are instead doomed to repeating the errors of prior civilizations of this continent. We will get to that in the coming days, but for now we remain interested in the definition and destiny of the "remnant" of the prior occupants.

(What an interesting text this Book of Mormon proves to be. It makes one wonder why it would ever suffer from neglect.)

3 Nephi 21: 29

> **"And they shall go out from all nations; and they shall not go out in haste, nor go by flight, for I will go before them, saith the Father, and I will be their rearward."**

When the time comes to redistribute the survivors to their respective promised lands of inheritance, they will not flee, nor will the process be hurried. No one will pursue them. They will at last be free to go to their homes without being molested along the way.

The Father will go before them. The Father will be on their rear guard. His glory and His presence will be their shield and protection.

How will the earth respond to such a passage? Psalms 48: 1-4 gives some idea of this great and joyful procession.[210] Psalms 67 is another great anthem of this event.

Though the days before were terrible, in their wake all be comforted, for to know the Great Comforter is to know at last peace. Isaiah could not refrain from adding to the anthems of praise of this future event: "Thus saith the Lord, In an acceptable time have I heard thee, and in a day of salvation have I helped thee: and I will preserve thee, and give thee for a covenant of the people, to establish the earth, to cause to inherit the desolate heritages; That thou mayest say to the prisoners, Go forth; to them that are in darkness, Shew yourselves. They shall feed in the ways, and their pastures shall be in all high places. They shall not hunger nor thirst; neither shall the heat nor sun smite them: for he that hath mercy on them shall lead them, even by the springs of water shall he guide them. And I will make all my mountains a way, and my highways shall be exalted. Behold, these shall come from far: and, lo, these from the north and from the west; and these from the land of Sinim. Sing, O heavens; and be joyful, O earth; and break forth into singing, O mountains: for the Lord hath comforted his people, and will have mercy upon his afflicted." (Isa. 49: 8-13.)

---

[210] Ps. 48: 1-4: "Great is the Lord, and greatly to be praised in the city of our God, in the mountain of his holiness. Beautiful for situation, the joy of the whole earth, is mount Zion, on the sides of the north, the city of the great King. God is known in her palaces for a refuge. For, lo, the kings were assembled, they passed by together."

This ultimate triumph was always intended to be the outcome. The end will be joyful. Though His covenant people may pass through the trials and rigors of mortality, the fruit offered to them is delicious even in times of tragedy and distress.[211] To make it through what is coming and endure to the final comfort, it will be necessary to come and plant that seed inside you now. Unless you do so, you will not have the strength to lay hold on the promises of the Lord.

The end will be worth all the shame and bitterness endured while the world still lies in sin and error.[212] The final triumph will be won by those who can endure the presence of the Father. This requires more than enduring the presence of the Son. Those who can rise to this glory must be sealed by the Holy Spirit of Promise, and become kings and priests, holding that same priesthood and bearing that same right which was in the beginning and is named after the Son of God. They will be everlasting, for they came from everlasting and have reconnected with that while here in mortality.

The Book of Mormon is a message of hope and triumph. But to win that triumph and possess that hope requires the reader to follow the same path and take the same steps as all others who went before. There simply is not a way to avoid the rigors of the journey. It must change YOU. The work of the Father is to develop YOU. To do so it will require you to cooperate with Him. It is His work and His glory, but you must choose to let Him bring you along. Read Nephi's remarkable summary: "Behold, the Lord hath created the earth that it should be inhabited; and he hath created his children that they should possess it. And he raiseth up a righteous nation, and destroyeth the nations of the wicked. And he leadeth away the righteous into precious lands, and the wicked he destroyeth, and curseth the land unto them for their sakes. He ruleth high in the heavens, for it is his throne, and this earth is his footstool. And **he loveth those who will have him to be their God**. Behold, he loved our fathers, and he covenanted with them, yea, even Abraham, Isaac, and Jacob; and he remembered the covenants which he had made;" (1 Ne. 17: 36-40, emphasis added.) Can you not see the pleading, the meekness and the humility in this description of our God?

---

[211] Alma 32: 28: "Now, we will compare the word unto a seed. Now, if ye give place, that a seed may be planted in your heart, behold, if it be a true seed, or a good seed, if ye do not cast it out by your unbelief, that ye will resist the Spirit of the Lord, behold, it will begin to swell within your breasts; and when you feel these swelling motions, ye will begin to say within yourselves—It must needs be that this is a good seed, or that the word is good, for it beginneth to enlarge my soul; yea, it beginneth to enlighten my understanding, yea, it beginneth to be delicious to me."

[212] 2 Ne. 9: 18: "But, behold, the righteous, the saints of the Holy One of Israel, they who have believed in the Holy One of Israel, they who have endured the crosses of the world, and despised the shame of it, they shall inherit the kingdom of God, which was prepared for them from the foundation of the world, and their joy shall be full forever."

Great is His wisdom and endless His mercy and the extent of His doings no man can find out! He makes Himself known to those who seek after Him, and those who cry out they do not know Him is only because they have chosen to ignore His plea!

We will return then to Nephi's writings and continue this effort to understand what great covenants the Book of Mormon lay before us if we choose to receive them.

A home or Temple is called "sacred space" because the Lord may come and dwell there. It is a place of refuge and peace. It would be good to have such a house right now. But, if not, "know ye not that ye are the Temple of God?" God can come and dwell with you, even if others will not permit Him. Since you are the Temple, you may become the sacred space to which He comes. The blood on the posts and lentil saved the occupants, for the sake of the righteous. For the want of a few Sodom was destroyed. Be the few. Be the leaven. Be the salt. If you are the Temple you preserve more than yourself.

What makes any of you think you can become redeemed without bringing others with you? Why would you think that those given to associate with you are not a gift from God, deliberately in your life to permit you the high honor and great responsibility of showing by a godly walk what redemption can bring? Why shrug off others, thinking they will fail when you will succeed? You will only succeed if you minister to them in patience, all the while seeking their redemption even before your own. Christ came not to be ministered to, but to minister. Why would it be different for His servants?

We're still in a discussion which began June 7th to try and make sense of the present and future of Zion.

We have seen how priestly authority is more complex than a list of names on a page showing some connection to the Prophet Joseph Smith. We have examined how necessary it is to reconnect with heaven itself to have not just authority, but also power in the priesthood. That connection of power in the priesthood comes from the hand of God, not from another man. The powers of the priesthood are inseparably connected with the powers of heaven and the hand of God.[213]

Men do not make priests, God does. For those who have eyes to see, God's hand in priestly authority has been seen by endowed Latter-day Saints from Nauvoo onward. Men do not make prophets. God has reserved that right for Himself.[214] God will call them whether or not men accept or recognize them.

---

[213] D&C 121: 36: "That the rights of the priesthood are inseparably connected with the powers of heaven, and that the powers of heaven cannot be controlled nor handled only upon the principles of righteousness."

[214] Num. 12: 6: "And he said, Hear now my words: If there be a prophet among you, I the Lord will make myself known unto him in a vision, and will speak unto him in a dream."

We think we have a hope in membership in the church, but the scriptures offer us no reason for that hope. Hope lies in Christ.

We have seen how carefully the Book of Mormon distinguishes between the "remnant" to inherit great promises, and "gentiles" who must align themselves with Christ to become inheritors of those promises. We have seen how members of The Church of Jesus Christ of Latter-day Saints are always identified with the gentiles[215], and not the remnant.

We have seen how the gentiles will be given authority over the remnant, and will be permitted to abuse and tread upon them for a season. We have seen that the promises once given the remnant will be given conditionally and for a season to the gentiles, who will receive the book written by the remnant's forebearers. The gentiles will become a great nation, and will be protected and powerful. They will be greater than any other nation on the earth. We have read how that will result in pride and foolishness.

We have seen that the gentiles will be swept away, just as the remnant was swept away. But those gentiles who will repent and receive Christ will receive a covenant entitling them to also belong to and possess this land as a place of inheritance.

Those gentiles who enter into this covenant, repent, come to Christ and receive Christ's presence will be preserved as the remainder of the gentiles' probation ends. When the time of the gentile dominance ends, they will be swept away.

We have seen that the gentiles who do not possess the covenant will become trodden under foot just as the remnant. The world will descend into darkness, as the Spirit and the Light of Christ withdraws from all but those who are chosen heirs. The wicked will destroy the wicked. The gathered faithful will have the Lord's Spirit as a protection and shield. The wicked will fear and not go near them, for they will be "terrible" to the wicked.

The covenant people will be gathered in the "tops of the mountains" where there will be a refuge and the Lord will be among them. When the destruction ends and the wicked have been swept away, the Father will return these gathered covenant people to their lands of promise. When He does, His hand will be over them, and will be their rear guard. Nothing and no-one will hurt or make them afraid.

This orients us to begin to consider more carefully what the gentiles have done and will do with their opportunity. So we return to Nephi's writings to look more carefully at ourselves and the perils we face.

All of this is an experiment to see if it is possible to have this kind of discussion take place on a blog. I used to teach a weekly Book of Mormon class where we examined the text carefully. In those ten years

---

215 D&C 109: 60: "Now these words, O Lord, we have spoken before thee, concerning the revelations and commandments which thou hast given unto us, who are identified with the Gentiles."

we were able to go from 1 Nephi 1:1 to Jarom 1: 4. I know the material could be taught in that setting because the people were in front of me and I could take in what they were receiving as I taught. This is an alien way to teach, where disembodied words are put into a blog to be read by those who may or may not be attentive, diligent, prayerful and prepared. I cannot gage the effectiveness of this as well except from how the Lord assists me at my end. At the reader's end I am divided by circuitry, time and space and cannot measure as I could if you were in front of me.

I will continue the experiment, but remain doubtful that this will work as well as a book or a meeting would. In the end, the reader (or listener) must have the Spirit to be able to take in any light taught. So you will determine for yourself if you will receive what is offered. So, we will see…

2 Nephi 28

2 Nephi 28: 1-2

> **"And now, behold, my brethren, I have spoken unto you, according as the Spirit hath constrained me; wherefore, I know that they must surely come to pass. And the things which shall be written out of the book shall be of great worth unto the children of men, and especially unto our seed, which is a remnant of the house of Israel."**

Nephi, as any prophetic writer, says what "the Spirit hath constrained" him to say. This is the very definition of using the Lord's name with permission and not using His name in vain.[216]

Nephi held power from God in the words he used. Therefore he could "know that they must surely come to pass" because he sealed them as he wrote them.[217] For any person holding the sealing authority (which is an indispensable part of the Patriarchal Priesthood discussed earlier), the authority requires an alignment between the prophet, the Lord and the Lord's will. (See D&C 132: 45-49, in particular verse 48 which mentions "by my word and according to my law"—which required Joseph to align himself with the Lord before using

---

[216] Ex. 20: 7: "Thou shalt not take the name of the Lord thy God in vain; for the Lord will not hold him guiltless that taketh his name in vain."

[217] D&C 1: 38: "What I the Lord have spoken, I have spoken, and I excuse not myself; and though the heavens and the earth pass away, my word shall not pass away, but shall all be fulfilled, whether by mine own voice or by the voice of my servants, it is the same."

that power.[218] Those who have this authority will not do anything contrary to the will of the Lord.[219] It is because of this trust between the Lord and His messenger that the power is given to the man. Nephi was such a man. His book contained a seal upon it bearing the power of God.

Nephi knew. Knowledge came from Christ. Nephi knew Christ.[220]

Notice how Nephi refers to the "remnant" who are "our seed." Nephi refers to the remnant variously as:

- descendants of his father Lehi[221]

---

[218] D&C 132: 45-49: "For I have conferred upon you the keys and power of the priesthood, wherein I restore all things, and make known unto you all things in due time. And verily, verily, I say unto you, that whatsoever you seal on earth shall be sealed in heaven; and whatsoever you bind on earth, in my name and by my word, saith the Lord, it shall be eternally bound in the heavens; and whosesoever sins you remit on earth shall be remitted eternally in the heavens; and whosesoever sins you retain on earth shall be retained in heaven. And again, verily I say, whomsoever you bless I will bless, and whomsoever you curse I will curse, saith the Lord; for I, the Lord, am thy God. And again, verily I say unto you, my servant Joseph, that whatsoever you give on earth, and to whomsoever you give any one on earth, by my word and according to my law, it shall be visited with blessings and not cursings, and with my power, saith the Lord, and shall be without condemnation on earth and in heaven. For I am the Lord thy God, and will be with thee even unto the end of the world, and through all eternity; for verily I seal upon you your exaltation, and prepare a throne for you in the kingdom of my Father, with Abraham your father."

[219] Hel. 10: 5: "And now, because thou hast done this with such unwearyingness, behold, I will bless thee forever; and I will make thee mighty in word and in deed, in faith and in works; yea, even that all things shall be done unto thee according to thy word, for thou shalt not ask that which is contrary to my will."

[220] 2 Ne. 11: 3: "And my brother, Jacob, also has seen him as I have seen him; wherefore, I will send their words forth unto my children to prove unto them that my words are true. Wherefore, by the words of three, God hath said, I will establish my word. Nevertheless, God sendeth more witnesses, and he proveth all his words."

[221] 1 Ne. 13: 34: "And it came to pass that the angel of the Lord spake unto me, saying: Behold, saith the Lamb of God, after I have visited the remnant of the house of Israel—and this remnant of whom I speak is the seed of thy father—wherefore, after I have visited them in judgment, and smitten them by the hand of the Gentiles, and after the Gentiles do stumble exceedingly, because of the most plain and precious parts of the gospel of the Lamb which have been kept back by that abominable church, which is the mother of harlots, saith the Lamb—I will be merciful unto the Gentiles in that day, insomuch that I will bring forth unto them, in mine own power, much of my gospel, which shall be plain and precious, saith the Lamb."

- descendants of his brethren[222]
- his family's descendants or "our seed"[223]
- a mixture of Nephi's descendants who are among his brother's descendant's[224]

Nephi's primary line of descendants would be destroyed, but that destruction would not include all. There would remain a mixture of blood that would include partial descent from Nephi.[225] The various bloodlines remained identified as Nephites, Jacobites, Josephites, Zoramites, Lamanites, Lemuelites and Ishmaelites.[226] Although it would

---

[222] 1 Ne. 13: 38-39: "And it came to pass that I beheld the remnant of the seed of my brethren, and also the book of the Lamb of God, which had proceeded forth from the mouth of the Jew, that it came forth from the Gentiles unto the remnant of the seed of my brethren. And after it had come forth unto them I beheld other books, which came forth by the power of the Lamb, from the Gentiles unto them, unto the convincing of the Gentiles and the remnant of the seed of my brethren, and also the Jews who were scattered upon all the face of the earth, that the records of the prophets and of the twelve apostles of the Lamb are true."

[223] 1 Ne. 15: 13-14: "And now, the thing which our father meaneth concerning the grafting in of the natural branches through the fulness of the Gentiles, is, that in the latter days, when our seed shall have dwindled in unbelief, yea, for the space of many years, and many generations after the Messiah shall be manifested in body unto the children of men, then shall the fulness of the gospel of the Messiah come unto the Gentiles, and from the Gentiles unto the remnant of our seed—And at that day shall the remnant of our seed know that they are of the house of Israel, and that they are the covenant people of the Lord; and then shall they know and come to the knowledge of their forefathers, and also to the knowledge of the gospel of their Redeemer, which was ministered unto their fathers by him; wherefore, they shall come to the knowledge of their Redeemer and the very points of his doctrine, that they may know how to come unto him and be saved."

[224] 1 Ne. 13: 30: "Nevertheless, thou beholdest that the Gentiles who have gone forth out of captivity, and have been lifted up by the power of God above all other nations, upon the face of the land which is choice above all other lands, which is the land that the Lord God hath covenanted with thy father that his seed should have for the land of their inheritance; wherefore, thou seest that the Lord God will not suffer that the Gentiles will utterly destroy the mixture of thy seed, which are among thy brethren."

[225] 1 Ne. 13: 30-31: "Nevertheless, thou beholdest that the Gentiles who have gone forth out of captivity, and have been lifted up by the power of God above all other nations, upon the face of the land which is choice above all other lands, which is the land that the Lord God hath covenanted with thy father that his seed should have for the land of their inheritance; wherefore, thou seest that the Lord God will not suffer that the Gentiles will utterly destroy the mixture of thy seed, which are among thy brethren. Neither will he suffer that the Gentiles shall destroy the seed of thy brethren."

[226] Mormon 1: 8: "And it came to pass in this year there began to be a war between the Nephites, who consisted of the Nephites and the Jacobites and the Josephites and the Zoramites; and this war was between the Nephites, and the Lamanites and the Lemuelites and the Ishmaelites."

be impossible, without revelation, for us to determine which of these lines a person might belong to today, the Lord nevertheless revealed in 1828 that these various divisions remain identified to Him.[227] No doubt, in time, He will restore to the remnant descendants this knowledge of their sacred paternity and eternal identity.

Their blood may be mixed, but the remnant remains. Nephi may have referred to them more often as descendants of his "brethren," but they have within them some of his blood as well. In the day of redemption and restoration, the promises will all be fulfilled. The whole of the family of Lehi will be represented in the remnant.

Notice Nephi's prophecy is that "words which shall be written out of the book" rather than the book itself. This is, of course, exactly what we have. The actual book has been withheld. Only words from the book have been given us. But those words are intended to be of great worth to mankind, and in particular to the remnant.

This process is sacred, the promises are from the Lord. These words are given to us by Him, through a servant possessing authority to seal them up. We cannot prevent them from happening. We can, however, align ourselves with them and in turn be saved as well.

2 Nephi 28: 3

> **" For it shall come to pass in that day that the churches which are built up, and not unto the Lord, when the one shall say unto the other: Behold, I, I am the Lord's; and the others shall say: I, I am the Lord's; and thus shall every one say that hath built up churches, and not unto the Lord—"**

The Book of Mormon will become available to the remnant in a day when there will be "churches which are built up, and not unto the Lord." Generally this is interpreted by Latter-day Saints to mean OTHER churches, but not ours. However, the context requires all, including our own church, to be considered at risk as well. Here are the questions bearing on whether we (LDS) are among those being warned:

---

227 D&C 3: 16-19: "Nevertheless, my work shall go forth, for inasmuch as the knowledge of a Savior has come unto the world, through the testimony of the Jews, even so shall the knowledge of a Savior come unto my people—And to the Nephites, and the Jacobites, and the Josephites, and the Zoramites, through the testimony of their fathers—And this testimony shall come to the knowledge of the Lamanites, and the Lemuelites, and the Ishmaelites, who dwindled in unbelief because of the iniquity of their fathers, whom the Lord has suffered to destroy their brethren the Nephites, because of their iniquities and their abominations. And for this very purpose are these plates preserved, which contain these records—that the promises of the Lord might be fulfilled, which he made to his people;"

- Is the prophecy limited to the time before the Book of Mormon comes forth? (No; it will reach until the time when other records of the Lost Tribes are to come forth—a future event.[228])

- Is the prophecy about only those churches created by man, and not one intended to become Zion? (No.[229])

- Can a church established by the Lord become one which is not built up to Him? (Of course.[230])

- Does the promise that the Lord will never abandon His latter-day work[231] mean that the church He established will not drift into condemnation?

Should we, therefore, consider these warnings to be equally applicable to us as Latter-day Saints as to the larger community of churches?

Nephi warns that each church will claim it is the Lord's. Do we do that? Each will claim divine authority and approval. Do we do that?

---

228 2 Ne. 29: 13-14: "And it shall come to pass that the Jews shall have the words of the Nephites, and the Nephites shall have the words of the Jews; and the Nephites and the Jews shall have the words of the lost tribes of Israel; and the lost tribes of Israel shall have the words of the Nephites and the Jews. And it shall come to pass that my people, which are of the house of Israel, shall be gathered home unto the lands of their possessions; and my word also shall be gathered in one. And I will show unto them that fight against my word and against my people, who are of the house of Israel, that I am God, and that I covenanted with Abraham that I would remember his seed forever."

229 2 Ne. 28: 21-24: "And others will he pacify, and lull them away into carnal security, that they will say: All is well in Zion; yea, Zion prospereth, all is well—and thus the devil cheateth their souls, and leadeth them away carefully down to hell. And behold, others he flattereth away, and telleth them there is no hell; and he saith unto them: I am no devil, for there is none—and thus he whispereth in their ears, until he grasps them with his awful chains, from whence there is no deliverance. Yea, they are grasped with death, and hell; and death, and hell, and the devil, and all that have been seized therewith must stand before the throne of God, and be judged according to their works, from whence they must go into the place prepared for them, even a lake of fire and brimstone, which is endless torment. Therefore, wo be unto him that is at ease in Zion!"

230 Ezek. 44: 10: "And the Levites that are gone away far from me, when Israel went astray, which went astray away from me after their idols; they shall even bear their iniquity."
Isa. 53: 6: "All we like sheep have gone astray; we have turned every one to his own way; and the Lord hath laid on him the iniquity of us all."
John 5: 39: "Search the scriptures; for in them ye think ye have eternal life: and they are they which testify of me."

231 D&C 138: 44: "Daniel, who foresaw and foretold the establishment of the kingdom of God in the latter days, never again to be destroyed nor given to other people;"

Each will assert it belongs to the Lord. Do we do that? But the question Nephi focuses upon is whether it is "unto the Lord."

What does it mean for a church to be "unto the Lord?" What would the opposite be?

How certain are we that what we do as a church is building up to the Lord? Do the procurement practices of the church "build up unto the Lord?" Does the auditor's report in General Conference even begin to allow you to make that determination? If some of the large and well-connected Latter-day Saint families own the businesses which contract with the church and have become wealthy by reason of trading with the church, is there some question which ought to be considered about "building up unto the Lord" in how business is conducted?

I explained how the church distinguishes between tithing money and "investment income" in a post on April 1, 2010. Does this seem consistent with the Lord's parable about the talents?[232] If in the parable, all returns realized on the money were the Lord's, why does the return on the Lord's tithing now become investment money to be used for commercial projects developing condominiums, shopping malls, banks, and other income-producing ventures? Who is benefiting? What careers and fortunes are being made? What families are being benefited? Are they the Lord?

Assuming the purpose of a church were to "build up unto the Lord" what single purpose would be most important? In the Book of Mormon, as I've explained earlier, the writers seek to have you trade unbelief for belief; then to trade belief for faith; then to come beyond faith and receive knowledge. The knowledge it would have you obtain is of Christ.[233]

The lack of knowledge condemns a people who claim to be the Lord's. Nephi quoted Isaiah in 2 Nephi 15: 13: [You will not understand Nephi's purpose in quoting Isaiah if you are unacquainted with *Nephi's Isaiah*.] *"Therefore, my people are gone into captivity, because they have no knowledge; and their honorable men are famished, and their multitude dried up with thirst."* Captivity comes from a lack of knowledge. Joseph Smith warned that "a man is saved no faster than he gains knowledge." (DHC 5: 588.) The ones who are considered "honorable" are "famished" because they lack knowledge. The

---

232 Luke 19: 20-23: "And another came, saying, Lord, behold, here is thy pound, which I have kept laid up in a napkin: For I feared thee, because thou art an austere man: thou takest up that thou layedst not down, and reapest that thou didst not sow. And he saith unto him, Out of thine own mouth will I judge thee, thou wicked servant. Thou knewest that I was an austere man, taking up that I laid not down, and reaping that I did not sow: Wherefore then gavest not thou my money into the bank, that at my coming I might have required mine own with usury?"

233 Ether 3: 19: "And because of the knowledge of this man he could not be kept from beholding within the veil; and he saw the finger of Jesus, which, when he saw, he fell with fear; for he knew that it was the finger of the Lord; and he had faith no longer, for he knew, nothing doubting."

"multitude" who follow the "honorable men" are in turn "dried up with thirst" because they are not taught enough to become saved.[234]

If the Lord promises to never abandon His latter-day work[235], does that mean men cannot abandon Him? Although men may abandon Him, can He work with you individually and "remember" His promises? Even if others are without knowledge, can you still obtain knowledge from Him? Though others may be "dried up with thirst" can you still obtain "living waters" from Him?

Can you rely upon the assertions from any church today that it is "built up unto the Lord?" How can you be "built up unto the Lord" even if you do not have any institution you can trust to bring to you that knowledge? Was the Lord always intended to be directly involved in your life?[236]

If "captivity" comes from a lack of knowledge, and Joseph Smith tied knowledge to salvation, then why is the correlated curriculum of the church focusing less and less on doctrine? Why was the Relief Society and Priesthood Manual on *Teachings of the Presidents* volume on Joseph Smith carefully edited by the Correlation Department so as to support meanings somewhat different than Joseph's? If you think meanings were not changed, then go to the sources quoted in the *History of The Church* and read each of the whole statements made by Joseph from which the excerpts were taken. I leave it to you to decide if the edited versions in the church manual were or were not both incomplete and misleading. [Personally, I was dismayed. But I have a sensitivity to words that is quite acute, and therefore something left out that is important to me may not be significant to you. You must decide that question for yourself. You will find it an interesting exercise even if you disagree with my conclusion.]

If a church claims to be built up to the Lord, but does not attempt to confer knowledge of the Lord upon people, then how are you to seek after this knowledge? [We are going to be discussing Nephi's instruction to us about this very subject for the coming weeks. So keep the question in mind as we go forward.]

---

234 2 Ne. 28: 14: "They wear stiff necks and high heads; yea, and because of pride, and wickedness, and abominations, and whoredoms, they have all gone astray save it be a few, who are the humble followers of Christ; nevertheless, they are led, that in many instances they do err because they are taught by the precepts of men."

235 D&C 138: 44: "Daniel, who foresaw and foretold the establishment of the kingdom of God in the latter days, never again to be destroyed nor given to other people;"

236 Matt. 11: 27-30: "All things are delivered unto me of my Father: and no man knoweth the Son, but the Father; neither knoweth any man the Father, save the Son, and he to whomsoever the Son will reveal him. Come unto me, all ye that labour and are heavy laden, and I will give you rest. Take my yoke upon you, and learn of me; for I am meek and lowly in heart: and ye shall find rest unto your souls. For my yoke is easy, and my burden is light."

Remember this is the promised day when all are intended to grow into knowledge of the Lord, from the least to the greatest.[237] "Those who remain" will remain because they have "knowledge" that will save them. Hence Joseph's teaching about the link between "knowledge" and "salvation." Also, the captivity spoken of by Nephi because people lack knowledge.

Go back to the post on Lecture 6 of the *Lectures on Faith*, April 21, 2010. If your church encourages you to become part of a broad mainstream without asking for the sacrifice of all things, then it is not requiring you to take the steps necessary to develop faith to save you. Rest assured, however, the Lord still has the same requirements, and He will work directly with you to develop you into a person who has the required knowledge. It was always intended to be individual. It is your quest. Others may encourage you along, but you must confront the process for yourself.

[Now, as a complete aside, I want to address the misapplication and overreaching misinterpretation of the idea one is "evil speaking" when a person explains something that concerns them. First, we are dealing with the souls of men. We are addressing salvation itself. If there is an error in doctrine or practice, everyone has an obligation to speak up, from the least to the greatest. (D&C 20: 42, 46-47, 50-51, 59, among other places.) Second, the "truth" cannot ever be "evil." Though the truth may cut with a two edged sword, truth is not and cannot be "evil." Therefore, if someone should say something that is untrue or in error, then correct their doctrine, show the error, but do not claim what is good to be evil, nor support what is evil by calling it good.[238] Using a broad generalization to stifle a discussion of the truth is a trick of the devil, who is an enemy to your soul. It is not the way of our Lord. He was always open to questions, always willing to answer questions, ever willing to speak the truth even when it caused those with authority over Him to be pained by His words. We must follow Him, and not men, in

---

[237] JS-H 1: 41: "He also quoted the second chapter of Joel, from the twenty-eighth verse to the last. He also said that this was not yet fulfilled, but was soon to be. And he further stated that the fulness of the Gentiles was soon to come in. He quoted many other passages of scripture, and offered many explanations which cannot be mentioned here."
Joel 2: 28-29: "And it shall come to pass afterward, that I will pour out my spirit upon all flesh; and your sons and your daughters shall prophesy, your old men shall dream dreams, your young men shall see visions: And also upon the servants and upon the handmaids in those days will I pour out my spirit."
D&C 84: 96-97: "For I, the Almighty, have laid my hands upon the nations, to scourge them for their wickedness. And plagues shall go forth, and they shall not be taken from the earth until I have completed my work, which shall be cut short in righteousness—"

[238] 2 Ne. 15: 20: "Wo unto them that call evil good, and good evil, that put darkness for light, and light for darkness, that put bitter for sweet, and sweet for bitter!"

that example. Even if we would personally prefer to not endure insults but remain silent. So, rather than condemn something as "evil speaking" that you believe to be wrong, explain the error and bring us all into greater understanding. But if something is true, then even if it disturbs your peace of mind, it cannot be evil.]

2 Nephi 28: 4

> **"And they shall contend one with another; and their priests shall contend one with another, and they shall teach with their learning, and deny the Holy Ghost, which giveth utterance."**

Nephi foresees that churches in our day will argue over the claim to have truth. When it comes to the Latter-day Saints, the relentless accusation made against us is that we aren't "Christian." This accusation is made by those who claim the right to define the word "Christian" to necessarily include acceptance of the creeds of Historic Christianity. These creeds are an amalgam of Neo-Platonic philosophy mingled with scripture.

We just ought to concede the point. We should proudly acknowledge we are NOT part of Historic Christianity. We disagree with Historic Christianity, and at a fundamental level we denounce it as false. We are a restoration of Primitive Christianity. We do not share in accepting the creeds which Christ Himself denounced as "an abomination in His sight."[239]

Oddly, from our end, we try and avoid the argument, fit in, claim we are "good Christians too," and part of the larger community of churches. There isn't as much fight left in us as there was once. Or, perhaps more correctly, our arguments are focused instead, toward those who attempt to preserve practices from the early part of the Restoration. In other words, we try to make ourselves seem more like Historic Christianity, and avoid or discard what once set us apart. We have inverted the picture from where we began. (Nephi will address that, as well.)

Although there are numerous examples of how we have altered our views to become more like other faiths, we can take just one to illustrate the point. We have abandoned plural marriage. But it is hard for us to claim the doctrine is false because it remains in Section 132 of the Doctrine and Covenants. While we do not practice it, and believe those who do have failed to stay on track, we cannot gainsay that the doctrine is true. Yet no other church is so vehement in denouncing and persecuting those who practice plural marriage. It is as if we want to

---

[239] JS-H 1: 19: "I was answered that I must join none of them, for they were all wrong; and the Personage who addressed me said that all their creeds were an abomination in his sight; that those professors were all corrupt; that: 'they draw near to me with their lips, but their hearts are far from me, they teach for doctrines the commandments of men, having a form of godliness, but they deny the power thereof'."

lead the argument against the practice in order to distract people from the fact that the practice is approved in our scriptures.

Let me be clear that I do not advocate the practice nor recommend it. Nor do I think those who continue the practice do so either with approval or authority. I've explained the defects in their arguments to authority in *Beloved Enos,* and I am confident in the explanation given there. They do not possess the keys to continue that practice. Their own position is self-defeating.

Nor do I think these people will be given the hand of fellowship until Zion returns. But when it does, I do not expect those who follow the practice if plural marriage in a humble and devout way, having real intent, and proceeding prayerfully will be excluded from the gathering. It also seems self-evident that if John D. Lee, who was executed for the Mountain Meadows Massacre, has been reinstated to the privileges of the church, that those practicing plural marriage after the 1905 letter from President Joseph F. Smith will some day not also be reinstated to church membership.

Well, that was an aside merely to illustrate a point. We fail to contend about errors of other faiths, fail to defend our unique status, and in turn attack doctrines that we know to be true.

What Nephi will focus on in his prophecy is not the contention, but the absence of guidance from the Holy Ghost. This criticism will become the theme of the coming chapters. This collection of chapters at the end of 2 Nephi are his final warnings in which he tells us the great themes of prophecy that rest so heavily upon his soul. He is most alarmed that, in our day, men will " teach with their learning, and deny the Holy Ghost, which giveth utterance." What do you suppose it means to "teach with their learning?"

We know that other churches employ trained theological experts to professionally teach them as a paid clergy. We have always been critical of that approach because once a minister has been to college and been trained for the ministry, they mingle the philosophies of men with scripture. We have always been taught that even a child with the Spirit can edify a congregation in Sacrament by speaking with the influence of the Holy Ghost. We intend our meetings to be directed in word and thought by the Holy Ghost. But how much of what we are taught in our meetings and conferences are the result of man's learning? Of focus group opinion gathering? Of opinion polling? Of careful study of trends and development of data bases from social sciences? (See *Slippery* on February 22, 2010.)

How much of what we are taught is from the "Spirit which giveth utterance?" How often are we fed as the Lord directed in D&C 84: 85 through entirely spontaneous utterance?[240] If Joseph was commanded to

---

[240] D&C 84: 85: "Neither take ye thought beforehand what ye shall say; but treasure up in your minds continually the words of life, and it shall be given you in the very hour that portion that shall be meted unto every man."

speak spontaneously so the Spirit could direct him[241] then why is a Correlation Department allowed to control talks today and prevent any spontaneous speaking in our conferences?

I know the purpose behind correlation was to insure false doctrine was not taught. They seem to have instead insured that no doctrine is taught.

In my view, correlation has failed in its purpose. It has stifled the Spirit and stripped us of doctrine which should be prized and taught. Furthermore, it has not insured the doctrine it permits to be taught is true or consistent with scripture or earlier teachings.

Even though correlation has not prevented us from having errors of doctrine I do not believe an error of doctrine makes a person a bad man. Joseph Smith said: "I did not like the old man being called up for erring in doctrine. It looks too much like the Methodist, and not like the Latter-day Saints. Methodists have creeds which a man must believe or be asked out of their church. I want the liberty of thinking and believing as I please. It feels so good not to be trammeled. It does not prove that a man is not a good man because he errs in doctrine." (DHC 5: 340.) I do not believe anyone should ever be subject to church discipline for believing false doctrine. The false teaching should be overcome by teaching the truth, not by stifling discussion. The quickest way for truth to triumph is to allow free discussion. When we are open, the truth will always win out.

I agree with Joseph Smith that teaching false doctrine does not prove "that a man is not a good man." Take the Proclamation on the Family, for example. It states: "All human beings —male and female—are created in the image of God. Each is a beloved spirit son or daughter of heavenly parents, and, as such, each has a divine nature and destiny. Gender is an essential characteristic of individual pre-mortal, mortal, and eternal identity and purpose." This statement conflicts with what President Joseph Fielding Smith taught in the arrangement prepared by Bruce R. McConkie (and therefore undoubtedly approved by Elder McConkie as well): "Some of the functions in the celestial body will not appear in the terrestrial body, neither in the telestial body, and the power of procreation will be removed. I take it that men and women will, in these kingdoms, be just what the so-called Christian world expects us all to be: **neither man nor woman,** merely immortal beings having received the resurrection. (Doctrines of Salvation 2:287-288; emphasis

---

[241] D&C 100: 5-6: "Therefore, verily I say unto you, lift up your voices unto this people; speak the thoughts that I shall put into your hearts, and you shall not be confounded before men; For it shall be given you in the very hour, yea, in the very moment, what ye shall say."

D&C 24: 5-6: "And thou shalt continue in calling upon God in my name, and writing the things which shall be given thee by the Comforter, and expounding all scriptures unto the church. And it shall be given thee in the very moment what thou shalt speak and write, and they shall hear it, or I will send unto them a cursing instead of a blessing."

added.) In another place President Smith taught, "Is not the sectarian world justified in their doctrine generally proclaimed, that **after the resurrection there will be neither male nor female sex**? It is a logical conclusion for them to reach and apparently is in full harmony with what the Lord has revealed regarding the kingdoms into which evidently the vast majority of mankind is likely to go." (Answers to Gospel Questions, Vol 4, p.66—a set that was also edited by Elder Bruce R. McConkie.)

If it is a grave offense to now err in doctrine, either President Smith and his son-in-law Elder McConkie should be condemned, or those who signed the *Proclamation on the Family* in September 1995 (the entire First Presidency and Quorum of the Twelve) should be condemned. They contradict one another. The Apostle Paul would seem to agree with President Smith and Elder McConkie.[242] The "Christian" world, of course, denounces marriage in eternity precisely because they disbelieve sexual identity ends with mortality. They base this upon Luke 20: 34-35, Matt. 22: 30, and Mark 12: 25 as well as Paul's statement in Galatians.

It appears to me that someone errs in doctrine. Despite that, I absolutely DO NOT BELIEVE that either the First Presidency and Quorum of the Twelve in 1995, nor President Joseph Fielding Smith and Bruce R. McConkie are bad men. Nor do I think that the contradiction should be managed by the Correlation Department. I think it should stand and become something on which each of us consider, ponder, pray and reach some conclusion for ourselves. It isn't necessary for us to always have controversies taken away from us, particularly at the expense of losing our doctrine.

The approach now is to prevent spontaneous talks from being delivered under the influence of the Holy Spirit because of fear that we would excite criticism by contradicting one another. I think this is wrong. If we want to be cautious about doctrine, then we ought to call men who understand and teach doctrine to preside. I see trustworthy men and women on KBYU discussing doctrine all the time. Elder Packer was a Seminary Instructor before his call to be a General Authority, and he has always been reliable on doctrine. I would love to hear him speak spontaneously every time he speaks. Elder Scott, also, seems to me to be a man who, if allowed to speak without a prepared text would have a great deal to share. It would be delightful to hear him speak extemporaneously. There is something valuable enough when an inspired man does this that the D&C admonished Joseph Smith to only address the Saints in this manner. If that was the Lord's desire for Joseph, and it remains in the D&C, then it is little wonder we pay a price as a result of the correlation process.

This is what the verse we are considering here it telling us SHOULD be the case. We cannot help but "deny the Holy Ghost, which giveth

---

242 Gal. 3: 28: "There is neither Jew nor Greek, there is neither bond nor free, there is neither male nor female: for ye are all one in Christ Jesus."

utterance" when we do not permit the Holy Ghost the opportunity to inspire by giving spontaneous utterance.

President Brigham Young:"What a pity it would be if we were led by one man to utter destruction! Are you afraid of this? I am more afraid that this people have so much confidence in their leaders that they will not inquire of themselves of God whether they are led by Him. I am fearful they will settle down in a state of blind self-security, trusting their eternal security in the hands of their leaders with a reckless confidence that in itself would thwart the purposes of God in their salvation, and weaken that influence they could give to their leaders, did they know for themselves, by the revelations of Jesus Christ, that they are led in the right way." (JD 9: 149-50.)

Joseph Smith cautioned about trusting to much in the prophet and neglecting the duties devolving upon the Saints individually. And George Q. Cannon also taught the principle that you cannot trust leadership to save you.

"It makes no difference what is written or what anyone has said, if what has been said is in conflict with what the Lord has revealed, we can set it aside. My words, and the teachings of any other m ember of the Church, high or low, if they do not square with the revelations, we need not accept them. Let us have that matter clear." (Doctrines of Salvation 3:203, emphasis in original.)

2 Nephi 28: 5

> **"And they deny the power of God, the Holy One of Israel; and they say unto the people: Hearken unto us, and hear ye our precept; for behold there is no God today, for the Lord and the Redeemer hath done his work, and he hath given his power unto men;"**

The defect Nephi terms "deny the power of God" is an interesting matter to ponder. What do you suppose denying that power involves? How would it manifest itself in the way religious people go about their lives? Is praying without seeking an answer "denying" God's power? Is presuming you have an answer when your own desires are all you are considering perhaps also "denying" God's power?

I reflect on how many times I've learned something surprising, unanticipated, or which had never before entered into my mind. I think, too, about Joseph's comment before his First Vision that "it had never entered i nto [his] heart that all were wrong"[243], but the answer from God informed him otherwise. God's answers are quite often:

---

[243] JS-H 1: 18: "My object in going to inquire of the Lord was to know which of all the sects was right, that I might know which to join. No sooner, therefore, did I get possession of myself, so as to be able to speak, than I asked the Personages who stood above me in the light, which of all the sects was right (for at this time it had never entered into my heart that all were wrong)—and which I should join."

- unanticipated

- never something you would have considered

- inconvenient

- requiring of you something you would prefer not to give or do

- clear and unequivocal

- enough to make your frame shake as it penetrates to your soul.

When prayer gets through to God and provokes an answer from Him, it is offered with a sincere heart, having real intent.[244] If a prayer is offered without a sincere heart, and while lacking real intent, is this "denying" the power of God?

If a minister lacks real intent, and does not go to God in mighty prayer, has never become acquainted with the "power of God," but proceeds to teach with their own learning anyway, do they deny the power of God?

In place of preaching what the Lord reveals, men will claim they teach correct "precepts." They have all the revelation they need, and they are now proceeding with the authority given them by God. But they don't hear from Him, don't have new revelation to deliver from Him, and do not expect God to be involved any longer.

In effect, God has become so distant that "there is no God today." He finished His work. He's given His authority to men.

Whether the claim is based on Protestant claims that authority is derived from the New Testament, and all men who believe have authority from God, or it is a Catholic claim to have a line of authority back to Jesus Christ, it is the same. Without some involvement from God in the church itself, the teachings end in the same conclusion: "God has given His power unto men." The institution has taken over. The claim is always that "the church is true" without regard to whether the Lord remains involved, revealing Himself to the church. This is what the Catholic Church has claimed for centuries God has finished His work and surrendered the "keys of authority" to the church. Now God has transmuted into a church, a Holy Roman Church, to which you may confess your sins, obtain absolution for your sins, and have entry into heaven provided to you.

With such a claim, why ask God for help? Why turn to a priesthood advancing such claims? Why make the difficult, inner changes that bring about real intent and faith in Christ? Why seek for and come into

---

[244] Moroni 10: 4: "And when ye shall receive these things, I would exhort you that ye would ask God, the Eternal Father, in the name of Christ, if these things are not true; and if ye shall ask with a sincere heart, with real intent, having faith in Christ, he will manifest the truth of it unto you, by the power of the Holy Ghost."
James 1: 5: "If any of you lack wisdom, let him ask of God, that giveth to all men liberally, and upbraideth not; and it shall be given him."

contact with "the power of God" if a church can be an adequate substitute?

How like the Catholics have we become?

Was Nephi only warning about Catholic error? Do his warnings apply equally to all?

2 Nephi 28: 6

> **"Behold, hearken ye unto my precept; if they shall say there is a miracle wrought by the hand of the Lord, believe it not; for this day he is not a God of miracles; he hath done his work."**

This lack of faith in receiving answers to prayer from God leads to skepticism about any other manifestation by God. If the leader isn't having any experience with God, then they distrust claims by anyone else. Everyone is a fraud, if the leader can't receive an answer to prayer.

The root of this is jealousy and envy. But it is completely unfounded. Revelation received by another person has no limiting effect on what personal revelation you can receive. The Lord is willing to share with all. However, it is predicated on the same principle. If the leader were willing to humble himself and seek in the prescribed manner, he would receive the same result. Everyone is invited. No one is excluded.

Nicodemus came to Christ in the dark, and Christ taught him the same way He taught others. There are some sources which suggest Nicodemus was ultimately converted. If he was, there is little doubt that after his conversion, the spiritual life he had as one of the Lord's disciples was greater than that of a member of the Sanhedrin. The Lord was not unwilling to share with the Sanhedrin, but they were unwilling to receive Him. When one (Nicodemus) changed his heart, the Lord came to him.

This seething distrust and accusation of any who claim to experience the miraculous leads in turn to denouncing the gifts of God. When denounced, such gifts depart from us. We no longer hear about miracles, healings, visions, tongues, visitations, or other gifts experienced by those we read of in scripture. Therefore, when the presence of the gifts end, the record of scriptures ends. There is nothing to add, and so nothing is added.

Eventually the end of this spiritual journey into the dark is to denounce all things coming from the "hand of God." No "miracle wrought by the hand of God" will be acknowledged, but will be denounced instead. The position becomes unalterable: "God is not a God of miracles anymore." You must trust leaders and leadership. You will be deceived if you profess revelation or the miraculous. And so the approach into hell is carefully laid by argument, emotion and fear.

Nephi foresaw this. He is warning us against it. We should not be seduced into thinking God has finished His work. He hasn't. He is in the middle of fulfilling promises made generations ago to the "fathers." We inherit from the Lord the promises He made to them. Now is a great day of miracles, visits, visitations, dreams, and healings. The heavens are open, if you will ask with a sincere heart having real intent, He will manifest the truth unto you. God remains the same. His blessings remain predicated upon the same conditions.

Seek. Ask. Knock. It will all be unfolded to you. He is no respecter of persons.

2 Nephi 28: 7-8

> **"Yea, and there shall be many which shall say: Eat, drink, and be merry, for tomorrow we die; and it shall be well with us. And there shall also be many which shall say: Eat, drink, and be merry; nevertheless, fear God—he will justify in committing a little sin; yea, lie a little, take the advantage of one because of his words, dig a pit for thy neighbor; there is no harm in this; and do all these things, for tomorrow we die; and if it so be that we are guilty, God will beat us with a few stripes, and at last we shall be saved in the kingdom of God."**

This notion that religion should always encourage merriment and feasting has so taken hold that it becomes impossible to cry repentance. Anything that challenges a happy outlook is thought to be negative and of the devil. It creates the misunderstanding that the right to feel good about one's self is a higher obligation than the duty to teach repentance and forsaking sin.

If you are laden with sin[245], it is of no consequence, for God intends that you be happy. It is of little matter that happiness cannot be found in sin[246], the gospel of positive attitude and flattery will triumph with the ungodly every time when it competes with a warning to repent and return to Christ.

The whole system has been worked out for us. The odds are you're going to be exalted. Deseret Book has taken a firm stand on that very subject. We have it from God, you see. Because Deseret Book is owned by the church, the church has been headed by a prophet, the prophet can't lead you astray, and therefore the odds are you're going to be exalted—Or so the reasoning goes.

If Nephi's warning is urged against the tide of permissiveness, supported by this false gospel of positive attitude and false hope, then the message must surely be meant by Nephi for someone other than us. We cannot possibly be among those who incorrectly believe the Lord will justify us in committing a little sin. We do not believe in the utility

---

245 Isa. 1: 4: "Ah sinful nation, a people laden with iniquity, a seed of evildoers, children that are corrupters: they have forsaken the Lord, they have provoked the Holy One of Israel unto anger, they are gone away backward."

246 Alma 41: 10: "Do not suppose, because it has been spoken concerning restoration, that ye shall be restored from sin to happiness. Behold, I say unto you, wickedness never was happiness."

of a little lie, do we? We do not use words to take advantage of others do we?

What pits have we dug for our neighbors?

By what measure do we advocate to live life pleasantly and not fear death or judgment? How could we be taken with the notion that a little guilt will result in merely a "few stripes" from an irritated, but ultimately tolerant, and permissive God? What doctrine is it we advance that suggests all of us will, at last, be saved in the kingdom of God?

Assuming this was meant to be a warning to US, ***the readers of the Book of Mormon****, and not to another audience* ***who will never read the book*** *because they aren't converted to it*, then how do we fit into this warning? Do we have a mistaken view of God's plan? What do we say, preach or believe that would provoke this warning from Nephi? Have you scrutinized the recent manuals from the Correlation Department to see if there is any basis for concern? Have you read the General Conference talks for hints of these teachings? Do you find them there?

How many articles do you find in the LDS Church News, Ensign and New Era which are positive, flattering and reassuring? How many articles confront you, call you to repent, warn you of the judgment and the duration of eternity?[247]

Why is the Book of Mormon constantly calling upon us to repent? Why are we not called relentlessly to repentance by our current leaders? Is there a disconnection between the message of the Book of Mormon and our modern messages? Has the Lord changed His mind? Was Nephi just a crank? Is the Book of Mormon a negative book not relevant to an enlightened people who are specially chosen by God for endless happiness and promised they will never be led astray? Why would the Book of Mormon be a message for us? Why do we have a book so negative in tone, pessimistic in its view of us, while we sit atop the promises of never again having to face an apostasy?

What accounts for this disparity?

An interlude by Bobby McFerrin: "Hmmmmmm, hmm, hmm, hmm, hmm, hmm, hmmmm, hmmmm, hm-hum-hm-hm... Don't worry. Be happy."

He's Mormon now, isn't he? I heard someone's friend's boyfriend baptized him when serving a mission in Southern California...

Poets and artists have been proclaiming the coming apocalypse in songs, art and movies for several decades. Nephi gives us the same message. But we spin happily out of control, loosed from the moorings and tossed by the approaching hurricane, all the while promising one

---

[247] Enos 1: 23: "And there was nothing save it was exceeding harshness, preaching and prophesying of wars, and contentions, and destructions, and continually reminding them of death, and the duration of eternity, and the judgments and the power of God, and all these things—stirring them up continually to keep them in the fear of the Lord. I say there was nothing short of these things, and exceedingly great plainness of speech, would keep them from going down speedily to destruction. And after this manner do I write concerning them."

another that it will all turn out right. We are special. We are chosen by God. Surely He will not judge us, nor hold us to account for what we believe. If we're mistaken, He owes it to us to give us a warning, and an opportunity to repent. Other than that sad account of the prior occupants of this land, He hasn't done that…

Oh. The Book of Mormon is important, isn't it?

The foolishness of the doctrines that Nephi is denouncing provokes such dismay that our own foolishness needs to be paraded out in all its stupidity. We just don't seem to get it. We're reading Nephi's warnings to us and pretending they were meant for everyone other than us. They aren't—they are aiming at us. Read the verse again and try to see our own teachings being laid bare. We are his target. We are his audience. We are being warned.

2 Nephi 28: 9

> **"Yea, and there shall be many which shall teach after this manner, false and vain and foolish doctrines, and shall be puffed up in their hearts, and shall seek deep to hide their counsels from the Lord; and their works shall be in the dark."**

The alarming use of the word "many" suggests this is to be a widespread problem in our time. These teachings are denounced as "false and vain and foolish." We should look at each:

What does "false" mean? Does something have to be thoroughly and completely wrong to be false? Is it enough to be off by enough to rob the teaching of power? How many truths will a liar tell while trying to get you to believe an ultimate lie? How well does a deception work if there isn't some truth included in the message? So, then, how difficult will detecting the error be? May the very elect be deceived?[248] How will one be able to decide between a false and a true teaching?[249]

What does "vain" mean? Is the best meaning "futile" or "without power?" If a teaching robs you of power, deprives you of the Spirit, is that "vain?" What would you trade in exchange for having power in the Spirit? If a little flattery is enough, would you take the assurance that God loves you, and will never let you be deceived enough to get you to

---

[248] Matt. 24: 24: "For there shall arise false Christs, and false prophets, and shall shew great signs and wonders; insomuch that, if it were possible, they shall deceive the very elect."
JS-Matt. 1: 22: "For in those days there shall also arise false Christs, and false prophets, and shall show great signs and wonders, insomuch, that, if possible, they shall deceive the very elect, who are the elect according to the covenant."

[249] Moroni 10: 5: "And by the power of the Holy Ghost ye may know the truth of all things."

let go of the responsibility to ever have His Spirit to be with you?[250] If the current President of the Quorum of the Twelve has lamented our lack of power, is it really a lament about our vain beliefs? If so, what can you do about it? How can you avoid having your faith become vain?

What does "foolish" mean? Would something that is so poorly based, so weak and powerless to save, and utterly false be foolish? What about trusting a man to save you, rather than the Lord? What about the notion that there is a man who will be perfectly unable to ever lead you astray? How foolish is it to trust your salvation to the inerrancy of a man?

What kind of a heart is "puffed up?" How would these false, vain and foolish doctrines result in a proud following? Why would they think themselves better than they are because of these doctrines?

What does it mean to "seek deep to hide their counsels from the Lord?" What does it mean to "seek deeply?" What foolish men would think they could ever "hide their counsel from the Lord?" Who would believe that God would be bound to follow what a man dictates—because they have keys to bind Him—rather than recognizing that the Lord alone holds all authority to judge and will alone determine all judgment?[251] How foolish is it to become a sycophant of priestly pretenders, hoping that they will save you in the day of judgment? Will appeasing an LDS authority be of any more value than kissing a Cardinal's ring when you are standing before the Lion of Israel to be judged? How well will the vain ceremonies and guarded conspiracies work in the day when everything is shouted from the rooftops?

What does it mean to have "works" which "shall be in the dark?" Does this just mean hidden? Does "darkness" also include the quality of the works? What kinds of work are "dark?" Can obliterating part of a sacred ceremony remove light and replace it with dark? Does curtailing the Saints' ability to discuss true principles, exercising control and dominion and compulsion to prevent knowledge from spreading all contribute to darkness in the minds of the Saints?

When is the last time you were encouraged in the Temple to understand and discuss the meaning of the Temple ceremonies? When was the last time you were told NOT to discuss the Temple meaning inside the Temple? If you can't discuss it inside the Temple, and you covenanted not to discuss it outside the Temple, then where can you discuss its meaning? How will you learn if you are unable to share ideas

---

250 Moroni 5: 2: "O God, the Eternal Father, we ask thee, in the name of thy Son, Jesus Christ, to bless and sanctify this wine to the souls of all those who drink of it, that they may do it in remembrance of the blood of thy Son, which was shed for them; that they may witness unto thee, O God, the Eternal Father, that they do always remember him, that they may have his Spirit to be with them. Amen."

251 3 Ne. 27: 27: "And know ye that ye shall be judges of this people, according to the judgment which I shall give unto you, which shall be just. Therefore, what manner of men ought ye to be? Verily I say unto you, even as I am."

about the symbols and their meaning? Is it "dark" when the light of teaching is closed to view?

I don't know if any of you recall that Hugh Nibley was given access to the chapel in the Provo Temple to speak to waiting patrons about the meaning of the Temple for a number of years. While waiting for a session to begin, patrons could listen to and ask questions of Hugh Nibley in an atmosphere of sharing and getting answers. Today, in contrast, they discourage you from discussing anything about the Temple even inside the Temple. I refer to an incident in the Jordan River Temple in *The Second Comforter*. I was told to not discuss meanings while in the Celestial Room speaking with full time missionaries assigned to my stake. I presided over the missionary work of the stake and worked closely with these wonderful young men. But I was told to stop teaching them. This is common today. It ought to end. We will only understand sacred symbols if we are able to teach one another about what we have learned. When I think of the library of material I have had to get through to be able to understand, I am left to wonder at how difficult the process has been made for those who would sincerely and humbly like to seek after further light and knowledge by teaching one another.

We should welcome as much light and truth in our exchanges with one another as we have to offer; in the right setting and with the right Spirit. It is not casting pearls before swine when the audience is prepared, worthy and interested in obtaining knowledge for the right reason. Now even if you have the very best of audiences, in the most sacred setting, we are told to not discuss what may be of vital interest to a soul seeking to gain further light and knowledge by conversing with the Lord through the veil.

How little discarding of light must one cause before they are doing "works in the dark?" It is such a terrible question with such fearful results that I would hesitate to be the one who limits the Saints' ability to seek into truth.

Now, to balance things somewhat, I want to affirm several fundamental truths:

- We are accountable for our own search into the truth.
- No one can limit you if you are searching with real intent having a contrite spirit and broken heart.
- There is no conflict between fulfilling your duties to the church on the one hand and your responsibilities to the Lord on the other.
- You cannot blame anyone else if you have not been diligent about your own search.
- In the end, whether there is active opposition or active assistance provided to you, it is necessary for you to make the internal changes and to follow the path.

No outside party will control what is yours alone to control. But the first step to be taken is to realize you really are personally responsible. You can't depend on others nor on an institution to do the work for you. But as you awaken to that recognition, you should not lose heart or become discouraged. Nothing has been lost collectively which you may not still lay claim upon for yourself.

I do think we could make a greater overall gentile success with a different, more benign attitude as a group. But even if you must work against a corrosive environment, you can still do it. You have the greatest tool in your hands. You truly can get closer to the Lord through the Book of Mormon than any other means. It is a guidebook written for us and for now.

2 Nephi 28: 10-12

> **"And the blood of the saints shall cry from the ground against them. Yea, they have all gone out of the way; they have become corrupted. Because of pride, and because of false teachers, and false doctrine, their churches have become corrupted, and their churches are lifted up; because of pride they are puffed up."**

Why does this mention the "blood of the saints?" What does it mean for their "blood to cry from the ground?" I've discussed this before, speaking of the earth's own spirit.

What does "all" include? Even us? If "they have all gone out of the way; they have become corrupted" includes us, what does that mean? How could we also be "out of the way?" Is Nephi right? What about Wilford Woodruff's claim that we would never be led astray? Can someone who promises to not lead you astray then lead you astray? How solid a guarantee does any man offer to you?

What does it mean to "have become corrupted?" Can a church be "true" and still be "corrupted?"[252]

What "pride" can religion impose upon people who believe false traditions? Does your faith make you "proud" to belong? Do you think it makes you better than others? Do you believe you're saved while others will be damned, because they don't share your faith? Does that make

---

[252] D&C 84: 53-58: "And by this you may know the righteous from the wicked, and that the whole world groaneth under sin and darkness even now. And your minds in times past have been darkened because of unbelief, and because you have treated lightly the things you have received—Which vanity and unbelief have brought the whole church under condemnation. And this condemnation resteth upon the children of Zion, even all. And they shall remain under this condemnation until they repent and remember the new covenant, even the Book of Mormon and the former commandments which I have given them, not only to say, but to do according to that which I have written—That they may bring forth fruit meet for their Father's kingdom; otherwise there remaineth a scourge and judgment to be poured out upon the children of Zion."

you lose sleep at night, and want to cry out to save them—or to relax and enjoy your security?

What does it mean that the faiths are "all out of the way?" Is there only one "way?" If so, how would you recognize the right "way" from the wrong one?

Who are "false teachers" that teach "false doctrine?" Does "false" include omission of important truths? If one teaches truths about Christ, but does not teach you how to return to His presence, is the teacher "false?" What would qualify someone to be "true" and teach the right "way?" How would you distinguish between true and false teachers? Between true and false doctrine?

How can "false teachers" corrupt a church? Can they corrupt any church? Even ours?

Why does becoming "puffed up" and "pride" follow false teachings? What is it about false religion that brings pride to its followers? How does false security caused by corrupt doctrine lead to "pride?"

What would the opposite religious attitude be for "pride?" Would humility, a broken heart and a contrite spirit be different than "pride?" What kind of teaching would cause a listener to become contrite, humble, meek and submissive? What kind of teaching would defeat pride and break a person's heart? Can you have both? Can you be "humble" and "broken hearted" and also be proud of your religion? If you cannot, then can you think deeply about your faith, your meetings, your conferences, your private as well as public conversations and ask yourself if the teachers to whom you listen lead you to pride? Lead you to humility? Lead you to contrition and repentance?

Who is Nephi describing? Is it possible it could apply to us along with all other organized faiths?

I have often heard my fellow-Saint speak of the sense of pride the Conference Center gives them. It is a great, spacious and technologically advanced center. I've thought the ceiling of that building looks somewhat like that very successful evangelist Joel Osteen's amazing church. I've wondered if the architectural firm took hints from other successful mega-churches when designing the Conference Center. Have you noticed how the dimmed lights and the magnified images, magnified voices and focus upon the great pulpit is designed to use all the modern audio-visual technology to create heroic images within the building for the audience? It is a technical marvel. Really state of the art. It is hard for me not to take some pride in it all. Anyone who wonders if our church is respectable, successful, powerful or advanced, who visits the facility will no doubt leave with the conclusion that, despite our humble origins, we certainly have made a success in the world for ourselves. It is a story of overcoming and prospering.

If those whose bloodstained footprints covered our westward migration could see what we've become, I wonder what delight (or disappointment) they would feel. Would they have any mixed emotions at seeing this monument in granite, glass, brass and walnut? The third-of-a-billion dollars we spent on it produced a landmark of splendor for the ages. Poor Joseph had only an open air bowery to use. Adam, too, used the open plains of Adam-Ondi-Ahman to meet. We are, of course, blessed with more resources to use as part of our "worship."

2 Nephi 28: 13

> **"They rob the poor because of their fine sanctuaries; they rob the poor because of their fine clothing; and they persecute the meek and the poor in heart, because in their pride they are puffed up."**

You must keep the prior verse in mind as you read this one. They are a continuation of thought.

It is an interesting thought to equate "fine sanctuaries" with "robbing the poor." Why do you suppose Nephi would make that equation? Does it give us any pause?

What "duty" would be owed to the poor that entitles them to come before a "fine sanctuary?"

Is there a duty to care for the poor that comes before the right of someone to wear "fine clothing?"

What does it mean to "persecute the meek?" Can you "persecute the meek" just by ignoring them? By neglecting them? Does any religion owe some duty to the meek? What obligation is owed to the meek by people of faith?

Who is "poor in heart?" What obligation do we all owe to the poor in heart?

Now look at the last phrase. It begins with "because." Isn't Nephi saying that our defects are all due to "our pride." That is, "because of their pride they are puffed up" and this is the reason we "rob the poor." This is the reason we "persecute the meek." This is the reason we "persecute the poor in heart." Or, in other words, we are proud and puffed up and therefore we cannot help but cause these other offenses.

We necessarily ignore our obligations to the poor and meek because we are filled with pride. We don't give a second thought to what we're doing with resources entrusted to us to bless and benefit others, because we believe we are entitled to have "fine sanctuaries." We just presume we are justified in our "fine clothing" without regard to what we may owe others.

There is a moment in film that helps illustrate this verse. It is in the closing of the movie *Schindler's List*. The Allies had overrun the area and the Nazi rule had ended. As Schindler was receiving the gratitude of those who had been saved by his efforts, he was struck by what more he could have done. He was less interested in receiving gratitude than he was guilt ridden by how many more lives could have been saved had he parted with a ring. Had he parted with a car it would have secured other lives. The thought filled him with guilt. He had done some, it was undoubtedly true. But his conscious was filled with remorse because he could have done more. And in that setting, doing more was saving lives. He preferred a ring to another man's life. He preferred a car to a family's lives. It tormented him. If you can harrow up your mind to remember this scene, then think of what we might have done with the great resources we have been given in place of some of the monuments we have built.

Why do we need chapels at all? Why not meet in homes? What good could be done with the money we have invested in the chapels we have built? Joseph Smith built temples; he did not build chapels. General Conference was held in an outdoor bowery. Do we have anything to apologize for in how we use our resources? Were or are there poor toward whom the Lord would have preferred us to show mercy, and do more? There are families who have supplied church leadership from their large construction companies who have built projects for the church. I am told these relationships are natural. They call who they know and associate with, after all. I suppose that is true.

Nephi seems troubled by his view of us. We seem untroubled by his words. At least we don't seem to change our behavior much because of Nephi's counsel. We deflect it, and point to others as his real target.

Well, Nephi is nothing if not relevant to almost everything going on today.

2 Nephi 28: 14

> **"They wear stiff necks and high heads; yea, and because of pride, and wickedness, and abominations, and whoredoms, they have all gone astray save it be a few, who are the humble followers of Christ; nevertheless, they are led, that in many instances they do err because they are taught by the precepts of men."**

This is so sobering and relevant a verse that it is the first thing quoted in the dedication of the first book I wrote, *The Second Comforter: Conversing With the Lord Through the Veil.* This is our moment. Inside this foolish age there are nevertheless a "few, who are the humble followers of Christ." These are the salt which preserve the world. These are the leaven who keep us still from destruction.

"Stiff necks" do not bow in prayer and praise before a Lord to whom they regard themselves as unworthy. They are undaunted by their unworthiness. They think themselves justified, and therefore without any need to bow in reverence.

"High heads" do not tilt down to behold the less fortunate to whom they might have provided relief. They ignore the destitute and needy, preferring only to see those who are on their standing or above. Who can help elevate them? Who can give them an advantage? Who is a good contact to keep? The "high heads" will be careful about what social advantages come from associations, and will always pick carefully those whom they deign to notice.

But these stiff necks and high heads belong to those carrying a burden of sin. They are prideful, wicked, given to abominations and whoredoms. These are the ones who sit upon the labors of others, and fare sumptuously here. So long as your neck remains stiff and your head held high, you will never notice Lazarus lying at your gate.

But what of the "few, who are the humble followers of Christ?" What of them?

It is clear in this verse that they do NOT lead, but are instead being led. They are "led that in many instances they do err." That is, those who qualify to be called the "few, who are the humble followers of Christ" are not themselves leaders. They are being led by others.

The others who lead them "cause them to err." And why do they cause this? "Because they are taught by the precepts of men." Therefore, the humble true followers are misled into accepting false, foolish and vain (or powerless) beliefs because the ones who preside over them are only able to offer the "precepts of men." These "precepts of men" are unable to bring the "humble followers of Christ" to the knowledge of Him.

Keep in mind that the "precepts of men" are repeated by Nephi in this written sermon more than any other phrase. The learning used to lead is distracting, even damning, whenever it fails to lead to the Lord. Men's precepts cannot rescue us.

Why are not the "humble followers of Christ" doing the leading? Because they do not have the "stiff necks and high heads" to become noticed, to be added to the group of insiders. Their clothes are not costly, their home "sanctuaries" are insufficiently ornate. They are not the stuff of renown and recognition. They are, in a word, *the least.*

It is a troubling image which begins to emerge from Nephi's words. They are shocking for us to consider. If the alternatives are what Nephi seems to leave us, then how much better is it to be among the "few, who are the humble followers of Christ" than among those with the authority to lead them?

I do not believe any of us are in a position to fully understand our times. We live inside a cultural fog that makes our judgments inside the bubble distorted in ways Nephi did not experience from his vantage point. The Lord can give us a clearer perspective through revelation, as He did for Nephi. But we are not equipped to fully recognize our peril standing inside this age and culture.

The one thing that is abundantly clear is that Joseph Smith was right about the need to reconnect with God. His first and primary message remains the testimony of James 1: 5: If we lack wisdom, we should ask of God. God will give liberally to those who ask with a sincere heart, having real intent. Whether you believe Joseph's account or not, Joseph was pointing us to James and testifying James made a promise which God will fulfill. So test James. Ask with real intent. Perhaps you will begin to see how Nephi's words of warning are exactly what is needed to save us from our peril. At a minimum, the petition will make you closer to being one of the "few, who are the humble followers of Christ" because of your desire to know from Him the truth of your plight.

He always intends to save those who wait upon Him. Those who serve Him and do as He asks will never be forsaken. All that is required to qualify is to repent and come to Christ with sincere intent. No matter what else is going on, the Lord can take your life's circumstances and make them work to fulfill His work. And His work is your salvation and exaltation.

The first step is to recognize the peril you face. The second is to then do something about it. To take the first step without the second is worse than meaningless. It inspires fear and pessimism. That is wrong. Happiness is the goal of our existence. That comes from Christ. So do not just notice your plight, but make the necessary flight back to Him.

2 Nephi 28: 15

> **"O the wise, and the learned, and the rich, that are puffed up in the pride of their hearts, and all those who preach false doctrines, and all those who commit whoredoms, and pervert the right way of the Lord, wo, wo, wo be unto them, saith the Lord God Almighty, for they shall be thrust down to hell!"**

Now we reach a terrible point. Nephi records an inspired condemnation. For a person in Nephi's position, recording words of condemnation holds terrible significance. They are not written unless they are instructed to do so, because their words will be fulfilled. I've explained this in *Beloved Enos.*

Nephi pronounces three "wo's." This is a three fold condemnation. It goes beyond this life. It will follow them into the hereafter.

Associated with the three "wo's" are three names used for God: "Lord God Almighty." It is a three fold assertion of divine authority. "Lord" refers to the Savior as Guide. "God" refers to Divine right and authority. "Almighty" refers to the irrevocable nature of the word used by God, and in turn the words given to Nephi. When you are confronted with all three, the "wo's" are pronounced by a power that cannot be altered.

This is more than a setback in the hopes of the "learned, and the rich" who are being condemned. This is a condemnation which reaches into hell itself. It is so significant a pronouncement that when you read it you should pause and think of the dreadful import for anyone who fits into the curse.

Those, who in their pride, use the precepts of men as the basis for their "preaching false doctrines," are not just wrong, they are damned for this perversion of the religion entrusted to them to preach in purity and truth.

In effect, they were given a precious and eternally significant treasure, and they have diverted it into something that makes them rich, puffed up, and powerful. It is tragic. It is pitiful—meaning it should inspire pity in each of us. These could be well meaning people who have fallen into this error. But they claim to preach the truth, using God's name in vain, while they spread a vain religion which cannot bring people to the knowledge of Christ.

Who would wish such a condemnation upon others? Who can read these words and not be moved with compassion and alarm for those who have fallen under this condemnation? Who would not remove it from those who are condemned if they could?

Nephi could not make a greater plea for the salvation of all those involved. The pronouncement is terrible and its implications eternal. Yet this verse seems to have escaped notice.

Who alone claims they are speaking for God Himself when they preach? Who could possibly qualify for this level of condemnation? This should make all of us think long and hard about any utterance we speak before we make our assertions "in the name of Jesus Christ." The thoughtlessness which accompanies that expression among the Saints is contrary to the seriousness of the condemnation we invite if we preach false doctrine while puffed up in pride; thereby perverting the right way of the Lord.

In an example which is chilling to read, the first anti-Christ we encounter in the Book of Mormon (Sherem) uses this phrase to justify his preaching. He accuses Jacob of "perverting the right way of God."[253] He brings himself under Nephi's curse. It was a small thing, therefore, for Jacob to reiterate the condemnation of Nephi against Sherem.[254] Jacob was merely repeating what Nephi had already pronounced. And since Nephi had sealed the condemnation, it would be Nephi, not Jacob, who was responsible for the cursing.

This three fold wo, and use of three titles for God all suggest that teaching false doctrine and using man's learning, while being filled with pride is so grave an offense that great care should always be taken before teaching, preaching or expounding on the Gospel. Only a fool would undertake to do so without knowing their words are approved of God. You cannot take cover using a Correlation Department, or a commentary, or a scholar's words, or a selected bibliography. When you presume to preach the truth, you need to realize how serious a matter you are undertaking. Joseph Smith wrote from Liberty Jail:

---

[253] Jacob 7: 7: "And ye have led away much of this people that they pervert the right way of God, and keep not the law of Moses which is the right way; and convert the law of Moses into the worship of a being which ye say shall come many hundred years hence. And now behold, I, Sherem, declare unto you that this is blasphemy; for no man knoweth of such things; for he cannot tell of things to come. And after this manner did Sherem contend against me."

[254] Jacob 7: 14: "And I said unto him: What am I that I should tempt God to show unto thee a sign in the thing which thou knowest to be true? Yet thou wilt deny it, because thou art of the devil. Nevertheless, not my will be done; but if God shall smite thee, let that be a sign unto thee that he has power, both in heaven and in earth; and also, that Christ shall come. And thy will, O Lord, be done, and not mine."

> "The things of God are of deep import; and time, and experience, and careful and ponderous and solemn thoughts can only find them out. Thy mind, O man! if thou wilt lead a soul unto salvation, must stretch as high as the utmost heavens, and search into and contemplate the darkest abyss, and the broad expanse of eternity—thou must commune with God. How much more dignified and noble are the thoughts of God, than the vain imaginations of the human heart! None but fools will trifle with the souls of men.
>
> "How vain and trifling have been our spirits, our conferences, our councils, our meetings, our private as well as public conversations—too low, too mean, too vulgar, too condescending for the dignified characters of the called and chosen of God, according to the purposes of His will, from before the foundation of the world!" (DHC 3: 295-6.)

When we speak about Christ and His Gospel with others, we should do so with a sense of terrible awe and fear. If we have doubts about our message, we should remain silent rather than risk proclaiming what may be an error. It is a burden to be carefully undertaken.

As Nephi warns about our day, there will be many who will teach vain, foolish and false things coming from the precepts of men.

I believe these words from Nephi are primarily directed at the leaders, and only secondarily relevant to those who are following. The trends and direction are always set by leaders.

I know there are humble people reading this who want to condemn themselves and justify leaders. But taken in context, Nephi's condemnation must necessarily be primarily aimed at those who lead.

I wish it were otherwise. I cannot tell you how these words cause me grief. I take no delight in this.

It would be easier to stop than to go on. But this Book of Mormon is something we must study if we are going to remove our condemnation. And it seems as if no one is willing to face its words. So the burden remains upon us.

On "evil speaking" the following are relevant:

First, it is not "evil" to say what is true.

Second, it cannot be "evil speaking" when it comes from an accepted prophet (Nephi) and is found in the scriptures.

Third, if the Spirit underlays the concept or thought, it is not you speaking it is the Spirit. If the message which comes from the Lord, or the Spirit, then it is not even you speaking. You are voice, but it is another who speaks.

Fourth, a call to repent is not "evil" speaking; because if it were then we could never be urged to repentance. Because the issues involved in repentance are always going to be somewhat personal, cutting and difficult.

In the narrowest sense "the Lord's anointed" would be those whom the Lord anoints. It would be those whom the Lord makes His, sealing them up to eternal life.

In the broadest sense it would be anyone who has been through the Temple to receive their washings and anointings.

It is NOT the Lord. As to Him, there are other commandments which relate to using His name in vain, His status as our Savior, and other appropriate rules for respecting and worshiping Him. But it only takes a moment of reflection to see the Lord's anointed would be those whom He has anointed.

My guess is that the most natural reaction to the critique of Nephi of our modern-day church and its foibles tends to be defensive because have testimonies of the divine role the organization plays. Any criticism must be attempting to pry us away from membership in the organization. I don't think that's what's involved here at all.

Perhaps we fall slightly into the trap of first declaring that we need to stop assuming infallibility and perfection of leaders and organization and start getting our answers for ourselves from the Lord.

Unfortunately, next we then hold up the leaders and organization against the measure of infallibility and perfection are then tempted to examine the failings in detail and lament the error and failings we find.

Well, what did we expect, we just said that we don't assume perfection in leaders and earthly institutions. They haven't changed with this new revelation to us, but maybe we need to change our approach to them. We don't throw them out because of their failings, we turn to the Lord and put our faith *there.* He can tell us through his Spirit the truth of all things, including the truth of the the teachings of those who stand as his imperfect legal administrators on earth.

2 Nephi 28: 16-17

> **"Wo unto them that turn aside the just for a thing of naught and revile against that which is good, and say that it is of no worth! For the day shall come that the Lord God will speedily visit the inhabitants of the earth; and in that day that they are fully ripe in iniquity they shall perish. But behold, if the inhabitants of the earth shall repent of their wickedness and abominations they shall not be destroyed, saith the Lord of Hosts."**

Nephi warns against "turning aside the just for a thing of naught." A "thing of naught" means something without value. To "turn aside" is to leave or move away from. So he is telling you to be careful to not walk away from the truth being taught by a "just" or true source, and instead follow after something of no value.

This rejection of a true messenger and following after a false one inevitably results in "reviling that which is good." When you reject the truth you normally have to deal with a troubled conscious. The way to calm it is to "revile against" the thing you have rejected. Not only do people "revile against" the message, but they go on to "say that it is of no worth!"

Think about the general reception given to the Lord's messengers throughout scripture. They are always the object of criticism and reviling. Nephi is describing a syndrome here which always attaches to the true message and true messenger. They aren't valued, but thought "a thing of naught." The argument is always: "If what they had to say were important, it would come from someone more important." Content is ignored in favor of status.

Now the Lord allows this to go on and always has. But, as Nephi reminds us, there does come a time when the limit has been reached. When the limit has been reached, the end "will speedily visit the inhabitants of the earth." That is, when the time has come, the turn will be so swift that they cannot repent any longer. Judgment will overtake them too quickly.

The moment when they have reached the limit is described by Nephi as "fully ripe in iniquity." That means they will no longer even listen to the truth. They have completely closed minds. It would do no good to extend them further opportunity, because they will not take any advantage of it.

So they are scheduled for destruction.

BUT, Nephi reminds us, they can repent. If they will change their minds and come to Christ, He will forgive them and heal them. If they repent, they will be preserved from the destruction. However, as has already become clear, their destruction is due to the fact they are "fully ripe." So although repentance remains theoretically possible, and the Lord will accept even late return to Him, the offenders are committed to their offense. They are not likely to take advantage of the opportunity.

How humble it is for the Lord to be willing to accept the reluctant, tardy and slow to repent. Nevertheless, He is willing to accept even them. He suffered for all, and will redeem as many as will come to Him. Initially, He won't destroy them with the wicked. Ultimately the outcome will depend upon how committed they are to the process of repentance. For to repent is to come to Him. They decide if His open arms will be where they finally embrace Him; of if they will stand afar off and think it too hard to surrender their sins and go further.

2 Nephi 28: 18-19

> **"But behold, that great and abominable church, the whore of all the earth, must tumble to the earth, and great must be the fall thereof. For the kingdom of the devil must shake, and they which belong to it must needs be stirred up unto repentance, or the devil will grasp them with his everlasting chains, and they be stirred up to anger, and perish;"**

Remember that this comes at the end of Nephi's ministry. He saw the vision of the great and abominable church at the beginning of his journey into the wilderness. There has been over forty years between the time of the earlier visions and the time of this summary of his great teachings.[255])

Between the time Nephi saw the visions (set out beginning in 1 Nephi 11) and the time of this final instruction, Nephi has had decades to ponder on the things he was shown in vision. He has, in fact, spent those years reflecting constantly upon the visions he received.[256] It is foolish to believe that Nephi, Joseph Smith, or any prophet understood what they saw the day they saw it. Only time, careful, solemn and ponderous thought can unravel what a person is shown in vision by the Lord. The understanding of a prophet is not static. It unfolds. Joseph's first impression of the first vision was personal. He thought it was a message to him about himself. By the time he had finished translating the Book of Mormon, organizing the church, and collecting a following, Joseph realized the first vision was not his, but it belonged at a minimum to a larger community of believers. Eventually he would come to see it belonged to the world. The version we have in the Pearl of Great Price reflects that changing understanding. In it he gives the first understanding in what he told his mother the day it happened: He learned that Presbyterianism was not true.[257]

So this statement goes back forty years earlier and Nephi's vision of the fall of the great whore. This universal false religion will fail. It will "fall." The "fall" will be "great." It will "tumble to the earth"—meaning that it will no longer stand on its own, but will altogether collapse.

The purpose of this great calamity is to bring about repentance. The purposes of God, even in punishment, are to elevate and save others.

Notice the devil's tool that will be used in opposition to repentance: they will "be stirred up to anger, and perish." That is, to harden hearts and to blind eyes, anger will be the most effective tool. Rather than being humbled by the fall of the great whore, those who will continue to resist repentance will be angry for the losses. They will lament the loss of what they held so dearly.

---

[255] 2 Ne. 5: 34: "And it sufficeth me to say that *forty years had passed away, and we had already had wars and contentions with our brethren."

[256] 2 Ne. 4: 16: "Behold, my soul delighteth in the things of the Lord; and my heart pondereth continually upon the things which I have seen and heard."

[257] JS-H 1: 20: "He again forbade me to join with any of them; and many other things did he say unto me, which I cannot write at this time. When I came to myself again, I found myself lying on my back, looking up into heaven. When the light had departed, I had no strength; but soon recovering in some degree, I went home. And as I leaned up to the fireplace, mother inquired what the matter was. I replied, "Never mind, all is well—I am well enough off." I then said to my mother, "I have learned for myself that Presbyterianism is not true." It seems as though the adversary was aware, at a very early period of my life, that I was destined to prove a disturber and an annoyer of his kingdom; else why should the powers of darkness combine against me? Why the opposition and persecution that arose against me, almost in my infancy?"

This, then, is how the groups break down—For those who repent, the difficulties they encounter bring humility and contrition. For those who refuse to repent, they respond with anger at their trials.

This is the great watershed test. If your set backs in life humble you, then your heart is soft and you are a candidate for repentance. If you become angry, accuse God of causing evil, and refuse to be comforted, you are not a candidate for repentance. Your anger is a tool used to blind you. The one employing the tool is the enemy to your soul.

The trials and difficulties are gifts to stir you up to repentance. That is how you ought to respond. The only way to approach the Lord is through humility. Anything that aids you in becoming humble is good, merciful and just. You should view it as a gift. No matter the difficulty. Christ descended below it all; and none of us are greater than He.[258]

2 Nephi 28: 20

> **"For behold, at that day shall he rage in the hearts of the children of men, and stir them up to anger against that which is good."**

One of the most effective ways to end thought or discussion is to get angry. Lawyers use anger as a tool to turn witnesses into thoughtless and emotional pawns. People make very bad decisions when they are angry. I've mentioned before my father's saying that he never spoke a word in anger than he did not later regret.

This is a time of great anger. Anger about religious ideas flows from insecurity and feeling threatened by the idea. It is not possible to have a discussion when people are insecure, angry and unwilling to be thoughtful about ideas.

This is the work of the devil. He succeeds when people close their minds and fill with anger at teachings which introduce ideas that challenge assumptions.

This is why the Jews wanted Christ killed. This is why they wanted to kill Lehi when he spoke of Christ. The teachings ran contrary to the presumptions, and as a result the response was emotional, angry and closed down thought and discussion.

Using fear to shut down people's ability to consider, ponder and pray is a technique used with amazing success. When you hear the argument that something will put you in peril, jeopardize your salvation, and to be afraid of the idea or discussion, you ought to ask yourself whether the notion that shutting down discussion seems right or not. Is it merely using fear to cause rage and anger? Can it be a tool to cause you to turn "against that which is good?"

---

[258] D&C 122: 8: "The Son of Man hath descended below them all. Art thou greater than he?"

All kinds of ideas need to be considered to bring you to the Lord. Closing down because of fear will hinder the process, as the devil knows.[259]

The tool of anger is the other side of fear.

The object of this is always to cheat your soul, close your mind, keep you from learning the truth.

Now is the great day of anger. Have you noticed how much of the discourse in public life is based upon fear and anger? Those larger social dynamics invade the community of Saints, as well. We are as vulnerable to this technique as the rest of society.

Be slow to anger, quick to forgive; open and prayerful. The great plan to cheat your soul will not succeed with you if you remain humble and open.

2 Nephi 28: 21

> **"And others will he pacify, and lull them away into carnal security, that they will say: All is well in Zion; yea, Zion prospereth, all is well—and thus the devil cheateth their souls, and leadeth them away carefully down to hell."**

Now we have reached a point where the audience becomes unavoidably identified with the gentiles of the last days who claim to be assembling as "Zion." This term gets applied in the Book of Mormon in a highly selective way. It includes the following:

- Last days time frame;
- Post-restoration of the Book of Mormon;
- People who are either claiming or who have actually assembled together as Zion.

We are the only ones who fit this definition. Therefore the application of these verses to include us is required. We cannot point to others and say we are not among those being warned.

What does "pacify" mean?

What does "lull" mean?

What does "carnal security" mean?

If you have people who are pacified, lulled with carnal security, what kind of people are you speaking about?

Why would these people think they were "Zion?" What possible basis could people who are pacified, and lulled with carnal security have for thinking they are "Zion?"

---

259 D&C 38: 30: "I tell you these things because of your prayers; wherefore, treasure up wisdom in your bosoms, lest the wickedness of men reveal these things unto you by their wickedness, in a manner which shall speak in your ears with a voice louder than that which shall shake the earth; but if ye are prepared ye shall not fear."

What does it mean that "all is well in Zion?" What does it mean "Zion prospereth?" Does "all is well in Zion" mean the same thing as "Zion prospereth?" If not, what is the difference? Is one "spiritual" and the other "carnal?"

Can one be an attitude, while the other is a measurement or statistic? Can "all be well in Zion" mean that we have comfortable controls and guarantees in place which will protect us?

Can "Zion prospereth" mean new converts, new buildings, new numbers, more tithing receipts, growth and political influence? What else might it mean?

Do we satisfy the notion that "all is well in Zion?" That is, can you see a reason to say that Zion is well at present? Do our people say that?

Do we satisfy the notion that "Zion prospereth?" That is, can you see any reason to say that Zion is presently prospering? Do our people say that?

Why would it "cheat souls" to make them think "all is well in Zion" and that "Zion prospereth?"

Why would it lead people "carefully down to hell" for them to believe all is well and Zion prospers?

Can Zion ever relent? Can Zion tolerate a little sin? Does it cheat us if we are good, decent people, and we recognize we are good and decent? Even if we are good and honorable, can we be deceived?[260] How does prosperity blind us? Do John's words to the Laodiceans tell us how we can err?[261]

What quality does the devil employ to mislead us? Does being led away "carefully" mean it is harder to recognize the peril? Should it be hard to avoid deception? Why do those who take the Holy Spirit as their guide avoid this kind of deception?[262]

Can anyone qualify to receive guidance from the Holy Spirit?[263]

Can anyone qualify to receive Christ as their guide?[264]

---

260 D&C 76: 75: "These are they who are honorable men of the earth, who were blinded by the craftiness of men."

261 Rev. 3: 17: "Because thou sayest, I am rich, and increased with goods, and have need of nothing; and knowest not that thou art wretched, and miserable, and poor, and blind, and naked:"

262 D&C 45: 57: "For they that are wise and have rcceived the truth, and have taken the Holy Spirit for their guide, and have not been deceived—verily I say unto you, they shall not be hewn down and cast into the fire, but shall abide the day."

263 Moroni 10: 5: "And by the power of the Holy Ghost ye may know the truth of all things."

264 D&C 93: 1: "Verily, thus saith the Lord: It shall come to pass that every soul who forsaketh his sins and cometh unto me, and calleth on my name, and obeyeth my voice, and keepeth my commandments, shall see my face and know that I am;"

What good does it do to follow even a true messenger, if you do not receive a testimony from Christ?[265]

To whom should you look for salvation?

Does part of the problem Nephi relates here grow out of the notion that being part of a group will matter? If you accept baptism and other saving ordinances from those with authority to minister them, but you do not come to Christ, will the ordinances alone save you? Since the ordinances do matter[266], what must you do after receiving them?[267] Is part of enduring to the end helping others within your own ward family? Can you just walk away from your obligations to the church after entering into the covenant of baptism?[268]

2 Nephi 28: 22

> **"And behold, others he flattereth away, and telleth them there is no hell; and he saith unto them: I am no devil, for there is none —and thus he whispereth in their ears, until he grasps them with his awful chains, from whence there is no deliverance."**

How can the devil "flatter" someone? Why would it be "flattery" to tell someone "there is no hell?" What does it mean that "there is no hell?" Have you ever heard this idea taught? Historic Christians are fully

---

[265] D&C 76: 98-101: "And the glory of the telestial is one, even as the glory of the stars is one; for as one star differs from another star in glory, even so differs one from another in glory in the telestial world; For these are they who are of Paul, and of Apollos, and of Cephas. These are they who say they are some of one and some of another—some of Christ and some of John, and some of Moses, and some of Elias, and some of Esaias, and some of Isaiah, and some of Enoch; But received not the gospel, neither the testimony of Jesus, neither the prophets, neither the everlasting covenant."

[266] Mark 16: 16: "He that believeth and is baptized shall be saved; but he that believeth not shall be damned."
2 Ne. 9: 23: "And he commandeth all men that they must repent, and be baptized in his name, having perfect faith in the Holy One of Israel, or they cannot be saved in the kingdom of God."

[267] D&C 20: 25: "That as many as would believe and be baptized in his holy name, and endure in faith to the end, should be saved—"

[268] Mosiah 18: 8-10: "And it came to pass that he said unto them: Behold, here are the waters of Mormon (for thus were they called) and now, as ye are desirous to come into the fold of God, and to be called his people, and are willing to bear one another's burdens, that they may be light; Yea, and are willing to mourn with those that mourn; yea, and comfort those that stand in need of comfort, and to stand as witnesses of God at all times and in all things, and in all places that ye may be in, even until death, that ye may be redeemed of God, and be numbered with those of the first resurrection, that ye may have eternal life—Now I say unto you, if this be the desire of your hearts, what have you against being baptized in the name of the Lord, as a witness before him that ye have entered into a covenant with him, that ye will serve him and keep his commandments, that he may pour out his Spirit more abundantly upon you?"

persuaded of the existence of hell. We, on the other hand, have three degrees of GLORY in which the idea of hell is sometimes lost.

So, is there a "hell?"[269] Do those who go there suffer? How difficult is the suffering?[270]

How can it be flattery for the devil to tell someone "I am no devil?" Would his appearance to someone as an "angel of light" be flattery?[271] Did the devil attempt to do this with Joseph Smith?[272] How was Joseph able to determine the devil was the devil, rather than an "angel of light" when he appeared? Did Joseph learn something about detecting evil spirits from this encounter? What did Michael do to teach Joseph how to detect the devil? What did Joseph later teach about how to detect the devil?[273] What kind of a handshake would you expect to be used to detect a true messenger?

---

[269] D&C 19: 15: "Therefore I command you to repent—repent, lest I smite you by the rod of my mouth, and by my wrath, and by my anger, and your sufferings be sore —how sore you know not, how exquisite you know not, yea, how hard to bear you know not."

[270] D&C 19: 16-18: "For behold, I, God, have suffered these things for all, that they might not suffer if they would repent; But if they would not repent they must suffer even as I; Which suffering caused myself, even God, the greatest of all, to tremble because of pain, and to bleed at every pore, and to suffer both body and spirit—and would that I might not drink the bitter cup, and shrink—"

[271] 2 Ne. 9: 9: "And our spirits must have become like unto him, and we become devils, angels to a devil, to be shut out from the presence of our God, and to remain with the father of lies, in misery, like unto himself; yea, to that being who beguiled our first parents, who transformeth himself nigh unto an angel of light, and stirreth up the children of men unto secret combinations of murder and all manner of secret works of darkness."

[272] D&C 128: 20: "And again, what do we hear? Glad tidings from Cumorah! Moroni, an angel from heaven, declaring the fulfilment of the prophets—the book to be revealed. A voice of the Lord in the wilderness of Fayette, Seneca county, declaring the three witnesses to bear record of the book! The voice of Michael on the banks of the Susquehanna, detecting the devil when he appeared as an angel of light! The voice of Peter, James, and John in the wilderness between Harmony, Susquehanna county, and Colesville, Broome county, on thc Susquehanna river, declaring themselves as possessing the keys of the kingdom, and of the dispensation of the fulness of times!"

[273] D&C 129: 8: "If it be the devil as an angel of light, when you ask him to shake hands he will offer you his hand, and you will not feel anything; you may therefore detect him."

Have others been confronted by Satan appearing as an angel?[274] Now if one were deceived by the devil, thinking him an angel of light, would the devil teach them false doctrines?[275]

Would the false doctrines make them and those hearing from them feel secure, or would it stir them up to repentance?

What does it mean for the devil to claim "there is none?" I'm reminded of Peter asking a minister if he knew who he (the minister) worked for. The minister did not know, and so Peter informed him he worked for the devil. We don't think about that much anymore, but it is nonetheless the case that there are many people offering instruction who are really either in the employ of the devil, or using the precepts of men as the fodder (food for livestock) for their teaching.

What comes to mind with the image of the devil "whispering in their ears?" How close must the devil come to be whispering into a person's ears? How attentive must the devil become to his target?

Why "awful chains" and not just "chains?" Are there "chains" that are not "awful?" Why would these particular chains always become "awful?"[276]

What does it mean that "there is no deliverance" from these chains? Why would there be no more deliverance provided?

The verses we are considering are part of a careful message and cannot be separated from each other. They blend together. So when considering this portion of the message you must also keep in mind the other things that went before in Nephi's sermon.

I am awestruck by this great prophet's message. It inspires fear for my fellow man when I read it. The plight in which some men find themselves by the traditions handed to us seem to be such a trap as to defy escape. What can I say to liberate them? What can I do to help them escape? Who am I to even dare think I can make any difference?

---

[274] Moses 1: 12: "And it came to pass that when Moses had said these words, behold, Satan came tempting him, saying: Moses, son of man, worship me."

[275] Alma 30: 53: "But behold, the devil hath deceived me; for he appeared unto me in the form of an angel, and said unto me: Go and reclaim this people, for they have all gone astray after an unknown God. And he said unto me: There is no God; yea, and he taught me that which I should say. And I have taught his words; and I taught them because they were pleasing unto the carnal mind; and I taught them, even until I had much success, insomuch that I verily believed that they were true; and for this cause I withstood the truth, even until I have brought this great curse upon me."

[276] Alma 12: 11: "And they that will harden their hearts, to them is given the lesser portion of the word until they know nothing concerning his mysteries; and then they are taken captive by the devil, and led by his will down to destruction. Now this is what is meant by the chains of hell."
2 Ne. 1: 13: "O that ye would awake; awake from a deep sleep, yea, even from the sleep of hell, and shake off the awful chains by which ye are bound, which are the chains which bind the children of men, that they are carried away captive down to the eternal gulf of misery and woe."

What petitions might I weary the Lord with to help avert this end for others?

We seem to all be asleep and incapable of noticing this terrible warning. Why cannot we all awake and arise and put on the beautiful garments, going forth to meet with the Bridegroom?[277]

Perhaps some of you may make a difference in this battle. All of our souls are at risk and we seem more interested in preserving our current circumstances than in understanding them.

This Book of Mormon is alarming when we consider it a warning for us. Not at all the docile and superficial text we can turn it into when studying 8 chapters in a single 50 minute Gospel Doctrine class—reduced by the time taken for announcement, opening and closing prayers, and witty banter exchanged among affable Saints as part of our renewal of weekly fellowship. Those things are good, of course, but the book commands deeper attention.

If I had to say one thing has done more to bring me into harmony with the Lord than any other thing it would be this: I have taken the Book of Mormon seriously. I have assumed it is an authentic and ancient text written by prophetic messengers whose words ought to be studied for how they can change my life. Though all the world may treat it lightly, I have tried to not do so. For that I believe the Lord's approval has been given to an otherwise foolish, vain, error-prone and weak man.

Take the Book of Mormon seriously. Apply it to yourself. Not as a means to judge others, but as a means to test your own life. It is one thing to evaluate our circumstances, which the book compels us to do, but we needn't go further than to realize our terrible plight. From that moment the warning should work inside ourselves to help us improve within, see more clearly our day, think more correctly about what is going on, and act more consistent with the Lord's purposes.

The Book of Mormon is the most correct book available. A person can get closer to God by abiding its precepts than with any other book.

2 Nephi 28: 23

> **"Yea, they are grasped with death, and hell; and death, and hell, and the devil, and all that have been seized therewith must stand before the throne of God, and be judged according to their works, from whence they must go into the place prepared for**

---

[277] Moroni 10: 31: "And awake, and arise from the dust, O Jerusalem; yea, and put on thy beautiful garments, O daughter of Zion; and strengthen thy stakes and enlarge thy borders forever, that thou mayest no more be confounded, that the covenants of the Eternal Father which he hath made unto thee, O house of Israel, may be fulfilled."
D&C 133: 10: "Yea, let the cry go forth among all people: Awake and arise and go forth to meet the Bridegroom; behold and lo, the Bridegroom cometh; go ye out to meet him. Prepare yourselves for the great day of the Lord."

them, even a lake of fire and brimstone, which is endless torment."

This is a continuation of the warning. Nephi wants us to take quite seriously his warnings.

When you read words like these it becomes apparent the only safe way to measure his warning is to apply it directly and personally to ourselves. To think this was meant only for "others" is too complacent.

When the truth has made you angry, and you have forfeited the option of repentance extended to you, the "grasp of death" is upon you. You will remain subject to "death and hell." Being "seized" by these two things, as you stand before the "throne of God" you will be certain that there will be, for you, a continuation of "the deaths."[278]

Judgment is based "according to their works."[279] Joseph ties sealing power to these "works" which must be done under this authority and then recorded to become binding. This is the practice of the church. It is and has always been the practice of those having such authority. They

---

[278] D&C 132: 25: "Broad is the gate, and wide the way that leadeth to the deaths; and many there are that go in thereat, because they receive me not, neither do they abide in my law."

[279] Rev. 20: 12-13: "And I saw the dead, small and great, stand before God; and the books were opened: and another book was opened, which is *the book* of life: and the dead were judged out of those things which were written in the books, according to their works. And the sea gave up the dead which were in it; and death and hell delivered up the dead which were in them: and they were judged every man according to their works."
D&C 128: 6-8: "And further, I want you to remember that John the Revelator was contemplating this very subject in relation to the dead, when he declared, as you will find recorded in Revelation 20: 12—*And I saw the dead, small and great, stand before God; and the books were opened; and another book was opened, which is the book of life; and the dead were judged out of those things which were written in the books, according to their works.* You will discover in this quotation that the books were opened; and another book was opened, which was the book of life; but the dead were judged out of those things which were written in the books, according to their works; consequently, the books spoken of must be the books which contained the record of their works, and refer to the records which are kept on the earth. And the book which was the book of life is the record which is kept in heaven; the principle agreeing precisely with the doctrine which is commanded you in the revelation contained in the letter which I wrote to you previous to my leaving my place—that in all your recordings it may be recorded in heaven. Now, the nature of this ordinance consists in the power of the priesthood, by the revelation of Jesus Christ, wherein it is granted that whatsoever you bind on earth shall be bound in heaven, and whatsoever you loose on earth shall be loosed in heaven. Or, in other words, taking a different view of the translation, whatsoever you record on earth shall be recorded in heaven, and whatsoever you do not record on earth shall not be recorded in heaven; for out of the books shall your dead be judged, according to their own works, whether they themselves have attended to the ordinances in their own *propria persona,* or by the means of their own agents, according to the ordinance which God has prepared for their salvation from before the foundation of the world, according to the records which they have kept concerning their dead."

not only perform the work, but upon having done so they create a record of having done so.

Upon being judged, they go "into the place prepared for them." This place is, for those who are grasped with "death and hell" called "a lake of fire and brimstone." A lake because it engulfs them so tightly they are flooded with the guilt. Fire because it is designed to purge and refine. Brimstone because of the bitterness of the experience. The torment there is "endless" meaning from God.[280]

This purging does not confer blessings, but merely balances out the claims of justice for those who would not accept mercy.[281]

Crying repentance is to warn, so the claims of justice may be avoided by obtaining mercy through Christ. Christ's mercy is offered to all, but will only be received in full by few. All will be resurrected because of His sacrifice[282], and those who died without law will not be punished for their ignorance[283], but to receive the full benefit of His atonement must do as He commands.[284]

---

[280] D&C 19: 4-12: "And surely every man must repent or suffer, for I, God, am endless. Wherefore, I revoke not the judgments which I shall pass, but woes shall go forth, weeping, wailing and gnashing of teeth, yea, to those who are found on my left hand. Nevertheless, it is not written that there shall be no end to this torment, but it is written *endless torment.* Again, it is written *eternal damnation;* wherefore it is more express than other scriptures, that it might work upon the hearts of the children of men, altogether for my name's glory. Wherefore, I will explain unto you this mystery, for it is meet unto you to know even as mine apostles. I speak unto you that are chosen in this thing, even as one, that you may enter into my rest. For, behold, the mystery of godliness, how great is it! For, behold, I am endless, and the punishment which is given from my hand is end Endless punishment is God's punishment."

[281] D&C 19: 15-19: "Therefore I command you to repent—repent, lest I smite you by the rod of my mouth, and by my wrath, and by my anger, and your sufferings be sore—how sore you know not, how exquisite you know not, yea, how hard to bear you know not. For behold, I, God, have suffered these things for all, that they might not suffer if they would repent; But if they would not repent they must suffer even as I; Which suffering caused myself, even God, the greatest of all, to tremble because of pain, and to bleed at every pore, and to suffer both body and spirit—and would that I might not drink the bitter cup, and shrink—Nevertheless, glory be to the Father, and I partook and finished my preparations unto the children of men."

[282] 1 Cor. 15: 22: "For as in Adam all die, even so in Christ shall all be made alive."

[283] D&C 76: 71-72: "And again, we saw the terrestrial world, and behold and lo, these are they who are of the terrestrial, whose glory differs from that of the church of the Firstborn who have received the fulness of the Father, even as that of the moon differs from the sun in the firmament. Behold, these are they who died without law;". See also D&C 45 and D&C 54.

[284] D&C 132: 22-23: "For strait is the gate, and narrow the way that leadeth unto the exaltation and continuation of the lives, and few there be that find it, because ye receive me not in the world neither do ye know me. But if ye receive me in the world, then shall ye know me, and shall receive your exaltation; that where I am ye shall be also."

Those who love others and want their eternal welfare will invite everyone to repent and come to Christ. The prospect of others suffering needlessly because they would not repent is a great horror to them. This is why Nephi's words are at times so blunt. This is why he wants to stir us all up to our terrible situation. It is merciful to speak to us in these frank terms.

I know some who have read these words of counsel from Nephi and find them objectionable. However, Isaiah spoke against those whose words were "smooth" but filled with deceit.[285] To people who are content and filled with pride, it takes a great deal of candor to bring them to their senses.[286] Nephi's warnings are intended to save as many of the gentiles who read his record from self-destruction as he can bring to repentance. It is better for us to take counsel from his hand than to dismiss his teachings. **He can only warn his readers. Since we are his readers, he must be speaking to us.**

2 Nephi 28: 24-25

> **"Therefore, wo be unto him that is at ease in Zion! Wo be unto him that crieth: All is well!"**

The word "therefore" ties all that went before to this warning about "Zion." The threat of damnation, the pronouncement of "wo's," and the cautions about false teachers spreading false teachings are all designed to cause unease to Zion. That would be us. Or it would be what we claim about ourselves.

It is foolish to turn Nephi's message into a warning to some other latter-day group. The gentiles, who have received the Book of Mormon, and who claim they are better than others, puffed up with conceit about being chosen and highly favored of God, are the ones who would identify themselves as "Zion" in Nephi's prophecy. Not others. Us.

If you have reacted to the previous discussion with the notion that the interpretation given is really just my "opinion," and not an actual warning targeting the Latter-day Saints, you should reconsider. Although Nephi's message has been construed to apply to other faiths, (and the language certainly permits it) this part of Nephi's sermon makes the conclusion inevitable. He is not warning others. He is not primarily targeting the world of the last days. He is warning and

---

[285] Isa. 30: 10: "Which say to the seers, See not; and to the prophets, Prophesy not unto us right things, speak unto us smooth things, prophesy deceits:"

[286] Enos 1: 23: "And there was nothing save it was exceeding harshness, preaching and prophesying of wars, and contentions, and destructions, and continually reminding them of death, and the duration of eternity, and the judgments and the power of God, and all these things—stirring them up continually to keep them in the fear of the Lord. I say there was nothing short of these things, and exceedingly great plainness of speech, would keep them from going down speedily to destruction. And after this manner do I write concerning them."

attempting to save the souls of those who receive his writings and self-identify themselves as "Zion."

This means if we are "Zion" we can never be "at ease." We can never relent. Self-praise and assuring words that make us relax are not only false, they cheat us whenever they remove the burden of repentance we must bear.

There can be no ease. There can be no determination that "all is well" until we have repented and come to Christ. When Christ has forgiven us, we can know we are forgiven. When Christ has promised us eternal life, we can know we have eternal life. Until then, we remain at risk and in jeopardy every hour we are here.[287] When, however, you know you are sealed up to eternal life, you have the more sure word of prophecy or the testimony of Jesus.[288]

When can a person know they have a part in Zion? When the Lord Himself has made them a citizen. When the description given below is the description of their lives, then they may know it will be well with them:

> "They are they who received the testimony of Jesus, and believed on his name and were baptized after the manner of his burial, being buried in the water in his name, and this according to the commandment which he has given—That by keeping the commandments they might be washed and cleansed from all their sins, and receive the Holy Spirit by the laying on of the hands of him who is ordained and sealed unto this power; And who overcome by faith, and are sealed by the Holy Spirit of promise, which the Father sheds forth upon all those who are just and true. They are they who are the church of the Firstborn. They are they into whose hands the Father has given all things—They are they who are priests and kings, who have received of his fulness, and of his glory; And are priests of the Most High, after the order of Melchizedek, which was after the order of Enoch, which was after the order of the Only Begotten Son. Wherefore, as it is written, they are gods, even the sons of God—Wherefore, all things are theirs, whether life or death, or things present, or things to come, all are theirs and they are Christ's, and Christ is God's. And they shall overcome all things." (D&C 76: 51-60.)

These are they who have been told by the voice of God from heaven that they have eternal life. They are those who have obtained a hope in Christ.

When the Gospel of Christ is taught, it is always the purpose to bring people to this point. It is not Christ's Gospel when the teachings fall

---

[287] 1 Cor. 15: 30: "And why stand we in jeopardy every hour?"

[288] D&C 131: 5: "(May 17th, 1843.) The more sure word of prophecy means a man's knowing that he is sealed up unto eternal life, by revelation and the spirit of prophecy, through the power of the Holy Priesthood."

short of declaring this to the audience. Nephi was not trying to get you to improve your behavior or to become a good citizen. He was not attempting to make you a conservative, mainstream American. He was warning you to flee from this corrupt and failing society to a higher place where you can obtain communion with the Church of the Firstborn. A place where you join the household of God.

Zion is not and has never been the product of an institutional organization on this earth. It is a byproduct of there being citizens of heaven living here. Zion is the only way such persons can live with one another. First obtain a hope in Christ, and then all things will be added to you.

Why, then, should there be no ease among us? Because we have too few for the Lord to bring again Zion. Until then we do not have Zion, and our false claims to it only serve to make us at ease while there remains yet a great unfinished labor to perform.

It is Nephi's love for us, his desire to see us saved and happy, that causes him to use such harsh words of warning. He knows what we lack. He wants us to overcome it all and join him in the chorus singing anthems of praise, because our joy cannot be expressed without such songs![289]

2 Nephi 28: 26

> **"Yea, wo be unto him that hearkeneth unto the precepts of men, and denieth the power of God, and the gift of the Holy Ghost!"**

---

[289] D&C 84: 98-102: "Until all shall know me, who remain, even from the least unto the greatest, and shall be filled with the knowledge of the Lord, and shall see eye to eye, and shall lift up their voice, and with the voice together sing this new song, saying:
The Lord hath brought again Zion;
The Lord hath redeemed his people, Israel,
According to the election of grace,
Which was brought to pass by the faith
And covenant of their fathers.
The Lord hath redeemed his people;
And Satan is bound and time is no longer.
The Lord hath gathered all things in one.
The Lord hath brought down Zion from above.
The Lord hath brought up Zion from beneath.
The earth hath travailed and brought forth her strength;
And truth is established in her bowels;
And the heavens have smiled upon her;
And she is clothed with the glory of her God;
For he stands in the midst of his people.
Glory, and honor, and power, and might,
Be ascribed to our God; for he is full of mercy,
Justice, grace and truth, and peace,
Forever and ever, Amen."

Now we return to Nephi's theme. Don't listen to the "precepts of men." This warning is not for the teachers or leaders. Nephi is not saying to them: "don't teach with your own learning." He has already consigned them to hell.[290] Now he is speaking to the "few, who are the humble followers of Christ."[291] In place of three "wo's" there is only one.

Nephi pronounces a "wo" upon those who "hearken" or accept the "precepts of men." They will be condemned. Their hopes will not be realized. They will suffer setbacks in their progression and will not attain to the hopes they might have otherwise attained. But their offense is less than that of the "lead them" and "cause them to err."[292]

If you "hearken" to the "precepts of men," you are denying "the power of the God, and the gift of the Holy Ghost." It is necessary for you to both deny God's power and rebel against the gift of the Holy Ghost in order for you to "hearken to the precepts of men." God's power was designed to keep you from making these errors. The gift of the Holy Ghost was given to lead you to the knowing the truth of all things.[293] When, therefore, you hearken to men's precepts you are not confirming through the Spirit that what is being taught is merely man's precepts.

With a tool like the Holy Ghost available to you, you are accountable for what teachings you accept. It is possible for you to listen to a teacher whose precepts are dark and to know as he speaks that the Spirit does not ratify his words. It is your responsibility to weigh all things and hold onto only those things which are good.[294]

When Jesus was asked about two witnesses He said He was one, the other was His Father, who also bore witness of Him. If they did not listen to the power of the Father, nor incline their hearts to receive the witness of the Spirit, then they could not know the Father, and could not

---

290 2 Ne. 28: 15: "O the wise, and the learned, and the rich, that are puffed up in the pride of their hearts, and all those who preach false doctrines, and all those who commit whoredoms, and pervert the right way of the Lord, wo, wo, wo be unto them, saith the Lord God Almighty, for they shall be thrust down to hell!"

291 2 Ne. 28: 14: "They wear stiff necks and high heads; yea, and because of pride, and wickedness, and abominations, and whoredoms, they have all gone astray save it be a few, who are the humble followers of Christ; nevertheless, they are led, that in many instances they do err because they are taught by the precepts of men."

292 2 Ne. 28: 14: "They wear stiff necks and high heads; yea, and because of pride, and wickedness, and abominations, and whoredoms, they have all gone astray save it be a few, who are the humble followers of Christ; nevertheless, they are led, that in many instances they do err because they are taught by the precepts of men."

293 Moroni 10: 5: "And by the power of the Holy Ghost ye may know the truth of all things."

294 1 Thes. 5: 21: "Prove all things; hold fast that which is good."

receive that second witness.[295] Nephi is saying the same thing. That is, no man teaching the precepts of men should be able to deceive you. Rather, for every teaching and every teacher, there should be a second witness coming from above which bears witness to you that you are hearing the truth.

So many Latter-day Saint teachers resort to sentimentality and emotion in their teaching, talks, books and testimonies. Some are fooled into thinking an emotional reaction is the same as a witness of the Spirit. Emotions rarely communicate light and truth or intelligence. The Spirit bears witness of the truth, conveys light and intelligence, and may not at all be emotional. Or, if emotions are involved, it may be fear[296], dread[297], or even horror at what you encounter.[298] Mere sentimentality is a false substitute for the witness of the Spirit. Joseph Smith explained it this way: "When you feel pure intelligence flowing into you, it may give you sudden strokes of ideas, so that by noticing it, you may find it fulfilled the same day or soon; (i.e.) those things that were presented unto your minds by the Spirit of God, will come to pass; and thus by learning the Spirit of God and understanding it, you may grow into the principle of revelation, until you become perfect in Christ Jesus." (TPJS p. 151.)

The warning from Nephi about how you deny the power of God, you reject the gift of the Holy Ghost whenever you "hearken to the precepts of men" is based on this principle. You have the tools to detect when you are being taught by men using the arm of flesh to advance an idea or

---

[295] John 8: 17-19: "It is also written in your law, that the testimony of two men is true. I am one that bear witness of myself, and the Father that sent me beareth witness of me. Then said they unto him, Where is thy Father? Jesus answered, Ye neither know me, nor my Father: if ye had known me, ye should have known my Father also."

[296] Isa. 6: 5: "Then said I, Woe *is* me! for I am undone; because I *am* a man of unclean lips, and I dwell in the midst of a people of unclean lips: for mine eyes have seen the King, the Lord of hosts."

[297] Gen. 28: 17: "And he was afraid, and said, How dreadful *is* this place! this *is* none other but the house of God, and this *is* the gate of heaven."

[298] Gen. 15: 12-18: "And when the sun was going down, a deep sleep fell upon Abram; and, lo, an horror of great darkness fell upon him. And he said unto Abram, Know of a surety that thy seed shall be a stranger in a land *that is* not theirs, and shall serve them; and they shall afflict them four hundred years; And also that nation, whom they shall serve, will I judge: and afterward shall they come out with great substance. And thou shalt go to thy fathers in peace; thou shalt be buried in a good old age. But in the fourth generation they shall come hither again: for the iniquity of the Amorites *is* not yet full. And it came to pass, that, when the sun went down, and it was dark, behold a smoking furnace, and a burning lamp that passed between those pieces. In the same day the Lord made a covenant with Abram, saying, Unto thy seed have I given this land, from the river of Egypt unto the great river, the river Euphrates:"

notion. You are accountable, hence the "wo" pronounced on you by Nephi.

Ask yourself the following questions as you hear a teacher:

- Does he teach you to come to Christ?
- Do the teachings convey intelligence upon you, or just sentiment?
- Do they awaken inside you light and truth that you hadn't considered before?
- Are the teachings based on the revelations of heaven, or some study, analysis or tool developed by academics?
- Are you encouraged to seek for a confirmation from the Spirit?
- Did you learn something new, but find yourself feeling you have known it before?
- Whether it causes dread, fear or even horror, does the Spirit tell you, nonetheless, it is of God?
- Are you more inclined to get on your knees and call upon God because of what you have learned?
- Does the speaker merely want you to honor her, or an institution?
- Does the speaker hold him/herself out as an expert or someone with impressive credentials?
- Does he rely on status or office as the reason to trust his teaching, or instead rely on the truthfulness of his message? No power or influence can or ought to be exerted by virtue of office or position, only by persuasion and pure knowledge.[299]
- Are the words noble and great, despite your view of the person who is delivering them?

You may be surprised when you ask such questions at what you learn. Nephi is saying it is your own responsibility if you allow yourself to be taken in by the precepts of men. Wo unto you if you do.

2 Nephi: 28: 28

> **"And in fine, wo unto all those who tremble, and are angry because of the truth of God! For behold, he that is built upon the rock receiveth it with gladness; and he that is built upon a sandy foundation trembleth lest he shall fall."**

---

[299] D&C 121: 41-42: "No power or influence can or ought to be maintained by virtue of the priesthood, only by persuasion, by long-suffering, by gentleness and meekness, and by love unfeigned; By kindness, and pure knowledge, which shall greatly enlarge the soul without hypocrisy, and without guile—"

This is the constant problem. People do not care about religion. So when someone like Nephi delivers a message to the audience that is threatening because it contradicts their presumptions, they get upset. They are fearful. They "tremble, and are angry." When Nephi puts out the message, he knows those he addresses are going to react in a very negative way. He will become the object of their distrust and dislike.

But Nephi reminds the audience that it isn't him they have a problem with. It is "the truth of God."

There are two reactions: One is anger, because it condemns them. The other is gladness. Those who are "built upon the rock"—-meaning Christ—have their hope and faith in Him, for He is the "Rock of Heaven"[300] and they "receive it with gladness."

Those who are "built upon a sandy foundation" will "tremble." This would mean they are struck with fear. They are afraid of the message. They fear because they begin to realize their religious convictions may be wrong. They are afraid they "shall fall," or in other words, if the message is true then they may be doomed and their high hopes dashed.

They would rather be angry and try and suppress the message than to receive it and repent. If someone has a good heart, then any warning is appreciated. Even if it informs them they are mistaken. They want truth. So a warning is appreciated when it permits them to correct their errors. These people are built upon the Rock, because truth alone determines what they will accept. They "hearken to the truth" because they are interested in knowing truth.

This message from Nephi reminds all of us about the difference between those who are grounded in the testimony of Jesus (the Rock) and those who hope their brand of religion will aid them (the sand). False hopes are quickly threatened when exposed to the truth. Knowledge that you are built upon the testimony of Jesus, however, cannot be shaken. Critics will be ground into dust by such a stone, but will not damage it.[301] Those with such knowledge would suffer death, but not deny the Lord.[302] Though called upon to suffer for His name,

---

300 Moses 7: 53: "And the Lord said: Blessed is he through whose seed Messiah shall come; for he saith—I am Messiah, the King of Zion, the Rock of Heaven, which is broad as eternity; whoso cometh in at the gate and climbeth up by me shall never fall; wherefore, blessed are they of whom I have spoken, for they shall come forth with songs of everlasting joy."

301 Daniel 2: 45: "Forasmuch as thou sawest that the stone was cut out of the mountain without hands, and that it brake in pieces the iron, the brass, the clay, the silver, and the gold; the great God hath made known to the king what shall come to pass hereafter: and the dream *is* certain, and the interpretation thereof sure."

302 Mosiah 17: 1-0: "Yea, and I will suffer even until death, and I will not recall my words, and they shall stand as a testimony against you. And if ye slay me ye will shed innocent blood, and this shall also stand as a testimony against you at the last day."

they will not submit, but choose to die secure in the knowledge they have of Christ.[303]

This kind of faith requires sacrifice, as explained in the Lectures on Faith previously posted. The Book of Mormon calls it "knowledge" and that lecture requires you "actually know the course you are pursuing is pleasing to God." That is, whether you call it "faith" as the Lectures do, or "knowledge" as the Book of Mormon does, it is the same. You must come to know Christ has accepted your sacrifices. You should re-read that if you want to reacquaint yourself with the requirements for gaining such faith.

2 Nephi 28: 29

> **"Wo be unto him that shall say: We have received the word of God, and we need no more of the word of God, for we have enough!"**

This general principle is addressed first. Nephi will build on it in the following verses. But the first statement is the broadest.

An earlier "wo" was pronounced upon those who rely on the uninspired teachings of men who use their own precepts. Now he adds a second "wo" to those who also deny the need for continuing revelation. We claim we are unlike all other faiths because we believe in the concept of continuing revelation. However, that notion is greatly modified by us to the point where the continuation of revelation is so limited, so curtailed, and so distrusted that we are generally unacquainted with any new revelation.

Do we hear of visions and visitations? Not much, if at all. We think that such things are reserved for leaders. For example, if Elijah were to return with a message to someone, we would expect the person with whom he would visit would be the church President. If it were someone other than the church President, we would instantly be suspicious because Elijah wasn't following the "chain of authority" **as we expect**. [Interestingly, as soon as you know Elijah was involved you should consider that another line of authority may be created.] So even if we heard from Elijah, it would cause us trouble and likely be rejected as too irregular. This would be true of other heavenly messengers, as well.

What visitations could we tolerate? Pretty much we'd only think it appropriate for an ancestor to visit with a descendant to give a family message. A deceased great-grandfather coming to bring a message about one of his descendants would seem to fit within the whole "chain of authority" model we have created. Family business. Seems to be acceptable. However, even then, we would expect the person involved

[303] D&C 138: 13-14: "And who had offered sacrifice in the similitude of the great sacrifice of the Son of God, and had suffered tribulation in their Redeemer's name. All these had departed the mortal life, firm in the hope of a glorious resurrection, through the grace of God the Father and his Only Begotten Son, Jesus Christ."

to "keep it to themselves" because it was inappropriate to share things like that. Too personal. Too sacred. Too much information of a deeply personal nature to warrant talking about it with others.

What if the great-grandfather were Abraham? Would that fit the model? What if his concerns ran to all who are living? Would that family be large enough to warrant talking about it with almost anyone? Oops, we're back to the whole "chain of authority" argument again, and would expect Abraham to limit his visit to the chief Mormon-in-charge. So a visit by Abraham would be suspect as well.

What if the message were from John the Beloved? He has a continuing ministry to visit with people and bring them to salvation. In fact, his ministry includes visiting with those who will be "heirs of salvation who dwell on the earth."[304] Still, if a person had him minister to him, we would not want to hear about it, would question the propriety, and wonder why John would come when other perfectly authoritative men are living on the earth inside the church holding the same keys as John. So, that would be questioned and regarded as irregular as well.

So as Latter-day Saints we believe in the continuation of revelation, visitations, visions, etc. so long as they conform to our limited model, come to the right person, and don't disturb anything we have going on at the present. Which is to say we don't believe in continuing revelation much at all.

What about Christ? Can He visit with anyone whom He deigns to visit? That's a little closer call, because He seems to have promised to come to all. He also displayed remarkably democratic tendencies both on the day of His resurrection, and when visiting the Nephites. (I've explained His disregard for the church hierarchy He established on the day of His resurrection in *Come, Let Us Adore Him.*) He seems much less interested in respecting established religious authority than we do. So we might allow the Lord to visit with someone, but, then we wouldn't want to hear many details because that would be wrong for some reason. Probably "casting pearls before swine" or "profaning" or

---

[304] D&C 7: 1-6: "And the Lord said unto me: John, my beloved, what desirest thou? For if you shall ask what you will, it shall be granted unto you. And I said unto him: Lord, give unto me power over death, that I may live and bring souls unto thee. And the Lord said unto me: Verily, verily, I say unto thee, because thou desirest this thou shalt tarry until I come in my glory, and shalt prophesy before nations, kindreds, tongues and people. And for this cause the Lord said unto Peter: If I will that he tarry till I come, what is that to thee? For he desired of me that he might bring souls unto me, but thou desiredst that thou mightest speedily come unto me in my kingdom. I say unto thee, Peter, this was a good desire; but my beloved has desired that he might do more, or a greater work yet among men than what he has before done. Yea, he has undertaken a greater work; therefore I will make him as flaming fire and a ministering angel; he shall minister for those who shall be heirs of salvation who dwell on the earth."

"disrespecting the line of authority" or something. Not sure which one, but there's got to be a prohibition against it somewhere.

So we have tendencies that are difficult to put into a hard and fast rule, but I'm going to attempt it.

Rule 1: We believe in continuing revelation; predicated upon the following:

(a) Mostly to the President of the church,

(b) but with others whenever:

- It is a grandparent who lived sometime during the restoration or had some unique reason to be coming back, but never:
  - an ancestor so long back they would be Biblical, because that puts us back into (a) above;
  - if they have a message which would be of general interest, because that puts us back into (a) above;
  - if the visit involves knowing something or clarifying something which might be sacred, because such things are wrong to discuss or acknowledge.
- It is the Lord, but that's because He pretty much gets to do what He wants to do; except if it's important we'd want Him to explain why He didn't follow (a) above—-and it better be a pretty good reason or else we'll have to question the report.

Well, We believe all that God has revealed to authorized people in positions of authority, all that He does now reveal, and we believe that He will yet reveal to the proper channels many great and important things pertaining to the Kingdom of God; and that once it has been reviewed by the Correlation Department and published by Deseret Book it will become something which we can all accept as being from an authorized source and reliable.

Until that happens, we have absolutely received enough of the word of God and we don't need any more of the word of God. And, by damn, if someone comes claiming revelation or an independent apostolic witness of the Lord's resurrection we will want them to cut off an arm or some other member of the body and then restore it again, so that we may know he has come with power. I'm quite confident that ought to satisfy our need to see a sign before we will believe a proposition.

Now we know for certain Nephi's warning is to those **other faiths** that do not accept continuing revelation and not to us. However, as to those, Nephi has pronounced a prior "wo" for their acceptance of the precepts of men, and now a second "wo" upon them for their refusal to accept continuing revelation. These begin to mount up and ought to worry those to whom these concerns are addressed, ***whoever*** they may be. Perhaps Nephi should have written his book for those people, instead of us good folks who read the book and know for certain that we're alright.

2 Nephi 28: 30

> **"For behold, thus saith the Lord God: I will give unto the children of men line upon line, precept upon precept, here a little and there a little; and blessed are those who hearken unto my precepts, and lend an ear unto my counsel, for they shall learn wisdom; for unto him that receiveth I will give more, and from them that shall say, We have enough, from them shall be taken away even that which they have."**

Here Nephi shows he is the prophetic precedent upon which others would build. We often quote Alma for this idea, because Alma lays it out more completely. But Alma's teaching has its root in Nephi's warning here.[305]

Notice the Lord's promise that He will "give unto the children of men." He is liberal and does not upbraid us for asking.[306] Indeed, He admonishes us to seek, ask and knock.[307]

Notice that "unto him that receiveth" is the singular. It isn't "those" but "him." Meaning each of us individually may come to Him and ask

---

[305] Alma 12: 9-11: "And now Alma began to expound these things unto him, saying: It is given unto many to know the mysteries of God; nevertheless they are laid under a strict command that they shall not impart only according to the portion of his word which he doth grant unto the children of men, according to the heed and diligence which they give unto him. And therefore, he that will harden his heart, the same receiveth the lesser portion of the word; and he that will not harden his heart, to him is given the greater portion of the word, until it is given unto him to know the mysteries of God until he know them in full. And they that will harden their hearts, to them is given the lesser portion of the word until they know nothing concerning his mysteries; and then they are taken captive by the devil, and led by his will down to destruction. Now this is what is meant by the chains of hell."

[306] James 1: 5-6: "If any of you lack wisdom, let him ask of God, that giveth to all *men* liberally, and upbraideth not; and it shall be given him. But let him ask in faith, nothing wavering. For he that wavereth is like a wave of the sea driven with the wind and tossed."

[307] Matt. 7: 7-11: "Ask, and it shall be given you; seek, and ye shall find; knock, and it shall be opened unto you: For every one that asketh receiveth; and he that seeketh findeth; and to him that knocketh it shall be opened. Or what man is there of you, whom if his son ask bread, will he give him a stone? Or if he ask a fish, will he give him a serpent? If ye then, being evil, know how to give good gifts unto your children, how much more shall your Father which is in heaven give good things to them that ask him?"
D&C 88: 63: "Draw near unto me and I will draw near unto you; seek me diligently and ye shall find me; ask, and ye shall receive; knock, and it shall be opened unto you."

and receive. However, "from them that shall say, We have enough" is plural. Meaning, there are many who could have been taught, had they not shut the doors. The collective will resist new revelation, even when it continues. They will shut their minds and not tolerate learning of truths.

When, however, groups close their minds it becomes impossible to keep what they have. It is inevitable that "from them shall be taken away even that which they have." Meaning, that we are either in a process of restoration or apostasy. The instant we stop restoring truths, we begin to lose them. You cannot just keep what Joseph restored to you. That will be lost. You either continue on and receive on-going revelation and new visions, visitations and restoration, or else you begin to forfeit what you already have. So soon as you walk away from one precept, from one doctrine, from one ordinance, you have begun the process of apostasy or falling away.

This environment is not static. It is always in change. Either it is being built up, created and newly formed, or it is decaying, dying and falling apart. It never holds static. This is because the things of this world testify of Christ's Gospel.[308] The path is only upward. So soon as you stray from it, you lose the path. This is why you take the shoes from off your feet and put them on again as a symbol that you accept the path. You never remove them again, because once upon that path you are to remain so. The path is accompanied by greater light and truth, going from grace to grace until you receive a fullness.[309]

Nephi is telling us how to receive the fullness. It comes only through revelation and the opening of heaven. You may be anointed to become kings and priests, but the realization of these blessings depends upon your faithfulness. If you are true and faithful the time will come when you will be called up and anointed, whereas now it is all conditional. Only Christ can remove the conditions. To have Him do that requires Him, as the Word, to intercede on your behalf. It requires Him to confirm by His own voice from heaven that you are His, and to establish His covenant directly with you.

Whether it is the words of an old book or the words of an older ceremony it is the same. They can't save you. Only following the exact

---

308 Moses 6: 63: "And behold, all things have their likeness, and all things are created and made to bear record of me, both things which are temporal, and things which are spiritual; things which are in the heavens above, and things which are on the earth, and things which are in the earth, and things which are under the earth, both above and beneath: all things bear record of me."

309 D&C 93: 19, 26-28: "I give unto you these sayings that you may understand and know how to worship, and know what you worship, that you may come unto the Father in my name, and in due time receive of his fulness. …The Spirit of truth is of God. I am the Spirit of truth, and John bore record of me, saying: He received a fulness of truth, yea, even of all truth; And no man receiveth a fulness unless he keepeth his commandments. He that keepeth his commandments receiveth truth and light, until he is glorified in truth and knoweth all things."

same path as the ancients followed can result in arriving at the same end. As the Sixth Lecture from the *Lectures on Faith* states:

"When a man has offered in sacrifice all that he has for the truth's sake, not even withholding his life, and believing before God that he has been called to make this sacrifice, because he seeks to do his will, he does know most assuredly that God does and will accept his sacrifice and offering, and that he has not nor will not seek his face in vain. Under these circumstances then, he can obtain the faith necessary for him to lay hold on eternal life. It is in vain for persons to fancy to themselves that they are heirs with those, or can be heirs with them, who have offered their all in sacrifice, and by this means obtained faith in God and favor with him so as to obtain eternal life, unless they in like manner offer unto him the same sacrifice, and through that offering obtain the knowledge that they are accepted of him."

What role does revelation play? Without it no person can be saved.

Who must receive the revelation? Each person for themselves.

What happens when revelation stops? To the person for whom revelation has ended, there is no salvation[310], and they will immediately begin to lose what they were previously given. To the people who refuse to receive more, "from them shall be taken away even that which they have."

Nephi has declared it, using authority from God to do so. We either accept his counsel and warnings or reject it at our peril.

2 Nephi 28: 31

> **"Cursed is he that putteth his trust in man, or maketh flesh his arm, or shall hearken unto the precepts of men, save their precepts shall be given by the power of the Holy Ghost."**

Now we move beyond the wo's to cursing. Cursing by one holding authority to seal is a terrible thing to encounter. However, we should expect that one having that authority, possessing correct knowledge, along with the ability to lead into light and truth, would do all he could to be clear about a matter so those who read what he has said will understand unmistakably the responsibilities they face. Nephi is discharging a duty, and doing so with our best interests in mind. We shouldn't take offense. We should be grateful even if it is painful to read.

---

[310] Moroni 7: 37-38: "Behold I say unto you, Nay; for it is by faith that miracles are wrought; and it is by faith that angels appear and minister unto men; wherefore, if these things have ceased wo be unto the children of men, for it is because of unbelief, and all is vain. For no man can be saved, according to the words of Christ, save they shall have faith in his name; wherefore, if these things have ceased, then has faith ceased also; and awful is the state of man, for they are as though there had been no redemption made."

So again we confront the phrase "trust in man" along with "maketh flesh his arm." Have you considered the meaning of these terms? Have you thought about them as symbols?

"Trust in man" is another way of describing reliance on man to save. Man's theories or hopes or vain formulas as the path to God is another way to describe "trust in man." Do you want a preacher who will give you the philosophies of men mingled with scripture?

Something from *Bartlett's Familiar Quotations* to "flesh out" the meaning of a phrase in scripture? A little story of personal experience from your own life, to personalize the meaning of a verse from the Bible? Will you trade that for an inspired warning that your soul is in jeopardy and you are cursed because of what you accept in place of the power of the Holy Ghost as your guide?

"Maketh flesh his arm" is another way of saying the "strength" of man, rather than the "strength" of God. The arm is also the means by which a sign or covenant might be set forth. By putting the "flesh his arm" rather than the signs of priestly authority from a true messenger, the implication is that any surrogate for God will do if they just have a few bona-fides. Credentials will be enough. Have they been to college and received training for the ministry? A man cannot preach unless he's been trained for the ministry, you see. Are they a scholar? We like to defer to them. We quote them, study them, and believe in their techniques and methods.

But Nephi keeps thundering back: No man's precepts should be accepted when they do not originate in revelation and the Holy Ghost. Without a connection to revelation and the Holy Ghost, the teachings are all the arm of flesh. If you want to trust in that, you will be cursed.

Nephi puts it into two, opposing camps. There are only two. There are either inspired teachings, given by revelation and confirmed by the Holy Ghost, or they are man's understanding. The first will save you. The other will curse you. There is no happy marriage. You cannot have both. This sword cuts both ways, and forces you to make a decision. Your eternity will be affected by the decision. So either you find the right way and follow it, or you are relying upon men and will in the end be cursed.

Interesting choice. Terrible dilemma. Glad we are absolutely guaranteed that the men we trust to lead us cannot ever lead us astray. Or the majority of them won't anyway. Because if we had to rely only on something as flimsy as the Holy Ghost to choose we would be forced to fast and pray, be humble and penitent to solve this terrible dilemma for us; working out our salvation with fear and trembling before God.[311]

I'm glad we don't have to go through that. We're the best of heaven and have come down to strut and fret our hour upon the stage, all the

---

311 Philip. 2: 12: "Wherefore, my beloved, as ye have always obeyed, not as in my presence only, but now much more in my absence, work out your own salvation with fear and trembling."

while enwrapped in several layers of guaranteed eternal life insurance policies paid for by the blood of martyrs and pioneers who suffered so we might be able to live comfortably. We are just GOOD people. They envied us. Everyone has, you know. The prophets all looked down from antiquity and longed to live among us, the favored few…

Oh, wait a minute, I got carried away. I forgot we were trying to understand Nephi's message. For a minute there I was too wrapped up in our own message. Well, to return to Nephi—someone's going to be cursed for trusting in men. Only those whose precepts and teachings originate in the Holy Ghost are going to be saved. It is a terrible burden to confront. It almost makes us want to turn away in sorrow rather than continue on following our Lord.[312] But, then again, who else has the words of eternal life other than Him?

2 Nephi 28: 32

> **"Wo be unto the Gentiles, saith the Lord God of Hosts! For notwithstanding I shall lengthen out mine arm unto them from day to day, they will deny me; nevertheless, I will be merciful unto them, saith the Lord God, if they will repent and come unto me; for mine arm is lengthened out all the day long, saith the Lord God of Hosts."**

After all these warnings, the mention of Zion, the foolishness of following the "precepts of men" Nephi turns again to identifying the most relevant group being warned. It is "the gentiles" (or us). As he considers our collective effort and how we allow the "precepts of men" to be our guide, he states his overall conclusion about our performance: "Wo be unto the Gentiles, saith the Lord God of Hosts!"

This is the third wo. And it is accompanied by a three name title. This time incorporating the "Hosts" or Family of God. This is the Father's judgment upon us. His status as the "Lord God of Hosts" is clearly intended to let us know those proud gentiles who rely upon the sparks of their own fire as their light will lay down in sorrow.[313]

When the Lord's open arm is extended all the day, they reject Him and walk away. They prefer their own false ideas to the truth found in Christ. In the end they have "denied the Lord" because all His efforts toward them have been rejected.

---

[312] John 6: 65-67: "And he said, Therefore said I unto you, that no man can come unto me, except it were given unto him of my Father. From that *time* many of his disciples went back, and walked no more with him. Then said Jesus unto the twelve, Will ye also go away?"

[313] Isa. 50: 11: "Behold, all ye that kindle a fire, that compass *yourselves* about with sparks: walk in the light of your fire, and in the sparks *that* ye have kindled. This shall ye have of mine hand; ye shall lie down in sorrow."
2 Ne. 7: 11: "Behold all ye that kindle fire, that compass yourselves about with sparks, walk in the light of your fire and in the sparks which ye have kindled. This shall ye have of mine hand—ye shall lie down in sorrow."

Still, despite all these failings, and all the wo's pronounced upon them, it is NOT the Lord's failure. It is the gentiles. Even now the Lord would welcome them "if they will repent and come to Him." His arm is yet "lengthened out all the day long." So long as life remains, He is pleading for our repentance. So long as we are here, He will welcome our repentance. And, so we do not miss the point, He also uses a three-name title when extending the plea to us for our repentance. He is speaking on behalf of, and as the chief among, all the "Hosts of heaven." The entire council would welcome us back, if we would but return.

Can you not sense the agony of this plea? Can you not feel the mercy God would grant to any penitent soul? Despite this, men prefer their arrogance, their own precepts, their own false teachings to being taught by the Holy Spirit. We refuse to repent because we prefer our false teachings. We prefer our traditions that build up our pride, and tell us we are going to be exalted because we are good and deserve God's favor. We've put up with tithing, and with faithful meeting attendance, and followed faithfully all kinds of leaders in every ward and stake we've ever attended. We've passed temple recommend interviews and attended faithfully our tithing settlement meetings—in short we think we've done everything God could possibly ask of us.

Except we have NOT repented and come to Christ. Had we done that, we would have been embraced in those opened arms of our Lord. In five points of contact with a loving God, we would have heard unspeakable things and know we escaped the wo's pronounced by Nephi.

Nephi's assessment of the gentile performance is consistently pessimistic. Coupled with Nephi's description of a consistently open and accepting Lord who would welcome us at any time were we willing to repent.

Nephi's message gets mangled in our distorted cultural rewriting of meanings. When someone points out what he's saying, it produces anger and resentment. The result is not particularly encouraging for the gentiles. Not merely because of Nephi's prophetic words, but also because of our reaction to them.

In the preceding verses Nephi has changed from giving his own advice and counsel to quoting the Lord. He began in verse 30 with the words: "behold, thus saith the Lord" and continues quoting Him through the end of that chapter and into the next.

The third "wo" was pronounced by Nephi as a quote from the Lord. The "cursing of the gentiles" was pronounced by Nephi as a quote from the Lord.

Now I didn't point that out as we went through the materials. It is significant enough that it requires additional attention.

Christ has divided judgment up into two separate functions. For those who will be blessed, He will delegate the honor of blessing to others, including His twelve at Jerusalem[314] and twelve Nephite disciples. Their judgment is honorary, however, because they are given no discretion in the matter. The Lord will decide the judgment. It is His alone, so as to insure it will be the right decision.[315] For those who are to be cursed, however, Christ will be the one who pronounces the judgment.[316]

It is of terrible significance that these statements come from the Lord who alone holds the right to judge. He sacrificed His life for all, and is the Savior and Redeemer, seeking to save all who will come to Him. This is the same Lord who pronounces the words through Nephi: *"Cursed is he that putteth his trust in man, or maketh flesh his arm, or shall hearken unto the precepts of men, save their precepts shall be given by the power of the Holy Ghost. Wo be unto the Gentiles, saith the Lord God of Hosts!"* (2 Ne. 28: 31-32.)

The message is delivered by Nephi. The words are the Lord's. The merciful and loving Christ who suffered for all that they might not suffer if they would repent[317] is announcing His pessimism about the latter-day gentile effort to obtain repentance. Why do we seem destined to fail? Why is repentance so difficult for us? What terrible "precepts of men" hold us bound in chains that we cannot break free.

Several have made comments on the question of how we are to repent and come to Christ. There is a fundamental first step to be taken which the Lord has explained repeatedly in His teachings. I have written about this often, including in my first and last books.

In the chapter on the Atonement in *Come, Let Us Adore Him* there is an explanation given of what Christ suffered and what obligations are devolving on us as a result. We must do as He did, suffer in like manner, and forgive all offenses. His infinite suffering cannot be replicated in one sense, but in our own sphere and time we do suffer offenses and

---

[314] Matt. 19: 28: "And Jesus said unto them, Verily I say unto you, That ye which have followed me, in the regeneration when the Son of man shall sit in the throne of his glory, ye also shall sit upon twelve thrones, judging the twelve tribes of Israel."
1 Ne. 12: 9: "And he said unto me: Thou rememberest the Twelve Apostles of the Lamb? Behold they are they who shall judge the twelve tribes of Israel; wherefore, the twelve ministers of thy seed shall be judged of them; for ye are of the house of Israel."

[315] 3 Ne. 27: 27: "And know ye that ye shall be judges of this people, according to the judgment which I shall give unto you, which shall be just. Therefore, what manner of men ought ye to be? Verily I say unto you, even as I am."

[316] D&C 29: 27-29: "And the righteous shall be gathered on my right hand unto eternal life; and the wicked on my left hand will I be ashamed to own before the Father; Wherefore I will say unto them—Depart from me, ye cursed, into everlasting fire, prepared for the devil and his angels. And now, behold, I say unto you, never at any time have I declared from mine own mouth that they should return, for where I am they cannot come, for they have no power."

[317] D&C 19: 16: "For behold, I, God, have suffered these things for all, that they might not suffer if they would repent;"

abuses. We are required to forgive as He forgave. It is our own forgiveness of others that qualifies us to receive forgiveness from Him. When we harbor grudges and resentments, we cut ourselves off from His Atonement. IF we are to be forgiven we must in turn FORGIVE others. In *The Second Comforter* it is shown how we must make intercession on behalf of others, even our enemies, if we are to have a hope in Christ. We must lay down the burden of sin to enter into His presence. Much of that "sin" in each of our lives has been the offenses against us, and the resentment and anger we hold from these abuses. There are people who have done you wrong. There are some who did so intentionally. When you forgive them, and plead on their behalf for the Lord to also forgive them in sincerity and love, you are not far from the Kingdom of Heaven. Your Lord did this. You must do as He did to be like Him. It is the only way to understand your Lord. In this, you must suffer as He did, choosing to forgive offenses rather than to seek justice. When you show mercy, you merit mercy. The beginning of repentance is found in forgiving others.

Your just claims for retribution must be surrendered. Your worthy desire to have vindication must be abandoned. Your right to have judgment against the ones who abused you must be forfeited. And you must go on to pray for their forgiveness.

If you have read all I have written you already know this. I am disappointed to have those who have not read what I've written trying to make sense of this blog. It will make absolutely no sense if it is not seen as an extension of what I've already covered. Even this brief statement about the relationship between your own salvation and redemption through following Christ is a brief note, a cryptic signal, and altogether inadequate to explain the matter. The careful, patient and fulsome explanation has been laid out elsewhere in what I've written. You must go there to see why, along with the many places in scripture where the Lord has made the matter clear.

Nephi takes no delight in pronouncing these wo's and writing the "cursing" the latter-day gentiles face. The Lord takes even less. He suffered and died to make salvation possible for these very same latter-day gentiles. He would save them all. But to do so it is absolutely necessary to bluntly warn those whom He loves. Enos recorded his own ministry and how it was affected by the audience he addressed: "And there was nothing save it was exceeding harshness, preaching and prophesying of wars, and contentions, and destructions, and continually reminding them of death, and the duration of eternity, and the judgments and the power of God, and all these things—stirring them up continually to keep them in the fear of the Lord. I say there was nothing short of these things, and exceedingly great plainness of speech, would keep them from going down speedily to destruction. And after this manner do I write concerning them."[318]

Why would a joyful Lord, who delights in our own happiness, speak in terms of "wo's" and "cursing" to us? What is it about us as His audience that compels Him to rebuke us? Have you thought of the standard in Section 121 ("reproving betimes with sharpness when moved upon by the Holy Ghost") as part of this rebuke?

He so completely loves us that John equated Him with love.[319] Can you imagine the frustration it causes our Lord to have to speak in these terms to us?

Why do we not repent? Why do we harbor and protect our sins? Why do we worship men rather than God? Why do we cleave to the precepts of men rather than the Holy Ghost? Why do we resist the truth when it is declared to us. Why do we demand that the truth be conformed to our understanding of the precepts of men? Why do we measure the things of God against our own traditions? Why do we not abandon instantly our false notions, and stop arguing against the truth which is in Christ? Why do we think any institution, fellowship, association or man can lead us to salvation instead of Christ alone who can save?[320]

How long will you harden your heart against your Lord, whose pleas are aimed only at saving your soul? Why turn away and say that you prefer membership in a great and spacious building, pointing an

---

[318] Enos 1: 23: "And there was nothing save it was exceeding harshness, preaching and prophesying of wars, and contentions, and destructions, and continually reminding them of death, and the duration of eternity, and the judgments and the power of God, and all these things—stirring them up continually to keep them in the fear of the Lord. I say there was nothing short of these things, and exceedingly great plainness of speech, would keep them from going down speedily to destruction. And after this manner do I write concerning them."

[319] 1 John 4: 8: "He that loveth not knoweth not God; for God is love."

[320] 2 Ne. 31: 19: "And now, my beloved brethren, after ye have gotten into this strait and narrow path, I would ask if all is done? Behold, I say unto you, Nay; for ye have not come thus far save it were by the word of Christ with unshaken faith in him, relying wholly upon the merits of him who is mighty to save."

accusing finger at those who would lead you to eternal life?[321] Our awards and honors are nothing. Your recognition and praise is corrosion. Everything here is doomed to decay, rot and fail.[322] This is the Telestial Kingdom. Everything here, every institution, organization and order is Telestial. None of it will survive death.[323] Even the one association intended to endure (the family) will not endure unless it is through the Holy Spirit of Promise.

If you are going to be rescued from this Telestial Kingdom, it will be Christ who rescues you. His arm has been stretched out to you as long as you have been here, and it will remain stretched out until you depart here. If you are not saved, it will be because of your rejection of Him, not His rejection of you. He has done all He could. He has sent stern warnings, warm invitations, cheerful messengers, the dignified and the undignified, to show in all things He is willing to meet you more than

---

[321] 1 Ne. 8: 26-31: "And I also cast my eyes round about, and beheld, on the other side of the river of water, a great and spacious building; and it stood as it were in the air, high above the earth. And it was filled with people, both old and young, both male and female; and their manner of dress was exceedingly fine; and they were in the attitude of mocking and pointing their fingers towards those who had come at and were partaking of the fruit. And after they had tasted of the fruit they were ashamed, because of those that were scoffing at them; and they fell away into forbidden paths and were lost. And now I, Nephi, do not speak all the words of my father. But, to be short in writing, behold, he saw other multitudes pressing forward; and they came and caught hold of the end of the rod of iron; and they did press their way forward, continually holding fast to the rod of iron, until they came forth and fell down and partook of the fruit of the tree. And he also saw other multitudes feeling their way towards that great and spacious building."

[322] Matt. 6: 19-20: "Lay not up for yourselves treasures upon earth, where moth and rust doth corrupt, and where thieves break through and steal: But lay up for yourselves treasures in heaven, where neither moth nor rust doth corrupt, and where thieves do not break through nor steal:"

[323] D&C 132: 7: "And verily I say unto you, that the conditions of this law are these: All covenants, contracts, bonds, obligations, oaths, vows, performances, connections, associations, or expectations, that are not made and entered into and sealed by the Holy Spirit of promise, of him who is anointed, both as well for time and for all eternity, and that too most holy, by revelation and commandment through the medium of mine anointed, whom I have appointed on the earth to hold this power (and I have appointed unto my servant Joseph to hold this power in the last days, and there is never but one on the earth at a time on whom this power and the keys of this priesthood are conferred), are of no efficacy, virtue, or force in and after the resurrection from the dead; for all contracts that are not made unto this end have an end when men are dead."

half way. Those who reject these widely different invitations are accountable for their failure.[324]

[324] Matt. 11: 7-24: "And as they departed, Jesus began to say unto the multitudes concerning John, What went ye out into the wilderness to see? A reed shaken with the wind? But what went ye out for to see? A man clothed in soft raiment? behold, they that wear soft *clothing* are in kings' houses. But what went ye out for to see? A prophet? yea, I say unto you, and more than a prophet. For this is *he,* of whom it is written, Behold, I send my messenger before thy face, which shall prepare thy way before thee. Verily I say unto you, Among them that are born of women there hath not risen a greater than John the Baptist: notwithstanding he that is least in the kingdom of heaven is greater than he. And from the days of John the Baptist until now the kingdom of heaven suffereth violence, and the violent take it by force. For all the prophets and the law prophesied until John. And if ye will receive *it,* this is Elias, which was for to come. He that hath ears to hear, let him hear. But whereunto shall I liken this generation? It is like unto children sitting in the markets, and calling unto their fellows, And saying, We have piped unto you, and ye have not danced; we have mourned unto you, and ye have not lamented. For John came neither eating nor drinking, and they say, He hath a devil. The Son of man came eating and drinking, and they say, Behold a man gluttonous, and a winebibber, a friend of publicans and sinners. But wisdom is justified of her children. Then began he to upbraid the cities wherein most of his mighty works were done, because they repented not: Woe unto thee, Chorazin! woe unto thee, Bethsaida! for if the mighty works, which were done in you, had been done in Tyre and Sidon, they would have repented long ago in sackcloth and ashes. But I say unto you, It shall be more tolerable for Tyre and Sidon at the day of judgment, than for you. And thou, Capernaum, which art exalted unto heaven, shalt be brought down to hell: for if the mighty works, which have been done in thee, had been done in Sodom, it would have remained until this day. But I say unto you, That it shall be more tolerable for the land of Sodom in the day of judgment, than for thee."

The Lord continually asks: "What more could I have done?"[325]

Apparently we will only accept the "precepts of men" and trust the "arm of flesh" and therefore merit the coming disappointments.

---

[325] Jacob 5: 41, 47, 49, 75: "And it came to pass that the Lord of the vineyard wept, and said unto the servant: What could I have done more for my vineyard? ...But what could I have done more in my vineyard? Have I slackened mine hand, that I have not nourished it? Nay, I have nourished it, and I have digged about it, and I have pruned it, and I have dunged it; and I have stretched forth mine hand almost all the day long, and the end draweth nigh. And it grieveth me that I should hew down all the trees of my vineyard, and cast them into the fire that they should be burned. Who is it that has corrupted my vineyard? ...And it came to pass that the Lord of the vineyard said unto the servant: Let us go to and hew down the trees of the vineyard and cast them into the fire, that they shall not cumber the ground of my vineyard, for I have done all. What could I have done more for my vineyard? ...And it came to pass that when the Lord of the vineyard saw that his fruit was good, and that his vineyard was no more corrupt, he called up his servants, and said unto them: Behold, for this last time have we nourished my vineyard; and thou beholdest that I have done according to my will; and I have preserved the natural fruit, that it is good, even like as it was in the beginning. And blessed art thou; for because ye have been diligent in laboring with me in my vineyard, and have kept my commandments, and have brought unto me again the natural fruit, that my vineyard is no more corrupted, and the bad is cast away, behold ye shall have joy with me because of the fruit of my vineyard."
2 Ne. 15: 4: "What could have been done more to my vineyard that I have not done in it? Wherefore, when I looked that it should bring forth grapes it brought forth wild grapes."

2 NEPHI 29

2 Nephi 29: 1-2

> **"But behold, there shall be many—at that day when I shall proceed to do a marvelous work among them, that I may remember my covenants which I have made unto the children of men, that I may set my hand again the second time to recover my people, which are of the house of Israel; And also, that I may remember the promises which I have made unto thee, Nephi, and also unto thy father, that I would remember your seed; and that the words of your seed should proceed forth out of my mouth unto your seed; and my words shall hiss forth unto the ends of the earth, for a standard unto my people, which are of the house of Israel;"**

The thought "there shall be many" will be concluded in verse 3, and will be discussed there.

The day of the Lord's "marvelous work" will be when He "remembers [His] covenants" made previously to "the children of men." Those covenants to "the children of men" are all inclusive. This will include promises made to all mankind, without regard to their status as Israel, gentile, heathen, or even if they are living or dead as the work begins. It is the Lord's covenants made in the pre-earth councils, and is for all mankind.

As fulfillment of these complete covenants, the Lord will "set [His] hand again the second time to recover my people." Now the focus moves from "the children of men" to a sub-set of those He calls "my people." His people are, by definition, necessarily affiliated with "the house of Israel" through covenant. These would include those called the "remnant" as well as those believing "gentiles" who accept the covenant and return through repentance to Christ.

Why do we see layers of covenants or promises referred to here? Why the covenants made "unto the children of men?" Why then further "the house of Israel?" Why further "promises made unto Nephi?" Why still further "thy father" [meaning Lehi]? Why a work which will affect all these groups? And, finally, why does all of the foregoing return to "remembering Nephi's seed?" What role does Nephi's seed, or remnant fulfill in the promises made to all mankind?

Why does the Lord make a covenant with all humanity, but then reiterate the covenant with Abraham? Why do the covenants get repeated through Isaac and Jacob, the last of whom supplies the name of the covenant people "Israel?" Why, after all those covenant recipients do the covenants get renewed with Lehi? Why immediately following Nephi do the covenants get renewed yet again in Nephi? Why does the Lord engage in this covenant making process to tie together the events of history and the lives of men? Can He still do this today? Does He still expect or want to enter into covenants with men today to further His purposes? Do those covenants necessarily get confined to an institution or priestly process rather than through Him, directly? Why not?

When we get to Nephi's descendants, why are they the ones who are to provide "a standard unto my people, which are of the house of Israel?" What does this say about the significance of the Book of Mormon? Why is it the "standard unto the Lord's people?" What does that do to clarify the condemnation resting upon the church under D&C 84: 57?[326] How important is "the standard" established by the Lord? Why would Joseph Smith say the "fullness of the gospel" is contained in the Book of Mormon?

Why does the title page of the Book of Mormon, which was part of the translated record, contain this description: "Which is to show unto the remnant of the House of Israel what great things the Lord hath done for their fathers; and that they may know the covenants of the Lord, that they are not cast off forever—And also to the convincing of the Jew and Gentile that Jesus is the Christ, the Eternal God, manifesting himself unto all nations."

What does it mean that these words shall "hiss forth to the ends of the earth?"

Did you notice the Lord taking personal credit for the words of the Book of Mormon? What does the phrase "the words of your seed should proceed forth **out of my mouth** unto your seed; and **my words** shall hiss forth unto the ends of the earth?" How does the Lord taking personal credit for these words affect the Book of Mormon's significance?

2 Nephi 29: 3

> **"And because my words shall hiss forth—many of the Gentiles shall say: A Bible! A Bible! We have got a Bible, and there cannot be any more Bible."**

---

[326] D&C 84: 57: "And they shall remain under this condemnation until they repent and remember the new covenant, even the Book of Mormon and the former commandments which I have given them, not only to say, but to do according to that which I have written—"

This is one of the great missionary scriptures. It is used to show the Book of Mormon already anticipated an argument against it, and as a result shows there is no reason to reject the Book of Mormon because there is already an existing, recognized volume of scripture.

The gentiles are prone to prefer the Bible to the Book of Mormon. We emphasized the Book of Mormon for a few years, but found that other faiths were critical because we were not using the Bible as we should. So there has been a conscious effort to re-emphasize the Bible and de-emphasize the Book of Mormon. This has been done to broaden our appeal to members of other faiths.

The gravamen of the argument is in the words: "there cannot be any more Bible." The idea there are other words of God, requiring equal respect to the words in the Bible, is a shocking heresy for many of the gentiles. Remember that first phrase in the first verse: "Behold there shall be many" who are going to say this. The "many" are the gentiles, and their criticism will be Bible-based.

So, how are we doing with this idea? Do we prefer the Biblical teachings to those of the Book of Mormon? Do we spend more time with the Bible than the Book of Mormon in our own individual study? If we had to choose one as the "standard for our people" which one would we choose? The Book of Mormon (as verse 2 suggests) or the Bible (as verse 3 suggests)? The Lord's standard is the Book of Mormon. The gentile standard will be the Bible. Once again we are at odds with Historic Christianity.

This is not to say we disrespect the Bible. We don't. We accept it as scripture. It is an admittedly valuable standard work, to be used in study and receiving knowledge of the things of God. Indeed, among other things the Book of Mormon testifies of the truth of the Bible. Therefore the Bible is certainly accepted as a work of importance and value to us in matters of faith. But only one can assume primacy. The primary one for us is the Book of Mormon.

We may be justified in our attachment to and affection for the Bible. But the Book of Mormon must be preeminent. Our respect and affection for the Doctrine and Covenants, Temple and church organization is also well placed and should inform our understanding and behavior. But the Book of Mormon was intended to be the primary means for the Lord to impart understanding to us.

Much has has been written and said about this volume of scripture, but we are only now beginning to understand what we are looking at.

In *Eighteen Verses* I have shown how little we have done so far with this book of scripture. I have never attempted to be exhaustive in any discussion about the book. In a decade of teaching weekly about the book, where I only went from 1 Nephi 1: 1 to Jarom 1: 4, the discussion was not exhaustive.

This book was a gift to us. We ought not think the Bible has more to offer than what we find in "the most correct book" because a "man can get closer to God by abiding the precepts [of the Book of Mormon] than any other book," just as Joseph Smith said.

The primary text of scripture I have used in *The Second Comforter*, *Nephi's Isaiah* and *Eighteen Verses* has been the Book of Mormon. The primary text used in this blog is the Book of Mormon.

Until we understand that book, I fail to see why we think we should have more. There is more in that book than we've noticed. The first step ought be to notice what we have. Then things will be added. However, until we have taken the Book of Mormon seriously, I fail to see why the most important message for us—-found within that book—should not be the first thing to be understood.

2 Nephi 29: 4-5

> **"But thus saith the Lord God: O fools, they shall have a Bible; and it shall proceed forth from the Jews, mine ancient covenant people. And what thank they the Jews for the Bible which they receive from them? Yea, what do the Gentiles mean? Do they remember the travails, and the labors, and the pains of the Jews, and their diligence unto me, in bringing forth salvation unto the Gentiles? O ye Gentiles, have ye remembered the Jews, mine ancient covenant people? Nay; but ye have cursed them, and have hated them, and have not sought to recover them. But behold, I will return all these things upon your own heads; for I the Lord have not forgotten my people."**

If you wonder at the Lord's patience and willingness to forgive you have an answer here. The Lord's respect for and defense of the "Jews" as His "ancient covenant people" is unmitigated by any criticism of them. Instead He points to their "travails, and the labors, and the pains of the Jews" experienced in bringing forth this Biblical record.

The Jews deserve our thanks, our gratitude and our respect for this great work of preserving the record.

Twice the Lord calls the Jews His "ancient covenant people." The Bible is a record of rebellion, persecution of the righteous, and slaying of prophets. It is a record of a fallen people who were often in apostasy, resisting true prophets calling for repentance, and suffering the judgment and condemnation of God. When the New Testament record (also a product of Jewish writers—even in the case of Luke who, though born to gentile parents, was converted to Judaism) came into existence it was the Jews who resisted and persecuted the Lord. Yet He still calls them His "ancient covenant people." He insists we have been ungrateful to the Jews for their work on the Bible.

This is the Lord speaking in the first person. Nephi is quoting Him. These are the same people Lehi taught would be the only ones "who would crucify their God."[327] Yet despite that, Christ refers to them as His "ancient covenant people" to whom we owe a debt of gratitude! How merciful is our Lord?

Now, those who produced the Bible text are not merely the believers, true prophets, and victims of Jewish hostility and persecution. The text may have originated with the prophets, but it passed quickly into the hands of the priests and Levites, scholars and Rabbis. These others may not have had the same divine inspiration and association with angels, but they nevertheless attended with strict discipline to preserving the record of the prophets. Even those who directly challenged the Lord included the scribes who worked to preserve the records of the prophets. These "labors" and "pains" and "diligence" have produced gratitude from the Lord!

If He is willing to thank them, how generous is our Lord in His thanks to mankind! How ungrateful are we?

We tend to see those with whom we differ as enemies. But the Lord does not want us to approach religious disagreement in this way. Instead he would have us "recover" them. He says: "ye have cursed them, and have hated them, and have not sought to recover them." As Joseph Smith's History recounts, his persecutors ought "to have treated me kindly, and if they supposed me to be deluded to have endeavored in a proper and affectionate manner to have reclaimed me."[328] That is the only way to obtain agreement—persuasion, gentleness, meekness and love unfeigned.[329] Instead of "holding a court" against someone, we

---

[327] 2 Ne. 10: 3: "Wherefore, as I said unto you, it must needs be expedient that Christ—for in the last night the angel spake unto me that this should be his name—should come among the Jews, among those who are the more wicked part of the world; and they shall crucify him—for thus it behooveth our God, and there is none other nation on earth that would crucify their God."

[328] JS-H 1: 28: "During the space of time which intervened between the time I had the vision and the year eighteen hundred and twenty-three—having been forbidden to join any of the religious sects of the day, and being of very tender years, and persecuted by those who ought to have been my friends and to have treated me kindly, and if they supposed me to be deluded to have endeavored in a proper and affectionate manner to have reclaimed me—I was left to all kinds of temptations; and, mingling with all kinds of society, I frequently fell into many foolish errors, and displayed the weakness of youth, and the foibles of human nature; which, I am sorry to say, led me into divers temptations, offensive in the sight of God. In making this confession, no one need suppose me guilty of any great or malignant sins. A disposition to commit such was never in my nature. But I was guilty of levity, and sometimes associated with jovial company, etc., not consistent with that character which ought to be maintained by one who was called of God as I had been. But this will not seem very strange to any one who recollects my youth, and is acquainted with my native cheery temperament."

[329] D&C 121: 41-42: "No power or influence can or ought to be maintained by virtue of the priesthood, only by persuasion, by long-suffering, by gentleness and meekness, and by love unfeigned; By kindness, and pure knowledge, which shall greatly enlarge the soul without hypocrisy, and without guile—"

ought to preach the Gospel to them and teach them the truth with love and meekness. It is clear the Lord is showing by example how our attitudes ought to be displayed with those who persecute and reject us. But, then again, He taught the same thing in the Sermon on the Mount (Matt. 5, 6, 7) and in how He lived[330] and died[331]. Oddly we would convict and excommunicate the adulterer, but our Lord would not. Nor does He who holds the greatest claim to condemn the Jews condemn them. Instead He says we ought to have gratitude for their pains, labors and diligence.

What does our ingratitude merit us? It merits us judgment. For the same judgment we apply to them will in turn be applied to us. We will see it used as the basis for His rejection of us: "I will return all these things upon your own heads; for I the Lord have not forgotten my people."

Being a religious people is fine; but being a self-righteous people has always been perilous. It is no different today. We should use the scriptures to inform our inner life. It is meant for internal use only. External application is likely to cause burning.

In the early church of this dispensation, the purpose of a church court was to obtain a confession. If someone confessed during the court, or immediately before, they would be forgiven and the court would end. If someone got excommunicated because of a sin, and they confessed the next day, they would be reinstated the next day. Once the confession was made, forgiveness was more or less immediate. Take a look at that early history. It is interesting.

For those who are excommunicated, we rarely see them again. The numbers are overwhelming against their return. So essentially an excommunication means the end of that person, oftentimes also his/her immediate family, and the descendants of those.

Sin is wrong, and needs to result in repentance and change. But for the most part that is between the person and the Lord. When it involves others, it also includes them, too. But we sometimes cause a great deal of unintended consequences to even the unborn when we excommunicate.

2 Nephi 29: 6-7

> **"Thou fool, that shall say: A Bible, we have got a Bible, and we need no more Bible. Have ye obtained a Bible save it were by the Jews? Know ye not that there are more nations than one? Know**

---

[330] Jon 8: 10-11: "When Jesus had lifted up himself, and saw none but the woman, he said unto her, Woman, where are those thine accusers? hath no man condemned thee? She said, No man, Lord. And Jesus said unto her, Neither do I condemn thee: go, and sin no more."

[331] Luke 23: 34: "Then said Jesus, Father, forgive them; for they know not what they do. And they parted his raiment, and cast lots."

> **ye not that I, the Lord your God, have created all men, and that I remember those who are upon the isles of the sea; and that I rule in the heavens above and in the earth beneath; and I bring forth my word unto the children of men, yea, even upon all the nations of the earth?"**

This is a continuing statement made to Nephi by the Lord. Besides the sermons delivered in the New Testament and Third Nephi, this is one of the most extensive revelations to be found given by Christ. Given its length, and the fact it is a quote from the Lord, we are compelled to take note. The Lord is doing all He can to draw our attention to the fact that the Book of Mormon MUST be valued above the Bible. It MUST take its place in latter-day study of God's acts among men.

To say you have enough information from God is foolish. God "created all men," and as a result He "remembers all men." He will "bring forth [His] word unto the children of men" in whatever place, time and circumstance as He decides. He cannot be circumscribed by our preferences or false understanding. He can and does exercise the prerogative to speak to whomever He decides.

When the Book of Mormon came forth, all people were startled at the idea God had more to say. They thought it an odd thing for anyone to claim there was yet more scripture. Joseph was persecuted and hated for announcing he had a new volume of scripture.

Now, some 180 years later we think the Lord is bound to talk to a specific person, in a specific way, and that anyone else or anywhere else is beyond the Lord's capacity to accomplish. In our own way, we are also bound to a tradition which excludes the Lord's prerogatives; we just redefine the box we confine the Lord.

He "brings forth His word" without regard to our views, and to "all the nations of the earth." Now "nations" is not the same thing as we regard it today. The "nations" at the time of the Book of Mormon were something we would call "people" or "ethnicity" like the Israelites.

The definition of an "isle of the sea" includes everything that is not part of the great Euro-Asian-African land mass. Although we regard North America as a continent, in the Book of Mormon vernacular it is an "isle of the sea."[332] Further, most of Israel was relocated onto

---

[332] 2 Ne. 10: 20: "And now, my beloved brethren, seeing that our merciful God has given us so great knowledge concerning these things, let us remember him, and lay aside our sins, and not hang down our heads, for we are not cast off; nevertheless, we have been driven out of the land of our inheritance; but we have been led to a better land, for the Lord has made the sea our path, and we are upon an isle of the sea."

the isles of the sea.[333] So when the Lord affirms He speaks to those on the "isles of the sea" He is confirming that there are multiple locations, involving multiple parties, each one of which has received sacred communication from Him. There are, in short, still a great deal of His words which have not as yet come to our attention. They are coming. When they do, we are warned to take care in what we choose to reject.

When I was first investigating the church, this argument was presented to me by the missionaries in one of the first discussions. I have to admit the proposition made such sense to me that I found it completely persuasive. The idea that God would not be in communication with the vast majority of mankind living separate from Palestine during the Lord's life seemed to be a sort of abandonment by the Lord. If He is the God of all mankind, then ought He not speak to all mankind?

The "wise men from the east" were not locals to Palestine. Yet they remained both connected to, and watching for signs involving the birth of the Lord. If them, why not others? The Book of Mormon answers this query. This idea was too persuasive for me to find doubt.

If God does remember all mankind, and speaks to the various nations over time, then the failure to keep the information intact is also explained. The Book of Mormon shows what and how a society's faith fails and is lost. It explains how very careless mankind is with knowledge given by God.

Riddles of history are better answered both directly and indirectly in the Book of Mormon than any other text, including the Bible.

2 Nephi 29: 8

> **"Wherefore murmur ye, because that ye shall receive more of my word? Know ye not that the testimony of two nations is a witness unto you that I am God, that I remember one nation like unto another? Wherefore, I speak the same words unto one nation like unto another. And when the two nations shall run together the testimony of the two nations shall run together also."**

Why would anyone complain or murmur because God has spoken? We do. Somehow we get offended at the very idea God can or has spoken further. It is disturbing. It requires us to learn more, and may require us to change. It is inconvenient. It is troubling.

But new information from God should always be welcomed. It should be exciting and delightful, even if it requires us to change.

---

333 1 Ne. 22: 4: "And behold, there are many who are already lost from the knowledge of those who are at Jerusalem. Yea, the more part of all the tribes have been led away; and they are scattered to and fro upon the isles of the sea; and whither they are none of us knoweth, save that we know that they have been led away."

Not only does the Lord remember all nations, but He "speaks the same words unto one nation like unto another." Meaning two things: First, the records are going to agree on doctrine, ordinances and practice. There will not be some shocking departure from what we have already learned. But, second, we may find that other records have done a better job of preserving deeper insight into the history or truths than have we.

At one time the record written by Moses contained what is now in the P earl of Great Price. At one time the record written by Abraham also found in the Pearl of Great Price was among the Biblical record. However, they were lost until they were restored through Joseph Smith. At one time the Biblical record contained the prophecies of Zenos and Zenock, only a small portion of which are still available through the Book of Mormon.

Although the records will agree, that does not mean there will not be significant additions to our understanding as a result of these becoming available. Even the record of the Nephites is sealed, and that of the Jaredites only partially translated.[334] Joseph and Sidney were forbidden to give the full account of the vision of the afterlife.[335] So you must not presume that "the same words" will be identical to the teachings preserved in our records. They may include much more.

It is also interesting how the Book of Mormon contains so much more information upon close inspection that it appears to have in a quick read. It is a measure of how seriously we take the Lord's words as to how carefully we search the text.

As I've pointed out, most of the Book of Mormon scholarship is devoted to the question of the book's authenticity. Word studies, Jewish idioms, internal consistencies, author variances and other examinations of the book have dominated the Book of Mormon library we have produced. I have proceeded from the premise that the book is authentic, that it is what it claims to be, and worthy of respect. Then, based on that premise, I've asked what the book teaches. The result has been more than edifying, it has been at times shocking. I've found that most of the deepest doctrines taught by Joseph Smith can be found in the Book of Mormon. When his revelations reach the greatest heights, the Book of Mormon equals what is revealed.

---

334 Ether 1: 4-5: "Therefore I do not write those things which transpired from the days of Adam until that time; but they are had upon the plates; and whoso findeth them, the same will have power that he may get the full account. But behold, I give not the full account, but a part of the account I give, from the tower down until they were destroyed."

335 D&C 76: 114-115: "But great and marvelous are the works of the Lord, and the mysteries of his kingdom which he showed unto us, which surpass all understanding in glory, and in might, and in dominion; Which he commanded us we should not write while we were yet in the Spirit, and are not lawful for man to utter;"

We tend to view the Book of Mormon as a "basic" version of doctrine, because we all know there are sealed portions yet to be revealed. However, I think that attitude is wrong. Everything in the sealed portion is already in the book we have in front of us. But to find it we must look more carefully at the text than we generally do.

I keep hoping that by showing respect to the text we can accomplish two things: First, please the Lord and remove our condemnation from neglecting this valuable ancient record. Second, increase our respect for the value of doctrine. Without the unique doctrines restored through the Book of Mormon, we may as well be Presbyterian or Methodist.

These verses promise us that the testimonies of differing nations will agree. They will all testify both of Jesus Christ as Redeemer and Savior, and provide the means by which we can come to Him and be saved.

The numerous examples of the Book of Mormon all converge on knowing Christ. Indeed, the text has more examples of Christ ministering through the veil to mortal men than any other record, including His Judean ministry. It is a veritable treasure of Second Comforter experiences. If you want to know Christ, the Book of Mormon is your best guide.

2 Nephi 29: 9

> **"And I do this that I may prove unto many that I am the same yesterday, today, and forever; and that I speak forth my words according to mine own pleasure. And because that I have spoken one word ye need not suppose that I cannot speak another; for my work is not yet finished; neither shall it be until the end of man, neither from that time henceforth and forever."**

The assurance to us by the Lord that He is the "same yesterday, today and forever" appears often in scripture. (See, e.g., four times by Nephi including 1 Ne. 10: 18; 2 Ne. 2: 4; 2 Ne. 27: 23, and above; Alma 31: 17; Mormon 9: 9; Moroni 10: 19; D&C 20: 12; and D&C 35: 1, among other places.) Why do you suppose the Lord wants us to trust in this idea? What is it about the Lord's "sameness" that is important for us to understand?

Are the Lord's expectations different from one generation to the next? Are His teachings? Are His ordinances? Can we discard what He has given us and be justified? If His expectations are as unchanged as He is, then how important is it for us to study and retain all that He has given by revelation to mankind? How important is it to keep ordinances entirely intact?

If the Lord does not change, and the story of the Nephite people is a story of temporary success followed by ultimate failure, then how relevant is that account for us? Does temporary success in repentance guarantee constant favor from the Lord? When the Book of Mormon follows splinter groups in the narrative, because the splinters kept the commandments of God better, does that preserve a relevant lesson for those reading the book today? If so, how?

If the Lord "speaks forth [His] own words according to [His] own pleasure" then how can we control to whom and when He is permitted to speak? If He reserves to Himself this right, what effect does our system of recognizing an authoritative message from Him have upon His right to speak? Did the revelation given to Oliver Cowdery that told him that he could not write commandments, but only according to wisdom, and never command Joseph Smith who presided over Oliver, establish a binding precedent on the Lord?[336] If so, what limit does that place on the Lord? Does the limitation on someone being sent forth as a missionary to preach the Gospel, and the requirement they be "regularly ordained by the heads of the church" limit the Lord's ability to speak His own words?[337] If so, in what way?

Does the revelation to Joseph Smith informing the Church in 1831 that no one other than Joseph Smith is to receive commandments and revelations for the Church limit the Lord's ability to speak to anyone else?[338] In particular, what of the Lord's counsel that this limitation was intended as "a law unto you, that ye receive not the teachings of any that shall come before you as revelations or commandments; And this I give unto you that you may not be deceived, that you may know they are not of me." (Id. verses 5-6.) Does that prevent Him from speaking "according to His own pleasure?"

What about the 1830 revelation given to Joseph Smith that no one other than Joseph Smith is to receive revelations and commandments in

---

[336] D&C 28: 4-6: "And if thou art led at any time by the Comforter to speak or teach, or at all times by the way of commandment unto the church, thou mayest do it. But thou shalt not write by way of commandment, but by wisdom; And thou shalt not command him who is at thy head, and at the head of the church;"

[337] D&C 42: 11: "Again I say unto you, that it shall not be given to any one to go forth to preach my gospel, or to build up my church, except he be ordained by some one who has authority, and it is known to the church that he has authority and has been regularly ordained by the heads of the church."

[338] D&C 43: 1-6: "O hearken, ye elders of my church, and give ear to the words which I shall speak unto you. For behold, verily, verily, I say unto you, that ye have received a commandment for a law unto my church, through him whom I have appointed unto you to receive commandments and revelations from my hand. And this ye shall know assuredly—that there is none other appointed unto you to receive commandments and revelations until he be taken, if he abide in me. But verily, verily, I say unto you, that none else shall be appointed unto this gift except it be through him; for if it be taken from him he shall not have power except to appoint another in his stead. And this shall be a law unto you, that ye receive not the teachings of any that shall come before you as revelations or commandments; And this I give unto you that you may not be deceived, that you may know they are not of me."

the church?[339] Does that limit the Lord's ability to speak according to His own pleasure?

Do the promises given to Joseph Smith apply directly and continually as the binding precedent and complete limitation on the Lord's capacity to speak to us? If so, then can He still speak to individual members of the church but without providing a "revelation and commandment" to the entire church? For example, do we expect only President Monson to receive revelation on the individual members of your own family? How is President Monson supposed to be doing that for the families of some 13 million church members? If that isn't possible, then what about the approximate 2,000 stakes? Do we expect only President Monson to receive revelation about each of these divisions? If the stake presidents have been delegated responsibility, then can the stake president receive all revelation for each family within the stake? Can the stake president alone receive revelation for the families of his stake?

If each person is intended to receive some revelation for themselves, is that an absolute bar to receiving revelation for another? If, for example, someone were not in your ward, not in your stake, not even living in your state, but asked you to give them a blessing because of illness or injury, are you entitled to receive revelation while giving the blessing? Even if you have no connection to this person by family or church calling? Should you proceed with the blessing? If so, would you expect the Lord to assist, give revelation, and even inspire a commandment to the person if it were appropriate?

How hard and fast are the rules we impose on the Lord? Does His statement that He alone will decide when and to whom He speaks according to "His own pleasure" need to be weighed as part of the equation? If He cannot speak to anyone other than Joseph Smith, then did Joseph's death prevent Him from speaking further? If He cannot speak to anyone other than Joseph's successors in the office of President of the High Priesthood, then what if the occupant of that office is ill, infirm, or disabled?

Would the "system" govern, or the Lord's "own pleasure" govern? If it is "His own pleasure" then how can we possibly know when He speaks? What about the Lord's house being a house of order? Once He has a church established, should we trust He will confine His efforts to that church alone?

I suppose all these questions are answered by the Lord adding to "His own pleasure" that "because that I have spoken one word ye need not suppose that I cannot speak another; for my work is not yet finished; neither shall it be until the end of man, neither from that time henceforth and forever."

---

339 D&C 28: 2: "But, behold, verily, verily, I say unto thee, no one shall be appointed to receive commandments and revelations in this church excepting my servant Joseph Smith, Jun., for he receiveth them even as Moses."

In the final analysis, it is left to us to fast, pray, seek the guidance of the Spirit, and to find where the Lord's own pleasure in speaking is to be found. I do not expect someone other than the presiding authorities to conduct the affairs of the church. Nor would I expect anyone would organize a ward or stake other than someone having authority over that responsibility, regularly recognized by the church. I would not expect to either pay tithing to, nor be asked to pay tithing to, someone other than a Bishop in the church. But, just as Elder F. Enzio Busche encountered gifted sisters with the gift of prophecy and visions, I do not believe revelation is or can be confined to any single office, person, or group. (See F. Enzio Busche's book, *Yearning for the Living God*.) While serving in various church leadership positions, including as a General Authority, he encountered gifted women with spiritual capacities who astonished him. But, to his credit, he did not doubt them.

God speaks according to His own pleasure. He cautions you that just because He says one thing at one time, He is never limited in what He may say at another time; even if you think it contradicts His earlier statements. He is living and He has the final decision in what He says and to whom He speaks. We must not forget that principle. Even though we may not like the uncertainty this introduces to our trusted systems. He alone will remain in control.

2 Nephi 29: 10-11

> **"Wherefore, because that ye have a Bible ye need not suppose that it contains all my words; neither need ye suppose that I have not caused more to be written. For I command all men, both in the east and in the west, and in the north, and in the south, and in the islands of the sea, that they shall write the words which I speak unto them; for out of the books which shall be written I will judge the world, every man according to their works, according to that which is written."**

Within the Book of Mormon, as a new volume of scripture, is the caution that even it is incomplete. What a marvel that is if you think about it. Here's a new revelation telling us that there are other revelations that aren't included in either the Book of Mormon or the Bible.

Everyone nation, from time to time, received sacred messages from the Lord! No matter where they are—east, west, north or south, He's been in touch. They have written it down. The records are sacred, and He watches over them. They will be revealed. And, the good/bad news is that from their content we will be judged.

We are judged "according to our works," but measured against "that which is written." Think about that for a moment.

What if they haven't come to light yet? Are they still written? Are they still going to be used to measure us? If we haven't seen these words, why would it be appropriate for them to be used as a measuring stick for our conduct? Was the Book of Mormon's standards binding upon us even before the record came forth?

Why does He assure us He is unchangeable? Why does He assure us He is the same yesterday, today and forever? Is the standard going to change from ancient record to ancient record? If it does not change, then are we accountable for the same standard of conduct no matter when or where we live? How can we be held to account for things that are yet to be revealed?

If we cannot be judged against something we do not know,[340] how can these words set a standard for judging even before they are published?

I want to propose a concept that appeals to my mind. When we are trying to "prove" a proposition, it is possible to set up an experiment where we control all variables but one, then see what that one variable does. How it acts, or reacts. Life here is like that, I think. A fallen Telestial Kingdom, "or the world in which you presently reside"—to quote an authoritative source—is the same place for Able and Cain, Enoch and Noah, Abraham and Nimrod, Moses and Pharaoh, Jesus and Ciaphus, Jacob and Sherem, Alma and Nehor, Joseph Smith and Thomas Sharp. Same place with all of these contemporaries. But with the exception of Enoch and Noah, (who took different routes, but nonetheless were both favored by God) all the other pairs had dramatically different outcomes? Why?

This world is a fallen, but controlled environment. We get introduced here with free will and the capacity to change. Inside that environment of a fallen world, there have been people who have come and lived with all the same limitations that we have, but who have grown to know God. Their lives are proof that it can happen. Their testimonies and records of success are part of the "proof" of God's fairness and of mankind's freedom to return to Him.

If the Bible and the Book of Mormon both attest to the fact that it is possible for mankind to overcome by faith and return to God's presence, then we have the proof needed to see how this life should be lived. We have the evidence of God's willingness to receive us, and of our own capacity to overcome and return to Him.

Testimony after testimony, experience after experience are recounted in the Book of Mormon. We have enough "proof" that this process is available and works. If we were to have more, in a different record, reaffirming the same thing involving other people, would it add any different proof than is already in our possession? If not, then can we be judged by the same standard without having the specific life stories before us to illustrate in another hundred ways how men have triumphed and men have failed?

---

[340] Mosiah 3: 11: "For behold, and also his blood atoneth for the sins of those who have fallen by the transgression of Adam, who have died not knowing the will of God concerning them, or who have ignorantly sinned."

Is it possible there are others, some of whom are still living, who may also have recorded unspeakable things? Do their words count? Are they binding upon us for no other reason than to prove that in this contemporary world of sin it remains still possible to return to God's presence?

What interesting things the Book of Mormon raises for our pondering and edification. It is a revolutionary book, in the sense it revolutionizes our understanding of how God deals with mankind.

2 Nephi 29: 12

> **"For behold, I shall speak unto the Jews and they shall write it; and I shall also speak unto the Nephites and they shall write it; and I shall also speak unto the other tribes of the house of Israel, which I have led away, and they shall write it; and I shall also speak unto all nations of the earth and they shall write it."**

This is more than interesting. The Lord speaks, various people write what He speaks to them. These groups include:

1. Jews—we get that and it's the Bible, right?
2. Nephites—we get that too, the Book of Mormon, right?
3. Other tribes— how many? Who? When? Where? What?
4. All the nations of the earth—Now it's just too broad. What does "all the nations" mean, exactly?

So, let's take this a bit by bit, going through each one:

1. Jews: We have a Bible. But we DON'T have all the writings of the Jews, do we? We already referred to missing prophets Zenos and Zenok, and there are others. Look in your Bible Dictionary for "Missing Scripture" and you'll see a list. (I'm pulling your leg. If you look that up it'll refer you to "Lost Books" so go there.)

[That reminds me of a joke I tell: If I get a tattoo it'll say "Leviticus 19: 28."[341] But you probably won't think that's funny.]

Anyway, the Jews recorded more both in the Old Testament and in the New Testament than we have currently. So don't get all certain the Bible is the final word from the ancient Jews. It isn't. Never was. There's more coming.

2. Nephites: Clearly more coming. Sealed material has not been revealed, and will be some day. Providing, of course, we were to actually merit the disclosure. So, I suppose that means don't hold your breath.

3. Other Tribes: We got nothing. Not even a number. The one chance we had to get a number was blown by both the disciples in Jerusalem and the Nephites. I've written about this in *The Second Comforter*. So

[341] Lev. 19: 28: "Ye shall not make any cuttings in your flesh for the dead, nor print any marks upon you: I *am* the Lord."

the only way to triangulate is to either take the allegory of the Olive Tree in Jacob 5 and try to estimate—a risky proposition since it was intended to convey an overall meaning not a number—or we can work backwards from the crucifixion to the approximate 11 1/2 months later when Jesus appeared to the Nephites. Take the time spent with the Nephites, then estimate He's been busy doing that same ministry elsewhere. Divide the time taken to minister into the available time and you get something between 10 and 18 other potential groups out there depending on your estimate of the time used. The record attempts to prevent us from being too accurate because it identifies three days specifically, then resorts to just "many times" to cover what may have been days or weeks.[342] However, when you read of the Nephite disciples "journeying and preaching" but coming together in "mighty prayer and fasting" and the Lord's appearance again there, it seems closer to the 10 number than the 18.[343] Well, you work it out. It's just an unknown plural number which might be greater than just a couple. And for these we have no record at all.

4. All nations: Nothing here, either. And no basis from which to compile an estimate.

So, from the foregoing we can see that we have some tiny fragment of the whole, and cannot even begin to construct an outline of what we are missing. But despite our ignorance, the Lord spoke to them, they wrote it, and it is available for some group to eventually read. Apparently not us. We do not even get the rest of the record written on

[342] 3 Ne. 26: 13: "Therefore, I would that ye should behold that the Lord truly did teach the people, for the space of three days; and after that he did show himself unto them oft, and did break bread oft, and bless it, and give it unto them."

[343] 3 Ne. 27: 1: "And it came to pass that as the disciples of Jesus were journeying and were preaching the things which they had both heard and seen, and were baptizing in the name of Jesus, it came to pass that the disciples were gathered together and were united in mighty prayer and fasting."

parchment and hidden by John, (referred to in the headnote to Section 7 of the D&C). We only get a part of the information from it.[344]

So, there's a lot to be had. We don't have it...But what we do have we won't study. Well, maybe there is a cause and effect...

Seems to me, you don't want to talk about it. Seems to me, you just turn your pretty head and walk away. (Joe Walsh, from the James Gang era, before the heaviest toll was taken.)

So the Lord wants us to know there's ever so much out there. That we have a tiny fraction of what was once available. And we just don't seem to care. We'd rather reduce the volume of topics we study and eliminate the "mysteries" from our diet of Gospel study, so as to relieve ourselves of any responsibility for what we already possess. We are beyond dumbing down the Gospel. We're discarding it by the week. Tighter and tighter, until you are left alone, without God in the world. There's a brilliant phrase. It comes from the Book of Mormon. It is found at Mosiah 27: 31; Alma 41: 11 and Mormon 5: 16.[345] Of all the phrases turned in the Book of Mormon this is the most solitary, profound and descriptive of the fall from grace mankind experiences. It is perfect, even if what it describes is perfectly horrid.

---

[344] D&C 7: 1-8: "And the Lord said unto me: John, my beloved, what desirest thou? For if you shall ask what you will, it shall be granted unto you. And I said unto him: Lord, give unto me power over death, that I may live and bring souls unto thee. And the Lord said unto me: Verily, verily, I say unto thee, because thou desirest this thou shalt tarry until I come in my glory, and shalt prophesy before nations, kindreds, tongues and people. And for this cause the Lord said unto Peter: If I will that he tarry till I come, what is that to thee? For he desired of me that he might bring souls unto me, but thou desiredst that thou mightest speedily come unto me in my kingdom. I say unto thee, Peter, this was a good desire; but my beloved has desired that he might do more, or a greater work yet among men than what he has before done. Yea, he has undertaken a greater work; therefore I will make him as flaming fire and a ministering angel; he shall minister for those who shall be heirs of salvation who dwell on the earth. And I will make thee to minister for him and for thy brother James; and unto you three I will give this power and the keys of this ministry until I come. Verily I say unto you, ye shall both have according to your desires, for ye both joy in that which ye have desired."

[345] Mosiah 27: 31: "Yea, every knee shall bow, and every tongue confess before him. Yea, even at the last day, when all men shall stand to be judged of him, then shall they confess that he is God; then shall they confess, who live without God in the world, that the judgment of an everlasting punishment is just upon them; and they shall quake, and tremble, and shrink beneath the glance of his all-searching eye."
Alma 41: 11: "And now, my son, all men that are in a state of nature, or I would say, in a carnal state, are in the gall of bitterness and in the bonds of iniquity; they are without God in the world, and they have gone contrary to the nature of God; therefore, they are in a state contrary to the nature of happiness."
Mormon 5: 16: "For behold, the Spirit of the Lord hath already ceased to strive with their fathers; and they are without Christ and God in the world; and they are driven about as chaff before the wind."

2 Nephi 29: 13

> **"And it shall come to pass that the Jews shall have the words of the Nephites, and the Nephites shall have the words of the Jews; and the Nephites and the Jews shall have the words of the lost tribes of Israel; and the lost tribes of Israel shall have the words of the Nephites and the Jews."**

Well, happily the Jews "shall" get the Nephite words. Some day. Currently for the most part they don't want them. And, even if they did, the "words of the Nephites" will include the sealed portion, because they are certainly part of the "words" the Nephites recorded. So this will be future, even if there were Jews interested in taking the offer today.

The Nephites also "shall" have the words of the Jews. However, once again as we have seen, the words include a great volume of material spoken by Christ, recorded by the Jews, and not in anyone's current possession. So this, too, must be in the future. For now we aren't even sure of who these "Nephites" are.

The Nephites and the Jews "shall" get the words of the lost tribes of Israel. This is a category, not a number. Remember that. So once again, future event. Don't know when. Don't know how many records. Don't even know how many groups will be included.

But all these records are inevitably to come forth. Just not yet. Why?

Read Mormon's explanation: "But behold the plates of Nephi do contain the more part of the things which he taught the people. And these things have I written, which are a lesser part of the things which he taught the people; and I have written them to the intent that they may be brought again unto this people, from the Gentiles, according to the words which Jesus hath spoken. And when they shall have received this, which is expedient that they should have first, to try their faith, and if it shall so be that they shall believe these things then shall the greater things be made manifest unto them. And if it so be that they will not believe these things, then shall the greater things be withheld from them, unto their condemnation. Behold, I was about to write them, all which were engraven upon the plates of Nephi, but the Lord forbade it, saying: I will try the faith of my people. Therefore I, Mormon, do write the things which have been commanded me of the Lord. And now I,

Mormon, make an end of my sayings, and proceed to write the things which have been commanded me."[346]

What if I do believe these things? What if I will accept the things which He offers? What if my faith has been tried and I am found to be deserving of more information? Can a person come out from under the condemnation referred to above, even if the rest of mankind fails to acquit themselves? Alma comes with the reply: "Yes."[347] So, as it turns out, ignorance is voluntary.

Well, shut my mouth! (That's a pun, you see.)

[Can you do puns in a religious blog? Or will the long faced and dour be offended? Well, they don't get it anyway. Hey! Why are you reading this if it offends you? Stop it!]

What do you suppose it would take for the Lord to respond to us removing the condemnation that we labor under? How should we go about trying to make that happen? I don't see it happening, do you? I'm sort of persuaded by Nephi's pessimism of the gentiles of our day. Even this mild blog discussion I am attempting has provoked ire in many readers. How we fix our collective disinterest seems a monumental enterprise beyond human ability. I fear it would take some great

---

[346] 3 Ne. 26: 7-12: "But behold the plates of Nephi do contain the more part of the things which he taught the people. And these things have I written, which are a lesser part of the things which he taught the people; and I have written them to the intent that they may be brought again unto this people, from the Gentiles, according to the words which Jesus hath spoken. And when they shall have received this, which is expedient that they should have first, to try their faith, and if it shall so be that they shall believe these things then shall the greater things be made manifest unto them. And if it so be that they will not believe these things, then shall the greater things be withheld from them, unto their condemnation. Behold, I was about to write them, all which were engraven upon the plates of Nephi, but the Lord forbade it, saying: I will try the faith of my people. Therefore I, Mormon, do write the things which have been commanded me of the Lord. And now I, Mormon, make an end of my sayings, and proceed to write the things which have been commanded me."

[347] Alma 12: 9-11: "And now Alma began to expound these things unto him, saying: It is given unto many to know the mysteries of God; nevertheless they are laid under a strict command that they shall not impart only according to the portion of his word which he doth grant unto the children of men, according to the heed and diligence which they give unto him. And therefore, he that will harden his heart, the same receiveth the lesser portion of the word; and he that will not harden his heart, to him is given the greater portion of the word, until it is given unto him to know the mysteries of God until he know them in full. And they that will harden their hearts, to them is given the lesser portion of the word until they know nothing concerning his mysteries; and then they are taken captive by the devil, and led by his will down to destruction. Now this is what is meant by the chains of hell."

calamity to unfold before we would change. Then again, I think the Lord has already told us that.[348]

2 Nephi 29: 14

> **"And it shall come to pass that my people, which are of the house of Israel, shall be gathered home unto the lands of their possessions; and my word also shall be gathered in one. And I will show unto them that fight against my word and against my people, who are of the house of Israel, that I am God, and that I covenanted with Abraham that I would remember his seed forever."**

Now we have an estimate of the time when a general disclosure of the records of these various nations will occur. It's set in the time when the people who have survived the great distresses and wars of the last days will leave the New Jerusalem and return to their lands of possessions. That is, post-New Jerusalem, post-destruction of the wicked, and after the time when the Lord has come among them. When they are sent into their respective lands of possessions, then at last the entire record of the Lord's dealings with each nation will be "gathered in one."

So this won't be anytime soon. Well, if soon, it will be after some more dramatic events, which will take our minds off the issue of missing scripture.

What is interesting is the Lord's emphasis on those who "fight against my word." He puts this first. The fight, as He puts it, is against both "my word and my people," but it is the fight against His "word" that He lists first. This is important.

You will recall there were two different reactions to the two parts of Lehi's message. When it was repentance from their wickedness, the Jews mocked him. But when it was a message of the coming Christ, they wanted to kill him.[349] This is the war against His "word" in a

---

[348] D&C 1: 17: "Wherefore, I the Lord, knowing the calamity which should come upon the inhabitants of the earth, called upon my servant Joseph Smith, Jun., and spake unto him from heaven, and gave him commandments;"
D&C 45: 50: "And calamity shall cover the mocker, and the scorner shall be consumed; and they that have watched for iniquity shall be hewn down and cast into the fire."

[349] 1 Ne. 1: 18-19: "Therefore, I would that ye should know, that after the Lord had shown so many marvelous things unto my father, Lehi, yea, concerning the destruction of Jerusalem, behold he went forth among the people, and began to prophesy and to declare unto them concerning the things which he had both seen and heard. And it came to pass that the Jews did mock him because of the things which he testified of them; for he truly testified of their wickedness and their abominations; and he testified that the things which he saw and heard, and also the things which he read in the book, manifested plainly of the coming of a Messiah, and also the redemption of the world."

nutshell. The message of hope and redemption found in Christ is what the enemies of God always seek to suppress.

First, distort, suppress and exclude His word. Then it follows that He has no people, because they cannot find their way back to Him.

Remember this is the great fight. It is relentlessly underway. So soon as His word becomes available, there will be forces, enemies, alliances, even good-intentions used to suppress, discard and alter His words. This is the great work of the adversary. This is the fight that gets waged first.

When the victory is won against His word, then the victory against the people is over. There cannot be any "people" belonging to Him if they do not possess His words in clarity, fullness, and with power.

What significance is there then in changing His words? Discarding His revelations? Suppressing His ordinances? Altering what He has revealed? Designating some of His word as "mysteries" that ought to be feared or avoided? Why would Joseph Smith advise us to search deeper and deeper into the mysteries of God? Why would we be told to avoid them today? What has happened in the fight against the Lord's word among us?

The purpose of His word is to establish His people. When people have His word, and obtain the light and truth that flows from it, then they are inevitably turned in their hearts to the fathers. Primarily among those fathers is the one mentioned here: Abraham. For in Abraham we see a return to the original order which preceded the flood. He inherited what "came down from the beginning" and restored the original ancient order.[350] When the "word" and "people" are again here, they are directly linked to Abraham, Isaac and Jacob and are heirs to the covenant and priesthood they held. It is a return. It is a resurrection of an ancient order, where men know God and are His friends and companions while living here in this fallen world.

The results of having the Lord's "word" is to then create a "people" who in turn are linked to "Abraham." These things all follow in turn. The fight against it is begun at the "word" to prevent the others who follow. If you can choke people off and get them to refuse His "words" then you can prevent them from ever becoming His "people" and realizing the association which brings their hearts to the fathers.

---

[350] Abr. 1: 2-3: "And, finding there was greater happiness and peace and rest for me, I sought for the blessings of the fathers, and the right whereunto I should be ordained to administer the same; having been myself a follower of righteousness, desiring also to be one who possessed great knowledge, and to be a greater follower of righteousness, and to possess a greater knowledge, and to be a father of many nations, a prince of peace, and desiring to receive instructions, and to keep the commandments of God, I became a rightful heir, a High Priest, holding the right belonging to the fathers. It was conferred upon me from the fathers; it came down from the fathers, from the beginning of time, yea, even from the beginning, or before the foundation of the earth, down to the present time, even the right of the firstborn, or the first man, who is Adam, or first father, through the fathers unto me."

It is a consistent plan and a predictable fight. How's it going in our time? What good things have we done to preserve His word? Have we kept intact everything He handed us through Joseph? Do we possess all of the word He intended us to have, study and live? Are we thereby made into new creations, His people? Do we show the fruits of being His people? Do the visions of heaven flow over us, and angels minister to us? Do we possess knowledge of God in the sense used in the Book of Mormon? Are we in possession of all the rights and powers conferred upon Abraham?

It is an interesting interconnection the Lord refers to here. Worth reflection at a minimum. Fasting, prayer and seeking as well, perhaps.

2 Nephi 30

2 Nephi 30: 1

> **"And now behold, my beloved brethren, I would speak unto you; for I, Nephi, would not suffer that ye should suppose that ye are more righteous than the Gentiles shall be. For behold, except ye shall keep the commandments of God ye shall all likewise perish; and because of the words which have been spoken ye need not suppose that the Gentiles are utterly destroyed."**

This is troubling if you understand what is said here. Let's see if we can pull it apart.

Nephi adds this direct comment to his descendants, the forebears of the remnant. Although they are the target of covenants and beneficiaries of the restoration, they too need to keep to the path. Though they are "beloved brethren" to Nephi, they are not given any unconditional promises. No one is. Everything we receive is based on what we do, think and say.[351]

Note that this is not about the actual remnant, but about the Nephites who would be destroyed. These people would have access to Nephi's record until the time of Mormon, when they would be destroyed. You can see the time frame in the word usage, "Ye are" as to the Nephites, in contrast to "the Gentiles who shall be." This message is addressed to the Nephites in a time before the gentile.

What is particularly distressing is the comparison Nephi is making. He is saying that the Nephites, who possess the land of promise, needn't think themselves "more righteous than the Gentiles shall be" because if

---

[351] Alma 12: 14: "For our words will condemn us, yea, all our works will condemn us; we shall not be found spotless; and our thoughts will also condemn us; and in this awful state we shall not dare to look up to our God; and we would fain be glad if we could command the rocks and the mountains to fall upon us to hide us from his presence."
D&C 130: 20-21: "There is a law, irrevocably decreed in heaven before the foundations of this world, upon which all blessings are predicated—And when we obtain any blessing from God, it is by obedience to that law upon which it is predicated."

these Nephite descendants do "not keep the commandments of God" then they "shall all likewise perish." If the Nephites do not keep the commandments, they will, like the gentiles, perish.

This means that Nephi is confirming again his prophecy of the destruction of the gentiles. They are doomed. And the Nephites are similarly doomed unless they are obedient.

Despite this warning we know what happened to the Nephites. They were destroyed. The gentiles will be destroyed also.

In the case of the Nephites and the gentiles, "ye need not suppose that the Gentiles are utterly destroyed." That is, neither all the Nephites have been, nor all the gentiles will be "utterly destroyed."

Well, this is happy news indeed. Some tiny fragment of the gentiles will actually survive the destruction of the coming days! So we ought to rejoice! All is well with us after all! And coming from Nephi we know that we have a promise from one holding sealing authority who will, as I have previously pointed out, seal this prophecy.[352]

Interestingly Nephi warns his own descendants about their pride and haughtiness. He says that these Nephite descendants, heirs of the covenant, should not think of themselves as righteous. "I, Nephi, would not suffer that ye should suppose that ye are more righteous than the Gentiles shall be." Nephi's prophecy is clear to him, and clear to his descendants. They both regarded the gentiles with pessimism. They (we) are doomed. So they saw us as something dreadful to be compared to. When Nephi confirms they ought not think themselves better than us, he is giving a strong warning indeed. The odd thing is that we read these same records, this same prophecy, and we think we're better than them! We have inverted the picture! We're good, they were bad! But Nephi is using us as the dreadful comparison, the stark warning, the terrible warning that if the Nephites do not repent they will be like us and perish.

When you pick these words apart and see the message it makes you wonder how we could have come to our inverted view. Arrogance and pride really do blind us. Almost completely. What more could Nephi have said to get us to understand?[353]

---

[352] 2 Ne. 33: 13-15: "And now, my beloved brethren, all those who are of the house of Israel, and all ye ends of the earth, I speak unto you as the voice of one crying from the dust: Farewell until that great day shall come. And you that will not partake of the goodness of God, and respect the words of the Jews, and also my words, and the words which shall proceed forth out of the mouth of the Lamb of God, behold, I bid you an everlasting farewell, for these words shall condemn you at the last day. For what I seal on earth, shall be brought against you at the judgment bar; for thus hath the Lord commanded me, and I must obey. Amen."

[353] 2 Ne. 32: 8: "And now, my beloved brethren, I perceive that ye ponder still in your hearts; and it grieveth me that I must speak concerning this thing. For if ye would hearken unto the Spirit which teacheth a man to pray ye would know that ye must pray; for the evil spirit teacheth not a man to pray, but teacheth him that he must not pray."

2 Nephi 30: 2

> **"For behold, I say unto you that as many of the Gentiles as will repent are the covenant people of the Lord; and as many of the Jews as will not repent shall be cast off; for the Lord covenanteth with none save it be with them that repent and believe in his Son, who is the Holy One of Israel."**

To the extent that gentiles "will repent" they may become part of the Lord's "covenant people." They are not the remnant, but they may join in the covenant. If they do, then by virtue of the covenant they become "covenant people."

What is required for the gentiles to repent?

What covenant must they enter into or receive so they may be numbered among the "covenant people?" Is membership in The Church of Jesus Christ of Latter-day Saints the only thing needed to "repent" and become a "covenant people?" If not, then what else would be required?

To the extent that "the Jews will not repent" then they will be "cast off." Although history has shown how the Jews have been treated (as Nephi put it), "ye have cursed them, and have hated them, and have not sought to recover them."[354] These difficulties suffered by the Jews are preliminary. The Lord always watched over and preserved them from complete destruction. However, when the Gospel is offered to them in the last days, in the final offering to the last (who had once been first[355]), they will reject the offered renewal of the covenant at their peril. If they reject it, they "shall be cast off" because that will sever the covenant. "The Lord covenanteth with none save it be with them that repent and believe in his Son, who is the Holy One of Israel."

Although we know the Lord will extend every opportunity to the descendants for the sake of a covenant with those who have become the friends of God, there are limits. God will do all He has promised to do. He will forbear, entreat, beseech, send messengers, labor alongside with His messengers, and do all He can to reclaim the heirs for the covenant's sake. In the end, however, the heirs must either accept what He offers, or be cast off.

It is extraordinary how long the Lord will extend His hand to reclaim His people. But everyone must choose to follow Him. We have our agency. We cannot be forced to follow Him. Even though He may be

---

354 2 Ne. 29: 5: "O ye Gentiles, have ye remembered the Jews, mine ancient covenant people? Nay; but ye have cursed them, and have hated them, and have not sought to recover them. But behold, I will return all these things upon your own heads; for I the Lord have not forgotten my people."

355 1 Ne. 13: 42: "And the time cometh that he shall manifest himself unto all nations, both unto the Jews and also unto the Gentiles; and after he has manifested himself unto the Jews and also unto the Gentiles, then he shall manifest himself unto the Gentiles and also unto the Jews, and the last shall be first, and the first shall be last."

long-suffering and patient, He cannot compel any to be saved.[356] Unless a person is free to choose for themselves, there is no existence.[357]

If you remove the right to choose, it is not only agency that is obliterated, but it is existence itself. Though we are utterly dependent on God for our very existence, sustained from moment to moment by Him loaning us the ability to move, breathe and act[358], because we are free to make choices we exist. If you destroy the right to choose you have ended the personality of the person. [I have explained this in the beginning of *Beloved Enos* .]

Well, all of this is of no import if the gentiles do not "repent." Whenever we brush up against that subject we wind up engaged in discussions about justice, mercy, vengeance and restitution. I've written about this process in both *The Second Comforter* and *Come, Let Us Adore Him* . Briefly, here are some of the most important points: To be forgiven we must forgive. Not just forgive, but plead for mercy for those who have offended us. The role of accusing is left to "the accuser of the brethren" or Satan.[359] When we accuse others we interfere with their salvation. If we are the one who was offended, and we make no accusation against them, then we become their savior. Satan's right to accuse is inferior to ours as victims of the offense. We suffer in the flesh the wrongs of others. If we make no claim for justice, surrender those and seek instead for mercy on behalf of others, then Satan's accusations can have no claim upon them. We mimic Christ, follow His example, and in our own limited way also atone for the sins of others. Joseph Smith was trying to get us to understand this concept when he taught:

---

356 Moses 4: 1-3: "And I, the Lord God, spake unto Moses, saying: That Satan, whom thou hast commanded in the name of mine Only Begotten, is the same which was from the beginning, and he came before me, saying—Behold, here am I, send me, I will be thy son, and I will redeem all mankind, that one soul shall not be lost, and surely I will do it; wherefore give me thine honor.

2 But, behold, my Beloved Son, which was my Beloved and Chosen from the beginning, said unto me—Father, thy will be done, and the glory be thine forever.

3 Wherefore, because that Satan rebelled against me, and sought to destroy the agency of man, which I, the Lord God, had given him, and also, that I should give unto him mine own power; by the power of mine Only Begotten, I caused that he should be cast down;"

357 D&C 93: 30: "All truth is independent in that sphere in which God has placed it, to act for itself, as all intelligence also; otherwise there is no existence."

358 Mosiah 2: 21: "I say unto you that if ye should serve him who has created you from the beginning, and is preserving you from day to day, by lending you breath, that ye may live and move and do according to your own will, and even supporting you from one moment to another—I say, if ye should serve him with all your whole souls yet ye would be unprofitable servants."

359 Rev. 12: 10: "And I heard a loud voice saying in heaven, Now is come salvation, and strength, and the kingdom of our God, and the power of his Christ: for the accuser of our brethren is cast down, which accused them before our God day and night."

"If you do not accuse each other, God will not accuse you. If you have no accuser you will enter heaven, and if you will follow the revelations and instructions which God gives you through me, I will take you into heaven as my back load. If you will not accuse me, I will not accuse you. If you will throw a cloak of charity over my sins, I will over yours —for charity covereth a multitude of sins." (DHC. 4:445)

I have explained this at length in what I've written in *Come, Let Us Adore Him*. Christ said this in His ministry repeatedly. He lived it. He showed by His own example the way to obtain forgiveness for every wrong you have ever done. It is in the same way He went about atoning for sins. It is by suffering offenses and returning good. It is by forgiving those who despitefully use and abuse you. It is through loving those who are your enemies. It is by becoming sons and daughters of God. And it can be done in no other way.[360] If you do not forgive others, you cannot be forgiven.[361] This is why Christ, in teaching us to pray, told us we are only forgiven as we forgive others.[362] It is as we forgive that we obtain forgiveness.

The way is strait and narrow, and cannot permit you to pass through while carrying any burden of accusation, desire for revenge or even just complaint about others. When you lay down what you might justly claim against others and seek nothing for their offenses, then you are able to enter in. To be blessed, we must seek peace with those who would make war against us.[363] When we judge all others with mercy, it is with mercy alone we will be judged.[364]

---

[360] Matt. 5: 38-48: "Ye have heard that it hath been said, An eye for an eye, and a tooth for a tooth: But I say unto you, That ye resist not evil: but whosoever shall smite thee on thy right cheek, turn to him the other also. And if any man will sue thee at the law, and take away thy coat, let him have *thy* cloke also. And whosoever shall compel thee to go a mile, go with him twain. Give to him that asketh thee, and from him that would borrow of thee turn not thou away. Ye have heard that it hath been said, Thou shalt love thy neighbour, and hate thine enemy. But I say unto you, Love your enemies, bless them that curse you, do good to them that hate you, and pray for them which despitefully use you, and persecute you; That ye may be the children of your Father which is in heaven: for he maketh his sun to rise on the evil and on the good, and sendeth rain on the just and on the unjust. For if ye love them which love you, what reward have ye? do not even the publicans the same? And if ye salute your brethren only, what do ye more *than others?* do not even the publicans so? Be ye therefore perfect, even as your Father which is in heaven is perfect."

[361] Matt. 6: 14-15: "For if ye forgive men their trespasses, your heavenly Father will also forgive you: But if ye forgive not men their trespasses, neither will your Father forgive your trespasses."

[362] Matt. 6: 12: "And forgive us our debts, as we forgive our debtors."

[363] Matt. 5: 9: "Blessed *are* the peacemakers: for they shall be called the children of God."

[364] Matt. 7: 2: "For with what judgment ye judge, ye shall be judged: and with what measure ye mete, it shall be measured to you again."

For the most part, the gentiles will not repent. They will hold courts, use their time judging, exact conditions, set limits, and annotate their permanent records with notes showing what discipline a person has undergone. And happily employ control, compulsion and dominion over one another[365] right up to the time when the trumpet sounds and it is everlastingly too late. Others will justify this failure to forgive, shout praises to the abuse, and claim all compulsion and dominion is necessary to protect us from the evil. Even though our Master told us not to resist the evil, but forgive it.[366]

For the most part, the gentiles will demand they be judged by a law they cannot satisfy. Some few, however, will forgive and plead for the weaknesses and failings of others. They will forgive, and thereby be forgiven. They will obtain for themselves a judgment based only on mercy, for they have shown mercy to others. This atoning act of love and intercession will be the hallmark by which the children of God are identified in the Day of Judgment.[367] Only the peacemakers can be trusted to live in peace with one another. All others are unfit for the presence of God.

2 Nephi 30: 3

> **"And now, I would prophesy somewhat more concerning the Jews and the Gentiles. For after the book of which I have spoken shall come forth, and be written unto the Gentiles, and sealed up again unto the Lord, there shall be many which shall believe the words which are written; and they shall carry them forth unto the remnant of our seed."**

Nephi speaks again prophetically about our time. He makes no distinction between the Jews and "the remnant of our seed," or Nephite remnant in what he says here. The "book of which I have spoken" is the record of the Nephites. It will come forth, written as a warning to the gentiles. Here is another attempt to establish a time frame for a prophecy. It will be after the record exists, gets brought forth "unto the gentiles" and then is "sealed up again unto the Lord." We are in that era now. The record exists, even if part of it is sealed. It has come forth, at least in that part intended to be released at the point of this prophecy.

---

365 D&C 121: 37: "That they may be conferred upon us, it is true; but when we undertake to cover our sins, or to gratify our pride, our vain ambition, or to exercise control or dominion or compulsion upon the souls of the children of men, in any degree of unrighteousness, behold, the heavens withdraw themselves; the Spirit of the Lord is grieved; and when it is withdrawn, Amen to the priesthood or the authority of that man."

366 Matt. 5: 39: "But I say unto you, That ye resist not evil: but whosoever shall smite thee on thy right cheek, turn to him the other also."

367 Matt. 5: 9: "Blessed *are* the peacemakers: for they shall be called the children of God."

And it has been "sealed up again unto the Lord." We don't have possession of it at present.

I've addressed the cover story that the Angel Moroni still has the plates in what I've written before. Briefly, the Book of Mormon tells Joseph Smith to "seal them up unto the Lord" in detail in three places. This is one of them. The other two are 2 Nephi 27: 22 (giving the most detailed instruction to Joseph)[368] and Ether 5: 1-4[369]. All of these instructions are to the same effect. Once the Book of Mormon has been translated, to the extent it is to come forth in our day, the plates are to be "sealed up again" by Joseph. Since he did everything else in the way he was instructed, there is no reason to believe he wouldn't have sealed up the record and hid it again.

Here Nephi prophesies that "there shall be many which shall believe the words which are written." Meaning that those words "written unto the gentiles" or what we have in print now, will in fact be believed by "many." They "shall believe the words." Nephi has assured us of that. Therefore, it is necessary that some group from among the gentiles distinguish itself by actually believing the words of the Book of Mormon. It will be this group which "shall carry them forth unto the remnant of" Nephi's seed. Notice that they will "believe" in the book. (That will require them to have a correct understanding of the book's content, otherwise they would have unbelief.)

Those who do not believe (or have unbelief) in the Book of Mormon will not, indeed cannot, bring the words to the remnant. They aren't qualified. They would not be able to convert any of the remnant. It will be those who actually believe in and accept the precepts of the Book of Mormon who will carry them forth unto the remnant.

Considering the otherwise direful predictions about the gentiles, this is the one way where hope may come to them. The group that believes in the Book of Mormon will necessarily have to be preserved to fulfill their responsibility to carry the words to the remnant. This is a subset of

---

368 2 Ne. 27: 22: "Wherefore, when thou hast read the words which I have commanded thee, and obtained the witnesses which I have promised unto thee, then shalt thou seal up the book again, and hide it up unto me, that I may preserve the words which thou hast not read, until I shall see fit in mine own wisdom to reveal all things unto the children of men."

369 Ether 5: 1-4: "And now I, Moroni, have written the words which were commanded me, according to my memory; and I have told you the things which I have sealed up; therefore touch them not in order that ye may translate; for that thing is forbidden you, except by and by it shall be wisdom in God. And behold, ye may be privileged that ye may show the plates unto those who shall assist to bring forth this work; And unto three shall they be shown by the power of God; wherefore they shall know of a surety that these things are true. And in the mouth of three witnesses shall these things be established; and the testimony of three, and this work, in the which shall be shown forth the power of God and also his word, of which the Father, and the Son, and the Holy Ghost bear record—and all this shall stand as a testimony against the world at the last day."

the Saints, and clearly not all of the members of the Church of Jesus Christ of Latter-day Saints. For the church itself, there remains a condemnation because of their unbelief in the book.[370] This condemnation of the church was repeated by President Benson and again by Elder Oaks.

If, therefore, you would like to be preserved, the manner in which that will happen, according to Nephi's prophecy, will necessarily require you to abandon the condemnation of the larger church, and become one of those who believe in the Book of Mormon. Not only to say, but to do; as Section 84 above requires.

It is surprising how much information the Book of Mormon has for us. It is even more surprising that with such detail available to us, we have done so little to understand and teach it. The words of this prophecy by Nephi ought to be proclaimed among us. However, very little attention has been given to it.

One of the effects of pride is blindness. We can't see what our pride prevents us from seeing. We have to come down to the depths of humility (to use a phrase Nephi coined in 2 Ne. 9: 42). Interestingly it is only the Book of Mormon which tells us to "come down in the depths of humility."[371] Once Nephi coined the phrase, Mormon used it twice in his abridgment. It is a good phrase. It does tell us what we must do.

The great work of the Lord in this day revolves around the Book of Mormon. More instruction, prophecy and promises are contained in that book for our day than any other. You can get closer to God by abiding its precepts than any other book.

Joseph Smith didn't write it. It was written by ancient prophets, sealed up to come forth in our day, and translated by the gift and power of God.

---

[370] D&C 84: 54-57: "And your minds in times past have been darkened because of unbelief, and because you have treated lightly the things you have received—Which vanity and unbelief have brought the whole church under condemnation. And this condemnation resteth upon the children of Zion, even all. And they shall remain under this condemnation until they repent and remember the new covenant, even the Book of Mormon and the former commandments which I have given them, not only to say, but to do according to that which I have written—"

[371] 2 Ne. 9: 42: "And whoso knocketh, to him will he open; and the wise, and the learned, and they that are rich, who are puffed up because of their learning, and their wisdom, and their riches—yea, they are they whom he despiseth; and save they shall cast these things away, and consider themselves fools before God, and come down in the depths of humility, he will not open unto them."
Hel. 6: 5: "Yea, and many did preach with exceedingly great power and authority, unto the bringing down many of them into the depths of humility, to be the humble followers of God and the Lamb."
3 Ne. 12: 2: "And again, more blessed are they who shall believe in your words because that ye shall testify that ye have seen me, and that ye know that I am. Yea, blessed are they who shall believe in your words, and come down into the depths of humility and be baptized, for they shall be visited with fire and with the Holy Ghost, and shall receive a remission of their sins."

It is a perilous book. We neglect it at the risk of failure. Don't let it remain a "sealed book" for you. Anyone can come to believe in it if they are willing.

2 Nephi 30: 4-5

"And then shall the remnant of our seed know concerning us, how that we came out from Jerusalem, and that they are descendants of the Jews. And the gospel of Jesus Christ shall be declared among them; wherefore, they shall be restored unto the knowledge of their fathers, and also to the knowledge of Jesus Christ, which was had among their fathers."

Once the remnant obtain a copy of the Book of Mormon, from a believing gentile hand, they will realize they are originally come out of Jerusalem. They will realize also that they are "descendants of the Jews."

It comes full circle. Those who were lost have returned again. The "prodigal" will return.[372] There will be joy at the return.

---

[372] Luke 15: 11-32: "And he said, A certain man had two sons: And the younger of them said to *his* father, Father, give me the portion of goods that falleth *to me.* And he divided unto them *his* living. And not many days after the younger son gathered all together, and took his journey into a far country, and there wasted his substance with riotous living. And when he had spent all, there arose a mighty famine in that land; and he began to be in want. And he went and joined himself to a citizen of that country; and he sent him into his fields to feed swine. And he would fain have filled his belly with the husks that the swine did eat: and no man gave unto him. And when he came to himself, he said, How many hired servants of my father's have bread enough and to spare, and I perish with hunger! I will arise and go to my father, and will say unto him, Father, I have sinned against heaven, and before thee, And am no more worthy to be called thy son: make me as one of thy hired servants. And he arose, and came to his father. But when he was yet a great way off, his father saw him, and had compassion, and ran, and fell on his neck, and kissed him. And the son said unto him, Father, I have sinned against heaven, and in thy sight, and am no more worthy to be called thy son. But the father said to his servants, Bring forth the best robe, and put *it* on him; and put a ring on his hand, and shoes on *his* feet: And bring hither the fatted calf, and kill *it;* and let us eat, and be merry: For this my son was dead, and is alive again; he was lost, and is found. And they began to be merry. Now his elder son was in the field: and as he came and drew nigh to the house, he heard musick and dancing. And he called one of the servants, and asked what these things meant. And he said unto him, Thy brother is come; and thy father hath killed the fatted calf, because he hath received him safe and sound. And he was angry, and would not go in: therefore came his father out, and intreated him. And he answering said to *his* father, Lo, these many years do I serve thee, neither transgressed I at any time thy commandment: and yet thou never gavest me a kid, that I might make merry with my friends: But as soon as this thy son was come, which hath devoured thy living with harlots, thou hast killed for him the fatted calf. And he said unto him, Son, thou art ever with me, and all that I have is thine. It was meet that we should make merry, and be glad: for this thy brother was dead, and is alive again; and was lost, and is found."

This will happen as a preliminary to "the gospel of Jesus Christ [being] declared among them." The Gospel being declared requires a true message, true messengers, authority, and ordinances. That will follow the remnant receiving the Book of Mormon. To what extent the gentiles bring those things and to what extent it will require heaven's direct involvement, remains to be seen. But when the remnant reconnects, they will reconnect in every respect. The "gospel of Jesus Christ shall be declared among them!"

As a result of these events, the remnant "shall be restored unto the knowledge of their fathers." What does it mean to be restored? What knowledge? Which fathers? The Nephites, and Lehi, or to the earlier "fathers" as well? Does this include Abraham, Isaac and Jacob?

What does it mean they will be "also [restored] to the knowledge of Jesus Christ?" What does this "knowledge" involve? What kind of relationship with Christ does this imply?

If we wonder at the "knowledge" the remnant will obtain, we have a parallel given to us: The future remnant knowledge of Christ shall be akin to that "which was had among their fathers." Meaning they will grow to know what the earlier Nephite disciples and peoples knew. What kind of knowledge does that include?

When the right target receives the right Gospel, the results are dramatic. When the wrong group is entrusted with the Gospel, they tend to let it atrophy, grow dim, and become a social order without the power of godliness. The restoration was intended to cure that problem. But as with any gift from God, we must do more than to "take no thought but to ask."[373] We must pursue knowledge and act with alacrity when it is given.

If we do not do this, then the result is not a blessing, but a cursing.[374] No matter what we are offered by the Lord, we must act consistent with His will to receive the blessings offered. When we fail to fulfill the obligation He appoints to us, then we fail to obtain what was offered.[375]

---

[373] D&C 9: 6-7: "Do not murmur, my son, for it is wisdom in me that I have dealt with you after this manner. Behold, you have not understood; you have supposed that I would give it unto you, when you took no thought save it was to ask me."

[374] D&C 124: 47-48: "And it shall come to pass that if you build a house unto my name, and do not do the things that I say, I will not perform the oath which I make unto you, neither fulfil the promises which ye expect at my hands, saith the Lord. For instead of blessings, ye, by your own works, bring cursings, wrath, indignation, and judgments upon your own heads, by your follies, and by all your abominations, which you practise before me, saith the Lord."

[375] D&C 124: 31-32: "But I command you, all ye my saints, to build a house unto me; and I grant unto you a sufficient time to build a house unto me; and during this time your baptisms shall be acceptable unto me. But behold, at the end of this appointment your baptisms for your dead shall not be acceptable unto me; and if you do not these things at the end of the appointment ye shall be rejected as a church, with your dead, saith the Lord your God."

Once they have been given the gospel, the remnant will not fail. Their reconnection will be as a nail in a sure place, not to be moved. Their knowledge will grow into the perfect day, just as it might with anyone who is willing to receive what Christ offers.[376] Noon at the summer solstice is a symbol of the perfect day. This year, in contrast, at midnight of the winter solstice there will be an eclipse. This would be a symbol in the heavens of the opposite of the perfect day. When it arrives it undoubtedly is a sign relevant to the time. (Those things are never accidents or mere happenstance.)

The ideas begin to accumulate. Darkness and light. Free will and acceptance of what is offered by God. So many divergent roads that are offered in place of the one that remains strait and narrow, but nevertheless in a straight course before you.[377]

2 Nephi 30: 6

> **"And then shall they rejoice; for they shall know that it is a blessing unto them from the hand of God; and their scales of darkness shall begin to fall from their eyes; and many generations shall not pass away among them, save they shall be a pure and a delightsome people."**

Once the remnant is in possession of the Gospel, they will "rejoice." What does that mean? What form would "rejoicing" take as a result of receiving the Gospel?

What does it mean to "know that it is a blessing unto them from the hand of God?" How would they recognize that?

What are the "scales of darkness" which cover eyes? How would the scales have been over their eyes in the first place? What does it mean to have the scales "begin to fall from their eyes?" Does "begin to fall" mean something about a gradual process, rather than a single quick event? How do scales continue to remain in place, even as they "begin to fall?" What does that imply about the difficulty in overcoming errors because of false understanding or traditions? Even the remnant will struggle to fully remove the "scales of darkness."

Why are there "not many generations" involved in this process? Do you need "generations" to pass away in order to fully remove darkness?

Why is it not possible to accomplish this in a single generation?

---

376 D&C 50: 24: "That which is of God is light; and he that receiveth light, and continueth in God, receiveth more light; and that light groweth brighter and brighter until the perfect day."

377 2 Ne. 9: 41: "O then, my beloved brethren, come unto the Lord, the Holy One. Remember that his paths are righteous. Behold, the way for man is narrow, but it lieth in a straight course before him, and the keeper of the gate is the Holy One of Israel; and he employeth no servant there; and there is none other way save it be by the gate; for he cannot be deceived, for the Lord God is his name."

If the Lord's purposes in redeeming the remnant will take "not many generations" then why do we think we can accomplish it in one? How gradual a process is involved?

What does it mean to become a "pure and delightsome people?" (For many editions of the Book of Mormon, this phrase used to be "white and delightsome." It was changed back to the original "pure" rather than "white" in the 1980 edition.)

Why does purity and being "delightsome" to the Lord go together?

If this process is going to involve "not many generations" then how far away are we from this unfolding?

When we read prophecy like this, we should realize we are looking at unfolding history from the Lord's perspective. We want to know what will happen in our single lifetime. We are impatient. He is interested in having us know the truth.

Nephi's prophecy gives us a perspective that helps put our own time into context. We are in a hurry. History is not. There is a great deal left to do. There is a great deal left to happen. Nephi is letting us see this lengthy agenda.

2 Nephi 30: 7-8

> **"And it shall come to pass that the Jews which are scattered also shall begin to believe in Christ; and they shall begin to gather in upon the face of the land; and as many as shall believe in Christ shall also become a delightsome people. And it shall come to pass that the Lord God shall commence his work among all nations, kindreds, tongues, and people, to bring about the restoration of his people upon the earth."**

Nephi has circled back and is reiterating his earlier prophecy, assuring us that this is the order, these are the priorities and this work is indeed universal.

The scattered Jews will begin to believe in Christ, and as they do they will be gathered again. These will also be among the people destined to become "delightsome" as a result of the Gospel.

Again, we have the reminder of the universal nature of this work. Every nation, kindred, tongue and people will be invited. The invitation is to result in a "restoration of His people upon the earth." That is, the purpose of the creation was to produce God's people. By and large that hasn't happened.

From the rebellion of Adam's children, through the almost universal rebellion at the time of Noah, mankind has been unwilling to become His people. The times when we find a "people of God" upon the earth is the exception, not the rule.

The desire to see Zion return is not the same thing as seeing its return.

I sometimes wonder if people who speak of Zion have any clue of the tremendous gulf between what that will require and who we are as a people. Having a vocabulary is not the same thing as having the heart to produce Zion.

How do people live with one another in peace? Without any poor among them? While seeking the best interest of all, and without ambition. Why would we believe we can get that great task done in a short effort in our day? There is no precedent living in anything like Zion, in this or the last seven generations.

Having the Gospel understood is the first step, of course. As a group, there is such a poor command of the scriptures that we have some considerable study before us. Passing familiarity with some scriptures is not of much use. They are the standard given to us to help reveal the basis for becoming a covenant people.

I notice how the subject of "calling and election" gets mentioned from time to time. It would be better to learn about the fundamentals of the Gospel that we are not living than to attempt to understand what lies at the end of the struggle.

Losing ourselves implies something quite distant from the self-centered worry that grows out of not knowing your standing before God. The first step is to pray in sincerity, asking God to soften your heart that you may believe. The steps Nephi followed are described in first few chapters of *The Second Comforter*. Those steps are not given to us merely to contemplate. They are given for us to follow.

As we see Nephi wrapping up his two books of scripture, he turns to the distant view of a return upon the earth of a "people of God." We could have been that people. We even fancy ourselves as being likely to be among such a people. But if we lived that kind of life, we would already associate with such beings here, in the flesh. We would know we have part with them, because we would be associating with heaven now, as they will do then.

There is no one else who you need to look to other than the Lord. There is enough revealed in the Book of Mormon to tell you what you must do to become part of His people. You don't need me, or a program, or a leader, other than Christ. He has offered the opportunity for each of us to become part of His people.

2 Nephi 30: 9-10

> **"And with righteousness shall the Lord God judge the poor, and reprove with equity for the meek of the earth. And he shall smite the earth with the rod of his mouth; and with the breath of his lips shall he slay the wicked. For the time speedily cometh that the Lord God shall cause a great division among the people, and the wicked will he destroy; and he will spare his people, yea, even if it so be that he must destroy the wicked by fire."**

Nephi quotes Isaiah to weave a second witness into this end-of-times description of the Lord's agenda.

Righteousness for the poor. Equity for the meek. Smiting for the earth. Death to the wicked. For the poor, why "righteousness?" For the meek, why "equity?" For the earth, why shall it be "smitten?" What is the "rod of His mouth" to be used to smite the earth?

For the wicked, it is the "breath of His lips" which will slay. Have you considered what this means? Why His "breath" when that is the mechanism that brings life to Adam,[378] and the Spirit to His disciples?[379] Does the word "breath" imply the converse of bringing life, and the removal of the Holy Spirit? If so, how do those ideas affect the meaning of the Lord's decision to "slay the wicked?" In what sense will they be "slain?"

What does it mean that "the time speedily cometh?" From what point is the measure taken to decide the "speed" of His coming? Is it from Nephi's prophecy, or from the time in which the prophecy is set?

What does it mean there will be "caused a great division?" How would that "division" manifest itself? Is it first spiritual, then physical? Or is it both from the start? If it is first a great spiritual division, followed at some point in a physical gathering together of these two groups into separate locations, how would it unfold?

How will the wicked be "destroyed?"[380] Will they also be able to destroy the people whom the Lord identifies as "His people?"[381]

What does it mean that the Lord "will spare His people, yea, even if it so be that He must destroy the wicked by fire?" Is that true? Would the Lord personally intervene to protect His people? Has He done anything like that before? If so, when? Why? Can He still do that today? In a time of tremendous upheaval and destruction, can He selectively

---

[378] Gen. 2: 7: "And the Lord God formed man *of* the dust of the ground, and breathed into his nostrils the breath of life; and man became a living soul."

[379] John 20: 22: "And when he had said this, he breathed on *them,* and saith unto them, Receive ye the Holy Ghost:"

[380] Mormon 4: 5: "But, behold, the judgments of God will overtake the wicked; and it is by the wicked that the wicked are punished; for it is the wicked that stir up the hearts of the children of men unto bloodshed."

[381] 1 Ne. 22: 16: "For the time soon cometh that the fulness of the wrath of God shall be poured out upon all the children of men; for he will not suffer that the wicked shall destroy the righteous."

preserve His people?[382] What protection is there from such forces of destruction?

Have you noticed how things seem to be speeding up? Business cycles that used to take generations now play themselves out in a few years. Political dynasties are crumbling and institutions which were once impervious to change are being forced to change. Cultural norms

---

382 3 Ne. 9: 1-13: "And it came to pass that there was a voice heard among all the inhabitants of the earth, upon all the face of this land, crying: Wo, wo, wo unto this people; wo unto the inhabitants of the whole earth except they shall repent; for the devil laugheth, and his angels rejoice, because of the slain of the fair sons and daughters of my people; and it is because of their iniquity and abominations that they are fallen! Behold, that great city Zarahemla have I burned with fire, and the inhabitants thereof. And behold, that great city Moroni have I caused to be sunk in the depths of the sea, and the inhabitants thereof to be drowned. And behold, that great city Moronihah have I covered with earth, and the inhabitants thereof, to hide their iniquities and their abominations from before my face, that the blood of the prophets and the saints shall not come any more unto me against them. And behold, the city of Gilgal have I caused to be sunk, and the inhabitants thereof to be buried up in the depths of the earth; Yea, and the city of Onihah and the inhabitants thereof, and the city of Mocum and the inhabitants thereof, and the city of Jerusalem and the inhabitants thereof; and waters have I caused to come up in the stead thereof, to hide their wickedness and abominations from before my face, that the blood of the prophets and the saints shall not come up any more unto me against them. And behold, the city of Gadiandi, and the city of Gadiomnah, and the city of Jacob, and the city of Gimgimno, all these have I caused to be sunk, and made hills and valleys in the places thereof; and the inhabitants thereof have I buried up in the depths of the earth, to hide their wickedness and abominations from before my face, that the blood of the prophets and the saints should not come up any more unto me against them. And behold, that great city Jacobugath, which was inhabited by the people of king Jacob, have I caused to be burned with fire because of their sins and their wickedness, which was above all the wickedness of the whole earth, because of their secret murders and combinations; for it was they that did destroy the peace of my people and the government of the land; therefore I did cause them to be burned, to destroy them from before my face, that the blood of the prophets and the saints should not come up unto me any more against them. And behold, the city of Laman, and the city of Josh, and the city of Gad, and the city of Kishkumen, have I caused to be burned with fire, and the inhabitants thereof, because of their wickedness in casting out the prophets, and stoning those whom I did send to declare unto them concerning their wickedness and their abominations. And because they did cast them all out, that there were none righteous among them, I did send down fire and destroy them, that their wickedness and abominations might be hid from before my face, that the blood of the prophets and the saints whom I sent among them might not cry unto me from the ground against them. And many great destructions have I caused to come upon this land, and upon this people, because of their wickedness and their abominations. O all ye that are spared because ye were more righteous than they, will ye not now return unto me, and repent of your sins, and be converted, that I may heal you?"

are changing so quickly that change is itself the new culture. The days seem to be shortening, don't they.[383]

2 Nephi 30: 11-15

> **"And righteousness shall be the girdle of his loins, and faithfulness the girdle of his reins. And then shall the wolf dwell with the lamb; and the leopard shall lie down with the kid, and the calf, and the young lion, and the fatling, together; and a little child shall lead them. And the cow and the bear shall feed; their young ones shall lie down together; and the lion shall eat straw like the ox. And the sucking child shall play on the hole of the asp, and the weaned child shall put his hand on the cockatrice's den. They shall not hurt nor destroy in all my holy mountain; for the earth shall be full of the knowledge of the Lord as the waters cover the sea."**

These words, again borrowed from Isaiah, are familiar to all of us. The time frame puts it inside the larger Nephi prophecy regarding the fulfillment of covenants made to the "fathers."

What is interesting for us is the narrative of end-of-times peace and return of righteousness. This includes a "people of God" returning to inhabit the earth set inside the Book of Mormon narrative prophecy. The Book of Mormon remnant figure centrally into the progression. It (the book) comes forth, and from that time until the fulfillment of the return of righteousness and peace, the book's involvement is central. The gentiles receive custody of it. Don't do much with it. Some few actually believe it. They will eventually take it to the remnant. The remnant begin to come onboard with their conversion. They increase, the gentiles decrease, the momentum builds. The gentiles ultimately get swept away, while the remnant begin to grow into the fullness of the Gospel in all its rights, ordinances, and return to the knowledge of Christ.

As the culmination of these trends, which begin small, but gain momentum as they roll forth, we see the final product for what it was always intended to become: Zion. Once the stone cut out of the mountain without hands begins to roll forth, it will not stop until it has filled the whole earth.

Among those who are destined to fulfill these events, they will "not hurt nor destroy in all" the Lord's "holy mountain." What does it mean to "not hurt?" What does it mean to "not destroy?" Why a "holy mountain?"

The earth itself will be "full of the knowledge of the Lord as the waters cover the sea." What "knowledge of the Lord" is referred to

---

383 Matt. 24: 22: "And except those days should be shortened, there should no flesh be saved: but for the elect's sake those days shall be shortened."
JS-Matt. 1: 20: "And except those days should be shortened, there should none of their flesh be saved; but for the elect's sake, according to the covenant, those days shall be shortened."

here? How completely does the water cover the sea? Will there be any need for one man to say to another "know ye the Lord" in that day, or will all who remain know Him?[384]

We imagine that day, but do not live for it. We think ourselves qualified to be part of that group. But ask yourself, do you make others hurt? Do others who hurt find relief from their pain by what you are willing to suffer, without returning evil for evil, but good for evil? Or do you believe such ideas to be "weird?" Because they are, indeed, for all we do, all we say, all we live and all we are, so alien to us that they are weird indeed.

From inside that culture, looking back at us and our time, reading our foolishness, observing our entertainment, they will think us more than "weird." They will think us utterly insane. And they will be right. We are the madmen, claiming ourselves to be righteous, while dwelling in raw sewage and celebrating revenge, discord, hatred and anger. We speak of Zion while marketing Babylon. We ask "what will sell" before we undertake any project. We study the trends of the fallen, wicked and perverse in order to adapt our faith, our words, and our conversations to appeal to Babylon. The social statistics of Latter-day Saints run about 7 years behind the larger population.

We're all headed to hell, but console ourselves that we remain "peculiar" because we are slower in our descent than the larger population. It never occurs to us that a complete break will be needed.

The Lord plans to provide that break. The question then will be whether we join with those who lament the fall of Babylon[385], or among

---

384 Jer. 31: 34: "And they shall teach no more every man his neighbour, and every man his brother, saying, Know the Lord: for they shall all know me, from the least of them unto the greatest of them, saith the Lord: for I will forgive their iniquity, and I will remember their sin no more."
D&C 84: 96-99: "For I, the Almighty, have laid my hands upon the nations, to scourge them for their wickedness. And plagues shall go forth, and they shall not be taken from the earth until I have completed my work, which shall be cut short in righteousness—Until all shall know me, who remain, even from the least unto the greatest, and shall be filled with the knowledge of the Lord, and shall see eye to eye, and shall lift up their voice, and with the voice together sing this new song, saying:
The Lord hath brought again Zion;
The Lord hath redeemed his people, Israel,
According to the election of grace,
Which was brought to pass by the faith
And covenant of their fathers."

385 Rev. 18: 9-11: "And the kings of the earth, who have committed fornication and lived deliciously with her, shall bewail her, and lament for her, when they shall see the smoke of her burning, Standing afar off for the fear of her torment, saying, Alas, alas, that great city Babylon, that mighty city! for in one hour is thy judgment come. And the merchants of the earth shall weep and mourn over her; for no man buyeth their merchandise any more:"

those who will rejoice at the coming of Zion[386] Perspective is affected by what our hearts value. Unfortunately, the choice is "either-or," and not both.[387]

Well this is indeed "getting weird"...

2 Nephi 30: 16-17

> **"Wherefore, the things of all nations shall be made known; yea, all things shall be made known unto the children of men. There is nothing which is secret save it shall be revealed; there is no work of darkness save it shall be made manifest in the light; and there is nothing which is sealed upon the earth save it shall be loosed."**

This is another confirmation by Nephi of what was written before. The Nephites will have the records of the Jews and lost tribes of Israel, and the Jews and the lost tribes will have the records of the Nephites. "The things of all nations" will include these various Divine messages and teachings given to the various nations/people of the earth. The "children of men" in that day will have available to them the records that allow them to see how the knowledge of the Lord will cover the earth as the waters cover the sea. They will realize that these distant

---

[386] D&C 84: 96-102: "For I, the Almighty, have laid my hands upon the nations, to scourge them for their wickedness. And plagues shall go forth, and they shall not be taken from the earth until I have completed my work, which shall be cut short in righteousness—Until all shall know me, who remain, even from the least unto the greatest, and shall be filled with the knowledge of the Lord, and shall see eye to eye, and shall lift up their voice, and with the voice together sing this new song, saying:
The Lord hath brought again Zion;
The Lord hath redeemed his people, Israel,
According to the election of grace,
Which was brought to pass by the faith
And covenant of their fathers.
The Lord hath redeemed his people;
And Satan is bound and time is no longer.
The Lord hath gathered all things in one.
The Lord hath brought down Zion from above.
The Lord hath brought up Zion from beneath.
The earth hath travailed and brought forth her strength;
And truth is established in her bowels;
And the heavens have smiled upon her;
And she is clothed with the glory of her God;
For he stands in the midst of his people.
Glory, and honor, and power, and might,
Be ascribed to our God; for he is full of mercy,
Justice, grace and truth, and peace,
Forever and ever, Amen."

[387] Luke 16: 13: "No servant can serve two masters: for either he will hate the one, and love the other; or else he will hold to the one, and despise the other. Ye cannot serve God and mammon."

echoes of the Gospel which appear in other faiths, traditions and sacred texts were, at one time, an authentic communication from the Lord or His servants.

So much of what appears to contradict will be found to have a common root. The things that have been sealed and kept from public discourse will become part of the public dialogue. We will not have the same requirement for "secrets" to be kept. But "nothing which is secret" will remain so. It will all "be revealed."

When the truth is unsealed, so are the conspiracies, the foolishness and the ambitions that have worked to keep the truth from becoming known. None of the "work of darkness" which has been afoot will be kept from public view, but "it shall be manifest in the light." Whatever excuses men have had to suppress the truth, deny the Spirit, and employ the "arm of flesh" as their guide will be exposed for what they are. They will put on display. The wisdom of the wise will be seen for the foolishness it was. The strength of man's arm, the studied foolishness gained from social sciences, opinion polling, focus groups and other attempts to figure out where the ignorant are going and jump in front of the trend to feign leadership, will be seen for what it was. The endless praise and adoration given to these foolish and weak political, governmental, business, educational and "moral" leaders will be seen for what it was.

Oh the wisdom of God and the foolishness of men! When men are educated they think they are wise.[388] All the studied ignorance of men will be recognized as foolishness, rather than as wisdom as it is now.[389] Then the fools will at last shut their mouths and cease to thunder out their errors.[390]

You can almost feel Nephi's relief as he contemplates this outcome. The final vindication of the truth. The final conquest of the foolishness of men. It is consoling to consider that this odd and corrupt world we find ourselves in will at some point finally end. The truth will be vindicated. The errors and evil we enshrine in our institutions and art will collapse. We will emerge from behind the scales of darkness covering our eyes and at last see things as they are in the light of heaven.

---

388 2 Ne. 9: 28: "O that cunning plan of the evil one! O the vainness, and the frailties, and the foolishness of men! When they are learned they think they are wise, and they hearken not unto the counsel of God, for they set it aside, supposing they know of themselves, wherefore, their wisdom is foolishness and it profiteth them not. And they shall perish."

389 1 Cor. 3: 19: "For the wisdom of this world is foolishness with God. For it is written, He taketh the wise in their own craftiness."

390 Isa. 52: 15: "So shall he sprinkle many nations; the kings shall shut their mouths at him: for *that* which had not been told them shall they see; and *that* which they had not heard shall they consider."

…I'm thinking the most common reaction will be "oops" or some four letter equivalent…

You realize you can fix that today, right? You know the Gospel intends to take you out of this fallen world and into that kind of light even now, right? That was what Christ was trying to do all along. That is why He's provided the scriptures (primarily the Book of Mormon for us) to help us catch on before the terrible end is upon us. So you can do something about all this.

Or you can think it just "weird," remain as you are, and enjoy the decline. 'Cuz lotsa folks is do'in just that, ya know…

2 Nephi 30: 18

> **"Wherefore, all things which have been revealed unto the children of men shall at that day be revealed; and Satan shall have power over the hearts of the children of men no more, for a long time. And now, my beloved brethren, I make an end of my sayings."**

The truth will be revealed. But truth of this nature will involve something else. Satan will have no power. When we gather enough light and truth, Satan's influence and power ends. We find that Satan is "cast out" because he can no longer deceive.

His primary tool is the lie. When there is enough truth, there is no longer any reason to believe or teach a lie. Therefore, he has lost power.

His secondary tool is the lusts and appetites of the flesh. When these are controlled, he is rendered completely ineffective. He is bound.

Once the lies are exposed and the appetites of the flesh are subdued, the hearts of men are freed from captivity. Nephi is describing a future day when this will be the the common situation for mankind.

Of course, this doesn't have to be a future day. It is possible to gain enough light and truth today so the lies are exposed to your view. It is also possible to subdue the appetites of the flesh. In any event, the desires, appetites and passions ought to be kept within the bounds which the Lord prescribes. We say that, but we don't often do that. Most people are not willing to actually subdue their desires, passions and appetites. It seems weird to suppress the desire for revenge, to actually turn the other cheek, and to return good for evil. In short, it would appear the Savior's conduct in willingly going to His death without accepting Peter's offer to use the sword in His defense was a bit nutty. At least from the perspective of the damned. (They can't even stop watching pornography. Latter-day "**Saint**" indeed. What's saintly about the vengeful, lustful, and gluttonous? But that's an aside…)

Binding Satan so he has no "power over the hearts of the children of men" is an interesting phrase. Why "power?" Why "power over the hearts?" Why "children of men" rather than sons of God? (See the dialogue between Moses and Satan where Moses refers to himself as a "son of God" but Satan calls him a "son of man" in Moses 1: 12-13.)[391] Isn't that interesting?

Why is it that such power over the hearts of the children of men will be lost? It is as if entry into a Terrestrial World will bring about the binding of Satan, even before becoming a "son of God," and beginning the final journey into the Lord's presence. This is interesting—as if Nephi understood the Temple itself.[392]

Satan's power is lost for a "long time" but not forever. Why? How will Satan be loosed again?[393] I've described this event and the reasons in "The Great Competition" in *Ten Parables*.

The final phrase is because Nephi was through with his message for a while. He may have intended to take his writing up again, but the final phrase indicates he was done for the time. We cannot tell how long it was between the last verse of Chapter 30 and the first verse of Chapter 31. When he takes up his writing again, he is clearly ending his ministry. How long he took to compose his final thoughts is undisclosed. But this will be an old man, finishing his mortal warning to us.

---

[391] Moses 1: 12-13: "And it came to pass that when Moses had said these words, behold, Satan came tempting him, saying: Moses, son of man, worship me. And it came to pass that Moses looked upon Satan and said: Who art thou? For behold, I am a son of God, in the similitude of his Only Begotten; and where is thy glory, that I should worship thee?"

[392] 2 Ne. 5: 16: "And I, Nephi, did build a temple; and I did construct it after the manner of the temple of Solomon save it were not built of so many precious things; for they were not to be found upon the land, wherefore, it could not be built like unto Solomon's temple. But the manner of the construction was like unto the temple of Solomon; and the workmanship thereof was exceedingly fine."

[393] Rev. 20: 7: "And when the thousand years are expired, Satan shall be loosed out of his prison,"
D&C 43: 31: "For Satan shall be bound, and when he is loosed again he shall only reign for a little season, and then cometh the end of the earth."
D&C 88: 110: "And so on, until the seventh angel shall sound his trump; and he shall stand forth upon the land and upon the sea, and swear in the name of him who sitteth upon the throne, that there shall be time no longer; and Satan shall be bound, that old serpent, who is called the devil, and shall not be loosed for the space of a thousand years."

2 NEPHI 31

2 Nephi 31: 1

> **"And now I, Nephi, make an end of my prophesying unto you, my beloved brethren. And I cannot write but a few things, which I know must surely come to pass; neither can I write but a few of the words of my brother Jacob."**

Don't make any mistakes, Nephi was a prophet. He knew he was a prophet. He also knew his testimony and explanations were indeed prophesy. So, in case you were wondering, here he removes any doubt. He is "making an end of my prophesying unto you." And he identifies "you" to mean his "beloved brethren." Who would that be? Could gentiles be included as his "beloved brethren?" What would a gentile have to do or be in order to qualify for that description? Then why aren't you doing that?

Why "cannot" he "write but a few things" further? Is there a limit put upon his prophecy for us?[394] Would he have liked to have said more? Does he assure us what he did write is true and complete as far as permitted to be written?[395]

What does it mean that he knows it "must surely come to pass?" How can he know that? What does it mean about the information we have in his record? How closely was the information given in conformity with what the Lord wanted him to reveal? How seriously should we take the record or prophecy of Nephi?

---

394 1 Ne. 14: 28: "And behold, I, Nephi, am forbidden that I should write the remainder of the things which I saw and heard; wherefore the things which I have written sufficeth me; and I have written but a small part of the things which I saw."

395 1 Ne. 14: 30: "And now I make an end of speaking concerning the things which I saw while I was carried away in the spirit; and if all the things which I saw are not written, the things which I have written are true. And thus it is. Amen."

Why does Nephi refer again to his brother Jacob? What did Nephi and Jacob have in common in their faith and knowledge?[396] What does this imply about the validity of their testimony, their prophecy, their commission to deliver words of warning? What level of attention should their words attract from us? If we give them strict heed, will they lead us in the way of life and salvation?

As he ends his record, an aging and dying prophet, whose journey began on another continent is pleading to us to save ourselves. He has been such a significant source of faith in moments of despair, that when the Lord was reminding Joseph Smith of faith in troubled times, He drew directly from Nephi's life. Joseph was in Liberty Jail, abandoned by force of arms by his people, who had been evicted from Missouri. The governor had ordered the extermination of Mormons if they remained. Joseph's people had been killed, mobbed, evicted, driven in the snow from Missouri, their property pillaged, their women abused, and their houses burned. In a dungeon cell, Joseph was lamenting his plight. He felt abandoned by the Saints, and by God. As he pled for relief, the Lord told him to face adversity without complaint, because it would ultimately be for his good. When the Lord spoke and reminded Joseph of moments of despair over which faith and hope triumphed, one of the moments used was taken from Nephi's life:

"if the billowing surge conspire against thee; if fierce winds become thine enemy; if the heavens gather blackness, and all the elements combine to hedge up the way; and above all, if the very jaws of hell shall gape open the mouth wide after thee, know thou, my son, that all these things shall give thee experience, and shall be for thy good."[397]

---

[396] 2 Ne. 11: 2-3: "And now I, Nephi, write more of the words of Isaiah, for my soul delighteth in his words. For I will liken his words unto my people, and I will send them forth unto all my children, for he verily saw my Redeemer, even as I have seen him. And my brother, Jacob, also has seen him as I have seen him; wherefore, I will send their words forth unto my children to prove unto them that my words are true. Wherefore, by the words of three, God hath said, I will establish my word. Nevertheless, God sendeth more witnesses, and he proveth all his words."

[397] 1 Ne. 18: 13-16: "Wherefore, they knew not whither they should steer the ship, insomuch that there arose a great storm, yea, a great and terrible tempest, and we were driven back upon the waters for the space of three days; and they began to be frightened exceedingly lest they should be drowned in the sea; nevertheless they did not loose me. And on the fourth day, which we had been driven back, the tempest began to be exceedingly sore. And it came to pass that we were about to be swallowed up in the depths of the sea. And after we had been driven back upon the waters for the space of four days, my brethren began to see that the judgments of God were upon them, and that they must perish save that they should repent of their iniquities; wherefore, they came unto me, and loosed the bands which were upon my wrists, and behold they had swollen exceedingly; and also mine ankles were much swollen, and great was the soreness thereof. Nevertheless, I did look unto my God, and I did praise him all the day long; and I did not murmur against the Lord because of mine afflictions."

It was no accident that the 116 pages were lost, compelling the use of Nephi's full record to begin the Book of Mormon. It was a "wise purpose" indeed.[398] These words were always destined to come to us unabridged, from the hand of Nephi unaltered, translated by the gift and power of God into our language by Joseph Smith. Now they confront us, inform us, elevate us, warn us and deliver to us the means of obtaining the fullness of the Gospel of Jesus Christ.

2 Nephi 31: 2

> **"Wherefore, the things which I have written sufficeth me, save it be a few words which I must speak concerning the doctrine of Christ; wherefore, I shall speak unto you plainly, according to the plainness of my prophesying."**

Nephi has been pondering for over four decades about the great revelations given to him in the Arabian Peninsula.[399] His creation of, and inscription on the plates were after these long deliberations and reflections.

When he says "the things which I have written sufficeth me," he is putting a punctuation mark on his plates. He is saying he has finished his ministry, finished his prophecy. He has refined and set out his message in a deliberate, careful way. These books of Nephi are not internet blogs undertaken daily. They are not rapid-fire responses, nor stream-of-consciousness statements. They were planned for the ages. Born from pondering, inspired by revelation, described as prophecy by the author, and filled with light and truth if considered with care by any reader. Nephi's pronouncement that they "sufficeth me" is a powerful statement by an aging prophet.

Years of preparation and reflection allow him to "speak plainly" to us. There's no need to be vague. No reason to hide our plight from us. He wants us to understand. When he attempts to "speak unto you plainly, according to the plainness of my prophesying," we read into it the wrong definitions, associate his words with others who will never read the book, and consider ourselves blessed and vindicated instead of condemned, and called to repentance. We do that a lot. What good is it to read things which tell you to be proud? Why follow a religion that tells you you've no reason to repent? Everyone but you is going to hell,

---

[398] Words of Mormon 1: 6-7: "And it came to pass that I, being *eleven years old, was carried by my father into the land southward, even to the land of Zarahemla. The whole face of the land had become covered with buildings, and the people were as numerous almost, as it were the sand of the sea."

[399] 2 Ne. 4: 16: "Behold, my soul delighteth in the things of the Lord; and my heart pondereth continually upon the things which I have seen and heard."
2 Ne. 5: 34: "And it sufficeth me to say that *forty years had passed away, and we had already had wars and contentions with our brethren."

right?[400] (Alma 31: 17-18.) Because so long as you remain affiliated with the broad mainstream of your church, God will save you. And if there's any hint of error, He will beat you with a few stripes and all will be well. Nephi has already condemned that as an error, hasn't he?[401]

If his words were plain and intended to be taken at face value, why read into them justification for yourself and your sins? Why think they condemn everyone but you? Why are they speaking in disparaging terms about **those who will never have the book**? Why did Nephi write a book **condemning only those who will never read it**? Surely, if he was in fact "plain" in his meaning, then we ought not read anything into it other than what it says and how it says it. **It must be a message to us**.

If it is addressed to us, then we have more than one "wo" pronounced upon us by Nephi. We have been warned. We need to change what we are doing. The gentiles with whom we are identified[402] are collectively condemned. We need to separate ourselves by our behavior from theirs. We need to repent.

Now, just in case you think, as a recent comment has asserted, that the Lord has sent another message vindicating us as a collective gentile body/church in D&C 1: 30,[403], I would remind you that revelation came from the Lord in 1831. In the following year the Lord gave

---

[400] Alma 31: 17-18: "But thou art the same yesterday, today, and forever; and thou hast elected us that we shall be saved, whilst all around us are elected to be cast by thy wrath down to hell; for the which holiness, O God, we thank thee; and we also thank thee that thou hast elected us, that we may not be led away after the foolish traditions of our brethren, which doth bind them down to a belief of Christ, which doth lead their hearts to wander far from thee, our God. And again we thank thee, O God, that we are a chosen and a holy people. Amen."

[401] 2 Ne. 28: 8: "And there shall also be many which shall say: Eat, drink, and be merry; nevertheless, fear God—he will justify in committing a little sin; yea, lie a little, take the advantage of one because of his words, dig a pit for thy neighbor; there is no harm in this; and do all these things, for tomorrow we die; and if it so be that we are guilty, God will beat us with a few stripes, and at last we shall be saved in the kingdom of God."

[402] D&C 109: 60: "Now these words, O Lord, we have spoken before thee, concerning the revelations and commandments which thou hast given unto us, who are identified with the Gentiles."

[403] D&C 1: 30: "And also those to whom these commandments were given, might have power to lay the foundation of this church, and to bring it forth out of obscurity and out of darkness, the only true and living church upon the face of the whole earth, with which I, the Lord, am well pleased, speaking unto the church collectively and not individually—"

another revelation that put the church under condemnation.[404] We know that condemnation was not lifted, because of comments by President Benson and Elder Oaks.

More troubling still is the Lord's threat to reject the gentile church altogether in January of 1841 if the church did not follow His strict appointment and complete building a temple in the time He provided.[405] The warning was given that even if the temple were built, we would still be condemned if we failed to do what He said.[406]

Did we keep the appointment given us? The Nauvoo Temple was not completed before Joseph Smith died. The endowment was not completed by Joseph, but Brigham Young was told he had to finish it.[407] Did we keep the appointment? Have we been able to avoid being rejected as a church? Have our covenants been fulfilled?

Why do we repeat endlessly the praise from 1831 but ignore the threatened rejection that came in 1841? From January of 1841, until Joseph's death in June of 1844, we had three and a half years to complete the Nauvoo Temple. Was that "sufficient time" to do what was required of us? If so, we did not complete it. Why was Joseph taken? Was that any indication about when the "sufficient time" expired? If so, what then? Where would that leave us?

Is our best hope to be found in the messages and warnings of the Book of Mormon? Can there be gentiles found who will believe its message? How carefully ought we study it?

Did you know the church had almost no use for the Book of Mormon until Hugh Nibley's efforts? (You know that if you've read *Eighteen*

---

[404] D&C 84: 54-58: "And your minds in times past have been darkened because of unbelief, and because you have treated lightly the things you have received—Which vanity and unbelief have brought the whole church under condemnation. And this condemnation resteth upon the children of Zion, even all. And they shall remain under this condemnation until they repent and remember the new covenant, even the Book of Mormon and the former commandments which I have given them, not only to say, but to do according to that which I have written—That they may bring forth fruit meet for their Father's kingdom; otherwise there remaineth a scourge and judgment to be poured out upon the children of Zion."

[405] D&C 124: 31-32: "But I command you, all ye my saints, to build a house unto me; and I grant unto you a sufficient time to build a house unto me; and during this time your baptisms shall be acceptable unto me. But behold, at the end of this appointment your baptisms for your dead shall not be acceptable unto me; and if you do not these things at the end of the appointment ye shall be rejected as a church, with your dead, saith the Lord your God."

[406] D&C 124: 47-48: "And it shall come to pass that if you build a house unto my name, and do not do the things that I say, I will not perform the oath which I make unto you, neither fulfil the promises which ye expect at my hands, saith the Lord. For instead of blessings, ye, by your own works, bring cursings, wrath, indignation, and judgments upon your own heads, by your follies, and by all your abominations, which you practise before me, saith the Lord."

[407] See previous commentary on 1 Ne. 13: 33-34.

Verses.) Hugh Nibley, by his efforts beginning in the 1950's, practically discovered the Book of Mormon for the church. He's gone now.

Even though Moses was taken from ancient Israel, and with him the authority of the priesthood,[408] the ancient Israelites remained the Lord's people. He still worked through them and sent them messengers from time to time. These messengers were rarely the High Priest. Although in Samuel's case he displaced the High Priest.[409] They were sent from time to time. Their qualifications were private, as the Lord told Moses they would be.[410] I have no doubt Hugh Nibley was sent to us. If you've paid close attention, his departure has created an intellectual collapse at the

---

408 D&C 84: 25-26: "Therefore, he took Moses out of their midst, and the Holy Priesthood also; And the lesser priesthood continued, which priesthood holdeth the key of the ministering of angels and the preparatory gospel;"

409 1 Sam. 3: 1-21: "And the child Samuel ministered unto the Lord before Eli. And the word of the Lord was precious in those days; *there was* no open vision. And it came to pass at that time, when Eli *was* laid down in his place, and his eyes began to wax dim, *that* he could not see; And ere the lamp of God went out in the temple of the Lord, where the ark of God *was,* and Samuel was laid down *to sleep;* That the Lord called Samuel: and he answered, Here *am* I. And he ran unto Eli, and said, Here *am* I; for thou calledst me. And he said, I called not; lie down again. And he went and lay down. And the Lord called yet again, Samuel. And Samuel arose and went to Eli, and said, Here *am* I; for thou didst call me. And he answered, I called not, my son; lie down again. Now Samuel did not yet know the Lord, neither was the word of the Lord yet revealed unto him. And the Lord called Samuel again the third time. And he arose and went to Eli, and said, Here *am* I; for thou didst call me. And Eli perceived that the Lord had called the child. Therefore Eli said unto Samuel, Go, lie down: and it shall be, if he call thee, that thou shalt say, Speak, Lord; for thy servant heareth. So Samuel went and lay down in his place. And the Lord came, and stood, and called as at other times, Samuel, Samuel. Then Samuel answered, Speak; for thy servant heareth. And the Lord said to Samuel, Behold, I will do a thing in Israel, at which both the ears of every one that heareth it shall tingle. In that day I will perform against Eli all *things* which I have spoken concerning his house: when I begin, I will also make an end. For I have told him that I will judge his house for ever for the iniquity which he knoweth; because his sons made themselves vile, and he restrained them not. And therefore I have sworn unto the house of Eli, that the iniquity of Eli's house shall not be purged with sacrifice nor offering for ever. And Samuel lay until the morning, and opened the doors of the house of the Lord. And Samuel feared to shew Eli the vision. Then Eli called Samuel, and said, Samuel, my son. And he answered, Here *am* I. And he said, What *is* the thing that *the Lord* hath said unto thee? I pray thee hide *it* not from me: God do so to thee, and more also, if thou hide *any* thing from me of all the things that he said unto thee. And Samuel told him every whit, and hid nothing from him. And he said, It *is* the Lord: let him do what seemeth him good. And Samuel grew, and the Lord was with him, and did let none of his words fall to the ground. And all Israel from Dan even to Beer-sheba knew that Samuel *was* established *to be* a prophet of the Lord. And the Lord appeared again in Shiloh: for the Lord revealed himself to Samuel in Shiloh by the word of the Lord."

410 Num. 12: 6: "And he said, Hear now my words: If there be a prophet among you, *I* the Lord will make myself known unto him in a vision, *and* will speak unto him in a dream."

center of the faith, with various egos contending to be noticed. They aspire to put upon them Hugh Nibley's mantle. They are not made of the same stuff, called with the same calling, nor endowed with the same capacities.

I doubt we'll see someone like him again. Perhaps we may someday see someone with an equally important message, but among those born in this dispensation, there is none to compare to Brother Nibley.

2 Nephi 31: 3

"For my soul delighteth in plainness; for after this manner doth the Lord God work among the children of men. For the Lord God giveth light unto the understanding; for he speaketh unto men according to their language, unto their understanding."

This raises an interesting side issue. Nephi's explanation of how God speaks to different people "according to their language" is something worth explaining. We have a great example in the visit of John the Baptist to Joseph and Oliver found in JS-H 1: 68-70 and Oliver's account in the footnote there[411]. The language they quote from John the Baptist is phrased differently by each of them, although both are quoting the angel. Angel's leave an impression. Notwithstanding Joseph Fielding Smith's teaching that memory from such things fade with time, my experience tells me quite the contrary. Such things are distinct and memorable. Often, if you need to hear a quote, the person who received it can quote word-for-word what they were told many years later; particularly when the quote is a declarative statement of what is to be or what is conferred. When, therefore, Joseph and Oliver give two different accounts of the quote, I understand this not to be a contradiction, but an example of the thing Nephi is referring to in this verse.

The communication of angels is not usually verbal in the traditional sense of verbal communication. That is, no air is being vibrated. Rather, the form the communication takes is for the angel to "speak" by delivering to the mind of the person spoken to the concept or declaration to be understood. Then the person, receiving the concept or declaration

---

[411] JS-H 1: 68-70: "We still continued the work of translation, when, in the ensuing month (May, 1829), we on a certain day went into the woods to pray and inquire of the Lord respecting baptism for the remission of sins, that we found mentioned in the translation of the plates. While we were thus employed, praying and calling upon the Lord, a messenger from heaven descended in a cloud of light, and having laid his hands upon us, he ordained us, saying: *Upon you my fellow servants, in the name of Messiah, I confer the Priesthood of Aaron, which holds the keys of the ministering of angels, and of the gospel of repentance, and of baptism by immersion for the remission of sins; and this shall never be taken again from the earth until the sons of Levi do offer again an offering unto the Lord in righteousness.* He said this Aaronic Priesthood had not the power of laying on hands for the gift of the Holy Ghost, but that this should be conferred on us hereafter; and he commanded us to go and be baptized, and gave us directions that I should baptize Oliver Cowdery, and that afterwards he should baptize me."

into their mind, is obliged to convert into words the message received. If the vocabulary of the recipient is German, they will use German to reduce the message to words. If English, they will use English. If their vocabulary is rich and complex, the words may be more exact. If their vocabulary is simple, the words may be simple.

However one comes into the presence of God or His angelic ministers, once there, the thoughts that come to the person will conform to their understanding, their vocabulary, their manner of phrasing. The underlying purpose is always the same: to make the communication plain to the understanding of the person visited.

It is also true that the Lord "giveth light unto the understanding" and does so according to the heed and diligence we give to what we have already received.[412] We cannot understand some things even if they are explained to us if we do not have the necessary light to permit that understanding. Light and truth attract one another.

When we approach God, we do so by degrees not merely by study. We find ourselves gaining light that quickens our understanding. What we cannot understand at first, gains clarity only after a period of living true to the things we already have.

The commandments are not something we follow to please God, but something we do to understand God. Living true to what we believe He expects of us, allows us to gain an appreciation for what kind of Being He truly is. In that sense, the commandments are not so much burdens to bear, but revelations to understand.

The greatest understanding, of course, does not lie in strict conformity to the letter of any law or commandment, but the insight obtained from the underlying principle you discover as you follow it. Commandments should soften or break your heart, not harden it. When a commandment hardens the heart of the follower, they have misunderstood the commandment altogether. This was the case with the accusers of Christ, who followed the underlying intent with perfection, while breaking the superficial requirements regularly.

None of it will become "plain" to the follower until they have done and understood what the commandments were attempting to reveal to them. When, however, you encounter a Nephi, you have someone who now sees the issues plainly. It was meant for us all to see them plainly.

---

[412] Alma 12: 9: "And now Alma began to expound these things unto him, saying: It is given unto many to know the mysteries of God; nevertheless they are laid under a strict command that they shall not impart only according to the portion of his word which he doth grant unto the children of men, according to the heed and diligence which they give unto him.
D&C 50: 24: "That which is of God is light; and he that receiveth light, and continueth in God, receiveth more light; and that light groweth brighter and brighter until the perfect day."

2 Nephi 31: 4

"Wherefore, I would that ye should remember that I have spoken unto you concerning that prophet which the Lord showed unto me, that should baptize the Lamb of God, which should take away the sins of the world."

This puts us back into the narrative Nephi wrote much earlier in his first book. He described this in 1 Nephi 11: 27.[413] Although the Lord's mortal ministry was future, and separated by more than half-a-millennium, Nephi witnessed it. The Lord is able to make witnesses of His mortal ministry even of someone who lived at another time and place, as He has done with Nephi.

During that vision, Nephi saw more than the Lord's mortal ministry. He was shown the entire history of the world through the end of time. However, Nephi was only permitted to bear selective testimony of what he saw. Others were given responsibility for testifying to portions of what Nephi saw, but was not permitted to record. He saw it all. He was to record only some of what he saw. He was told at a certain point that the responsibility for recording it became John the Beloved's and not

[413] 1 Ne. 11: 27: "And I looked and beheld the Redeemer of the world, of whom my father had spoken; and I also beheld the prophet who should prepare the way before him. And the Lamb of God went forth and was baptized of him; and after he was baptized, I beheld the heavens open, and the Holy Ghost come down out of heaven and abide upon him in the form of a dove."

Nephi's.[414] Nephi saw it, John the Beloved saw it, and others, including Isaiah, also saw it.[415] I've explained this in *Nephi's Isaiah*.

Here Nephi returns to the Lord's baptism to begin an explanation of "the doctrine of Christ"[416] so that Nephi's testimony refocuses the reader on the path required for salvation. Since Nephi's primary reason for writing is to save others, he cannot finish without a final direct appeal for all to understand the "doctrine of Christ."

What is the difference between "the doctrine of Christ" and the "Gospel of Jesus Christ?" How do they relate to one another?

Here Nephi has linked together four distinct thoughts: First he has 1) already described the prophet which 2) the Lord had shown to Nephi. This was the earlier vision described above. That prophet 3) should baptize the Lamb of God during the Lord's mortal ministry. The Lord, who is the Lamb of God 4) should take away the sins of the world.

This is a specific time and setting. It involves a specific event and two persons: John the Baptist and Jesus Christ. Nephi has seen the event, and reminds us of it as a baseline from which to reconstruct the "doctrine of Christ."

Remember that the Jews who confronted John the Baptist did not ask him what ordinance he was performing. They did not ask why he was performing the ordinance. They only asked what authority permitted

---

[414] 1 Ne. 14: 19-28: "And I looked and beheld a man, and he was dressed in a white robe. And the angel said unto me: Behold one of the twelve apostles of the Lamb. Behold, he shall see and write the remainder of these things; yea, and also many things which have been. And he shall also write concerning the end of the world. Wherefore, the things which he shall write are just and true; and behold they are written in the book which thou beheld proceeding out of the mouth of the Jew; and at the time they proceeded out of the mouth of the Jew, or, at the time the book proceeded out of the mouth of the Jew, the things which were written were plain and pure, and most precious and easy to the understanding of all men. And behold, the things which this apostle of the Lamb shall write are many things which thou hast seen; and behold, the remainder shalt thou see. But the things which thou shalt see hereafter thou shalt not write; for the Lord God hath ordained the apostle of the Lamb of God that he should write them. And also others who have been, to them hath he shown all things, and they have written them; and they are sealed up to come forth in their purity, according to the truth which is in the Lamb, in the own due time of the Lord, unto the house of Israel. And I, Nephi, heard and bear record, that the name of the apostle of the Lamb was John, according to the word of the angel. And behold, I, Nephi, am forbidden that I should write the remainder of the things which I saw and heard; wherefore the things which I have written sufficeth me; and I have written but a small part of the things which I saw."

[415] 1 Ne. 14: 26: "And also others who have been, to them hath he shown all things, and they have written them; and they are sealed up to come forth in their purity, according to the truth which is in the Lamb, in the own due time of the Lord, unto the house of Israel."

[416] 2 Ne. 31: 2: "Wherefore, the things which I have written sufficeth me, save it be a few words which I must speak concerning the doctrine of Christ; wherefore, I shall speak unto you plainly, according to the plainness of my prophesying."

him to be performing an ordinance which they already understood and undoubtedly already practiced. Why would John baptize if he were not Christ, or Elias (in that context meaning Elijah), or another returning prophet who already had the authority.[417] The inquisitors already understood the ordinance.

Baptism was a pre-Christian ordinance. Because of historic interests which conflict with one another, both the Jews and the Christians downplay or ignore that truth.

Look at the wording above and ask yourself: Why, when the vision is shown to Nephi, is Christ identified as "the Lord?" Then, when Nephi beholds His baptism, why does he refer to Christ as "the Lamb of God?" The same person, at first identified as "the Lord," and then identified as "the Lamb of God." Why these two identities? Why would it be so clear to Nephi that the Lord holds these two identities that he would use them in this single verse to make Christ's identity and deeds clear to the reader? How do the different names/titles help us to better understand Christ?

Why is a pre-Christian prophet commissioned to know and write about these things? Why would the Nephite descendants from the time of this writing through the time of Moroni all be entitled to know about this event? What importance is it for us to understand this about Christ?

Well, let's push further into the "doctrine of Christ" to see what it may persuade us to do or believe.

2 Nephi 31: 5

> **"And now, if the Lamb of God, he being holy, should have need to be baptized by water, to fulfill all righteousness, O then, how much more need have we, being unholy, to be baptized, yea, even by water!"**

This is a missionary proof text, used to persuade everyone to get baptized. They used it on me. It worked. I got baptized.

How undeniably essential is baptism as a result of this argument? Does it seem to you that if Christ Himself needed to be baptized that

---

417 John 1: 19-28: "And this is the record of John, when the Jews sent priests and Levites from Jerusalem to ask him, Who art thou? And he confessed, and denied not; but confessed, I am not the Christ. And they asked him, What then? Art thou Elias? And he saith, I am not. Art thou that prophet? And he answered, No. Then said they unto him, Who art thou? that we may give an answer to them that sent us. What sayest thou of thyself? He said, I *am* the voice of one crying in the wilderness, Make straight the way of the Lord, as said the prophet Esaias. And they which were sent were of the Pharisees. And they asked him, and said unto him, Why baptizest thou then, if thou be not that Christ, nor Elias, neither that prophet? John answered them, saying, I baptize with water: but there standeth one among you, whom ye know not; He it is, who coming after me is preferred before me, whose shoe's latchet I am not worthy to unloose. These things were done in Bethabara beyond Jordan, where John was baptizing."

without it it would not be possible for anyone to please God? If Christ needed it, then undoubtedly all of Christ's inferiors need it as well. The only exception seems to be those children who are not accountable, and for whom Christ's atonement will be applied because of the justice and mercy applied to such unaccountable young souls.[418] They need no baptism. But all of us do. Without it we have no hope for redemption.

It is indisputable from this verse that baptism is essential. But the question remains "why?" Why would this ordinance be required for residing in God's presence in the eternal worlds? We know, of course, that all such matters were ordained before the foundation of the world, and cannot be changed now.[419] But that does not answer the question of "why?"

Have you ever inquired to know why? It is not answered in scripture. It is only implied. Sometimes the best place to look for an answer is to go back to the beginning. Reading the account of Adam's baptism (who was the first to receive the ordinance in mortality) we find a few things. By the water we keep the commandment.[420] The first man was taken by the Spirit and baptized, put under the water and brought forth out of the water again.[421] After he had been buried in the water and brought forth again, he was told he had been born again of the Spirit.[422] Before any of the ordinance happened, however, Adam was told this: *"behold, all things have their likeness, and all things are created and made to bear record of me, both things which are temporal, and things which are spiritual; things which are in the heavens above, and things which are on the earth, and things which are in the earth, and things which*

[418] Moroni 8: 20-22: "And he that saith that little children need baptism denieth the mercies of Christ, and setteth at naught the atonement of him and the power of his redemption. Wo unto such, for they are in danger of death, hell, and an endless torment. I speak it boldly; God hath commanded me. Listen unto them and give heed, or they stand against you at the judgment-seat of Christ. For behold that all little children are alive in Christ, and also all they that are without the law. For the power of redemption cometh on all them that have no law; wherefore, he that is not condemned, or he that is under no condemnation, cannot repent; and unto such baptism availeth nothing—"

[419] D&C 130: 20-21: "There is a law, irrevocably decreed in heaven before the foundations of this world, upon which all blessings are predicated—And when we obtain any blessing from God, it is by obedience to that law upon which it is predicated."

[420] Moses 6: 60: "For by the water ye keep the commandment; by the Spirit ye are justified, and by the blood ye are sanctified;"

[421] Moses 6: 64: "And it came to pass, when the Lord had spoken with Adam, our father, that Adam cried unto the Lord, and he was caught away by the Spirit of the Lord, and was carried down into the water, and was laid under the water, and was brought forth out of the water."

[422] Moses 6: 65: "And thus he was baptized, and the Spirit of God descended upon him, and thus he was born of the Spirit, and became quickened in the inner man."

are under the earth, both above and beneath: all things bear record of me." (Moses 6: 63.) Did you catch that?

Just before Adam's baptism the Lord explains to Adam that the reason for "all things" being as they are is "to bear record of me [meaning Christ]." Baptism is designed to bear testimony of Christ. How so? In what way does baptism tell us about Christ?

Christ died, was buried, and on the third day arose from the dead.[423] He said He would do that before His crucifixion.[424] His disciples did not understand this prophecy.[425]

Baptism is a reenactment of Christ's death and resurrection. Once you have been placed under the water you are cut off from the breath of life. If you remain under the water for too long, you will die. While there, you are only able to survive by holding your breath. You retain the power to live, if you return to the surface soon enough, but your life is dependent upon the one performing the ordinance. They must lift you back to return you to life. Just as Christ needed the power of His Father, we also need the power of the officiator to raise us back to life. It is as if the life of Christ has been beautifully choreographed. Christ was sent to lay down His life and take it up again. That is what He did. As Joseph Smith explained in the King Follett Discourse: "The scriptures inform us that Jesus said, as the Father hath power in himself, even so hath the Son power—to do what? Why, what the Father did. The answer is obvious—in a manner to lay down his body and take it up again. Jesus, what are you going to do? To lay down my life as my Father did, and take it up again. Do you believe it? If you do not believe it you do not believe the Bible. The scriptures say it, and I defy all the learning and wisdom and all the combined powers of earth and hell together to refute it. Here, then, is eternal life—to know the only wise and true God; and you have got to learn how to be gods yourselves, and to be kings and priests to God, the same as all gods have done before you, namely, by going from one small degree to another, and from a small capacity to a great one; from grace to grace, from exaltation to exaltation, until you attain to the resurrection of the dead, and are able to dwell in everlasting burnings, and to sit in glory, as do those who sit enthroned in everlasting power."

First we receive an ordinance which shows us the way by symbols. We are shown the way back to redemption and resurrection, but must

---

[423] D&C 20: 23: "He was crucified, died, and rose again the third day;"

[424] Mark 8: 31: "And he began to teach them, that the Son of man must suffer many things, and be rejected of the elders, and *of* the chief priests, and scribes, and be killed, and after three days rise again."
Luke 18: 33: "And they shall scourge *him,* and put him to death: and the third day he shall rise again."

[425] Luke 18: 34: "And they understood none of these things: and this saying was hid from them, neither knew they the things which were spoken."

see it with the eyes of faith, before we behold it as it truly is.[426] If we are to rise from the dead and have eternal life in Christ, we must first enact that event through the ordinance which points to the reality of our future rise from the dead.

Ordinances are the preliminary act, designed to bear testimony of the real event. They are not the real thing, but a "type" of the real thing. They must be seen through the eyes of faith[427] to allow us to gain the faith necessary to obtain the real thing. Before you are resurrected in a whole, complete and glorified fashion you must first voluntarily agree to enact that future event, looking forward in faith to that future day. Before you enter into the Lord's presence, you must first enact that in the Temple, looking forward in faith to that future day.

All things point to Christ. However, only those who have the faith to see within them the underlying reality with the "eyes of faith" will obtain to the final promises and covenants intended for all of us to obtain.

2 Nephi 31: 6-7

> **"And now, I would ask of you, my beloved brethren, wherein the Lamb of God did fulfill all righteousness in being baptized by water? Know ye not that he was holy? But notwithstanding he being holy, he showeth unto the children of men that, according to the flesh he humbleth himself before the Father, and witnesseth unto the Father that he would be obedient unto him in keeping his commandments."**

Although Christ was the one mortal upon whom death could make no claim (He being holy), He nonetheless obeyed the same conditions as everyone else. Notwithstanding His holiness, His right to face judgment and not be condemned, He set the example. No one else could face the judgment and pass. Therefore, everyone other than Him would require baptism for repentance and remission of their sins. He did not. He determined to obey anyway so everyone could see the strait path by which they can obtain hope.

He was flesh. He was mortal. He could (and did) die. Though death could not claim Him, He was to die. Baptism is the great symbol of death and resurrection, and He is the resurrection. He lived the symbol as well as the reality, so all others could have part in that victory. The

---

[426] Ether 12: 19: "And there were many whose faith was so exceedingly strong, even before Christ came, who could not be kept from within the veil, but truly saw with their eyes the things which they had beheld with an eye of faith, and they were glad."

[427] Ether 12: 19: "And there were many whose faith was so exceedingly strong, even before Christ came, who could not be kept from within the veil, but truly saw with their eyes the things which they had beheld with an eye of faith, and they were glad."

symbol to point the way. The reality to open the way. We are in turn "shown the way" by what He did.

He also "witnesses" before "the Father that he would be obedient unto Him."

Think about the command of understanding Nephi is exhibiting here. He is telling us that Christ's mortal ministry would include these very specific events for these very specific reasons. This was what he was permitted to tell us. What other information was within his knowledge which he was forbidden from sharing? Does this level of understanding by Nephi tell you something about what can be learned from the Lord if you are diligent in following His path? Why, if you can see what may be available, would you not be willing to do whatever is asked of you in order to receive something similar in your own life?

Well, the foundation of the "doctrine of Christ" begins by seeing Christ's example, learning of the necessity of baptism and obedience to the will of God. That is where everyone must begin. If you start right, you are likely to continue in the right way. But if you do not begin aright, then you are not likely to have any ability to return and find the right way. You cannot enter in by some other way. If you enter in the right way, you will begin to recognize the True Shepherd's voice.[428] This is the beginning. It is as important to the doctrine of Christ as all that will follow.

2 Nephi 31: 8-9

> **"Wherefore, after he was baptized with water the Holy Ghost descended upon him in the form of a dove. And again, it showeth unto the children of men the straitness of the path, and the narrowness of the gate, by which they should enter, he having set the example before them."**

This is an interesting cause-and-effect. Once Christ was baptized, "the Holy Ghost descended upon Him" as a result of the baptism. Now, true enough an ordinance was instituted by which hands are laid upon a person, post-baptism, where the "gift of the Holy Ghost" is bestowed.

---

[428] John 10: 1-5: "Verily, verily, I say unto you, He that entereth not by the door into the sheepfold, but climbeth up some other way, the same is a thief and a robber. But he that entereth in by the door is the shepherd of the sheep. To him the porter openeth; and the sheep hear his voice: and he calleth his own sheep by name, and leadeth them out. And when he putteth forth his own sheep, he goeth before them, and the sheep follow him: for they know his voice. And a stranger will they not follow, but will flee from him: for they know not the voice of strangers."

This practice was instituted by Christ.[429] However, in the case of Christ's own baptism, no hands were put upon Him. He was baptized. The Holy Ghost descended upon Him.

It is clear that baptism is a gate through which all must pass. Immediately after the ordinance, the Holy Ghost must become the companion of those who are redeemed.

Christ set the example. We are obligated to follow the example.

Receiving baptism without also receiving the Spirit renders the event incomplete. Nephi will explain the essential nature of the Holy Ghost in the redemption process in a few more verses. It is clear that the Holy Ghost is the instrumentality by which redemption itself comes. The Spirit is the guide which will lead back to the Lord's presence. Without the guide, the doctrine of Christ is incomplete.

The water is something that we must pass through to keep the law. It is the companionship of the Spirit which makes you justified, by leading you to do what is right. It is the resulting application of Christ's blood on your behalf that will sanctify you.[430] You cannot receive sanctification without first receiving baptism and then also the Holy Ghost.

If there is no other way, and all must comply, then the way is both "strait" and "narrow."

Christ's example is the only one for us to follow to obtain hope for our own salvation. He is the "prototype of the saved man" (Lecture 7, *Lectures on Faith*, paragraph 9). If it was necessary for Him, it is the more necessary for us.

Baptism is one thing, accepting the Holy Ghost is another. The one is objective, and openly visible when the act happens. The other is internal, involving welcoming a member of the Godhead into your life.

I remember kneeling on an Atlantic beach in the cool sand at the setting of the sun on the day of my baptism. The Atlantic is cold in September, and I was chilled from the ordinance, still wet while kneeling, and shivering as the elders began the ordinance. When, however, they said: "receive the Holy Ghost" I remember becoming warm, beginning at my scalp and flowing downward until my entire body was warm and calm. It was palpable. It was physical. To me the experience was no less dramatic than the descent of the Holy Ghost "in the form of a dove" on the day of Christ's baptism. It was every bit as

---

429 Acts 8: 14-17: "Now when the apostles which were at Jerusalem heard that Samaria had received the word of God, they sent unto them Peter and John: Who, when they were come down, prayed for them, that they might receive the Holy Ghost: (For as yet he was fallen upon none of them: only they were baptized in the name of the Lord Jesus.) Then laid they *their* hands on them, and they received the Holy Ghost."

430 Moses 6: 60: "For by the water ye keep the commandment; by the Spirit ye are justified, and by the blood ye are sanctified;"

objective, as physical and as memorable as any other distinct event in my life.

More importantly, I began to experience the fruits of that event immediately. What followed for me, within the hour of my baptism, was akin to what Joseph and Oliver experienced.[431] Within days I found also that the scriptures began to have far more distinct and clear meaning than ever before, again just as Joseph and Oliver found.[432]

It was clear to me that the Holy Ghost imparts something altogether more significant than what I alone could do, understand, or accomplish. It expanded capacity, enlightened and informed the mind, and led to understanding things which were unknown and unknowable before.

This process is not just mandatory. It is a far superior way to experience life than to live alone, without God in the world.[433] It is a blessing, a gift. The "gift of the Holy Ghost" is, without question, the great "gift" coming from God to aid us in our return to Him.

2 Nephi 31: 10-11

> **"And he said unto the children of men: Follow thou me. Wherefore, my beloved brethren, can we follow Jesus save we shall be willing to keep the commandments of the Father? And the Father said: Repent ye, repent ye, and be baptized in the name of my Beloved Son."**

Notice the "prophetic-perfect" tense, where Nephi speaks of the Lord's future conduct as if it were in the past. This is what happens when a prophet speaks in prophecy. To the prophet, the events are in the past because he was shown it **before** writing it. Although the event has

---

[431] JS-H 1: 73: "Immediately on our coming up out of the water after we had been baptized, we experienced great and glorious blessings from our Heavenly Father. No sooner had I baptized Oliver Cowdery, than the Holy Ghost fell upon him, and he stood up and prophesied many things which should shortly come to pass. And again, so soon as I had been baptized by him, I also had the spirit of prophecy, when, standing up, I prophesied concerning the rise of this Church, and many other things connected with the Church, and this generation of the children of men. We were filled with the Holy Ghost, and rejoiced in the God of our salvation."

[432] JS-H 1: 74: "Our minds being now enlightened, we began to have the scriptures laid open to our understandings, and the true meaning and intention of their more mysterious passages revealed unto us in a manner which we never could attain to previously, nor ever before had thought of. In the meantime we were forced to keep secret the circumstances of having received the Priesthood and our having been baptized, owing to a spirit of persecution which had already manifested itself in the neighborhood."

[433] Alma 41: 11: "And now, my son, all men that are in a state of nature, or I would say, in a carnal state, are in the gall of bitterness and in the bonds of iniquity; they are without God in the world, and they have gone contrary to the nature of God; therefore, they are in a state contrary to the nature of happiness."

not occurred yet, the prophet remembers it in his mind and to him it is a past event.

This "remembering" the future makes the mind of the prophet akin to the mind of God.

Nephi again addresses his "beloved brethren" in this plea. Can we "follow Jesus" and not keep commandments? Is "be willing to keep the commandments" the same as "keeping the commandments?" Are all commandments to be kept? What about those that create conflict? How did Christ resolve the conflict between the commandment to do good and honor God on the Sabbath, with the commandment to do no work on the Sabbath? Are some commandments objective and without conflict (like baptism) while others may conflict with each other? Can you keep them all? Do you think you even know them all? How do you resolve conflicts? How do you make up for the wrongs you do in ignorance?[434]

Notice the quote Nephi reports from "the Father." Again, Nephi is telling us something about his associations. He says the Father has stated: "Repent ye, repent ye, and be baptized in the name of my Beloved Son." You can search all the scriptures and you will find this quote appears in this one place. Nephi is quoting the Father. Where did Nephi get the quote from if it does not otherwise appear in scripture?

What does that tell you about Nephi? What does it tell you about the Father's view of baptism? What does it tell you about the actions of Christ and the will of the Father? Why does the Father refer to Christ as "my Beloved Son" while speaking of baptism?

With what emotion does the Father express Himself about Christ? Does that emotion attach to any of those who do as Christ did? Does it please the Father when we are baptized? Why?

What is God's work?[435] How does baptism relate to this work? How do we "follow Christ" without seeking to do everything He did? Can we do all He did? Why did Joseph say we must go from one exaltation to another? What does Joseph refer to when he explained: "you have got to learn how to be gods yourselves, and to be kings and priests to God, the same as all gods have done before you, namely, by going from one small degree to another, and from a small capacity to a great one; from grace to grace, from exaltation to exaltation, until you attain to the resurrection of the dead, and are able to dwell in everlasting burnings, and to sit in glory, as do those who sit enthroned in everlasting power." (King Follett Discourse.) This was long after Joseph received the Vision of the Three Degrees of Glory found in Section 76. Section 76 was received February 16, 1832 while the King Follett Discourse was given April 7, 1844.

---

434 Mosiah 3: 11: "For behold, and also his blood atoneth for the sins of those who have fallen by the transgression of Adam, who have died not knowing the will of God concerning them, or who have ignorantly sinned."

435 Moses 1: 39: "For behold, this is my work and my glory—to bring to pass the immortality and eternal life of man."

Remember that all of what was seen in the vision was not recorded by Joseph: "But great and marvelous are the works of the Lord, and the mysteries of his kingdom which he showed unto us, which surpass all understanding in glory, and in might, and in dominion; Which he commanded us we should not write while we were yet in the Spirit, and are not lawful forman to utter."[436] Why would some things be known to a prophet but "not lawful" for him to reveal to others?

What does the idea of "following Christ" imply, if it were taken to its fullest extent? Why would that require someone to go "from one small degree to another?" What would be involved for someone to pass "from exaltation to exaltation," as Joseph mentions in this discourse in April 1844? How fully must we follow Christ?

If it is God's work to bring to pass immortality and eternal life for His children, then must God work out salvation for His children to confer upon them immortality and eternal life? If another becomes "like God" will they undertake the same work? Will it require the same price to be paid? Is there another way?

2 Nephi 31: 12

> **"And also, the voice of the Son came unto me, saying: He that is baptized in my name, to him will the Father give the Holy Ghost, like unto me; wherefore, follow me, and do the things which ye have seen me do."**

Notice that immediately following the quote from the Father, Nephi adds a quote from the Son. Here Nephi makes it clear that the Father said to Nephi what is quoted in verse 11, because he adds, "And also, the voice of the Son came unto me, saying..." As soon as the Father stopped speaking, the Son added the comment he now quotes.

This contradicts what is an often referred to Mormon legend. Our legend is that the Father does nothing other than introduce the Son. This comes from a misreading of the Joseph Smith Translation of John 1: 18. This verse is rendered in the JKV as follows: **"No man hath seen God at any time; the only begotten Son, which is in the bosom of the Father, he hath declared *him.*"** In the JST it is changed to read: **"No man hath seen God at any time except he hath borne record of the Son; the only begotten Son, which is in the bosom of the Father, he hath declared *him.*"** This is the basis for asserting the Father doesn't ever speak, apart from introducing and bearing testimony of the Son. It is clearly a false notion, however, as the Father has many quoted words in the Book of Mormon. The fact the myth exists is, once

[436] D&C 76: 114-115: "But great and marvelous are the works of the Lord, and the mysteries of his kingdom which he showed unto us, which surpass all understanding in glory, and in might, and in dominion; Which he commanded us we should not write while we were yet in the Spirit, and are not lawful for man to utter;"

again, evidence of how little we have as a people studied the Book of Mormon.

Well, returning to this verse, we find that the promise of the Holy Ghost is made by the Father! That is, Christ is saying when the Holy Ghost is sent, it is a gift from "the Father." Indeed it is! The Father of our spirits[437] has given us all that spirit which dwells within us.[438]

First the Father tells us to be baptized and follow Christ. Then Christ adds to it the plea: If you do that you will receive the Holy Ghost as a gift from the Father. So "follow me, and do the things which ye have seen me do."

How seamless the will of the Father is with the desire of His Son!

How eager are both the Father and the Son for us to come to them!

How consistent is the message we receive from both the Father and the Son!

There is no other record in all scripture that puts together the promises of the Father and the plea of the Son like Nephi has done here!

How great a prophet was Nephi! How trusted and familiar must he have been with both the Father and the Son to be able to deliver this message to us!

Let it sink in. Let it be understood. Then, realize Nephi was a man just like you and I. He suffered, toiled, was rejected, fled and worked in obscurity to follow God against the active opposition of his own brothers. His knowledge and experiences are open to all. If you have not realized before, now you should realize why Nephi forms the bedrock example in *The Second Comforter* to lay out the process of returning to God's presence. Among prophets, Nephi was a pillar of light, whose understanding reached into heaven itself.

Perhaps we should have been giving him more attention for the last 180 years. Well, it's not too late for you to begin to do so now.

2 Nephi 31: 13

> **"Wherefore, my beloved brethren, I know that if ye shall follow the Son, with full purpose of heart, acting no hypocrisy and no deception before God, but with real intent, repenting of your sins, witnessing unto the Father that ye are willing to take upon you the name of Christ, by baptism—yea, by following your Lord and your Savior down into the water, according to his word, behold, then shall ye receive the Holy Ghost; yea, then cometh the baptism of fire and of the Holy Ghost; and then can**

---

437 Heb. 12: 9: "Furthermore we have had fathers of our flesh which corrected *us,* and we gave *them* reverence: shall we not much rather be in subjection unto the Father of spirits, and live?"

438 D&C 130: 22: "The Father has a body of flesh and bones as tangible as man's; the Son also; but the Holy Ghost has not a body of flesh and bones, but is a personage of Spirit. Were it not so, the Holy Ghost could not dwell in us."

ye speak with the tongue of angels, and shout praises unto the Holy One of Israel."

Now we get the explanation of what it means to "follow Christ." It is not merely the act itself, but the underlying intent of the act. To follow Him requires:

- Full purpose of heart. What does that imply or require?
- Acting no hypocrisy. How so?
- No deception before God. Can a man deceive God?
- Real intent. What does "real intent" include?
- Repenting of your sins. How does one repent of their sins?
- Witnessing unto the Father: How do you witness to Him?
- Willing to take upon you the name of Christ. How?

The only way I can think to touch upon Nephi's meaning is to get personal about this process. It is by how I have lived that I have come to understand Nephi's meaning.

I remember as the missionaries were teaching me that I came to the conviction that the restoration of the Gospel had indeed happened. It was not a happy thought. I did NOT want to become a Mormon. It seemed like a terrible change to attempt to make, in what was an otherwise content life at the time. As a lifestyle some of it seemed to have merit. Not drinking, smoking and living a higher moral standard certainly made some sense to me. But the association with Mormons had no appeal to me at the time. I thought them shallow and artificial in many ways, and did not want to become immersed in a society that seemed to be either a pretense, or if not, then living a standard I could never attain.

I reluctantly accepted baptism, not because I wanted to become Mormon, but because I truly believed it was the restored Gospel of Jesus Christ. However humiliating it may be to associate with a social group I had practically nothing in common, it was the right thing to do before God. I told God that I was doing this because of Him, and that I doubted I could live these standards, doubted I could be happy among these odd people, that I did not know if they were really sincere, but that I was. I intended to try to leave such sins behind as I understood I was committing, and to attempt to become part of the artificial life-form known as "Mormon." But I doubted my capacity to continue on to the end. In all this I was absolutely sincere, but completely hopeless about what it would result in over the long run.

I was, in fact, willing to take upon me these obligations as a matter between me and God. However badly it may turn out between me and other Mormons, I expected that as between me and God it would be better than alright. I thought it would please Him.

So I was baptized.

Oddly, upon baptism things changed. A great deal, in fact. What seemed unlikely for me to be able to do under my own capacity, became almost second-nature. These people who I feared I could never fit in with became my brothers and sisters. It took a surprisingly short time and I found that what I feared most was the lightest of burdens to carry. Associating with other Mormons was delightful. I found that I loved the Mormons and I loved being one of them. It ceased to be "them" and "me" but turned into "us" and "we."

And, by damn, we are a peculiar lot. We're the oddest people on the planet. Peculiar doesn't even begin to capture our quirkiness, phobias, longings, hopes, aspirations, misunderstandings, convictions, genius mixed with stupidity, juxtapositions of truth and error, traditions and deep doctrines. We're a cacophony, really. But underlying it all is a hope that we are on the right track and a conviction that we're going to please God even if it requires us to offend Him.

I appreciate the faith restored through Joseph at a whole different level than the one which brought me into the fold. It IS true. Abidingly and without any failing, the faith restored through Joseph is the Gospel of Jesus Christ.

The sad truth is, however, that faith has not been preserved as Joseph brought it back. Even from the time I was baptized in the waning four months of President Lee's administration until today, the faith has undergone a radical revisionism. Today it isn't even what President Kimball presided over. It is becoming increasingly altered, bureaucratized, regimented and turning into a religious product managed by an increasingly menacing middle-management which prefers rules and regulations to the Spirit and truth. They manage it as if it is another Fortune 500 company whose product line is religion and religious paraphernalia. The Spirit increasingly withdraws from our councils, our conferences, our private as well as public conversations, because it is grieved, and not many people seem to notice as it does so.

The faith I joined still exists. But it is covered by layers of sediment making it progressively more difficult to breathe life into it. That original faith, the one that attracted me, was always meant to connect the believer to Christ. Directly, and without intermediaries. Each Saint was to be a prophet, because the testimony of Jesus is the spirit of prophecy, according to John the Beloved.

But I began this process "acting no hypocrisy" and I will finish it remaining so. My "real intent" is before God, and the resistance, opposition and criticism of men will not alter that. Indeed, it cannot. As soon as I respect the opinions of men more than the "full purpose of heart" required of me, I cease to be "willing to take upon me the name of Christ."

I understand Nephi's words. I live them. I cannot do otherwise at this point. It is for that reason, therefore, that I have been privileged to receive "the baptism of fire and of the Holy Ghost;" which has permitted me from time to time to "speak with the tongue of angels, and shout praises unto the Holy One of Israel." It has not been easy. It is certainly not what I wanted when missionaries interrupted a content life, and introduced this inconvenient faith to a reluctant 19-year old. It was not what I expected when the journey began before baptism, nor what I thought would then follow immediately after I was baptized. I find now, as I survey the altered and altering faith practiced by the Church I belong to, there are increasingly more troubles in living and acting with:

- Full purpose of heart
- Acting no hypocrisy
- No deception before God
- Real intent
- Repenting of my sins
- Witnessing unto the Father
- Willing to take upon me the name of Christ

But that will always remain a matter between the Father, the Lord and myself. Nephi lived these things, too. It was for that reason he understood them and was able to set them out with clarity in writing. Light and truth, which is intelligence, only come as a consequence of living it.

I will never stop being Mormon, nor forsake the faith I have accepted. I love associating with the Saints. I'm also glad to not be a part of leadership. I wouldn't want the condemnation that accompanies leading these people in the course that we are currently set. It is better to practice the faith as I understand it, explain it to those who care to listen, support those who try to keep my ward family at peace with one another, and raise my children to respect the light and truth.

I am content. More than content, I am filled with joy and hope for what lies ahead for myself and all those who have the testimony of Jesus.

2 Nephi 31: 14

> **"But, behold, my beloved brethren, thus came the voice of the Son unto me, saying: After ye have repented of your sins, and witnessed unto the Father that ye are willing to keep my commandments, by the baptism of water, and have received the baptism of fire and of the Holy Ghost, and can speak with a new tongue, yea, even with the tongue of angels, and after this should deny me, it would have been better for you that ye had not known me."**

Nephi first gave us his personal testimony and witness of the principles. Having done so, now he adds the testimony and promise of Christ. Christ's promise and covenant are slightly different than Nephi's formula. But the two are nevertheless in complete harmony.

The "voice of the Son" declares to Nephi, and Nephi testifies to us, that "after ye have repented of you sins" and you have "witnessed unto the Father that ye are willing to keep [Christ's] commandments" by receiving "baptism of water" and then have received "baptism of fire and the Holy Ghost" you will speak with "a new tongue."

How can a man speak with a "new tongue?" What does "a new tongue" mean?

Think of Isaiah's meeting with the Lord in the Temple. He confessed how unworthy his speech had been, and how much regret he felt at having been a man of "unclean lips".[439] His lips were unclean because of the low, mean, vulgar and unworthy things that occupied daily conversation. Or, as Joseph put it: "How vain and trifling have been our spirits, our conferences, our councils, our meetings, our private as well as public conversations—too low, too mean, too vulgar, too condescending for the dignified characters of the called and chosen of God, according to the purposes of His will, from before the foundation of the world!" (Letter from Liberty Jail.)

To speak with a new tongue is to speak worthily of sacred things. It is to correctly weigh the truth of a matter, know by the power of the Spirit that what is said is true and in conformity with God's will and then to speak it. It is to render sacred the vessel by the things it holds.

To speak with a new tongue is to be able to speak with the tongue of an angel because you have become an angel; or a companion of angels anyway. It is to elevate your thoughts, and then what proceeds forth from your mouth, because of what is in your thoughts. It is to reveal truth by the things you are authorized or commissioned to speak. It is to have a right to speak in the name of the Lord by His consent, His authority, His will. It is to "know, nothing doubting" that He is your Lord.[440] It is to say, without hypocrisy, without guile, without hesitation and in truth, that the power of salvation is found in Christ and that you are His. That He has entrusted to you words of life, and that salvation can be found only in Him and His words. It is to have the Word of God within you.

Can an angel fall from grace? Only by being cast out of heaven.[441] When an angel falls he becomes a devil. For these it would be better if they had never known Christ, for they have decided to crucify Him anew. Because after having had the Holy Spirit make great things known unto them they have turned against the Lord by their knowing

---

[439] Isa. 6: 5: "Then said I, Woe *is* me! for I am undone; because I *am* a man of unclean lips, and I dwell in the midst of a people of unclean lips: for mine eyes have seen the King, the Lord of hosts."

[440] Ether 3: 19: "And because of the knowledge of this man he could not be kept from beholding within the veil; and he saw the finger of Jesus, which, when he saw, he fell with fear; for he knew that it was the finger of the Lord; and he had faith no longer, for he knew, nothing doubting."

[441] 2 Ne. 2: 17: "And I, Lehi, according to the things which I have read, must needs suppose that an angel of God, according to that which is written, had fallen from heaven; wherefore, he became a devil, having sought that which was evil before God."

rebellion against Him.[442] They are sons of perdition, and the heavens weep over them.[443] These are they who know the battle is and always has been the Lord's, and they either align themselves with Him or against Him.

You cannot speak with the tongue of angels without having knowledge of certain things given you. The clarity with which you can declare truth is distinct from what others say or claim to know. Light and truth, which is intelligence or the glory of God[444], is not a mystery but an understood and appreciated experience where darkness has fled and God's own glory has been upon you.[445]

This is what the Gospel of Christ was intended to confer. Not just belief, or faith, but knowledge and understanding. The journey back to God's presence was always the outcome intended by the Gospel. The Gospel message is and always has been that you should receive further light and knowledge by conversing with the Lord through the veil. Not through an intermediary, but in your own behalf, face to face.

The entirety of the process may be reduced to just a few words: You are intended to receive baptism of fire and the Holy Ghost, which purges you from all sin. After being made clean, every whit, which is suggested by "fire" then through the instrumentality of the "Holy Ghost" which dwells within you you may be brought into remembrance of all things.

These then are the words of both Nephi and Christ. They agree. They are the two witnesses of this doctrine and truth. Therefore, it is so.

2 Nephi 31: 15

> **"And I heard a voice from the Father, saying: Yea, the words of my Beloved are true and faithful. He that endureth to the end, the same shall be saved."**

The dialogue continues. It is clear the conversation being reported by Nephi is one where both the Son and the Father spoke to Nephi, and contributed to the dialogue. A question was posed about whether Nephi heard this in connection with his vision of Christ's mortal baptism by

---

442 D&C 76: 35: "Having denied the Holy Spirit after having received it, and having denied the Only Begotten Son of the Father, having crucified him unto themselves and put him to an open shame."

443 D&C 76: 26, 31-32: "And was called Perdition, for the heavens wept over him—he was Lucifer, a son of the morning."

444 D&C 93: 36: "The glory of God is intelligence, or, in other words, light and truth."

445 Moses 1: 11: "But now mine own eyes have beheld God; but not my natural, but my spiritual eyes, for my natural eyes could not have beheld; for I should have withered and died in his presence; but his glory was upon me; and I beheld his face, for I was transfigured before him."

John the Baptist. He certainly beheld that event.[446] However, the testimony and teaching of both the Father and Son regarding baptism, as reported by Nephi in this final sermon, are separate from that event. They are an independent revelation and explanation to Nephi, where both the Father and Son taught the importance of baptism.

We also have the important condition set out of "enduring to the end" as a requisite for salvation. A while ago there was a question about the concept of "enduring to the end" and the Second Comforter. They are directly linked. You cannot have a great season of concentrated effort, followed by abandonment of purpose. If it is in you to abandon the journey, then you will never qualify to receive these blessings. The Lord knows the intent of the heart. The preceding verses describe how the Lord measures the heart. You cannot deceive Him.

The Lord also knows whether it is in you to "endure to the end." Whether the end has come is irrelevant to Him. He beholds all things, past, present and future.[447] Therefore, He knows if you are willing to "endure to the end" before your life has been lived.

Enduring to the end, or the fixed purpose to always serve God so that you may always have His spirit to be with you, is essential to salvation. You claim this is your determination every time you take the sacrament.[448] Whether you take this commitment seriously or not determines whether you are destined for salvation or not. It also determines if you are qualified to receive His personal ministry and comfort.

The Father declares: "Yea, the words of my Beloved are true and faithful." The reason Christ is the Father's "Beloved" is directly related

---

[446] 1 Ne. 11: 27: "And I looked and beheld the Redeemer of the world, of whom my father had spoken; and I also beheld the prophet who should prepare the way before him. And the Lamb of God went forth and was baptized of him; and after he was baptized, I beheld the heavens open, and the Holy Ghost come down out of heaven and abide upon him in the form of a dove."

[447] D&C 130: 7: "But they reside in the presence of God, on a globe like a sea of glass and fire, where all things for their glory are manifest, past, present, and future, and are continually before the Lord."

[448] D&C 20: 76-79: "And the elder or priest shall administer it; and after this manner shall he administer it—he shall kneel with the church and call upon the Father in solemn prayer, saying: O God, the Eternal Father, we ask thee in the name of thy Son, Jesus Christ, to bless and sanctify this bread to the souls of all those who partake of it, that they may eat in remembrance of the body of thy Son, and witness unto thee, O God, the Eternal Father, that they are willing to take upon them the name of thy Son, and always remember him and keep his commandments which he has given them; that they may always have his Spirit to be with them. Amen. The manner of administering the wine—he shall take the cup also, and say: O God, the Eternal Father, we ask thee in the name of thy Son, Jesus Christ, to bless and sanctify this wine to the souls of all those who drink of it, that they may do it in remembrance of the blood of thy Son, which was shed for them; that they may witness unto thee, O God, the Eternal Father, that they do always remember him, that they may have his Spirit to be with them. Amen."

to His words being "true and faithful." That is, Christ only does and says what He knows represents the Father's will. He has done this "from the beginning."[449] He represents the "Word" of the Father because you can find in Christ's words and deeds the very word of the Father.[450]

It is this that qualified Christ to be the Redeemer. His words are faithful and true. So are Nephi's. The words are the Lord's though they were delivered by a man.

Nephi, having been true and faithful in all things, was able to converse with the Father and the Son through the veil and receive from them further instruction, counsel, warning, and comfort because of the things he learned. This is the pattern for all of us. This is the culminating message of the Gospel of Christ.

2 Nephi 31: 16

> **"And now, my beloved brethren, I know by this that unless a man shall endure to the end, in following the example of the Son of the living God, he cannot be saved."**

What does it mean to "endure to the end?" It is to put up with all the difficulties of mortality? Are we simply supposed to overcome boredom, irritation, trials of our patience, and the offenses caused by others? Is that what it means to "endure?"

What about "endure to the end in following the example of the Son of the living God?" Is that something different?

What if you see errors and mistakes all around you? Is it "enduring" to keep your mouth shut? Do you need to speak up?

What about the changes that have been made or are being made which alarm you? Is it "enduring" to stay silent in the face of things that suggest this is harmful?

When I first went through the Temple, it was the understood and longstanding practice of the Saints to hold prayer circles in their homes, invoking the "True Order of Prayer" as taught in the Temple. President Kimball sent a letter to the Stake Presidents terminating that practice. I have a copy of that letter. It said that prayer circles were no longer to be practiced outside the Temple—by anyone in the church.

Then in 1990 the True Order of Prayer was altered again, with the elimination of penalties. Thereafter the name changed to the "Order of Prayer" rather than the "True Order of Prayer."

Those who went through the Temple before 1990 would know about how to conduct a prayer circle involving the True Order of Prayer. But

---

[449] 3 Ne. 11: 11: "And behold, I am the light and the life of the world; and I have drunk out of that bitter cup which the Father hath given me, and have glorified the Father in taking upon me the sins of the world, in the which I have suffered the will of the Father in all things from the beginning."

[450] D&C 93: 8: "Therefore, in the beginning the Word was, for he was the Word, even the messenger of salvation—"

they were instructed not to do so outside the Temple. Those who went through after 1990 would not know how to conduct a True Order of Prayer circle, because they were not instructed in the Temple in anything other than the Order of Prayer.

It was still possible for those who knew the pre-1990 form to communicate the process in the Temple to others. However, recently there has begun a practice of hushing any discussions seen taking place inside the Celestial Rooms of the Temples.

It is as if those who are in control are opposed to keeping the earlier information, and working to keep it from being preserved by others. Is it "enduring to the end" to watch these changes and say nothing? Or is it "enduring" to actually endure, to preserve, to persevere against opposition and to keep as an enduring feature of the faith, information you received if you went through the Temple before 1990? Does a person who, in all sincerity before God, believes that Isaiah's prophecy warned against this[451] "endure" if he remains silent? Or must he speak up? If so, how and to who? Which is enduring? Which is enduring to the end in following the example of the Son of the Living God? What example did Christ set in relation to this kind of a conflict? Did Christ submit, or resist authority? If He did both, how does one endure while appropriately weighing those things they will submit to, and those things they will resist?

What about Nephi's warning that you "cannot be saved" if you fail to do the right kind of "enduring" to the end? If salvation itself hinges upon solving this riddle, then how carefully must you weigh what you resist and what you submit to?

It is for this reason we work out our salvation before God as Nephi has explained, acting no hypocrisy, with real intent, having faith in God, but also with fear and trembling.[452]

Indeed, God has given us a test worthy of a God. And only those worthy of becoming among the gods will be able to solve the riddle. Because only they will humble themselves, come with a contrite spirit and broken heart to offer upon the altar a sacrifice worthy of being accepted. Others will proceed in ignorance and arrogance to proudly proclaim: "I know my culture is true!" "I know all is well in Zion!" "I follow a broad and safe mainstream into a great and spacious building

---

[451] Isa. 24: 5: "The earth also is defiled under the inhabitants thereof; because they have transgressed the laws, changed the ordinance, broken the everlasting covenant."

[452] Mormon 9: 27: "O then despise not, and wonder not, but hearken unto the words of the Lord, and ask the Father in the name of Jesus for what things soever ye shall stand in need. Doubt not, but be believing, and begin as in times of old, and come unto the Lord with all your heart, and work out your own salvation with fear and trembling before him."
Philip. 2: 12: "Wherefore, my beloved, as ye have always obeyed, not as in my presence only, but now much more in my absence, work out your own salvation with fear and trembling."

where there is peace, pride, success, prosperity and assurance that I am saved while all around me there are those who will be cast down to hell!" Or similar such nonsense... Warmed over Evangelical gibberish, with a vague Mormonesque vocabulary applied to it. Having a form of godliness, but without power. This new form of ungodliness will not be lacking in body, parts and passions, for the image of the idol raised will be the very image of the person looking in the mirror. They will think themselves destined to rule and reign over principalities, dominions, heights, depths and others. They are their own idols! What irony it all invokes! It must make the devil look up to heaven and laugh still. (Moses 7: 26.) Perhaps we ought to see some humor in it as well. ...Or, since we're speaking of the loss of men's souls, maybe it can never be humorous. Only tragedy. Only disappointment. Only foolishness.

Where is the hope? Is there none? Yes, in repentance! Changing our course! Remembering God again! Restoring what has been lost! Returning and repenting! That's right! And Nephi has invited us to do just that.

So "enduring to the end in following the example of the Son of the living God" is not easy. Even understanding the meaning of these words is challenging. Thank you Nephi. You have proven yet again how prayerful we all must be. Let us, therefore, repent!

2 Nephi 31: 17

"Wherefore, do the things which I have told you I have seen that your Lord and your Redeemer should do; for, for this cause have they been shown unto me, that ye might know the gate by which ye should enter. For the gate by which ye should enter is repentance and baptism by water; and then cometh a remission of your sins by fire and by the Holy Ghost."

You must "do the things which I have told you I have seen that your Lord and your Redeemer should do." You must "follow Him." There is no other way nor name given under heaven to obtain salvation.[453]

It was for this reason Nephi was "shown" these things. The Lord and His Father taught Nephi so he could in turn teach others, including us. The message was intended to save many, not just Nephi. But we must give heed to the message when we hear it.

The "gate by which ye should enter is repentance and baptism by water." You must repent first. Then, having repented, receive baptism by water. When this is done, "then cometh a remission of your sins by fire and by the Holy Ghost."

[453] Mosiah 5: 8: "And under this head ye are made free, and there is no other head whereby ye can be made free. There is no other name given whereby salvation cometh; therefore, I would that ye should take upon you the name of Christ, all you that have entered into the covenant with God that ye should be obedient unto the end of your lives."

Without the "fire" to purge the sacrifice upon the altar, it is not cleansed. It cannot become holy unless exposed to that fire.

But note—this is automatic. It is not by the laying on of hands. The laying on of hands for the gift of the Holy Ghost is not required in this teaching. Nephi, with elaboration from the Father and the Son, is teaching that this is an event that follows the process of "repentance and baptism by water." That is, the ordinance of baptism, when accompanied by repentance and done right, is the reason for this event.

Laying on of hands is for "the gift of the Holy Ghost" so there may be a companion and guide for a person. This is an ordinance. It is also the moment one is confirmed a member of the church. But it is not necessarily co-equal with receiving "fire and the Holy Ghost" as described here. There is nothing that excludes it from being coincidental in time, however. They may happen at the same moment. That is, after baptism, and while receiving the laying on of hands, one may receive both the gift of the Holy Ghost, and also fire and the Holy Ghost. As a result one is renewed in the manner described in this chapter. They are not co-equal.

Laying on of hands does not appear to be an ordinance in the Book of Mormon until the coming of Christ in 3 Nephi. The only potential exception is found in Alma 31: 36, where Alma "clapped his hands upon them who were with him" and they received the Holy Ghost. This is similar to the Lord "breathing" the Holy Ghost upon His disciples.[454] They were instructed to lay on hands, and would perform that act rather than breathing upon those who were to receive the Holy Ghost. The ordinance is different from "clapping" or from "breathing" and involves the process we follow in the church today.[455]

The baptism of fire and the Holy Ghost promised here is given without man's involvement, comes from heaven, is promised by both the Father and the Son. It is a signal of redemption, purification and holiness. It is included in the "gate" for entering into God's presence. For God is a "consuming fire" and those who enter into that presence must be able to endure that fire.[456] Without the capacity to do so, a person would be consumed by the flames.[457] The fire and the Holy Ghost are also given as a sign to the recipient that they may know it is

---

[454] John 20: 22: "And when he had said this, he breathed on *them,* and saith unto them, Receive ye the Holy Ghost:"

[455] D&C 33: 15: "And whoso having faith you shall confirm in my church, by the laying on of the hands, and I will bestow the gift of the Holy Ghost upon them."

[456] Heb. 12: 29: "For our God *is* a consuming fire."
Deut. 4: 24: "For the Lord thy God *is* a consuming fire, *even* a jealous God."

[457] Lev. 10: 1-2: "And Nadab and Abihu, the sons of Aaron, took either of them his censer, and put fire therein, and put incense thereon, and offered strange fire before the Lord, which he commanded them not. And there went out fire from the Lord, and devoured them, and they died before the Lord."

safe for them to enter into God's presence and not be consumed. In earlier versions of the First Vision, Joseph described the "pillar of light" as a "pillar of fire" which gradually descended. He wondered if the trees would be consumed as it descended, but seeing they were not he thought it safe for him to be exposed to it as well. When it fell upon him, the vision opened up and he saw the Father and the Son.

Christ also entered into this glorious light on the Mount of Transfiguration.[458]

We are to do as Nephi instructs, "do the things which I have told you I have seen that your Lord and your Redeemer should do; for, for this cause have they been shown unto me, that ye might know the gate by which ye should enter."

We live below the standard Christ set for us. We needn't. Have faith. Press forward feasting on His words. You can and will find Him there.

2 Nephi 31: 18

> **"And then are ye in this strait and narrow path which leads to eternal life; yea, ye have entered in by the gate; ye have done according to the commandments of the Father and the Son; and ye have received the Holy Ghost, which witnesses of the Father and the Son, unto the fulfilling of the promise which he hath made, that if ye entered in by the way ye should receive."**

This is the path to "eternal life." It is "strait and narrow," but it is the way to eternal life. What is eternal life?

Why is the path "strait and narrow?" Is it to deprive you of something, or is it to direct you toward the only path where abundance can be obtained? If you become connected to the "true vine," are you then able to "bear fruit?"[459] If you bear fruit, what can you ask of Him that He will not give to you?[460] What does that mean? Have you read *Beloved Enos*? If so you will understand what is being discussed.

---

[458] Matt. 17: 1-2: "And after six days Jesus taketh Peter, James, and John his brother, and bringeth them up into an high mountain apart, And was transfigured before them: and his face did shine as the sun, and his raiment was white as the light"

[459] John 15: 4-7: "Abide in me, and I in you. As the branch cannot bear fruit of itself, except it abide in the vine; no more can ye, except ye abide in me. I am the vine, ye *are* the branches: He that abideth in me, and I in him, the same bringeth forth much fruit: for without me ye can do nothing. If a man abide not in me, he is cast forth as a branch, and is withered; and men gather them, and cast *them* into the fire, and they are burned. If ye abide in me, and my words abide in you, ye shall ask what ye will, and it shall be done unto you."

[460] John 15: 7: "If ye abide in me, and my words abide in you, ye shall ask what ye will, and it shall be done unto you."

By doing as the Father and Son have asked, you "receive the Holy Ghost." What does it mean to have the Holy Ghost dwell within you?[461] How does a spirit dwell inside a person? How does that spirit become "Holy" and the third member of the Godhead? If the scriptures say, and Christ taught that those who receive God's word are gods, what does it mean?[462]

Did you notice the Father and Son promise the Holy Ghost, and when you receive it the Holy Ghost bears witness of the Father and Son? The first promise to you provides the last, and the last bears witness of the first. In one eternal round, the doctrine of Christ includes all members of the Godhead combined into a witness that will come to you, take up residence within you, and make you a vessel of the promises fulfilled. You are to return home, and take your abode again. Or, more correctly, permit Them to take up Their abode with you.[463]

You become the record of God's dealings with mankind. You become the promise of God's presence, for you fulfill "the promise which He hath made."

You receive the "record of heaven" or, more correctly, the Record of Heaven, for it is a proper name and title.[464] When it has come to you, then this Record of Heaven will abide with you. You will be the one who possess the "peaceable things of immortal glory." You will know "the truth of all things" for it will reside within you.[465] You will understand wisdom, for she will be with you. You will know mercy, possess truth, and be capable of performing judgment, for the judgment

---

[461] D&C 130: 22: "The Father has a body of flesh and bones as tangible as man's; the Son also; but the Holy Ghost has not a body of flesh and bones, but is a personage of Spirit. Were it not so, the Holy Ghost could not dwell in us."

[462] John 10: 34-36: "Jesus answered them, Is it not written in your law, I said, Ye are gods? If he called them gods, unto whom the word of God came, and the scripture cannot be broken; Say ye of him, whom the Father hath sanctified, and sent into the world, Thou blasphemest; because I said, I am the Son of God?"

[463] John 14: 23: "Jesus answered and said unto him, If a man love me, he will keep my words: and my Father will love him, and we will come unto him, and make our abode with him."

[464] Moses 6: 61: "Therefore it is given to abide in you; the record of heaven; the Comforter; the peaceable things of immortal glory; the truth of all things; that which quickeneth all things, which maketh alive all things; that which knoweth all things, and hath all power according to wisdom, mercy, truth, justice, and judgment."

[465] Moses 6: 61: "Therefore it is given to abide in you; the record of heaven; the Comforter; the peaceable things of immortal glory; the truth of all things; that which quickeneth all things, which maketh alive all things; that which knoweth all things, and hath all power according to wisdom, mercy, truth, justice, and judgment."

you judge will not be yours but will be given to you.[466] God will dwell within you.

When He appears to you, you will see Him as He is, for you will be at last like Him.[467] If you can understand this, then you will purify yourself to receive it.[468] For the baptism of fire and the Holy Ghost will purge and purify, refining you with that holy fire.[469]

This doctrine of Christ will bring you in contact with God. You were meant to return to the Family you came from. It is the homecoming you have always felt was needed. You do not belong here. There is something higher, something more holy calling to you. It is not found in an institution, or program, or award, or office. It is only found in God, who is your home.

The doctrine of Christ is the doctrine of God's return to be with you and abide with you. It is Him coming to sup with you. He has been knocking at the door all these years seeking entry into your life.[470] If you let Him come in, He will prepare a throne for you.[471] Only those who have descended will be permitted to rise. Only those who humble themselves can be exalted.[472] While all those who rule rather than serve, will be disappointed. These are they who declare themselves worthy to be followed and insist they can use compulsion. They pretend to be on the Lord's errand while they are on their own. They crave dominion

---

[466] 3 Ne. 27: 27: "And know ye that ye shall be judges of this people, according to the judgment which I shall give unto you, which shall be just. Therefore, what manner of men ought ye to be? Verily I say unto you, even as I am."

[467] 1 John 3: 1-2: "Behold, what manner of love the Father hath bestowed upon us, that we should be called the sons of God: therefore the world knoweth us not, because it knew him not. Beloved, now are we the sons of God, and it doth not yet appear what we shall be: but we know that, when he shall appear, we shall be like him; for we shall see him as he is."

[468] 1 John 3: 3: "And every man that hath this hope in him purifieth himself, even as he is pure."

[469] Mal. 3: 2: "But who may abide the day of his coming? and who shall stand when he appeareth? for he *is* like a refiner's fire, and like fullers' soap:"

[470] Rev. 3: 20: "Behold, I stand at the door, and knock: if any man hear my voice, and open the door, I will come in to him, and will sup with him, and he with me."

[471] Rev. 3: 21-22: "To him that overcometh will I grant to sit with me in my throne, even as I also overcame, and am set down with my Father in his throne. He that hath an ear, let him hear what the Spirit saith unto the churches."

[472] Matt. 23: 12: "And whosoever shall exalt himself shall be abased; and he that shall humble himself shall be exalted."

over others but will be cast down. They will be denied priesthood, and be left begging for water to cool their tongues for the torment of it all.[473]

How much better is it, then, for us to repent? It seems foolish to do otherwise. I find I'm persuaded by Nephi.

2 Nephi 31: 19-20

> **"And now, my beloved brethren, after ye have gotten into this strait and narrow path, I would ask if all is done? Behold, I say unto you, Nay; for ye have not come thus far save it were by the word of Christ with unshaken faith relying wholly upon the merits of him who is mighty to save. Wherefore, ye must press forward with a steadfastness in Christ, having a perfect brightness of hope, and a love of God and of all men. Wherefore, if ye shall press forward, feasting upon the word of Christ, and endure to the end, behold, thus saith the Father: Ye shall have eternal life. in him,**

"Once on the narrow path, are you done? Have you "arrived?" Is there "rest?"

No, you are on the path, but you cannot turn back. If you even look back, you risk moving on an uneven path.[474] You could not get this far if you hadn't followed "the word of Christ" and therefore you can only continue by following the word of Christ along the journey.

Your path is not just based on Christ's words, but also "with unshaken faith in Him." What is "unshaken faith?"

---

473 D&C 121: 37: "That they may be conferred upon us, it is true; but when we undertake to cover our sins, or to gratify our pride, our vain ambition, or to exercise control or dominion or compulsion upon the souls of the children of men, in any degree of unrighteousness, behold, the heavens withdraw themselves; the Spirit of the Lord is grieved; and when it is withdrawn, Amen to the priesthood or the authority of that man."
Luke 16: 23-24: "And in hell he lift up his eyes, being in torments, and seeth Abraham afar off, and Lazarus in his bosom. And he cried and said, Father Abraham, have mercy on me, and send Lazarus, that he may dip the tip of his finger in water, and cool my tongue; for I am tormented in this flame."

474 Luke 9: 62: "And Jesus said unto him, No man, having put his hand to the plough, and looking back, is fit for the kingdom of God."

What does it mean to rely "wholly upon the merits of Him who is mighty to save?" Can you take any pride in what you have done? Can you boast of something about yourself?[475]

What does it mean to "press forward with a steadfastness in Christ?" How would "steadfastness" be lived?

What is a "perfect brightness of hope?" I've defined that kind of "hope" in *Eighteen Verses*.

How does any person come into possession of "a love of God and of all men?" Would that come from within, or as a gift from God? Moroni prayed for the gentiles to receive grace that they might obtain charity.[476] The Lord replied that if the gentiles lack charity it would not cause any loss to Moroni, for he was saved.[477] [Once again reflecting the pessimism which the latter-day gentiles are consistently viewed by the Book of Mormon.]

Why "press forward?"

What does it mean for us to be "feasting upon the word of Christ?" Is "feasting" something more than participating in a gospel doctrine class discussion once a week? What would it require for you to "feast" upon the "word of Christ?" Is scripture study alone enough? Would you need to receive anything directly from Him to be included in the "feast?" How would that be obtained?

Did you notice once again we are reminded we must "endure to the end?" Once again, you must determine how "enduring" is to be accomplished, and what "enduring" will require.

If, however, you do these things then "behold, thus saith the Father: Ye shall have eternal life." Notice the promise of eternal life comes from the office of "the Father." It is because this final step comes from the

---

475 Mosiah 2: 22-25: "And behold, all that he requires of you is to keep his commandments; and he has promised you that if ye would keep his commandments ye should prosper in the land; and he never doth vary from that which he hath said; therefore, if ye do keep his commandments he doth bless you and prosper you. And now, in the first place, he hath created you, and granted unto you your lives, for which ye are indebted unto him. And secondly, he doth require that ye should do as he hath commanded you; for which if ye do, he doth immediately bless you; and therefore he hath paid you. And ye are still indebted unto him, and are, and will be, forever and ever; therefore, of what have ye to boast? And now I ask, can ye say aught of yourselves? I answer you, Nay. Ye cannot say that ye are even as much as the dust of the earth; yet ye were created of the dust of the earth; but behold, it belongeth to him who created you."

476 Ether 12: 36: "And it came to pass that I prayed unto the Lord that he would give unto the Gentiles grace, that they might have charity."

477 Ether 12: 37: "And it came to pass that the Lord said unto me: If they have not charity it mattereth not unto thee, thou hast been faithful; wherefore, thy garments shall be made clean. And because thou hast seen thy weakness thou shalt be made strong, even unto the sitting down in the place which I have prepared in the mansions of my Father."

authority to make you a son. His office is the only one which can declare "this day have I begotten thee."[478]

2 Nephi 31: 21:

> **"And now, behold, my beloved brethren, this is the way; and there is none other way nor name given under heaven whereby man can be saved in the kingdom of God. And now, behold, this is the doctrine of Christ, and the only and true doctrine of the Father, and of the Son, and of the Holy Ghost, which is one God, without end. Amen."**

This is "the way" to salvation. Nephi adds: "and there is none other way." What does it mean there "is none other way?" Does that mean any religious system, institution, process, explanation or additional doctrine cannot save you? Is it true that you either enter in through this method or you cannot be saved? Is the purpose of the other rites, rituals, ordinances and teachings merely to bring you into this one true "way and there is none other way?" Or do you need to look for additional things, helps, ordinances, confirmations, and blessings to be conferred?

What of the other Gospel rites? They did come from God, didn't they? How are we to understand the relationship between other ordinances, even "higher ordinances" and this "doctrine of Christ" being explained by Nephi?

Clearly the "doctrine of Christ" is intended to give you the underlying basis for all salvation. There is no other "name given under heaven whereby man can be saved in the kingdom of God" apart from Jesus Christ. He is the one who, by His obedience and sacrifice, put power into the plan of salvation. We know this to be true from everything declared by the prophets of God. But what about "this is the way; and there is none other way." What does that mean? Does it exclude other ordinances or processes? Does it make the Law of Moses no longer binding upon Nephi and his posterity?

Clearly following Nephi's ministry, his descendants did not abandon the Law of Moses.[479] And so, if there is "none other way," it did not mean that the Nephites were to abandon practice of the ordinances then

---

[478] Ps. 2: 7: "I will declare the decree: the Lord hath said unto me, Thou *art* my Son; this day have I begotten thee."

[479] Jarom 1: 5: "And now, behold, *two hundred years had passed away, and the people of Nephi had waxed strong in the land. They observed to keep the law of Moses and the sabbath day holy unto the Lord. And they profaned not; neither did they blaspheme. And the laws of the land were exceedingly strict."
Alma 25: 15: "Yea, and they did keep the law of Moses; for it was expedient that they should keep the law of Moses as yet, for it was not all fulfilled. But notwithstanding the law of Moses, they did look forward to the coming of Christ, considering that the law of Moses was a type of his coming, and believing that they must keep those outward performances until the time that he should be revealed unto them."

in effect. Nor does it mean that we abandon the ordinances now in effect in our day.

It is not that the ordinances are essential, but that the **purpose** of the ordinances are essential. The underlying meaning is essential. The "doctrine of Christ" becomes possible to understand, live and receive as you follow the ordinances. They are "helps" to bring you into this correct path. You will honor them, conform to them, seek for them, in order that you may inherit the blessings of the "doctrine of Christ."

Why are ordinances instituted? They are to bring you to the point where you inherit in your body and spirit these great blessings of the "doctrine of Christ." They prepare you. Their effect is to qualify you, instruct you, advance you toward this goal of receiving the blessings found in the doctrine of Christ as expounded by Nephi in this chapter. Once ordinances have been adopted, it is then unlikely you can ignore them and receive what is promised by the "doctrine of Christ." How can you refuse what is offered and still accept the underlying gift? How can you mix ingratitude and gratitude?

Is it important, therefore, to keep the ordinances intact? If changed does some of the communication involved in preparing you to receive the "doctrine of Christ" lose something?

For example, without the shedding of blood there can be no covenant. Christ's blood is the culminating event which shed blood to activate a covenant between God and man. However, even after Christ's sacrifice, we are still required to offer sacrifice, and even the return of animal sacrifice will happen at some point in this final dispensation. The Law of Moses was fulfilled and will not return. However, the sacrifice of blood by animals which was before the Law of Moses will return. As Joseph Smith taught: ""These [animal] sacrifices, as well as every ordinance belonging to the Priesthood, will, when the Temple of the Lord shall be built, and the sons of Levi be purified, be fully restored and attended to in all their powers, ramifications, and blessings. This ever did and ever will exist when the powers of the Melchizedek Priesthood are sufficiently manifest; else how can the restitution of all things spoken of by the Holy Prophets be brought to pass. It is not to be understood that the law of Moses will be established again with all its rites and variety of ceremonies; this has never been spoken of by the prophets; but those things which existed prior to Moses' day, namely, sacrifice, will be continued." (TPJS, p. 173, D.H.C 4:212)

When the penalties existed in the Temple ceremonies of our dispensation, we were reminded of the shedding of blood required for a covenant. When removed, we lose some of that memory. How would penalties involving the shedding of blood prepare people for the return of animal sacrifice? Would it help remind them that shedding blood is required to establish a covenant? Even this final Dispensation of the

Fullness of Time could not be an effective covenant without the shedding of blood to seal the testament or covenant.[480]

Does the Gospel of Jesus Christ require the sacrifice of all things? (We've explained this before in relation to the Lectures on Faith.) If so, then how do we obtain the blessings we desire from the hand of God without being willing to make a similar sacrifice? If it is required, then how do we qualify to receive this baptism of fire spoken of by Nephi that will purge us from all sin and permit us to speak with a new tongue? How is this sacrifice made apart from the irrevocable commitment made within yourself to "endure to the end" by laying upon the altar everything you have, even your own life if necessary, to build up His kingdom? How, in a fallen world filled with sin, in a day where there is no sacrifice or consecration being made by others; how do you do that? What does the "doctrine of Christ" allow you to do without regard to the sins and errors you find all around you? Even if all the world is content to remain Telestial, or some few encourage only a Terrestrial law be followed, can you still find and live the "doctrine of Christ?" Does Nephi's teachings require you to be anything or anyone special or noteworthy in this life? Can you do this in private, between you and God? Can you follow the "doctrine of Christ" by what you think, ponder, pray, say, do and believe?

This statement, which concludes the exposition on "the doctrine of Christ" is concluded using the names of "the only and true doctrine of the Father, and of the Son, and of the Holy Ghost, which is one God, without end. Amen." Although only a few will recognize this, it is a formula used when using the sealing authority. If you are aware of this, then you would realize what Nephi has done is declared that he possesses the Patriarchal Priesthood authority, which invariably includes the power to seal. He will mention "sealing" his testimony again before he concludes. But if you know this is a formula employed in connection with this authority, you will recognize it. Within the ordinances of the church, we use this formula when baptizing and again when sealing a marriage in the Temple. All other intermediate ordinances are done "in the name of Jesus Christ."

---

480 D&C 135: 3: "Joseph Smith, the Prophet and Seer of the Lord, has done more, save Jesus only, for the salvation of men in this world, than any other man that ever lived in it. In the short space of twenty years, he has brought forth the Book of Mormon, which he translated by the gift and power of God, and has been the means of publishing it on two continents; has sent the fulness of the everlasting gospel, which it contained, to the four quarters of the earth; has brought forth the revelations and commandments which compose this book of Doctrine and Covenants, and many other wise documents and instructions for the benefit of the children of men; gathered many thousands of the Latter-day Saints, founded a great city, and left a fame and name that cannot be slain. He lived great, and he died great in the eyes of God and his people; and like most of the Lord's anointed in ancient times, has sealed his mission and his works with his own blood; and so has his brother Hyrum. In life they were not divided, and in death they were not separated!"

Baptism has been specifically authorized to be performed "in the name of the Father, and of the Son, and of the Holy Ghost." That authorization came from the Lord, by revelation.[481] That authorization is important and allows the formula to be used. Then, in the Temple, it is once again prescribed for use. I point it out deliberately, and knowing that the authorization of the formula is deliberate, noteworthy and important to consider as a matter of meaning.

---

[481] D&C 20: 73: "The person who is called of God and has authority from Jesus Christ to baptize, shall go down into the water with the person who has presented himself or herself for baptism, and shall say, calling him or her by name: Having been commissioned of Jesus Christ, I baptize you in the name of the Father, and of the Son, and of the Holy Ghost. Amen."

2 Nephi 32

2 Nephi 32: 1-2

> **"And now, behold, my beloved brethren, I suppose that ye ponder somewhat in your hearts concerning that which ye should do after ye have entered in by the way. But, behold, why do ye ponder these things in your hearts? Do ye not remember that I said unto you that after ye had received the Holy Ghost ye could speak with the tongue of angels? And now, how could ye speak with the tongue of angels save it were by the Holy Ghost?"**

It is the program of the Gospel that communication and understanding of God's will should be obtained through revelation. That revelation comes from contact with, and communication by, the Holy Ghost. The Holy Ghost is able to tell you "all things."[482]

You don't need another source once you are in contact with the Holy Ghost. It possesses the "record of heaven."[483]

Nephi is assuring us that we can come into possession of the fullness of truth by the means he has been explaining as the "doctrine of Christ." As a central, active part of that doctrine, the line of communication between you and God is opened. It is another reminder of counsel found in Deuteronomy 30: 11-14: "For this commandment which I command thee this day, it is not hidden from thee, neither is it far off. It is not in heaven, that thou shouldest say, Who shall go up for us to heaven, and

---

482 Moses 6: 61: "Therefore it is given to abide in you; the record of heaven; the Comforter; the peaceable things of immortal glory; the truth of all things; that which quickeneth all things, which maketh alive all things; that which knoweth all things, and hath all power according to wisdom, mercy, truth, justice, and judgment."
Moroni 10: 4: "And when ye shall receive these things, I would exhort you that ye would ask God, the Eternal Father, in the name of Christ, if these things are not true; and if ye shall ask with a sincere heart, with real intent, having faith in Christ, he will manifest the truth of it unto you, by the power of the Holy Ghost."

483 Moses 6: 61: "Therefore it is given to abide in you; the record of heaven; the Comforter; the peaceable things of immortal glory; the truth of all things; that which quickeneth all things, which maketh alive all things; that which knoweth all things, and hath all power according to wisdom, mercy, truth, justice, and judgment."

bring it unto us, that we may hear it, and do it? Neither is it beyond the sea, that thou shouldest say, Who shall go over the sea for us, and bring it unto us, that we may hear it, and do it? But the word is very nigh unto thee, in thy mouth, and in thy heart, that thou mayest do it."

Forget all the cultural assumptions and extras you hang on to. Leave them all behind and keep it simple:

You were a spirit before you were born.[484] You were there when some were chosen to be "rulers," or in other words, teachers.[485] You have within you a spirit that was in that group. You saw and participated in what went on, and have that somewhere still inside you. It is kept from you by the "veil of flesh" now covering your spirit.[486] Somewhere within you lies the "record of heaven." Or more correctly, the Record of Heaven.[487] If you gain access to it, it has the capacity to teach you the "truth of all things."[488] Within it is such an abundance of truth that the things of God are not hidden from you, neither far off. It is not in heaven, so that you ask: who will go to heaven to bring it to us. It is not beyond the sea that you should ask who can go to bring it to us? But it is

---

[484] Abr. 3: 22-28: "Now the Lord had shown unto me, Abraham, the intelligences that were organized before the world was; and among all these there were many of the noble and great ones; And God saw these souls that they were good, and he stood in the midst of them, and he said: These I will make my rulers; for he stood among those that were spirits, and he saw that they were good; and he said unto me: Abraham, thou art one of them; thou wast chosen before thou wast born. And there stood one among them that was like unto God, and he said unto those who were with him: We will go down, for there is space there, and we will take of these materials, and we will make an earth whereon these may dwell; And we will prove them herewith, to see if they will do all things whatsoever the Lord their God shall command them; And they who keep their first estate shall be added upon; and they who keep not their first estate shall not have glory in the same kingdom with those who keep their first estate; and they who keep their second estate shall have glory added upon their heads for ever and ever. And the Lord said: Whom shall I send? And one answered like unto the Son of Man: Here am I, send me. And another answered and said: Here am I, send me. And the Lord said: I will send the first. And the second was angry, and kept not his first estate; and, at that day, many followed after him"

[485] 2 Ne. 5: 19: "And behold, the words of the Lord had been fulfilled unto my brethren, which he spake concerning them, that I should be their ruler and their teacher. Wherefore, I had been their ruler and their teacher, according to the commandments of the Lord, until the time they sought to take away my life."

[486] Heb. 10: 20: "By a new and living way, which he hath consecrated for us, through the veil, that is to say, his flesh;"

[487] Moses 6: 61: "Therefore it is given to abide in you; the record of heaven; the Comforter; the peaceable things of immortal glory; the truth of all things; that which quickeneth all things, which maketh alive all things; that which knoweth all things, and hath all power according to wisdom, mercy, truth, justice, and judgment."

[488] Ibid.

very close to you, in your own mouth, in your own heart, that you can do what is asked of you.[489]

Hence the saying of Christ that the Comforter will bring things to your remembrance.

Christ taught the kingdom of God is within you.

Why is it that the body is animated, with power of thought and communication, alive and vital while there is a spirit within it? But when the spirit departs, what then of the body? The power to live and breathe and move and do according to your will is gone at that point. But from whence came that power?[490] If it is God who is "lending you that power" then how closely are you connected to God? How immediate is His presence within you?

If you can gain access to God, will you need to go out, or will you instead need to go within?

Our minds are corrupted. I've spent time dealing with the corrosive influence of cultures from Babylon to today in *Nephi's Isaiah*. All that must be "ground to dust" and blown away.[491] That will occur within you. You are the battleground where the conflict is being fought. You are potentially the Temple of God.[492]

Awake and arise! Come to yourself and realize who you are. This "doctrine of Christ" will teach you all things you must know for life and salvation. But you ought not look to another to find what you already have. You must instead repent and return to God, who is your home.

---

489 Deut. 30: 11-14: "For this commandment which I command thee this day, it *is* not hidden from thee, neither *is* it far off. It *is* not in heaven, that thou shouldest say, Who shall go up for us to heaven, and bring it unto us, that we may hear it, and do it? Neither *is* it beyond the sea, that thou shouldest say, Who shall go over the sea for us, and bring it unto us, that we may hear it, and do it? But the word *is* very nigh unto thee, in thy mouth, and in thy heart, that thou mayest do it."

490 Mosiah 2: 21: "I say unto you that if ye should serve him who has created you from the beginning, and is preserving you from day to day, by lending you breath, that ye may live and move and do according to your own will, and even supporting you from one moment to another—I say, if ye should serve him with all your whole souls yet ye would be unprofitable servants."

491 Dan. 2: 34-35: "Thou sawest till that a stone was cut out without hands, which smote the image upon his feet *that were* of iron and clay, and brake them to pieces. Then was the iron, the clay, the brass, the silver, and the gold, broken to pieces together, and became like the chaff of the summer threshingfloors; and the wind carried them away, that no place was found for them: and the stone that smote the image became a great mountain, and filled the whole earth."

492 1 Cor. 3: 16: "Know ye not that ye are the temple of God, and *that* the Spirit of God dwelleth in you?"

2 Nephi 32: 3

> **"Angels speak by the power of the Holy Ghost; wherefore, they speak the words of Christ. Wherefore, I said unto you, feast upon the words of Christ; for behold, the words of Christ will tell you all things what ye should do."**

Nephi makes these three things equal:

1. The power of the Holy Ghost to give words, which

2. Are the same as what angels would speak, which in turn

3. Are the same as the words of Christ.

Holy Ghost/words of angels/words of Christ. They are all the same as "the words of Christ" which will "tell you all things what ye should do."

If you will "feast upon the words of Christ" then you will know "all things what ye should do."

How do you unlock this power that potentially exists inside you? What tools have been given to us to receive access to this great inner record of truth?

Why are we given ordinances? If we will follow them and receive them, what do ordinances allow the Lord to open up for us?

You know if you are doing as you should. You cannot lie to yourself. You cannot deceive yourself about whether you will follow God with full purpose of heart, acting no deception, repenting of your sins, and with real intent.[493] If you do these things there is a law irrevocably decreed which permits you to receive what is offered.[494] You actually know if you have offered the correct sacrifice. (Lecture 6, in *Lectures on Faith* discussed here.) Just as you know when you are unworthy before Him[495], you also know when your confidence before God grows

---

[493] 2 Ne. 31: 13: "Wherefore, my beloved brethren, I know that if ye shall follow the Son, with full purpose of heart, acting no hypocrisy and no deception before God, but with real intent, repenting of your sins, witnessing unto the Father that ye are willing to take upon you the name of Christ, by baptism—yea, by following your Lord and your Savior down into the water, according to his word, behold, then shall ye receive the Holy Ghost; yea, then cometh the baptism of fire and of the Holy Ghost; and then can ye speak with the tongue of angels, and shout praises unto the Holy One of Israel."

[494] D&C 130: 20-21: "There is a law, irrevocably decreed in heaven before the foundations of this world, upon which all blessings are predicated—
21 And when we obtain any blessing from God, it is by obedience to that law upon which it is predicated."

[495] Mormon 9: 4-5: "Behold, I say unto you that ye would be more miserable to dwell with a holy and just God, under a consciousness of your filthiness before him, than ye would to dwell with the damned souls in hell. For behold, when ye shall be brought to see your nakedness before God, and also the glory of God, and the holiness of Jesus Christ, it will kindle a flame of unquenchable fire upon you."

naturally inside you and you follow the path to return to the light[496]. It is extraordinary and even miraculous, but it is also absolutely natural.

The conditions were set before the foundation of the world and all you must do to obtain these blessings is to follow the path. You KNOW if you are in the right way. You cannot lie to God, and as we have seen in the discussion of the preceding verses, God is within you.

Do you keep the commandments? Why? Are you doing so with real intent, following the "doctrine of Christ" or just to be "seen of men?"[497] When you do these things in secret, your Father (and you) know it and then come the rewards of having your heart right with God.[498]

At the end of the long search into all the universe to find God, you will discover the search leads you back to what was inside you all along. You came from Him, and He is with you. But to find Him you must return. The scriptures and teachings of Christ are filled with this journey and the battleground has always been within you. You need to remember. The Holy Ghost, the third member of the godhead, dwells inside you, provided you will receive it.

The laws irrevocably decreed are the very principles which permeate life itself. You are not separate from this "doctrine of Christ" but a living embodiment of it. If you live it, you will prove it. You are here to be proven.[499] What have you determined to prove with your life?

Nephi spoke in plainness to us. He could not find simpler language to describe this process. I have tried to be plain using other scriptures and language. But the great lesson can be reduced to this: Do what you have been taught. When you do it, the light will increase within you. That light is truth. It is intelligence, or light and truth, or the power of

---

[496] D&C 121: 45-46: "Let thy bowels also be full of charity towards all men, and to the household of faith, and let virtue garnish thy thoughts unceasingly; then shall thy confidence wax strong in the presence of God; and the doctrine of the priesthood shall distil upon thy soul as the dews from heaven. The Holy Ghost shall be thy constant companion, and thy scepter an unchanging scepter of righteousness and truth; and thy dominion shall be an everlasting dominion, and without compulsory means it shall flow unto thee forever and ever."

[497] Matt. 6: 1, 5: "Take heed that ye do not your alms before men, to be seen of them: otherwise ye have no reward of your Father which is in heaven. …And when thou prayest, thou shalt not be as the hypocrites *are:* for they love to pray standing in the synagogues and in the corners of the streets, that they may be seen of men. Verily I say unto you, They have their reward."

[498] Matt. 6: 4, 6: "That thine alms may be in secret: and thy Father which seeth in secret himself shall reward thee openly. …But thou, when thou prayest, enter into thy closet, and when thou hast shut thy door, pray to thy Father which is in secret; and thy Father which seeth in secret shall reward thee openly."

[499] Abr. 3: 25: "And we will prove them herewith, to see if they will do all things whatsoever the Lord their God shall command them;"

God.[500] All you must do to activate that light, gain that intelligence, and behold the glory of God is to keep His commandments.[501] If you want to receive a "fullness" then the immediate door through which you pass is to keep the commandments.[502]

Most importantly, you must "follow the Son, with full purpose of heart, acting no hypocrisy and no deception before God, but with real intent, repenting of your sins, witnessing unto the Father that ye are willing to take upon you the name of Christ."[503] You alone will know if you have done this. Or rather, you and the Lord will know. When you are satisfied that there is no hypocrisy and no deception between you and God, that you have come to Him with real intent and repenting of your sins, witnessing through the ordinances (baptism and sacrament) that you will take upon you the name of Christ, then you qualify. If you do not, then you are not qualified.

I am completely satisfied that the people who gain such access, receive the blessings, or obtain a hope in Christ are ordinary people. They are not distinguished by their great intellect or powerful positions. They are typified only by the singleness of their heart and true devotion. There is not a whit of difference between what they believe and how they live. They do not excuse themselves from doing what they know to be right, even if it is painful, uncomfortable, or something they would never do on their own. They invariably do what the "words of Christ" bid them to do. No matter the price, they will follow Him; not a leader. Indeed, almost all of His servants are at odds with leadership. You know how completely He was at odds if you have read *Come, Let Us Adore Him*. To follow Him is to have that same contention between you and the larger religious community of any age or dispensation. Stop trying to please men and start following Christ.

I do not know what more can be said than Nephi has been saying. Let's press on.

---

500 D&C 93: 36: "The glory of God is intelligence, or, in other words, light and truth."

501 D&C 93: 28: "He that keepeth his commandments receiveth truth and light, until he is glorified in truth and knoweth all things."

502 D&C 93: 20: "For if you keep my commandments you shall receive of his fulness, and be glorified in me as I am in the Father; therefore, I say unto you, you shall receive grace for grace."

503 2 Ne. 31: 13: "Wherefore, my beloved brethren, I know that if ye shall follow the Son, with full purpose of heart, acting no hypocrisy and no deception before God, but with real intent, repenting of your sins, witnessing unto the Father that ye are willing to take upon you the name of Christ, by baptism—yea, by following your Lord and your Savior down into the water, according to his word, behold, then shall ye receive the Holy Ghost; yea, then cometh the baptism of fire and of the Holy Ghost; and then can ye speak with the tongue of angels, and shout praises unto the Holy One of Israel."

2 Nephi 32: 4-5

> **"Wherefore, now after I have spoken these words, if ye cannot understand them it will be because ye ask not, neither do ye knock; wherefore, ye are not brought into the light, but must perish in the dark. For behold, again I say unto you that if ye will enter in by the way, and receive the Holy Ghost, it will show unto you all things what ye should do."**

Comprehension of the "doctrine of Christ" is not based on command of a vocabulary or mastery of an argument. It is based on gathering light. Light is gathered by heed (obedience) and diligence alone.[504] By following the light you have received already, you grow in light.[505] This process leads to the "perfect day" where the light has chased away all darkness. This is how we, like Christ, can grow from grace to grace until we also receive a fullness.[506]

If you do not do this, then you may acquire a vocabulary with which to discuss the subject, but you will not have the light to comprehend it. Light can be shining all around you, but if you do not acquire light within yourself by your actions, you cannot comprehend the light. (See, e.g., D&C 6: 21; D&C 10: 58; D&C 34: 2; D&C 39: 2; D&C 45: 7; and D&C 88: 49.)

If it perplexes you, then ask God for understanding. He will tell you what to do. Follow His instruction. In this way you qualify to receive further light and knowledge by conversing with the Lord. He knows perfectly what you lack, and by the Holy Ghost within you will tell you what you must do.

If you will not humble yourself and ask for this to be made known to you, then you cannot be brought into the light. Then the only result will be to perish in the dark.

If you will follow the steps with the required real intent, acting no deception before God as you do, then you will receive the Holy Ghost. It will be unlocked to tell you what you lack and what you need to do. This inner light is a powerful source which can literally tell "you all things what ye should do."

It is in the doing that you find the learning. It is in the act of following Him that you learn to be like Him. Obedience is the means by which you gather light. The commandments are revelations of the inner

---

504 D&C 130: 19: "And if a person gains more knowledge and intelligence in this life through his diligence and obedience than another, he will have so much the advantage in the world to come."

505 D&C 50: 24: "That which is of God is light; and he that receiveth light, and continueth in God, receiveth more light; and that light groweth brighter and brighter until the perfect day."

506 D&C 93: 20: "For if you keep my commandments you shall receive of his fulness, and be glorified in me as I am in the Father; therefore, I say unto you, you shall receive grace for grace."

person you ought to become. They are how you grow in the flesh to comprehend God in the Spirit. Your body is a veil that keeps you from Him. By subordinating the will of the flesh to the will of the Spirit, you gain light and truth.

Do it to understand it.

Once you understand you will be able to tell when someone speaks with the power of the Spirit words of eternal life, or if they are, as Nephi puts it: "perishing in the dark." There are many who claim to speak on the Lord's behalf who declare false, vain and foolish things. While they will be held to account for that, the point is not to condemn them. They may yet see the light, and repent and return. The point is that you must avoid being misled by those who would lead you astray. The few humble followers of Christ are warned that they will be taught the precepts of men and must use caution to avoid being misled.[507] We've discussed that already.

The proportions and the balances required to see things aright are too fine, too subtle and too difficult to put into words. They are harmony. Nephi's teachings are woven into one great whole. There are not isolated strains to be taken from the great whole and then given undeserved importance. They must fit together. You can only accomplish that when you see the whole by the light of the Holy Ghost within you.

Nephi is both pleading and warning in these two verses. He wants you to go to the source and be directed from there. To have the words of Christ available to you. To hear the words of angels as you draw near to the light. If you do not, then it is because you refuse to follow the steps he has described.

You must act to know. Without following through in your heart (which you cannot ever deceive) you can't draw near to the light. The discussion in *The Second Comforter* walks through line upon line that walk back into the light, and ultimately into Christ's presence. It is a modern manual to find Him.

2 Nephi 32: 6

> **"Behold, this is the doctrine of Christ, and there will be no more doctrine given until after he shall manifest himself unto you in the flesh. And when he shall manifest himself unto you in the flesh, the things which he shall say unto you shall ye observe to do."**

This is the totality of the matter: the doctrine of Christ.

Receive the Comforter and it will tell you what you must do.

---

507 2 Ne. 28: 14: "They wear stiff necks and high heads; yea, and because of pride, and wickedness, and abominations, and whoredoms, they have all gone astray save it be a few, who are the humble followers of Christ; nevertheless, they are led, that in many instances they do err because they are taught by the precepts of men."

It will in turn lead you to the Second Comforter. He will then take you further still.

What does it mean that Christ "shall manifest Himself unto you in the flesh?" Is this speaking of the time when Christ appeared to the Nephites (3 Nephi 11: 1-41, where He did declare doctrine)? Or is this speaking of Him appearing to each individual?[508] Is it both?

What does it mean that "the things which He shall say unto you shall ye observe to do?" What takes primacy—your culture, respected peers, leaders of society or government or church, or the Lord and His sayings? Why?

What does it mean that "no more doctrine" will be given until Christ "shall manifest Himself unto you in the flesh?" Was there more doctrine given to later Nephite prophets before Christ appeared in 3 Nephi? What about the very next writer-prophet of the Book of Mormon and his testimony of revelation from Christ?[509] Was his ministry one that included the Lord "manifesting Himself unto [Jacob] in the flesh?"[510]

How and what is to be revealed? Although you may receive Christ "in the flesh," does it mean you may tell others all things you learn as a result? Or are you constrained and limited in what and how you measure

---

508 John 14: 23: "Jesus answered and said unto him, If a man love me, he will keep my words: and my Father will love him, and we will come unto him, and make our abode with him."
D&C 130: 3: "John 14:23—The appearing of the Father and the Son, in that verse, is a personal appearance; and the idea that the Father and the Son dwell in a man's heart is an old sectarian notion, and is false."

509 Jacob 1: 4, 6: "And if there were preaching which was sacred, or revelation which was great, or prophesying, that I should engraven the heads of them upon these plates, and touch upon them as much as it were possible, for Christ's sake, and for the sake of our people. ...And we also had many revelations, and the spirit of much prophecy; wherefore, we knew of Christ and his kingdom, which should come."
Jacob 4: 6: "Wherefore, we search the prophets, and we have many revelations and the spirit of prophecy; and having all these witnesses we obtain a hope, and our faith becometh unshaken, insomuch that we truly can command in the name of Jesus and the very trees obey us, or the mountains, or the waves of the sea."
Jacob 7: 5: "And he had hope to shake me from the faith, notwithstanding the many revelations and the many things which I had seen concerning these things; for I truly had seen angels, and they had ministered unto me. And also, I had heard the voice of the Lord speaking unto me in very word, from time to time; wherefore, I could not be shaken."

510 2 Ne. 11: 3: "And my brother, Jacob, also has seen him as I have seen him; wherefore, I will send their words forth unto my children to prove unto them that my words are true. Wherefore, by the words of three, God hath said, I will establish my word. Nevertheless, God sendeth more witnesses, and he proveth all his words."

to others? Who decides what is appropriate to include in your testimony, you or the Lord?[511]

If "what He shall say unto you shall ye observe to do," then what of criticism? What of those who will not accept your testimony? What if your testimony of Christ is dismissed as merely your "claims?" What if things done in meekness and humility are misconstrued and said instead to be done to get notice and popularity? Should you expect to be without criticism?

What does it mean that "the things which he shall say unto you shall ye observe to do?" Does it mean others will even understand why you do what you do? Does it mean it will be welcomed? Does it mean you will have some credential the world will recognize? Or will only those who hear the Master's voice respond?[512] If it is the Master's voice which should be heard, then how do you avoid introducing your own voice in His place? What if the words are a rebuke or warning? Should you hesitate?[513]

If you only have your testimony to offer, how likely is it to be persuasive in this world where rank, position, acclaim and popularity define influence? What if, as Bob Dylan penned: *"All I got is this red guitar, three chords and the truth."* What then? Is the truth resilient enough to endure in this hurricane of deceit and worldliness? It will, even if only with a few.

At your core, you love and respect Jesus Christ. When given the choice before your were born, you accepted and agreed to follow Him. That is why you are here. If you followed Him then, you ought to be willing to follow Him now. If you can find Him. I believe that anyone who can find the Master's words, no matter how unlikely a source by which they come, will follow them. The only means authorized to

---

[511] Alma 12: 9-10: "And now Alma began to expound these things unto him, saying: It is given unto many to know the mysteries of God; nevertheless they are laid under a strict command that they shall not impart only according to the portion of his word which he doth grant unto the children of men, according to the heed and diligence which they give unto him. And therefore, he that will harden his heart, the same receiveth the lesser portion of the word; and he that will not harden his heart, to him is given the greater portion of the word, until it is given unto him to know the mysteries of God until he know them in full."

[512] John 10: 27: "My sheep hear my voice, and I know them, and they follow me:"

[513] 3 Ne. 30: 1-2: "Hearken, O ye Gentiles, and hear the words of Jesus Christ, the Son of the living God, which he hath commanded me that I should speak concerning you, for, behold he commandeth me that I should write, saying: Turn, all ye Gentiles, from your wicked ways; and repent of your evil doings, of your lyings and deceivings, and of your whoredoms, and of your secret abominations, and your idolatries, and of your murders, and your priestcrafts, and your envyings, and your strifes, and from all your wickedness and abominations, and come unto me, and be baptized in my name, that ye may receive a remission of your sins, and be filled with the Holy Ghost, that ye may be numbered with my people who are of the house of Israel."

declare them is through persuasion, gentleness, meekness, love and pure knowledge.[514] As it turns out, that is enough. Those who have kept the Light of Christ shining within them will recognize His voice.[515]

2 Nephi 32: 7

> **"And now I, Nephi, cannot say more; the Spirit stoppeth mine utterance, and I am left to mourn because of the unbelief, and the wickedness, and the ignorance, and the stiffneckedness of men; for they will not search knowledge, nor understand great knowledge, when it is given unto them in plainness, even as plain as word can be."**

Nephi has reached the limit of what he can say. He has alluded to the Second Comforter, or the appearance of Christ to you in the flesh, but then his message ends. He "cannot say more." But he has told you that when Christ appears to you that you should do what Christ tells you to do.

Then Nephi laments our unbelief, wickedness, ignorance and stiffneckedness. You have already been told that in the vocabulary of the Book of Mormon the word "unbelief" means that you do not understand correct doctrine. You accept false notions, or your understanding is so incomplete as to make it wrong.

What is "wicked" about not following the "doctrine of Christ" so that you can receive the tongue of an angel? What is wicked about not pressing forward in the light of the Holy Ghost to the point where you receive Christ in the flesh? Why would that failing be "wicked?"[516]

Why are we "ignorant?" Is it because of our lack of learning or sophistication, or instead because of it? Studied ignorance is the most indelible kind. It prevents someone from ever casting away unbelief. It enshrines unbelief.

These conditions are all culminated by "stiffneckedness." Meaning that we are not only in error, but we are decidedly committed to remaining so. We won't budge. Won't humble ourselves and ask the Lord to remove our scales of darkness. We just remain devoted disciples of unbelief, leading in turn to our wickedness, borne upon the shoulders of our ignorance. What a spectacle we are when seen in the light of the Holy Ghost—that is, through the eyes of a prophet like Nephi.

What is interesting is this comment comes at the very end of Nephi's ministry. It is an aged prophet carving his last message targeted to the

---

[514] D&C 121: 41: "No power or influence can or ought to be maintained by virtue of the priesthood, only by persuasion, by long-suffering, by gentleness and meekness, and by love unfeigned;"

[515] John 10: 27: "My sheep hear my voice, and I know them, and they follow me:"

[516] D&C 88: 33: "For what doth it profit a man if a gift is bestowed upon him, and he receive not the gift? Behold, he rejoices not in that which is given unto him, neither rejoices in him who is the giver of the gift."

last day audience of first gentiles, then secondarily the remnant, and finally the Jews. And to this latter-day audience beginning with us, Nephi is rebuking us. It must be because of his love for us. It must be motivated by the love of Christ, because it follows immediately after explaining to us the "doctrine of Christ." So whether it seems to be the case or not, this is a loving, kind, light-filled warning from someone who knows what we lack.

Soberly, however, this rebuke should be compared to the rebuke he leveled at Laman and Lemuel. He told them to stop debating the meaning of a revelation given to their father, and start asking God for answers. Compare Nephi's earlier warning and rebuke to his brothers with this verse addressed to us:

"And they said: Behold, we cannot understand the words which our father hath spoken concerning the natural branches of the olive-tree, and also concerning the Gentiles. And I said unto them: **Have ye inquired of the Lord?** And they said unto me: We have not; for the Lord maketh no such thing known unto us. Behold, I said unto them: **How is it that ye do not keep the commandments of the Lord? How is it that ye will perish, because of the hardness of your hearts?** Do ye not remember the things which the Lord hath said?—If ye will not harden your hearts, and ask me in faith, believing that ye shall receive, with diligence in keeping my commandments, surely these things shall be made known unto you."[517] We read that and think ourselves better than Laman and Lemuel because we identify ourselves with Nephi. Nephi, on the other hand, sees our day, and identifies us with Laman and Lemuel. What a profound disconnect our arrogance causes between Nephi's meaning and our reading.

He is being as plain as words can be. And we are being as obstinate and obtuse as unbelief, wickedness, ignorance and stiffneckedness can cause. You can feel the irony.

2 Nephi 32: 8

> **"And now, my beloved brethren, I perceive that ye ponder still in your hearts; and it grieveth me that I must speak concerning this thing. For if ye would hearken unto the Spirit which teacheth a man to pray ye would know that ye must pray; for the evil spirit**

[517] 1 Ne. 15: 7-11: "And they said: Behold, we cannot understand the words which our father hath spoken concerning the natural branches of the olive-tree, and also concerning the Gentiles. And I said unto them: Have ye inquired of the Lord? And they said unto me: We have not; for the Lord maketh no such thing known unto us. Behold, I said unto them: How is it that ye do not keep the commandments of the Lord? How is it that ye will perish, because of the hardness of your hearts? Do ye not remember the things which the Lord hath said?—If ye will not harden your hearts, and ask me in faith, believing that ye shall receive, with diligence in keeping my commandments, surely these things shall be made known unto you."

teacheth not a man to pray, but teacheth him that he must not pray."

Again we are called "beloved brethren" despite having just reminded us of our unbelief, wickedness, ignorance and stiffneckedness. His motive is our welfare. He doesn't care a whit about flattering us. He wants us saved.

Still you wonder if this can be true. Still you doubt and think it too much. Still you are left not knowing if the message comes from the Lord. But those doubts are because of your failure to pray. You just won't listen to the Spirit which teaches everyone they must pray. "For if ye would hearken unto the Spirit which teacheth a man to pray ye would know ye must pray."

Nephi knows this because he is a man of prayer. Nephi, as a man of prayer, is struck by the foolishness of deciding matters without prayer. To him it is amazingly obvious that prayer will rescue you from doubt. But Nephi knows why you won't pray to know the truth of things.

You want an authority to tell you.

You want the truth to become popular so it is easy to find.

You want certifications, scholarly support and widespread recognition of the truth.

You want someone whose position you respect to tell you what is true. And until they do, you feel confident you don't need to study it out and pray to know for yourself if it is true.

But Nephi catches you in the act and tells you this is because you are listening to "the evil spirit" which is the one who "teacheth not a man to pray, but teacheth him that he must not pray." So you are following the spirit. But it is an evil spirit you follow.

God's Spirit will always teach you to pray and to ask Him about the truth. And if you ask with a sincere heart, with real intent, He will manifest the truth unto you. He can tell you the truth of all things if you will ask and permit the Holy Ghost to respond.[518]

If the only way to find the truth is to search prayerfully for it before receiving a witness from the Holy Ghost that it is indeed true, what happens to you as a result? Do you gain a testimony of the process? Do you grow in light and truth by what you have experienced? Was this always meant to be direct between you and God? Is the method itself necessarily always to involve God?

Nephi is a prophet. And he's working to make others like him. That's the way it is, you see. Those who have something are eager to have others join them. They are not interested in praise or recognition. Instead

[518] Moroni 10: 4-5: "And when ye shall receive these things, I would exhort you that ye would ask God, the Eternal Father, in the name of Christ, if these things are not true; and if ye shall ask with a sincere heart, with real intent, having faith in Christ, he will manifest the truth of it unto you, by the power of the Holy Ghost. And by the power of the Holy Ghost ye may know the truth of all things."

they are interested in seeing other souls redeemed. Hence Nephi's blunt message and plain words. They are merciful indeed.

2 Nephi 32:9

> **"But behold, I say unto you that ye must pray always, and not faint; that ye must not perform any thing unto the Lord save in the first place ye shall pray unto the Father in the name of Christ, that he will consecrate thy performance unto thee, that thy performance may be for the welfare of thy soul."**

Another significant reminder by a prophet of what is needed.

The great passage from Alma on prayer is an echo of Nephi.[519] Nephi said it first.

What is involved with "performing anything unto the Lord?" How much of what we do in our daily responsibilities ought to be performed "unto the Lord?"

Do not "perform any thing" for the Lord until you have "in the first place" prayed to consecrate your performance. Here Nephi teaches you how to live the law of consecration. You don't need others to join you. You don't need a city to live where all things are held in common. You only need your own pure intent, acting no hypocrisy, consecrating your performance to the Lord for the welfare of your soul.

If you "must not perform any thing unto the Lord" before praying and consecrating it "for the welfare of thy soul," then how should you proceed? How much thought should you take about the Lord and your relationship with Him daily? How careful should you be about your words, thoughts and works?[520] It is again, a reminder that we should

---

[519] Alma 34: 17-27: "Therefore may God grant unto you, my brethren, that ye may begin to exercise your faith unto repentance, that ye begin to call upon his holy name, that he would have mercy upon you; Yea, cry unto him for mercy; for he is mighty to save. Yea, humble yourselves, and continue in prayer unto him. Cry unto him when ye are in your fields, yea, over all your flocks. Cry unto him in your houses, yea, over all your household, both morning, mid-day, and evening. Yea, cry unto him against the power of your enemies. Yea, cry unto him against the devil, who is an enemy to all righteousness. Cry unto him over the crops of your fields, that ye may prosper in them. Cry over the flocks of your fields, that they may increase. But this is not all; ye must pour out your souls in your closets, and your secret places, and in your wilderness. Yea, and when you do not cry unto the Lord, let your hearts be full, drawn out in prayer unto him continually for your welfare, and also for the welfare of those who are around you."

[520] Alma 12: 14: "For our words will condemn us, yea, all our works will condemn us; we shall not be found spotless; and our thoughts will also condemn us; and in this awful state we shall not dare to look up to our God; and we would fain be glad if we could command the rocks and the mountains to fall upon us to hide us from his presence."

always remember Him, and keep His commandments which He has given us, that we may have His Spirit to be with us.[521]

What does it mean to "pray always, and not faint?" What does "praying" have to do with "fainting?" What does it mean to "faint?" Can you "faint" in your spiritual life? Is a physical "faint" merely an example of what happens to us in the spirit? If so, what must you do to avoid becoming "faint" in your prayers?

How many of your prayers have ended by your mind drifting away? No certain conclusion to the prayer, just a distracted mind becoming occupied by something other than the prayer being offered? Is that to "faint?"

What does "fainting" tell you about your vulnerability? What precautions do you need to take to be able to "pray always" and not be vulnerable to "fainting?"

Is the primary difference between the outcome of the lives of Nephi and Jacob on the one hand, and Laman and Lemuel on the other, how they regarded prayer?

What does having prayer as a priority say about an individual?

---

[521] D&C 20: 77: "O God, the Eternal Father, we ask thee in the name of thy Son, Jesus Christ, to bless and sanctify this bread to the souls of all those who partake of it, that they may eat in remembrance of the body of thy Son, and witness unto thee, O God, the Eternal Father, that they are willing to take upon them the name of thy Son, and always remember him and keep his commandments which he has given them; that they may always have his Spirit to be with them. Amen."

2 NEPHI 33

2 Nephi 33: 1-2

> **"And now I, Nephi, cannot write all the things which were taught among my people; neither am I mighty in writing, like unto speaking; for when a man speaketh by the power of the Holy Ghost the power of the Holy Ghost carrieth it unto the hearts of the children of men. But behold, there are many that harden their hearts against the Holy Spirit, that it hath no place in them; wherefore, they cast many things away which are written and esteem them as things of naught."**

Nephi would like to teach us (his readers) all he taught those who lived with him and heard him speak. But he could not. Even the things he was able to etch in the metal record he left was incomplete when compared to the body of teachings he preached to his people.

There is also a significant difference between speaking and writing. When you speak there are many tools of speech—emphasis, movement, presence, and radiation of the Spirit to help the speaker measure the effect of the message on the audience. When Nephi taught by the power of the Holy Ghost, he was able to see how his audience was receiving it. He knew when it penetrated "unto the hearts of the children of men."

Writing was another matter. Particularly when it would be translated from one language to another before the gentiles would receive the words. The distance and language between Nephi and his audience is so great that Nephi came to the sad realization that a reader who is not already prepared to have the Spirit with them as they read will miss the power of the message.

In their presence Nephi could use the power of the Holy Ghost to affect the spirit of those who were listening. However, a reader separated by language and culture, and more than two millennia would have to have the Spirit first before being able to understand his message.

It was the recognition that many gentiles would read this record without possessing the Spirit that made Nephi acknowledge the gap between his spoken ministry and his written one. Those with "hard hearts" may be affected by his presence and preaching. Those with "hard hearts" who only have his written record, however, are going to "cast things away which are written and esteem them as things of naught." They won't recognize that they were from God, written by a prophet who knew God, and were the result of a commission to preach given by God. Instead they will think him "a thing of naught."

Nephi's message will mean far more to those who are prepared. For those who are not prepared, the message will be meaningless. Nothing. A thing of "naught" to be "cast away."

That is always the case. The Lord commissions someone with a message and the audience has a role in receiving the message. Powerful public ministries do not convince everyone. Even Nephi failed to convert Laman, Lemuel and the majority of those who were living together at the time of Lehi's death. Then, immediately upon Nephi's death, there were struggles in the society he helped found.

The process of salvation is always a work between God, His children, appropriately sent messages, and adversity and opposition. Nephi is reminding us how vital having the Spirit is to the success of understanding his written message. We should ask ourselves often if our hearts are open to receiving truth, no matter how it comes to us, and no matter how it may challenge our presumptions, pride and foolish traditions.

What a terrible thing it will be for some to realize they "esteemed as things of naught" the very words which might have saved them had they given heed.

2 Nephi 33: 3

> **"But I, Nephi, have written what I have written, and I esteem it as of great worth, and especially unto my people. For I pray continually for them by day, and mine eyes water my pillow by night, because of them; and I cry unto my God in faith, and I know that he will hear my cry."**

Nephi's single-minded focus was life-long. Now, as he writes advanced in age, with a retrospective knowledge, and prophetic foreknowledge of revelation, he confirms what he has written is "of great worth." When a prophet like Nephi appraises the work as "of great worth," it is important to realize that your disagreement with the assessment is a reflection on you, not him. It is a reflection of your own level of understanding rather than on the work itself.

Are Nephi's two books "of great worth" to you? Why? Can you articulate the reasons they have this "great worth" in everything you think and do in your daily life? How have they changed you? If there is nothing you can point to of value, then perhaps you have not yet found the "great worth" Nephi believed his writing to hold.

Why "especially unto [Nephi's] people?" Who are Nephi's "people?" Why would they be more valuable to them? Why would they have a special value to them, above the value to the gentiles?

When Nephi says he "prays continually for them," who is the group he identifies as "them?" Why does he pray for "them?"

Why does Nephi cry into his pillow at night because of "them?" Who are they and what did Nephi know would be the end of "them?"[522]

Nephi knew his cries to the Lord would not go unheard. He knew the Lord would keep a covenant made with Nephi concerning "them."[523] The remnant of Nephi's seed would not be utterly destroyed. Nevertheless, the future destruction would be near absolute, leaving only a remnant.

Despite this foreknowledge, Nephi nevertheless reports he made it a practice to nightly "cry unto my God in faith, and I know that he will hear my cry."

Nephi kept faith in the face of certain destruction of his descendants. Hope in the face of looming apostasy by his seed. Charity toward those who would reject the Lord.

He has ceased to be exclusively a prophet, and has risen to the role of intercessor and advocate for the unworthy. He has become covenantal father, and presiding Patriarch over a lineage whose redemption will come through his covenant with the Father. He has joined the ranks of the "fathers" toward whom hearts must turn in order to avoid cursing at the Lord's return.[524]

The circle has closed and the eternal round is completed. Nephi has godly feelings and godly empathy for a doomed posterity. We behold at last the veil removed. We see such nobility of character, and greatness of soul that we are compelled to accept his role as teacher and ruler. He has taught righteousness all his days. Though his older brothers refused to acknowledge or accept him, we should not. His parting message suggests, however, that more of those who will read his record have the

---

[522] 1 Ne. 12: 19: "And while the angel spake these words, I beheld and saw that the seed of my brethren did contend against my seed, according to the word of the angel; and because of the pride of my seed, and the temptations of the devil, I beheld that the seed of my brethren did overpower the people of my seed."
1 Ne. 15: 5: "And it came to pass that I was overcome because of my afflictions, for I considered that mine afflictions were great above all, because of the destruction of my people, for I had beheld their fall."

[523] 1 Ne. 13: 30: "Nevertheless, thou beholdest that the Gentiles who have gone forth out of captivity, and have been lifted up by the power of God above all other nations, upon the face of the land which is choice above all other lands, which is the land that the Lord God hath covenanted with thy father that his seed should have for the land of their inheritance; wherefore, thou seest that the Lord God will not suffer that the Gentiles will utterly destroy the mixture of thy seed, which are among thy brethren."

[524] Mal. 4: 6: "And he shall turn the heart of the fathers to the children, and the heart of the children to their fathers, lest I come and smite the earth with a curse."

same spirit as Laman and Lemuel than will have the necessary spirit to recognize and "esteem of great worth" what he has provided to us.

It is almost too great to take in for the few who are the humble followers of Christ. However, they can avoid being led into error by recognizing in Nephi the teacher and ruler who was sent to deliver a message of salvation to a doomed people. For those who now live under the same prophetic doom,[525] Nephi represents a lifeline offered to those humble enough to accept his message. They will gladly recognize their plight, awake and arise and become people of prayer.

2 Nephi 33: 4

> **"And I know that the Lord God will consecrate my prayers for the gain of my people. And the words which I have written in weakness will be made strong unto them; for it persuadeth them to do good; it maketh known unto them of their fathers; and it speaketh of Jesus, and persuadeth them to believe in him, and to endure to the end, which is life eternal."**

Nephi makes a practical application and provides us with an example of his teaching of "consecration." He knows the Lord God will "consecrate" his "prayers for the gain of [Nephi's] people." Notice that the benefit of that consecration is not for the welfare of Nephi's soul, but the welfare of others. Once again Nephi follows his teaching, and then elevates the purpose from "the welfare of [his own] soul" to the welfare of others.[526] His concerns are selfless, sacrificial and intercessory. He has become a man of charity and full of love for others. These whom he calls his "beloved brethren" and his "people" are, in fact, those who will destroy and supplant his own descendants. Although a "mixture" of his seed will be there, these people for whom he is consecrating his petitions to God are the Lamanite victors over his posterity. If you have

---

[525] 3 Ne. 16: 15: "But if they will not turn unto me, and hearken unto my voice, I will suffer them, yea, I will suffer my people, O house of Israel, that they shall go through among them, and shall tread them down, and they shall be as salt that hath lost its savor, which is thenceforth good for nothing but to be cast out, and to be trodden under foot of my people, O house of Israel."
3 Ne. 20: 16: "Then shall ye, who are a remnant of the house of Jacob, go forth among them; and ye shall be in the midst of them who shall be many; and ye shall be among them as a lion among the beasts of the forest, and as a young lion among the flocks of sheep, who, if he goeth through both treadeth down and teareth in pieces, and none can deliver."
3 Ne. 21: 12: "And my people who are a remnant of Jacob shall be among the Gentiles, yea, in the midst of them as a lion among the beasts of the forest, as a young lion among the flocks of sheep, who, if he go through both treadeth down and teareth in pieces, and none can deliver."

[526] 2 Ne. 32: 9: "But behold, I say unto you that ye must pray always, and not faint; that ye must not perform any thing unto the Lord save in the first place ye shall pray unto the Father in the name of Christ, that he will consecrate thy performance unto thee, that thy performance may be for the welfare of thy soul."

read *Beloved Enos* you will see the elements of redemption playing out in Nephi's words similar to how they play out in Enos' words. Charity is the end result of this consecrated life.

Nephi's words were "written in weakness" but he knows the Lord God will make them "strong unto them." Who is "them?" How does the Lord God make "words strong" to someone? What power communicates the strength of Nephi's words?

What does Nephi mean by "it persuadeth them to do good?" Why is persuading to do good part of the way to recognize words from God?

What does Nephi mean "it maketh known unto them of their fathers?" Which "fathers?" Does the reference to "their fathers" help you identify who "them" is referring to?

Why do words which will become strong always focus upon "Jesus, and persuade to believe in Him?" Can words which speak of something else, or other programs, initiatives, organizations and events ever "become strong?" Must the message focus upon Christ before it is possible for it to "become strong?"

Why must you "endure to the end, which is eternal life?" What end? We've asked that before, but not answered it. How long must the enduring last, if it is to result in "eternal life?" Will it be a great deal after this life before you have learned enough to be saved? Will you need to endure then, as now, for eternal life to be yours?

What else were you going to do after this life? Planning to play a harp and sit on a cloud somewhere with Captain Stormfield? Or were you planning to be engaged in a good cause, enduring to the end of all time and all eternity, worlds without end?

We encounter so much doctrine in Nephi's writing. It is almost impossible to understand this writer-prophet without some effort to learn the doctrine ourselves. Perhaps we de-emphasize doctrine at the peril of losing the very message Nephi wrote.

2 Nephi 33: 5-6

> **"And it speaketh harshly against sin, according to the plainness of the truth; wherefore, no man will be angry at the words which I have written save he shall be of the spirit of the devil. I glory in plainness; I glory in truth; I glory in my Jesus, for he hath redeemed my soul from hell."**

Nephi's writings "speaketh harshly against sin." This is because of "plainness of the truth." If you're going to speak plainly about sin, the words are necessarily harsh, because there's no other way to be plain about it. Warning against sin and pride is offensive.[527]

---

[527] 2 Ne. 4: 13: "And it came to pass that not many days after his death, Laman and Lemuel and the sons of Ishmael were angry with me because of the admonitions of the Lord."

Those who become angry at the truth have "the spirit of the devil" in them. That is, they are under the devil's influence and deceived. Nephi understood this principle because of his older brothers' reactions.[528] So when someone becomes angry at the truth, they are in darkness.

Christ gave this as one of the signs of the deceived. They argue against the truth and become angry.[529]

Those who are Christ's, however, join with Nephi in glorying in plainness, even if it cuts or requires repentance. They appreciate the plain direction which allows them to follow in the true path. They appreciate truth, even when it condemns their acts and requires them to change. They glory in Christ, preferring Him to unbelief, traditions of men, and the arm of flesh.

Nephi knew Christ had redeemed his soul from hell, for He had declared it to Nephi. The reason Nephi understood the fullness of Christ's Gospel, could declare the doctrine of Christ, and was a prophet given a commission to teach was because he had been taught by the Lord.[530] The return to Christ's presence was not merely a spectacular event to write in a journal, or a bragging point to claim among others. Indeed, much of what Nephi obtained from the Lord was never recorded for us or Nephi's posterity. The return was to obtain light and truth, or intelligence, which is the glory of God. It was to be ministered to by the Perfect Teacher. This, in turn, made Nephi the great minister he became.

The Greatest Servant teaches servants to serve. They are not chosen to be idolized. They are not chosen so a band can strike up "Hail to the Chief" when they enter a room, as everyone rises in adoration and respect. Nor are they chosen to wear silk robes, with subservient sycophants kissing their ring in adoration, hoping for favors. They are chosen instead to serve, while being discarded, challenged, rejected and scorned. Yet in this they only follow their Master, who came not to be

---

[528] 1 Ne. 16: 1-2: "And now it came to pass that after I, Nephi, had made an end of speaking to my brethren, behold they said unto me: Thou hast declared unto us hard things, more than we are able to bear. And it came to pass that I said unto them that I knew that I had spoken hard things against the wicked, according to the truth; and the righteous have I justified, and testified that they should be lifted up at the last day; wherefore, the guilty taketh the truth to be hard, for it cutteth them to the very center."

[529] 3 Ne. 11: 29: "For verily, verily I say unto you, he that hath the spirit of contention is not of me, but is of the devil, who is the father of contention, and he stirreth up the hearts of men to contend with anger, one with another."

[530] 2 Ne. 11: 2: "And now I, Nephi, write more of the words of Isaiah, for my soul delighteth in his words. For I will liken his words unto my people, and I will send them forth unto all my children, for he verily saw my Redeemer, even as I have seen him."

served, but to serve. Christ disparaged us gentiles because we submit to abuse and call our abusers our benefactors.[531]

We hardly understand the Gospel of Jesus Christ at all because we utterly reject its principles. We won't live them to know if they are true. Then in our ignorant darkness we judge the light.[532] All the while Nephi's words invite us to choose a different route, act with real intent, with full purpose of heart, repenting of our sins to find our way back into the light. Instead, we cling to the false traditions of our fathers, claiming for ourselves the prerogatives of God Himself, believing we are better than others, and failing to see the burden of sin we carry in our blind ignorance.

Nephi may have gloried in plainness, but we glory in positive messages telling us we will be saved in our sins. Nephi may have gloried in Jesus, but we use His name to endorse our products and ratify our false teachings. Nephi may have urged the plainness of truth itself, but we market based on focus group tested and opinion polled results so our product line should get good market acceptance.

Nephi's way would work better, you know. The truth attracts those who seek truth. No matter how utterly it may fail in market testing, truth sells. Truth attracts. At least it attracts the Master's sheep, and we'll never be able to save any others anyway. So we should offer the truth to make a clarion call to those sheep. When we dilute it with the theories of marketing, the arm of flesh, salesmanship and branding, the sheep have no idea that there is any truth under the slick presentation. How can you hear the Master's voice in such a cacophony of Wall Street gibberish? Truth alone wins, prevails, succeeds against all opposition and will have its final vindication in the triumph of the Lamb!

I appreciate Nephi's plainness and preference for the truth. I think I may join him in that view. I suppose, however, it'll make some folks angry.

2 Nephi 33: 7-9

"I have charity for my people, and great faith in Christ that I shall meet many souls spotless at his judgment-seat. I have

---

[531] Luke 22: 25-27: "And he said unto them, The kings of the Gentiles exercise lordship over them; and they that exercise authority upon them are called benefactors. But ye *shall* not *be* so: but he that is greatest among you, let him be as the younger; and he that is chief, as he that doth serve. For whether *is* greater, he that sitteth at meat, or he that serveth? *is* not he that sitteth at meat? but I am among you as he that serveth."

[532] D&C 58: 30-33: "Who am I that made man, saith the Lord, that will hold him guiltless that obeys not my commandments? Who am I, saith the Lord, that have promised and have not fulfilled? I command and men obey not; I revoke and they receive not the blessing. Then they say in their hearts: This is not the work of the Lord, for his promises are not fulfilled. But wo unto such, for their reward lurketh beneath, and not from above."

charity for the Jew—I say Jew, because I mean them from whence I came. I also have charity for the Gentiles. But behold, for none of these can I hope except they shall be reconciled unto Christ, and enter into the narrow gate, and walk in the strait path which leads to life, and continue in the path until the end of the day of probation."

It is necessary to read all three verses to see what Nephi is saying. What distinctions does he make? Is his charity to his people unequivocal? Is his charity to the Jews unequivocal? Is his charity to the gentiles equivocal? Why?

Does the condition that appears in the final verse apply to the preceding group (gentiles) or to all three groups? How do the remarks made by Nephi in the prior verses we have looked at modify or explain which group the final limitation should be applied?

What has Nephi foreseen or said to suggest he has hope for his own people? What has he done to seek charity by his consecrated petitions for his own people? What has he said about the future inheritance of the covenant blessings for both his people and the Jews?

On the other hand, how little promise has he shown for the gentiles? How conditional are their latter-day rights? How much failure has been prophesied regarding the gentiles?

Since we've been discussing this for months, I am not going to repeat it. You can look to see the scope of Nephi's declarations for his people, for the Jews and for the gentiles. After you've done that, it becomes plain that Nephi has:

Charity for his people. Charity for the Jews, from whence he came.

Charity for the Gentiles, but he cannot hope for the gentiles except they shall be reconciled to Christ, enter into the narrow gate, walk in the strait path, and continue to do so until the end of the day of probation.

We are reminded again of the Savior's own prophecy of the failure of the gentiles.[533] We are reminded of the Lord's promise to take the fullness from us in 1841 if we did not complete the construction of the Nauvoo Temple within the allotted time given.[534] If we failed, we would be rejected. We did not complete the Nauvoo Temple in the three and a half years allotted after that revelation while Joseph was alive. Then

---

[533] 3 Ne. 16: 10: "And thus commandeth the Father that I should say unto you: At that day when the Gentiles shall sin against my gospel, and shall reject the fulness of my gospel, and shall be lifted up in the pride of their hearts above all nations, and above all the people of the whole earth, and shall be filled with all manner of lyings, and of deceits, and of mischiefs, and all manner of hypocrisy, and murders, and priestcrafts, and whoredoms, and of secret abominations; and if they shall do all those things, and shall reject the fulness of my gospel, behold, saith the Father, I will bring the fulness of my gospel from among them."

[534] D&C 124: 32: "But behold, at the end of this appointment your baptisms for your dead shall not be acceptable unto me; and if you do not these things at the end of the appointment ye shall be rejected as a church, with your dead, saith the Lord your God."

Joseph was taken, much like Moses was taken.[535] What the Lord threatened we would lose permanently at the end of our appointment was the fullness of the priesthood, which He had already removed from us in 1841.[536] So the gentiles sit in a precarious position indeed.

You must answer for yourself the questions posed by Nephi's teaching:

- Have we been reconciled to Christ?
- Have we entered into the narrow gate?
- Do we walk in the strait path?
- If so, have we done so as a people until the end of our days of probation?

To be able to rcstore again that which we lost before 1841 would require someone truly mighty in Spirit. Fortunately, we have been promised that lifeline will be extended to us again at some point.[537] However even he will not be able to help a gentile who has not been diligent having their name written in the book of the law of God.

The mothers who minister to their children in patience and love will undoubtedly be among those whom the Lord will remember in that day. The first parable, *The Busy Young Man*, is about those little acts through which we find our Lord. *The Weathered Tree* is about the enduring power of a mother's love, and how like the Lord's own sacrifice, this often under appreciated calling has been and continues to be.

Mothers oftentimes do not take time to study because they are too busy engaged in the **actual work** of charity, love and service. Some may not be able to construct a scripture-based explanation or exposition, but they recognize truth by the light acquired within by their fidelity to the Lord's system of conferring light and truth.

I have been far more impressed with mothers in Zion than with the tattered remains of what is now called Zion by the gentiles. The pride and foolish traditions which claim authority while lamenting the lack of power are the expected results of the latter-day gentile stewardship according to Nephi.

---

535 D&C 84: 25: "Therefore, he took Moses out of their midst, and the Holy Priesthood also;"

536 D&C 124: 28: "For there is not a place found on earth that he may come to and restore again that which was lost unto you, or which he hath taken away, even the fulness of the priesthood."

537 D&C 85: 7: "And it shall come to pass that I, the Lord God, will send one mighty and strong, holding the scepter of power in his hand, clothed with light for a covering, whose mouth shall utter words, eternal words; while his bowels shall be a fountain of truth, to set in order the house of God, and to arrange by lot the inheritances of the saints whose names are found, and the names of their fathers, and of their children, enrolled in the book of the law of God;"

The good news, and the thing we should rejoice over, is that Nephi does extend to us gentiles an opportunity to be saved. All we must do to join in the blessings is to:

- Be reconciled to Christ.

- Enter into the narrow gate.

- Walk in the strait path.

- Endure to the end of our days of probation.

So we do have a choice. No matter what failings have occurred or things we lack.

It was Lifehouse who sang an anthem to yearning:

> Desperate for changing, starving for truth, … / Letting go of all I've held onto, I'm standing here until you make me move / I'm hanging by a moment here with you… / Forgetting all I'm lacking, Completely incomplete / I'll take your invitation, You take all of me…

I like that song. It is strangely applicable to the condition we find ourselves. But our yearning of course ought to be for the Redeemer who alone can save us.

2 Nephi 33: 10

> **"And now, my beloved brethren, and also Jew, and all ye ends of the earth, hearken unto these words and believe in Christ; and if ye believe not in these words believe in Christ. And if ye shall believe in Christ ye will believe in these words, for they are the words of Christ, and he hath given them unto me; and they teach all men that they should do good."**

After the conditional statement warning the gentiles of their need to be reconciled to Christ, Nephi speaks to his "beloved brethren" and the "Jews," but omits specific mention of the gentiles. Instead he refers to "all ye ends of the earth." This would include all those who are neither Jew, nor Israelite, nor gentile. This is a lot of people who are called "heathen" because they have little direct prophetic mention. Nephi, for example, only refers to them once in his writings.[538] In that single reference Nephi promises all, if they will repent and return to Christ, can be saved. All are invited. All can come. Everyone may learn of Christ, find Him and be saved.

---

[538] 2 Ne. 26: 33: "For none of these iniquities come of the Lord; for he doeth that which is good among the children of men; and he doeth nothing save it be plain unto the children of men; and he inviteth them all to come unto him and partake of his goodness; and he denieth none that come unto him, black and white, bond and free, male and female; and he remembereth the heathen; and all are alike unto God, both Jew and Gentile."

There is a distinction between God's absolute willingness to accept all who will come to Him, on the one hand, and the prophetic foreknowledge of who would accept the invitation, on the other. The opportunity is open for all. There will be few who will accept.

Nephi's testimony is based on Christ and employs both Christ's doctrine and teachings. He assures us as readers that if we are willing to accept his writings we are, in fact, accepting the words of Christ. If you believe Christ, you will believe Nephi. For almost everything Nephi has written comes directly or indirectly from Christ. To believe in Nephi's words is to believe in Christ, and to believe in Christ is to accept Nephi's words.

Think about that for a moment. Nephi does not leave you wondering if the message will save you or not, whether he has some special inside information or not, or whether he has seen the Lord or not. He is direct and does not require you to guess. He has not adopted any equivocal or carefully studied words or phrases to tell you about Christ. He is blunt, even plain. His words offend those who are unwilling to surrender their sins and repent. He says what he has written "are the words of Christ." This means that before he taught, before he wrote, before he concluded his testimony, he consulted with and obtained approval from Christ.

There is nothing vague in Nephi's warnings, nor unclear in his message.

He openly invites the gentiles to repent. He does so repeatedly. He tells us that with the exception of only a few, we are condemned and will fail in our dispensation. As to those few, he warns us that we will be prone to err because of the things we are taught.[539] He offers us a clear, light filled body of teachings that will clarify for us the body of doctrine that will save us. However, we must take his warnings seriously and study them with care.

Imagine how much effort and thought went into preparing to carve into the metal plates. Imagine the amount of thought he employed before undertaking the final, permanent etchings to complete his ministry. His brother commented about how arduous the process was during his writing on the same plates.[540]

Nephi saw our day, and knew how difficult it would be for us. He wrote a message to be preserved and available no matter who would lead us, no matter what messages we would hear, no matter what confusion would develop. He gave us a message to announce the

---

[539] 2 Ne. 28: 14: "They wear stiff necks and high heads; yea, and because of pride, and wickedness, and abominations, and whoredoms, they have all gone astray save it be a few, who are the humble followers of Christ; nevertheless, they are led, that in many instances they do err because they are taught by the precepts of men."

[540] Jacob 4: 1: "Now behold, it came to pass that I, Jacob, having ministered much unto my people in word, (and I cannot write but a little of my words, because of the difficulty of engraving our words upon plates) and we know that the things which we write upon plates must remain;"

conditions of salvation over the heads of any foolish, vain or false teachings. They are a lifeline extended to the gentiles, as well as his beloved mixed blood descendants (the remnant), and the Jews.

Nephi knows his words will teach anyone who accepts them "to do good."

The gentile problem is not in reading his words, but in "believing in them." Gentile interpretation almost always involves unbelief. We do not let his words hold their "plain meaning" but want to construe them, read into them praise, and remove from them the blunt warnings given us. We want to make ourselves justified by the words that warn, condemn and challenge us to do more. Our unbelief separates us from Nephi's message even as we read his words.

It does no good to argue with him. It does no good to juxtapose his words of counsel and warning with other words of comfort and reassurance. He is alarmed by our condition and warns us to flee from error. We want to read into these words other ideas Nephi never intended.

When we began back with Alma Chapter 13, it was with the idea we would let the words speak for themselves. We were going to try and see what was being said apart from our own desires or hopes. We've been trying to let Nephi have his own words and meanings as we've been looking at his teachings, as well.

An inspired teacher will not offer their own words and pretend they come from Christ. They are not going to dare speak in the name of Christ if they offer only their suppositions, hopes, and understanding. They know, as Nephi, that to do so is to take the Lord's name in vain, and to preach for doctrines the commandments of men. It is often the case, however, that men will urge their own views hoping to make them more convincing, while using the name of Christ. Surely every such teacher will be held to account before Christ for every idle word spoken in His name without His authority or approval.

Nephi knew this doctrine. Nephi understood how weighty a matter it was to use the Lord's name in connection with teaching doctrine. Nephi writes in the full confidence that the Lord has approved his message, inspired his words, and will vindicate them to those who will believe them.

Personally, I would hardly dare to teach doctrine if I did not know what I say to be true. Nephi's example is perhaps more important in this respect than in any other. He is surely worthy to be called a "teacher and a ruler" by all of us.[541]

2 Nephi 33: 11-12

---

541 2 Ne. 5: 19: "And behold, the words of the Lord had been fulfilled unto my brethren, which he spake concerning them, that I should be their ruler and their teacher. Wherefore, I had been their ruler and their teacher, according to the commandments of the Lord, until the time they sought to take away my life."

> **"And if they are not the words of Christ, judge ye—for Christ will show unto you, with power and great glory, that they are his words, at the last day; and you and I shall stand face to face before his bar; and ye shall know that I have been commanded of him to write these things, notwithstanding my weakness. And I pray the Father in the name of Christ that many of us, if not all, may be saved in his kingdom at that great and last day."**

You judge. You decide. If you don't believe, Christ will vindicate Nephi's teachings, and you will learn just how wrong your judgment was. For Nephi will be at the judgment bar with Christ. You will stand "face to face" with Nephi as you stand before Christ. You will see, along with all those who abuse and treat true messengers as "things of naught," that you have rejected Christ when you rejected His words delivered by one authorized to speak in His name. Nephi invites you to judge his words with the confidence of knowing that he was given power to say all he said. And he had the Lord's confidence because he didn't say anything about what the Lord instructed him not to speak about.

You will one day know Nephi was "commanded of [Christ] to write these things." Nephi was commanded despite his "weakness." In this context "weakness" is a relative thing. Because Nephi had seen the Lord his perspective allowed him to measure himself against perfection. It allowed him to assess the difference between the Lord as Teacher, and Nephi as servant.

The holiness, majesty and power of God were known to Nephi. He had already had the experience of seeing the absolute standard of holiness in Christ. For most people this will come at the last day, and will result in them understanding, for the first time, that they should have repented.[542] Nephi had already been able to reconcile himself to Christ. Therefore Nephi knew of his own "weakness" and of the power of redemption found through Christ.

Nephi's prayer was for the redemption of all. He hoped that "many of us, if not all, may be saved in his kingdom at that great and last day." Nephi knew he had been redeemed. Yet he identifies with all of us who read his words, and hoped all may be saved.

The measure of a prophet's ministry is in the salvation of others. Nephi does not celebrate his own redemption. He agonizes over the salvation of others. He labors for the redemption of "many...if not all"

---

542 Mormon 9: 3-5: "Then will ye longer deny the Christ, or can ye behold the Lamb of God? Do ye suppose that ye shall dwell with him under a consciousness of your guilt? Do ye suppose that ye could be happy to dwell with that holy Being, when your souls are racked with a consciousness of guilt that ye have ever abused his laws? Behold, I say unto you that ye would be more miserable to dwell with a holy and just God, under a consciousness of your filthiness before him, than ye would to dwell with the damned souls in hell. For behold, when ye shall be brought to see your nakedness before God, and also the glory of God, and the holiness of Jesus Christ, it will kindle a flame of unquenchable fire upon you."

of the rest of mankind. This is the pattern. Redemption causes the redeemed to work for the salvation of others. Perhaps it might be better put that the reason someone obtains the kind of redemption Nephi obtained is because they are of a character to work for the redemption of others. There is no reason to withhold the promise of eternal life from them, because others will be redeemed as a result of their redemption. They will labor, preach, teach, intercede, seek, pray, and work tirelessly to bring others to the tree of life. They become a fellow-servant with Christ and labor alongside Him in the work of redeeming others. This is one of the reasons for the parable of The Busy Young Man in *Ten Parables*.

Nephi is working directly toward redemption of others. There is no secondary or indirect route being taught. There is no attempt to get some kind of "activity" started, or to introduce a program to do anything apart from bringing you to repentance. He wants you to approach Christ directly through the power of the baptism of fire and the Holy Ghost, which will teach you all things you should do. He wants you to hear and speak with the tongues of angels. He does not want to entertain, distract, or emotionally move you. He wants you to come to Christ. Nephi only tells you the minimum about himself, giving only such information as may be relevant to his message concerning Christ. To the extent he is able, Nephi consistently draws your focus to the Lord.

There is great understanding of how a true friend of Christ lives, acts and thinks found in Nephi's writings. They are a urim and thummim into what you find in a man of God. Imitations will always exist. But the real thing is going to be far more like Nephi than Joel Osteen. More sleeves rolled up and fewer cuff-links.

I do hope we may all join Nephi and are saved in the kingdom at that last day. I hope we recognize how great Nephi's teachings are, and how they address our day with the message we need to hear and heed.

2 Nephi 33: 13

> **"And now, my beloved brethren, all those who are of the house of Israel, and all ye ends of the earth, I speak unto you as the voice of one crying from the dust: Farewell until that great day shall come."**

When Nephi paraphrased Isaiah 29 in 2 Nephi 27, he appropriated Isaiah's words to the coming forth of the Book of Mormon. He adapted them making a paraphrase rather than a quote. (I explain the reasons for this in *Nephi's Isaiah.*) Here he uses the Isaiah materials again to identify who he (Nephi) is: "the voice of one crying from the dust." The primary audience for his writings will be those who come to read the book in the last days; when mankind will be in possession of the record which has been printed and distributed to the masses.

Nephi's primary audience for his teachings are those who, like us, live in the last days after the Book of Mormon has come to light.

Although Nephi's descendants would have access to these same records, their greatest work and worth would be in the last days. Hence Nephi identifying himself as a "voice of one crying from the dust."

There is also a secondary meaning. Because Nephi was mortal, he was made of the "dust of the ground."[543] He was a man testifying to the truthfulness, as a witness in mortality, of the great things which exist beyond the veil. He is one of us, and yet able to tell us of things to come. Therefore, his witness is given in mortal weakness, but with the power of God behind it. His own strength is dust. The power of Christ to redeem, however, is without limit.

Three distinct groups are addressed in the message: Nephi's descendants, called his "beloved brethren." They are "brethren" rather than "children" because they would descend primarily from his brother's seed who would overcome his. But there would be a mixture of his among them. So they were his "brethren."

The second are called "those who are of the house of Israel." These are the Jews, or others who keep their identity with Israel. Not the gentiles, who have been lost and must gain covenant status one by one, and thereafter live true to the covenant in order to be redeemed. "Those who are of the house of Israel" have been previously identified and discussed by Nephi in 2 Nephi 28.

The final group is "all ye ends of the earth." That is, the gentiles, heathen, and those who are not otherwise included even in prophetic mention. All mankind. All the ends of the earth may receive what is offered and attain to covenant status, if they repent, acting no deception, without hypocrisy, following Christ. And all are included in the broad sweep of Nephi's invitation to come to Christ.

His "farewell" is "until that great day shall come." That day is when you see the Lord in judgment with Nephi there beside Him. At that time you will be "face to face" with Nephi, accounting for your heed or neglect of his message. He just mentioned that in the prior verses. He now bids you good-by until that moment. So you should look forward to meeting Nephi at this point. Although you need to take his message seriously if you intend to enjoy the moment.

What other prophets have warned us that their message will confront us in the presence of Christ while he, the prophet-messenger, is there with us at the moment of judgment? Nephi is in a very small group of qualified messengers whose words should be taken with soberness and respect. He is a towering figure when measured by the correct standard. We seldom encounter such a man. When we do, we would be well advised to take counsel from him.

---

[543] Moses 3: 7: "And I, the Lord God, formed man from the dust of the ground, and breathed into his nostrils the breath of life; and man became a living soul, the first flesh upon the earth, the first man also; nevertheless, all things were before created; but spiritually were they created and made according to my word."

What more can he have said to alert us to the importance of his message?

2 Nephi 33: 14

> **"And you that will not partake of the goodness of God, and respect the words of the Jews, and also my words, and the words which shall proceed forth out of the mouth of the Lamb of God, behold, I bid you an everlasting farewell, for these words shall condemn you at the last day."**

From Nephi's perspective, if you deny his message, reject what is taught, and walk away from his teachings, then you "will not partake of the goodness of God." You have been offered fruit from the tree of life, and you're just unwilling to "partake of that goodness." It is ingratitude and foolishness.[544]

This word "partake" hearkens back to the tree in Lehi's and Nephi's dream. (Lehi's version is found in 1 Nephi 8.) People prefer to go join in a crowd inside a building. The building is a symbol of man's work. The "arm of flesh" is used to build such structures. No matter how "great" or "spacious" such work may be[545], it is nonetheless the product of human labor. In the dream, those who enter into the building do so to join the multitude in mocking and scorn of those who choose the tree instead.[546] In contrast to this, the tree bearing fruit is a product of nature—God's product. Man's labors do not produce trees. Without God, trees do not exist. Man cannot take credit for either the tree or its fruit. It is a gift given to him.

Now the gift must be obtained by coming to the tree. You cannot partake of its fruit while standing at a distance. You must go to the tree, take the fruit in your hand, and "partake of the goodness of God" before you are able to realize how "delicious" this goodness truly is.[547] So Nephi's invitation to "partake of the goodness of God" is a reminder at

---

[544] D&C 88: 33: "For what doth it profit a man if a gift is bestowed upon him, and he receive not the gift? Behold, he rejoices not in that which is given unto him, neither rejoices in him who is the giver of the gift."

[545] 1 Ne. 8: 31: "And he also saw other multitudes feeling their way towards that great and spacious building."

[546] 1 Ne. 8: 33: "And great was the multitude that did enter into that strange building. And after they did enter into that building they did point the finger of scorn at me and those that were partaking of the fruit also; but we heeded them not."

[547] 1 Ne. 8: 10-12: "And it came to pass that I beheld a tree, whose fruit was desirable to make one happy. And it came to pass that I did go forth and partake of the fruit thereof; and I beheld that it was most sweet, above all that I ever before tasted. Yea, and I beheld that the fruit thereof was white, to exceed all the whiteness that I had ever seen. And as I partook of the fruit thereof it filled my soul with exceedingly great joy; wherefore, I began to be desirous that my family should partake of it also; for I knew that it was desirable above all other fruit."

the end of his record of the visions he received at the beginning of the record. Come, partake, be saved.

What would you need to do in order to "respect the words of the Jews, and also [Nephi's] words?" Why does he add "and the words which shall proceed forth out of the mouth of the Lamb of God?" Does this mean that if you have "respect" for Nephi's words and the Bible, you will receive other words? Words from "the mouth of the Lamb of God?" Does it suggest you will speak directly with Christ? That part of the fullness of this process is to once again speak to and hear from "the Lamb of God?" Will it result in Christ speaking to you in the flesh?[548]

Why will Nephi's words "condemn you at the last day?" Why does Nephi bid an "everlasting farewell" to those who won't "partake of the goodness of God?"

Is Nephi uncharitable? Are his words harsh, unkind or intemperate? Should he be praising us more and condemning us less? Is this a "hard thing" he has spoken to us?[549] If it is not harsh, unkind, or intemperate, then should this kind of warning be given by anyone who is concerned for the salvation of your soul? Why? If your messengers don't challenge you to repent, but instead use smooth words, reassuring you in your present course, would their message conflict with Nephi's message? What would you make of such a conflict between their praise and reassurance, and Nephi's stark warnings?

2 Nephi 33: 15

> **"For what I seal on earth, shall be brought against you at the judgment bar; for thus hath the Lord commanded me, and I must obey. Amen."**

Another reminder of Nephi's status. Not only does he preach the words of Christ, but he also has the authority and power to "seal on earth" his message. He obtained this directly from the Lord. He is a trusted servant, acting in the similitude of the Savior Himself. Holding the power to seal, he proceeds to do so. Those with eyes to see will realize this is an important punctuation mark on the the final statement he leaves for us in his message.

The power to seal and "the Lord commanded me, and I must obey" go hand in hand. One simply does not receive this kind of authority if they will begin to freelance. They are to use it only in the manner the

---

[548] 2 Ne. 32: 6: "Behold, this is the doctrine of Christ, and there will be no more doctrine given until after he shall manifest himself unto you in the flesh. And when he shall manifest himself unto you in the flesh, the things which he shall say unto you shall ye observe to do."

[549] 1 Ne. 16: 2: "And it came to pass that I said unto them that I knew that I had spoken hard things against the wicked, according to the truth; and the righteous have I justified, and testified that they should be lifted up at the last day; wherefore, the guilty taketh the truth to be hard, for it cutteth them to the very center."

Lord would use it. Although the power is theirs to use, they are governed by their character to use it only according to the Lord's command. Nephi, for example, received this acknowledgment when given the power to seal: "that all things shall be done unto thee according to thy word, for thou shalt not ask that which is contrary to my will."[550]

When Joseph Smith received this power it was given in connection with his calling and election made sure. It happened between 1829 and 1832, the exact date is unknown. It was reduced to writing in 1843 in D&C 132. It is my view that the revelation making mention of it was not a single event, but rather as many as five different revelations related to the same subject, all of which were dictated at the same time and included in Section 132. I've explained this earlier in a series of posts about Section 132. Go back and look here, here, here, here, here, and here if you don't remember it.

Joseph received this power, and this fullness between 1829 and 1832. However, by 1841 Joseph was no longer able to use it because it had been "taken from [the church]."[551] It would not affect Joseph individually, for his calling and election was made sure.[552] But if "taken," it would affect the church.

Nephi's power to "seal" his writings at the command of the Lord, and his own obedience, now make his words binding on all of us. They become covenantal. Hence the reference to remembering "the new covenant, even the Book of Mormon."[553] It is not merely interesting doctrine, nor even prophecy, but has reached covenantal status by virtue of the priestly seal placed upon it by Nephi. We ignore it at our peril. We define it as just a volume of scripture at our loss. It was intended to be studied and followed as the means to reassert a covenant between

---

550 Hel. 10: 4-5: "Blessed art thou, Nephi, for those things which thou hast done; for I have beheld how thou hast with unwearyingness declared the word, which I have given unto thee, unto this people. And thou hast not feared them, and hast not sought thine own life, but hast sought my will, and to keep my commandments. And now, because thou hast done this with such unwearyingness, behold, I will bless thee forever; and I will make thee mighty in word and in deed, in faith and in works; yea, even that all things shall be done unto thee according to thy word, for thou shalt not ask that which is contrary to my will."

551 D&C 124: 28: "For there is not a place found on earth that he may come to and restore again that which was lost unto you, or which he hath taken away, even the fulness of the priesthood."

552 D&C 132: 49: "For I am the Lord thy God, and will be with thee even unto the end of the world, and through all eternity; for verily I seal upon you your exaltation, and prepare a throne for you in the kingdom of my Father, with Abraham your father."

553 D&C 84: 57: "And they shall remain under this condemnation until they repent and remember the new covenant, even the Book of Mormon and the former commandments which I have given them, not only to say, but to do according to that which I have written—"

ourselves and God. By following its precepts we can return to God's presence where we are endowed with light and truth, receive intelligence and understanding. Each of us is invited to make that return. Nephi lived it, and as a result was able to teach it. We should do the same. That is, live it to be able to understand and then teach it. ***It is the doing that leads to the understanding***.

There is a great deal of what Nephi taught that we have not considered.

THE REMNANT

When I started, I doubted a blog was an appropriate venue to address a topic like the "remnant" of the Book of Mormon. This is still an experiment.

If you're new to this blog, you need to go back and start reading sometime in April. Then you'll have the foundation for understanding this topic as we move forward.

Undoubtedly there will be those who don't bother to read what has been written previously. They will make comments here about something that was thoroughly discussed in earlier posts. Just grin and bear it. For the most part, I will be ignoring it.

I've tried to remain focused even when there have been questions good enough to answer. But to start answering even very good questions is to hijack the topic and run afield. There have been occasional asides, but that's because of human weakness and the inability to resist temptation.

We are trying to fit our traditions about the remnant and their role into the framework of the Book of Mormon. From what we've seen so far, it should be clear that we, the Latter-day Saints, are identified as "gentiles" in the Book of Mormon. We are not ever identified as the "remnant." As a result, the prophecies about the "remnant" are not prophecies about us. They are primarily descendants of the Lamanites, but have some mixed blood of Nephi as well. They are grouped by the Lord into several different clans, and remain identified as "Nephites, and the Jacobites, and the Josephites, and the Zoramites… the Lamanites, and the Lemuelites, and the Ishmaelites." (D&C 3: 17-18.) These are those who, though diminished in numbers, are still with us. They retain both a separate identity before the Lord and prophetic inheritance from previous covenants. They are not us and we are not them.

There are two great books which discuss two different views of where the Book of Mormon geography took place. One is by Sorenson, titled *An Ancient American Setting for the Book of Mormon*. The other is *Prophecies and Promises* by Meldrum and Porter. Sorenson says Central America, Porter and Meldrum say North America.

It is not necessary to resolve the question of Book of Mormon geography in order to have a discussion of this topic. The place could be either Central or North America. The result of the last genocidal wars was that the fighting spread into the Finger Lakes region of New York, with Moroni ultimately placing the plates in the Hill Cumorah, where Joseph Smith recovered them. Therefore, there were descendants of these people located in the North American area by the time the Book of Mormon record ends. Furthermore, during the time between 400 a.d., when the record ends, and the time of post-Revolutionary American in 1805, when Joseph Smith was born, there were many undocumented migrations of people we know nothing about other than what anthropology tells us, which is not much.

So when we get to Joseph Smith and his comments about the "descendants of the Book of Mormon" he is speaking at a time disconnected from the events in the Book of Mormon. I take Joseph's comments at face value, and presume them to be correct. When Joseph talks about the ancestors of the American Indians being the Book of Mormon people, I accept that.

Also, I think it is better to let the words of prophecy speak for themselves and not impose our own beliefs or traditions on them. We tend to see in the words meanings that are harmonious with our own preconceptions. It is better to abandon those preconceptions and see if the words give us any better or different explanation of what is to happen. That way we are not misinformed by the traditions of men, even if they come to us from very good men.

I do not judge what others believe, explain or teach. They are entitled to their beliefs. But each of us are entitled to believe and take at face value the words of prophecy in scripture, even if they collide with some other notions. I think it better to abandon the ideas which collide with scripture than it is to wrestle the scriptures to conform with the ideas. But you can do as you choose. I really do claim the privilege of worshiping Almighty God according to the dictates of my own conscience, and believe it my duty to allow all men the same privilege. I will let them worship how, where, or what they may. That's not a hollow statement for me. I believe in complete freedom of conscience for you and for me. We are accountable to God only for what we believe. Until the COB correlates that out of the Articles of Faith by editing instead of by conduct, I will continue to believe in, and practice the principle of freedom of belief. [That is why so many comments critical of me appear in this blog and why relatively few of those praising me are allowed through.]

So, with that brief introduction, we turn to the trail we've been on for some time. The remnant…

Part 2

The first statement about the existence of the Book of Mormon in our day was made by Moroni to Joseph Smith. Moroni stated, among other things: "he was a messenger sent from the presence of God to me, and that his name was Moroni; that God had a work for me to do; and that my name should be had for good and evil among all nations, kindreds, and tongues, or that it should be both good and evil spoken of among all people. He said there was a book deposited, written upon gold plates, giving an account of the former inhabitants of this continent, and the source from whence they sprang. He also said that the fulness of the everlasting Gospel was contained in it, as delivered by the Savior to the ancient inhabitants".[554] The "former inhabitants of this continent" would necessarily be North America.

The remnant came from people who frequently received a place called "this land" in the prophecies. For example: "we have obtained a land of promise, a land which is choice above all other lands; a land which the Lord God hath covenanted with me should be a land for the inheritance of my seed. Yea, the Lord hath covenanted this land unto me, and to my children forever, and also all those who should be led out of other countries by the hand of the Lord."[555] The relevant "land" is one which the ancestors of the remnant were promised would be choice above all other lands. A land of inheritance for the remnant. And one to which people would be "led out of other countries by the hand of the Lord" to later occupy. This is a reference to Nephi's earlier vision wherein the unfolding history of the Americas were shown to him. That included the following:

There would be a man separated by "many waters" who would be wrought upon by the Spirit of God and make the journey across the "many waters" to the remnant "seed of my brethren, who were in the promised land."[556] This identifies Columbus, whose original landfall was in the West Indies of the Caribbean. However, the prophecy continues with greater details, increasingly focusing on a North American setting.

---

[554] JS-H 1: 33-34: "He called me by name, and said unto me that he was a messenger sent from the presence of God to me, and that his name was Moroni; that God had a work for me to do; and that my name should be had for good and evil among all nations, kindreds, and tongues, or that it should be both good and evil spoken of among all people. He said there was a book deposited, written upon gold plates, giving an account of the former inhabitants of this continent, and the source from whence they sprang. He also said that the fulness of the everlasting Gospel was contained in it, as delivered by the Savior to the ancient inhabitants;"

[555] 2 Ne. 1: 5: "But, said he, notwithstanding our afflictions, we have obtained a land of promise, a land which is choice above all other lands; a land which the Lord God hath covenanted with me should be a land for the inheritance of my seed. Yea, the Lord hath covenanted this land unto me, and to my children forever, and also all those who should be led out of other countries by the hand of the Lord."

[556] 1 Ne. 13: 12: "And I looked and beheld a man among the Gentiles, who was separated from the seed of my brethren by the many waters; and I beheld the Spirit of God, that it came down and wrought upon the man; and he went forth upon the many waters, even unto the seed of my brethren, who were in the promised land."

After the original discovery by the man wrought upon by the Spirit of God (Columbus), the same "Spirit of God... wrought upon other Gentiles" who also made the migration across the "many waters."[557] Again it is not unequivocal because migration included and still includes both North and South America.

When the gentile waves of immigration overtake the promised land, they are humbled, fleeing from captivity[558], and the power of God was upon them.[559] They were delivered by the power of God out of the hands of all other nations.[560] These gentile people are then "lifted up by the power of God above all other nations, upon the face of the land which is choice above all other lands, which is the land that the Lord God hath covenanted with thy father that his seed should have for the land of their inheritance."[561] That description seems to identify the United States, for there is no historic basis for saying Canada, Mexico, Guatemala, Honduras, Cuba, Columbia or Peru are or ever have been "lifted up by the power of God above all other nations." The United States, however, as the world's single recognized "superpower" has fit this description. If it is the area of the United States being identified, then this is the "land that the Lord God hath covenanted with thy father that his seed should have for the land of their inheritance." Or, in other words, this is where one should expect to find remains of the remnant who inherited and will inherit again the land as their promise from the Lord.

The gentiles who inherited the area of the United States waged a continuing campaign to dispossess the native people, succeeding in

---

[557] 1 Ne. 13: 13: "And it came to pass that I beheld the Spirit of God, that it wrought upon other Gentiles; and they went forth out of captivity, upon the many waters."

[558] 1 Ne. 13: 16: "And it came to pass that I, Nephi, beheld that the Gentiles who had gone forth out of captivity did humble themselves before the Lord; and the power of the Lord was with them."

[559] Ibid.

[560] 1 Ne. 13: 19: "And I, Nephi, beheld that the Gentiles that had gone out of captivity were delivered by the power of God out of the hands of all other nations."

[561] 1 Ne. 13: 30: "Nevertheless, thou beholdest that the Gentiles who have gone forth out of captivity, and have been lifted up by the power of God above all other nations, upon the face of the land which is choice above all other lands, which is the land that the Lord God hath covenanted with thy father that his seed should have for the land of their inheritance; wherefore, thou seest that the Lord God will not suffer that the Gentiles will utterly destroy the mixture of thy seed, which are among thy brethren."

causing them to dwindle, but not be utterly destroyed.[562] It is in the United States, beginning in upper New York State that the gentiles are given the chance to remove the "awfūl state of blindness" through the restoration of the Gospel.[563] The coming forth of the Book of Mormon was a North American event, coming to the gentiles who are occupying the land covenanted to the fathers and upon which we would find the remnant.[564]

There is enough, therefore, in Nephi's prophecy to identify the area where the remnant would initially be found. That area is inside the United States. This is where the remnant would initially be swept away, smitten and afflicted by the gentiles. But they would not be utterly destroyed. A small fraction of them would be preserved, so the promises could be realized.[565]

---

562 1 Ne. 13: 30-31: "Nevertheless, thou beholdest that the Gentiles who have gone forth out of captivity, and have been lifted up by the power of God above all other nations, upon the face of the land which is choice above all other lands, which is the land that the Lord God hath covenanted with thy father that his seed should have for the land of their inheritance; wherefore, thou seest that the Lord God will not suffer that the Gentiles will utterly destroy the mixture of thy seed, which are among thy brethren. Neither will he suffer that the Gentiles shall destroy the seed of thy brethren."

563 1 Ne. 32, 34: "Neither will the Lord God suffer that the Gentiles shall forever remain in that awful state of blindness, which thou beholdest they are in, because of the plain and most precious parts of the gospel of the Lamb which have been kept back by that abominable church, whose formation thou hast seen. …And it came to pass that the angel of the Lord spake unto me, saying: Behold, saith the Lamb of God, after I have visited the remnant of the house of Israel—and this remnant of whom I speak is the seed of thy father—wherefore, after I have visited them in judgment, and smitten them by the hand of the Gentiles, and after the Gentiles do stumble exceedingly, because of the most plain and precious parts of the gospel of the Lamb which have been kept back by that abominable church, which is the mother of harlots, saith the Lamb—I will be merciful unto the Gentiles in that day, insomuch that I will bring forth unto them, in mine own power, much of my gospel, which shall be plain and precious, saith the Lamb."

564 1 Ne. 13: 35-36: "For, behold, saith the Lamb: I will manifest myself unto thy seed, that they shall write many things which I shall minister unto them, which shall be plain and precious; and after thy seed shall be destroyed, and dwindle in unbelief, and also the seed of thy brethren, behold, these things shall be hid up, to come forth unto the Gentiles, by the gift and power of the Lamb. And in them shall be written my gospel, saith the Lamb, and my rock and my salvation."

565 1 Ne. 13: 30-31: "Nevertheless, thou beholdest that the Gentiles who have gone forth out of captivity, and have been lifted up by the power of God above all other nations, upon the face of the land which is choice above all other lands, which is the land that the Lord God hath covenanted with thy father that his seed should have for the land of their inheritance; wherefore, thou seest that the Lord God will not suffer that the Gentiles will utterly destroy the mixture of thy seed, which are among thy brethren. Neither will he suffer that the Gentiles shall destroy the seed of thy brethren."

So they were here. And some of them remain still. So, when we begin to identify who they are, the initial proof of their identity is found in Nephi's prophecy and our own history. I do not think it was intended to be particularly difficult to see what was prophesied or who was involved. But we need to pay some attention or we miss the information lying before us.

Joseph Smith also made statements identifying the former occupants of the area that is now the United States where the Book of Mormon people were situated. From his mother, Lucy Mack Smith, we have the following description of what Joseph told the family during the four years he was being educated by Moroni in the annual visits to the Hill Cumorah before obtaining possession of the plates: "During our evening conversations, Joseph would occasionally give us some of the most amusing recitals that could be imagined. He would describe the ancient inhabitants of this continent, their dress, mode of traveling, and the animals upon which they rode; their cities, their buildings, with every particular; their mode of warfare; and also their religious worship. This he would do with as much ease, seemingly, as if he had spent his whole life among them." The reference to "this continent" being a reference to North America.

There are other references by Joseph Smith, as well. In looking at this I am not trying to identify where Book of Mormon events occurred. Instead I am only interested in the subject of whether at the time of dispossession of the land, the people who were dispossessed were descendants who had promises extended to them in the Book of Mormon. It seems evident that is the case. It seems almost undeniable that the promised people who are yet to receive the benefit of an earlier covenant with Lehi and Nephi, Jacob and Enos, include those who were occupants of the area of the United States during the early years of American conquest.

Part 3

To understand our own history and prophecies, we have to look at the events taking place during the time of the revelations. The composition of people and geography were dynamic, and changing. They were anything but static. So when you look at events at a specific moment in time, you have to look at the composition of the land and people to understand what was occurring. If you miss it by a decade, you miss what was revealed.

From the beginning of the United States the Indians were a political problem in need of a solution for both State and Federal government. Various conflicts and battles resulted in temporary solutions. By the time we reach the end of the 1820's, a more general solution was needed. Andrew Jackson came to office with a plan to deal with the problem.

Andrew Jackson wanted the Indians removed from the eastern portion of the United States, from Maine to Florida and from the Atlantic to the Mississippi. He wanted them all relocated. Congress responded and passed the Indian Relocation Act of 1830, forcibly removing all Native Americans to the area owned by the United States and acquired from France in the Louisiana Purchase. The land used for the relocation was just beyond the western border of Missouri. In fact, the border town of Independence was located immediately adjacent to, and in the center of the relocated Indian tribes. You couldn't get any closer, and you couldn't be any more in the center than in Independence, Missouri.

Joseph Smith, expressing that "one of the most important points in the faith of the Church of the Latter-day Saints…is the gathering of Israel (of whom the Lamanites constitute a part)" seemed pleased that the American government was assisting in a gathering of the Lamanites, anticipating that it would facilitate their reception of the gospel. He even included in his history a positive statement expressing President Jackson's views on the Native Americans (*History of the Church* 2: 357–60).

By 1831, after the relocation was well underway, the closest a white man could get to the Indians was Independence, Missouri. When you left Independence heading west, you would encounter the line dividing the land and establishing the territory the Federal Government exercised control over for the benefit of the tribes located there. It was for this reason the revelation given in 1831 refers to the "line running directly between Jew and Gentile."[566] The "Jew" being the American Indian tribes located across the border, and the "gentile" being the Americans, including the LDS missionaries at the time.

In 1830 the first missionary to the "Lamanites" was called. Oliver Cowdery was told, among other things, the following: "And now, behold, I say unto you that you shall go unto the Lamanites and preach my gospel unto them; and inasmuch as they receive thy teachings thou shalt cause my church to be established among them; and thou shalt have revelations, but write them not by way of commandment. And now, behold, I say unto you that it is not revealed, and no man knoweth where the city Zion shall be built, but it shall be given hereafter. Behold, I say unto you that it shall be on the borders by the Lamanites."[567]

Later the same month, Peter Whitmer was told to join Oliver in this first mission to the Lamanites. That revelation states: "Behold, I say unto you, Peter, that you shall take your journey with your brother

566 D&C 57: 4: "Wherefore, it is wisdom that the land should be purchased by the saints, and also every tract lying westward, even unto the line running directly between Jew and Gentile;"

567 D&C 28: 8-9: "And now, behold, I say unto you that you shall go unto the Lamanites and preach my gospel unto them; and inasmuch as they receive thy teachings thou shalt cause my church to be established among them; and thou shalt have revelations, but write them not by way of commandment. And now, behold, I say unto you that it is not revealed, and no man knoweth where the city Zion shall be built, but it shall be given hereafter. Behold, I say unto you that it shall be on the borders by the Lamanites."

Oliver; for the time has come that it is expedient in me that you shall open your mouth to declare my gospel; therefore, fear not, but give heed unto the words and advice of your brother, which he shall give you. And be you afflicted in all his afflictions, ever lifting up your heart unto me in prayer and faith, for his and your deliverance; for I have given unto him power to build up my church among the Lamanites;"[568] Both Oliver and Peter Whitmer were assigned to find these Lamanites, preach the Gospel, and at some point a place where the city of Zion would be built would be revealed. So the Lamanite conversion and revealing of the city of Zion were to happen together. The remnant being required for Zion to be built.

You will recall we discussed earlier how the gentiles will only "assist" in building the city. The remnant will do most of the work.[569] (3 Nephi 21: 23, discussed already.) So this mission was to locate the relevant group, and also locate the relevant spot where the remnant would construct the city of Zion.

In addition to Oliver and Peter, Parley Pratt and Ziba Peterson were called to serve this same mission. They went to Indians in New York, passed through Kirtland, and wound up in Independence at the end of the journey some time later. The Kirtland detour resulted in a large conversion, including Sidney Rigdon. Kirtland was the largest LDS congregation.

Well, the asides are interesting, but the point is that the search for Lamanites began in New York, and moved along until its end in a location center of the relocated tribes. It is immediately next to the boundary separating the Indians and whites, or in the language of revelation, "the Jews and gentiles."

By the following year, Joseph came to visit the area. With the large relocated group of Lamanite nations across the border, and Independence the site from which all of them could be reached, Joseph received this revelation in July, 1831: "Hearken, O ye elders of my church, saith the Lord your God, who have assembled yourselves together, according to my commandments, in this land, which is the land of Missouri, which is the land which I have appointed and consecrated for the gathering of the saints. Wherefore, this is the land of promise, and the place for the city of Zion. And thus saith the Lord your God, if you will receive wisdom here is wisdom. Behold, the place which is

---

568 D&C 30: 5-6: "Behold, I say unto you, Peter, that you shall take your journey with your brother Oliver; for the time has come that it is expedient in me that you shall open your mouth to declare my gospel; therefore, fear not, but give heed unto the words and advice of your brother, which he shall give you. And be you afflicted in all his afflictions, ever lifting up your heart unto me in prayer and faith, for his and your deliverance; for I have given unto him power to build up my church among the Lamanites;"

569 3 Ne. 21: 23: "And they shall assist my people, the remnant of Jacob, and also as many of the house of Israel as shall come, that they may build a city, which shall be called the New Jerusalem."

now called Independence is the center place; and a spot for the temple is lying westward, upon a lot which is not far from the courthouse. Wherefore, it is wisdom that the land should be purchased by the saints, and also every tract lying westward, even unto the line running directly between Jew and Gentile; And also every tract bordering by the prairies, inasmuch as my disciples are enabled to buy lands. Behold, this is wisdom, that they may obtain it for an everlasting inheritance." (D&C 57: 1-5.)

At that moment in time we had everything in one convenient place. A land to build Zion, the remnant next door, central location, approval from God, and the permission to proceed with establishing a temple.

People, places, opportunities and events would all change between the early 1830's and the mid 1840's. Dramatically. And so we will follow a few of those events and the accompanying revelations which reflect the dynamic changes among both the Saints and the Lamanites.

Part 4

You should already be familiar with the history of the problems the Saints experienced in Missouri. Independence was hostile, and the Saints were driven away from Jackson County into surrounding areas. By 1833 the possibility of building in Independence was lost. A revelation assured the Saints that the place for Zion was not moved. The consoling revelation states: "Therefore, let your hearts be comforted concerning Zion; for all flesh is in mine hands; be still and know that I am God. Zion shall not be moved out of her place, notwithstanding her children are scattered. They that remain, and are pure in heart, shall return, and come to their inheritances, they and their children, with songs of everlasting joy, to build up the waste places of Zion—And all these things that the prophets might be fulfilled." (D&C 101: 16-19.)

Zion was intended to be built in the center of the last part of Lamanite land available in 1831. The fact that the gentiles were expelled does not mean the site for building Zion was automatically changed. The Lord reiterated Zion wasn't changed. The gentile children may be scattered, but the site would remain. More importantly, the Lamanite children were being scattered as well. The picture was changing on both sides of the line separating "Jew from gentile" in the years following the 1831 revelation.

By 1838 the conflict between Mormons and Missourians had escalated to the point that it was called the "Mormon War." The election battle at Gallatin on August 6, 1838 is at one end, and Joseph Smith's surrender at Far West in November, 1838 at the other.

Missouri was lost to the Saints. The natives voted to expel them, and Governor Lilburn Boggs signed the Extermination Order on October 27, 1838 requiring Mormons to be exterminated or driven from the State of Missouri; a curious piece of Americana that was not rescinded until some 137 years later on June 25, 1976 by Missouri Governor Christopher Bond.

The immediate aftermath of the Extermination Order was the battle at Haun's Mill, ultimately leading to the surrender in November by Joseph Smith. He was subsequently tried by a military tribunal and sentenced to death, but the death sentence was not carried out.

Joseph spent the winter of 1838-39 in the Liberty Jail, and in March, 1839 wrote a letter from which we have taken three sections of the Doctrine and Covenants, Sections 121, 122 and 123. The possibility of building in Missouri was lost, at least for the time.

The Saints moved to Commerce, renamed it Nauvoo, and started a new city. This one was also identified not only as "Zion" but as the "cornerstone of Zion."[570] So, although "Zion" was not to be moved, by 1841 the "cornerstone of Zion" was now in Nauvoo. This is not a contradiction. Zion has never been moved. But the Lamanites were moving, the Saints were moving, and the opportunity to locate it in the places where it could have been constructed earlier were no longer relevant.

We read the words of Section 101 to mean that the location remains in Independence, Jackson County. It is possible, however, there is another meaning. That is, the location hasn't changed, although temporary opportunities existed earlier. It wasn't built earlier, and will be built, but when it is built, it will be at the place always prophesied for its construction. Zion was to be located on the top of the high mountains.[571] Jackson County has no mountains, no mountain range, no possibility of fulfilling the promised environs for establishing Zion.[572] Make the descriptions "spiritual" if you want, but a mountain setting is clearly required for the prophesied Zion. (Psalms 133: 3; Isa. 52: 7; Joel 3: 17; Micah 4: 2; 2 Ne. 12: 3; D&C 49: 25; among others.)

Zion was always intended to be built upon the mountain top. (Isa. 30: 17.) Even a valley location in Salt Lake cannot answer to the description given in prophecy. A valley floor is not the "top of the mountain" upon which the beacon will be set. Zion has never been moved. Nor will it. In the same revelation which confirms Zion will not be moved, the Lord spoke of the Saints profaning the land earlier identified as Zion. "For all those who will not endure chastening, but

---

[570] D&C 124: 2: "Your prayers are acceptable before me; and in answer to them I say unto you, that you are now called immediately to make a solemn proclamation of my gospel, and of this stake which I have planted to be a cornerstone of Zion, which shall be polished with the refinement which is after the similitude of a palace."

[571] Isa. 40: 9: "O Zion, that bringest good tidings, get thee up into the high mountain; O Jerusalem, that bringest good tidings, lift up thy voice with strength; lift *it* up, be not afraid; say unto the cities of Judah, Behold your God!"

[572] Isa. 2: 3: "And many people shall go and say, Come ye, and let us go up to the mountain of the Lord, to the house of the God of Jacob; and he will teach us of his ways, and we will walk in his paths: for out of Zion shall go forth the law, and the word of the Lord from Jerusalem."

deny me, cannot be sanctified. Behold, I say unto you, there were jarrings, and contentions, and envyings, and strifes, and lustful and covetous desires among them; therefore by these things they polluted their inheritances. They were slow to hearken unto the voice of the Lord their God; therefore, the Lord their God is slow to hearken unto their prayers, to answer them in the day of their trouble." (D&C 101: 5-7.)

So the location identified for building Zion was lost. It was lost because of the jarrings, contentions, envyings, strifes, lustful and covetous desires. This caused the land to be "polluted" and rendered it unfit for Zion. It is true, however, that in the same revelation making purchase of land in Jackson County was approved.[573] There is no doubt a glorious future for Jackson County. But that will be by and by. There is a gathering in the tops of the mountains which must precede that. If there is not a gathering in the mountains first, then ancient and modern prophecy will fail. There is to be a gathering within the boundaries of the everlasting hills.[574] Zion will flourish upon the mountains.[575] There aren't any places in Missouri that qualify for this preliminary gathering.

If jarring and contending can pollute Zion, are we ready for it now? If envy and strife will make it unacceptable, how prepared are we to gather to Zion now? If lustful and covetous desires will make it unfit for an inheritance, are we above those weaknesses now? So, how soon ought we expect the establishment of Zion to get underway?

All of this is an aside to the subject of the remnant. But it is an important aside. The remnant will build the city of Zion. In 1830, when the earlier inhabitants were relocated to the area immediately adjacent to Jackson County, had the city been built it would have been there. It wasn't time. It also wasn't the place. So, although the future of that place may be glorious at some point, the city of Zion to be built by the remnant, would necessarily be built where the remnant is located. Their location, if it answers to the description of prophecy, would be mountainous, in the top of the mountains, and a suitable place for refuge during a time of upheaval. We'll follow the events of the 1840's with that in mind.

---

573 D&C 101: 70-71: "Which saith, or teacheth, to purchase all the lands with money, which can be purchased for money, in the region round about the land which I have appointed to be the land of Zion, for the beginning of the gathering of my saints; All the land which can be purchased in Jackson county, and the counties round about, and leave the residue in mine hand."

574 D&C 133: 31-32: "And the boundaries of the everlasting hills shall tremble at their presence. And there shall they fall down and be crowned with glory, even in Zion, by the hands of the servants of the Lord, even the children of Ephraim."

575 D&C 49: 25: "Zion shall flourish upon the hills and rejoice upon the mountains, and shall be assembled together unto the place which I have appointed."

Part 5

Another principle that must be included in the mix of understanding the prophecies concerning the remnant is timing and patience.

When you speak of bloodlines and blessings, it is not possible to follow the details of interconnections across generations with any amount of accuracy. Even Joseph Smith, while certain of the remnant's existence and importance, was not certain of their identity. They needed to be found. Although some groups showed promise, they were not, and have not, been identified.

There were rumors of a people in the southwest, who made rugs, that may be the group.

There are those who are convinced the Hopi are the people. Hugh Nibley has spent time with the Hopi and written a great deal about them. He seemed satisfied they were likely the chosen remnant. He studied their year-end dance festivals and believed they contained elements of sacred narrative identifiable with the Gospel of Jesus Christ. I have LDS friends who have spent time among the Hopi who have the same view.

I do not believe it is necessary to identify who the remnant is. It is important to realize there is a prophetic destiny of a remnant, and to have a little humility about the limited gentile success which has been prophesied. But to go further than that is not always wise.

Everything in the Lord's plan is timed. You cannot change the timing. If, for example, you hurry to get where you think Zion will be established, and arrive before the burning and cleansing of that land, then you may have found the right spot, but you arrived at the wrong time. You will be killed, burned off the land as it is purged and prepared. The Lord alone controls timing. And timing is as important as any other portion of the Lord's plan.

Also, to identify the remnant beforehand is ill—advised. ***They will be identified in the ordinary course of events***. They will fulfill their prophetic destiny. As it unfolds, it will be natural, appropriate and in accordance with the hand of God. There will be no need to force Zion.

Those who are the remnant may well be Hopi. Or, they may come from Hopi blood, if that is indeed the remnant bloodline. But during the time between the closing of the Book of Mormon history and the opening of American history, how many from that bloodline departed or were captured and carried away to another place. If only one left and migrated into Canada, later to intermarry and leave descendants, who have now intermarried and live in Alberta, Montana and Idaho, then they may have long ago lost any identity with the Hopi. But they may still be heirs according to the bloodline that is theirs.

How do we know the remnant does not now include businessmen in Mexico City, families in Peru, a physician in San Francisco, or a housewife in Florida, all of whom have the blood of the remnant within them, but they are without any knowledge of it? Nor can we know if there were intermarriages and migrations which make northern Mexico and Arizona filled with people who are the remnant, heirs of the promises, and destined to one day return to the faith of Christ. Who knows but what the in-migration of those regarded as "illegal aliens" currently inside the United States are not in possession of the blood that qualifies them as heirs of the promises.

They exist. They are known to the Lord. There may be great areas and people, as well as disbursed and assimilated individuals who are among those who are heirs. It is not important to "find" them in one sense, but critical that they be found in another. They will self-identify. That is, those in whom the promises will be fulfilled will act consistent with the promises. They will become known as they engage in the prophesied conduct. They will convert. They will become reunited through the Gospel of Jesus Christ. They will shake off the dust of history, arise and become glorious. They will blossom as a rose and build the New Jerusalem. We will not control that. It will be them awakening, not us attempting to assimilate them into our culture and society. The Indian Placement Program didn't work because it was not the means by which they are to be found. Pushing our culture on them will only create errors their return is intended to cure. And so the timing and means are critical for this to unfold in accordance with the Lord's plan.

If you were to know for certain exactly who was to fulfill the prophecies, and to visit with them today, you may be profoundly disappointed. Until the time is right, they won't be ready either. They will awaken on time. But until that time, you cannot rouse from slumber those who are not ready to awaken. That it WILL happen is certain. But the time is as important as any other component of the event.

Do the remnant people even know they are the Lord's and heirs of promises in the Book of Mormon? Probably not. They, the remnant, are to learn of these things from the gentiles.[576] Therefore it is unlikely they will know anything about it until the record of the Book of Mormon is delivered to them by the gentiles. So if they are to learn about these things from the gentiles, the first step will be educational. Gentiles need to become converted to the beliefs of the Book of Mormon, then bring these correct beliefs to the remnant. The remnant may have a glorious destiny, but not until after first the gentiles who believe in the words take them to the remnant and teach them.

Even if you knew the Hopi were the right people, that does not accomplish what the promises foretell. The remnant must be taught the truth. That will be taught by believing gentiles. We don't have many of those yet. So to deliver a copy of the Book of Mormon to a Hopi and expect that to result in spontaneous combustion producing light, truth

---

576 2 Ne. 30: 3: "And now, I would prophesy somewhat more concerning the Jews and the Gentiles. For after the book of which I have spoken shall come forth, and be written unto the Gentiles, and sealed up again unto the Lord, there shall be many which shall believe the words which are written; and they shall carry them forth unto the remnant of our seed."

and glory is at best a naive notion and at worst absolute foolishness. It won't happen that way. The right people must be brought the right message by a believing gentile, preaching the fullness of the Gospel to them. When that happens, Nephi's prophecy may begin to unfold. We lack qualified gentile ministers at present. They labor under condemnation for not taking the Book of Mormon seriously or remembering the covenant made within it. So the first step is to convert a few gentiles.

Nevertheless, this is an important subject and worth taking time to understand. But with this, as with almost everything else in the Gospel, having it measured correctly and weighed in proportion is the only way to understand. So we proceed step by cautious step to try and dismantle false and corrupt notions, and to assemble the true ones. You must be patient to understand the Lord's plan. And therefore we proceed patiently in this subject, as well.

Patience is more than a virtue. It is critical to participating in the Lord's plan.

Part 6

A few additional statements by Joseph Smith and others add weight to the identity of the existing American Indian population at the time of the prophecies given to Joseph Smith.

When Joseph and Oliver went to seek answers about baptism on May 15, 1829, they explained the motivation for the inquiry. They report they were inspired "after writing the account given of the Savior's ministry to the remnant of the seed of Jacob, upon this continent." (*Messenger and Advocate*, Vol. 1, p. 15, October 1834.)

"The Book of Mormon is a record of the forefathers of our western Tribes of Indians," Smith wrote to N. C. Saxton, editor of a Rochester, New York, newspaper. "The land of America is a promised land unto them," where they would be instrumental in building a New Jerusalem." [Taken from Ronald Walker's paper: *Seeking the Remnant*; one of the first publications to take the role of the remnant found in the American Indians as a serious matter of study.]

On their mission to the Lamanites, Oliver and Parley were interviewed by newspapers as they went on their journey. *The Telegraph* published in Painesville, Ohio, on 16 and 30 November 1830, made the following mention about Oliver's interview: "He proclaims destruction upon the world in a few years. We understand that he is bound for the regions beyond the Mississippi, where he contemplates founding a 'City of Refuge' for his followers, and converting the Indians, under his prophetic authority." Cowdery also reportedly spoke of an about-to-rise Indian prophet, who would bring these events to pass.

Parley Pratt's autobiography discusses the Mission to the Lamanites. He describes how the missionaries didn't even hesitate in their mission after their tremendous success at Kirtland. They changed the entire center of gravity for the Church by the Kirtland conversions. But they retained their focus on the target of the remnant, whom they had been sent to teach. This was the first organized missionary effort after the organization of the church, and the target was the Lamanites. The priority and focus was remarkable, when you consider the abundance of potential white converts all around the tiny start-up church. It gives some indication of how important Joseph regarded the Lamanite remnant to be as an obligation for the restored church.

Winter did not slow their journey toward the western frontier and border with the relocated American Indian tribes. Here's a brief excerpt from Parley's writings:

"We halted for a few days in Illinois, about twenty miles from St. Louis, on account of a dreadful storm of rain and snow, which lasted for a week or more, during which the slow fell in some places near three feet deep...In the beginning of 1831 we renewed our journey; and, passing through St. Louis and St. Charles, we traveled on foot for three hundred miles through vast prairies and through trackless wilds of snow —no beaten road; houses few and far between; and the bleak northwest wind always blowing in our faces with a keenness which would almost take the skin off the face. ...We often ate our frozen bread and pork by the way, when the bread would be so frozen that we could not bite or penetrate any part of it but the outside crust.

"After much fatigue and some suffering we all arrived in Independence, in the county of Jackson, on the extreme western frontiers of Missouri, and the United States." (*Autobiography of Parley P. Pratt*, p. 40.)

Parley's account continues and explains how two of the missionaries took employment as tailors in Independence while the others crossed the boundary and "commenced a mission among the Lamanites, or Indians." (*Id.* p. 41.) They taught the Shawnees, then the Delaware, including the chief over ten tribes of Delaware. The sermon delivered to the gathering called by the chief, delivered by Oliver Cowdery, is set out on pp. 42-43 where it is clear Oliver understood the Delaware were descended from the Book of Mormon people. The chief replied: "We feel truly thankful to our white friends who have come so far, and been at such pains to tell us good news, and specially this new news concerning the Book of our forefathers; it makes us glad in here—placing his hands on his own heart."

Although the Indian reaction was favorable, the Indian Agents were alarmed at the Mormon success. In particular they did not want the upstart religion to gain a foothold among the relocated Indians, and began to interfere with the missionary efforts.

Of interest to us, however, is Oliver's mention of the Rocky Mountains as the ultimate destination of the missionary effort, to be "with the Indians." (*The Telegraph*, Painesville, 18 January 1831, cited by Walker, above, on p. 9.) Walker writes: "Smith gave a revelation requiring Sidney Gilbert to open a store in western Missouri that would allow 'clerks employed in his service' to go unto the Lamanites and 'thus the gospel may be preached unto them.' He also issued a confidential revelation that presaged the introduction of plural marriage. This latter statement promised that the elders would intermarry with the native women, making the red man's posterity 'white, delightsome, and just.'" (*Seeking the Remnant*, p. 10, Citations omitted.)

This early focus on the duty to find and preach to the remnant was not a passing concern. It was far more central to the early efforts than we realize as we review the events today. Today the view of the Lamanite remnant's role is, if anything, superficial. To the earliest converts, they were central. They would remain a focus of interest throughout not only Joseph's life, but also into the early part of the western migration. Indeed, the western movement of the church itself was related to locating the remnant.

Now there are a number of prophecies given in the Book of Mormon or Doctrine and Covenants which relate to why the remnant were a priority for Joseph Smith and the early church of this dispensation. The further we get from those times, however, the more we seem to forget the underlying reasons. We have become so successful as an organization, and prosper in every economic, political and social measure that it is hard to remember things. When Presidential candidates, the leader of the United States Senate, the Ambassador to China, business and educational leaders are members of the church, we do not relate as well to the promised cataclysms. Where once we may have welcomed destruction to end our persecutions, now we fear what we would lose. Our former poverty made us fear nothing in the destruction of the world, but now we have a great deal to lose and therefore we want to continue as we are. We have even redefined the term "remnant" to mean us, the Latter-day Saints, as if redefining it will remove the prophetic threat posed to the gentiles. (See *Children of the Covenant*, May, 1995 Ensign, the General Conference talk by Russell M. Nelson; in particular the interpretation given in footnote 15.) The careful distinctions between the remnant of the Book of Mormon on the one hand, and the gentiles on the other, has been forgotten, or altogether lost in our modern teachings. But that does not alter what Nephi or Christ meant in their prophecies that we still read in the Book of Mormon text.

We've worked to establish a basis for understanding the distinctions for several months now. With that foundation we will continue our search for understanding where we find ourselves in history, what group we are identified with and what we should expect in the coming calamities.

Onward, then…

Part 7

When Joseph had made a sufficient "offering" and "acknowledgments," the Lord gave another opportunity for the Saints to receive again what had been taken from them, that is the "fullness of the priesthood."[577]

To be permitted to undertake this, however, there would be a limited time appointed. After that appointment, the church would be rejected.[578] The time is not specified, but the work was to be undertaken by sending "swift messengers,"[579] and gathering all the Saints together with their gold, silver, antiquities, and precious things to construct this Temple.[580]

The Saints gathered to Nauvoo and by 1844 the population had swollen to 12,000. There were shops, brick homes, stores, and a Masonic Hall constructed in Nauvoo. There was a gunsmith shop, a university, library and wide streets. Unlike other frontier towns with adobe and log homes, Nauvoo boasted brick houses and affluence. This community was superior to anything else along the western boundary of the United States at the time.

When Joseph and Hyrum were killed on June 27, 1844, the Temple walls were not completed and no portion had been dedicated. After Joseph's death, the Saints rededicated themselves to finish the Temple. The exterior walls were completed in December, 1844 and the final sunstone put into place with some considerable difficulty.

On March 16, 1845 Brigham Young asked the Saints to rededicate themselves to building the Temple, promising them blessings if they would redouble their efforts to complete the building. On the following

---

[577] D&C 124: 1, 28: "Verily, thus saith the Lord unto you, my servant Joseph Smith, I am well pleased with your offering and acknowledgments, which you have made; for unto this end have I raised you up, that I might show forth my wisdom through the weak things of the earth. …For there is not a place found on earth that he may come to and restore again that which was lost unto you, or which he hath taken away, even the fulness of the priesthood."

[578] D&C 124: 31-32: "But I command you, all ye my saints, to build a house unto me; and I grant unto you a sufficient time to build a house unto me; and during this time your baptisms shall be acceptable unto me. But behold, at the end of this appointment your baptisms for your dead shall not be acceptable unto me; and if you do not these things at the end of the appointment ye shall be rejected as a church, with your dead, saith the Lord your God."

[579] D&C 124: 26: "And send ye swift messengers, yea, chosen messengers, and say unto them: Come ye, with all your gold, and your silver, and your precious stones, and with all your antiquities; and with all who have knowledge of antiquities, that will come, may come, and bring the box-tree, and the fir-tree, and the pine-tree, together with all the precious trees of the earth;"

[580] D&C 124: 26-27: "And send ye swift messengers, yea, chosen messengers, and say unto them: Come ye, with all your gold, and your silver, and your precious stones, and with all your antiquities; and with all who have knowledge of antiquities, that will come, may come, and bring the box-tree, and the fir-tree, and the pine-tree, together with all the precious trees of the earth; And with iron, with copper, and with brass, and with zinc, and with all your precious things of the earth; and build a house to my name, for the Most High to dwell therein."

day 105 extra laborers showed up to help. (History of the Church 7: 385-87.) It was not until 24 May 1845 that the capstone would be laid.

Joseph was dead for 18 months before the endowment was administered in the Nauvoo Temple on December 10th, 1845. Those who had been given some instruction regarding the Temple in Joseph's brick store, used what they had learned before Joseph's death to perform the ceremonies. A portion of the attic was temporarily dedicated for this work, even though the structure was incomplete. The final endowments were performed on February 7, 1846. On February 8, 1846 the Twelve prayed in the Temple to be able to finally complete and formally dedicate the Temple. The following day the Temple caught fire, damaging the area that had been used for the endowment requiring repairs to be made. A week later Brigham Young's party departed Nauvoo with the Temple still incomplete, but Nauvoo was a magnificent city that showed enormous culture, prosperity and success.

If you have visited Nauvoo since the beginning of the Church-sponsored Nauvoo Restoration, Inc. work, you know how amazing the city was when abandoned by the Saints. It was a tribute to labor, dedication, and perseverance. The Temple was incomplete and still under construction—not at all ready for dedication, but the city was a marvel. As the church leadership departed to the west, they left instruction to complete the Temple even though it would not be used.

Finally, on April 29, 1846 the Nauvoo Temple was complete enough to dedicate. The following day a private dedication service was conducted by Wilford Woodruff, Orson Hyde and about twenty others. The prayer was offered by Joseph Young, Brigham's brother. The next day a public dedication service was held with those attending charged $1.00 entrance fee to help pay those who had worked in completing the structure. In this dedication ceremony Elder Hyde offered the prayer and included the following: *"By the authority of the Holy Priesthood now we offer this building as a sanctuary to Thy Worthy Name. We ask Thee to take the guardianship into Thy hands..."*

The following Sunday Elder Hyde explained that the Temple needed to be completed for the church to be accepted by the Lord with our dead. He commented that the work had only been accomplished "by the skin of our teeth." (*Wilford Woodruff's Journal* 3: 43.)

By September, 1846 a mob overran Nauvoo, and the caretakers gave the keys to the Temple doors to the mob. The mob was eventually shamed into returning the Temple to the caretakers and on October 20th the keys were returned to Brother Paine. The trustees of Nauvoo then tried to sell the Temple, but the best offer received was $100,000. A Missouri newspaper reported that the Temple was sold in June, 1847 to the Catholic Church for $75,000, but that the sale failed because of a defect in the title to the property.

On October 9, 1848 the Nauvoo Temple was destroyed by an arsonist.

In March, 1849 the French Icarians purchased the hollow shell of the destroyed Temple. On May 27, 1850 a storm blew down the north wall and made the structure so dangerous that it was further torn down to make it safe. Pieces of the blockwork were then sold and some of them were transported to be used in building projects outside the community, including to St. Louis. By 1865 the city removed what little remained. The site was then used for saloons, slaughter houses, hotels, grocery and drug stores, pool halls and private houses. ("The Nauvoo Temple", *The Instructor*, March 1965.)

From the time of Nauvoo until the present day, every President of The Church of Jesus Christ of Latter-day Saints either lived in Nauvoo between January 1841 and June 1844, or descended from those who lived there during the time. (Although some were called on missions and abandoned families who resided there for some of that time.)

Church history takes the view that Nauvoo was a triumph, and the Saints succeeded in accomplishing all that was required of them, and more. The stories of heroism, sacrifice and devotion that focus on the Nauvoo era are endless. Those families who trace their genealogy to ancestors in Nauvoo at that time defend the notion that the they are specially favored as families, and are among the noble and great chosen to lead others in mortality because of their great devotion and sacrifice.

The promise of a remnant holding authority and performing a central work in the establishment of Zion, as prophesied by the Book of Mormon and Doctrine and Covenants, would be a dramatic change in course for the church. This is something that will occur in any event. Indeed, coalitions, conspiracies and man's arm will be powerless to prevent it. Unlikely history is the stuff of scripture.

Prophecies will be fulfilled. Despite vanity and foolishness, error and unbelief, prophecies will be fulfilled.

Part 8

We've seen some of what the remnant is defined to mean. We've seen the definition in the Book of Mormon excludes gentiles. We've seen the converted gentiles comprising the Latter-day Saints are still defined as gentiles after conversion.

We've seen that the first formal mission called after the establishment of the church was sent to the Lamanites to find the remnant. We've seen how the mission went no further than the boundary where the Indian Nations were relocated by the US Government in 1830. What we haven't discussed is the interest Joseph Smith had in locating the remnant throughout his life.

When he was fleeing Nauvoo in late June, he intended to go to the Rocky Mountains. That was the location chosen precisely because it was where he hoped to find the remnant. He was talked into returning by those who claimed it was cowardly for him to flee. They used the Lord's analogy about the false shepherd who would flee when the flock was in danger.[581] He reportedly said "if my life is of no value to my friends, it is of no value to myself." He returned. With that, Joseph's attempt to locate and identify the remnant came to an end. However, before his final surrender, his intention was to go to the Rocky Mountains to locate the remnant.

The following entry appears on June 22, 1844 in Vol. 6, page 547 of the DHC: "About 9 p.m. Hyrum came out of the Mansion and gave his hand to Reynolds Cahoon, at the same time saying, 'A company of men are seeking to kill my brother Joseph, and the Lord has warned him to flee to the Rocky Mountains to save his life. Good-bye, Brother Cahoon, we shall see you again.' In a few minutes afterwards Joseph came from his family. His tears were flowing fast. He held a handkerchief to his face, and followed after Brother Hyrum without uttering a word."

In his final public address Joseph said, among other things: "You will gather many people into the vastness of the Rocky Mountains as a center for the gathering of the people …you will yet be called upon to go forth and call upon the free men from Main to gather themselves together to the Rocky Mountains; and the Redmen from the West and all people from the North and from the South and from the East, and go to the West, to establish themselves in the strongholds of their gathering places, and there you will gather with the Redmen to their center from their scattered and dispersed situation, to become the strong arm of Jehovah, who will be a strong bulwark of protection from your foes." ("A Prophecy of Joseph the Seer", found in The Fate of the Persecutors of the Prophet Joseph Smith, p. 154, 156.)

There is a well known quote that speaks volumes when considered as a whole: "I want to say to you before the Lord that you know no more concerning the destinies of this Church and Kingdom than a babe upon its mother's lap. You don't comprehend it. It is only a little handful of Priesthood you see here tonight, but this Church will fill North and South America—it will fill the world. It will fill the Rocky Mountains. There will be tens of thousands of Latter-day Saints who will be gathered in the Rocky Mountains, and there they will open the door for the establishing of the Gospel among the Lamanites…This people will go into the Rocky Mountains; they will there build temples to the Most High. They will raise up a posterity there, and the Latter-day Saints who dwell in these mountains will stand in the flesh until the coming of the Son of Man. The Son of Man will come to them while in the Rocky Mountains." (Millennial Star, Vol. 54 (1852), p. 605.)

We've seen how the primary effort to build the city of Zion will be the remnant's, and the gentiles will merely "assist" in the construction.

---

[581] John 10: 11-13: "I am the good shepherd: the good shepherd giveth his life for the sheep. But he that is an hireling, and not the shepherd, whose own the sheep are not, seeth the wolf coming, and leaveth the sheep, and fleeth: and the wolf catcheth them, and scattereth the sheep. The hireling fleeth, because he is an hireling, and careth not for the sheep."

To see the remnant's role is more important than to understand their identity. Their identity will come. But their role is distinct and important. We are not them, and they have a destiny appointed them by covenant and promise. We cannot substitute ourselves for them. Nor can we fulfill the prophetic promises without them.

3 Nephi 20

Christ had some specific teachings about the remnant we have not yet examined. We'll turn to that to add to our understanding of the remnant role:

3 Nephi 20: 11

> **"Ye remember that I spake unto you, and said that when the words of Isaiah should be fulfilled—behold they are written, ye have them before you, therefore search them—"**

Christ is speaking and will turn to the future destiny of the Nephites. By the time this statement was made, however, the Nephites were mingled with all other bloodlines. There were shortly to be no more "ites" but only one people.[582]

The destiny of the future remnant will unfold in conformity with words spoken by Isaiah. They are adequate to foretell the future of the events involving the people on this, the American land. But we are supposed to "search them" to be able to get an understanding of what will unfold.

There is a plan. It was all foreseen. It will happen as the prophecies describe. However we need to trust the language and not impose other ideas upon the words.

3 Nephi 20: 12

> **"And verily, verily, I say unto you, that when they shall be fulfilled then is the fulfilling of the covenant which the Father hath made unto his people, O house of Israel."**

Isaiah's prophecies concerning the Israelite covenant will happen at the same time as the fulfillment of the covenants for the Nephite

---

[582] 4 Ne. 1: 17: "There were no robbers, nor murderers, neither were there Lamanites, nor any manner of -ites; but they were in one, the children of Christ, and heirs to the kingdom of God."

remnant. So things will develop simultaneously for all the chosen people. Not just locally, but globally.

Notice the reference to the "Father" and to "His people." Why is it the "Father's people" in this scripture? What significance is there to the covenant being fulfilled for the Father's people? Are they different from others? Can others have a covenant with Christ? Why is it the Father's people who will see the fulfillment of their covenants in this final, winding up of history?

How are "O house of Israel" and the "Father's people" related? Are they the same? Why or why not?

Why would all covenants come to a fulfillment at the same time? What is there of general historical development which requires all of these to be fulfilled simultaneously?

How would you prepare for the time when the fulfillment of all the covenants are to occur? Is there some kind of storage you should be assembling? What about things that put "oil" in a "lamp?" How would you go about getting that put together?

If the judgments of God will begin on His own house[583], then how do you prepare to avoid that judgment?

There is an upside to every prophecy, even in those predicting calamity. The upside consists in two things: First, avoiding the judgment by being prepared for it.[584] Second, recognizing it so as to not be alarmed or lose faith because of it.[585]

---

[583] D&C 112: 24-26: "Behold, vengeance cometh speedily upon the inhabitants of the earth, a day of wrath, a day of burning, a day of desolation, of weeping, of mourning, and of lamentation; and as a whirlwind it shall come upon all the face of the earth, saith the Lord. And upon my house shall it begin, and from my house shall it go forth, saith the Lord; First among those among you, saith the Lord, who have professed to know my name and have not known me, and have blasphemed against me in the midst of my house, saith the Lord."

[584] D&C 38: 30: "I tell you these things because of your prayers; wherefore, treasure up wisdom in your bosoms, lest the wickedness of men reveal these things unto you by their wickedness, in a manner which shall speak in your ears with a voice louder than that which shall shake the earth; but if ye are prepared ye shall not fear."

[585] D&C 1: 3: "And the rebellious shall be pierced with much sorrow; for their iniquities shall be spoken upon the housetops, and their secret acts shall be revealed.And the rebellious shall be pierced with much sorrow; for their iniquities shall be spoken upon the housetops, and their secret acts shall be revealed."

When you see the distresses which are to come, recognize them as signs given by the Lord and take comfort.[586]

Christ uses Isaiah as His source because Isaiah was inspired in what he wrote. We also have a record of his prophecy. Therefore, the Lord could speak in the first person and have us quote Him. However, He pays tribute to His own prophet by quoting the words of Isaiah. This is meekness indeed. Our Lord is not and never has been prideful. He is meek, and willing to let others have credit, share in triumph, and be treated as equals. How unlike Him are the gentile leaders who love to lord it over one another, holding each other as subservients. Christ, however, made Himself a servant of all.[587] He puts that same meekness on display again here, as he quotes from Isaiah. This shows the Lord's respect for Isaiah.

Interesting the things which become apparent the closer you look at our Lord. Interesting how much the Book of Mormon adds to the picture of our Lord. What a great volume of scripture we have been given.

3 Nephi 20: 13

> **"And then shall the remnants, which shall be scattered abroad upon the face of the earth, be gathered in from the east and from the west, and from the south and from the north; and they shall be brought to the knowledge of the Lord their God, who hath redeemed them."**

Notice "remnants" is plural. This is Christ speaking, and the scope of the message is universal. It is not local. It includes local events, to be sure. But the time of this fulfillment will be global. All the "remnants" will be affected.

It will not matter if the particular "remnant" is anywhere "upon the face of the earth" they will be "gathered in."

Why would they necessarily be "gathered?" What is the purpose of "gathering?"

---

[586] Luke 21: 8-13: "And he said, Take heed that ye be not deceived: for many shall come in my name, saying, I am *Christ;* and the time draweth near: go ye not therefore after them. But when ye shall hear of wars and commotions, be not terrified: for these things must first come to pass; but the end *is* not by and by. Then said he unto them, Nation shall rise against nation, and kingdom against kingdom: And great earthquakes shall be in divers places, and famines, and pestilences; and fearful sights and great signs shall there be from heaven. But before all these, they shall lay their hands on you, and persecute *you,* delivering *you* up to the synagogues, and into prisons, being brought before kings and rulers for my name's sake. And it shall turn to you for a testimony."

[587] Mark 10: 42-44: "But Jesus called them *to him,* and saith unto them, Ye know that they which are accounted to rule over the Gentiles exercise lordship over them; and their great ones exercise authority upon them. But so shall it not be among you: but whosoever will be great among you, shall be your minister: And whosoever of you will be the chiefest, shall be servant of all"

Why "gather" merely to then return them to their lands of inheritance?[588]

Which is more important, to gather physically or to gather "to the knowledge of the Lord their God?"

How could people gather "to the knowledge of the Lord their God?" What kind of "knowledge of the Lord God" will be involved? Do you get that knowledge by supporting men in their callings? Do men and their callings even matter? Can you grow in knowledge of God by following, even memorizing, a handbook; following, memorizing talks and inspirational literature? What does a person need to follow, to do, to abide by in order to gain "knowledge of the Lord their God?" What about those who testify to you about programs and personalities, but never preach about Christ and Him crucified?

Do true messengers speak about one another, or about their Lord? How can a man, any man, save you? Who alone has the capacity to redeem you? Is "knowledge of the Lord their God" related also to knowledge that He "hath redeemed them?" Can you "know" Christ and not acquire in the process of knowing Him the knowledge that He "hath redeemed" you?

Do you come to understand He has redeemed you by also coming to know Him?

Do Joseph's remarks about the Lord coming to visit with the remnant in the Rocky Mountains explain how both those coming from the four corners of the compass will gain "knowledge of the Lord their God" and also know He "hath redeemed them?"

Do you begin to see a pattern of consistent prophetic foreknowledge of the last days? Do Christ's words in this message of the Book of Mormon give any greater reason to believe in the promises?

If these promises are made by Him, should you expect it possible for you to go ahead and "gather in" to Him even before there are others willing to do so? Can this "gathering in" occur in your lifetime, for you? If God is no respecter of persons, then what would you need to do today to obtain the same blessings others will receive as they "gather in" in perhaps greater numbers in the future? Is it possible to do that? Are you willing to try?

It seems to me this doctrine is important in a macro sense in understanding prophetic promises and future gatherings. But it is perhaps more important in the micro sense, in that anything promised to anyone in any age is always available on the same principles to anyone willing to abide them at any time.[589] Do you really believe these teachings of our Lord? Then why not act on them?

---

588 See discussion of 3 Nephi 21: 27-28.

589 D&C 130: 20-21: "There is a law, irrevocably decreed in heaven before the foundations of this world, upon which all blessings are predicated—And when we obtain any blessing from God, it is by obedience to that law upon which it is predicated."

I know these things are truly within the reach of almost all of you. The overwhelming majority of readers of this blog have lived better lives than I have You are almost all better qualified than I was. I believed these things, trusted the Lord, acted on His promises. As a result, I am among those who has been "gathered in" and I "know the Lord my God," having been "redeemed by Him." It is more than possible for you.

3 Nephi 20: 14-15

> **"And the Father hath commanded me that I should give unto you this land, for your inheritance. And I say unto you, that if the Gentiles do not repent after the blessing which they shall receive, after they have scattered my people—"**

Christ is speaking to a group of people and their descendants when making these remarks. The Father has commanded Christ to confirm to the Nephites they are given this land. "This land." So now the question of where Christ was while making these comments becomes important.

Where were they at the moment Christ spoke to them? That affects things, doesn't it? Was it Guatemala? Or the United States?

There are two ways of trying to determine the answer to this question. One would be to study the internal content of the Book of Mormon and try to reconstruct a location based on the clues there. This has been done with varying results. The two leading works on the two leading theories have been referred to in this post. There is another theory that the area was in the Gulf of Mexico. The land was completely reformed, broken up, and altered as a result of the upheavals of the 3 Nephi destruction, and the land no longer appears as it did once. It is now underwater. You can work and justify a number of locations based on the content of the Book of Mormon.

The other way is to take other sources that presumably knew, and accept what they said about the location. I've already quoted from both Moroni and Joseph Smith about the location. Both have placed the events in the area now known as the United States. Moroni's description of the Book of Mormon, and its people, was as follows: "He said there was a book deposited, written upon gold plates, giving an account of the former inhabitants of this continent, and the source from whence they sprang." (JS-H 1: 34.) I presume Moroni knew, and that Joseph had no reason to misstate what he said. It would appear that the continent referred to by Christ using the words, "this land" was North America. And the promise from the Father, made by covenant, was with "the former inhabitants of this continent."

So the remnant was (at the moment Christ was speaking to this audience, and confirmed this covenant of the Father) located in North America. This does not mean they weren't mobile and subsequently moved about. This does not mean they did not disburse and occupy other portions of the North and South American land masses. This does not mean that other migrations of these people which scattered them elsewhere into the world have not occurred. Even if you confine everything to a North American venue for the entirety of the Book of Mormon account, there is still a gap between 400 a.d. when the narrative draws to a conclusion and the 1820's when the record comes to light again. Nothing closes that gap.

So if Moroni's comments to Joseph Smith can be trusted, then originally the people from whom the remnant came were people who lived on "this continent" at some time in history.

The gentiles are mentioned again here. They are reminded of the blessings they have received. They are reminded they were given the responsibility of scattering the remnant and disciplining them for the remnant's failings. But, once the gentiles are blessed, once they have scattered the remnant and destroyed most of them (leaving only a remnant of what was here before), then the gentiles are warned. They must repent. Without repentance the fate of the gentiles will be a similar holocaust of destruction, scattering and treading down; leaving only a remnant of the gentiles still upon the land.

So the roles will reverse. At first, the gentiles dominate and the remnant recedes, at last the remnant will dominate and the gentiles recede.

The remnant's role and the gentiles' pride are interconnected with one another. It is for this reason, if no other, the subject of the remnant is important to know something about.

So, we continue.

3 Nephi 20: 16

> **"Then shall ye, who are a remnant of the house of Jacob, go forth among them; and ye shall be in the midst of them who shall be many; and ye shall be among them as a lion among the beasts of the forest, and as a young lion among the flocks of sheep, who, if he goeth through both treadeth down and teareth in pieces, and none can deliver."**

The descendants of Christ's audience remaining after the holocaust of gentile destruction (i.e., the "remnant of the house of Jacob") would be used by God to deliver judgment upon the gentiles. First the descendants are to be reduced to a remnant by the gentiles, but then the fortunes would be reversed. Initially the gentiles would be the very embodiment of the "wrath of God" to "scatter" and "smite" the descendants.[590] Following that, the gentiles are favored of God and

---

590 1 Ne. 13: 14: "And it came to pass that I beheld many multitudes of the Gentiles upon the land of promise; and I beheld the wrath of God, that it was upon the seed of my brethren; and they were scattered before the Gentiles and were smitten."

"prosper." This land becomes the temporary land of inheritance for the gentiles, as well.[591]

But the gentiles would occupy the land on condition. They would need to serve the God of the land, who is Jesus Christ.[592]

Ultimately, they will need to repent, or they will fill the measure of their own cup of wrath by rejecting the fullness of the Gospel. The gentiles would not continue in their humility, but would be offered the fullness of the Gospel, reject it, then turn to their own pride, even more proud of themselves than any comparable people upon the earth. As Christ describes the latter-day gentiles, they will be full of mischief, lyings, deceits, hypocrisy and priestcrafts. Indeed, they will be full of all this and will also reject the fullness of the Gospel offered them by the Lord.[593]

When they do, Christ will "bring the fullness of my Gospel from among them."[594] Upon removing the fullness, and the gentiles being filled with their pride, priestcrafts, deceits and hypocrisy, the Lord will use the remnant who remain to return judgment upon the gentiles in the same manner the gentiles had earlier returned judgment upon the remnant.[595]

As Christ states above, using the words of Isaiah, "a remnant of the house of Jacob" will "go forth among them; and ye shall be in the midst of them who shall be many; and ye shall be among them as a lion among the beasts of the forest, and as a young lion among the flocks of sheep, who, if he goeth through both treadeth down and teareth in pieces, and none can deliver."

---

591 1 Ne. 13: 15: "And I beheld the Spirit of the Lord, that it was upon the Gentiles, and they did prosper and obtain the land for their inheritance; and I beheld that they were white, and exceedingly fair and beautiful, like unto my people before they were slain."

592 Ether 2: 12: "Behold, this is a choice land, and whatsoever nation shall possess it shall be free from bondage, and from captivity, and from all other nations under heaven, if they will but serve the God of the land, who is Jesus Christ, who hath been manifested by the things which we have written."

593 3 Ne. 16: 10: "And thus commandeth the Father that I should say unto you: At that day when the Gentiles shall sin against my gospel, and shall reject the fulness of my gospel, and shall be lifted up in the pride of their hearts above all nations, and above all the people of the whole earth, and shall be filled with all manner of lyings, and of deceits, and of mischiefs, and all manner of hypocrisy, and murders, and priestcrafts, and whoredoms, and of secret abominations; and if they shall do all those things, and shall reject the fulness of my gospel, behold, saith the Father, I will bring the fulness of my gospel from among them."

594 Ibid.

595 3 Ne. 16: 15: "But if they will not turn unto me, and hearken unto my voice, I will suffer them, yea, I will suffer my people, O house of Israel, that they shall go through among them, and shall tread them down, and they shall be as salt that hath lost its savor, which is thenceforth good for nothing but to be cast out, and to be trodden under foot of my people, O house of Israel."

We've discussed the "beasts of the forest" and the "flocks of sheep" before. Both categories of gentiles will be swept away. None can deliver them from this coming judgment. The remnant will be the Lord's instrument of judgment upon the gentiles, and the gentile pride, priestcrafts, lyings, deceits will all come crashing down upon them in judgment. Their idols will be trodden down and torn in pieces, for they are their own idols imagining in their own hearts themselves to be greater than any other people. Their image of themselves as high and lifted up will be brought down low, into the dust.[596] How like their master Mahon these gentiles have become. But then rejecting the fullness of the Gospel when it has been offered to a people always carries a heavy price.

The remnant will be doing the work of the Father in that day. For the judgment is the Lord's and not the remnant's. The remnant are only the means by which the judgment is delivered.

Cleansing precedes the blessing. And this blessed land will be Zion. But not while occupied by filthy people who idolize themselves, reject the fullness, support priestcrafts, lyings, deceit and hypocrisy calling it righteousness, truth and beauty. They cannot see their own condition, and will not trust the Lord to reveal it to them. They will say the Lord does not speak any more, and we have enough of the revelations of God.[597] They will say God has finished His work of restoring truth, given His power to men, and now we must follow men to be saved.[598]

But the Lord will prove that He had more to say when the gentiles learn, too late, they trusted in the arm of flesh rather than in the Spirit

---

[596] Compare Isa. 14: 12-17: "How art thou fallen from heaven, O Lucifer, son of the morning! *how* art thou cut down to the ground, which didst weaken the nations! For thou hast said in thine heart, I will ascend into heaven, I will exalt my throne above the stars of God: I will sit also upon the mount of the congregation, in the sides of the north: I will ascend above the heights of the clouds; I will be like the most High. Yet thou shalt be brought down to hell, to the sides of the pit. They that see thee shall narrowly look upon thee, *and* consider thee, *saying, Is* this the man that made the earth to tremble, that did shake kingdoms; *That* made the world as a wilderness, and destroyed the cities thereof; *that* opened not the house of his prisoners?"

[597] 2 Ne. 28: 27-29: "Yea, wo be unto him that saith: We have received, and we need no more! And in fine, wo unto all those who tremble, and are angry because of the truth of God! For behold, he that is built upon the rock receiveth it with gladness; and he that is built upon a sandy foundation trembleth lest he shall fall. Wo be unto him that shall say: We have received the word of God, and we need no more of the word of God, for we have enough!"

[598] 2 Ne. 28: 5: "And they deny the power of God, the Holy One of Israel; and they say unto the people: Hearken unto us, and hear ye our precept; for behold there is no God today, for the Lord and the Redeemer hath done his work, and he hath given his power unto men;"

which saves.[599] At that day, despite all the gentile petitions for relief from that God whose fullness they rejected, none will deliver.

The interplay between the gentiles and the remnant is a fascinating subject, with prophetic details given so as to allow us to appreciate the peril we find ourselves as gentiles in these last days. It is good we Latter-day Saints know we are safe and are part of a great, saved and favored community to be preserved against the coming judgments, isn't it? It is good we do not need to repent much if at all to be saved, because as we hear so very often: All is well. All is well.

"And he said, Go, and tell this people, Hear ye indeed, but understand not; and see ye indeed, but perceive not. Make the heart of this people fat, and make their ears heavy, and shut their eyes; lest they see with their eyes, and hear with their ears, and understand with their heart, and convert, and be healed."[600]

This is not about psychology. In fact using the tools of psychology to understand the invitation to come to Christ won't help.

Repentance is love. It is coming to Him. But coming to Him by learning of Him. It is not fear; though approaching God is indeed fearful. That fear in the approach arises from your own inner worthiness before Him. It is unavoidable because none of us are worthy apart from Him. Therefore the dread of being before God will remain until He removes it by an act of His mercy.

The Lord and His prophets teach plainly what we all understood and all agreed upon before the world was begun. The plan we have is tried, true, and is the path by which all those who have ever ascended to heaven have made that ascent.

Focusing upon whether one's motivation is based upon fear or love is unhelpful. Focusing upon what the Lord says, and then what is meant by what the Lord says, is helpful. The inner man must change. The change is mandatory, and comes from knowing Him and learning of Him. But until the moment of relief is granted by Him, there will always be discomfort because of our fallen state and tendency to sin. This is why He is a "Comforter"—because He removes from us the discomfort we feel from sin. But we surely do feel (ALL of us feel) dread and fear because of what we lack as we approach the throne of grace. He "Comforts" us by freeing us from that terrible burden. But such freedom comes on His terms, based upon the eternal plan for removing sin, or it does not happen at all.

---

[599] 2 Ne. 28: 31: "Cursed is he that putteth his trust in man, or maketh flesh his arm, or shall hearken unto the precepts of men, save their precepts shall be given by the power of the Holy Ghost."

[600] Isa. 6: 9-10: "And he said, Go, and tell this people, Hear ye indeed, but understand not; and see ye indeed, but perceive not. Make the heart of this people fat, and make their ears heavy, and shut their eyes; lest they see with their eyes, and hear with their ears, and understand with their heart, and convert, and be healed."

3 Nephi 20: 17-19

> **"Thy hand shall be lifted up upon thine adversaries, and all thine enemies shall be cut off. And I will gather my people together as a man gathereth his sheaves into the floor. For I will make my people with whom the Father hath covenanted, yea, I will make thy horn iron, and I will make thy hoofs brass. And thou shalt beat in pieces many people; and I will consecrate their gain unto the Lord, and their substance unto the Lord of the whole earth. And behold, I am he who doeth it."**

The remnant will be the instruments of Divine retribution against the gentiles. It will be the remnant's "hand" which "shall be lifted up upon thine adversaries." And it will be "all [the remnant's] enemies [which] shall be cut off." So, who will be the remnant's "adversaries?" Who will be their "enemies?"

The Lord promises to "gather my people together"—-and the only ones He has called His people are the Nephite audience, never the gentiles.[601] The Lord's people to be gathered, the promised inheritors of the land, the chosen and covenant people are the remnant. This prophecy

[601] 3 Ne. 16: 8-9: "But wo, saith the Father, unto the unbelieving of the Gentiles—for notwithstanding they have come forth upon the face of this land, and have scattered my people who are of the house of Israel; and my people who are of the house of Israel have been cast out from among them, and have been trodden under feet by them; And because of the mercies of the Father unto the Gentiles, and also the judgments of the Father upon my people who are of the house of Israel, verily, verily, I say unto you, that after all this, and I have caused my people who are of the house of Israel to be smitten, and to be afflicted, and to be slain, and to be cast out from among them, and to become hated by them, and to become a hiss and a byword among them—"

3 Ne. 20: 15, 27: "And I say unto you, that if the Gentiles do not repent after the blessing which they shall receive, after they have scattered my people— …And after that ye were blessed then fulfilleth the Father the covenant which he made with Abraham, saying: In thy seed shall all the kindreds of the earth be blessed—unto the pouring out of the Holy Ghost through me upon the Gentiles, which blessing upon the Gentiles shall make them mighty above all, unto the scattering of my people, O house of Israel."

3 Ne. 21: 2: "And behold, this is the thing which I will give unto you for a sign—for verily I say unto you that when these things which I declare unto you, and which I shall declare unto you hereafter of myself, and by the power of the Holy Ghost which shall be given unto you of the Father, shall be made known unto the Gentiles that they may know concerning this people who are a remnant of the house of Jacob, and concerning this my people who shall be scattered by them;"

is about them. The gentiles are only included to the extent that a few of them will repent.[602]

The "sheaves into the floor" is a harvest image. It is an end-of-times view, because it involves harvest time. "Gathering the sheaves into the floor" is a reference to latter-day Zion, where a group is first "gathered" before the burning of the fields that always follows.

Again the Lord calls the remnant "my people" while clarifying that His people are those "with whom the Father hath covenanted." To covenant with the Father is to receive a Father. The Father does not covenant with strangers. His covenants are with His household. So this is the Family of God.

The "iron horn" and the "brass hoofs" are also symbolic images. What does a "horn" represent? In the context of judgment, does the "horn" hold additional meaning? Why is the horn said to be "iron?" What do the hoofs represent? In the context of judgment do the "hoofs" have additional meaning? Why are they "brass?" How stern and unrelenting will the judgment be? How complete will it become for the "people" to be "beat in pieces?" How terrible will the pouring out of judgment become?

Why would judgment be so severe upon a people who claim to be godly? Think about the introduction to Joseph Smith at the time the restoration of all things was offered.[603] Compare that to the statement made by the mortal Christ when the Pharisees were confronting Him about violating the rituals and practices of the religious hierarchy at the time.[604] Christ offered them the fullness of His Gospel and they rejected it. The judgment which followed was unlike anything that went before.

---

[602] 3 Ne. 16: 13: "But if the Gentiles will repent and return unto me, saith the Father, behold they shall be numbered among my people, O house of Israel."
3 Ne. 21: 6: "For thus it behooveth the Father that it should come forth from the Gentiles, that he may show forth his power unto the Gentiles, for this cause that the Gentiles, if they will not harden their hearts, that they may repent and come unto me and be baptized in my name and know of the true points of my doctrine, that they may be numbered among my people, O house of Israel;"

[603] JS-H 1: 19: "I was answered that I must join none of them, for they were all wrong; and the Personage who addressed me said that all their creeds were an abomination in his sight; that those professors were all corrupt; that: 'they draw near to me with their lips, but their hearts are far from me, they teach for doctrines the commandments of men, having a form of godliness, but they deny the power thereof'."

[604] Mark 7: 5-9: "Then the Pharisees and scribes asked him, Why walk not thy disciples according to the tradition of the elders, but eat bread with unwashen hands? He answered and said unto them, Well hath Esaias prophesied of you hypocrites, as it is written, This people honoureth me with *their* lips, but their heart is far from me. Howbeit in vain do they worship me, teaching *for* doctrines the commandments of men. For laying aside the commandment of God, ye hold the tradition of men, *as* the washing of pots and cups: and many other such like things ye do. And he said unto them, Full well ye reject the commandment of God, that ye may keep your own tradition."

Christ warned them it would be so.[605] Nevertheless, they refused to accept the fullness offered them, continued on in their religious traditions, and were besieged by Roman legions and slain en masse. The account from Josephus is difficult and shocking to read. Mothers cannibalizing their infants to satiate their hunger pains. It is as if hell itself opened upon Jerusalem.

Rejection of the fullness of Christ's Gospel carries terrible consequences. We have seen it before. And, when it was rejected before, it was done in preference to traditions from men. The arm of flesh and a religion multiplied the commandments of men until every aspect of life was controlled by religion. How one dressed, what they ate, how they observed the Sabbath, what things were considered clean and unclean, how to appear in public in order to conform to the right look, vocabulary and conduct. These were very religious people. I've discussed them in *Come, Let Us Adore Him*. I assume you're familiar with that.

Thank goodness we are not like them. We have the fullness, don't we? We are safe and in the right path and none can molest us or make us afraid. For we are the chosen people.

Well those other people (not us) who rejected the fullness of the Gospel, those are the ones who will be broken into pieces. Then their "gain" and their "substance" will be consecrated to the Lord. So they will live the law of consecration after all! Only it will be postmortem. That is, once killed, the Lord can use their gain and substance to provide for His people.

Lest any forget the author and finisher of our faith, He speaks to us anew to remind us who is responsible for these deeds: "And behold, I am he who doeth it."

The Lord is, after all, the same yesterday, today and tomorrow. When He invites us in meekness to come to Him, we should realize that failure to come risks the judgments that have always been terrible to bear. Those Old Testament events we have a difficult time associating with Christ will become associated with Christ again. Just as His New Testament judgments were His and terrible to behold. He is the same. We should expect that when the time ends and we have not met our appointment, we actually do risk rejection and judgment.

3 Nephi 20: 20

"And it shall come to pass, saith the Father, that the sword of my justice shall hang over them at that day; and except they repent it shall fall upon them, saith the Father, yea, even upon all the nations of the Gentiles."

---

605 Matt. 24: 21: "For then shall be great tribulation, such as was not since the beginning of the world to this time, no, nor ever shall be."

Again the reminder is made to the gentiles. We who are associated with the gentiles[606] are numbered among "all the nations of the gentiles."

So this is Divine judgment, aimed at the gentiles who were offered, and then rejected the fullness of His Gospel. These are those who will be receiving the "sword of [His] justice." Even now, the "sword of [His] justice ...hangs over us." For we are "at that day" now. So the sword "shall fall upon them, saith the Father" unless we "repent."

How does one repent when they have rejected the fullness? Would it have been easier to have accepted it when first offered? When did we neglect receiving it? If taken, how was it taken? How do we obtain it anew?

These seem to be important issues. They seem to involve the very subject of life and death, both mortally and eternally. Why, if so important, do we go about telling one another "odds are you're going to be exalted" when such alarms as these exist in Christ's own words in the Book of Mormon? What foolishness have we been given in place of the "plain words" of truth which Nephi and Christ Himself taught?

Do we get angry at the truth like Laman and Lemuel?[607] Do we take the truth to be a hard thing? Why do we get angry at the truth? Do we accept truth and welcome it, or think it is a terrible thing when we hear it?[608] Do those who are offended at the truth really have the spirit of the devil?[609]

The key for gentile survival is repentance. Time and time again the words "repent" or "repentance" are used to let the gentiles know there is an escape. But that escape does not come from receiving a hollow form

---

606 D&C 109: 60: "Now these words, O Lord, we have spoken before thee, concerning the revelations and commandments which thou hast given unto us, who are identified with the Gentiles."

607 2 Ne. 1: 26: "And ye have murmured because he hath been plain unto you. Ye say that he hath used sharpness; ye say that he hath been angry with you; but behold, his sharpness was the sharpness of the power of the word of God, which was in him; and that which ye call anger was the truth, according to that which is in God, which he could not restrain, manifesting boldly concerning your iniquities."

608 2 Ne. 28: 28: "And in fine, wo unto all those who tremble, and are angry because of the truth of God! For behold, he that is built upon the rock receiveth it with gladness; and he that is built upon a sandy foundation trembleth lest he shall fall."

609 2 Ne. 33: 5: "And it speaketh harshly against sin, according to the plainness of the truth; wherefore, no man will be angry at the words which I have written save he shall be of the spirit of the devil."

of godliness without any power.[610] What is "priesthood" if there is no power in it?

Well the Book of Mormon continues to invite listening gentiles to repent. Over the heads of all responsible for failure, the Book of Mormon preaches repentance and truth. It preaches against priestcraft which teaches gentiles to worship man and rely upon the arm of flesh, the Book of Mormon invites gentiles to come and receive pure religion and knowledge of their Redeemer.

The Book of Mormon is the cornerstone of our religion; the cornerstone of the religion of Jesus Christ. It is the most correct book. A man can get closer to God by abiding its precepts than any other book. We have had it warning and inviting us for 180 years and we still have not actually either learned its precepts nor begun to abide by them.

The times of the gentiles are drawing to a close. If there is to be any significant gentile repentance, it must happen soon or the sword of the Lord's justice, which hangs over us, will surely fall on us.

So this topic of remnant destiny and gentile destiny are intertwined. It is little wonder why Joseph found reason to send the first missionaries to find them; and sought to flee to the Rocky Mountains himself to find them the last week of his life. Our current proximity does not matter, however, if our hearts are far from the Lord's invitation to repent.

3 Nephi 20: 21-22

> **"And it shall come to pass that I will establish my people, O house of Israel. And behold, this people will I establish in this land, unto the fulfilling of the covenant which I made with your father Jacob; and it shall be a New Jerusalem. And the powers of heaven shall be in the midst of this people; yea, even I will be in the midst of you."**

The Lord will establish His people, including all of the "house of Israel." The plan is global. But when it comes to the Americas, His people are those in the audience at the moment He was speaking to "this people." And the land of promise for them is "this land." Meaning that wherever it was that Christ was speaking involved two things: The ancestors of the remnant, and the land of promise.

Now the statement gets interesting because Christ refers to a covenant He made personally with "your father Jacob." Which "Jacob" is this referring to? And, if the Old Testament father whose name was changed to Israel, then why refer to him by his earlier name ("Jacob") rather than by his new name ("Israel")? I've described the reasons for

---

610 JS-H 1: 19: "I was answered that I must join none of them, for they were all wrong; and the Personage who addressed me said that all their creeds were an abomination in his sight; that those professors were all corrupt; that: 'they draw near to me with their lips, but their hearts are far from me, they teach for doctrines the commandments of men, having a form of godliness, but they deny the power thereof'."

distinguishing between these two names for a single man in *Nephi's Isaiah*. It is relevant here and I'd remind you of that discussion.

In Jacob's final blessing to his sons, he blessed Joseph as one "separate from his brethren" to inherit a land "unto the utmost bound of the everlasting hills."[611] The covenant between Christ and Jacob affected this blessing given Joseph. It is in the "utmost bound of the everlasting hills" that Zion or the New Jerusalem is to be built. And it will be Jacob's posterity, the remnant visited by Christ, who will build it. Christ's visit to these people reaffirms the prior covenant, and reconfirms the Lord's intent to fulfill His covenant with Jacob. It is for Jacob's sake this is done. Covenants between the Lord and His sons are always fulfilled; for the Lord takes His word very seriously. His word cannot be broken.[612] But, as I have explained in *Beloved Enos*, these are the words of His covenants. It is not merely vain words spoken using His name as authority by those whom He did not authorize to speak such words.[613]

Since the statement involves global gathering of all the "house of Israel," it would appear this reference to "Jacob" is a reference to the global, overall covenant for the entire collection of remnants (plural) throughout the world, wherever they are scattered. However, the crowning portion of the covenant, the capstone which Jacob was given for his posterity in his covenant, was the promise of the New Jerusalem. When that New Jerusalem has come again, it will be "unto the fulfilling of the covenant which [Christ] made with your father Jacob."

Implicit in the return of a New Jerusalem is the redemption of a worthy assembly of Jacob's posterity. It is the culmination of history. It is the final redemption of a people among whom the Lord may take up His residency.

This New Jerusalem will involve "the powers of heaven" being "in the midst of this people." Also, the Lord "will be in the midst of you." For the Lord to take up His residence with people requires them to be saved, clean every whit, and to receive at last the "fullness of the Gospel of Jesus Christ." These are not pretenders who claim, but do not do.

---

[611] Gen. 49: 26: "The blessings of thy father have prevailed above the blessings of my progenitors unto the utmost bound of the everlasting hills: they shall be on the head of Joseph, and on the crown of the head of him that was separate from his brethren."

[612] D&C 1: 38: "What I the Lord have spoken, I have spoken, and I excuse not myself; and though the heavens and the earth pass away, my word shall not pass away, but shall all be fulfilled, whether by mine own voice or by the voice of my servants, it is the same."

[613] Matt. 7: 22-23: "Many will say to me in that day, Lord, Lord, have we not prophesied in thy name? and in thy name have cast out devils? and in thy name done many wonderful works? And then will I profess untot hem, I never knew you: depart from me, ye that work iniquity."

Even penitent harlots and publicans are preferred to the self-righteous who claim to be something they are not.[614]

Why are "the powers of heaven" mentioned first? Must the "powers of heaven" precede the Lord's presence? Is that why they are mentioned by the Lord first, and His dwelling among them is mentioned second? What does that suggest about the manner in which we proceed into the presence of the Lord? How do we experience the "powers of heaven?" What is that power? Is a "form of godliness without any power" a sufficient substitute for the "powers of heaven?"[615]

Do the "powers of heaven" invariably precede and in turn lead to the Lord's presence? Why?

Reading these words you begin to see how our Lord is consistent and determined. His covenants matter. For the sake of those who have obtained a covenant with Him, He will always deliver what He promises. For those who break their covenants with Him, there is no promise. He has always been the same.[616]

Read again the words of condemnation given against us, which remain in effect still today:

> 49 And the whole world lieth in sin, and groaneth under darkness and under the bondage of sin.
>
> 50 And by this you may know they are under the bondage of sin, because they come not unto me.
>
> 51 For whoso cometh not unto me is under the bondage of sin.

---

[614] Matt. 21: 28-32: "But what think ye? A *certain* man had two sons; and he came to the first, and said, Son, go work to day in my vineyard. He answered and said, I will not: but afterward he repented, and went. And he came to the second, and said likewise. And he answered and said, I *go,* sir: and went not. Whether of them twain did the will of *his* father? They say unto him, The first. Jesus saith unto them, Verily I say unto you, That the publicans and the harlots go into the kingdom of God before you. For John came unto you in the way of righteousness, and ye believed him not: but the publicans and the harlots believed him: and ye, when ye had seen *it,* repented not afterward, that ye might believe him."

[615] JS-H 1: 19: "I was answered that I must join none of them, for they were all wrong; and the Personage who addressed me said that all their creeds were an abomination in his sight; that those professors were all corrupt; that: 'they draw near to me with their lips, but their hearts are far from me, they teach for doctrines the commandments of men, having a form of godliness, but they deny the power thereof'."

[616] Lev. 26: 15-17: "And if ye shall despise my statutes, or if your soul abhor my judgments, so that ye will not do all my commandments, *but* that ye break my covenant: I also will do this unto you; I will even appoint over you terror, consumption, and the burning ague, that shall consume the eyes, and cause sorrow of heart: and ye shall sow your seed in vain, for your enemies shall eat it. And I will set my face against you, and ye shall be slain before your enemies: they that hate you shall reign over you; and ye shall flee when none pursueth you."

> 52 And whoso receiveth not my voice is not acquainted with my voice, and is not of me.
>
> 53 And by this you may know the righteous from the wicked, and that the whole world groaneth under sin and darkness even now.
>
> 54 And your minds in times past have been darkened because of unbelief, and because you have treated lightly the things you have received—
>
> 55 Which vanity and unbelief have brought the whole church under condemnation.
>
> 56 And this condemnation resteth upon the children of Zion, even all.
>
> 57 And they shall remain under this condemnation until they repent and remember the new covenant, even the Book of Mormon and the former commandments which I have given them, not only to say, but to do according to that which I have written—
>
> 58 That they may bring forth fruit meet for their Father's kingdom; otherwise there remaineth a scourge and judgment to be poured out upon the children of Zion. (D&C 84: 49-58.)

It is not that we haven't been warned. It is that we just will not allow the warnings to inform us. We prefer to pretend rather than to do. We certainly have a form of godliness, but we lament even in General Conference about the lack of power in that form.

3 Nephi 20: 23

> **"Behold, I am he of whom Moses spake, saying: A prophet shall the Lord your God raise up unto you of your brethren, like unto me; him shall ye hear in all things whatsoever he shall say unto you. And it shall come to pass that every soul who will not hear that prophet shall be cut off from among the people."**

If there were any doubt about who was meant in Deuteronomy 18: 15-19[617], Christ clarifies it here. He, Christ, was always meant to be the ultimate Law-Giver. He is the one who must be followed. He may send

---

[617] Deut. 18: 15-19: "The Lord thy God will raise up unto thee a Prophet from the midst of thee, of thy brethren, like unto me; unto him ye shall hearken; According to all that thou desiredst of the Lord thy God in Horeb in the day of the assembly, saying, Let me not hear again the voice of the Lord my God, neither let me see this great fire any more, that I die not. And the Lord said unto me, They have well *spoken that* which they have spoken. I will raise them up a Prophet from among their brethren, like unto thee, and will put my words in his mouth; and he shall speak unto them all that I shall command him. And it shall come to pass, *that* whosoever will not hearken unto my words which he shall speak in my name, I will require *it* of him."

prophets, but it is Christ alone who is to be followed. Those who draw attention away from Him and turn attention to themselves will always lead astray. For the Lord alone can save. No man can.

We've been trying to make the matter clear for some time. Not merely in this blog, but by my writing and your reading the six books I've written before beginning this effort. The Lord alone is the one to whom each of us must look for hope and salvation. He is the one with whom you can covenant to receive salvation.

In the middle of this prophecy of remnant return and gentile holocaust, comes the reminder again of the Lord's primacy. Look to Him. Him alone. He is the one raised up to save mankind. He is the gentile hope.

The judgments the gentiles have merited by their refusal to accept the fullness of Christ's Gospel is not an impediment to you, if you will come to Him. It was always meant to be a singular event anyway. There is no collective salvation. Each person comes to Him one at a time. Even when He redeems a group, He visits with them individually.[618]

Those who will not "hear Him" will be "cut off from among the people." What does it mean to "hear Him?" How do you go about accomplishing that?

What does it mean to be "cut off from among the people?" What "people?" Why is being cut off from those people a curse? Where are you sent if you are not among the Lord's people? How do you go about rectifying that—joining in to be among those who "hear Him" and are part of His people?

Can you do it now? Do you have to wait till some distant future time or place? Why aren't you doing more about it now, then?

3 Nephi 20: 24

> **"Verily I say unto you, yea, and all the prophets from Samuel and those that follow after, as many as have spoken, have testified of me."**

The Lord chose and established Israel. He would remain committed to them, although they went whoring after other gods.

---

618 3 Ne. 11: 13-17: "And it came to pass that the Lord spake unto them saying: Arise and come forth unto me, that ye may thrust your hands into my side, and also that ye may feel the prints of the nails in my hands and in my feet, that ye may know that I am the God of Israel, and the God of the whole earth, and have been slain for the sins of the world. And it came to pass that the multitude went forth, and thrust their hands into his side, and did feel the prints of the nails in his hands and in his feet; and this they did do, going forth one by one until they had all gone forth, and did see with their eyes and did feel with their hands, and did know of a surety and did bear record, that it was he, of whom it was written by the prophets, that should come. And when they had all gone forth and had witnessed for themselves, they did cry out with one accord, saying: Hosanna! Blessed be the name of the Most High God! And they did fall down at the feet of Jesus, and did worship him."

Moses held the fullness of the priesthood. He conferred blessings upon others. Although Moses was taken from Israel, the blessings of the priesthood remained. Moses blessed Joshua, and Joshua held the blessings of the priesthood for so long as he lived. But the fullness of the priesthood, that portion which permitted a man to see God face to face, was taken with Moses.[619]

When Joshua died, both the priesthood that left with Moses, and the blessings from that priesthood were lost. What remained thereafter was a lesser form of priesthood called the Levitical or Aaronic Priesthood. This continued to be ministered from Moses until Jesus Christ.

The prophets, however, were something different. They came through diverse families and from unexpected places. They were not part of the leading Levitical families and not even from that tribe on occasion. Their priesthood was not reckoned by what was then on the earth, but was given to them directly from heaven itself. Joseph Smith taught: *"All priesthood is Melchizedek, but there are different portions or degrees of it. That portion which brought Moses to speak with God face to face was taken away; but that which brought the ministry of angels remained. All the prophets had the Melchizedek Priesthood and were ordained by God himself"* (*TPJS*, pp. 180-81).

The men who held the higher form of priesthood, the fullness that made it possible for them to behold God face to face, were "all the prophets from Samuel and those that followed after." Having this form of priesthood they could behold God face to face and live.[620]

The power to see God face to face is not real if the man does not actually behold God face to face. It is powerless. It is theory. It is a notion and not a reality. This priesthood the revelation speaks about is not a theoretical idea, but an actual, real power which allows the person holding it to behold God and live. Therefore, when Christ states that "all the prophets from Samuel and those that followed after" had "testified of [Christ]" this is more than rhetoric. They became prophets by reason of the Lord having appeared and spoken to them; having testified of Himself to them. Therefore their status as prophets and their witness of

---

619 D&C 84: 20-25: "Therefore, in the ordinances thereof, the power of godliness is manifest. And without the ordinances thereof, and the authority of the priesthood, the power of godliness is not manifest unto men in the flesh; For without this no man can see the face of God, even the Father, and live. Now this Moses plainly taught to the children of Israel in the wilderness, and sought diligently to sanctify his people that they might behold the face of God; But they hardened their hearts and could not endure his presence; therefore, the Lord in his wrath, for his anger was kindled against them, swore that they should not enter into his rest while in the wilderness, which rest is the fulness of his glory. Therefore, he took Moses out of their midst, and the Holy Priesthood also;"

620 D&C 84: 22-23: "For without this no man can see the face of God, even the Father, and live. Now this Moses plainly taught to the children of Israel in the wilderness, and sought diligently to sanctify his people that they might behold the face of God;"

Him were coequal. They sprang from the very same thing—the same event. This, then, formed the basis for their service as the Lord's prophets. They knew Him. They could testify of what they knew, heard and saw, rather than what they believed to be true from what others had said. God had made Himself known to them.

Christ was confirming that these prophets had testified of Him because He was the one who had called them. He was the one who qualified them. He was the one whose witness and message they bore to others. The testimony of Jesus is the spirit of prophecy![621] Here He confirms again that those prophets sent by Him have testified they know Him. They do not testify of themselves, but of Him. They do not point to themselves, but they point to Him. They do not promise salvation through themselves, but invite others to come to Christ and be saved. They will understate rather than overstate their calling and standing before God.

3 Nephi 20: 25-27

> **"And behold, ye are the children of the prophets; and ye are of the house of Israel; and ye are of the covenant which the Father made with your fathers, saying unto Abraham: And in thy seed shall all the kindreds of the earth be blessed. The Father having raised me up unto you first, and sent me to bless you in turning away every one of you from his iniquities; and this because ye are the children of the covenant—And after that ye were blessed then fulfilleth the Father the covenant which he made with Abraham, saying: In thy seed shall all the kindreds of the earth be blessed—unto the pouring out of the Holy Ghost through me upon the Gentiles, which blessing upon the Gentiles shall make them mighty above all, unto the scattering of my people, O house of Israel."**

These verses connect a single doctrine. That doctrine is at the heart of "turning of the hearts of the children to the fathers," which is the result of any restoration of the Gospel. The definition of "children of the prophets" is that one has accepted, believed, and followed the Lord's true messengers. They become children of Abraham and receive priestly authority sealing them into the family of God, joining the "fathers." From the time of Abraham until today, all who are redeemed have become a part of his household.

The phrase "turning the hearts of the children to the fathers" is a reference to the restoration of sealing authority, allowing a connection between man living on the earth, and the fathers (Abraham, Isaac and Jacob). In this dispensation, that restoration occurred when Joseph Smith was given the sealing authority and priesthood whereby he could

---

[621] Rev. 19: 10: "And I fell at his feet to worship him. And he said unto me, See *thou do it* not: I am thy fellowservant, and of thy brethren that have the testimony of Jesus: worship God: for the testimony of Jesus is the spirit of prophecy."

ask and receive answers.[622] As discussed earlier, this was sometime between 1829 and 1833, though I think it was more likely the earlier date as I have explained. Coincident with receiving this authority, Joseph's calling and election was made sure.[623] I have explained this in *Beloved Enos*. This priesthood, having the hearts of the recipients turned to the fathers, and the promise of exaltation, are interconnected.

Abraham not only held this authority, but received the promise that all who received the Gospel after him would become his descendants. From the time of Abraham to the present, every saved soul has had their heart turned to him, become his son or daughter, and received that same priesthood.[624] When Joseph received this, he was not merely sealed up to eternal life, but he became part of the family of Abraham. If you remember the diagram of the celestial kingdom referred to earlier on this blog, you know Joseph became one of those who was grafted into the family tree, and would then in turn preside over others who were sealed up to eternal life thereafter.

The sealing authority used by Joseph in December, 1832, was to seal others up to eternal life.[625] This promise had been previously conferred upon Joseph in that portion of Section 132 referred to above. In fact,

---

[622] D&C 132: 45-47: "For I have conferred upon you the keys and power of the priesthood, wherein I restore all things, and make known unto you all things in due time. And verily, verily, I say unto you, that whatsoever you seal on earth shall be sealed in heaven; and whatsoever you bind on earth, in my name and by my word, saith the Lord, it shall be eternally bound in the heavens; and whosesoever sins you remit on earth shall be remitted eternally in the heavens; and whosesoever sins you retain on earth shall be retained in heaven. And again, verily I say, whomsoever you bless I will bless, and whomsoever you curse I will curse, saith the Lord; for I, the Lord, am thy God."

[623] D&C 132: 49: "For I am the Lord thy God, and will be with thee even unto the end of the world, and through all eternity; for verily I seal upon you your exaltation, and prepare a throne for you in the kingdom of my Father, with Abraham your father."

[624] Abr. 2: 10-11: "And I will bless them through thy name; for as many as receive this Gospel shall be called after thy name, and shall be accounted thy seed, and shall rise up and bless thee, as their father; And I will bless them that bless thee, and curse them that curse thee; and in thee (that is, in thy Priesthood) and in thy seed (that is, thy Priesthood), for I give unto thee a promise that this right shall continue in thee, and in thy seed after thee (that is to say, the literal seed, or the seed of the body) shall all the families of the earth be blessed, even with the blessings of the Gospel, which are the blessings of salvation, even of life eternal."

[625] D&C 88: 2-4: "Behold, this is pleasing unto your Lord, and the angels rejoice over you; the alms of your prayers have come up into the ears of the Lord of Sabaoth, and are recorded in the book of the names of the sanctified, even them of the celestial world. Wherefore, I now send upon you another Comforter, even upon you my friends, that it may abide in your hearts, even the Holy Spirit of promise; which other Comforter is the same that I promised unto my disciples, as is recorded in the testimony of John. This Comforter is the promise which I give unto you of eternal life, even the glory of the celestial kingdom;"

Joseph's use of that authority in December 1832 on behalf of others is evidence that the promise to him recorded in Section 132 was necessarily received earlier than December 1832. If it had not been received earlier, there would have been no need to make the statement in D&C 132: 49 to Joseph, because of what is in Section 88. Why tell Joseph his calling and election was sure in 1843 if it had happened already in 1832? This is another reason you can know Section 132, although recorded in 1843, was in fact a revelation received by Joseph much earlier. It was reduced to writing in 1843 at Hyrum's request.

The reference to "turning the hearts of the fathers to the children" made by Elijah was not because Elijah conferred those keys upon Joseph in the Kirtland Temple[626], for they arrived years earlier than 1836. Elijah was confirming that the keys were now all returned so the hearts of the children could turn to the fathers, and in turn the father's hearts to the children.[627] And, so as to signify he was a true messenger, Elijah also showed a sign by his hand to Joseph whereby Joseph could recognize a true messenger.[628]

In Christ's statement to the Nephite audience, He confirmed that they were "the children of the prophets" because they followed the prophets' teachings. Therefore, because of their obedience they were "of the house of Israel" and had realized that status because "of the covenant which the Father made with your fathers." That covenant was given "unto Abraham" promising to Abraham: "And in thy seed shall all the kindreds of the earth be blessed." All those after the day of Abraham who received this priesthood and sealing would become the seed of Abraham. They become heirs of the promise, and children of Abraham. They are sealed up to eternal life and therefore their hearts have turned to the fathers.

Christ was sent to these Nephites because "The Father having raised me up unto you first, and sent me to bless you in turning away every one of you from his iniquities; and this because ye are the children of the covenant." Realizing the promises, and being visited by the Lord are also connected. When enough are ready to enter into this order, have their hearts turned to the fathers, receive the covenant, then the Lord will bring again Zion.

---

626 D&C 110: 16: "Therefore, the keys of this dispensation are committed into your hands; and by this ye may know that the great and dreadful day of the Lord is near, even at the doors."

627 D&C 110: 15: "To turn the hearts of the fathers to the children, and the children to the fathers, lest the whole earth be smitten with a curse—"

628 D&C 2: 1: "Behold, I will reveal unto you the Priesthood, by the hand of Elijah the prophet, before the coming of the great and dreadful day of the Lord."

3 Nephi 20: 27-28

> **"...unto the pouring out of the Holy Ghost through me upon the Gentiles, which blessing upon the Gentiles shall make them mighty above all, unto the scattering of my people, O house of Israel. And they shall be a scourge unto the people of this land. Nevertheless, when they shall have received the fullness of my gospel, then if they shall harden their hearts against me I will return their iniquities upon their own heads, saith the Father."**

The reason the gentiles received access to the Holy Ghost was to fulfill the purposes of the Father. The remnant would reject the Gospel, and as a result merit judgment. Judgment would come through the gentiles. For that to occur, the Holy Ghost needed to inspire gentile successes.

The Spirit would be responsible for such great gentile success that they will be made "mighty above all, unto the scattering of my people." That is, no other people will be able to prevail against the gentiles of North America while the Holy Ghost was with the gentiles. They will be a "scourge" upon the remnant as a result of the Father's judgments implemented by Christ, using the Holy Ghost.

The Spirit will entitle the gentiles to be offered the fullness. They will qualify by their acts and obedience. When you receive light and stay true to it, you are offered more light. The gentiles will accept and pursue more light, and will merit an opportunity to receive the fullness of the Gospel.

Gentiles did have the fullness of the Gospel, which requires the fullness of the priesthood that was offered while Joseph Smith was here. It was given sometime between 1829 and 1832, and removed before 1841.[629]

When the gentiles were offered the fullness, they displayed little interest in it. Joseph remarked: ""I have tried for a number of years to get the minds of the Saints prepared to receive the things of God; but we frequently see some of them, after suffering all they have for the work of God, will fly to pieces like glass as soon as anything comes that is contrary to their traditions: they cannot stand the fire at all. How many will be able to abide a celestial law, and go through and receive their exaltation, I am unable to say, as many are called, but few are chosen." (DHC 6: 184-185).[630]

When the Saints were given a final opportunity to receive the offered fullness extended to all, they needed to show their willingness to accept

---

[629] D&C 132: 45: "For I have conferred upon you the keys and power of the priesthood, wherein I restore all things, and make known unto you all things in due time."
D&C 124: 28: "For there is not a place found on earth that he may come to and restore again that which was lost unto you, or which he hath taken away, even the fulness of the priesthood."

[630] See also D&C 121: 40: "Hence many are called, but few are chosen."

it by completing the Nauvoo Temple within a short time. They were given long enough to complete it, and if it was not completed in that appointed time, they would be rejected.[631] We have seen how the Saints proceeded to build Nauvoo and their own homes rather than the Nauvoo Temple from 1841 to June, 1844 when Joseph and Hyrum were killed. (See The Remnant Part VII.) When Joseph was taken, the Temple walls had not yet been completed to the second floor.

When the Twelve prayed in the Temple on February 8, 1846 that the Lord would bless the Saints to be able to complete the Temple, the Temple caught fire the next day.

Repairs and further work allowed a dedication to finally take place at the end of April, 1846, nearly two years after Joseph's death. The dedicatory prayer petitioned the Lord to "take guardianship into Thy hands," but by September the keys to the Temple doors were handed to a mob which had overrun Nauvoo. It was the position of Elder Hyde that the Saints performed as they were required "by the skin of our teeth," thereby escaping rejection by the Lord. (This was discussed in The Remnant Part VII.)

The prophecy of Christ, as commanded by the Father, foretells that if the gentiles do reject the fullness, then the Father will "return their iniquities upon their own heads." Meaning that the gentiles will, by reason of their rejection of what was offered them, merit condemnation for ingratitude.[632] They remain "filthy still" because that which would have cleansed them was not received in gratitude. It was rejected. When a people reject the Lord, the Lord, being governed by law, must reject them.

This is the reason the coming judgments are necessary. Where much is given (and we were offered everything) then much is expected.[633] When everything is rejected, then the punishment merited reflects

---

[631] D&C 124: 32: "But behold, at the end of this appointment your baptisms for your dead shall not be acceptable unto me; and if you do not these things at the end of the appointment ye shall be rejected as a church, with your dead, saith the Lord your God."

[632] D&C 88: 33-35: "For what doth it profit a man if a gift is bestowed upon him, and he receive not the gift? Behold, he rejoices not in that which is given unto him, neither rejoices in him who is the giver of the gift. And again, verily I say unto you, that which is governed by law is also preserved by law and perfected and sanctified by the same. That which breaketh a law, and abideth not by law, but seeketh to become a law unto itself, and willeth to abide in sin, and altogether abideth in sin, cannot be sanctified by law, neither by mercy, justice, nor judgment. Therefore, they must remain filthy still."

[633] Luke 12: 47-48: "And that servant, which knew his lord's will, and prepared not *himself,* neither did according to his will, shall be beaten with many *stripes.* But he that knew not, and did commit things worthy of stripes, shall be beaten with few *stripes.* For unto whomsoever much is given, of him shall be much required: and to whom men have committed much, of him they will ask the more."

complete rejection of the Lord. You must keep this in mind as you read the judgments Christ prophesies upon the gentiles.

And remember also that no matter what the collective gentile conduct may be (or fail to be), the Lord approaches each of us individually. The Book of Mormon is intended as the final opportunity for gentile salvation. The church is under condemnation for failing to remember its contents and take them seriously.[634] That scourge needn't be applied to you, if you will "repent and remember the new covenant" offered to you. There is, for any gentile who will repent and take the covenants offered in the Book of Mormon, an opportunity to yet become associated with the remnant and an heir of the preservation and salvation offered to them.

As we survey the condition of the gentile church today, there seems to be less and less made of the Book of Mormon's contents. The Correlation Department's teachings are insubstantial and becoming even less so. However, you have the Book of Mormon in front of you. You don't need anyone to prepare a manual for you. You have the text itself.

I am hoping what I've written, particularly in *The Second Comforter*, will show you how the Book of Mormon teaches you the return to the fullness. *Nephi's Isaiah* informs you of the Book of Mormon's prophecies of our days and our failures. *Eighteen Verses* shows how Book of Mormon doctrinal teachings address every major dilemma of our day. *Beloved Enos* shows what the fullness will confer upon you. I believe whatever merit the Lord has conferred upon me arises out of my serious study of the Book of Mormon. Though everyone may treat this covenant lightly, I have not. I would encourage you, therefore, to do the same, and prayerfully study the most correct volume of scripture we possess. It is a lifeline extended by the Lord to us. However, it cannot do you any good if you fail to act on its contents. Do the works, and you will know the doctrine. I suspect our universal failure to know doctrine today is because we do not live as we should. Understanding doctrine is tied to living it. The more you live it, the more you will comprehend it.[635] The less you live it, the more elusive it becomes to you. Until at last, you become like Deseret Book, incapable of offering anything other than romance novels, "inspirational" mush, and historical fiction, all

---

[634] D&C 84: 54-58: "And your minds in times past have been darkened because of unbelief, and because you have treated lightly the things you have received— Which vanity and unbelief have brought the whole church under condemnation. And this condemnation resteth upon the children of Zion, even all. And they shall remain under this condemnation until they repent and remember the new covenant, even the Book of Mormon and the former commandments which I have given them, not only to say, but to do according to that which I have written— That they may bring forth fruit meet for their Father's kingdom; otherwise there remaineth a scourge and judgment to be poured out upon the children of Zion."

[635] John 7: 16-17: "Jesus answered them, and said, My doctrine is not mine, but his that sent me. If any man will do his will, he shall know of the doctrine, whether it be of God, or *whether* I speak of myself."

with a veneer of Mormon vocabulary. Kitsch and superficiality, more distracting to the reader than edifying to their soul. Making one think there is some good being accomplished by participating, all the while forfeiting the days which might have been better spent.

THE REMNANT CONTINUED

The interplay between the latter-day gentiles and the remnant has been illustrated repeatedly in the Book of Mormon prophecies. We have seen Nephi's prophecies of the event, and Christ's affirmation and expansion on the event.

Gentiles would be offered the fullness and would reject it. Then the gentiles would take the gospel to the remnant who would receive it. The remnant would then blossom with the gospel, ultimately establishing the New Jerusalem. When the New Jerusalem is built by the remnant, a few gentiles who had received the fullness would be able to "assist" in bringing again Zion.[636]

We have at least a reasonable basis for fearing the gentiles rejected the fullness by not building the Temple in the "appointed time." Inside this Temple, the fullness was to be revealed.[637] Joseph Smith, who possessed the fullness, was taken 3 1/2 years after the revelation warning to act with speed in building the required Temple. When he died, the walls had not yet been completed to the second floor.

If we assume the worst, and the fullness was taken by the failure to complete the Temple in the permitted time, what then? Do the gentiles have no further use? Are the gentiles without a role in the latter-day

---

[636] 3 Ne. 21: 23-24: "And they shall assist my people, the remnant of Jacob, and also as many of the house of Israel as shall come, that they may build a city, which shall be called the New Jerusalem. And then shall they assist my people that they may be gathered in, who are scattered upon all the face of the land, in unto the New Jerusalem."

[637] D&C 124: 28, 32: "For there is not a place found on earth that he may come to and restore again that which was lost unto you, or which he hath taken away, even the fulness of the priesthood. ...But behold, at the end of this appointment your baptisms for your dead shall not be acceptable unto me; and if you do not these things at the end of the appointment ye shall be rejected as a church, with your dead, saith the Lord your God."

events? That is hardly the case. The gentiles continue to occupy a central role in the latter-days, despite their failures.

The gentiles will bring the Gospel to the remnant.[638] The gentiles will be commissioned to preach, teach, baptize, lay on hands for the gift of the Holy Ghost, carry the Book of Mormon forward throughout the world, and preserve truths which will enable others to be saved. The gentiles will shoulder a prophetic burden they alone will be able to bear off in the last days.

When Moses was taken, along with the higher priesthood he possessed, the Lord did not cease to recognize ancient Israel as His people. They were indeed His people, and the ones with whom He worked. He cared for, and watched over them, although we know in hindsight they were a hard hearted and foolish people who rejected something far greater than what they kept. If we rejected a fullness by our own failures, that does not mean we are cut off. We are the Lord's people. We have a form of priesthood, and the right to organize and preach the Gospel throughout the world. We are being watched over. We are the means through which the Lord will bring to pass all of His latter-day plans.

You should also not worry that our collective limitations apply to individuals. That has never been the case. There have always been those who have risen up, shed their sins, repented and come to the Lord individually and been redeemed. That pattern appears throughout scriptures. The Book of Mormon is a product of one family, led by one man who repented in a generation scheduled for destruction. He led his family, preached the Gospel, had sons who accepted the invitation to receive from the fruit of the tree of life, and established a righteous branch of Israel. The Book of Mormon at its foundation is a testimony that the Lord is ever willing to receive any who will come to Him.

The gentiles are integral to the Lord's work. We should never fear that The Church of Jesus Christ of Latter-day Saints is meaningless, irrelevant or without God's watchful care. It is the means by which people are invited to come to Christ today.

In *Eighteen Verses* I describe the phenomena of building a new religion inside the original one established by revelation through Joseph

---

638 1 Ne. 15: 13-14: "And now, the thing which our father meaneth concerning the grafting in of the natural branches through the fulness of the Gentiles, is, that in the latter days, when our seed shall have dwindled in unbelief, yea, for the space of many years, and many generations after the Messiah shall be manifested in body unto the children of men, then shall the fulness of the gospel of the Messiah come unto the Gentiles, and from the Gentiles unto the remnant of our seed—And at that day shall the remnant of our seed know that they are of the house of Israel, and that they are the covenant people of the Lord; and then shall they know and come to the knowledge of their forefathers, and also to the knowledge of the gospel of their Redeemer, which was ministered unto their fathers by him; wherefore, they shall come to the knowledge of their Redeemer and the very points of his doctrine, that they may know how to come unto him and be saved."

Smith. This new, false religion is designed to interfere with the Gospel, enshrine worship or adoration of a priestly class instead of the worship of Christ. The Correlation Department's effort to correlate teaching has created a new ambition to correlate power and control over everything. Part of that involves the adoration of a person, or as I explained it in Catholic terms—the cult of personality. This is a tried and true pattern for compromising the Gospel and rendering it a means for controlling and dominating socially, politically, religiously, and ultimately dictatorially.

The way the adversary works is always the same. It is not to destroy the work of God by annihilation, but to co-opt it and make it his. Satan wants to supplant God as the god of this earth. Therefore, anytime God has a work underway, Satan is eager to rush in and become the one the Lord's work follows. The "arm of flesh" as opposed to the "Holy Ghost" is the difference between following in the single, strait, narrow path which alone will bring people back to God, and the altered and compromised path that will take you elsewhere.

I thought President Uchtdorf's analogy about the airplane being only one degree off would become 500 miles separated from its target at the equator was particularly apt. (*A Matter of a Few Degrees*, May, 2008 Ensign.) This is how men and institutions fail. How can mortal man be vulnerable to err, and committees of mortal men are not? It is an almost universal truth that committees multiply errors, not decrease them. And who of you have ever sustained the Correlation Department?

We are fools to believe that the same pattern of compromising the truth that resulted in the apostasy of the church established by Christ will not relentlessly press against the restoration of our day. I know there are quotes saying otherwise—that the church cannot be led astray—but I cannot believe them, try as I might. Joseph, Brigham, John Taylor, President George Cannon **all said the exact opposite**. Even when Wilford Woodruff was claiming he would "not lead the church astray" he did not mean what we have attributed to his words. He was saying, in effect: "Don't worry, the Manifesto is a lie. We're not really abandoning plural marriage." The Manifesto did NOT stop plural marriage and it was not a revelation. He referred to it as "beating the Devil at his own game." Meaning it was intended to mislead the public. It was a press release designed to stop the persecution of the church and the threatened legislation to dis-incorporate and confiscate the Temples. Criticism by the eastern press resulted in it becoming part of the Doctrine & Covenants. Plural marriages continued from then until after President Joseph F. Smith testified before the Senate in the seating of Senator Smoot in 1905. When the excommunications of the Apostles Taylor and Cowley in 1911 happened, it was not based on the Manifesto, but on the letter of President Joseph F. Smith actually ending the practice. The fundamentalist groups know this history and use it to persuade others that their current practices are justified. Their practices today are wrong, as I've discussed in *Beloved Enos*. But their use of history to trouble the unaware has been effective in many cases. [Now this is entirely a side issue and I'm not interested in pursuing it at this moment. I'm only mentioning it in the context of another thought.]

So ask yourself which is better:

1. Presume that no man can err who becomes a President of the LDS Church in direct contradiction to what Joseph Smith, Brigham Young, John Taylor and George Q. Cannon taught?

2. Presume that without the ratification of the Holy Ghost bearing testimony to you that a matter is true, no man can be trusted and your salvation is based on what God alone tells you to be true?

If you believe the first, your religion is new, post-Correlation and will damn you. I do not intend to disassociate with you, and will gladly let you practice your faith if you will permit me to practice mine. If you believe the second, you are a Latter-day Saint who accepts accountability for what you believe and will work out your salvation with fear and trembling before God. You believe as I do, that Joseph was the means through which the Lord initiated a work for the salvation of mankind, and that work continues today. You believe in revelation and in God's continuing hand with us still today. You accept such good things as come through The Church of Jesus Christ of Latter-day Saints, rejoice in them, pay tithing to them, and are blessed by what things the church continues to preserve and practice. However, you are not deluded into worship of men.

The gentiles include both. The gentiles will be instrumental to the Lord's work in the last days, whether they are Saints or Brethrenites. The remnant will come to the faith, receive the Gospel and become acquainted with their fathers through the Book of Mormon delivered by gentile hands.[639] Without faithful gentile Saints, the work of the Father will not happen. Therefore, no matter the condition we find ourselves, we have an obligation to the Lord and the prophets who went before, to live as to bring these things to pass.

First, a slight detour because of comments or complaints. I am a member of The Church of Jesus Christ of Latter-day Saints. It is the only church I have ever joined. I owe to that church my knowledge of the truth. If you've read my original explanation of this blog, you would know that already. If you've read the books I've written, you'd know that

---

[639] 2 Ne. 30: 3-5: "And now, I would prophesy somewhat more concerning the Jews and the Gentiles. For after the book of which I have spoken shall come forth, and be written unto the Gentiles, and sealed up again unto the Lord, there shall be many which shall believe the words which are written; and they shall carry them forth unto the remnant of our seed. And then shall the remnant of our seed know concerning us, how that we came out from Jerusalem, and that they are descendants of the Jews. And the gospel of Jesus Christ shall be declared among them; wherefore, they shall be restored unto the knowledge of their fathers, and also to the knowledge of Jesus Christ, which was had among their fathers"

already. I haven't changed my position. I'm still what I was all along—a faithful, active Latter-day Saint.

It is from the church I have received the ordinances of baptism and laying on of hands for the gift of the Holy Ghost.

It is from the church I have received the scriptures, other ordinances, and authority.

I pay tithing to the church, attend regular meetings with other members, and receive the Sacrament weekly. I raise my children to attend and be faithful to the church. I am grateful to the church for its programs for children.

I listen to General Conference, and attend a large gathering on the BYU campus with my sons every six months during the Priesthood Session of Conference. I drive my children by the conference center during conference to see the protesters and read their anti-Mormon signs. This reminds my children that, although we are in the majority here, we are not liked by the majority elsewhere.

I have no intention of ever leaving the church. I see no reason to ever do so. I know the church welcomes me and my family. I know they are grateful that I attend, pay tithing and support the programs as we are asked to do.

I mention that only to make certain that some of those who read here are not misled. I have no ambition to lead the church or any person other than my family. I am grateful others are called to do so. I pray for them and do not think I could do any better job than is being done. On the contrary, I think I would make things worse.

I love my fellow Latter-day Saints. Even those with whom I have deep disagreements over doctrine. I enjoy associating with people who can discuss some of the important issues facing us, even if we hold very different views of what the solutions should be. At the end of the day, in order for the church to survive, it needs to have a mechanism to bring debate to an end and make a decision. That mechanism is in place and I respect it. If it were to be altered, it would likely break the entire system. The system is essential for the church's survival.

I sustain President Monson and do not think anyone other than him has final decision-making authority in The Church of Jesus Christ of Latter-day Saints. Think about what it would mean if his decisions could be vetoed endlessly from his office down to the lay members. This would cease to be a meaningful organization.

We have tremendous problems facing the church at present. I think they are all due to the abandonment of a pattern originally restored, in favor of innovations recommended by social sciences. The Correlation Department has accelerated this metamorphosis of the church and now leads it. The possibility remains that the church will return to an earlier pattern, but that seems quite unlikely at this point. To paraphrase Deseret Book: "Doctrine doesn't sell now." Doctrine does not matter as it once did, and as a result, the gentiles are not even aware of the content of the scriptures, the messages addressed to **us**, the responsibilities which have been laid upon **us**, and the warnings about how **we** are proceeding. The prophetic pessimism of the Book of Mormon prophets is not found in the modern messages. In fact, the feel-good messages seem to be denounced by the Book of Mormon and foretold as a sign of **our own** erring.

As a single, private member of the church, the only tool available to me approved by scripture is persuasion. If what I write does not persuade, I own no office, hold no calling, and command no position from which to insist you trust, believe or accept what I write. Oddly, no priesthood position in the church, from the least to the greatest, is entitled to insist you trust, believe or accept what they say. (D&C 121: 41.) I see very little demanding when it comes to actual presiding authorities. But I see a lot of that being urged vicariously, on behalf of presiding authorities, and in their names. It appears that between the Brethren who preside, and the common members, there is a disconnection wherein the Correlation Department has inserted themselves. Into that arena they have brought increasingly more intolerant and strict rule-making. I think there are talks every General Conference intended to work against that mischief. But, alas, the COB is a difficult beast to ride. It will take a grizzly bear to wrestle it into submission, I suspect.

In any event, the gentiles must fulfill their own destiny. Although there will be failings, limitations, foolishness and apostasy by the gentiles rejecting what is offered them, they will perform a great act. They will be the means of bringing back the remnant. There will be those who believe the Book of Mormon, teach correctly to the remnant about their own fathers, and assist in bringing about the New Jerusalem.

This interplay between gentile and remnant destinies is very real, and requires a work of the gentiles not yet completed.

I do not know how much further to pursue this topic. There are prophecies Joseph made about the Rocky Mountain gathering. There is the controversial "horse-shoe prophecy" about the travel of the Saints before the New Jerusalem would be founded. There is Joseph's finger on the map pointing where he suspected the New Jerusalem would be built. And the fellow who saw the pointing who speculated it was around where Snowflake, Arizona is presently located. However, the map had no borders, no states, and Snowflake didn't exist at the time. So a finger on a map could be hundreds of miles away from Snowflake. I'm not inclined to do much with that right now. I'm more inclined to take up some other stuff and leave the remnant alone for the time being.

As I said when this started, it was going to take a while. I'm thinking it might be better to change topics for a while and turn attention to some other things. The remnant will reappear in its own natural order as we move along in any direction we take. Their appearance is so widespread in latter-day prophecy that it is unavoidable. Many of you hadn't noticed it before. Now you have some background and ought to be able to pick up the matter on your own and see it for yourselves.

Text of the Supplemental Readings Mentioned

A Remarkable Prophecy By President John Taylor As Told by Edward Lunt, An Ordinance Worker in the Mesa Temple:

He said that faithful Latter-day Saints would go to the south and would form a circle something like a horseshoe, before they return to Jackson County, Missouri. Said he, "Those only will be privileged to help build Jackson County who will be found willing and glad to obey the counsel and advice of the authorities who will be placed over them, and who will seek counsel that they may be guided and protected from dire want and distress."

President Taylor also said that we will assist the Lamanites in building the New Jerusalem in Jackson county. He said that the vision to him appeared so terrible that he besought the Lord to close it up, but he saw that those who would keep the commandments and adhere to the authorities of the church would be the ones who would survive and not be destroyed. And that the lord would protect them as he did the children of Israel."

Journal of Mosiah Hancock:

Placing his (Joseph Smith's) finger on the map (I should think about where Snowflake, Arizona, is situated, or it could have been Mexico) he said, "The government will not receive you with the laws God designed that you should live, and those who are desirous to live the laws of God will have to go south. You will live to see men arise in power in the Church who will seek to put down your friends and the friends of our Lord and Savior, Jesus Christ. Many will be hoisted because of their money and the worldly learning which they seem to be in possession of; and many who are the true followers of our Lord and Savior will be cast down because of their poverty."

3 Nephi 11

I have always wanted to do something with Christ's sermons to the Nephites. It seems to me that we've been running through prophecies and warnings which serve one purpose, and leaving another one neglected. Balance requires us to return to another important purpose of the Book of Mormon. Namely, testifying that Jesus is the Christ, the Savior and Redeemer of Israel and the whole world.

So for that part, we'll turn attention to Christ's Nephite sermons. I've already dealt with what I have termed the "Ceremony of Recognition" involved in Christ's initial appearance. That is covered in *The Second Comforter* and won't be repeated here. So I'm going to skip to these verses:

3 Nephi 11: 18-20

> **"And it came to pass that he spake unto Nephi (for Nephi was among the multitude) and he commanded him that he should come forth. And Nephi arose and went forth, and bowed himself before the Lord and did kiss his feet. And the Lord commanded him that he should arise. And he arose and stood before him."**

The Lord has appeared, is identified and recognized by those who were at the Bountiful Temple. (This is probably an open air temple much like what we find in the Parowan Gap. If you consider the entirety of the description, it is not likely a closed structure like we build.) And those who are there have engaged in an Hosanna shout.[640] When the ceremony has ended and the place has become sanctified by His presence, and the body there recognizes and accepts Him as who and what He is, the stage has been set for a further ceremonial event.

Christ speaks to Nephi. He calls his name. Important stuff. Being called by name by the Son of God! Now we're seeing something really important. For those whose names are called by God are not merely

---

640 3 Ne. 11: 17: "Hosanna! Blessed be the name of the Most High God! And they did fall down at the feet of Jesus, and did worship him."

being addressed. They are, the instant the Lord calls out their name, "called." That is, the Lord will never speak one's name to them unless He calls them to a work. So when we read that the Lord speaks to Nephi we know the Lord has both called Nephi's name and called the bearer of that name to do a work. Nephi knew it. The crowd knew it. All present would have understood that Nephi just became the chief prophet of those present.

Nephi is told to "come forth." It instantly puts us in mind of Lazarus being called forth from the tomb.[641] Like Lazarus, who rose from the dead by the speaking of those words, Nephi now goes forth to a new life. Resurrected from his prior status and put into a minister's role by the Lord of all mankind.

Called, commanded to "come forth," and endowed immediately with the Lord's anointing voice, which bestows power and authority upon a man[642], Nephi arises from his kneeling position and steps forward.

Every knee remains bowed except Nephi's. For a brief moment, as he walks forward, he alone, of all those assembled in the crowd, is the one who stands in the presence of the Lord.[643] Others kneel, Nephi stands. It is honor, glory and privilege being displayed in this ceremony. Christ as King and Lord calls, His chief servant rises while all others remain kneeling. We are getting informed about the Lord and His ways in detailed ceremony conveying vast information in passing movement. It is too wonderful for words.

Nephi knows what he must do. For the servant who has been called to stand above his peers must then descend below them. Pride is unthinkable when in the presence of such a meek and humble figure as our Lord. It is required that the balance be restored. Nephi, who has been made to rise, must on his own choose to descend and abase himself. Those who seek their own glory will fall, while those who seek to humble themselves will rise again. So Nephi does what any person filled with light and truth would do in these circumstances. He comes to the Lord, falls below all, and descends to kiss the Master's feet. He kneels again, bows to the ground. And in an ultimate sign of humility, he kisses His feet, which on any other being is the symbol of uncleanliness itself. Nephi can do nothing more to show his own submission to the Lord. He can do nothing further in ceremonial activity to say he is

---

641 John 11: 43: "And when he thus had spoken, he cried with a loud voice, Lazarus, come forth."

642 D&C 132: 46: "And verily, verily, I say unto you, that whatsoever you seal on earth shall be sealed in heaven; and whatsoever you bind on earth, in my name and by my word, saith the Lord, it shall be eternally bound in the heavens; and whosesoever sins you remit on earth shall be remitted eternally in the heavens; and whosesoever sins you retain on earth shall be retained in heaven."

643 Luke 1: 19: "And the angel answering said unto him, I am Gabriel, that stand in the presence of God; and am sent to speak unto thee, and to shew thee these glad tidings."

nothing and the Lord is everything. He can show no greater respect and gratitude. Here is a servant indeed. A chief servant to the Servant of servants! A Master and servant whose hearts are alike. Nephi is, above all else, showing to us all how we ought be.

The gentiles love those who rule over and exploit them.[644] But Christ's true followers do not crave chief seats. They desire to serve. They will hold others up, even if it requires them to descend below to lift them. Nephi is not a gentile, nor one who would ever exercise unrighteous dominion over others.[645]

The ceremony now requires the abased to respond to the Lord's command again. Nephi is commanded to "arise." It was not enough to "come forth" to the new life. Now, having been chosen, Nephi must also "arise." It is a terrible burden. How can man "arise?" How can a man assume his position alongside His Lord? How can one who feels more suited to kneel and kiss his Master's feet, rise up and look his Lord in the face? It is all too much. One hardly can bear the burden and difficulty to "arise" when it is the Lord's own countenance you must confront. Too much. Too difficult. Too heavy a burden to lay upon mere man. How does Nephi dare to respond to the command to "arise?"

Through the swirling anxiety following the command, Nephi doesn't have the strength to do so until the realization that "arising" is the Master's will. It is the Master's command. It can be done through faith in Him. For He gives no command without having prepared the means to accomplish it.[646] It must be possible for Nephi to actually arise. Though a lifetime's dread and remorse says to remain on your knees, it is the Master's will that you nonetheless arise. And so you begin the dreadful effort, and your trembling knees respond. To your own surprise you find it possible to arise and look into the face of Him who is compassion itself. There can be no pride in this, for rising is by His command, and not by your own will. You may want to join in Moses' chorus that "for this cause you know man is nothing!"[647] But it isn't necessary to voice the thought. It is enough to understand the thought.

---

644 Matt. 20: 25: "But Jesus called them *unto him,* and said, Ye know that the princes of the Gentiles exercise dominion over them, and they that are great exercise authority upon them."

645 D&C 121: 39: "We have learned by sad experience that it is the nature and disposition of almost all men, as soon as they get a little authority, as they suppose, they will immediately begin to exercise unrighteous dominion."

646 1 Ne. 3: 7: "And it came to pass that I, Nephi, said unto my father: I will go and do the things which the Lord hath commanded, for I know that the Lord giveth no commandments unto the children of men, save he shall prepare a way for them that they may accomplish the thing which he commandeth them."

647 Moses 1: 10: "And it came to pass that it was for the space of many hours before Moses did again receive his natural strength like unto man; and he said unto himself: Now, for this cause I know that man is nothing, which thing I never had supposed."

No man assumes this honor for himself. He must be called by God to stand in His presence.

And so Nephi arose, and stood before His Lord.

3 Nephi 11: 22

> **"And again the Lord called others, and said unto them likewise; and he gave unto them power to baptize. And he said unto them: On this wise shall ye baptize; and there shall be no disputations among you."**

Space was limited and the mechanics of writing was difficult for Mormon. Therefore, in his abridgement of the account, for all others "the Lord called," and the ceremony was repeated for each. In the process, He "said likewise" unto each of them. Every individual person was acknowledged by the Lord as having conferred upon each of them "power to baptize" by the Lord.

None of those who received this power had any doubt about their authority to act in this ordinance in the Lord's name. None of them lacked the "power" to baptize others. None of those who were present, and still kneeling during the ceremony, or who overheard the Lord's words had any doubts about those who held a commission from Christ to baptize them. Finally, none of those present would have any doubts about the need to be baptized by this newly bestowed power.

Although every one of them had been baptized previously, it becomes apparent that once new power to baptize has been given by Christ, that power ought to be used. It is not given to be neglected. Nor can power endure through neglect. So when given, the power is to be used, and all who were present are candidates for baptism.

Then comes the instruction from Christ as to the manner for performing the ordinance. "On this wise shall ye baptize…" begins the instruction. If the Lord provides the power and then gives the instruction, can the ordinance be changed? What if someone else says they hold the keys, and we all accept the person does in fact hold the keys, can such a person change the manner of baptism? If there is a potential convert who is infirm, ill or elderly and is unable to be baptized in the prescribed manner, can the ordinance be changed in form to accommodate the need? That is exactly how the ordinance was changed after the New Testament times. A reasonable need, and accommodation for that need, resulted in an exception. Then the exception became the rule, and the original manner was forgotten.

If the Lord's instruction regarding the manner of baptism in this verse cannot be changed, even by one holding keys and authority to do so, then what about other ordinances? Can other ordinances be changed by one who holds keys if they choose to do them differently? Why not? What happens when the one in a recognized position to perform ordinances decides to make changes to the ordinances?

Assume for a moment the Lord instructs Nephi on how to perform baptism, but Nephi decides thereafter to make a change to it. How would that reflect on Nephi? How would that reflect on the Lord? How would it reflect on the Lord's instruction? What about Joseph Smith's statement: **"Ordinances instituted in the heavens before the foundation of the world, in the priesthood, for the salvation of men, are not to be altered or changed."** (TPJS p. 308) If the Lord gave Nephi the "power" to baptize, does that carry with it the "power" to change it as well?

Well, the purpose behind the Lord giving instructions was that "there shall be no disputations among you." Does the instruction given by the Lord end as soon as we begin to see "disputations among" followers? Can an opinion poll that shows a majority of those who practice the ordinances don't relate to them anymore and want to see them altered, create a "disputation" that allows the instruction from the Lord to be altered?

As stupid as these questions may seem, there are people who are genuinely confused by them. So I ask them. You must decide if the Lord's instructions deserve respect and ought to be followed. Apparently men of good faith, honest hearts, and sincere desires can by reason of their status alone, contradict the Lord's instructions and people won't even blink. That's the beauty of the claim that Rome makes to having Peter's keys and the ability to seal on earth and in heaven. The Catholics can change anything and no one doubts they had the authority to do it. To allow the possibility that God would not support the Pope would be to entertain the unthinkable. So don't even hold that thought.

3 Nephi 11: 23

> **"Verily I say unto you, that whoso repenteth of his sins through your words, and desireth to be baptized in my name, on this wise shall ye baptize them—Behold, ye shall go down and stand in the water, and in my name shall ye baptize them."**

The candidate for baptism must first qualify themselves by "repent[ing] of his sins." That's an interesting *pre*-condition in the Lord's instruction. Until one has determined to abandon their sins, they are not fit for baptism. They first decide to lay things behind, move forward in following the Lord, determined to serve Him. This decision to make a change must come "through your words." Meaning that before someone can repent, they must first learn the conditions for repentance and following the Lord.

This is much like the instructions given by revelation to this dispensation about how baptism is to be performed. We were told, "All those who humble themselves before God, and desire to be baptized, and come forth with broken hearts and contrite spirits, and witness before the church that they have truly repented of all their sins, and are willing to take upon them the name of Jesus Christ, having a determination to serve him to the end, and truly manifest by their works that they have received of the Spirit of Christ unto the remission of their sins, shall be received by baptism into his church."[648]

After having made the decision to be baptized with a broken heart and contrite spirit, confessing before the church that you have repented of your sins (or be willing to change and follow Christ), determined to endure to the end, a person receives from the Spirit of Christ a witness that changes their behavior. Their works show they are penitent. At this point a person is ready for baptism. Until then, they are not ready and the ordinance is not appropriate.

Now the instructions in Section 20 are more complete than the abbreviated statement in Christ's instructions to His Nephite disciples, but it is to the same effect. When this pattern is followed, people are converted and follow Christ. Their baptism matters and will change them. When these instructions are not followed, the ordinance is relatively meaningless and people drift off into inactivity. I believe today the numbers evidence that approximately 10% of those who are baptized are actually converted. The rest are just names and numbers used as membership statistics to be reported and proclaimed each April in a worldwide conference.

The Gospel of Christ is quite exact and it works whenever it is tried. It is tried today in about 10% of the cases of those who are baptized by our missionaries.

Perhaps the ordinance ought to be offered to more of our adults as they come to recognize that they may not have actually been prepared to receive the ordinance when given to them. No matter, there's always the Alma exception. (That's when in the course of baptizing someone else, you go ahead and take the covenant yourself.[649]) Clearly Alma was baptizing Helam at the time, and added himself for good measure; he (Alma) feeling the need for the ordinance himself. He went ahead and

---

[648] D&C 20: 37: "*And again, by way of commandment to the church concerning the manner of baptism*—All those who humble themselves before God, and desire to be baptized, and come forth with broken hearts and contrite spirits, and witness before the church that they have truly repented of all their sins, and are willing to take upon them the name of Jesus Christ, having a determination to serve him to the end, and truly manifest by their works that they have received of the Spirit of Christ unto the remission of their sins, shall be received by baptism into his church."

[649] Mosiah 18: 13-15: "And when he had said these words, the Spirit of the Lord was upon him, and he said: Helam, I baptize thee, having authority from the Almighty God, as a testimony that ye have entered into a covenant to serve him until you are dead as to the mortal body; and may the Spirit of the Lord be poured out upon you; and may he grant unto you eternal life, through the redemption of Christ, whom he has prepared from the foundation of the world. And after Alma had said these words, both Alma and Helam were buried in the water; and they arose and came forth out of the water rejoicing, being filled with the Spirit. And again, Alma took another, and went forth a second time into the water, and baptized him according to the first, only he did not bury himself again in the water."

was baptized again for good measure. This seems to be a precedent that would allow for others to do likewise—perhaps when performing a vicarious baptism for the dead. I leave the Alma exception for your own consideration, and will stop short of advocating such a thing. I just notice things and share what I notice. I'm not trying to convince anyone to do anything.

In Christ's instructions, and in Section 20, the heavy lifting of repentance precedes baptism. Then, after determining to change and follow Christ, leaving behind the foolish errors of the past, the person is fit to be baptized. At that point the baptism symbolizes the new life being undertaken. The presence of the Holy Ghost then ratifies the purging of the repentant, now baptized convert. But that comes next in Christ's teaching.

3 Nephi 11: 24-25

> **"And now behold, these are the words which ye shall say, calling them by name, saying: Having authority given me of Jesus Christ, I baptize you in the name of the Father, and of the Son, and of the Holy Ghost. Amen."**

Christ prescribes the exact words to be used in the ordinance. However, the instruction we use today is slightly different in wording, but identical in meaning: Instead of: "Having authority given me of Jesus Christ" we say instead: "Having been commissioned of Jesus Christ."[650]

After giving these disciples "power to baptize" Christ's instructions require them to say they have "authority" (in 3 Nephi) or today, hold a "commission"[651] (in D&C 20). Is there a difference between "authority" to baptize and the "power" to baptize?

Why does the authorization come from Jesus Christ, but the ordinance get performed "in the name of the Father, and of the Son, and of the Holy Ghost?" The power to do the ordinance comes from the Son, but the ordinance is in the name of each member of the Godhead. Why?

Though they are one, the names show they occupy different roles and hold different responsibilities. (As to following and being sanctified

---

650 D&C 20: 73: "The person who is called of God and has authority from Jesus Christ to baptize, shall go down into the water with the person who has presented himself or herself for baptism, and shall say, calling him or her by name: Having been commissioned of Jesus Christ, I baptize you in the name of the Father, and of the Son, and of the Holy Ghost. Amen."

651 Ibid.

by different laws and receiving different kingdoms.)[652] We are in the fallen world where the primary means God communicates with man is through the Holy Ghost.[653] When, however, a person rises up through the merits of Jesus Christ to receive Him as a minister, they are living in a Terrestrial law and inherit Terrestrial blessings.[654] When He has finished His preparations with the person, and can bring them to the Father, the person is brought to a point where the Father can accept and acknowledge them as a son.[655] They are then begotten of the Father.[656] Through each of these steps, does baptism matter? Does one receive the companionship of the Holy Ghost without baptism? Do they come to Christ without baptism? Do they inherit what the Father has without baptism? Is baptism critical to the association with each member of the Godhead?

The point at which the person's journey is completed, and they may enter into the rest of the Lord is when the Lord declares by His own voice that the man's offering has been accepted and they are sealed up to eternal life. I've explained this on the blog as to Joseph Smith. I've explained it for Enos and others in *Beloved Enos*. The Gospel is the

---

[652] D&C 88: 21-26: "And they who are not sanctified through the law which I have given unto you, even the law of Christ, must inherit another kingdom, even that of a terrestrial kingdom, or that of a telestial kingdom. For he who is not able to abide the law of a celestial kingdom cannot abide a celestial glory. And he who cannot abide the law of a terrestrial kingdom cannot abide a terrestrial glory. And he who cannot abide the law of a telestial kingdom cannot abide a telestial glory; therefore he is not meet for a kingdom of glory. Therefore he must abide a kingdom which is not a kingdom of glory. And again, verily I say unto you, the earth abideth the law of a celestial kingdom, for it filleth the measure of its creation, and transgresseth not the law—Wherefore, it shall be sanctified; yea, notwithstanding it shall die, it shall be quickened again, and shall abide the power by which it is quickened, and the righteous shall inherit it."

[653] D&C 14: 8: "And it shall come to pass, that if you shall ask the Father in my name, in faith believing, you shall receive the Holy Ghost, which giveth utterance, that you may stand as a witness of the things of which you shall both hear and see, and also that you may declare repentance unto this generation."

[654] D&C 76: 77: "These are they who receive of the presence of the Son, but not of the fulness of the Father."

[655] D&C 76: 54-59, 92: "They are they who are the church of the Firstborn. They are they into whose hands the Father has given all things—They are they who are priests and kings, who have received of his fulness, and of his glory; And are priests of the Most High, after the order of Melchizedek, which was after the order of Enoch, which was after the order of the Only Begotten Son. Wherefore, as it is written, they are gods, even the sons of God—Wherefore, all things are theirs, whether life or death, or things present, or things to come, all are theirs and they are Christ's, and Christ is God's. ...And thus we saw the glory of the celestial, which excels in all things—where God, even the Father, reigns upon his throne forever and ever;"

[656] Ps. 2: 7: "I will declare the decree: the Lord hath said unto me, Thou *art* my Son; this day have I begotten thee."

same now, as always before. Therefore, no matter how you will receive blessings of the Lord in the afterlife, it will be through the Gospel of Jesus Christ and by the ordinances instituted for claiming blessings. These were established as law to govern man's conduct here even before the world was.[657]

Note also the person cannot receive the ordinance without also having their name stated. Why do you suppose it is necessary to first call out the name of the person before they receive an ordinance? Why would the Lord's instruction require a person to be "called" first? Though they are submitting to the ordinance voluntarily, why call their name?

Does it matter if the full legal name is used? We do that in the church, of course. But does it matter? If the Lord called Joseph by name at the time of the First Vision (and He did)[658], what name do you suppose was called? Was it "Joseph Smith, Jr."? Or was it "Joseph"? Or was it that name used by his most intimate friend at the time?

Whenever a name is given by an angel in an appearance to parents, the name is always the first name, or the name their friends would call them.[659] Similarly, when the Lord calls a man's name, He uses his first, given name.[660] The Lord does not use formal names, but uses intimate names when addressing His servants.

We call the person to be baptized by name. Our practice is to use the full, legal name.

3 Nephi 11: 26

"And then shall ye immerse them in the water, and come forth again out of the water."

---

[657] D&C 130: 20-21: "There is a law, irrevocably decreed in heaven before the foundations of this world, upon which all blessings are predicated—And when we obtain any blessing from God, it is by obedience to that law upon which it is predicated."

[658] JS-H 1: 17: "It no sooner appeared than I found myself delivered from the enemy which held me bound. When the light rested upon me I saw two Personages, whose brightness and glory defy all description, standing above me in the air. One of them spake unto me, calling me by name and said, pointing to the other—*This is My Beloved Son. Hear Him!*"

[659] Luke 1: 13: "But the angel said unto him, Fear not, Zacharias: for thy prayer is heard; and thy wife Elisabeth shall bear thee a son, and thou shalt call his name John."
Luke 1: 31: "And, behold, thou shalt conceive in thy womb, and bring forth a son, and shalt call his name JESUS."

[660] 1 Sam. 3: 4: "That the Lord called Samuel: and he answered, Here *am* I."
Ex. 3: 4: "And when the Lord saw that he turned aside to see, God called unto him out of the midst of the bush, and said, Moses, Moses. And he said, Here *am* I."

The manner of baptism is clearly by immersion. To perform the ordinance, they must be put under the water and then "come forth again out of the water" to follow the instruction given by Christ.

The purpose of baptism is to follow Christ's example.[661] It symbolizes the death of the old man of sin, and the resurrection into a new life in Christ.[662] That symbol cannot be mirrored by sprinkling. It must involve immersion.

In immersion we are placed below the surface of the water, in the same way as the dead are buried below ground.

In immersion the breath of life is cut off while under the water, and restored anew when you "come forth again out of the water."

In the case of the officiator, they are the one who immerses and then brings the recipient up out of the water. Performing this ordinance puts the officiator in the role of the Lord who holds the keys of death[663] and resurrection.[664]

Those who are baptized, and those who officiate, enact, by symbol, some eternal truths regarding the plan of salvation. In the very moment the ordinance is performed there is a renewal in symbol of life, innocence, forgiveness and resurrection. The earth itself is blessed by such things as baptism and other ordinances. The earth itself is defiled when the ordinances are not kept exactly as prescribed.[665]

The earth knows that God ordained the ordinances of heaven and earth.[666] As regular and reliable as the movements of the sun and moon

---

[661] John 10: 27: "My sheep hear my voice, and I know them, and they follow me:"
John 14: 15: "If ye love me, keep my commandments."

[662] Rom. 6: 4: "Therefore we are buried with him by baptism into death: that like as Christ was raised up from the dead by the glory of the Father, even so we also should walk in newness of life."

[663] Rev. 1: 18: "*I am* he that liveth, and was dead; and, behold, I am alive for evermore, Amen; and have the keys of hell and of death."

[664] 2 Ne. 2: 8: "Wherefore, how great the importance to make these things known unto the inhabitants of the earth, that they may know that there is no flesh that can dwell in the presence of God, save it be through the merits, and mercy, and grace of the Holy Messiah, who layeth down his life according to the flesh, and taketh it again by the power of the Spirit, that he may bring to pass the resurrection of the dead, being the first that should rise."

[665] Isa. 24: 5: "The earth also is defiled under the inhabitants thereof; because they have transgressed the laws, changed the ordinance, broken the everlasting covenant."
Moses 7: 28: "And it came to pass that the God of heaven looked upon the residue of the people, and he wept; and Enoch bore record of it, saying: How is it that the heavens weep, and shed forth their tears as the rain upon the mountains?"

[666] Jer. 33: 25: "Thus saith the Lord; If my covenant *be* not with day and night, *and if* I have not appointed the ordinances of heaven and earth;"

are, so too should the ordinances of the Lord be kept in their appointed ways.[667]

The heavens and earth rejoice when the ordinances are kept. They symbolize eternal hope, man's acceptance of God's plan, and a presence of righteousness in a fallen world. Our own participation in ordinances are vital to our own renewal, and the renewal of all creation through redemption of each individual soul.

The baptism ordinance, like all those that follow after, is intended not merely to fulfill an initiation rite. It is intended to communicate light and truth into the mind of the individual who is performing and receiving the ordinance. It is meant to enlighten.

I have discussed previously the meaning of "come forth" used by Christ in restoring life to Lazarus[668] and therefore won't repeat it again here. It is no accident the Lord employs the same meaning here as there. We are rising from the tomb of sin which imprisons us into the new life awaiting us in Christ.

The Lord is more than brilliant. He is filled with light and truth. The closer you draw to Him, the more light and truth you begin to receive from Him.

3 Nephi 11: 27

> **"And after this manner shall ye baptize in my name; for behold, verily I say unto you, that the Father, and the Son, and the Holy Ghost are one; and I am in the Father, and the Father in me, and the Father and I are one."**

The ordinance of baptism is to be done in the names of all three members of the Godhead. And, correspondingly, Christ wants us to understand the unity that exists between these three. They are "one" with each other.

The "oneness" of God the Father, His Son, and the Holy Ghost was discussed by Christ in His teachings of the New Testament. The Intercessory Prayer recorded in John 17, includes His expansion on the idea. There Christ taught: "Neither pray I for these alone, but for them also which shall believe on me through their word; That they all may be one; as thou, Father, art in me, and I in thee, that they also may be one in us: that the world may believe that thou hast sent me. And the glory which thou gavest me I have given them; that they may be one, even as we are one: I in them, and thou in me, that they may be made perfect in

---

[667] Jer. 31: 35-36: "Thus saith the Lord, which giveth the sun for a light by day, *and* the ordinances of the moon and of the stars for a light by night, which divideth the sea when the waves thereof roar; The Lord of hosts *is* his name: If those ordinances depart from before me, saith the Lord, *then* the seed of Israel also shall cease from being a nation before me for ever."

[668] John 11: 43: "And when he thus had spoken, he cried with a loud voice, Lazarus, come forth."

one; and that the world may know that thou hast sent me, and hast loved them, as thou hast loved me. Father, I will that they also, whom thou hast given me, be with me where I am; that they may behold my glory, which thou hast given me: for thou lovedst me before the foundation of the world."[669]

This unity between the Father, Son and Holy Ghost is a point of doctrine raised by Christ in this teaching. It is important for us to understand that the message we receive from the Holy Ghost will be the same as the message we would receive from Christ. It is also important for us to rely on and have faith in Christ and the Holy Ghost so that we may trust them to bring us to the Father.

It is also a model for us to follow. We are supposed to drop our fears and worries, shed our ambitions and desires, and come together in unity until we are "one." The non-competitive, fully cooperative manner the Father, Son and Holy Ghost are "one" is the model of Zion itself. Divisions and strifes are unthinkable between the members of the Godhead. In contrast, among us they are unavoidable.

The ideal is always the standard. We push toward perfection. The Father lives in absolutes. Therefore we strive for the absolute, all the while struggling with our relative and incremental improvement. We are in the process of being "added upon."[670] The Father, on the other hand, dwells where there is nothing but perfection.[671] So for us the Mediator and the Savior establish the bridge between where we are forbidden to enter in sin, and the borrowed cleanliness which momentarily lets us enter in.

We are to become "one" with Them. It is a distant goal, to be accomplished after being "added upon" for a long time. Joseph taught in the King Follett Discourse: "Here, then, is eternal life—to know the only wise and true God; and you have got to learn how to be gods yourselves, and to be kings and priests to God, the same as all gods have done before you, namely, by going from one small degree to another, and from a small capacity to a great one; from grace to grace, from

---

[669] John 17: 20-24: "Neither pray I for these alone, but for them also which shall believe on me through their word; That they all may be one; as thou, Father, *art* in me, and I in thee, that they also may be one in us: that the world may believe that thou hast sent me. And the glory which thou gavest me I have given them; that they may be one, even as we are one: I in them, and thou in me, that they may be made perfect in one; and that the world may know that thou hast sent me, and hast loved them, as thou hast loved me. Father, I will that they also, whom thou hast given me, be with me where I am; that they may behold my glory, which thou hast given me: for thou lovedst me before the foundation of the world."

[670] Abr. 3: 26: "And they who keep their first estate shall be added upon; and they who keep not their first estate shall not have glory in the same kingdom with those who keep their first estate; and they who keep their second estate shall have glory added upon their heads for ever and ever."

[671] D&C 1: 31: "For I the Lord cannot look upon sin with the least degree of allowance;"

exaltation to exaltation, until you attain to the resurrection of the dead, and are able to dwell in everlasting burnings, and to sit in glory, as do those who sit enthroned in everlasting power… When you climb up a ladder, you must begin at the bottom, and ascend step by step, until you arrive at the top; and so it is with the principles of the gospel—you must begin with the first, and go on until you learn all the principles of exaltation. But it will be a great while after you have passed through the veil before you will have learned them. It is not all to be comprehended in this world; it will be a great work to learn our salvation and exaltation even beyond the grave."

To become "one" will be to reach the end of a long journey. We can have promises of that end. We can receive covenants that will bring us there. But our arrival will "be a great while after [we] have passed through the veil" for "it is not all to be comprehended in this world." Moses was told that, also.[672] We may be initiated, but to enter in will be "a great work to learn our salvation and exaltation even beyond the grave."

So the ideal of "one" with the Father, Son and Holy Ghost for us is distant, to be sought, to be kept before us, but not to be obtained until some time later. But to be "one" with each other is another matter. Being "one" is required of us for Zion to return. Zion is required for the Lord to dwell among us again. He is going to return to a Zion, no matter how few may be involved. He will come even if only two or three gather in His name.[673] Zion may be small, but it will nonetheless be Zion before He can visit with her.

3 Nephi 11: 28-30

> **"And according as I have commanded you thus shall ye baptize. And there shall be no disputations among you, as there have hitherto been; neither shall there be disputations among you concerning the points of my doctrine, as there have hitherto been. For verily, verily I say unto you, he that hath the spirit of contention is not of me, but is of the devil, who is the father of contention, and he stirreth up the hearts of men to contend with anger, one with another. Behold, this is not my doctrine, to stir up the hearts of men with anger, one against another; but this is my doctrine, that such things should be done away."**

The Lord's elaboration on "disputations" and "contentions" is important and consistent enough that all three verses should be considered together.

---

672 Moses 1: 5: "Wherefore, no man can behold all my works, except he behold all my glory; and no man can behold all my glory, and afterwards remain in the flesh on the earth."

673 Matt. 18: 20: "For where two or three are gathered together in my name, there am I in the midst of them."

First, He clarifies that baptism must be done as He "commanded you." Deviations are not permitted and should not be asked for, or entertained. That is the thing about ordinances. When given, they are to be kept in exactly the manner they come from Him. When we change them we risk breaking the covenant between Him and ourselves.[674]

The Book of Mormon is silent about the "disputations" which existed among them over baptism. However, when Christ says there has "hitherto been" disputes, we know they existed. It becomes apparent from later passages that one practice which caused some of the argument was the issue of baptizing infants. There were likely others, as well. The Lord wants that to end. Perform the ordinances as He sets them out, and stop arguing about the manner.

The reason arguments arise is because men stop gathering light by righteous behavior. When they lose light they cease to understand the truth. They stray from the correct practice of the ordinance because they are unable to understand its importance. They see no reason to continue the ordinance in one form when another seems to work just as well. The result is a change to the ordinance. It is ever the same. By the time the change is made, the ones making it are unaware of any importance associated with the ordinance they change. They discard what they view is meaningless. It would require a good deal more light and truth for them to understand the importance of what was given them. But that light and truth has passed away from them because of their conduct.

Into the darkness the devil enters with arguments over the ordinances: Why do it that way? It really doesn't mean anything. It is arcane and outdated. It doesn't really matter as long as you still have faith in Christ. [That particular lie is very effective because it allows the person to presume they have faith, when in fact they haven't the faith sufficient to obey Christ.] People will get more out of the changes if we make them. People will have greater peace of mind if we baptize their infants. We'll save more souls, because by baptizing them when they're infants we include everyone who would die before getting baptized. Our numbers will increase. We'll look more successful by getting more followers by adding their numbers into the group. What we change isn't important, anyway. If it were important, we would know that, and since it doesn't seem important to us, it must, in fact, not be important. Those who rebel at change are not really faithful. This shows inspiration; it's faith affirming. Change is proof that God is still leading us. ...And other such arguments and persuasions from our adversary.

On the other hand, Christ is saying to keep the ordinances unchanged. And further, don't even begin to dispute them. They are off limits for argument, dispute and discussion. When you open the

---

674 Isa. 24: 5: "The earth also is defiled under the inhabitants thereof; because they have transgressed the laws, changed the ordinance, broken the everlasting covenant."

opportunity to dispute over the ordinances, you are allowing the devil an opportunity to influence the discussion and change the ordinances.

Disputes lead to contention, contention leads to anger, and anger is the devil's tool. So don't start down that road. Accept and understand the ordinances. If you are perplexed by them, then let those who understand speak, exhort, expound and teach concerning them. As they do, you will come into the unity of faith and become one. Perplexity cannot exist when there is light and truth. Light and truth comes from understanding the ordinances, not changing them. So do not begin the process through dispute. The purpose of discussion is not to dispute, which leads to contention, which leads to anger.

When the Gospel and its ordinances turn into something angry and contentious, then the Spirit has fled, and souls are lost. It is the devil's objective to prevent you from practicing the ordinances in the correct manner. But, more importantly, it is his objective to prevent you from becoming one. When he uses arguments over ordinances to cause disunity, he is playing with two tools at the same time. First, changing the ordinances brings about cursings, and second, encouraging contention and anger grieves the Spirit, and prevents the Saints from becoming one.

As a result, disputes or discussions over ordinances, which could lead to changing them, should not be entertained. As soon as the ordinances are open to dispute, reconsideration, alteration or to being changed, then you are opening the door to this whole process. It culminates in the souls of men being lost through apostasy. Once the ordinances are changed, the earth is cursed[675] and Israel is scattered rather than gathered.[676]

The devil knows this, even if men do not. Men are urged to take steps they presume have little effect, all the while being lied to by the enemy of their souls.

When men arrive at the point they are angry in their hearts with one another, they are not united by love as they are intended to be. These are the end results of the two paths. One leading to love and joy[677], and the other to anger and wrath.[678]

Disputes over ordinances are caused by the devil. Ordinances that preserve symbolic truths and have the power to save are turned into

---

675 Ibid.

676 Jer. 31: 36: "If those ordinances depart from before me, saith the Lord, *then* the seed of Israel also shall cease from being a nation before me for ever."

677 Hel. 5: 44: "And Nephi and Lehi were in the midst of them; yea, they were encircled about; yea, they were as if in the midst of a flaming fire, yet it did harm them not, neither did it take hold upon the walls of the prison; and they were filled with that joy which is unspeakable and full of glory."

678 D&C 76: 33: "For they are vessels of wrath, doomed to suffer the wrath of God, with the devil and his angels in eternity;"

tools for the devil by disputations. It is a complete victory when discussions about changing ordinances are allowed to take place. Even good men are taken in by such disputes.

3 Nephi 11: 31-32

> **"Behold, verily, verily, I say unto you, I will declare unto you my doctrine. And this is my doctrine, and it is the doctrine which the Father hath given unto me; and I bear record of the Father, and the Father beareth record of me, and the Holy Ghost beareth record of the Father and me; and I bear record that the Father commandeth all men, everywhere, to repent and believe in me."**

When the Lord proclaims there is a "doctrine" belonging to Him, it is important to take note. As He begins His doctrinal statement, He first reminds us again of the unity between Himself, His Father and the Holy Ghost. This reminder of unity has followed the admonition to avoid contention and anger—things which prevent our becoming one with each other.

To understand His doctrine you must first know and understand that the doctrine originates with the Father. Christ has completely accepted and advocates the doctrine. Moreover He embodies it.

The Father's doctrine is that "all men, everywhere, [must] repent and believe in [Christ]." This is what the whole of creation hangs on: the atonement of the Son. It is through the Son's sacrifice that the Father's plan became operational. Now, to return to the Father all must do so in reliance upon the merits of the Son.[679]

The Son preaches the doctrine of, and bears witness of the Father. The Father bears witness of the Son. The Holy Ghost bears record of the Father and Son.

When did the Father bear record of the Son? Did you notice that? The FATHER bears record of the Son! I'm not talking about Matthew or Luke's testimony that the Father bore record of the Son, because that is Matthew's and Luke's testimony. I'm not talking about Joseph Smith's record of the Father's testimony of the Son. I'm talking about the Father's testimony. When did you hear the Father bear record of the Son?

The Father **does** bear record of the Son. But you must go through the Son to get to the Father. When you do, acting in faith according to the conditions established for your salvation, then you will receive the Father's testimony or record of the Son for yourself. But implicit in this statement is the fact that access to the Father is possible by the means provided through the Son. That is a ratification of the fullness of the Gospel. It is an invitation to return to heaven and obtain from the Father a confirmation of your salvation.

---

[679] John 3: 16: "For God so loved the world, that he gave his only begotten Son, that whosoever believeth in him should not perish, but have everlasting life."

The Father's testimony is that our salvation comes through Christ. For us the Father has provided a Savior. If we repent, we can come back into the presence of God and enter into our salvation and exaltation. But it is through the means provided for us: A Savior, who is Christ the Lord.

We are commanded to:

1. Repent.
2. Believe in Christ.

To repent is to turn again to Him. To follow Him and leave behind your sinful ways. To abandon the world and worldliness and to choose to always remember Him, that you may have His spirit to be with you always.

To believe in Him is to accept, study, contemplate and ponder His teachings. It is not to just go along with a herd, but to rise up from your position and awaken from your slumber. It is to grow into knowledge about Him. Belief leads to faith and faith to knowledge. But the process is initiated by your belief (**correct understanding**) of His teachings.

The doctrine continues…

3 Nephi 11: 33-34

> **"And whoso believeth in me, and is baptized, the same shall be saved; and they are they who shall inherit the kingdom of God. And whoso believeth not in me, and is not baptized, shall be damned."**

Imagine the importance attached to the ordinance of baptism! It is an absolute minimum requirement. Upon the proper performance of this ordinance, hangs the difference between being "saved" and "inheriting the kingdom of God" on the one hand, and being "damned" on the other.

[As a complete aside: A few posts back there was a comment about what a burden it would be for "the church" and "the priesthood" if people seek re-baptism to renew commitments. It was made as we approached Christ's teachings on baptism. The comment was so immediate and so dark in tone and content it has caused me rethink the importance of this idea. Anytime an idea is confrontational and dark, I pause to consider why that is so. Here's what now occurs to me. What a terrible burden it would be to depart this life without the ordinance of baptism properly performed, by proper authority, in the proper manner, with repentance preceding the event. I would not want a dark and troubled soul to perform baptism for anyone, but a person filled with joy, hope and the Spirit, having a testimony in Christ like Nephi. These people would not find performing such an ordinance troubling.

If there is a hint of doubt held by any baptized member of the church, why would any right-thinking and charitable soul refuse them the right to be re-baptized? Now, I've suggested the Alma exception and how that might be accomplished in a time of reluctance and resistance to recommitment baptism. But it occurs to me upon further reflection that since the church doesn't recognize or record rebaptisms anyway, why would this concern the "heavy laden priesthood" which has no time for such things? Anyone holding authority, at any place where there is sufficient water to perform the rite, could accomplish it. Since the church doesn't record it, there is no need of witnesses. It could be done in private, at any time, or any place with sufficient water. It could be done by any person holding the office of Priest. It would be good practice for future missionaries if they were given the opportunity. I think the idea is one which ought to be acted upon with regularity, in private and without troubling the busy and overburdened church and priesthood. A close family member could take care of it, and I suspect all involved will soon recognize heaven's approval of the idea.]

Well, back to the subject at hand. Anciently the Jews practiced baptism in "living water." That is, in a naturally renewing body of water, like a river, lake or ocean. Living water was part of the symbol. We have fonts, and there is nothing wrong with that. But I have always cherished my baptism in the Atlantic Ocean.

Well, believing in Christ precedes baptism. In fact, belief in Christ causes baptism. The one results in the other. Without faith in Him, there is no need for baptism. This then makes the first step belief in Christ, and baptism the second step.

I've heard of those who obtain a testimony of Christ in adulthood, but who were baptized many years earlier at age 8. If belief in Christ is supposed to precede baptism, but in fact follows it, does that recommend repeating the ordinance? Does Christ's establishment of an order to these things, by the commandment of the Father, matter? If it matters, then why not try it? If tried and it "tastes good" then you have your answer. And if nothing changes, then you also have learned something, as well.

I was fortunate to be able to follow the proper sequence. I was 19 years old when I came to the church. I try to follow the proper sequence with my own children by teaching them before baptism and testifying of Christ to them in a way calculated to produce faith in Him. I would take no offense, however, if one of my children were to later want to be re-baptized as an affirmation of their continuing belief in Christ. I can't see why anyone would take offense.

What does it mean to "inherit the kingdom of God?" Would that be important to secure while alive? This work cannot be done after death, you know.[680] However, if offered the opportunity now and a person declines it, they cannot afterwards receive it and inherit the "kingdom of God." They inherit another kingdom.[681]

---

680 D&C 138: 33: "These were taught faith in God, repentance from sin, vicarious baptism for the remission of sins, the gift of the Holy Ghost by the laying on of hands,"

681 D&C 76: 74: "Who received not the testimony of Jesus in the flesh, but afterwards received it."

This is important enough a matter that I rather think the whole subject is worth careful consideration. Christ's teachings have been carefully preserved at great effort and come to us by way of revelation and direct inspiration from God. From a prophet to another prophet in composition, and through a prophet in translation. It holds a power for salvation in the kingdom of God. It is worth prayerful consideration. The outcome is the difference between the "kingdom of God" on the one hand and "damnation" on the other.

3 Nephi 11: 35

> **"Verily, verily, I say unto you, that this is my doctrine, and I bear record of it from the Father; and whoso believeth in me believeth in the Father also; and unto him will the Father bear record of me, for he will visit him with fire and with the Holy Ghost."**

Belief in Christ necessarily means belief in the Father. To believe Christ is to accept His message of the Father's primacy and authority.

You see in these three members of the Godhead a full establishment of interconnected roles and responsibilities.

The Father ordains the plan. It is He who presides.

The Son implements the plan. It is He who makes the required sacrifice to save us.

The Holy Ghost activates the plan. It is the "fire" of the Holy Ghost which makes new, cleanses and perfects the man's understanding.

These three are "one" and united. They provide mankind with the possibility for salvation and exaltation.

Christ "bears record of it from the Father." This means that Christ is the Father's messenger announcing the Father's plan. What of the need for two witnesses?[682] One of the criticisms of Christ's message was the absence of additional witnesses.[683] Is Christ doing that same thing here with the Nephites? Does His announcement that He speaks for the Father constitute one, or two witnesses? The Father first bore witness of Christ.[684] Now Christ bears witness of Him.

---

682 Matt. 18: 16: "But if he will not hear *thee, then* take with thee one or two more, that in the mouth of two or three witnesses every word may be established."

683 John 8: 13-14: "The Pharisees therefore said unto him, Thou bearest record of thyself; thy record is not true. Jesus answered and said unto them, Though I bear record of myself, *yet* my record is true: for I know whence I came, and whither I go; but ye cannot tell whence I come, and whither I go."

684 3 Ne. 11: 6-7: "And behold, the third time they did understand the voice which they heard; and it said unto them: Behold my Beloved Son, in whom I am well pleased, in whom I have glorified my name—hear ye him."

The Father's testimony always affirms the status of the Son as His Beloved, and of our need to "hear Him."[685] The Father can, and does, acknowledge others as His.[686] But, unlike the Son who has repeatedly visited this earth, walked upon it[687], been handled by people[688], and eaten here[689], the Father does not come into contact with this earth in its fallen state.[690] The only time the Father had contact with this earth was before the Fall, in the Paradisiacal setting of Eden—which was a Temple

---

[685] Matt. 17: 5: "While he yet spake, behold, a bright cloud overshadowed them: and behold a voice out of the cloud, which said, This is my beloved Son, in whom I am well pleased; hear ye him."
JS-H 1: 17: "It no sooner appeared than I found myself delivered from the enemy which held me bound. When the light rested upon me I saw two Personages, whose brightness and glory defy all description, standing above me in the air. One of them spake unto me, calling me by name and said, pointing to the other—*This is My Beloved Son. Hear Him!*"
Matt. 3: 17: "And lo a voice from heaven, saying, This is my beloved Son, in whom I am well pleased."

[686] Ps. 2: 7: "I will declare the decree: the Lord hath said unto me, Thou *art* my Son; this day have I begotten thee."

[687] Luke 24: 15-16: "And it came to pass, that, while they communed *together* and reasoned, Jesus himself drew near, and went with them. But their eyes were holden that they should not know him."

[688] Luke 24: 36-39: "And as they thus spake, Jesus himself stood in the midst of them, and saith unto them, Peace *be* unto you. But they were terrified and affrighted, and supposed that they had seen a spirit. And he said unto them, Why are ye troubled? and why do thoughts arise in your hearts? Behold my hands and my feet, that it is I myself: handle me, and see; for a spirit hath not flesh and bones, as ye see me have."
3 Ne. 11: 14-15: "Arise and come forth unto me, that ye may thrust your hands into my side, and also that ye may feel the prints of the nails in my hands and in my feet, that ye may know that I am the God of Israel, and the God of the whole earth, and have been slain for the sins of the world. And it came to pass that the multitude went forth, and thrust their hands into his side, and did feel the prints of the nails in his hands and in his feet; and this they did do, going forth one by one until they had all gone forth, and did see with their eyes and did feel with their hands, and did know of a surety and did bear record, that it was he, of whom it was written by the prophets, that should come."

[689] John 21: 13: "Jesus then cometh, and taketh bread, and giveth them, and fish likewise."

[690] Matt. 17: 5: "While he yet spake, behold, a bright cloud overshadowed them: and behold a voice out of the cloud, which said, This is my beloved Son, in whom I am well pleased; hear ye him."
JS-H 1: 17: "It no sooner appeared than I found myself delivered from the enemy which held me bound. When the light rested upon me I saw two Personages, whose brightness and glory defy all description, standing above me in the air. One of them spake unto me, calling me by name and said, pointing to the other—*This is My Beloved Son. Hear Him!*"

at the time.[691] Whenever there has been contact with the Father thereafter, He has been at a distance from this earth.[692]

There is a formality with the Father that does not exist with the Son. For example, the Son has eaten with mortal man while He was immortal, both before His ministry in the flesh[693] and after.[694] As our Redeemer, He is directly responsible for us and has contact with us to perform His redemptive service. The Father, on the other hand, is different in status, responsibility, glory and dominion. The Son can appear to mortal man without showing His glory or requiring any alteration of the mortal who beholds Him.[695] To behold the Father, to endure His presence, one must be transfigured.[696] Mortal man cannot behold the Father's works while mortal, for if you comprehend them you cannot afterward remain mortal in the flesh.[697]

---

[691] Gen. 3: 8: "And they heard the voice of the Lord God walking in the garden in the cool of the day: and Adam and his wife hid themselves from the presence of the Lord God amongst the trees of the garden."

[692] Moses 7: 24: "And there came generation upon generation; and Enoch was high and lifted up, even in the bosom of the Father, and of the Son of Man; and behold, the power of Satan was upon all the face of the earth."
1 Ne. 1: 8: "And being thus overcome with the Spirit, he was carried away in a vision, even that he saw the heavens open, and he thought he saw God sitting upon his throne, surrounded with numberless concourses of angels in the attitude of singing and praising their God."
Alma 36: 22: "Yea, methought I saw, even as our father Lehi saw, God sitting upon his throne, surrounded with numberless concourses of angels, in the attitude of singing and praising their God; yea, and my soul did long to be there."

[693] Ex. 24: 9-11: "Then went up Moses, and Aaron, Nadab, and Abihu, and seventy of the elders of Israel: And they saw the God of Israel: and *there was* under his feet as it were a paved work of a sapphire stone, and as it were the body of heaven in *his* clearness. And upon the nobles of the children of Israel he laid not his hand: also they saw God, and did eat and drink."

[694] Luke 24: 41-43: "And while they yet believed not for joy, and wondered, he said unto them, Have ye here any meat? And they gave him a piece of a broiled fish, and of an honeycomb. And he took *it,* and did eat before them."

[695] John 20: 15-17: "Jesus saith unto her, Woman, why weepest thou? whom seekest thou? She, supposing him to be the gardener, saith unto him, Sir, if thou have borne him hence, tell me where thou hast laid him, and I will take him away. Jesus saith unto her, Mary. She turned herself, and saith unto him, Rabboni; which is to say, Master. Jesus saith unto her, Touch me not; for I am not yet ascended to my Father: but go to my brethren, and say unto them, I ascend unto my Father, and your Father; and *to* my God, and your God."

[696] Moses 1: 2: "And he saw God face to face, and he talked with him, and the glory of God was upon Moses; therefore Moses could endure his presence."

[697] Moses 1: 5: "Wherefore, no man can behold all my works, except he behold all my glory; and no man can behold all my glory, and afterwards remain in the flesh on the earth."

The primary means to learn of Christ for mortal man is the Holy Ghost. It is this means which brings all things to your remembrance.[698] Once the learning has culminated in preparation of the individual, then the Savior has a continuing ministry.[699] The Savior's ministry is to bring the person redemption.

When this process is complete, then it is the responsibility of those who have been redeemed to cry repentance to their neighbors.[700] Indeed, the desire to bring others to receive redemption becomes their primary concern.[701]

The process then produces those who bear testimony of the Son. If they are called of God, they will use scriptures to testify of Christ. This has always been the pattern ordained by God.[702] They may understand the scriptures more clearly, because they have seen the same things as earlier prophets.[703] But their testimonies will draw from the scriptures and the words of their brothers in Christ who went before as they testify of Him.

It is through such signs as these you know the Father and Son are one, and the Holy Ghost and the Son are one, and the messengers sent by them will testify of the Father, Son and Holy Ghost. These three are the ones in whom faith must be focused for salvation. Though the

---

698 John 14: 26: "But the Comforter, *which is* the Holy Ghost, whom the Father will send in my name, he shall teach you all things, and bring all things to your remembrance, whatsoever I have said unto you."

699 John 14: 21: "He that hath my commandments, and keepeth them, he it is that loveth me: and he that loveth me shall be loved of my Father, and I will love him, and will manifest myself to him."

700 D&C 88: 74, 81: "And I give unto you, who are the first laborers in this last kingdom, a commandment that you assemble yourselves together, and organize yourselves, and prepare yourselves, and sanctify yourselves; yea, purify your hearts, and cleanse your hands and your feet before me, that I may make you clean; ... Behold, I sent you out to testify and warn the people, and it becometh every man who hath been warned to warn his neighbor."

701 Mosiah 28: 3: "Now they were desirous that salvation should be declared to every creature, for they could not bear that any human soul should perish; yea, even the very thoughts that any soul should endure endless torment did cause them to quake and tremble."

702 Jacob 7: 10-11: "And I said unto him: Believest thou the scriptures? And he said, Yea. And I said unto him: Then ye do not understand them; for they truly testify of Christ. Behold, I say unto you that none of the prophets have written, nor prophesied, save they have spoken concerning this Christ."

703 JS-H 1: 74: "Our minds being now enlightened, we began to have the scriptures laid open to our understandings, and the true meaning and intention of their more mysterious passages revealed unto us in a manner which we never could attain to previously, nor ever before had thought of. In the meantime we were forced to keep secret the circumstances of having received the Priesthood and our having been baptized, owing to a spirit of persecution which had already manifested itself in the neighborhood."

heavens may include hosts of others, saving faith must be focused in the Father, Son and Holy Ghost alone. Whenever attention and worship moves from the Father, Son and Holy Ghost, the result is invariably apostasy and false beliefs.[704]

The doctrine of Christ is to be strictly followed. It alone delivers from destruction. All other paths lead to error, foolishness and the dark, where you will perish.[705]

From following this process we obtain the necessary "fire and the Holy Ghost" which redeems, purges, purifies and changes us into a new creature in Christ.

I have said very little of my personal experiences because of how quickly people turn from following Christ to following men whenever attention is drawn to a man. Mankind is inclined toward idolatry. The church has become a great idol. I do not intend to supplant the Lord, nor to call attention to myself, nor to offer myself as an idol for others. **I cannot save anyone**. If not for Christ and His atonement, I would have only dread for my eternal state. The doctrine of Christ is what the Father ordained as the means for salvation. Anyone who interferes with the process, or offers another means for salvation, cannot deliver.[706] Whether it is an institution or an individual, no one other than Christ can save. Hence His title as Savior. For some reason mankind is so prone to error, so quick to leave the path, and so vulnerable to being deceived, that focus must remain on the Son, as empowered and sent by the Father, through the witness of the Holy Ghost, or we go astray. Joseph cautioned: "How much more dignified and noble are the thoughts of

---

[704] See Deut. 16, 18, 19, and 19. Also 1 Cor. 8: 5-6: "For though there be that are called gods, whether in heaven or in earth, (as there be gods many, and lords many,) But to us *there is but* one God, the Father, of whom *are* all things, and we in him; and one Lord Jesus Christ, by whom *are* all things, and we by him."
2 Kgs. 17: 13-16: "Yet the Lord testified against Israel, and against Judah, by all the prophets, *and by* all the seers, saying, Turn ye from your evil ways, and keep my commandments *and* my statutes, according to all the law which I commanded your fathers, and which I sent to you by my servants the prophets. Notwithstanding they would not hear, but hardened their necks, like to the neck of their fathers, that did not believe in the Lord their God. And they rejected his statutes, and his covenant that he made with their fathers, and his testimonies which he testified against them; and they followed vanity, and became vain, and went after the heathen that *were* round about them, *concerning* whom the Lord had charged them, that they should not do like them. And they left all the commandments of the Lord their God, and made them molten images, *even* two calves, and made a grove, and worshipped all the host of heaven, and served Baal."

[705] Deut. 8: 19: "And it shall be, if thou do at all forget the Lord thy God, and walk after other gods, and serve them, and worship them, I testify against you this day that ye shall surely perish."

[706] Mosiah 3: 17: "And moreover, I say unto you, that there shall be no other name given nor any other way nor means whereby salvation can come unto the children of men, only in and through the name of Christ, the Lord Omnipotent."

God, than the vain imaginations of the human heart! None but fools will trifle with the souls of men." (TPJS p. 137.)

3 Nephi 11: 36

> **"And thus will the Father bear record of me, and the Holy Ghost will bear record unto him of the Father and me; for the Father, and I, and the Holy Ghost are one."**

The phrase: "And thus will the Father bear record of me" is referring to the Father visiting "him with fire and the Holy Ghost." This means that to the recipient of the baptism of fire and the Holy Ghost comes a witness to the person of the Father. When the baptism of fire and the Holy Ghost come to you, so does the Father's testimony of the Son.

You cannot receive this baptism and not have a testimony given to you by the Father of the Son.

In the Book of Mormon we read accounts of conversion experiences which include visitations of angels or opening of the heavens.[707] These converts' experiences did not come after a lifetime of study or reading a library of scholarly works. Indeed, in some cases the only information they had before the encounter came from the words of a missionary testifying to the truth.

Becoming converted is a question of sincerity, real intent, and asking God. It is not about the library you have read. Indeed, approaching it on purely intellectual terms has never produced a single convert. I've written a chapter on this in *Eighteen Verses*.

The problem is always obtaining a connection to the Father, Son and Holy Ghost. It is not a matter of scholarship. Joseph was anything but a scholar when he encountered God in the First Vision. He was young and ignorant. He read the Bible, believed in God's existence, and trusted the promise by James that if he were to ask God he would not be upbraided

---

[707] See e.g., Mosiah 27: 11-24; Alma 22: 16-18, 23; Alma 19: 12-19.

but would be answered.[708] Therefore he decided to ask, with real intent, trusting in the promise.[709]

Because he asked, he met God. Walking into the grove near his home that morning he was a foolish and ignorant boy. Walking back he was a prophet. Though it would be many years following that encounter before he appreciated how far he would have to go to gain knowledge of godliness and the mysteries of salvation. But all of his study and effort was informed by the scriptures and revelation. In my view, this is how it should be.

Scriptures are an essential anchor of understanding. All truths should find a comfortable setting inside existing scripture. If a notion or teaching is jarringly contradictory of existing scripture, then there must be a very good reason or explanation before it should be accepted. It has been my experience that revelation does not contradict, but opens up meaning of the scriptures. This was Joseph's and Oliver's experience, as well.[710]

When I study other materials, I do so to inform my reading and understanding of scripture, not to supplant it. I spend as much time with scripture study as I do with other writings. Although I could recite things using my own words, I find the language of scripture describes truths better than new wordings and therefore often use the language of scripture even if I do not show them in quotes. I also make frequent reference to scripture in this blog to show the reader that the scriptures are an existing library of material dealing with every part of Christ's Gospel. Since we have scripture made available to us at great

[708] James 1: 5-6: "If any of you lack wisdom, let him ask of God, that giveth to all *men* liberally, and upbraideth not; and it shall be given him. But let him ask in faith, nothing wavering. For he that wavereth is like a wave of the sea driven with the wind and tossed."

[709] JS-H 1: 12-13: "Never did any passage of scripture come with more power to the heart of man than this did at this time to mine. It seemed to enter with great force into every feeling of my heart. I reflected on it again and again, knowing that if any person needed wisdom from God, I did; for how to act I did not know, and unless I could get more wisdom than I then had, I would never know; for the teachers of religion of the different sects understood the same passages of scripture so differently as to destroy all confidence in settling the question by an appeal to the Bible. At length I came to the conclusion that I must either remain in darkness and confusion, or else I must do as James directs, that is, ask of God. I at length came to the determination to "ask of God," concluding that if he gave wisdom to them that lacked wisdom, and would give liberally, and not upbraid, I might venture."

[710] JS-H 1: 74: "Our minds being now enlightened, we began to have the scriptures laid open to our understandings, and the true meaning and intention of their more mysterious passages revealed unto us in a manner which we never could attain to previously, nor ever before had thought of. In the meantime we were forced to keep secret the circumstances of having received the Priesthood and our having been baptized, owing to a spirit of persecution which had already manifested itself in the neighborhood."

effort from God and the prophets, it would be terribly ungrateful for us to fail to study what they have provided.

The "record" we already have of the Father's testimony of the Son, the Son's testimony of the Father, and the Holy Ghost's interaction with mankind is found in the scriptures. Although you may not see it fully without further revelation, it is nevertheless there. I have found the scriptures often open up further revelation. This is how Section 76, the First Vision, Section 138, Section 93, Section 132, and many other revelations have come to us. Search the meaning of scripture, and then ask God for what you do not see through your own effort. Appreciation for what has been given already produces further revelation.

The Father, Son and Holy Ghost are one. And the primary means for obtaining access to their "record" spoken of in this verse, is through the scriptures. Although I may try to shed additional light upon the meaning of scripture, I try to keep the scriptures an integral part of anything I write. (Excepting only the parables, where I felt free to let another tradition inform how and what I have written. And the proverbs; which I titled "Sayings" at the end of *The Second Comforter*; which was another tradition as well.)

3 Nephi 11: 37-38

> **"And again I say unto you, ye must repent, and become as a little child, and be baptized in my name, or ye can in nowise receive these things. And again I say unto you, ye must repent, and be baptized in my name, and become as a little child, or ye can in nowise inherit the kingdom of God."**

Repentance is not likely unless a person is willing to undergo a change to become more "childlike" in perspective and attitude. I've written a chapter on this in *The Second Comforter.* I used that as the basis for my comments at the recent Chiasmus Conference. It is more than just an analogy or good advice. It is a prerequisite. It is the only way you can "inherit the kingdom of God."

Children are open to change and willing to learn. They welcome new ideas for all ideas are new to them. The world is new to them. They feel their ignorance and are anxious to fill it with information and understanding. They know they are unable to cope with the world they live in unless they obtain more understanding than they have. So they relentlessly search to know more.

On the other hand, adults are generally closed. They believe they already know something, and therefore are unwilling to receive more.[711]

Adults learn disciplines of study and then think the Gospel should be viewed by the tools of the scholar. To the economist, all of the Gospel appears to be financial. To the philosopher, all of the Gospel appears to

---

[711] 2 Ne. 28: 29: "Wo be unto him that shall say: We have received the word of God, and we need no more of the word of God, for we have enough!"

be dialectic. To the lawyer it is a legal system. But the Gospel is separate from the understanding of men. It requires us to surrender our arrogance and foolishness and come as a child to learn anew everything about life and truth. This is why the Gospel always begins with creation, informs of the Fall, and preaches the Atonement.

We must "repent" because the foundation of accepting new truth begins with the realization that we're not getting anywhere by what we've already done. We need to abandon old ways and begin anew. Until we are open to the new truths offered through the Gospel, we can't even start the journey. We're headed in the wrong direction and don't even know it. First we need to realize our direction is wrong. Then stop going that way. When we turn to the new direction, we've begun repenting.[712]

From repentance comes light and truth. At first, just turning to face the new direction is a great revelation. But you've not seen anything until you walk in that direction for a while. As you move toward the light and receive more, the world itself changes meaning and nothing you used to think important remains important.[713]

Becoming as a little child, or repenting, must precede baptism if you are to be saved. Otherwise, you cannot "receive these things" or, in other words, you cannot accept the new truths and perspectives the Gospel will require you to know and accept. Unless these steps are taken you cannot "inherit the kingdom of God" because only such people will be able to enter.

Teachable. Open. Willing to receive more. Able to endure difficulties as a result of the changes which come to them. Patient. Submissive to God. And eager to learn more.[714]

Not arrogant. Not trying to fit the new truths into your existing framework of false notions.[715] Not resisting truth and arguing against

---

712 2 Cor. 5: 17: "Therefore if any man *be* in Christ, *he is* a new creature: old things are passed away; behold, all things are become new."

713 Isa. 65: 17: "For, behold, I create new heavens and a new earth: and the former shall not be remembered, nor come into mind."

714 Mosiah 3: 19: "For the natural man is an enemy to God, and has been from the fall of Adam, and will be, forever and ever, unless he yields to the enticings of the Holy Spirit, and putteth off the natural man and becometh a saint through the atonement of Christ the Lord, and becometh as a child, submissive, meek, humble, patient, full of love, willing to submit to all things which the Lord seeth fit to inflict upon him, even as a child doth submit to his father."

715 Mark 2: 22: "And no man putteth new wine into old bottles: else the new wine doth burst the bottles, and the wine is spilled, and the bottles will be marred: but new wine must be put into new bottles."

it.[716] Not proud or boastful, secure in your own salvation.[717] Not holding a testimony that you will be saved while others around you will be lost because they do not believe as you do.[718]

How few there will be who find it.[719] Most people are simply unwilling to repent. They have such truth as they are willing to receive already, and want nothing more.[720]

---

[716] 1 Tim. 6: 4-6: "He is proud, knowing nothing, but doting about questions and strifes of words, whereof cometh envy, strife, railings, evil surmisings, Perverse disputings of men of corrupt minds, and destitute of the truth, supposing that gain is godliness: from such withdraw thyself. But godliness with contentment is great gain."

[717] Luke 18: 11: "The Pharisee stood and prayed thus with himself, God, I thank thee, that I am not as other men *are,* extortioners, unjust, adulterers, or even as this publican."

[718] Alma 31: 14-18: "Therefore, whosoever desired to worship must go forth and stand upon the top thereof, and stretch forth his hands towards heaven, and cry with a loud voice, saying: Holy, holy God; we believe that thou art God, and we believe that thou art holy, and that thou wast a spirit, and that thou art a spirit, and that thou wilt be a spirit forever. Holy God, we believe that thou hast separated us from our brethren; and we do not believe in the tradition of our brethren, which was handed down to them by the childishness of their fathers; but we believe that thou hast elected us to be thy holy children; and also thou hast made it known unto us that there shall be no Christ. But thou art the same yesterday, today, and forever; and thou hast elected us that we shall be saved, whilst all around us are elected to be cast by thy wrath down to hell; for the which holiness, O God, we thank thee; and we also thank thee that thou hast elected us, that we may not be led away after the foolish traditions of our brethren, which doth bind them down to a belief of Christ, which doth lead their hearts to wander far from thee, our God. And again we thank thee, O God, that we are a chosen and a holy people. Amen."

[719] Matt. 7: 14: "Because strait *is* the gate, and narrow *is* the way, which leadeth unto life, and few there be that find it."
3 Ne. 14: 14: "Because strait is the gate, and narrow is the way, which leadeth unto life, and few there be that find it."
3 Ne. 27: 33: "And it came to pass that when Jesus had ended these sayings he said unto his disciples: Enter ye in at the strait gate; for strait is the gate, and narrow is the way that leads to life, and few there be that find it; but wide is the gate, and broad the way which leads to death, and many there be that travel therein, until the night cometh, wherein no man can work."
D&C 132: 22: "For strait is the gate, and narrow the way that leadeth unto the exaltation and continuation of the lives, and few there be that find it, because ye receive me not in the world neither do ye know me."

[720] 2 Ne. 28: 14-15: "They wear stiff necks and high heads; yea, and because of pride, and wickedness, and abominations, and whoredoms, they have all gone astray save it be a few, who are the humble followers of Christ; nevertheless, they are led, that in many instances they do err because they are taught by the precepts of men. O the wise, and the learned, and the rich, that are puffed up in the pride of their hearts, and all those who preach false doctrines, and all those who commit whoredoms, and pervert the right way of the Lord, wo, wo, wo be unto them, saith the Lord God Almighty, for they shall be thrust down to hell!"

Even Christ is unable to persuade them to accept His Gospel.

3 Nephi 11: 39

> **"Verily, verily, I say unto you, that this is my doctrine, and whoso buildeth upon this buildeth upon my rock, and the gates of hell shall not prevail against them."**

This is the reason for this doctrine. It will allow those who accept and follow it to endure against all enemies. It will allow them to prevail.

Even the "gates of hell shall not prevail against them." Meaning that death and hell can have no claim upon them. They will not be taken captive either in this world[721] or when they leave this world.[722]

When we consider the Father is to bear record of the Son, and the Son bears record of the Father, and the Holy Ghost bears record of the Father and Son, then we realize this doctrine of Christ is designed to put us in contact with all three members of the Godhead. We are to join them. We are to be one with them.

There is no separating us from God when we have the record of each given to us.

It is interesting that the "rock" upon which we build is the Father, Son and Holy Ghost. There is abundant evidence of other "gods" and of "goddesses." It is beyond dispute that the "image of God" includes both "male and female."[723] It is inescapable, therefore, that the God we worship includes a Father and a Mother. However, we are only to seek after the Father, Son and Holy Ghost as the "rock" upon which our salvation is to be built.

Oddly enough, mankind prefers a female deity over a male deity. Catholicism has reconciled this preference by the doctrine of Immaculate Conception and the cultic veneration of Mary. Pope John Paul II was an ardent believer in the Cult of Mary and made no secret of

---

[721] Alma 12: 11: "And they that will harden their hearts, to them is given the lesser portion of the word until they know nothing concerning his mysteries; and then they are taken captive by the devil, and led by his will down to destruction. Now this is what is meant by the chains of hell."

[722] Alma 40: 13: "And then shall it come to pass, that the spirits of the wicked, yea, who are evil—for behold, they have no part nor portion of the Spirit of the Lord; for behold, they chose evil works rather than good; therefore the spirit of the devil did enter into them, and take possession of their house—and these shall be cast out into outer darkness; there shall be weeping, and wailing, and gnashing of teeth, and this because of their own iniquity, being led captive by the will of the devil."

[723] Gen. 1: 27: "So God created man in his *own* image, in the image of God created he him; male and female created he them."
Moses 2: 27: "And I, God, created man in mine own image, in the image of mine Only Begotten created I him; male and female created I them."
Abr. 4: 27: "So the Gods went down to organize man in their own image, in the image of the Gods to form they him, male and female to form they them."

that veneration. It is almost beyond dispute that Mary's status is preferred over Christ's in the lives of the common Catholic.

In the Old Testament, the goddess Ashtoreth, (in her various iterations) was a leading figure in apostasies of ancient Israel. She was the female consort to Baal (who also had various spellings). The Egyptian counterpart being Hathor, whose image appears in figure 5 of Facsimile No. 2 in the Book of Abraham. The representation there being Egyptian—that is, emerging through the great cycle of life, afterlife and resurrection coming through the womb. An understanding of which Hugh Nibley was setting forth in *One Eternal Round.* This work was reduced in volume by half before publication. This resulted in problems with the published text. That, however, is another subject not relevant here.

Notwithstanding man's preference for the female god, for salvation we must anchor ourselves to the Father, Son and Holy Ghost. They are the "rock" upon which we must build to avoid the gates of hell, despite our knowledge of heaven, salvation and the necessary unity of the sexes before salvation is obtained.[724] It is through the union of the sexes that mortals imitate immortality, for all of us will die. Yet if joined together we will continue through the seed forever, as the gods.[725]

There is also the continuing trouble about polygamy which so often afflicted the discussions on this blog before comments were discontinued. Those who preach on the subject often speak out of the coarseness of ambition and insecurity (for those always go together), and without understanding how a marriage must work to warrant preservation beyond this life.

Ask yourself what kind of a relationship would be godlike? What association between a man and a woman would be something the heavens would want to preserve and continue? Is an ambitious man who looks upon a woman as someone to rule over worthy of heavenly preservation? Is such a man worthy of one wife, let alone several?

Wouldn't you expect the relationship between a man and woman worthy of eternal preservation to evidence such things as equality, respect, kindness, joyful and voluntary interchange of thoughts, and to be grounded in love? Wouldn't you expect such a marriage to be part of heaven, though the parties live as mortals on the earth? Why would you

---

[724] 1 Cor. 11: 11: "Nevertheless neither is the man without the woman, neither the woman without the man, in the Lord."

[725] D&C 132: 20-22: "Then shall they be gods, because they have no end; therefore shall they be from everlasting to everlasting, because they continue; then shall they be above all, because all things are subject unto them. Then shall they be gods, because they have all power, and the angels are subject unto them. Verily, verily, I say unto you, except ye abide my law ye cannot attain to this glory. For strait is the gate, and narrow the way that leadeth unto the exaltation and continuation of the lives, and few there be that find it, because ye receive me not in the world neither do ye know me."

expect a form of marriage, having as its chief output, unhappy but frequently pregnant women, having an absentee husband to be godlike?

Have you read the tenth parable in *Ten Parables*? If you have and still think you need a "brood" of women to become godlike, then you haven't understood the tenth parable.

Foolishness never was enlightenment. Ambition is unbecoming in a candidate for exaltation. We will keep going into Christ's sermons to the Nephites and, as we do, you will find He emphasizes how to become like Him through service and abasing yourself. By sacrifice and devotion to the best interests of others. Not by compulsion, dominion and ruling over others.

If you want to prevail against the gates of hell, then Christ's simple doctrines need to become yours. They need to be how you live and what you do. They are the only rock upon which you can build and have something which will endure the buffetings of hell itself.

If a man hasn't made a single woman happy, why would he be trusted to have more wives? Why would he want them? What does such a man think the purpose of marriage to be? Gratification? Industrial baby-production? What's the reason? If happiness is the end of our design by God, then wouldn't you need to find someone who can live in peace and happiness with another person as their husband as the first step? If that is true, then why isn't that challenge enough in a marriage between one man and one woman? Until that has been conquered, why should misery be multiplied by adding additional spouses into a failed interpersonal relationship?

Too many people are advocating too many alternatives which distract from the simplicity of what is really needed. There aren't enough marriages worthy of preservation. Make yours one of them. That is a very good work and challenge enough for all of us at present.

3 Nephi 11: 40

> **"And whoso shall declare more or less than this, and establish it for my doctrine, the same cometh of evil, and is not built upon my rock; but he buildeth upon a sandy foundation, and the gates of hell stand open to receive such when the floods come and the winds beat upon them."**

Here is Christ's explanation of why we must focus on these doctrines to be saved. I've heard more words of caution about speaking "more" than I've ever heard cautioning about "less." Both are a problem. It is more fashionable today to speak less about Christ's doctrine, or to circumscribe it into so narrow a meaning as to render it powerless in effect.

First, as to "more." When we "declare more" we are getting ahead of the process. We aren't to worship the "hosts of heaven," nor a heavenly mother. Despite all we may know about Her, that knowledge won't save. Other personages or ministers cannot save either. Gabriel will not.

Enoch will not. Michael will not. Only the Son will save; and the Father will bear testimony of Him. Interesting stories about individual spiritual encounters or experiences will not save. They are evidence that heaven is still attending to us, but the details are for the individual. The experiences that will save have already been recorded in scripture for our general instruction. Outside of scripture those individual experiences are only useful to the extent they shed light upon scriptural accounts. If a person can help you understand Daniel's visionary encounters by what they have been shown, then their personal experiences are not as important as the light they may shed upon Daniel's prophecy. Similarly what I've written is helpful only to understand scripture, and not otherwise. Even the account of Gethsemane is anchored in scripture and useful only to the extent it sheds light upon what has been given to us in the New Testament Gospels, Nephi's prophecy, Alma's testimony and D&C 19. I do think my account goes further to explain what occurred than any other writing which has come to my attention. Nevertheless the scriptures are needed as the primary tool for understanding our Lord's atonement. So the definition of "more" would include such things that supplant scripture or suggest anything is more important than the Father, Son and Holy Ghost; but things as may shed additional light on the meaning of scripture.

Interestingly enough, when we "declare less" we are also condemned. It works both ways. It's a two-edged sword. Not "more nor less" is permitted. We sometimes greet preaching "less" with applause, because we want less. But that is no better than missing the mark while preaching "more." Perhaps it is worse, because it represents a rejection of truth. It is active suppression of what needs to be proclaimed.

All of us must be concerned about declaring less. Deleting or omitting is as serious a matter as adding. Either will allow the gates of hell to prevail.

When you adopt creedal Historic Christianity and amalgamate the Father, Son and Holy Ghost into a single cosmic siamese-triplet construct, you are declaring them as less. The disembodiment of God the Father was a lie to supplant and replace Him by another disembodied pretender claiming to be the god of this world.

Christ's teaching here is preliminary to the Sermon that follows. In the coming Sermon we will read a better preserved version of the Sermon on the Mount from Jerusalem, called here the Sermon at Bountiful. But this explanation of doctrine is given by Christ first. The foundation of doctrine of the oneness of the Father, Son and Holy Ghost, the conferral of power to baptize, and manner of baptism come before the great Sermon. First we receive the instruction to avoid disputes. These disputes lead to contention that lays the foundation for anger between men. This doctrine is so foundational that Christ covers it before any other teaching. Therefore, you should realize its importance.

We will be captured by hell if we do not understand and follow these teachings. Though they are Christ's very first instructions, we almost never discuss them. You may want to re-read these verses again, and realize their fundamental importance.

Christ is saying it is "evil" to do more or less with His doctrine. It surely is, for ignoring, altering, omitting or enlarging leads to evil.

3 Nephi 11: 41

> **"Therefore, go forth unto this people, and declare the words which I have spoken, unto the ends of the earth."**

This is the charge given by Christ to the twelve whom He had called and given power to baptize. It was overheard by those who had been witnessing these events. But the charge is to the twelve.

The obligation to declare the doctrine of Christ, preach repentance, baptize with authority and make known the Father, Son and Holy Ghost is imposed upon the twelve. This burden, therefore, rests on them and is theirs to bear off "unto this people." They are to warn everybody of these obligations. Not just those who were there.

The extent of the duty runs "unto the ends of the earth." From where they were at the time Christ was preaching, to the entire North and South American continents and all those who may be living there at the time were the assigned mission field to whom the doctrine of Christ was to be declared.

The break between this portion of Christ's teachings and what would follow is interesting to consider. The remainder of His teachings will form the primary message foundational to Christianity. It is the new, higher law which replaces the earlier Law of Moses. Yet this portion, declared by Christ as His "doctrine" is the part to be taken first and declared everywhere. Why?

A fair conclusion to reach is that before you consider the new, higher law you must first:

- Repent

- Be Baptized

- Receive the Holy Ghost

- Have a correct understanding of God the Father, God the Son, and the Holy Ghost

These things precede His replacement of the older, lower law with His new, higher law. It is reasonable to conclude you will not comprehend His follow-on teachings if you have not first repented, been baptized, received the Holy Ghost, and understand the Godhead. Or, even more to the point: You will never be able to LIVE His new, higher law unless these steps are taken first. Until then you may aspire, but you will not be able to live them. They address the heart, rather than just conduct. They go to the deepest convictions inside you, what motivates you, and the reasons for your conduct. Your conduct will follow these precepts when you have been changed. For the required change, the tools discussed first must be acquired.

He will return to the themes of this opening statement, declaring nothing more or less than what He has taught should be given as His.[726]

So we turn from this introductory, first statement of His doctrine to His great foundational Sermon at Bountiful in which the higher law is first given in one, complete statement of what we are to become. It is not merely direction to us. It is also a revelation of what kind of person Christ was. He explains it Himself…

---

[726] 3 Ne. 18: 12-13: "And I give unto you a commandment that ye shall do these things. And if ye shall always do these things blessed are ye, for ye are built upon my rock. But whoso among you shall do more or less than these are not built upon my rock, but are built upon a sandy foundation; and when the rain descends, and the floods come, and the winds blow, and beat upon them, they shall fall, and the gates of hell are ready open to receive them."

3 Nephi 12

3 Nephi 12: 1

"And it came to pass that when Jesus had spoken these words unto Nephi, and to those who had been called, (now the number of them who had been called, and received power and authority to baptize, was twelve) and behold, he stretched forth his hand unto the multitude, and cried unto them, saying: Blessed are ye if ye shall give heed unto the words of these twelve whom I have chosen from among you to minister unto you, and to be your servants; and unto them I have given power that they may baptize you with water; and after that ye are baptized with water, behold, I will baptize you with fire and with the Holy Ghost; therefore blessed are ye if ye shall believe in me and be baptized, after that ye have seen me and know that I am."

Nephi and the other twelve heard and recorded the words we've been reviewing in Chapter 11. But here Christ makes certain all others who were present also knew the same doctrine. Notice the following:

"He stretched forth His hand." What does that mean? Why is it noted in the record? Why would the fact that He stretched forth His hand be significant enough to etch into metal plates?

Why does it say Christ "cried unto them?" How loud would He need to make His voice before it would be considered "crying" out to the audience? This suggests that what was covered in Chapter 11 was not loud enough for all those present to hear. But what follows He wants everyone to hear.

The Sermon at Bountiful begins with a new beatitude. "Blessed are ye if ye shall give heed unto the words of these twelve whom I have chosen from among you to minister unto you." A commenter recently suggested this means that any person ever called to any council of twelve is entitled to the same kind of status. Is that correct? Does membership in a group entitle someone to respect? Would receiving power directly from Christ entitle a person to respect? What if someone were to receive power from Christ, but not be included in some presiding group? For example, John the Baptist received power from an angel to overthrow the kingdom of the Jews at eight days old. He was never among a presiding group.[727] Paul was given power directly from heaven, calling himself "born out of due time" because he became a witness after Christ's resurrection and was not among the leadership when first visited.[728] Which does this apply to: those called to preside, or those called directly by the Lord (as the scriptures testify is sometimes the case)? Or does it only apply to the twelve disciples the Lord was referring to standing before the crowd on that day? Is limiting it to that narrow an application appropriate? Is expanding it to include anyone ever called to preside too broad an application? How are you to decide that question?

Is it appropriate for Christ to couple "minister to you" with "and to be your servants?" Can a "servant" exercise authority over you as the gentiles do?[729] Why not?

When Christ says these people have "power to baptize you" and then promises that He, Christ, "will baptize you with fire and with the Holy Ghost" does this promise mean that Christ will send the Holy Ghost if you are baptized by one having power from Him? Always? If it hasn't happened, does that mean the one who baptized you did not have this "power?" Why or why not? What is the relationship between the power to baptize, and the promise of the Holy Ghost? What role does your own repentance have to play? Christ has previously given the order of things, and included repentance first.

What does the statement mean: "blessed are ye if ye shall believe in me and be baptized, after that ye have seen me and know that I am." How likely would it be for you to "believe in [Christ] after that ye have seen [Him]?" Do you suspect any of those who were present would not believe in Him? Why?

Would you expect those present to believe in Him after seeing Him descend from heaven, hear the voice of the Father testify of Him, see His wounds, witness Him healing all their sick, and beholding angels minister in tongues of fire to their young children? Would you be able to do so? What about reading the record of the events in the Book of

---

727 D&C 84: 28: "For he was baptized while he was yet in his childhood, and was ordained by the angel of God at the time he was eight days old unto this power, to overthrow the kingdom of the Jews, and to make straight the way of the Lord before the face of his people, to prepare them for the coming of the Lord, in whose hand is given all power."

728 1 Cor. 15: 8-10: "And last of all he was seen of me also, as of one born out of due time. For I am the least of the apostles, that am not meet to be called an apostle, because I persecuted the church of God. But by the grace of God I am what I am: and his grace which *was bestowed* upon me was not in vain; but I laboured more abundantly than they all: yet not I, but the grace of God which was with me."

729 Luke 22: 25-26: "And he said unto them, The kings of the Gentiles exercise lordship over them; and they that exercise authority upon them are called benefactors. But ye *shall* not *be* so: but he that is greatest among you, let him be as the younger; and he that is chief, as he that doth serve."

Mormon; is that enough to testify of Him? Can you ask in prayer if these things about Christ are true and get a testimony of them for yourself? Have you done so? Have you acquired belief in Him as a result of praying to know if they are true? Can you then believe in Him? Are you "blessed" for it? Do you "know that He is?" What more do you need to do in order to "know that He is?" Why haven't you done that yet?

3 Nephi 12: 2

> **"And again, more blessed are they who shall believe in your words because that ye shall testify that ye have seen me, and that ye know that I am. Yea, blessed are they who shall believe in your words, and come down into the depths of humility and be baptized, for they shall be visited with fire and with the Holy Ghost, and shall receive a remission of their sins."**

Some people are given knowledge.[730] This would include the Prophet Joseph Smith. Others believe on their words and trust in Christ through what they have learned from witnesses of Him.[731] This would include President Thomas S. Monson, who in last General Conference testified he has no question about the testimonies of those who have seen Him. As President Monson testified: "I have read—and I believe—the testimonies of those who experienced the grief of Christ's Crucifixion and the joy of His Resurrection. I have read—and I believe—the testimonies of those in the New World who were visited by the same risen Lord. I believe the testimony of one who, in this dispensation, spoke with the Father and the Son in a grove now called sacred and who gave his life, sealing that testimony with his blood. Declared he: 'And now, after the many testimonies which have been given of him, this is the testimony, last of all, which we give of him: That he lives! For we saw him, even on the right hand of God; and we heard the voice bearing record that he is the Only Begotten of the Father.' The darkness of death can always be dispelled by the light of revealed truth. 'I am the resurrection, and the life,' spoke the Master. 'Peace I leave with you, my peace I give unto you.' Over the years I have heard and read testimonies too numerous to count, shared with me by individuals who testify of the reality of the Resurrection and who have received, in their hours of greatest need, the peace and comfort promised by the Savior." (He is Risen!, Sunday Morning Session, April 2010 Session; footnotes omitted.)

Why would someone be "more blessed" because they "believe in the words" of those who have "seen Christ" than those who have seen Him?

---

[730] D&C 46: 13: "To some it is given by the Holy Ghost to know that Jesus Christ is the Son of God, and that he was crucified for the sins of the world."

[731] D&C 46: 14: "To others it is given to believe on their words, that they also might have eternal life if they continue faithful."

What is it about believing on the words of those who **have seen** which is "more blessed" than the ones who see Him?

Notice once again the connection between having seen the Lord and "ye know that I am." Notice the use of "I am" in the statement of the Lord about Himself.

Now note too how the "believing in the words" is not enough, because He adds action to the belief. That is, those who "believe in your words" are required then to "come down into the depths of humility and be baptized" for the "blessing" to have any effect. It is not enough for someone to be moved to believe when they hear a witness of Christ, they must also respond to His invitation to be baptized. Before being baptized they need also to "come down into the depths of humility." The intention and inner meaning are everything. But the outward act confirms the inner change which takes place.

Action is married to belief and intent. Both are necessary.

When it is done in faith, sincerity, complying with the steps the Lord has prescribed, He promises to visit the obedient "with fire and with the Holy Ghost." This is how a person will know they have received "a remission of their sins."

The instructions of the Lord are intended to change lives. Change is repentance. And repentance leads to redemption. He expects our behavior to mirror our beliefs, because if behavior does not model our professed beliefs then we are hypocrites—not converts.

This is why commandments are given to us. They tell us how we can continue to receive and renew a continuing conversion to Christ's way of life. Commandments are not a burden to bear but a roadmap to follow. They are not a measuring stick to judge and then abuse others. It is a light for us to follow.

These explanations by Christ are beyond the question of "faith verses works" because Christ is telling us we act from our heart in faith, receive ordinances because of our faith, then have our hearts filled again. We proceed from grace to grace. This is how Christ received the fullness, and the only way we may receive the fullness.[732]

The task of knowing God always begins by trusting on the words of those who have seen Him. But it should never end there. Everyone is invited to lay aside their sins, call upon God in faith, obey His commandments, listen to the voice of inspiration and do as you are told, thereby coming to see Him face-to-face.[733] This is the reason for the book *The Second Comforter*. It is a manual for how any person can come back into the presence of the Lord and join those witnesses who can testify they have seen Him.

He lives. And He is the same, yesterday, today and forever.

3 Nephi 12: 3

> **"Yea, blessed are the poor in spirit who come unto me, for theirs is the kingdom of heaven."**

The blessing referred to for those who are "poor in spirit" comes as a result of "coming unto" Christ. Any who come to Christ will receive "the kingdom of heaven." However, to obtain it, you must "come unto [Christ]."

Christ is approachable. But the approach is determined by the Gospel. The earlier "doctrine of Christ" taught in Chapter 11 tells you how to "come unto Christ."

Belief on His teachings, then repentance and baptism are all essential prerequisites to coming to Him.

---

[732] D&C 93: 12-14, 19-29: "And I, John, saw that he received not of the fulness at the first, but received grace for grace; And he received not of the fulness at first, but continued from grace to grace, until he received a fulness; And thus he was called the Son of God, because he received not of the fulness at the first. …I give unto you these sayings that you may understand and know how to worship, and know what you worship, that you may come unto the Father in my name, and in due time receive of his fulness. For if you keep my commandments you shall receive of his fulness, and be glorified in me as I am in the Father; therefore, I say unto you, you shall receive grace for grace. And now, verily I say unto you, I was in the beginning with the Father, and am the Firstborn; And all those who are begotten through me are partakers of the glory of the same, and are the church of the Firstborn. Ye were also in the beginning with the Father; that which is Spirit, even the Spirit of truth; And truth is knowledge of things as they are, and as they were, and as they are to come; And whatsoever is more or less than this is the spirit of that wicked one who was a liar from the beginning. The Spirit of truth is of God. I am the Spirit of truth, and John bore record of me, saying: He received a fulness of truth, yea, even of all truth; And no man receiveth a fulness unless he keepeth his commandments. He that keepeth his commandments receiveth truth and light, until he is glorified in truth and knoweth all things. Man was also in the beginning with God. Intelligence, or the light of truth, was not created or made, neither indeed can be."

[733] D&C 93: 1: "Verily, thus saith the Lord: It shall come to pass that every soul who forsaketh his sins and cometh unto me, and calleth on my name, and obeyeth my voice, and keepeth my commandments, shall see my face and know that I am;"

What does it mean to be "poor in spirit?" Does that make you more open to Him? Have you ever had a season in which you felt "poor in spirit?" Were you more open to Him as a result?

Before I converted, though I did not consider myself a candidate to convert, I also felt a hollowness in life. There was something missing. The void inside us was meant to be there. Filling it was always the responsibility of the Gospel. We were all meant to feel "poor in spirit" until we find truth. Then, upon finding truth, we were meant to "come unto Christ" so the void may be filled. Coming to Christ is the return to life and light. It is the journey back to that light from where we originated.

Converting was more of a homecoming than anything else. The Gospel rings true and His sheep hear His voice [734] because these are things we long ago accepted and decided to follow.[735] Each of us needs to be converted. Even if you were raised in the church, you still need to convert. The steps Christ is outlining are the ones each of us are expected to follow. Whether you do so as an adult, or did so earlier in life, we are all required to "come unto Christ" and be converted.

We are not meant to remain "poor in spirit" but to "come to Christ" and move beyond that. Moving beyond it we find ourselves joyfully informed that "ours is the kingdom of heaven." We cannot claim it for ourselves. But Christ can claim it for us. This is how our poverty of spirit is to be cured. The Lord juxtaposes poverty with the riches of heaven itself. The contrast is designed to make us think, and to make us grateful. We were always intended to have joy. Above all else, Christ is a Deliverer from sorrow.[736]

3 Nephi 12: 4

> **"And again, blessed are all they that mourn, for they shall be comforted."**

This is unconditional. "All" are included. "All they that mourn" will be blessed.

Between sessions of conference Saturday I attended a friend's funeral. Mourning because of death is the first cause we associate with this promise. Over death, however, He has gained the victory. It was His mission and ministry to bring about victory over death. "And he will

[734] John 10: 27: "My sheep hear my voice, and I know them, and they follow me:"

[735] See Abraham 3.

[736] Rev. 7: 17: "For the Lamb which is in the midst of the throne shall feed them, and shall lead them unto living fountains of waters: and God shall wipe away all tears from their eyes."

take upon him death, that he may loose the bands of death."[737] This done now, though death continues to claim all of us. We know we will have part in His victory. Comfort from that victory will come to us all.

Death is not the only cause of mourning, however. We all experience afflictions, troubles, temptations, and pains while mortal. He has gained the victory over all of these also: "And he shall go forth, suffering pains and afflictions and temptations of every kind; and this that the word might be fulfilled which saith he will take upon him the pains and the sicknesses of his people. And he will take upon him death, that he may loose the bands of death which bind his people; and he will take upon him their infirmities, that his bowels may be filled with mercy, according to the flesh, that he may know according to the flesh how to succor his people according to their infirmities. Now the Spirit knoweth all things; nevertheless the Son of God suffereth according to the flesh that he might take upon him the sins of his people, that he might blot out their transgressions according to the power of his deliverance; and now behold, this is the testimony which is in me."[738]

Do you mourn because of afflictions? Temptations? Pains? Sickness? Infirmities? The troubles of the flesh? Sins and transgressions? It does not matter the cause of your mourning, Christ has suffered all these things so that He may understand the troubles of the flesh and, by understanding them to overcome them all. By overcoming them all, He then in turn can share the victory.

Your failures are not going to be reason to punish you. If you repent, they will be lessons from which to learn. The guilt will be removed, you will be comforted, and the lessons will remain. Your mortal trials will confer upon you the taste of the fruit of the tree of knowledge of good

---

737 Alma 7: 12: "And he will take upon him death, that he may loose the bands of death which bind his people; and he will take upon him their infirmities, that his bowels may be filled with mercy, according to the flesh, that he may know according to the flesh how to succor his people according to their infirmities."

738 Alma 7: 11-13: "And he shall go forth, suffering pains and afflictions and temptations of every kind; and this that the word might be fulfilled which saith he will take upon him the pains and the sicknesses of his people. And he will take upon him death, that he may loose the bands of death which bind his people; and he will take upon him their infirmities, that his bowels may be filled with mercy, according to the flesh, that he may know according to the flesh how to succor his people according to their infirmities. Now the Spirit knoweth all things; nevertheless the Son of God suffereth according to the flesh that he might take upon him the sins of his people, that he might blot out their transgressions according to the power of his deliverance; and now behold, this is the testimony which is in me."

and evil.[739] You will have learned from what you suffer the difference between the two, and have the benefit of Christ's atonement to remove all guilt.[740]

All will be comforted from every offense they have ever suffered. All that remains will be the choices you have made.[741] The offenses you suffered at the hands of others will be made up to you. All infirmities you have been plagued with while mortal will be removed.[742] Only your choices will remain as either a continuing blessing or continuing affliction. But that is your choice.[743]

---

[739] Gen. 3: 17-19: "And unto Adam he said, Because thou hast hearkened unto the voice of thy wife, and hast eaten of the tree, of which I commanded thee, saying, Thou shalt not eat of it: cursed *is* the ground for thy sake; in sorrow shalt thou eat *of* it all the days of thy life; Thorns also and thistles shall it bring forth to thee; and thou shalt eat the herb of the field; In the sweat of thy face shalt thou eat bread, till thou return unto the ground; for out of it wast thou taken: for dust thou *art,* and unto dust shalt thou return."

[740] 2 Ne. 2: 26: "And the Messiah cometh in the fulness of time, that he may redeem the children of men from the fall. And because that they are redeemed from the fall they have become free forever, knowing good from evil; to act for themselves and not to be acted upon, save it be by the punishment of the law at the great and last day, according to the commandments which God hath given."

[741] Moroni 7: 16-17: "For behold, the Spirit of Christ is given to every man, that he may know good from evil; wherefore, I show unto you the way to judge; for every thing which inviteth to do good, and to persuade to believe in Christ, is sent forth by the power and gift of Christ; wherefore ye may know with a perfect knowledge it is of God. But whatsoever thing persuadeth men to do evil, and believe not in Christ, and deny him, and serve not God, then ye may know with a perfect knowledge it is of the devil; for after this manner doth the devil work, for he persuadeth no man to do good, no, not one; neither do his angels; neither do they who subject themselves unto him."

[742] Alma 40: 23: "The soul shall be restored to the body, and the body to the soul; yea, and every limb and joint shall be restored to its body; yea, even a hair of the head shall not be lost; but all things shall be restored to their proper and perfect frame."

[743] Alma 41: 13-14: "O, my son, this is not the case; but the meaning of the word restoration is to bring back again evil for evil, or carnal for carnal, or devilish for devilish—good for that which is good; righteous for that which is righteous; just for that which is just; merciful for that which is merciful. Therefore, my son, see that you are merciful unto your brethren; deal justly, judge righteously, and do good continually; and if ye do all these things then shall ye receive your reward; yea, ye shall have mercy restored unto you again; ye shall have justice restored unto you again; ye shall have a righteous judgment restored unto you again; and ye shall have good rewarded unto you again."
Moroni 7: 18-19: "And now, my brethren, seeing that ye know the light by which ye may judge, which light is the light of Christ, see that ye do not judge wrongfully; for with that same judgment which ye judge ye shall also be judged. Wherefore, I beseech of you, brethren, that ye should search diligently in the light of Christ that ye may know good from evil; and if ye will lay hold upon every good thing, and condemn it not, ye certainly will be a child of Christ."

Earth's valuable lessons will remain with you, and inform you eternally with knowledge of good and evil. In this you will have become like God.[744] But the experiences you suffer, which are the means of learning good from evil, will all be removed. You will no longer "mourn" for anything. You will, however, remain accountable for your choices.

This is the perfectly balanced experience. Through it we learn and gain experience[745] but we are only burdened by what we voluntarily impose upon ourselves through our choices.[746] The promised "comfort" against our mourning will be complete if we have chosen to follow Christ, and incomplete if we have chosen to reject Him. Because He can only remove all the burdens of nature and mortality imposed as a condition of life here, He cannot remove those voluntarily assumed by wrong choice while living here.[747]

The balance between necessary experience and accountability is maintained. Through Christ are all things made possible.

3 Nephi 12: 5

"And blessed are the meek, for they shall inherit the earth."

---

[744] Gen. 3: 22: "And the Lord God said, Behold, the man is become as one of us, to know good and evil: and now, lest he put forth his hand, and take also of the tree of life, and eat, and live for ever:"

[745] See Abraham 3.

[746] 1 Ne. 15: 32-33: "And it came to pass that I said unto them that it was a representation of things both temporal and spiritual; for the day should come that they must be judged of their works, yea, even the works which were done by the temporal body in their days of probation. Wherefore, if they should die in their wickedness they must be cast off also, as to the things which are spiritual, which are pertaining to righteousness; wherefore, they must be brought to stand before God, to be judged of their works; and if their works have been filthiness they must needs be filthy; and if they be filthy it must needs be that they cannot dwell in the kingdom of God; if so, the kingdom of God must be filthy also."

[747] Mosiah 16: 8-13: "But there is a resurrection, therefore the grave hath no victory, and the sting of death is swallowed up in Christ. He is the light and the life of the world; yea, a light that is endless, that can never be darkened; yea, and also a life which is endless, that there can be no more death. Even this mortal shall put on immortality, and this corruption shall put on incorruption, and shall be brought to stand before the bar of God, to be judged of him according to their works whether they be good or whether they be evil—If they be good, to the resurrection of endless life and happiness; and if they be evil, to the resurrection of endless damnation, being delivered up to the devil, who hath subjected them, which is damnation—Having gone according to their own carnal wills and desires; having never called upon the Lord while the arms of mercy were extended towards them; for the arms of mercy were extended towards them, and they would not; they being warned of their iniquities and yet they would not depart from them; and they were commanded to repent and yet they would not repent. And now, ought ye not to tremble and repent of your sins, and remember that only in and through Christ ye can be saved?"

This earth abides by a Celestial Law.[748] Therefore, it is destined to become a Celestial Kingdom because it will be sanctified by a Celestial Law.[749] The destiny of the earth is glory.[750] Therefore, to "inherit the earth" is to inherit a Celestial Glory.

Since this is so, you need to understand the definition of "meekness." Elder Hales made these remarks about "meekness" in General Conference: "To be meek, as defined in Webster's dictionary, is 'manifesting patience and longsuffering: enduring injury without resentment.' Meekness is not weakness. It is a badge of Christian courage." (*Christian Courage: The Price of Discipleship*, October 2008 General Conference, Elder Robert D. Hales.)

I've given another explanation in *Beloved Enos*. There I explained it is necessary to be meek first before being trusted with great power. The power to seal on earth and in heaven is something which cannot be handled apart from meekness. Without meekness a man cannot be trusted with such a power. When Enos used the power, he did so meekly. He asked rather than pronounced. He petitioned rather than decreed. Though the Lord would hearken to his words, he refrained from acting.

This is because the proper way to use such authority is only and strictly in conformity with the Lord's will. The reason Nephi received the authority was because he was meek. The account of the conferral is also the account of his qualification:

> "Blessed art thou, Nephi, for those things which thou hast done; for I have beheld how thou hast with unwearyingness declared the word, which I have given unto thee, unto this people. And **thou hast not feared them, and hast not sought thine own life, but hast sought my will, and to keep my commandments**. And now, because thou hast done this with such unwearyingness, behold, I will bless thee forever; and I will make thee mighty in word and in deed, in faith and in works; yea, even that **all things shall be done unto thee**

---

[748] D&C 88: 25: "And again, verily I say unto you, the earth abideth the law of a celestial kingdom, for it filleth the measure of its creation, and transgresseth not the law—"

[749] D&C 88: 25-29: "And again, verily I say unto you, the earth abideth the law of a celestial kingdom, for it filleth the measure of its creation, and transgresseth not the law—Wherefore, it shall be sanctified; yea, notwithstanding it shall die, it shall be quickened again, and shall abide the power by which it is quickened, and the righteous shall inherit it. For notwithstanding they die, they also shall rise again, a spiritual body. They who are of a celestial spirit shall receive the same body which was a natural body; even ye shall receive your bodies, and your glory shall be that glory by which your bodies are quickened. Ye who are quickened by a portion of the celestial glory shall then receive of the same, even a fulness."

[750] D&C 84: 101: "The earth hath travailed and brought forth her strength;
And truth is established in her bowels;
And the heavens have smiled upon her;
And she is clothed with the glory of her God;
For he stands in the midst of his people."

> **according to thy word, for thou shalt not ask that which is contrary to my will**. Behold, thou art Nephi, and I am God. Behold, I declare it unto thee in the presence of mine angels, that ye shall have power over this people, and shall smite the earth with famine, and with pestilence, and destruction, according to the wickedness of this people. Behold, **I give unto you power, that whatsoever ye shall seal on earth shall be sealed in heaven; and whatsoever ye shall loose on earth shall be loosed in heaven**; and thus shall ye have power among this people. And thus, if ye shall say unto this temple it shall be rent in twain, it shall be done. And if ye shall say unto this mountain, Be thou cast down and become smooth, it shall be done. And behold, if ye shall say that God shall smite this people, it shall come to pass.**And now behold, I command you, that ye shall go and declare unto this people, that thus saith the Lord God, who is the Almighty: Except ye repent ye shall be smitten, even unto destruction**." (Helaman 10: 4-11.)

This is meekness. First, Nephi had conducted his life meekly. He did not fear others. He was not afraid to lose his standing, even his life. He kept God's commandments to him above all else. He possessed an iron will, his face like flint, unwilling to waiver from what the Lord would have him say and do. He could not be tempted to betray the Lord's will. Therefore, the Lord knew by the way Nephi lived his life that he would "not ask that which is contrary to [the Lord's] will." Never.

Therefore, when the Lord had tried him and determined he was willing to serve Him at all costs, he qualifies to receive trust from God. That trust allows the Lord to confer upon the man great power. (See also TPJS p. 150: "After a person has faith in Christ, repents of his sins, is baptized for the remission of his sins, and receives the Holy Ghost (by the laying on of hands), which is the first Comforter, then let him continue to humble himself before God, hungering and thirsting after righteousness and living by every word of God. The Lord will soon say unto him, 'Son, thou shalt be exalted.' When the Lord has thoroughly proved him and finds that the man is determined to serve him at all hazards, then the man will find his calling and election made sure.")

Meekness is required to qualify for great power. And you know a man is meek when, having great power, he uses it strictly in conformity with the Lord's will; never varying from the Lord's command, and never pursuing his own agenda. This kind of meekness is men is a rare thing. Nephi, after receiving that power, was instructed that he was to deliver the Lord's message: "thus saith the Lord God, who is Almighty: Except ye repent ye shall be smitten, even unto destruction." It is the Lord's judgment. It is a meek man who delivers it. But such judgments only come after the Lord has a meek soul upon whom He can place this trust.

For He has covenanted to always first employ such a servant before imposing judgments upon mankind.[751]

Therefore, when the Lord teaches the "meek shall inherit the earth" it is a statement which includes exaltation for the meek. It is one of the Lord's deepest teachings, and most profound descriptions of those who will be exalted and why.

3 Nephi 12: 6

> **"And blessed are all they who do hunger and thirst after righteousness, for they shall be filled with the Holy Ghost."**

This is not about hunger or poverty. This is about fasting and seeking after righteousness.

You qualify for this blessing by hungering "after righteousness." You qualify by thirsting "after righteousness." In other words, you receive the Holy Ghost in proportion to the hunger and thirst you display to receiving it.

Fasting is a promised means for increasing the Holy Ghost in your life. We read this about Alma when he served as High Priest over the church: "And this is not all. Do ye not suppose that I know of these things myself? Behold, I testify unto you that I do know that these things whereof I have spoken are true. And how do ye suppose that I know of their surety? Behold, I say unto you **they are made known unto me by the Holy Spirit of God. Behold, I have fasted and prayed many days that I might know these things of myself**. And now I do know of myself that they are true; for the Lord God hath made them manifest unto me by his Holy Spirit; and this is the spirit of revelation which is in me. And moreover, I say unto you that it has thus been revealed unto me, that the words which have been spoken by our fathers are true, even so according to the spirit of prophecy which is in me, which is also by the manifestation of the Spirit of God." (Alma 5: 45-47.)

Fasting and praying opens the Spirit. It allows you to know a matter through the power of the Holy Ghost. Again, we read this about the Sons of Mosiah who were completing their service as missionaries: "…Alma did rejoice exceedingly to see his brethren; and what added more to his joy, they were still his brethren in the Lord; yea, and they had waxed strong in the knowledge of the truth; for they were men of a sound understanding and they had searched the scriptures diligently, that they might know the word of God. But this is not all; **they had given themselves to much prayer, and fasting; therefore they had the spirit of prophecy, and the spirit of revelation, and when they taught, they taught with power and authority of God**." (Alma 17: 2-3) They not only searched the scriptures, but they also spent time

[751] Amos 3: 7: "Surely the Lord God will do nothing, but he revealeth his secret unto his servants the prophets."

praying and fasting, that they might show God their earnest commitment to know the truth. The result was the "spirit of prophecy, and the spirit of revelation." Or, in other words, they were filled with the Holy Ghost.

The Lord speaks in simple formulas. They work; when tried in sincerity, acting no hypocrisy, with real intent, they work. Half-hearted efforts are not so effective. But when a soul, any soul, hungers and thirsts after righteousness, they are filled with the Holy Ghost.

This sometimes presents a problem for those who have medical conditions which prevent them from fasting. In *The Second Comforter,* I've suggested there are other ways to subordinate the desires of the flesh as a way to "hunger and thirst" while keeping medical needs satisfied. Reducing calories, or doing without some other thing as a form of "fasting" can be substituted. The decision would be between you and the Lord, but there are always ways provided for meeting what the Lord asks, including fasting by those who are medically unable.[752]

This sermon is a blue-print of the Lord's new charter for mankind. It is the new, higher way ofliving. It is intended to result in a new spiritual life for those willing to live it. Therefore you should not dismiss "hunger and thirst for righteousness" as something trivial. If you are among those who does not believe the Lord speaks with them, take these invitations from the Lord seriously. They are designed to reconnect you with God. They have the power to accomplish it.

Also, in the case of the Sons of Mosiah, there was actual "power" which came through this means. These missionaries could teach "with power and authority of God" because of their fasting, prayer and study of scripture.

3 Nephi 12: 7

"And blessed are the merciful, for they shall obtain mercy."

The standard applied to us is the standard we apply to others. This is repeatedly set out in scripture:

Alma teaching his son Corianton recorded: "Therefore, my son, see that you are merciful unto your brethren; deal justly, judge righteously, and do good continually; and if ye do all these things then shall ye receive your reward; yea, ye shall have mercy restored unto you again; ye shall have justice restored unto you again; ye shall have a righteous judgment restored unto you again; and ye shall have good rewarded unto you again. For that which ye do send out shall return unto you again, and be restored; therefore, the word restoration more fully condemneth the sinner, and justifieth him not at all." (Alma 41: 14-15.)

---

752 1 Ne. 3: 7: "And it came to pass that I, Nephi, said unto my father: I will go and do the things which the Lord hath commanded, for I know that the Lord giveth no commandments unto the children of men, save he shall prepare a way for them that they may accomplish the thing which he commandeth them."

Moroni's final discussion about the Gospel included these words: "And now, my brethren, seeing that ye know the light by which ye may judge, which light is the light of Christ, see that ye do not judge wrongfully; for with that same judgment which ye judge ye shall also be judged." (Moroni 7: 18.)

Peter asked a practical question about the extent of forgiving others. He wanted a mathematical limit to be set. The Lord, however, raised the limit beyond an ability to reasonably count: "Then came Peter to him, and said, Lord, how oft shall my brother sin against me, and I forgive him? till seven times? Jesus saith unto him, I say not unto thee, Until seven times: but, Until seventy times seven." (Matt. 18: 21-22.)

There are others. I'd commend the chapter on the Atonement in *Come, Let Us Adore Him* for a more complete explanation of this doctrine.

If you want mercy from the Lord, you must give it to your fellow man. If you do not show mercy to your fellow man, the Lord cannot provide it to you. There is a law which binds the Lord to the same standard you set for yourself. It is an irrevocable law. Therefore, the Lord teaches us to show mercy so that we might merit mercy. We are the final beneficiaries of all the mercy we show to others.

It really is true that "what you send out shall return unto you again," to quote Alma. This is called "karma" in another faith. It is a true principle. Perhaps it operates within an larger time frame than just this life, but it operates, nonetheless. Alma knew the truth and was teaching it to his son.

It was Laban's judgment of Nephi and his brothers that got him killed. I've discussed this in *The Second Comforter*. It was his decision that a robber was worthy of death[753] which sealed his fate. For when he became a robber[754], then the Lord was free to show him the same judgment he had rendered.[755] Sometimes what you send out returns to you again in this life

3 Nephi 12: 8

"And blessed are all the pure in heart, for they shall see God."

---

[753] 1 Ne. 3: 13: "And behold, it came to pass that Laban was angry, and thrust him out from his presence; and he would not that he should have the records. Wherefore, he said unto him: Behold thou art a robber, and I will slay thee."

[754] 1 Ne. 3: 25: "And it came to pass that when Laban saw our property, and that it was exceedingly great, he did lust after it, insomuch that he thrust us out, and sent his servants to slay us, that he might obtain our property."

[755] 1 Ne. 4: 11: "And the Spirit said unto me again: Behold the Lord hath delivered him into thy hands. Yea, and I also knew that he had sought to take away mine own life; yea, and he would not hearken unto the commandments of the Lord; and he also had taken away our property."

This is a remarkable promise. Would you like to see God? Then first purify your heart.

Notice this is not just ritual purity, which had been the focus of the Law of Moses. Christ is replacing earlier ritual based purity with internal purity.

He speaks about the heart, rather than the hands and feet. Christ is speaking about beholding God, unlike the retreat Israel took from the offered opportunity at Sinai.[756] He is returning to the time of Moses, when a higher way might have been chosen.

Purity of the heart is a borrowed benefit from the Savior. Man cannot become clean before God without the necessary offering of a sacrifice. The Law of Moses taught this, but Christ would actually bring it to pass.[757]

Christ's atonement cleanses us.[758]

When we repent we turn to Christ and listen to and follow Him. Until then, we are not even facing the right direction in life.

Some reminders of how the heart may be purified:

- Let virtue constantly prevail in your thoughts.[759]

- Pray to the Father with a devoted heart.[760]

---

[756] D&C 84: 22-25: "For without this no man can see the face of God, even the Father, and live. Now this Moses plainly taught to the children of Israel in the wilderness, and sought diligently to sanctify his people that they might behold the face of God; But they hardened their hearts and could not endure his presence; therefore, the Lord in his wrath, for his anger was kindled against them, swore that they should not enter into his rest while in the wilderness, which rest is the fulness of his glory. Therefore, he took Moses out of their midst, and the Holy Priesthood also;"

[757] Alma 34: 36: "And this I know, because the Lord hath said he dwelleth not in unholy temples, but in the hearts of the righteous doth he dwell; yea, and he has also said that the righteous shall sit down in his kingdom, to go no more out; but their garments should be made white through the blood of the Lamb."

[758] Alma 13: 11: "Therefore they were called after this holy order, and were sanctified, and their garments were washed white through the blood of the Lamb."
Ether 13: 10: "And then cometh the New Jerusalem; and blessed are they who dwell therein, for it is they whose garments are white through the blood of the Lamb; and they are they who are numbered among the remnant of the seed of Joseph, who were of the house of Israel."

[759] D&C 121: 45: "Let thy bowels also be full of charity towards all men, and to the household of faith, and let virtue garnish thy thoughts unceasingly; then shall thy confidence wax strong in the presence of God; and the doctrine of the priesthood shall distil upon thy soul as the dews from heaven."

[760] Moroni 7: 48: "Wherefore, my beloved brethren, pray unto the Father with all the energy of heart, that ye may be filled with this love, which he hath bestowed upon all who are true followers of his Son, Jesus Christ; that ye may become the sons of God; that when he shall appear we shall be like him, for we shall see him as he is; that we may have this hope; that we may be purified even as he is pure. Amen."

- Repent and call upon God with a contrite spirit, asking the atonement to be applied to your sins.[761]
- Fast and pray often, that you may become humble.[762]
- Follow what light you have to receive more light, until you have the "perfect day" in which you are a vessel of light.[763]

It is also interesting that what must be "pure" is the "heart." There are so many other things one might measure. But what the Lord looks upon to determine purity is the "heart."

I've said that there is almost nothing about us that can become perfect in this life. The only thing that can approach perfection, however, is our intent. We can mean to follow God at all times. Even if the dilemmas of life make it impossible to actually do so, we can still intend to follow Him. We may not even know if what we are doing pleases Him, or how to resolve conflicting interests or commandments. We may even be making a mistake, but if our intent is right, our hearts may be pure.

This is also one of the reasons we cannot judge another. They may be weak, foolish and error prone, but if they intend to be doing the right then God alone can measure their heart and decide whether they are approved. It would take a God to know if the person's life, training, understanding and intent are pure before Him. I suspect there are those we look upon as deluded and even evil but the Lord views them with compassion and understanding. He may find their hearts to be perfect even before the heart of the proud who claim they have and follow the truth. Though a person may misunderstand a great deal, still if they have love for their fellow man, relieve suffering where they can, give

---

[761] Mosiah 4: 2: "And they had viewed themselves in their own carnal state, even less than the dust of the earth. And they all cried aloud with one voice, saying: O have mercy, and apply the atoning blood of Christ that we may receive forgiveness of our sins, and our hearts may be purified; for we believe in Jesus Christ, the Son of God, who created heaven and earth, and all things; who shall come down among the children of men."

[762] Hel. 3: 35: "Nevertheless they did fast and pray oft, and did wax stronger and stronger in their humility, and firmer and firmer in the faith of Christ, unto the filling their souls with joy and consolation, yea, even to the purifying and the sanctification of their hearts, which sanctification cometh because of their yielding their hearts unto God."

[763] D&C 50: 24: "That which is of God is light; and he that receiveth light, and continueth in God, receiveth more light; and that light groweth brighter and brighter until the perfect day."
D&C 93: 28: "He that keepeth his commandments receiveth truth and light, until he is glorified in truth and knoweth all things."

patience to the foolish and water to the thirsty, they may be perfect before God.[764]

There are so many illusions here. Some who are regarded as high and lifted up by God, temperate in their conduct, studying how they are seen by others before acting; are in fact wretched, miserable, poor and naked.[765] I say with authority that there are some regarded as the very chiefest of the righteous among the Latter-day Saints who are before God wretched, miserable, poor and naked. They cannot survive even a glance from His all seeing eye. Yet they pretend they share in His vision, when they do not.

How few hearts are pure before God. How rare a thing it is to contemplate such a person. How few we produce in this restoration of the Gospel. We remain as a people too low, too mean, too vulgar, too condescending to be called of God. No wonder we stumble and fall backward and many are taken in snares.[766]

3 Nephi 12: 9

> **"And blessed are all the peacemakers, for they shall be called the children of God."**

---

[764] Luke 18: 9-14: "And he spake this parable unto certain which trusted in themselves that they were righteous, and despised others: Two men went up into the temple to pray; the one a Pharisee, and the other a publican. The Pharisee stood and prayed thus with himself, God, I thank thee, that I am not as other men *are,* extortioners, unjust, adulterers, or even as this publican. I fast twice in the week, I give tithes of all that I possess. And the publican, standing afar off, would not lift up so much as *his* eyes unto heaven, but smote upon his breast, saying, God be merciful to me a sinner. I tell you, this man went down to his house justified *rather* than the other: for every one that exalteth himself shall be abased; and he that humbleth himself shall be exalted."

[765] Rev. 3: 14-17: "And unto the angel of the church of the Laodiceans write; These things saith the Amen, the faithful and true witness, the beginning of the creation of God; I know thy works, that thou art neither cold nor hot: I would thou wert cold or hot. So then because thou art lukewarm, and neither cold nor hot, I will spue thee out of my mouth. Because thou sayest, I am rich, and increased with goods, and have need of nothing; and knowest not that thou art wretched, and miserable, and poor, and blind, and naked:"

[766] Isa. 8: 11-17: "For the Lord spake thus to me with a strong hand, and instructed me that I should not walk in the way of this people, saying, Say ye not, A confederacy, to all *them to* whom this people shall say, A confederacy; neither fear ye their fear, nor be afraid. Sanctify the Lord of hosts himself; and *let* him *be* your fear, and *let* him *be* your dread. And he shall be for a sanctuary; but for a stone of stumbling and for a rock of offence to both the houses of Israel, for a gin and for a snare to the inhabitants of Jerusalem. And many among them shall stumble, and fall, and be broken, and be snared, and be taken. Bind up the testimony, seal the law among my disciples. And I will wait upon the Lord, that hideth his face from the house of Jacob, and I will look for him."

More often than not those who are "peacemakers" will be abused. They will at least have to endure aggression and give a soft word in return.[767] There will be no end to the peace which comes from Christ because there was no end to the suffering He was willing to endure.[768]

When we hearken to the Lord's commandments we have peace like a river flowing.[769] This is because the "Lord shall fight for you, and ye shall hold your peace." (Ex. 14: 14.) The Lord will fight Zion's battles.[770]

When a man is right before God, even his enemies are at peace with him.[771] At least until his time comes and his mission is completed.[772]

When the Lord was taken with violence and crucified, He was at peace.[773] He purchased peace through what He suffered. He alone can share that with all.[774]

Through Him, the "peacemakers" have found this peace. This is why they have become His "children" for He has begotten them.[775]

---

[767] Prov. 15: 1: "A Soft answer turneth away wrath: but grievous words stir up anger."

[768] Isa. 9: 7: "Of the increase of *his* government and peace *there shall be* no end, upon the throne of David, and upon his kingdom, to order it, and to establish it with judgment and with justice from henceforth even for ever. The zeal of the Lord of hosts will perform this."

[769] Isa. 48: 18: "O that thou hadst hearkened to my commandments! then had thy peace been as a river, and thy righteousness as the waves of the sea:"

[770] D&C 105: 14: "For behold, I do not require at their hands to fight the battles of Zion; for, as I said in a former commandment, even so will I fulfil—I will fight your battles."

[771] Prov. 16: 7: "When a man's ways please the Lord, he maketh even his enemies to be at peace with him."

[772] D&C 122: 9: "Therefore, hold on thy way, and the priesthood shall remain with thee; for their bounds are set, they cannot pass. Thy days are known, and thy years shall not be numbered less; therefore, fear not what man can do, for God shall be with you forever and ever."
John 19: 10-11: "Then saith Pilate unto him, Speakest thou not unto me? knowest thou not that I have power to crucify thee, and have power to release thee? Jesus answered, Thou couldest have no power *at all* against me, except it were given thee from above: therefore he that delivered me unto thee hath the greater sin."

[773] Luke 23: 24: "And Pilate gave sentence that it should be as they required."

[774] Isa. 53: 5: "But he *was* wounded for our transgressions, *he was* bruised for our iniquities: the chastisement of our peace *was* upon him; and with his stripes we are healed."

[775] Mosiah 27: 25: "And the Lord said unto me: Marvel not that all mankind, yea, men and women, all nations, kindreds, tongues and people, must be born again; yea, born of God, changed from their carnal and fallen state, to a state of righteousness, being redeemed of God, becoming his sons and daughters;"

In a world of violence and abuse, it is peace we seek. But that peace comes only to the children of God and only because they know they are the children of God. At their rebirth, they are at rest from the cares of this dreary world, and informed by a better promise of things to come.[776]

Those who bring peace bring hope to this world. This world is filled with tribulation, but the Lord has overcome this world.[777] Many have experienced this peace, become children of God, and then been persecuted, hated, reviled and killed.[778]

Peace is a gift from Christ, and His peace is for this world and for the world to come.[779]

---

[776] See discussion on Alma 13: 29.
Alma 13: 29: "Having faith on the Lord; having a hope that ye shall receive eternal life; having the love of God always in your hearts, that ye may be lifted up at the last day and enter into his rest."
Moroni 7: 3: "Wherefore, I would speak unto you that are of the church, that are the peaceable followers of Christ, and that have obtained a sufficient hope by which ye can enter into the rest of the Lord, from this time henceforth until ye shall rest with him in heaven."

[777] John 16: 33: "These things I have spoken unto you, that in me ye might have peace. In the world ye shall have tribulation: but be of good cheer; I have overcome the world."

[778] Heb. 11: 33-35: "Who through faith subdued kingdoms, wrought righteousness, obtained promises, stopped the mouths of lions, Quenched the violence of fire, escaped the edge of the sword, out of weakness were made strong, waxed valiant in fight, turned to flight the armies of the aliens. Women received their dead raised to life again: and others were tortured, not accepting deliverance; that they might obtain a better resurrection:"

[779] John 14: 27: "Peace I leave with you, my peace I give unto you: not as the world giveth, give I unto you. Let not your heart be troubled, neither let it be afraid."

But the promise of triumph is hereafter, when the world can no longer make any claim upon a child of God.[780]

Though a man may declare peace, the world will not be at peace until the Lord slays the wicked.[781] Peace, as all other sacred things in our day, must be internal. We live in a day of overwhelming ignorance, foolishness and wickedness. It is not possible to obtain peace except on the terms which allow it. If you live those, you will have peace. But the world will not live them with you.

Patrick Henry put the problem of peace in this world into immortal words: "Gentlemen may cry, Peace, Peace——but there is no peace. The war is actually begun! The next gale that sweeps from the north will bring to our ears the clash of resounding arms! Our brethren are already in the field! Why stand we here idle? What is it that gentlemen wish? What would they have? Is life so dear, or peace so sweet, as to be purchased at the price of chains and slavery? Forbid it, Almighty God! I

---

[780] D&C 122: 4: "And although their influence shall cast thee into trouble, and into bars and walls, thou shalt be had in honor; and but for a small moment and thy voice shall be more terrible in the midst of thine enemies than the fierce lion, because of thy righteousness; and thy God shall stand by thee forever and ever."
D&C 135: 6-7: "Hyrum Smith was forty-four years old in February, 1844, and Joseph Smith was thirty-eight in December, 1843; and henceforward their names will be classed among the martyrs of religion; and the reader in every nation will be reminded that the Book of Mormon, and this book of Doctrine and Covenants of the church, cost the best blood of the nineteenth century to bring them forth for the salvation of a ruined world; and that if the fire can scathe a green tree for the glory of God, how easy it will burn up the dry trees to purify the vineyard of corruption. They lived for glory; they died for glory; and glory is their eternal reward. From age to age shall their names go down to posterity as gems for the sanctified. They were innocent of any crime, as they had often been proved before, and were only confined in jail by the conspiracy of traitors and wicked men; and their *innocent blood* on the floor of Carthage jail is a broad seal affixed to "Mormonism" that cannot be rejected by any court on earth, and their *innocent blood* on the escutcheon of the State of Illinois, with the broken faith of the State as pledged by the governor, is a witness to the truth of the everlasting gospel that all the world cannot impeach; and their *innocent blood* on the banner of liberty, and on the *magna charta* of the United States, is an ambassador for the religion of Jesus Christ, that will touch the hearts of honest men among all nations; and their *innocent blood,* with the innocent blood of all the martyrs under the altar that John saw, will cry unto the Lord of Hosts till he avenges that blood on the earth. Amen."

[781] Rev. 19: 11-16: "And I saw heaven opened, and behold a white horse; and he that sat upon him *was* called Faithful and True, and in righteousness he doth judge and make war. His eyes *were* as a flame of fire, and on his head *were* many crowns; and he had a name written, that no man knew, but he himself. And he *was* clothed with a vesture dipped in blood: and his name is called The Word of God. And the armies *which were* in heaven followed him upon white horses, clothed in fine linen, white and clean. And out of his mouth goeth a sharp sword, that with it he should smite the nations: and he shall rule them with a rod of iron: and he treadeth the winepress of the fierceness and wrath of Almighty God. And he hath on *his* vesture and on his thigh a name written, KING OF KINGS, AND LORD OF LORDS."

know not what course others may take; but as for me, give me liberty or give me death!"

The war remains today, but now it is against all righteousness. We wrestle not against flesh and blood, but against spiritual wickedness in high places.[782] Elder Packer cannot even preach a sermon to a congregation of Saints belonging to a church over which he holds office without the anger and vilification of the homosexual community and others being aroused.

If you are to find peace, and to become a peacemaker here, then it is through the Gospel of Jesus Christ. The world will not know peace again until He returns. To be a child of God and know peace is, in our day, to cry repentance and to bring others to Christ.

3 Nephi 12: 10

> **"And blessed are all they who are persecuted for my name's sake, for theirs is the kingdom of heaven."**

It is not just persecution, but persecution "for [His] name's sake" that makes you blessed. When you are doing what you should for His name's sake, you are likely to provoke persecution. He will later explain this is almost inevitable. It won't be because you are provoking it by your obnoxious behavior. It is because people will question your sincerity and commitment. The world expects hypocrites. They regard everyone with suspicion. And, let's face it, most charlatans adopt religion as one of their cloaks. We'll get to that a little further into this sermon from the Lord.

The kind of persecution which produces the "kingdom of heaven" is, of course, martyrdom. Originally the word "martyr" meant witness, but so many of the early Christian witnesses were killed that it came to have the modern meaning, that is one who dies for their faith.

Martyrs were seen in John's vision below the altar of God.[783] This of course means they were holy because of their sacrifice. The heavenly altar being a symbol of them having shed their blood as witnesses.

---

[782] Eph. 6: 12: "For we wrestle not against flesh and blood, but against principalities, against powers, against the rulers of the darkness of this world, against spiritual wickedness in high *places.*"

[783] Rev. 6: 9: "And when he had opened the fifth seal, I saw under the altar the souls of them that were slain for the word of God, and for the testimony which they held:"

Joseph Smith and Hyrum joined those who qualified for such a witness.[784]

Zenos, author of the Olive Tree allegory,[785] prophet of the three days of darkness upon the isles of the sea, witness of the Lord's burial in a sepulcher[786] seven centuries before His birth, was slain for his testimony.[787]

Stephen was killed for his testimony but clearly inherited the kingdom of heaven.[788]

There are many others, including Able, Isaiah, Peter, Paul and Abinadi.

Blessed are those who are willing to endure persecution for His name's sake. For they are those who are willing develop faith which cannot be obtained in any other way. It is through the sacrifice of all things that faith necessary for salvation is developed. Read again the post on Lecture 6 of the Lectures on Faith on April 21, 2010.

---

[784] D&C 135: 7: "They were innocent of any crime, as they had often been proved before, and were only confined in jail by the conspiracy of traitors and wicked men; and their *innocent blood* on the floor of Carthage jail is a broad seal affixed to "Mormonism" that cannot be rejected by any court on earth, and their *innocent blood* on the escutcheon of the State of Illinois, with the broken faith of the State as pledged by the governor, is a witness to the truth of the everlasting gospel that all the world cannot impeach; and their *innocent blood* on the banner of liberty, and on the *magna charta* of the United States, is an ambassador for the religion of Jesus Christ, that will touch the hearts of honest men among all nations; and their *innocent blood,* with the innocent blood of all the martyrs under the altar that John saw, will cry unto the Lord of Hosts till he avenges that blood on the earth. Amen."

[785] Jacob 5: 1: "Behold, my brethren, do ye not remember to have read the words of the prophet Zenos, which he spake unto the house of Israel, saying:"

[786] And the God of our fathers, who were led out of Egypt, out of bondage, and also were preserved in the wilderness by him, yea, the God of Abraham, and of Isaac, and the God of Jacob, yieldeth himself, according to the words of the angel, as a man, into the hands of wicked men, to be lifted up, according to the words of Zenock, and to be crucified, according to the words of Neum, and to be buried in a sepulchre, according to the words of Zenos, which he spake concerning the three days of darkness, which should be a sign given of his death unto those who should inhabit the isles of the sea, more especially given unto those who are of the house of Israel.

[787] Hel. 8: 19: "And now I would that ye should know, that even since the days of Abraham there have been many prophets that have testified these things; yea, behold, the prophet Zenos did testify boldly; for the which he was slain."

[788] Acts 7: 55-59: "But he, being full of the Holy Ghost, looked up stedfastly into heaven, and saw the glory of God, and Jesus standing on the right hand of God, And said, Behold, I see the heavens opened, and the Son of man standing on the right hand of God. Then they cried out with a loud voice, and stopped their ears, and ran upon him with one accord, And cast *him* out of the city, and stoned *him:* and the witnesses laid down their clothes at a young man's feet, whose name was Saul. And they stoned Stephen, calling upon *God*, and saying, Lord Jesus, receive my spirit."

Beginning with faith to follow Him, then enduring persecution as a result, to offering the sacrifice necessary to develop faith, then inheriting the kingdom of heaven, the Gospel of Christ is one great whole.

Sometimes we bring persecution upon ourselves because we are unwise. The Lord will address that. We are to take offenses, but not give them. When we unwisely give offenses and cause persecution, that is not for His name's sake. There is a balance between wisdom and righteousness.

As an aside on the subject of persecution I wanted to add this:

I've thought about Elder Packer's talk and the homosexual community's reaction to it. Elder Packer was right, and he was addressing a community of believers who look to him for teachings like the ones given in that talk. Nobody ought to take offense at that. If you can prevent Elder Packer's teaching in that setting, then you can invade and stop talk in any setting on any subject.

However, nothing in that talk would encourage or justify invading the privacy and causing the shame visited upon the Rutgers University student who committed suicide. The invasion of his privacy was cruel, the act of publicizing it was a calculated act of terrible insult. His grief, despair and subsequent suicide are the fault of those who invaded his privacy and exposed his weakness. It was wrong. Elder Packer's talk was to benefit a community of believers, not to persecute an audience of unbelievers.

I have friends I ride Harley's with who have absolutely no interest in Mormonism. One of my dear friends hates my church, thinks it barbaric and unenlightened. But that does not stop our mutual friendship nor define the areas about which we find common ground. Another person's differing views are only offensive when they demand I accede to them. If they will suspend judgment against me because of my faith, I am willing to suspend judgment against them because of theirs. This ought to define the boundaries of conduct, not militant demands for conceding the argument on questions of faith and belief. I can believe that my friend's lifestyle is corrupt and even immoral. But so long as he does not expect me to join him, I am pleased to be a friend, share what we have in common, and leave our differences for polite disagreement.

There are some sins I simply do not understand. But if my friendship may help someone to understand my faith, then I would sooner be friends with someone of another faith than one of my own. I do not expect many people to accept what I believe. In fact, I think there are very few fellow Latter-day Saints who believe or understand the Gospel as I do. If I were to limit my friends to those with whom I have everything in common, then my wife and children alone would be my friends.

Elder Packer should have the right to speak and preach the truth as he understands it. Those who would censor him are wrong.

If he is mistaken, then point out his error in a kindly way and seek to reclaim him. But condemning, protesting and attacking only shows intolerance and coercion which all of us have a responsibility to resist and condemn. It is wrong when the homosexual community does it, and it is wrong when the church does it. Win the argument with persuasion and strong reasoning. Yelling, condemning and protesting only attempts to silence thought, not to provoke it into correct understanding.

Now I'm off topic…

3 Nephi 12: 11-12

> **"And blessed are ye when men shall revile you and persecute, and shall say all manner of evil against you falsely, for my sake; For ye shall have great joy and be exceedingly glad, for great shall be your reward in heaven; for so persecuted they the prophets who were before you."**

If your actions are misjudged, that is only normal. There have been charlatans using religion to cloak their evil deeds from the beginning of time. They are so widespread, so often exposed for what they really are, that humanity has a legitimate skepticism about those who come in the name of the Lord.

From Jimmy Swaggart's prostitutes to Ted Haggard's homosexual encounters, the evangelical world has been rocked by the sexual misconduct of ministers. Catholic priesthood sexual abuse has been so widespread that there is a whole legal industry devoted to bringing and defending claims from victims of that abuse. The LDS Church has quietly settled a number of claims on both coasts and adjusted how membership records are documented and what precautions are taken when calling a man to teach in Primary because of sexual misconduct and associated legal claims.

The Burt Lancaster film *Elmer Gantry* was based on the Sinclair Lewis novel and illustrated the life and deeds of a false prophet. Indeed, the term "prophet" is rarely used in modern vernacular outside of LDS circles unless coupled with the term "false." "False prophet" is expected. What is unexpected is the contrary.

So when first reactions are taken, it will always be to sneer, to jeer, to mock and to suspect those who come in the name of the Lord. They are right to do that. Everyone OUGHT to question motives. Everyone OUGHT to think you're a fraud. They should expect you are like all those others in whom society trusted. No one wants to follow Jim Jones to their death, drinking strychnine laced Kool-Aid in another mass-suicide. That has happened too often already. Indeed, the fruits of such false prophets have been so devastating, so evil, so wrong in spirit and result that only a fool would be eager to trust you even should you have a pure heart and a true message.

The first reaction should be skepticism which will result in an attempt to measure your sincerity. Until you've been tested by the world, there is no reason for the world to believe anything you have to say. They will revile you, thinking you just another fraud. They will persecute you as if a charlatan, though you are His disciple. They will say all manner of evil against you falsely, all the while thinking they are only giving you what you deserve.

This is how the world decides if you are following Him. They have seen and heard no end of those who have claimed to follow Him, and you are no different in their eyes. That is, until you have actually followed Him; borne their criticism, returned good for evil, and shown how devoted you are in fact, as Christ will address in coming verses. When you have proven your devotion, then some few will soften their hearts. Others will remain unwilling to admit the truth, even when it is apparent you are His.

This is the way in which Christ lived His life. These teachings are an explanation of Him. And, in turn, it is also an explanation of the lives of any who follow Him. To follow Him, and to learn of His ways always requires experiencing some of what He experienced. While He assumed a full measure of these teachings, we are required to experience some of what He did only to allow us to understand Him. But these teachings are meant to be lived. They are meant to be applied and tested. If you test them, you will discover Him through them.

You will also come to know and understand the prophets who went before. This is a timeless brotherhood. Some of them invariably also come to succor their fellow Saint. This is always the same when the fullness of the Gospel of Jesus Christ is lived on the earth.

3 Nephi 12: 13

> **"Verily, verily, I say unto you, I give unto you to be the salt of the earth; but if the salt shall lose its savor wherewith shall the earth be salted? The salt shall be thenceforth good for nothing, but to be cast out and to be trodden under foot of men."**

Salt is a preservative, but in this case it is for the culinary benefit. It produces "savor." That is, the taste of the whole is affected by the presence of a little.

You don't need much to preserve the whole. Abraham's negotiation to preserve Sodom demonstrated that only a little of the "salt" is required for an entire population to receive the Lord's blessings.[789] ***Progress*** is enough in our day.[790] As long as the wheat is still growing, it is enough.

How can salt "lose its savor" except through contamination or impurities? When that is lost, the salt cannot preserve. There is no remaining savor. Then the salt is nothing more than common dirt, to be cast aside and trodden under foot.

---

789 Gen. 18: 17-33: "And the Lord said, Shall I hide from Abraham that thing which I do; Seeing that Abraham shall surely become a great and mighty nation, and all the nations of the earth shall be blessed in him? For I know him, that he will command his children and his household after him, and they shall keep the way of the Lord, to do justice and judgment; that the Lord may bring upon Abraham that which he hath spoken of him. And the Lord said, Because the cry of Sodom and Gomorrah is great, and because their sin is very grievous; I will go down now, and see whether they have done altogether according to the cry of it, which is come unto me; and if not, I will know. And the men turned their faces from thence, and went toward Sodom: but Abraham stood yet before the Lord. And Abraham drew near, and said, Wilt thou also destroy the righteous with the wicked? Peradventure there be fifty righteous within the city: wilt thou also destroy and not spare the place for the fifty righteous that *are* therein? That be far from thee to do after this manner, to slay the righteous with the wicked: and that the righteous should be as the wicked, that be far from thee: Shall not the Judge of all the earth do right? And the Lord said, If I find in Sodom fifty righteous within the city, then I will spare all the place for their sakes. And Abraham answered and said, Behold now, I have taken upon me to speak unto the Lord, which *am but* dust and ashes: Peradventure there shall lack five of the fifty righteous: wilt thou destroy all the city for *lack of* five? And he said, If I find there forty and five, I will not destroy *it*. And he spake unto him yet again, and said, Peradventure there shall be forty found there. And he said, I will not do *it* for forty's sake. And he said *unto him,* Oh let not the Lord be angry, and I will speak: Peradventure there shall thirty be found there. And he said, I will not do *it,* if I find thirty there. And he said, Behold now, I have taken upon me to speak unto the Lord: Peradventure there shall be twenty found there. And he said, I will not destroy *it* for twenty's sake. And he said, Oh let not the Lord be angry, and I will speak yet but this once: Peradventure ten shall be found there. And he said, I will not destroy *it* for ten's sake. And the Lord went his way, as soon as he had left communing with Abraham: and Abraham returned unto his place."

790 Luke 13: 30: "And, behold, there are last which shall be first, and there are first which shall be last."

This is the gentile predicament in the last days. They will, of course, lose their savor. They will reject the fullness offered to them.[791] When they do, they will be torn apart and trodden under foot.[792]

Notice it is the Lord who "gives unto you to be the salt of the earth." This condition is a gift from God. Through repentance, or turning to Him, you can receive this. Without repentance you cannot become the salt.

There are no private lives. Every life counts. Your private devotions are more important than your public notice. The salt which preserves may be unknown, likely is unknown, to most people. But if you are the salt, then your private life of devotion to the Lord is saving the lives of many others. The angels want to begin the harvest. They are impatient to begin reaping and cutting down the wicked now.[793] There is only time given because of a few who deserve more time to grow in faith before the harvest begins.[794] Your growth is all that is keeping the harvest from beginning now. Therefore, how you proceed has consequences far beyond your own life.

When wheat is ripe it will be protected. When tares are ripe they will be burned. But the tender plants worthy of preservation are the only ones allowed more time.[795] I advocate for them and realize how tenuous

---

791 3 Ne. 16: 10: "And thus commandeth the Father that I should say unto you: At that day when the Gentiles shall sin against my gospel, and shall reject the fulness of my gospel, and shall be lifted up in the pride of their hearts above all nations, and above all the people of the whole earth, and shall be filled with all manner of lyings, and of deceits, and of mischiefs, and all manner of hypocrisy, and murders, and priestcrafts, and whoredoms, and of secret abominations; and if they shall do all those things, and shall reject the fulness of my gospel, behold, saith the Father, I will bring the fulness of my gospel from among them."

792 3 Ne. 20: 16: "Then shall ye, who are a remnant of the house of Jacob, go forth among them; and ye shall be in the midst of them who shall be many; and ye shall be among them as a lion among the beasts of the forest, and as a young lion among the flocks of sheep, who, if he goeth through both treadeth down and teareth in pieces, and none can deliver."
3 Ne. 21: 12: "And my people who are a remnant of Jacob shall be among the Gentiles, yea, in the midst of them as a lion among the beasts of the forest, as a young lion among the flocks of sheep, who, if he go through both treadeth down and teareth in pieces, and none can deliver."

793 D&C 86: 5: "Behold, verily I say unto you, the angels are crying unto the Lord day and night, who are ready and waiting to be sent forth to reap down the fields;"

794 D&C 86: 6-7: "But the Lord saith unto them, pluck not up the tares while the blade is yet tender (for verily your faith is weak), lest you destroy the wheat also. Therefore, let the wheat and the tares grow together until the harvest is fully ripe; then ye shall first gather out the wheat from among the tares, and after the gathering of the wheat, behold and lo, the tares are bound in bundles, and the field remaineth to be burned."

795 D&C 86: 4: "But behold, in the last days, even now while the Lord is beginning to bring forth the word, and the blade is springing up and is yet tender—"

a position humanity itself is in at present. But you are the ones in the balance and for whom time is granted. How much longer no one knows, but your sins are not private. Your repentance is critical to all of creation. Do not think your life is your own. All of us have a share in your good works.

Do not think the Savior's words are without cosmic significance. I define "cosmic" to include the cosmos or organized creation here. Even the earth itself longs to be freed from the burden of sin upon her face.[796] It is the Lord alone who has granted you time to repent. This current state of the creation we live is affected by the promise held in those who are repenting. As soon as that hope ends, and no further repentance is to occur, then the harvest will begin. Therefore, becoming salt has never been so important as it now is.

3 Nephi 12: 14-16

> **"Verily, verily, I say unto you, I give unto you to be the light of this people. A city that is set on a hill cannot be hid. Behold, do men light a candle and put it under a bushel? Nay, but on a candlestick, and it giveth light to all that are in the house; Therefore let your light so shine before this people, that they may see your good works and glorify your Father who is in heaven."**

Here, again, is a reference to Zion. Zion will be that city upon a hill which cannot be hidden. It will tower over the landscape, elevated both physically and spiritually. It will be the mountain of the Lord in the top

[796] Moses 7: 48: "And it came to pass that Enoch looked upon the earth; and he heard a voice from the bowels thereof, saying: Wo, wo is me, the mother of men; I am pained, I am weary, because of the wickedness of my children. When shall I rest, and be cleansed from the filthiness which is gone forth out of me? When will my Creator sanctify me, that I may rest, and righteousness for a season abide upon my face?"

of the mountains.[797] He will dwell there.[798] I've already addressed this and won't repeat it again here.

What is the "light" which you are to be to "this people?" Who are "this people?" What is to be a "light of this people?"

If you have light, how is it to be shared? Within The Church of Jesus Christ of Latter-day Saints the obligation to preach, teach, exhort and expound is imposed upon everyone having the office of Priest and above.[799] Members of both sexes were commanded in 1832 to teach one another the doctrines of the Gospel.[800] If you have light and refuse to share it with others, are you putting a candle under a bushel?

How do you let the light you have shine through "good works?" That is how it is supposed to be shown. Christ's teaching explains that people are to see your "good works" as the means for your light to shine. How would that be accomplished?

Most interesting of all is that upon seeing your good works, the glory is to be given "your Father who is in heaven." How would your works reflect on Him rather than on yourself? What would you need to do in order for those benefited by your efforts to turn their thanks to God, rather than to you?

If you were interested in your good works reflecting credit to "your Father who is in heaven" how many monuments would you want built to your memory? How many buildings would you want named after you? How many statutes would you want carved of your likeness and put on display for men to admire?

The light should point to the Lord, who can save. It is nevertheless the case that some have become subjects of adoration or veneration despite their inability to save anyone. Those who are distracted from following the Lord become Telestial and continue to suffer the deaths of

---

797 Isa. 2: 2-3: "And it shall come to pass in the last days, *that* the mountain of the Lord's house shall be established in the top of the mountains, and shall be exalted above the hills; and all nations shall flow unto it. And many people shall go and say, Come ye, and let us go up to the mountain of the Lord, to the house of the God of Jacob; and he will teach us of his ways, and we will walk in his paths: for out of Zion shall go forth the law, and the word of the Lord from Jerusalem."

798 2 Ne. 14: 5: "And the Lord will create upon every dwelling-place of mount Zion, and upon her assemblies, a cloud and smoke by day and the shining of a flaming fire by night; for upon all the glory of Zion shall be a defence."
D&C 76: 66: "These are they who are come unto Mount Zion, and unto the city of the living God, the heavenly place, the holiest of all."
D&C 84: 2: "Yea, the word of the Lord concerning his church, established in the last days for the restoration of his people, as he has spoken by the mouth of his prophets, and for the gathering of his saints to stand upon Mount Zion, which shall be the city of New Jerusalem."

799 D&C 20: 46: "The priest's duty is to preach, teach, expound, exhort, and baptize, and administer the sacrament,"

800 D&C 88: 77: "And I give unto you a commandment that you shall teach one another the doctrine of the kingdom."

false religion.[801] These are no better than the liars, adulterers and whoremongers.[802] They became these vessels of God's wrath because they worshiped men, rather than God. If, therefore, prophets such as Moses, Elias, John, Peter and Enoch have such followers despite preaching that salvation is in Christ alone, then how much worse is it for a man to intentionally cultivate adoration for himself? How much worse is it to deliberately invite this error?

What steps should you take to make certain there are no thunderous celebrations broadcast on television on your birthdays? How quick would you be to reaffirm you are nothing and no-one, and salvation is through Christ and not a man? How clear would you be about your own weakness, foolishness and inability to save another? How often would you point to the Lord who alone can save?

It is not enough to be religious. Hell will be filled with the religious. It is not enough to proclaim you have light if you do not live according to its principles. The sermon we are looking at now is the Lord's careful formulation of the principles which will save. He delivered it often during His mortal ministry. When He was resurrected and ministered to lost sheep, including the Nephites, He delivered the same address to them all.

Above all other sources of information about the path back to God, this is the greatest message of all. Within it are the very steps that are required for life and salvation, spoken by the author of salvation.

3 Nephi 12: 17-18

> **"Think not that I am come to destroy the law or the prophets. I am not come to destroy but to fulfil; For verily I say unto you, one jot nor one tittle hath not passed away from the law, but in me it hath all been fulfilled."**

The Lord sends ministers with a commission to transition from one dispensation of the Gospel to another. From Adam until Enoch there was an order, but with Enoch that order changed. Wickedness and rebellion required a new approach, and Enoch was commissioned to bring it

---

801 D&C 76: 99-101: "For these are they who are of Paul, and of Apollos, and of Cephas. These are they who say they are some of one and some of another—some of Christ and some of John, and some of Moses, and some of Elias, and some of Esaias, and some of Isaiah, and some of Enoch; But received not the gospel, neither the testimony of Jesus, neither the prophets, neither the everlasting covenant."

802 D&C 76: 103-104: "These are they who are liars, and sorcerers, and adulterers, and whoremongers, and whosoever loves and makes a lie. These are they who suffer the wrath of God on earth."

about.[803] Mankind was in such a state of rebellion that their time was to end. Enoch gathered together people upon a high mountain where he established a city which would survive the destruction by becoming Zion.[804]

Soon after Enoch was called, the Lord called another, giving him also a dispensation of the Gospel. He, however, was to remain on the earth.[805] With him a new covenant was made.[806]

Both Enoch and Noah were contemporaries, but each had been given a dispensation of the Gospel. The covenant with Enoch did not disannul the covenant with Adam. Nor did the covenant with Noah contradict the covenant with Enoch.

---

803 Moses 6: 32-34: "And the Lord said unto Enoch: Go forth and do as I have commanded thee, and no man shall pierce thee. Open thy mouth, and it shall be filled, and I will give thee utterance, for all flesh is in my hands, and I will do as seemeth me good. Say unto this people: Choose ye this day, to serve the Lord God who made you. Behold my Spirit is upon you, wherefore all thy words will I justify; and the mountains shall flee before you, and the rivers shall turn from their course; and thou shalt abide in me, and I in you; therefore walk with me."

804 Moses 7: 17-21: "The fear of the Lord was upon all nations, so great was the glory of the Lord, which was upon his people. And the Lord blessed the land, and they were blessed upon the mountains, and upon the high places, and did flourish. And the Lord called his people Zion, because they were of one heart and one mind, and dwelt in righteousness; and there was no poor among them. And Enoch continued his preaching in righteousness unto the people of God. And it came to pass in his days, that he built a city that was called the City of Holiness, even Zion. And it came to pass that Enoch talked with the Lord; and he said unto the Lord: Surely Zion shall dwell in safety forever. But the Lord said unto Enoch: Zion have I blessed, but the residue of the people have I cursed. And it came to pass that the Lord showed unto Enoch all the inhabitants of the earth; and he beheld, and lo, Zion, in process of time, was taken up into heaven. And the Lord said unto Enoch: Behold mine abode forever."

805 Moses 7: 42-43: "And Enoch also saw Noah, and his family; that the posterity of all the sons of Noah should be saved with a temporal salvation; Wherefore Enoch saw that Noah built an ark; and that the Lord smiled upon it, and held it in his own hand; but upon the residue of the wicked the floods came and swallowed them up."
Gen. 6: 12-14: "And God looked upon the earth, and, behold, it was corrupt; for all flesh had corrupted his way upon the earth. And God said unto Noah, The end of all flesh is come before me; for the earth is filled with violence through them; and, behold, I will destroy them with the earth. Make thee an ark of gopher wood; rooms shalt thou make in the ark, and shalt pitch it within and without with pitch."

806 Gen. 9: 8-9: "And God spake unto Noah, and to his sons with him, saying, And I, behold, I establish my covenant with you, and with your seed after you;"

Abraham also received a dispensation of the Gospel.[807] Moses also.[808]

Christ also received a dispensation of the Gospel in the same manner as all those who went before.[809]

Christ fulfilled all the law. Not merely the Law of Moses, which indeed pointed to Him,[810] but also every part of the Gospel from Adam to Christ's earthly ministry.[811] All have testified of Him and He has completed His ministry in strict conformity with all that was foreshadowed, all that was prophesied, all that was anticipated of Him. Just how completely He did this is not possible to understand with the current state of our scriptures. But He did fulfill all righteousness, complete every assignment, accomplish every task and live in conformity with every prophesy concerning Him.

Not one matter respecting Him was left undone. From His hair to His feet, all that was foreshadowed or prophesied was done by Him. He turned not His face from those who spit at Him.[812] He let Himself be shorn as a sheep and kept silent as it was done.[813]

---

[807] Abraham 2.

[808] Moses 1: 3-4: "And God spake unto Moses, saying: Behold, I am the Lord God Almighty, and Endless is my name; for I am without beginning of days or end of years; and is not this endless? And, behold, thou art my son; wherefore look, and I will show thee the workmanship of mine hands; but not all, for my works are without end, and also my words, for they never cease."

[809] Matt. 4: 11: "Then the devil leaveth him, and, behold, angels came and ministered unto him."
Matt. 17: 1-3: "And after six days Jesus taketh Peter, James, and John his brother, and bringeth them up into an high mountain apart, And was transfigured before them: and his face did shine as the sun, and his raiment was white as the light. And, behold, there appeared unto them Moses and Elias talking with him."

[810] Gal. 3: 24: "Wherefore the law was our schoolmaster *to bring us* unto Christ, that we might be justified by faith."

[811] Jacob 4: 4: "For, for this intent have we written these things, that they may know that we knew of Christ, and we had a hope of his glory many hundred years before his coming; and not only we ourselves had a hope of his glory, but also all the holy prophets which were before us."
Jacob 7: 11: "And I said unto him: Then ye do not understand them; for they truly testify of Christ. Behold, I say unto you that none of the prophets have written, nor prophesied, save they have spoken concerning this Christ."

[812] Isa. 50: 6: "I gave my back to the smiters, and my cheeks to them that plucked off the hair: I hid not my face from shame and spitting."
Matt. 26: 57: "And they that had laid hold on Jesus led *him* away to Caiaphas the high priest, where the scribes and the elders were assembled."

[813] Isa. 53: 7: "He was oppressed, and he was afflicted, yet he opened not his mouth: he is brought as a lamb to the slaughter, and as a sheep before her shearers is dumb, so he openeth not his mouth."

He inherited Kingship, but deferred His reign to another time.[814]

He fulfilled, but did not destroy. In this He was like those whom He sent before to complete and open anew. In one hinge point of history a dispensation closes and another opens. Enoch and Noah, Abraham and Moses were all commissioned to open and close. For the Lord, however, He divided the spoil. He sent John to close,[815] leaving it to Himself to open.[816] Mankind cannot measure humility or meekness, but in Christ was a fullness of both.

Men in their insecurity and vanity want honors, awards, recognition and fame. The Lord has hidden from us most of what He did, most of what He is. He is content to confine the record of His doings to the minimum necessary for our understanding so we may have faith in Him. But the extent of His doings mankind has yet to find out.[817] This is more than a tribute to Him. He has understated His accomplishments. He has hidden His glory from us. He has made less of Himself, that we may not be unable to identify with Him. He is meeker and more humble than mankind understands.

He can be trusted with all power because He will never abuse it.[818] He will use it to serve others.[819]

---

814 John 18: 36: "Jesus answered, My kingdom is not of this world: if my kingdom were of this world, then would my servants fight, that I should not be delivered to the Jews: but now is my kingdom not from hence."

815 D&C 84: 27-28: "Which gospel is the gospel of repentance and of baptism, and the remission of sins, and the law of carnal commandments, which the Lord in his wrath caused to continue with the house of Aaron among the children of Israel until John, whom God raised up, being filled with the Holy Ghost from his mother's womb. For he was baptized while he was yet in his childhood, and was ordained by the angel of God at the time he was eight days old unto this power, to overthrow the kingdom of the Jews, and to make straight the way of the Lord before the face of his people, to prepare them for the coming of the Lord, in whose hand is given all power."

816 John 8: 12: "Then spake Jesus again unto them, saying, I am the light of the world: he that followeth me shall not walk in darkness, but shall have the light of life."

817 D&C 76: 2: "Great is his wisdom, marvelous are his ways, and the extent of his doings none can find out."

818 Matt. 28: 18: "And Jesus came and spake unto them, saying, All power is given unto me in heaven and in earth."

819 Luke 22: 27: "For whether *is* greater, he that sitteth at meat, or he that serveth? *is* not he that sitteth at meat? but I am among you as he that serveth."

In Christ was all fulfilled. In Him is all fulfilled. In Him dwells the fullness of the Godhead bodily.[820] He is the light who came to His own, but we will not receive Him.[821]

He was, He is, and He has risen. Above all others and all else, He has risen. And because of this He has made it possible for others also to rise. Everything He has done was in fulfillment of the law, pointing for us the way. Now it is only left for us to follow, trusting in Him.

3 Nephi 12: 19

> **"And behold, I have given you the law and the commandments ofm y Father, that ye shall believe in me, and that ye shall repent of your sins, and come unto me with a broken heart and a contrite spirit. Behold, ye have the commandments before you, and the law is fulfilled."**

This hearkens back to the doctrine of Christ given preliminarily to the audience. Repent. Be baptized. Receive the Holy Ghost. These commandments are the foundation upon which all else is to be built.

To all that He explained before, He has added, "repent of your sins, and come unto me with a broken heart and a contrite spirit." Repenting will be accompanied by a broken heart and contrite spirit. When you turn to Him and see clearly for the first time how dark your ways have been, it should break your heart. You should realize how desperately you stand in need of His grace to cover you, lift you, and heal you. You can then appreciate the great gulf between you and Him.[822]

If you had to bear your sins into His presence it would make you burn with regret and fear.[823] Your own heart must break.

When you behold how little you have to offer Him, your spirit becomes contrite. He offers everything. And we can contribute nothing but our cooperation. And we still reluctantly give that, or if we give a little of our own cooperation we think we have given something

---

[820] Col. 2: 9: "For in him dwelleth all the fulness of the Godhead bodily."

[821] John 1: 10-11: "He was in the world, and the world was made by him, and the world knew him not. He came unto his own, and his own received him not."

[822] Moses 1: 10: "And it came to pass that it was for the space of many hours before Moses did again receive his natural strength like unto man; and he said unto himself: Now, for this cause I know that man is nothing, which thing I never had supposed."

[823] Mormon 9: 3-5: "Then will ye longer deny the Christ, or can ye behold the Lamb of God? Do ye suppose that ye shall dwell with him under a consciousness of your guilt? Do ye suppose that ye could be happy to dwell with that holy Being, when your souls are racked with a consciousness of guilt that ye have ever abused his laws? Behold, I say unto you that ye would be more miserable to dwell with a holy and just God, under a consciousness of your filthiness before him, than ye would to dwell with the damned souls in hell. For behold, when ye shall be brought to see your nakedness before God, and also the glory of God, and the holiness of Jesus Christ, it will kindle a flame of unquenchable fire upon you."

significant. We have not. Indeed, we cannot.[824] He honors us if He permits us to assist. We should proceed with alacrity when given the chance to serve.

How patiently He has proceeded with teaching us all. We have the law, we have the commandments. Still we hesitate. Still He invites and reminds us: Repent. Come to Him. Do what was commanded. The law is fulfilled, and He is its fulfillment. Look to Him and be saved.

The heart that will not break does not understand the predicament we live in. The proud spirit is foolish and blind. Our perilous state is such that we can forfeit all that we have ever been by refusing Christ's invitation to repent and turn again to Him.

But we still hesitate. We still hold back.

He really can save you. He has that power. He holds those keys. Even death and hell are conquered by Him.[825] But His victory cannot become ours unless we repent and turn again to Him.

Think of those you have lost to the grave. All those living will likewise be lost unless we come to Christ. We have hope only in Him.

It seems too simple a thing to achieve so great a result. It has always been like that.[826] Look to Him and be saved. Keep His commandments. Repent. He can and will lead you from wherever you find yourself at present back into the light. It really does not matter what foolish traps you have surrounding you. So soon as you turn to face Him, He will direct you back safely. Repent and keep His commandments and they will bring you to Him.

---

824 Mosiah 2: 20-21: "I say unto you, my brethren, that if you should render all the thanks and praise which your whole soul has power to possess, to that God who has created you, and has kept and preserved you, and has caused that ye should rejoice, and has granted that ye should live in peace one with another—I say unto you that if ye should serve him who has created you from the beginning, and is preserving you from day to day, by lending you breath, that ye may live and move and do according to your own will, and even supporting you from one moment to another—I say, if ye should serve him with all your whole souls yet ye would be unprofitable servants."

825 Mosiah 15: 7-9: "Yea, even so he shall be led, crucified, and slain, the flesh becoming subject even unto death, the will of the Son being swallowed up in the will of the Father. And thus God breaketh the bands of death, having gained the victory over death; giving the Son power to make intercession for the children of men—Having ascended into heaven, having the bowels of mercy; being filled with compassion towards the children of men; standing betwixt them and justice; having broken the bands of death, taken upon himself their iniquity and their transgressions, having redeemed them, and satisfied the demands of justice."

826 1 Ne. 17: 41: "And he did straiten them in the wilderness with his rod; for they hardened their hearts, even as ye have; and the Lord straitened them because of their iniquity. He sent fiery flying serpents among them; and after they were bitten he prepared a way that they might be healed; and the labor which they had to perform was to look; and because of the simpleness of the way, or the easiness of it, there were many who perished."

3 Nephi 12: 20

"Therefore come unto me and be ye saved; for verily I say unto you, that except ye shall keep my commandments, which I have commanded you at this time, ye shall in no case enter into the kingdom of heaven."

There goes the argument that all you need do to be saved is "confess Jesus." It doesn't work that way. You must keep His commandments. If you don't, then "ye shall in no case enter into the kingdom of heaven." It is not possible to "come unto [Him]" and "be saved" without also keeping His commandments. It is the only true measure of coming to Him. And "except ye shall keep [His] commandments... ye can in no case enter into the kingdom of heaven." Entry is barred unless you follow Him. If He needed baptism to enter, then clearly we do as well.[827]

There is no space between faith in Christ and behavior evidencing that faith. There is no dichotomy between "grace" and "works" because it is by our conduct we merit grace. Christ received grace by the things He did.[828] The manner by which we receive grace is through keeping His commandments.[829]

Grace, or power to move closer to God, is also an increase of light. Light grows only as you move closer to it. But you have choice, and must elect to move closer to the light.[830] The great proof text for salvation by confession of faith alone is Romans 10: 9: *"That if thou shalt confess with thy mouth the Lord Jesus, and shalt believe in thine heart that God hath raised him from the dead, thou shalt be saved."*

---

[827] 2 Ne. 31: 5: "And now, if the Lamb of God, he being holy, should have need to be baptized by water, to fulfil all righteousness, O then, how much more need have we, being unholy, to be baptized, yea, even by water!"

[828] D&C 93: 11-14: "And I, John, bear record that I beheld his glory, as the glory of the Only Begotten of the Father, full of grace and truth, even the Spirit of truth, which came and dwelt in the flesh, and dwelt among us. And I, John, saw that he received not of the fulness at the first, but received grace for grace; And he received not of the fulness at first, but continued from grace to grace, until he received a fulness; And thus he was called the Son of God, because he received not of the fulness at the first."

[829] D&C 93: 19-20: "I give unto you these sayings that you may understand and know how to worship, and know what you worship, that you may come unto the Father in my name, and in due time receive of his fulness. For if you keep my commandments you shall receive of his fulness, and be glorified in me as I am in the Father; therefore, I say unto you, you shall receive grace for grace."

[830] D&C 93: 27-28: "And no man receiveth a fulness unless he keepeth his commandments. He that keepeth his commandments receiveth truth and light, until he is glorified in truth and knoweth all things."
D&C 50: 23-25: "And that which doth not edify is not of God, and is darkness. That which is of God is light; and he that receiveth light, and continueth in God, receiveth more light; and that light groweth brighter and brighter until the perfect day. And again, verily I say unto you, and I say it that you may know the truth, that you may chase darkness from among you;"

This is offered as if Paul had priority over Christ, if the two conflict. However, Paul does not conflict, for in the same letter he teaches: *"Know ye not, that to whom ye yield yourselves servants to obey, his servants ye are to whom ye obey; whether of sin unto death, or of obedience unto righteousness? But God be thanked, that ye were the servants of sin, but ye have obeyed from the heart that form of doctrine which was delivered you."* (Romans 6: 16-17.) Righteousness comes by obedience. Obedience requires action. Without conforming conduct to the Lord's commandments, it is impossible to enter into the kingdom of heaven. Paul understood this, and lived his life accordingly. Who worked more than Paul to spread the Gospel? If his life was filled with works from the time of his conversion to the time of his martyrdom, then does not his example prove the necessity of obedience to the Lord's commandments? How then are his words twisted to mean confession alone, without obedience, can save? Even if someone were mistaken and in good faith sincerely believed Paul to justify salvation by confession alone, how did Paul become greater than Christ?

The Lord's instructions are clear and obedience to His and the Father's commandments are a threshold requirement for salvation. Without obedience to them you cannot enter the kingdom of heaven.

Grace is a gift, but the gift must be received. Only those willing to "receive" it, merit grace.[831] It is "received" in the way the Lord ordained and in no other way.[832]

Only the deceived or the wicked would contradict the Lord's teaching that "except ye keep [His] commandments" then "ye cannot enter into the kingdom of heaven." Yet there are those who both make this claim in the various Protestant denominations, and are trying to advance this position into the LDS faith, as well. We would be better served by forgetting how to make ourselves seem more Protestant, and instead accepting and teaching what Christ established as the sole basis for entering the kingdom of heaven.

---

[831] D&C 88: 32-35: "And they who remain shall also be quickened; nevertheless, they shall return again to their own place, to enjoy that which they are willing to receive, because they were not willing to enjoy that which they might have received. For what doth it profit a man if a gift is bestowed upon him, and he receive not the gift? Behold, he rejoices not in that which is given unto him, neither rejoices in him who is the giver of the gift. And again, verily I say unto you, that which is governed by law is also preserved by law and perfected and sanctified by the same. That which breaketh a law, and abideth not by law, but seeketh to become a law unto itself, and willeth to abide in sin, and altogether abideth in sin, cannot be sanctified by law, neither by mercy, justice, nor judgment. Therefore, they must remain filthy still."

[832] D&C 130: 21: "And when we obtain any blessing from God, it is by obedience to that law upon which it is predicated."

3 Nephi 12: 21-22

> **"Ye have heard that it hath been said by them of old time, and it is also written before you, that thou shalt not kill, and whosoever shall kill shall be in danger of the judgment of God; But I say unto you, that whosoever is angry with his brother shall be in danger of his judgment. And whosoever shall say to his brother, Raca, shall be in danger of the council; and whosoever shall say, Thou fool, shall be in danger of hell fire."**

Christ is elevating the Law of Moses by raising the expectation for human conduct. He moves from mere outward conduct into the inner soul of the man. You are not doing as you should if all you do is refrain from killing. Instead, you need to remove anger.

The prior obligation ("said by them of old") focused only on your conduct, now it is your motivation.

You can judge another based on conduct. They either do or do not do something. The conduct is observable, and therefore capable of being judged. Now, however, Christ moves the battleground inside a person. It is now in the heart. On such terrain as that, man is incapable of knowing, and therefore, of judging.

With anything involving truth and rules of conduct, there are always some reasons to depart from the rule. Christ departed from this rule. So we must consider the departures to understand the rule.

First, however, we need to know and understand the rule. The "judgment" which you are "in danger of" by being angry with your brother is not your brother's anger, but God's. The judgment of God is provoked by those who are angry with their brother.

We are not to be angry with our brother because that is the beginning of a whole sequence of events, the culmination of which may be killing. Before killing, however, there are other troubles and offenses along the way. Anger leads to abuse. It leads to discourtesy, dishonesty, and cheating. It justifies miserable conduct because you think it right to give offenses to another. It corrodes relationships and makes society sick.

If you can prevent this at the heart, you can heal society. Refrain from letting offenses turn into anger. Deal with them inside, showing forgiveness and compassion. He will stress this further in subsequent verses.

The terms "Raca" and "fool" are derisive names. Christ is saying that applying derisive names to others is wrong, even damning. He is not preventing you from identifying foolishness. He often spoke of fools and foolishness.[833] He would even use the term "foolish" in this same sermon.[834] So it is not at all inappropriate to use the term "fool" or "foolish" when discussing foolishness. What is wrong it to regard your fellow man with derision and use terms of derision to describe them.

Even with this rue of conduct, however, Christ applied a derisive term to King Herod. He called him "that fox."[835] This was a term of derision, but appropriately applied to a wicked king meriting derision. He was corrupt, evil and vile. Therefore, with respect to Herod, Christ's example allows for terms of derision to be appropriately applied to those who merit them. Christ was able to weigh the heart. For Him to make that conclusion was a matter of Divine prerogative. I suppose that we are equally entitled to apply such terms of judgment and condemnation, including terms of derision, if we obtain them by inspiration from the Lord. That is, if the Lord inspires such a term of derision to be used, then it would be appropriate despite this verse. For whatever we do, even if sharpness is involved, is appropriate when moved upon by the

---

[833] Matt. 23: 17: "*Ye* fools and blind: for whether is greater, the gold, or the temple that sanctifieth the gold? …*Ye* fools and blind: for whether *is* greater, the gift, or the altar that sanctifieth the gift?"
Matt. 25: 2-8: "And five of them were wise, and five *were* foolish. They that *were* foolish took their lamps, and took no oil with them: But the wise took oil in their vessels with their lamps. While the bridegroom tarried, they all slumbered and slept. And at midnight there was a cry made, Behold, the bridegroom cometh; go ye out to meet him. Then all those virgins arose, and trimmed their lamps. And the foolish said unto the wise, Give us of your oil; for our lamps are gone out."
Luke 12: 20: "But God said unto him, *Thou* fool, this night thy soul shall be required of thee: then whose shall those things be, which thou hast provided?"
Luke 24: 25 (after His resurrection): "Then he said unto them, O fools, and slow of heart to believe all that the prophets have spoken:"
2 Ne. 29: 4, 6: "But thus saith the Lord God: O fools, they shall have a Bible; and it shall proceed forth from the Jews, mine ancient covenant people. And what thank they the Jews for the Bible which they receive from them? Yea, what do the Gentiles mean? Do they remember the travails, and the labors, and the pains of the Jews, and their diligence unto me, in bringing forth salvation unto the Gentiles? …Thou fool, that shall say: A Bible, we have got a Bible, and we need no more Bible. Have ye obtained a Bible save it were by the Jews?"

[834] 3 Ne. 14: 26: "And every one that heareth these sayings of mine and doeth them not shall be likened unto a foolish man, who built his house upon the sand—"

[835] Luke 13: 31-32: "The same day there came certain of the Pharisees, saying unto him, Get thee out, and depart hence: for Herod will kill thee. And he said unto them, Go ye, and tell that fox, Behold, I cast out devils, and I do cures to day and to morrow, and the third *day* I shall be perfected."

Holy Ghost.[836] So, also, even killing another can be done when the Lord is the one deciding life and death.[837]

The tendency is to always think the exceptions allow your anger. I would suspect the best approach is to do as Nephi did. That is, insist upon following the one standard of conduct and always refrain. Always. Then, if the Lord is going to have it otherwise, leave it to the Lord to make that insistence so dramatic, so undeniable, so compelling, that you know it is the Lord's judgment and not your own. Removing anger from the heart is a difficult enough challenge to last the rest of your life. To start thinking any passing offense justifies an exception because it may be "inspired" is the way of a fool. Do as Christ bids you to do in this sermon. If He wants a different approach, you ought to require that to be made absolutely clear by Him before you depart from this standard.

Remember how often great souls have interceded for their fellow man. I've written about that so often in my books I won't repeat it again. However, intercession for your fellow man, including those who give offense to you, is one of the hallmarks of the saved soul. This is who Abraham was, and why he became a friend of God. I've hesitated to even discuss the exceptions to the rule because everyone wants the exceptions to apply to them. No one wants to comply with the rule. The higher way is, however, found in following the rule. It should be an absolute sacrifice, and a painful one at that, for the exception to be applied in your life. If an inspired condemnation is required at your hand and by your voice, then immediately afterwards you should make intercession with the Lord for those condemned. That is the way of those who know the Lord. Those who have been forgiven much—including those who have been forgiven everything—always love much in return.[838]

---

[836] D&C 121: 43: "Reproving betimes with sharpness, when moved upon by the Holy Ghost; and then showing forth afterwards an increase of love toward him whom thou hast reproved, lest he esteem thee to be his enemy;"

[837] 1 Ne. 4: 10-13: "And it came to pass that I was constrained by the Spirit that I should kill Laban; but I said in my heart: Never at any time have I shed the blood of man. And I shrunk and would that I might not slay him. And the Spirit said unto me again: Behold the Lord hath delivered him into thy hands. Yea, and I also knew that he had sought to take away mine own life; yea, and he would not hearken unto the commandments of the Lord; and he also had taken away our property. And it came to pass that the Spirit said unto me again: Slay him, for the Lord hath delivered him into thy hands; Behold the Lord slayeth the wicked to bring forth his righteous purposes. It is better that one man should perish than that a nation should dwindle and perish in unbelief."

[838] Luke 7: 47: "Wherefore I say unto thee, Her sins, which are many, are forgiven; for she loved much: but to whom little is forgiven, *the same* loveth little."

3 Nephi 12: 23-24

> **"Therefore, if ye shall come unto me, or shall desire to come unto me, and rememberest that thy brother hath aught against thee — Go thy way unto thy brother, and first be reconciled to thy brother, and then come unto me with full purpose of heart, and I will receive you."**

Notice the offense is taken by the brother, not by you. It is presumed that you haven't taken offense against him. If he, however, 'hath aught against thee"—meaning that if you have done anything to cause him an offense, you have steps to take.

Notice that your relationship with the Lord comes second, **after** you have made amends with any you have offended.

You can't bring "full purpose of heart" when there is a lingering offense you have not attempted to cure. This kind of mental distraction alters you.

If you realize you've offended someone it likely means you know your conduct has been uncharitable. You did something wrong. You hurt another.

Inventory of your conduct is something to be done before approaching the Lord. If you have offended someone you need to take the steps to free your conscience from it. Only then can you bring "full purpose of heart" in approaching God.

When the heart is right, then the Lord can "receive you." When the heart is not right, you cannot be received.

He's said this before, of course. His doctrine in the preceding chapter required repentance before baptism precisely so you could be right in the heart before the ordinance takes place.[839]

Other Book of Mormon writers said the same thing as well: "For behold, God hath said a man being evil cannot do that which is good; for if he offereth a gift, or prayeth unto God, except he shall do it with real intent it profiteth him nothing. … And likewise also is it counted evil unto a man, if he shall pray and not with real intent of heart; yea, and it profiteth him nothing, for God receiveth none such." (Moroni 7: 6, 9.) "Wherefore, my beloved brethren, I know that if ye shall follow the Son, with full purpose of heart, acting no hypocrisy and no deception before God, but with real intent, repenting of your sins, witnessing unto the Father that ye are willing to take upon you the name of Christ, by baptism—yea, by following your Lord and your Savior down into the water, according to his word, behold, then shall ye receive the Holy Ghost; yea, then cometh the baptism of fire and of the Holy Ghost; and then can ye speak with the tongue of angels, and shout praises unto the

---

839 3 Ne. 11: 23: "Verily I say unto you, that whoso repenteth of his sins through your words, and desireth to be baptized in my name, on this wise shall ye baptize them—Behold, ye shall go down and stand in the water, and in my name shall ye baptize them."

Holy One of Israel." (2 Nephi 31: 13.) "But as oft as they repented and sought forgiveness, with real intent, they were forgiven." (Moroni. 6: 8.)

You bring your whole heart to Him. That He can receive. That He can work with. Less than that, it is not possible for Him to offer you anything. You will invariably reject what He offers. Acting as the hypocrite will neither fool you or Him. Hence Nephi's counsel in 2 Nephi 31: 13 quoted above, and discussed previously in this blog.

3 Nephi 12: 25-26

> **"Agree with thine adversary quickly while thou art in the way with him, lest at any time he shall get thee, and thou shalt be cast into prison. Verily, verily, I say unto thee, thou shalt by no means come out thence until thou hast paid the uttermost senine. And while ye are in prison can ye pay even one senine? Verily, verily, I say unto you, Nay."**

This notion of agreeing with your adversaries is difficult for most people. It requires you to submit to what is sometimes unjust demands. He is saying to submit anyway. Do not rebel against the adversaries in life, but accommodate them.

Give to the unjust what they demand, so that they may see your good works and understand there is a higher way. Without your example, they cannot understand.

Retaliation continues the cycles. Someone eventually needs to lay down their just claim for retribution and simply take the injury without returning anything in return. This was what Christ did. He took everyone's injuries and returned only forgiveness.

Now He asks for His followers to do some of the same. The failure to tolerate injustice can spiral into continuing the conflict, until there is prison. The prison to fear is not one made by men. But if you are cast into that prison then you cannot come out until you have paid the highest price.[840] It is better to repent because this payment made even

---

[840] D&C 76: 84-85, 105, 106: "These are they who are thrust down to hell. These are they who shall not be redeemed from the devil until the last resurrection, until the Lord, even Christ the Lamb, shall have finished his work. These are they who suffer the vengeance of eternal fire. These are they who are cast down to hell and suffer the wrath of Almighty God, until the fulness of times, when Christ shall have subdued all enemies under his feet, and shall have perfected his work;"

God, the greatest of all, to tremble with pain and shrink from the burden.[841]

It is not possible to pay the price while in prison. The price must be paid by a person while in the flesh.[842] Any who are consigned to prison dwell in darkness, awaiting deliverance from Him whom they rejected while in the flesh.[843] They become dependent upon others working to pay the debt on their behalf.[844]

The sermon delivered by Christ is the foundation of how man ought to relate to fellow-man. It is the pattern on which it becomes possible to dwell in peace with one another. It is the groundwork for Zion.

We need to look at this sermon as the guideline for changing our internal lives, so we may become a fit and proper resident with others who are Saints. Even Saints will give inadvertent offenses. Even Saints will disappoint one another from time to time. To become "one" in the sense required for redeeming a people and restoring them again to Zion is beyond any person's reach if they cannot internalize this sermon.

The purpose of this sermon is not to equip you to judge others. It has no use for that. It is designed to change you. You need to become something different, something higher, something more holy. That will require you to reexamine your heart, your motivations, and your thoughts. It will require you to take offenses and deliberately lay them

---

[841] D&C 19: 15-18: "Therefore I command you to repent—repent, lest I smite you by the rod of my mouth, and by my wrath, and by my anger, and your sufferings be sore—how sore you know not, how exquisite you know not, yea, how hard to bear you know not. For behold, I, God, have suffered these things for all, that they might not suffer if they would repent; But if they would not repent they must suffer e ven as I; Which suffering caused myself, even God, the greatest of all, to tremble because of pain, and to bleed at every pore, and to suffer both body and spirit—and would that I might not drink the bitter cup, and shrink—"

[842] Luke 16: 22-26: "And it came to pass, that the beggar died, and was carried by the angels into Abraham's bosom: the rich man also died, and was buried; And in hell he lift up his eyes, being in torments, and seeth Abraham afar off, and Lazarus in his bosom. And he cried and said, Father Abraham, have mercy on me, and send Lazarus, that he may dip the tip of his finger in water, and cool my tongue; for I am tormented in this flame. But Abraham said, Son, remember that thou in thy lifetime receivedst thy good things, and likewise Lazarus evil things: but now he is comforted, and thou art tormented. And beside all this, between us and you there is a great gulf fixed: so that they which would pass from hence to you cannot; neither can they pass to us, that *would come* from thence."

[843] D&C 138: 20-22: "But unto the wicked he did not go, and among the ungodly and the unrepentant who had defiled themselves while in the flesh, his voice was not raised;

21 Neither did the rebellious who rejected the testimonies and the warnings of the ancient prophets behold his presence, nor look upon his face.

22 Where these were, darkness reigned, but among the righteous there was peace;"

[844] D&C 138: 33: "These were taught faith in God, repentance from sin, vicarious baptism for the remission of sins, the gift of the Holy Ghost by the laying on of hands,"

down without retaliation. When you do, you become someone who can live in peace with others. Living in peace with others is the rudimentary beginning of Zion. It will not culminate in a City set on the hilltop until there is a population worthy of dwelling in the high places, in peace, without poor among them.[845]

Christ's sermon is not merely a description of what kind of person He is. It is a description of what kind of person will qualify to live with Him.[846]

3 Nephi 12: 27-29

> **"Behold, it is written by them of old time, that thou shalt not commit adultery; But I say unto you, that whosoever looketh on a woman, to lust after her, hath committed adultery already in his heart. Behold, I give unto you a commandment, that ye suffer none of these things to enter into your heart;"**

Here it is again—the heart. It is the intent and not just the act. It is not enough that you stop short of doing the thing commanded in the Law of Moses. Christ is attacking the root cause, the internal trouble which causes the mistakes.

The Law of Moses is not being replaced with a new era of easy grace triggered by confession for salvation. The Head of the new Dispensation, Christ, is instead providing a much higher standard for mankind to adopt in place of carnal commandments.

You must raise your thoughts to a higher level. Sexual appetites and passions must be kept within the bounds the Lord has prescribed. For this new, higher standard, it is not enough to just refrain from immoral acts, but you must purge thoughts. Neither lust of a woman, nor any of "these things" should "enter into your heart." This uniform standard applies to all: male and female, married or single, without regard to who or what causes your lusts. It is universal.

The raging controversy going on at present over President Packer's last General Conference address entirely misses the point. Whether your sexual attraction is male or female, it is to be confined in thought and deed to the bounds prescribed by the Lord, and the Lord has rather clearly identified the bounds in this sermon.

The heart is where sin begins. So it is the heart which Christ would have us cleanse. All else will follow.

---

[845] Moses 7: 17-18: "The fear of the Lord was upon all nations, so great was the glory of the Lord, which was upon his people. And the Lord blessed the land, and they were blessed upon the mountains, and upon the high places, and did flourish. And the Lord called his people Zion, because they were of one heart and one mind, and dwelt in righteousness; and there was no poor among them."

[846] Luke 9: 23: "And he said to *them* all, If any *man* will come after me, let him deny himself, and take up his cross daily, and follow me."

No one knows how formidable an obstacle this is until they have confronted it themselves. Nor can a person who confronts this challenge succeed at the first attempt. C.S. Lewis made such a profound observation on this subject it is worth quoting here:

"No man knows how bad he is till he has tried very hard to be good. A silly idea is current that good people do not know what temptation means. This is an obvious lie. Only those who try to resist temptation know how strong it is. After all, you find out the strength of the German army by fighting against it, not by giving in. You find out the strength of a wind by trying to walk against it, not by lying down. A man who gives in to temptation after five minutes simply does not know what it would have been like an hour later. That is why bad people, in one sense, know very little about badness. They have lived a sheltered life by always giving in. We never find out the strength of the evil impulse inside us until we try to fight it: and Christ, because he was the only man who never yielded to temptation, is also the only man who knows to the full what temptation means—the only complete realist." (CS Lewis, Mere Christianity, Chapter 11.)

Those who would rather settle into a comfortable enjoyment of their sins find discomfort in being reminded they are wrong. So when President Packer reminds them of this, it is painful, and they want him to retract his words. It would be better to consider them, for whether he retracts them or not, it will not change the underlying problem of sin. Only by confronting and overcoming sins within us will we ever become people who will be preserved in the coming harvest.

Imagine, if you can, the idea of impurity being a compound which exists within you. A compound that could be identified by the Lord and burned away. Think of it like the fuller's soap or the refiner's fire, where impurity is removed and something pure and clean is left behind.[847] To survive that burning purge there must be so little to burn away that the injury from the burn will not threaten life. It is a useful way to examine what is inside you. And a useful way to reconsider your thoughts.

This leads to the final question: What is the difference between the mind and the "heart?" This commandment addresses the "heart" in you. What is the "heart?"

3 Nephi 12: 30

> **"For it is better that ye should deny yourselves of these things, wherein ye will take up your cross, than that ye should be cast into hell."**

---

[847] Mal. 3: 2-3: "But who may abide the day of his coming? and who shall stand when he appeareth? for he *is* like a refiner's fire, and like fullers' soap: And he shall sit *as* a refiner and purifier of silver: and he shall purify the sons of Levi, and purge them as gold and silver, that they may offer unto the Lord an offering in righteousness."

Each person's cross is individual. Carrying "your cross" is not the same as carrying mine. Therefore, when you "deny yourself of these things" what you surrender and what you take up will be "your cross" and never mine.

It is odd how we are able to spot from a distance the weaknesses of others. We have highly acute sensitivities about others' flaws. But we rarely appreciate the crosses they bear.

How hard a burden a man carries when he disciplines himself to rise daily, and work to sacrifice for his family, is not at all the same across the economic scale. Nor, for that matter, is the daily service carried on by mothers who have deprived themselves of other pursuits to raise sometimes ungrateful children.

But "hell" is where we are cast when we are pained by the regrets of having lived without discipline, having lived selfishly.[848] We will stand "naked" before God. All of what we want hidden will be before us, revealed and exposed to view.

The "hell" of it all will be our regret, for we are our own tormentor. The torment of a disappointed mind will be like fire and brimstone to the regretful. (TPJS p. 357.)

Christ is advising us in a kindly way how to prevent that moment of fear, regret and torment. He is telling us how to escape it. These teachings are not a threat addressed at us, but a caution about the future moment when these teachings apply to us all.

It is as if the Lord wants us to know clearly beforehand what we are going to wish we had done instead. Now, in mortality, while we can still change how things will turn out, He is telling us how to accomplish that. In an understatement, He advises: "it is better to deny yourself" than it will be to indulge. You may find it a "cross" as you do, but if you deny yourself now it will let you escape "hell" in the future. It is kindly advice, without a threat. It is a warning about the road you have taken, and guidance on how you can avoid the collision that is coming.

Whatever the "cross" is you take up in your daily effort to live inside the bounds prescribed by the Lord, it will be worth it. By heeding His counsel, you will become someone better and avoid becoming devilish.

The temptations each of us face are unique to the individual. What is universal, however, is the limit placed upon temptations. They are never too great to resist. There is always an escape provided by the Lord.[849]

---

848 Mormon 9: 4-5: "Behold, I say unto you that ye would be more miserable to dwell with a holy and just God, under a consciousness of your filthiness before him, than ye would to dwell with the damned souls in hell. For behold, when ye shall be brought to see your nakedness before God, and also the glory of God, and the holiness of Jesus Christ, it will kindle a flame of unquenchable fire upon you."

849 1 Cor. 10: 13: "There hath no temptation taken you but such as is common to man: but God *is* faithful, who will not suffer you to be tempted above that ye are able; but will with the temptation also make a way to escape, that ye may be able to bear *it.*"

Nor are you given any commandment you cannot obey.[850] However, that is not to say temptation is easily overcome. Weakness is our lot.[851]

What then are you to make of your cross? If you've tried to deny yourself and failed, does it mean you are hopeless? Is the persistent failure to lift the cross you have been called to bear proof that you are just unable to merit salvation? Does the relentless return to temptation mean you are lost? Are you necessarily doomed because you have not found the escape promised by Paul's writing to the Corinthians?

Life is filled with cycles. When we battle and fail one day, then join the battle again, but fail again; then another, and another and another, what is the use? What do we make of such persistent failure, such continuing weakness? Is the lesson that we are lost? Or is it that we are weak? Weaker than we had ever imagined. Weaker than you could ever suppose man to be.[852] Is this evidence that you are doomed? Or is it merely a patient God proving to your utter satisfaction that you are indeed in need of saving grace to rescue you from where you find yourself? Is this the moment when, while filling your belly with husks along with the swine you've descended to accompany, you wake up?[853] If you will finally surrender your pride, come forward with a broken heart and real intent, returning to your Father, He will joyfully receive

---

[850] 1 Ne. 3: 7: "And it came to pass that I, Nephi, said unto my father: I will go and do the things which the Lord hath commanded, for I know that the Lord giveth no commandments unto the children of men, save he shall prepare a way for them that they may accomplish the thing which he commandeth them."

[851] Ether 12: 27: "And if men come unto me I will show unto them their weakness. I give unto men weakness that they may be humble; and my grace is sufficient for all men that humble themselves before me; for if they humble themselves before me, and have faith in me, then will I make weak things become strong unto them."

[852] Moses 1: 10: "And it came to pass that it was for the space of many hours before Moses did again receive his natural strength like unto man; and he said unto himself: Now, for this cause I know that man is nothing, which thing I never had supposed."

[853] Luke 15: 11-17: "And he said, A certain man had two sons: And the younger of them said to *his* father, Father, give me the portion of goods that falleth *to me*. And he divided unto them *his* living. And not many days after the younger son gathered all together, and took his journey into a far country, and there wasted his substance with riotous living. And when he had spent all, there arose a mighty famine in that land; and he began to be in want. And he went and joined himself to a citizen of that country; and he sent him into his fields to feed swine. And he would fain have filled his belly with the husks that the swine did eat: and no man gave unto him. And when he came to himself, he said, How many hired servants of my father's have bread enough and to spare, and I perish with hunger!"

you still.[854] (Luke 15: 18-24.) There is joy in heaven over you when you awaken.

Weakness is nothing, for all are weak. It is a gift, given to break your heart. Your broken heart will qualify you for His company. Whether a leper, an adulteress, a tax collector or a blind man, He can heal it all. But what He cannot do, and you must alone bring to Him, is that broken heart required for salvation.

William Ernest Henley wrote *Invictus*:

Out of the night that covers me,
Black as the Pit from pole to pole,
I thank whatever gods may be
For my unconquerable soul.
In the fell clutch of circumstance
I have not winced nor cried aloud.
Under the bludgeonings of chance
My head is bloody, but unbowed.
Beyond this place of wrath and tears
Looms but the Horror of the shade,
And yet the menace of the years
Finds, and shall find, me unafraid.
It matters not how strait the gate,
How charged with punishments the scroll.
I am the master of my fate:
I am the captain of my soul.

Orson F. Whitney penned the response in *The Soul's Captain*:

Art thou in truth? Then what of him
Who bought thee with his blood?
Who plunged into devouring seas
And snatched thee from the flood?
Who bore for all our fallen race
What none but him could bear—
The God who died that man might live,
And endless glory share?
Of what avail thy vaunted strength,

---

[854] Luke 15: 18-24: "I will arise and go to my father, and will say unto him, Father, I have sinned against heaven, and before thee, And am no more worthy to be called thy son: make me as one of thy hired servants. And he arose, and came to his father. But when he was yet a great way off, his father saw him, and had compassion, and ran, and fell on his neck, and kissed him. And the son said unto him, Father, I have sinned against heaven, and in thy sight, and am no more worthy to be called thy son. But the father said to his servants, Bring forth the best robe, and put *it* on him; and put a ring on his hand, and shoes on *his* feet: And bring hither the fatted calf, and kill *it;* and let us eat, and be merry: For this my son was dead, and is alive again; he was lost, and is found. And they began to be merry."

Apart from his vast might?
Pray that his Light may pierce the gloom,
That thou mayest see aright.
Men are as bubbles on the wave,
As leaves upon the tree.
Thou, captain of thy soul, forsooth
Who gave that place to thee?
Free will is thine—free agency
To wield for right or wrong;
But thou must answer unto him
To whom all souls belong.
Bend to the dust that head "unbowed,"
Small part of Life's great whole!
And see in him, and him alone,
The Captain of thy soul.

We choose. We live with our choices. It is better to deny ourselves and take up our individual crosses.

3 Nephi 12: 31-32

> **"It hath been written, that whosoever shall put away his wife, let him give her a writing of divorcement. Verily, verily, I say unto you, that whosoever shall put away his wife, saving for the cause of fornication, causeth her to commit adultery; and whoso shall marry her who is divorced committeth adultery."**

First and foremost, this is a verse dealing with male conduct. The verse is masculine in orientation and word usage, and deals with a male's prerogative under the law that existed then. So applying this new, higher law, beyond that is not warranted, as will be more clearly seen in the discussion below.

The ease with which a divorce could be granted made the serious nature of the act unappreciated. Today it is still unappreciated. Divorce rates among Latter-day Saints have risen to practically mirror the population at large. We follow all the surrounding social trends, but are a little slower in getting there. We are not "peculiar" any longer. We are just slower.

Christ was re-enshrining the significance of marriage. It should not be easy to end a marriage. But, then again, perhaps the kind of marriage Christ is speaking of is one of a higher order and rarely exists here.

Although there are reasons for every marriage to be treated as sacred and worth preserving, it was always intended for there to be a higher purpose in marriage. It was intended to be an eternal union, inside of which sacred acts mirroring heaven itself take place. Bringing into this world new life by the loving union of two partners is a mirror of heaven. Such things are, or ought to be, most sacred.

But a higher kind of union, where love is the prevailing rule, is not often established here. More often than not, the marriages of this world are corrupted, just as society itself is corrupted.

I hardly dare offer a different view of these verses, because people think they know what they're reading in them. I'm not sure we have ever seen what Christ is actually speaking about. Though caution would suggest otherwise, I'm going to go ahead with offering a different view.

First, this is always interpreted to be discussing things which are coarse or material, but it comes immediately following a discussion about the inner or spiritual self. This suggests our normal reading of this language may be incorrect. When the focus of Christ's new and higher law is the inner man, then to read this as applying to outward behavior (fornication/adultery) may miss the point.

Second, notice the contrast between the only justified reason for terminating the marriage (fornication) and the subsequent results (adultery). Two different words are used, suggesting two different meanings are present.

I've consulted with John Hall about the New Testament language in the Matthew account of this sermon, where "**porneia**" is the typical rendering. There the meaning of the first word which we render "fornication" could be a variety of things including: prostitution, sexual permissiveness or merely a sexual act. But, if the word was "**poneria**" then it could, by broad measure, mean bad acts (with no sexual connotation at all).

There is a possibility that the correct way to read this could be rendered in this way: "Whoever puts away his wife for any reason other than the lack of marital intimacy..." That would mean the only justified reason to end the marriage is that the marriage has ended within the heart. There is no longer any love in the relation. It has died. It is no longer worthy of preservation, and therefore, the death of the heart justifies the death of the relation.

However, the focus is on the woman's heart. That is, if the woman still retains marital intimacy for the husband, he cannot be justified in putting her away. He is obligated to retain as his wife the woman who loves him. If he puts away such a wife, then he causes her to commit adultery.

This, then, raises the issue of the meaning of adultery. We tend to view it as a physical act involving sexual union with another. But adultery also holds the connotation of unfaithfulness, as in Israel becoming unfaithful and playing the part of an adulteress, worshiping other gods.[855] When forced away by the man she loves, a woman is then "adulterated" by the act of the man. He is accountable for the treachery involved in dissolving the marriage which the woman wanted, and

---

[855] Jer. 3: 8: "And I saw, when for all the causes whereby backsliding Israel committed adultery I had put her away, and given her a bill of divorce; yet her treacherous sister Judah feared not, but went and played the harlot also."

forcing her into the relation with either no one, or with another man. Either one is "adulterating" the marriage which she had with him. He is accountable for that uncharitable, unkind, and unjustified treatment of the woman.

On the other hand, when she has lost affection for him, and the union has become hollow and without love, then the marriage is dead and continuation of the relation is a farce. It is not a marriage. In fact, it is a pretense and an abomination unworthy of preservation. It will not endure. It is not eternal and not possible to preserve beyond the grave.

No union that has not been sealed by the Holy Spirit of Promise will endure beyond the grave.[856] The reason for sealing such a marriage by the promise of the Spirit is because it replicates the kind of holy union found in heaven. It is like unto the unions between gods and goddesses. It is worthy of preservation because it is eternal. It is enduring. It is worth preserving into all eternity. It is sealed because the gods recognize on the earth a mirror of what is found in heaven itself. Therefore heaven ratifies and approves the relationship. They do not create such relations in heaven, but instead recognize them here, and approve them for eternal duration. Without such a relationship, the parties are worthy of continuation as angels, but not as spouses, as Christ would put it elsewhere.[857]

It is true enough that the restored Gospel allows everyone the opportunity to come to the Temple and receive ordinances which hold

---

[856] References include, among others, D&C 132: 7, 18: "And verily I say unto you, that the conditions of this law are these: All covenants, contracts, bonds, obligations, oaths, vows, performances, connections, associations, or expectations, that are not made and entered into and sealed by the Holy Spirit of promise, of him who is anointed, both as well for time and for all eternity, and that too most holy, by revelation and commandment through the medium of mine anointed, whom I have appointed on the earth to hold this power (and I have appointed unto my servant Joseph to hold this power in the last days, and there is never but one on the earth at a time on whom this power and the keys of this priesthood are conferred), are of no efficacy, virtue, or force in and after the resurrection from the dead; for all contracts that are not made unto this end have an end when men are dead. …And again, verily I say unto you, if a man marry a wife, and make a covenant with her for time and for all eternity, if that covenant is not by me or by my word, which is my law, and is not sealed by the Holy Spirit of promise, through him whom I have anointed and appointed unto this power, then it is not valid neither of force when they are out of the world, because they are not joined by me, saith the Lord, neither by my word; when they are out of the world it cannot be received there, because the angels and the gods are appointed there, by whom they cannot pass; they cannot, therefore, inherit my glory; for my house is a house of order, saith the Lord God."

[857] Matt. 22: 30: "For in the resurrection they neither marry, nor are given in marriage, but are as the angels of God in heaven."
D&C 132: 17: "For these angels did not abide my law; therefore, they cannot be enlarged, but remain separately and singly, without exaltation, in their saved condition, to all eternity; and from henceforth are not gods, but are angels of God forever and ever."

the promise of an eternal union. But those are relationships where the parties are on probation. They are given as an opportunity to work out your salvation before God. They are given so that if you are true and faithful, the time may come when you are called up and chosen by the Holy Spirit of Promise to be kings and queens, priests and priestesses, whereas now you are only given opportunity to prove yourself worthy to become such.

There are many unhappy Latter-day Saint marriages which exist in name only. The notorious high record use of anti-depressants by women in Utah is driven in large part by unhappy marriages they believe ought to be preserved because of a misunderstanding of these verses. Yet the underlying reality that the union causes suffering rather than rejoicing cannot be escaped. So they alter their natural reaction to the unhappy union by altering the brain with chemicals. Such a marriage cannot endure into eternity. Though the woman may sacrifice herself to preserve her heart's desire to be a faithful, married mother, her unworthy marriage is not what will endure. It cannot be sealed by the Holy Spirit of Promise, though she may be otherwise qualified.

Now, to be clear, I do not advocate divorce, particularly where minor children are involved. But I do advocate a higher view of the marital union where the prevailing reason for the union is love. This should be the whole preparation for marriage. Before contracting the union, the parties should look for that spouse with whom they can find heaven on earth. Unhappy marriages might all be saved if the parties would repent. The higher ideal is not impossible for any union to seek and find. That is the right of every party here, if they will but seek after it. If however, after every effort has been made to both find, and cultivate such a union, it proves to be an impossibility, then the parties ought to use the precious time allotted to them in mortality to find a union which will be worthy of continuation. Not at the expense of their children, who are entitled to have both parents raise them. The Holy Spirit of Promise was intended to be shed upon many marriages, rather than a comparative few. Happiness was the design of our creation. When we avoid it by our misconduct and foolishness, we do not please heaven. Nor does gritting our teeth, putting up with miserable relationships, and enduring an unholy union please heaven or merit some eternal reward.

These words of Christ are speaking of a higher way to conduct our lives. To read into them exclusively outward behavior, when the whole import of the sermon addresses the inner-man, is out of context. I think we hardly understand the Lord's meaning. But, then again, perhaps it is best if we do not understand His full meaning until we are ready to see for ourselves what great things the Lord has in store for those who love

Him.[858] Perhaps it is best that man is not capable of making them known.

Now, as to the woman, there is another standard. He does not articulate it here, but can be found throughout scripture. A woman's love of and fidelity to her husband is more often than not a product of her nature. It takes quite a fool to turn a wife's natural affection for him into distrust and bitterness. But there are churlish men, as we know from scripture. Sometimes they marry an Abigail.[859]

3 Nephi 12: 33-37

> **"And again it is written, thou shalt not forswear thyself, but shalt perform unto the Lord thine oaths; But verily, verily, I say unto you, swear not at all; neither by heaven, for it is God's throne; Nor by the earth, for it is his footstool; Neither shalt thou swear by thy head, because thou canst not make one hair black or white; But let your communication be Yea, yea; Nay, nay; for whatsoever cometh of more than these is evil."**

This revokes the oath making of the earlier Dispensation. When an oath was taken it was to be performed without fail.[860] It was binding.

---

[858] D&C 76: 114-117: "But great and marvelous are the works of the Lord, and the mysteries of his kingdom which he showed unto us, which surpass all understanding in glory, and in might, and in dominion; Which he commanded us we should not write while we were yet in the Spirit, and are not lawful for man to utter; Neither is man capable to make them known, for they are only to be seen and understood by the power of the Holy Spirit, which God bestows on those who love him, and purify themselves before him; To whom he grants this privilege of seeing and knowing for themselves;"

[859] 1 Sam. 25: 3: "Now the name of the man *was* Nabal; and the name of his wife Abigail: and *she was* a woman of good understanding, and of a beautiful countenance: but the man *was* churlish and evil in his doings; and he *was* of the house of Caleb."

[860] Num. 30: 2: "If a man vow a vow unto the Lord, or swear an oath to bind his soul with a bond; he shall not break his word, he shall do according to all that proceedeth out of his mouth.

Ancient Israel relied on vows to govern their conduct.[861] Oaths were relied on because they bound your conduct before God.

Christ is putting an end to the practice. No further vow-making was to take place. In its place say "yea" or say "nay," but nothing further to bind your soul before God.

Swearing by men who possess nothing is foolish and prideful. Particularly when they swear by heaven, because it is not theirs to promise. Nor should they swear by the earth, because it is not theirs either. A man cannot even offer his own life, because it belongs to God who gave it. Indeed, there is nothing we own or can offer.[862]

The comment regarding the inability to make a single hair "black or white" is emphasizing how little control we really have over things. Even our own bodies will take a course assigned it by God. They will age, and eventually die. We have our body as a stewardship. It is ours for a season, then we will lay it down. Until then, we serve a probation in which we are given power over these elements we occupy. But that stewardship is one designed to "prove" us, and show what we really are.

---

[861] 1 Ne. 4: 33-37: "And I spake unto him, even with an oath, that he need not fear; that he should be a free man like unto us if he would go down in the wilderness with us. And I also spake unto him, saying: Surely the Lord hath commanded us to do this thing; and shall we not be diligent in keeping the commandments of the Lord? Therefore, if thou wilt go down into the wilderness to my father thou shalt have place with us. And it came to pass that Zoram did take courage at the words which I spake. Now Zoram was the name of the servant; and he promised that he would go down into the wilderness unto our father. Yea, and he also made an oath unto us that he would tarry with us from that time forth. Now we were desirous that he should tarry with us for this cause, that the Jews might not know concerning our flight into the wilderness, lest they should pursue us and destroy us. And it came to pass that when Zoram had made an oath unto us, our fears did cease concerning him."

[862] Mosiah 2: 20-25: "I say unto you, my brethren, that if you should render all the thanks and praise which your whole soul has power to possess, to that God who has created you, and has kept and preserved you, and has caused that ye should rejoice, and has granted that ye should live in peace one with another—I say unto you that if ye should serve him who has created you from the beginning, and is preserving you from day to day, by lending you breath, that ye may live and move and do according to your own will, and even supporting you from one moment to another—I say, if ye should serve him with all your whole souls yet ye would be unprofitable servants. And behold, all that he requires of you is to keep his commandments; and he has promised you that if ye would keep his commandments ye should prosper in the land; and he never doth vary from that which he hath said; therefore, if ye do keep his commandments he doth bless you and prosper you. And now, in the first place, he hath created you, and granted unto you your lives, for which ye are indebted unto him. And secondly, he doth require that ye should do as he hath commanded you; for which if ye do, he doth immediately bless you; and therefore he hath paid you. And ye are still indebted unto him, and are, and will be, forever and ever; therefore, of what have ye to boast? And now I ask, can ye say aught of yourselves? I answer you, Nay. Ye cannot say that ye are even as much as the dust of the earth; yet ye were created of the dust of the earth; but behold, it belongeth to him who created you."

When we gratify the body at the expense of others, or destroy our bodily temple housing our spirits by indulging uncontrolled appetites, we are unwise. We will lose these bodies before long and then, left with the same spiritual emptiness which caused the cravings in the first place, will find ourselves suffering. Whereas, if you discipline the body, keep it under control and subject to your spirit, then death can bring a release and freedom from suffering. It will be an odd reversal. One known only to those who go through it; at which point it is too late to change the outcome.

Additionally, Christ is suggesting that we speak in plain language, without the rhetoric of grand threats or promises. Speak simply. Speak out of an abundance of humility. Mean what you say, and do not obligate yourself to do what you cannot do.

Live simply, prepare to deal honestly with one another. And leave the heavens out of your promises if you cannot control them.

Do not commit yourself to do anything by swearing to God it shall be done. You have no control over when you will die, whether you will have another day of health to accomplish what you have vowed, or even if the thing about which you committed yourself will continue to be possible. Be humble about what you are given. Be grateful.

These verses address a social standard that needed to be left behind. Coming out of that should be a replacement of plain speaking, humility about what we are able to do, and caution about words we use.

In this reformation alone Christ proves Himself to be a sage. He was more than a wise teacher, He was the Great Teacher. This concept alone makes Him one of the greatest social reformers of the ancient world.

3 Nephi 12: 38-39

> **"And behold, it is written, an eye for an eye, and a tooth for a tooth; But I say unto you, that ye shall not resist evil, but whosoever shall smite thee on thy right cheek, turn to him the other also;"**

This is reforming the law of retaliation or lex talionis. When first adopted, the law of retaliation was designed to limit retribution. It was merciful in the context of the time. It prevented taking a life for an eye. The scope of the injury suffered put a limit on the scope of the retaliation permitted. I taught a class on this ancient law in the BYU Education Week some years ago. It is too much to cover in this post in order to fully understand the ramifications of this law.

The popular understanding of that law is quite a distortion. The injury permitted was not actually exacted under the law. "An eye for an eye" meant that the victim was entitled to take the eye of the one causing the injury. In practice the eye was not taken. The value of the eye was agreed upon between victim and perpetrator. They sealed the agreement before two witnesses in the gate of the city. Then the debtor was obligated to pay the agreed sum (called "satisfaction"). If he defaulted the elders could take the eye as penalty for the default in payment, which stood as collateral for the debt.

Payment of "satisfaction" was permitted and given for offenses under the *lex talionis* except in the case of a limited class of offenses, including murder.[863] In such cases it was considered too dangerous to allow satisfaction, and therefore the penalty needed to be carried out.

Here, Christ is replacing that entire body of law by substituting forgiveness and mercy for justice and recompense. The victim is being urged to seek nothing in return for his injury. Instead, the victim is to bear the injury and allow evil against themselves without retaliation for the offense.

This may seem odd, even wrong. However, there is an example of this in the Book of Mormon. Although many lives were lost in the process, it resulted in the salvation of many souls. The Anti-Lehi-Nephites were unwilling to take up arms to defend themselves, instead allowing their enemies to slay them. The result broke the hearts of those who were killing them, and many were converted by this example.[864]

---

[863] Num. 35: 31-32: "Moreover ye shall take no satisfaction for the life of a murderer, which *is* guilty of death: but he shall be surely put to death. And ye shall take no satisfaction for him that is fled to the city of his refuge, that he should come again to dwell in the land, until the death of the priest."

[864] Alma 24: 19-27: "And thus we see that, when these Lamanites were brought to believe and to know the truth, they were firm, and would suffer even unto death rather than commit sin; and thus we see that they buried their weapons of peace, or they buried the weapons of war, for peace. And it came to pass that their brethren, the Lamanites, made preparations for war, and came up to the land of Nephi for the purpose of destroying the king, and to place another in his stead, and also of destroying the people of Anti-Nephi-Lehi out of the land. Now when the people saw that they were coming against them they went out to meet them, and prostrated themselves before them to the earth, and began to call on the name of the Lord; and thus they were in this attitude when the Lamanites began to fall upon them, and began to slay them with the sword. And thus without meeting any resistance, they did slay a thousand and five of them; and we know that they are blessed, for they have gone to dwell with their God. Now when the Lamanites saw that their brethren would not flee from the sword, neither would they turn aside to the right hand or to the left, but that they would lie down and perish, and praised God even in the very act of perishing under the sword—Now when the Lamanites saw this they did forbear from slaying them; and there were many whose hearts had swollen in them for those of their brethren who had fallen under the sword, for they repented of the things which they had done. And it came to pass that they threw down their weapons of war, and they would not take them again, for they were stung for the murders which they had committed; and they came down even as their brethren, relying upon the mercies of those whose arms were lifted to slay them. And it came to pass that the people of God were joined that day by more than the number who had been slain; and those who had been slain were righteous people, therefore we have no reason to doubt but what they were saved. And there was not a wicked man slain among them; but there were more than a thousand brought to the knowledge of the truth; thus we see that the Lord worketh in many ways to the salvation of his people."

But the people of God were joined by more than the number who were slain.

The book by C. Terry Warner titled *The Bonds That Make Us Free: Healing Our Relationships, Coming to Ourselves* explains how the actions of those who forgive are able to break the hearts of those who are forgiven. There is not merely freedom in forgiving others, there is power in it as well. Terry Warner's book is an examination of the principles of sin and forgiveness, and worth reading if you have not done so before.

We gain power by what things we suffer for the Lord's sake. Christ who loved the most, sacrificed the most. Those two things are linked together.

This teaching was not only given by Christ, but it was lived by Him also. In this statement, as in no other, He is defining who He is and revealing what His conduct invariably will be. This is the Lord's standard. This is the Lord's manner. The choice of turning the other cheek is taken from the Messianic standard described by Isaiah.[865] We can also heal others by the things we willingly suffer. We can endure and forgive. As we do righteousness increases on the earth.

Saint Francis Assisi believed this, practiced it. In an age of darkness and apostasy, the Lord spoke with St. Francis, and sent angels to minister to him. He is appropriately referred to as a Saint. He lived the Sermon on the Mount. It is perhaps St. Francis, who above all others, proves a mortal may walk in the Lord's steps. Christ did it first and more completely than would any other. But St. Francis surely followed.

I have little doubt that the Lord's teachings are impractical in this world. But, then again, we are not called to live for this world, are we? The reason Zion always flees from this world is precisely because the Lord will not permit the world to overwhelm those who would surely be overthrown if not for His grace and protection. He will fight their battles to spare those in Zion from the necessity of becoming warlike.[866]

I am amused by the martial inclinations of the Latter-day Saints. When the lamb and lion lie down together I suppose many of the Latter-day Saints expect to be able to hunt them both.

3 Nephi 12: 40-42

> **"And if any man will sue thee at the law and take away thy coat, let him have thy cloak also; And whosoever shall compel thee to**

---

[865] Isa. 50: 6: "I gave my back to the smiters, and my cheeks to them that plucked off the hair: I hid not my face from shame and spitting."
Isa. 53: 5: "But he *was* wounded for our transgressions, *he was* bruised for our iniquities: the chastisement of our peace *was* upon him; and with his stripes we are healed."

[866] D&C 105: 14: "For behold, I do not require at their hands to fight the battles of Zion; for, as I said in a former commandment, even so will I fulfil—I will fight your battles."

go a mile, go with him twain. Give to him that asketh thee, and from him that would borrow of thee turn thou not away."

This is the point Mark Twain quipped included him in the Bible. He suggested "Go with him Twain" is Divine notice given him.

The cloak covers the cloak. If someone wants one, give them both. Without conflict. Without retaliation. Give those who demand.

The law allowed a Roman soldier to compel a civilian to bear a load for a mile. Christ said submit, and go a second mile to demonstrate you have not been compelled at all. You have chosen to give the service.

When asked, give. When someone needs to borrow, let them.

What a markedly different world this would be.

The results of an entire society behaving in this manner would be Zion itself. There would be no poor. Those with the means would share, those in need would ask. The resulting cooperation and mutual assistance would solve many social ills. But such a society would necessarily be voluntary. To attempt to level the economic circumstances of society by force would be an imprisonment, not a liberation. Government cannot impose it, but men can voluntarily implement it.

In our early post-Nauvoo distress, there was a brief time when we flirted with notions like these. We did some voluntary collective work on providing a social system to benefit everyone. Those ended because of the bickering and turmoil. We went back to tithing, which still today allows us to retain our individual fortunes and limit sharing our individual misfortunes.

The question is what happens when a society continues to suffer from all the ills of our own, but a single individual chooses to live these principles. What then? Can a person really live like this when he or she alone is guided by these principles?

Common agreement is that this sermon's admonitions are impractical. They won't work. They can't be lived by a single person acting alone, or a small group acting together, because a larger corrupt society will overwhelm and exploit them. Therefore, Christ is teaching what cannot be done. At least cannot be done by anyone who is unwilling to try it. Occasionally we get a Mother Teresa or a Saint Francis, but they're Catholic. Surely it can't work with Latter-day Saints who are busy studying Steven Covey's books, polishing their resumes and looking to find a secure middle-management position from which to launch their successful careers. Maybe a handful of good, believing Catholics will found Zion. Then we can come in and help manage the results after it becomes well enough established. After all, we have the true franchise from which Zion will be built. We even own a bank already named for the venture.

It makes you wonder why Christ would preach something which only a handful of Catholics have successfully accomplished in an individual setting.

3 Nephi 12: 43-45

> **"And behold it is written also, that thou shalt love thy neighbor and hate thine enemy; But behold I say unto you, love your enemies, bless them that curse you, do good to them that hate you, and pray for them who despitefully use you and persecute you; That ye may be the children of your Father who is in heaven; for he maketh his sun to rise on the evil and on the good."**

Loving the ones you care for, associate with, and live nearby is sometimes easy. Hating those who show you disrespect or cause you injury is normal. Nevertheless, Christ teaches to love enemies, bless those who are trying to do you harm, and pray for your persecutors.

This is the only way to become like Him. He is an intercessor. As I've explained in *The Second Comforter*, becoming an intercessor for others is part of development, through grace, to become as He is. It is through this that charity becomes a part of your character.[867] And charity is a necessary attribute in character.[868]

This treatment of enemies is how you prove your inner self. Only by suffering, do we learn if we are converted. If you receive only praise and adulation, authority and wealth, prestige and acceptance as a result of following Christ, then you've never been proven. It is through the sacrifice of your good name, reputation, position, wealth and social standing that you learn if you truly trust in Christ.

When you actually do sacrifice all earthly things for Him, you will have knowledge that the course of your life is pleasing to Him. Anything less than this will leave your mind in doubt.[869]

If you follow this teaching by Christ, you will convert yourself first, then others. No-one can doubt the goodness of a life lived as this teaching commends. Though such a life may not convert others immediately, it will triumph.

Sometimes people die teaching the truth. They surrendered all they were on the altar, thereby coming to know God. This teaching would allow anyone to do the same. You would have to not only accept the idea, you would need to implement it.

---

[867] Moroni 7: 46: "Wherefore, my beloved brethren, if ye have not charity, ye are nothing, for charity never faileth. Wherefore, cleave unto charity, which is the greatest of all, for all things must fail—"

[868] 2 Ne. 26: 30: "Behold, the Lord hath forbidden this thing; wherefore, the Lord God hath given a commandment that all men should have charity, which charity is love. And except they should have charity they were nothing. Wherefore, if they should have charity they would not suffer the laborer in Zion to perish."
Moroni 7: 47: "But charity is the pure love of Christ, and it endureth forever; and whoso is found possessed of it at the last day, it shall be well with him."

[869] See post on Lecture 6 of *Lectures on Faith* at http://denversnuffer.blogspot.com/2010/04/lectures-of-faith-no-6.html

Abinadi returned to bear witness of the truth, and then die. Alma was his only convert. But from the moment of Alma's conversion to the end of the Book of Mormon, every character who wrote in the plates descended from Abinadi's single convert.

Abinadi was a hinge character around whom the story of the Nephites would pivot from his life onward. But he had little success, and was killed by those to whom he ministered.

In some respects, dying for the cause of Christ is easier than living it. This teaching, however, shows how you can begin to live it.

It is not designed to be easy. As I discussed in *Beloved Enos*, sometimes it takes quite a bit of effort to come to terms with what the Lord requires of us. But that does not alter in the least the importance of doing it, or lessen the quality of the results obtained.

Keep in mind the Lord's admonition: "If ye love me, keep my commandments."[870]

Remember also the Lord's statement that the things He is teaching "at this time" are necessary to enter into the kingdom of Heaven.[871] These are not just sayings. They are meant to be acted on. It is in the doing of them you will meet Him. When you descend below where you are at the present, you will find the Lord. For He is condescending whenever He is seen.

Finally, Christ reminds us that the Lord blesses all with the sun, light, life and abundance. Both good and evil are blessed by Him. Therefore, the petty differences between the good and the bad are so insignificant when compared against an absolute standard of perfection that the relative goodness and relative badness is inconsequential. So inconsequential that for any of us to be redeemed will require the atonement. Therefore, we all owe everything to Him. Only the redeemed come to realize and accept that while here. Everyone will eventually grasp that reality.

Accepting Him is the means for healing us. His open invitation to all can be seen in the sun shining on "both the evil and on the good." Everyone is bidden to come to the throne and receive healing, grace and forgiveness. To merit it, you must first give it. To obtain forgiveness you must give forgiveness. To have Him suffer for your sins, you must first suffer and forgive others of their sins committed against you.

Every balanced life surrenders claims for justice and shows mercy, thereby making a claim for themselves upon mercy.

---

[870] John 14: 15: "If ye love me, keep my commandments."

[871] 3 Ne. 12: 20: "Therefore come unto me and be ye saved; for verily I say unto you, that except ye shall keep my commandments, which I have commanded you at this time, ye shall in no case enter into the kingdom of heaven."

3 Nephi 12: 46-47

> **"Therefore those things which were of old time, which were under the law, in me are all fulfilled. Old things are done away, and all things have become new."**

Christ will elaborate on this later as the audience puzzles over what is removed and what remains. But here Christ introduces the concept that the Law of Moses is now "fulfilled." Importantly, He says: "in me are all fulfilled."

When He walked on the Road to Emmaus on the day of His resurrection, He began with the Law of Moses and explained: "And beginning at Moses and all the prophets, he expounded unto them in all the scriptures the things concerning himself."[872] I've spoken on this and then published the talk in the Appendix to *Eighteen Verses*. The talk shows how the rites and temple of the Dispensation of Moses testified to the details of His life. It ought to be noted that the thing "under the law, in [Christ were indeed] all fulfilled." His life was foreshadowed by the rites of Moses. His healing and His ministry, His history and His sacrifice, all were foreshadowed by the Law of Moses.

Since the Law pointed to Him, and He came to live His mortal life in conformity with that Law, it was now completed. The signpost was no longer necessary. The event had happened.

When He says, "Old things are done away" it is not because they are terminated. It is because they were fulfilled. He completed the circle. He lived and died under the Law, fulfilling every jot and tittle of its requirements.

Now it was time to push the meaning of the earlier Law deeper into the souls of His audience. "All things have become new." It is a new beginning, a new Dispensation, a new message. This message was delivered by the author of the Law of Moses not through an intermediary. This message comes from the Author in person.

Dispensations have their bounds. Beforehand, the prophets give, through prophecy, a limit on the things which are to come. When the prophesied events have unfolded and the measure has been met, then one Dispensation comes to an end while another opens. John the Baptist closed the Dispensation of Moses. Christ opened the Dispensation of the Meridian of Time. He recognizes the transition in this statement.

Whenever things are "become new" again, it is important to recognize the signs of the time.[873] Those living contemporary with Christ who did not recognize the signs remained at Jerusalem and were

---

[872] Luke 24: 27: "And beginning at Moses and all the prophets, he expounded unto them in all the scriptures the things concerning himself."

[873] Matt. 16: 2-3: "He answered and said unto them, When it is evening, ye say, *It will be* fair weather: for the sky is red. And in the morning, *It will be* foul weather to day: for the sky is red and lowring, O *ye* hypocrites, ye can discern the face of the sky; but can ye not *discern* the signs of the times?"

destroyed.[874] It is important that you be on watch, for in the very hour you think it unlikely for Him to act He will act.[875]

Everything was fulfilled by Christ, and everything prophesied will happen before He comes again. There is no more scrupulous a follower of the prophetic promises than the Lord. He inspired the prophecies, and intends that they all come to pass. In Him have all things been fulfilled, and in Him will all things yet remaining be fulfilled.

3 Nephi 12: 48

> **"Therefore I would that ye should be perfect even as I, or your Father who is in heaven is perfect."**

In the Matthew text Christ unequivocally limited this to His Father.[876] Here "perfection" is achieved by both Christ and His Father.

Assuming the Matthew text is correct, the difference is significant. It is another confirmation that anyone who is mortal, including the Lord, stands in jeopardy every hour.[877] He simply could not claim perfection while in mortality because mortality is a time of change, challenge and temptation. After all, He was tempted while mortal just as every human soul is tempted.[878] Though He chose to give no heed to it, He was nevertheless tempted.[879]

---

[874] JS-Matt. 1: 13-18: "Then let them who are in Judea flee into the mountains; Let him who is on the housetop flee, and not return to take anything out of his house; Neither let him who is in the field return back to take his clothes; And wo unto them that are with child, and unto them that give suck in those days; Therefore, pray ye the Lord that your flight be not in the winter, neither on the Sabbath day; For then, in those days, shall be great tribulation on the Jews, and upon the inhabitants of Jerusalem, such as was not before sent upon Israel, of God, since the beginning of their kingdom until this time; no, nor ever shall be sent again upon Israel."

[875] JS-Matt. 1: 48: "Therefore be ye also ready, for in such an hour as ye think not, the Son of Man cometh."

[876] Matt. 5: 48: "Be ye therefore perfect, even as your Father which is in heaven is perfect."

[877] 1 Cor. 15: 30: "And why stand we in jeopardy every hour?"

[878] Heb. 4: 15: "For we have not an high priest which cannot be touched with the feeling of our infirmities; but was in all points tempted like as *we are, yet* without sin."

[879] D&C 20: 22: "He suffered temptations but gave no heed unto them."

While mortal He looked to the Father in all things.[880] After concluding His time in mortality, achieving the resurrection of the dead, He was given all power in heaven and on earth.[881]

Therefore, if the Matthew text is correct, and the differences are accounted for in what we have just reviewed, then the admonition of Christ for our own perfection is not just an earthly endeavor. It is an invitation to follow Him and His Father into a loftier state, as well.[882] One where the final realization will come only as we are able to endure greater glory than a mortal may possess.[883]

It is good we know this commandment is possible to accomplish.[884] It is hard to conceive of following the Son in this way. Yet it is He who pronounced it, and He who has promised to share the throne of His Father with all who will come to Him.[885]

I am not perfect, nor anything like it. I have seen Perfection, know what it is, and can confirm I am nothing like it.

A harmonious symmetry of light, majesty, holiness, glory and power are all around Him who is perfection. When I read the admonition to "be ye therefore perfect, even as I or your Father who is in Heaven is perfect" I can hardly grasp how that gulf between us could be bridged. I understand about the Lord's atonement. I have certainly been the beneficiary of it and will continue to be so. When I consider the infinite gulf between His and His Father's perfection, and my own imperfection, I am left completely stupefied at the idea it is even possible. Nevertheless, He gives no command which He does not provide means to obey. Therefore the means do exist.

When I hear from the casual observer of the LDS faith the stupidity about how we are going to "get exalted," I wonder at what the reaction will be when they finally realize how great the gulf separating us from that result is. I have some appreciation for what will be required, and know it will be eons before that end can be attained by any of us. It will

---

880 John 5: 30: "I can of mine own self do nothing: as I hear, I judge: and my judgment is just; because I seek not mine own will, but the will of the Father which hath sent me."

881 Matt. 28: 18: "And Jesus came and spake unto them, saying, All power is given unto me in heaven and in earth."

882 Abraham 3.

883 Moses 1: 5: "Wherefore, no man can behold all my works, except he behold all my glory; and no man can behold all my glory, and afterwards remain in the flesh on the earth."

884 1 Ne. 3: 7: "And it came to pass that I, Nephi, said unto my father: I will go and do the things which the Lord hath commanded, for I know that the Lord giveth no commandments unto the children of men, save he shall prepare a way for them that they may accomplish the thing which he commandeth them."

885 Rev. 3: 21: "To him that overcometh will I grant to sit with me in my throne, even as I also overcame, and am set down with my Father in his throne."

not be magic. It will be through incremental improvement, being added upon, growing in light and truth, and perfectly natural in the process. Joseph Smith put it in these words in the King Follett Funeral Sermon: *"When you climb up a ladder, you must begin at the bottom, and ascend step by step, until you arrive at the top; and so it is with the principles of the Gospel——you must begin with the first, and go on until you learn all the principles of exaltation. But it will be a great while after you have passed through the veil before you will have learned them. It is not all to be comprehended in this world; it will be a great work to learn our salvation and exaltation even beyond the grave."*

We are not left without warning about how great the gulf is we are to cover in this bridge we are to cross. Even now it seems the best use of our time would be to meditate on the things of God day and night. The revelations inform us that "Whatevcr principle of intelligence we attain unto in this life, it will rise with us in the resurrection. And if a person gains more knowledge and intelligence in this life through his diligence and obedience than another, he will have so much the advantage in the world to come."[886] Yet we seem collectively often pedestrians in a crowd milling aimlessly about presuming Christ will furnish us an easy time of it. His atonement removes from us all guilt and shame. But for perfection, we must acquire it bit by bit, grace for grace, line upon line, growing by accepting more until at last we have obtained what is needed. That will be our own doing. He provides the means, and His Father ordained the laws by which it can be done, and they provide us with free will and the capacity to choose, but we must choose. We must accept. We must press forward holding Their hands in order to arrive at last, after an infinitely long journey, in the courts of Heaven itself, fit to reside there.

Be ye therefore perfect. And start on that this moment. For you haven't another moment to spare.

---

[886] D&C 130: 18-19: "Whatever principle of intelligence we attain unto in this life, it will rise with us in the resurrection. And if a person gains more knowledge and intelligence in this life through his diligence and obedience than another, he will have so much the advantage in the world to come."

3 Nephi 13

3 Nephi 13: 1-4

> **"Verily, verily, I say that I would that ye should do alms unto the poor; but take heed that ye do not your alms before men to be seen of them; otherwise ye have no reward of your Father who is in heaven. Therefore, when ye shall do your alms do not sound a trumpet before you, as will hypocrites do in the synagogues and in the streets, that they may have glory of men. Verily I say unto you, they have their reward. But when thou doest alms let not thy left hand know what thy right hand doeth; That thine alms may be in secret; and thy Father who seeth in secret, himself shall reward thee openly."**

Giving should be done for its own sake, and not for a reward. Recognition for what a person has done is its own reward.

If this is a larger principle, and the reasoning underlying this applies throughout your service or good acts, then any recognition is your payment. In fact, the only way to reserve for yourself a blessing is to be either anonymous when you do it, or to be reviled, hated or persecuted for it. Otherwise you have your reward.

Applying this to like things it might be said that:

- When men name buildings after you for your achievements, you have your reward.
- When institutions heap awards upon you for your philanthropic acts, you have your reward.
- When they fill an auditorium up with people singing praises and paying tribute to you on your birthday, you have your reward.
- When honorary doctorate degrees are awarded to you for your life's work, you have your reward.
- When the Boy Scouts of America gives you a plaque, a title, and a commendation for your long support of their cause, you have your reward.

- When you sit at the head of a congregation, exciting envy from others wishing to hold your position, and are honored with praise, acknowledged as presiding and accepting deference for your status as local, area or regional leader, you may very well have your reward.
- If you minister to the downtrodden, the ill and infirm, then recount endlessly to others these acts, do you not "sound a trumpet before you" to be seen of men, and thereby collect your reward?

When Christ was called "good," He rebuked the one rendering praise with the retort: "Why callest thou me good? none is good, save one, that is, God."[887] He would accept their persecution, derision and shame, but discouraged any praise. He accepted Peter's confession of His status as "the Christ, the Son of the Living God" but followed up that confession of faith with the admonition to not speak of it: "Then charged he his disciples that they should tell no man that he was Jesus the Christ."[888]

How can His servants exalt themselves to be more than He? How can the Servant's own servants make themselves greater than He? When the Master came and lived the most common of lives, how can His disciples build monuments named for themselves, tolerate no criticism, accept honor, praise and adulation and expect to be counted as His?

How can any man redeem or rescue another? Are not all in need of rescuing by Him who alone can provide deliverance? Acclaim and praise in this life preclude recognition from the Lord in the afterlife. Therefore, only a fool would welcome praise, adulation and recognition for good things done in mortality. Indeed, such recognized deeds are often a veneer covering a malignant character. As a result, the Lord offers a test to prove sincerity: Do it in secret. Do it without notice or praise. Do it not to be seen of men. Do it as an act in private between you and the Lord alone, without any earthly party becoming aware of the deed. Then the beneficiary will indeed give glory to your Father which is in heaven, and not to another man.[889]

This new standard challenges not merely the acts of a person, but also the underlying reasons and intent for any acts that are done. Your conduct is not the measure. It is your heart. For that, it is best if men do not understand you. It is best if they misjudge you, attribute foul motive when motive is pure, ascribe evil to you when you are on the Lord's errand, and reject you though you are His. Only then can your heart

---

[887] Luke 18: 18-19: "And a certain ruler asked him, saying, Good Master, what shall I do to inherit eternal life? And Jesus said unto him, Why callest thou me good? none *is* good, save one, *that is,* God."

[888] Matt. 16: 20: "Then charged he his disciples that they should tell no man that he was Jesus the Christ."

[889] 3 Ne. 12: 16: "Therefore let your light so shine before this people, that they may see your good works and glorify your Father who is in heaven."

remain true to Him and uncompromised by the praise of your fellow-man.

It is this teaching, if followed, that will result in the anonymous acts and unrecognized deeds that exalt a person. It will make you private in your devotions and obscure to your fellow man.

3 Nephi 13: 5-6

> **"And when thou prayest thou shalt not do as the hypocrites, for they love to pray, standing in the synagogues and in the corners of the streets, that they may be seen of men. Verily I say unto you, they have their reward. But thou, when thou prayest, enter into thy closet, and when thou hast shut thy door, pray to thy Father who is in secret; and thy Father, who seeth in secret, shall reward thee openly."**

Like the previous verses, this verse is saying prayer ought to be private, not public. It should be between you and God. Others do not need to know of, see, or participate in your prayers. Most importantly, your prayers ought not be put on display for others to notice and admire.

There are public prayer occasions, of course. Those come every time a meeting opens and closes with a prayer. For such opportunities there will always be a prayer offered by one person, acting as the voice for those assembled. But the prayer is not the individual's. It is the prayer of all those assembled. This warning is about personal prayer, not group prayer.

These verses are confirming the principle that prayer should be kept private between you and God. It should not be put on public display to call attention to yourself. Those whose prayers are offered "for to be seen" are really not praying to God anyway. They are using the pretense of prayer to call attention to themselves. They want recognition. When they get recognition they have their reward. They got what they wanted: public notice.

As a result of this teaching I have some hesitation about praying at a public restaurant before a meal. If I do, it is private, unspoken, and only thought. I have always thought this teaching proscribed public prayer whenever it attracted notice.

This counsel, and the counsel immediately before, show just how solitary a journey it is back to the Lord's presence. It is not a group event. It is done in the privacy of your own heart, your own intent, and your own private conduct. It is your personal devotions which show the Lord who and what you are. By keeping these things secret between you and Him, you gain a power of familiarity with Him which will permit Him to comfort you.

I've tried to avoid ever speaking of personal matters, choosing instead to only focus on the Lord's teachings. Some people have expressed frustrations at the absence of personal details in what I've written or said. Those complaints reaffirm to me that I've weighed the matter correctly. It is not, and never has been about me or any man. It is about the Lord and His teachings. I have testified to His teachings and that they are both true and applicable to everyone. I've testified that high office and notoriety are not required, but the least are invited. When Zion finally comes, I doubt there will be many notable people there. It will be the man from Tennessee who is handy with mechanical repairs, whose calloused hands show dedication to labor for others It will be the patient Temple worker-couple who, despite the regimentation seen all around them, have pursued the Lord's will and found Him. It will be the patient and obscure people whose private devotion to the Lord is known to Him, acknowledged by His voice. The invitation to gather will come to them directly from Him.

It is in these teachings that I will be justified and required to end my public efforts. As they end, you will need to do as He has taught, and as I have endeavored to do. I will soon be ending this blog. I will be finishing up this phase of what I've been asked to do for the last several years, and hopefully be shown the courtesy of being allowed to return to my family and ward. The things I have written require a real person to stand behind them, to testify of them, and to take responsibility for what is said. I have allowed you to know who it is. But enough has been done. I look forward to returning to my own closet and laying down this more public effort.

Christ would have us all know the Father in the privacy of our individual lives. That is as true of Him as it is meant to be for us. How often He spent the night in private prayer. How often he separated Himself from His followers and prayed in secret to His Father. That is what we should accomplish more often. That is how we draw closest to Him.

You can as readily gratify your vain ambition by praying to be noticed as you can by aspiring and receiving a church position or rank. It is all vanity. There really is none who are good, except God alone.

3 Nephi 13: 7-8

> **"But when ye pray, use not vain repetitions, as the heathen, for they think that they shall be heard for their much speaking. Be not ye therefore like unto them, for your Father knoweth what things ye have need of before ye ask him."**

Here is wisdom indeed. There is no magic formula for communicating with God. No list of what is to be said or repeated. No vain —meaning ineffective—repetitions. He "gets it" even before you speak. So the act of prayer is a formal way of showing

- Respect (by doing what He has asked)

- Devotion (by showing submission to Him)

- Obedience (by keeping a commandment to pray always), and

- Companionship (by taking the time alone with Him).

He knows what you need before you ask. Indeed, sometimes the needs we think we have are not what He knows we need even before we pray.

We think we need to get a solution to interior lighting for 8 barges. We come to Him in prayer expecting to receive help for that. He knows what we really need is redemption from the Fall, instruction in the history of mankind, and knowledge of Him. He solves the lighting problem with a touch of His finger, but then goes on to reveal all things.

We think we need to know what church to join. So Joseph comes asking that one question in sincerity. He knows, however, the world needs a prophet to re-establish the long absent Church of Jesus Christ upon the earth.

We think we need to understand how to baptize. So Joseph and Oliver ask. He knows, however, the Aaronic Priesthood must be restored, and sends an angel to return it to the earth.

We think we need to know what our standing is before God. So Joseph asks, fully expecting to learn if his life has been acceptable. God knows, however, the time has come to send an angel having the everlasting Gospel to declare. So Mororni comes to declare the restoration of the book.

You take thought about what your cares are, but they are not what the Lord knows you need. Your cares are merely the tiniest of obstacles given you to remind you to pray. The Father operates on a much grander scale, dealing with the salvation of souls. He will use the man or woman of prayer as the means of accomplishing a great deal more then they imagined.

Pray. Ask simply. It is not necessary to be elaborate or long winded. State clearly what you believe you need. Accept what then comes in His answer. Trust He knows more than you. Trust He can give you what you need, even if you hadn't even thought about it as a need.

3 Nephi 13: 9-13

> **"After this manner therefore pray ye: Our Father who art in heaven, hallowed be thy name. Thy will be done on earth as it is in heaven. And forgive us our debts, as we forgive our debtors. And lead us not into temptation, but deliver us from evil. For thine is the kingdom, and the power, and the glory, forever. Amen."**

Simple. Direct. Plain.

Christ assures us that He is "Our Father" and not just His. We are all united in sharing that status with Christ. We are a family.

First He identifies the Father as "ours" and then, least we should presume too great a familiarity, He adds "hallowed be thy name." A name is important for many reasons. In the case of Deity, it was an ancient presumption that if you knew the name of an angel, demon, or god you could summon such a being by using that name. Here, however, Christ is applying sacred status to the Father's name. It is His Fatherhood that is emphasized, not His hallowed name.

The Father's will is not done on earth. Here, there is rebellion, rejection, chaos and despair. Here, order is imposed by the strong upon the weak. Men exploit, abuse and misrule. In heaven, however, the Father's rule establishes order, kindness and equity. Anyone who is aware of the fallen conditions here will ask for the Father's will to be done on earth, as it is in heaven.

That petition can also be read to mean: "Let me live on earth as if I were in heaven." Or, "let the Father's will come to earth by the life I live here." Or, "let me prove myself worthy of heaven's companionship, though I live here on earth."

The prayer links forgiving others to being forgiven. This is not merely a wise petition, it is also a statement of cause and effect. We merit forgiveness as we give it. It is by forgiving that we are forgiven.

We pay our debts by giving others forgiveness of their debts to us. I've written a chapter about this in *Come, Let Us Adore Him*. We merit what we give to others. We establish the criteria by which we will be judged as we decide how to treat others. He will return to this concept in 3 Nephi 14: 2.

When the Father leads you it will never be into temptation, but will always deliver you from evil. This is a petition which reminds us to be willing to be led. We are literally to ask the Father to help us be led by Him. Through Him we will obtain deliverance.

The Father owns the kingdom, the power and glory. Mankind does not confer that upon Him. It is His. But mankind can acknowledge it. By making that acknowledgement we are able to have confidence in Him. We can trust His power to deliver, His ability to bring again His kingdom, and to bear and share in His glory as He has promised.

Many of these simple statements are confessions of our own desires and clarify we have understanding. God's kingdom, power and glory exist independent of our prayers. But when our prayers attest that we understand this, we are making our submission and meekness known to Him. We are stating our trust in Him.

We acknowledge His kingdom is His, to be restored in His time, with His power. It is His to control. We do not envy that control, nor attempt to force Him to do our bidding. We acknowledge that His right exists, independent of man's will or ambition. He will decide and we will accept. We can ask, but He will determine the events that will take place and when they will unfold.

This prayer is an acknowledgement that we are not trying to control God, but instead are willing to be subject to Him. He is the sovereign, we are the subjects.

We ask, He decides. If He determines to do a work we defer to Him. The greater the recognition of His kingdom, power and glory, the greater the confidence we have in His decisions. The less we are inclined to argue with Him or to substitute our desires for His.

When the Lord decides to bring again Zion, it will be because the Father has decided it is time to do so. It will not be because a group has volunteered to accomplish it. When He decides, and He is the author of it, no power under heaven will stand against it. When men have ambition to create what is in His power alone to do, then they will not just fail but will be swept away.

This petition to the Father instructs us in patience and faith.

3 Nephi 13: 14-15

> **"For, if ye forgive men their trespasses your heavenly Father will also forgive you; But if ye forgive not men their trespasses neither will your Father forgive your trespasses."**

This is an absolute condition. It is mandatory.

If you forgive not men their trespasses, neither will your Father forgive you your trespass.

You can't be forgiven by the Father if you do not forgive others.

It can't be done.

That grudge you harbor prevents the Father from forgiving you.

Those resentments you think are justified are keeping you from being forgiven by the Father.

Those injustices imposed upon you by others who are unthinking or cruel must be surrendered.

The early Saints were victimized by mobs in Missouri and Illinois. They wanted revenge. Brigham Young implemented a covenant to seek vengeance upon the murderers of Joseph Smith until the third and fourth generation. They did not build Zion.

The opposite of this is forgiveness. If you forgive, your Heavenly Father WILL forgive you. Offenses are opportunities for you to gain forgiveness. All you need to do is forgive them.

It is a simple, direct cause and effect. It was ordained before the world was founded, and applies universally in all ages and among all people.

The world is in Satan's grip largely because the world seeks vengeance and refuses to forgive.

Zion, on the other hand, will be filled with those who forgive. Of course that puts an absolute limit on those who can dwell there. ...Very few indeed.

3 Nephi 13: 16-18

> **"Moreover, when ye fast be not as the hypocrites, of a sad countenance, for they disfigure their faces that they may appear unto men to fast. Verily I say unto you, they have their reward. But thou, when thou fastest, anoint thy head, and wash thy face; That thou appear not unto men to fast, but unto thy Father, who**

is in secret; and thy Father, who seeth in secret, shall reward thee openly."

Again our devotion is to be entirely private. Your inner struggle to come into God's presence should be yours. Private. Personal. Individual. Secret.

The time may come after you have found Him that He will bring you into contact with others. The journey back to Him will be individual, and private.

After you find Him, you will be His. He can do with you as He chooses. When He appears to you in the flesh, He will give you commandments.[890] He will teach you doctrine. He will direct what you should do. But that is later. Until then, the journey is private. There is nothing to announce. There should be no notice of your fasting, tithe paying, or praying. There are no notable deeds to be seen of men.

Men should see your washed face and never detect the fasting you are performing for Him alone.

Men should see your comfortable behavior and never appreciate what great things you have put on the altar in sacrifice to Him.

Men should never notice the mighty wrestle you are having with God.

When the wrestle has produced a covenant between you and God, even then the particulars of what you learn, what has been promised, what has been committed into your hands, and the things the Lord and you share should be kept between you and Him.

As I have said in *The Second Comforter*, some great things can be learned but not taught. Also, the Lord will never entrust truly sacred things to a person who is incapable of keeping them confidential. It is surprising how few people really believe in that principle. It is surprising how many people want that principle violated because they are curious, anxious and think it their right to receive what is purchased by someone else at a terrible personal price. It is surprising what things people will ask for and expect to be given, despite the fact that they haven't worked for them. It can't be shared by anyone other than you and the Lord. Whenever you disrespect that limitation by your questions, or demands you make to others, you postpone the time when you might have received greater things. You do not need a guru—You need the Lord. You do not need another John, Moses, Elias, Esaias, Isaiah, or Enoch.[891] You need Him.

---

[890] 2 Ne. 32: 6: "Behold, this is the doctrine of Christ, and there will be no more doctrine given until after he shall manifest himself unto you in the flesh. And when he shall manifest himself unto you in the flesh, the things which he shall say unto you shall ye observe to do."

[891] D&C 76: 100: "These are they who say they are some of one and some of another—some of Christ and some of John, and some of Moses, and some of Elias, and some of Esaias, and some of Isaiah, and some of Enoch;"

We see in scripture how easily and often messengers are made into idols. That is not what is to happen. It is even more of a perversion for men to set themselves up as idols, to be followed as if they were God. That is Satanic and evidence of a falling away.[892]

The private devotions of a sincere Saint are more worthy, more ennobling, more developing than any public display has ever been, or will ever be. Small gatherings when He directs may be of aid from time to time. But almost all the sacred events involving Him will take place between you and Him alone. When a few have approached Him by themselves—alone, then at some point it may possible for Him to gather with them in small numbers.[893]

Would you like to see Zion return? Then approach Him in private, keep your journey from the notice of others, gather to Him in secret. Then, when He has a few who can gather in His name, He will gather them. Ultimately there will need to be occupants for a city before a city will be founded by Him. But it all starts with these teachings we are presently reading.

This Sermon is first a description of Him.

It is also a description of His disciples.

It is a formula for returning to His presence.

It is the basis for the coming Zion.

---

[892] 2 Thes. 2: 3-4: "Let no man deceive you by any means: for *that day shall not come,* except there come a falling away first, and that man of sin be revealed, the son of perdition; Who opposeth and exalteth himself above all that is called God, or that is worshipped; so that he as God sitteth in the temple of God, shewing himself that he is God."

[893] Matt. 18: 22: "Jesus saith unto him, I say not unto thee, Until seven times: but, Until seventy times seven."

When the Father at last rewards you openly, it will be time for His arm to be revealed in terrible majesty.[894] He will reward you openly indeed!

3 Nephi 13: 19-21

> **"Lay not up for yourselves treasures upon earth, where moth and rust doth corrupt, and thieves break through and steal; But lay up for yourselves treasures in heaven, where neither moth nor rust doth corrupt, and where thieves do not break through nor steal. For where your treasure is, there will your heart be also."**

Things here are in constant change. There are two great forces always at work. Entropy and decay are affect everything. All things grow distant, cold and less organized. The opposite is the force that creates and brings anew. Between decay and recreation, we find ourselves in a world where our hold will eventually slip away, and we will no longer be found among the living.

What will endure?

The monuments men build to themselves and their causes break down, decay, rust, erode and fade. They all pass away. The most enduring things are not what we build with our hands, but the truth that we teach. Truth will endure for eternity. It may be lost, fought or suppressed, but it will return. Truth will triumph.

The closest thing we have to eternal living is found in the great ideas and great revelations of the prophets and poets, philosophers and sages. The things made in our minds are what change humanity and elevate us to be more godlike. It is not the structures where men craving

---

[894] D&C 105: 14: "For behold, I do not require at their hands to fight the battles of Zion; for, as I said in a former commandment, even so will I fulfil—I will fight your battles."

D&C 45: 67-75: "And the glory of the Lord shall be there, and the terror of the Lord also shall be there, insomuch that the wicked will not come unto it, and it shall be called Zion. And it shall come to pass among the wicked, that every man that will not take his sword against his neighbor must needs flee unto Zion for safety. And there shall be gathered unto it out of every nation under heaven; and it shall be the only people that shall not be at war one with another. And it shall be said among the wicked: Let us not go up to battle against Zion, for the inhabitants of Zion are terrible; wherefore we cannot stand. And it shall come to pass that the righteous shall be gathered out from among all nations, and shall come to Zion, singing with songs of everlasting joy. And now I say unto you, keep these things from going abroad unto the world until it is expedient in me, that ye may accomplish this work in the eyes of the people, and in the eyes of your enemies, that they may not know your works until ye have accomplished the thing which I have commanded you; That when they shall know it, that they may consider these things. For when the Lord shall appear he shall be terrible unto them, that fear may seize upon them, and they shall stand afar off and tremble. And all nations shall be afraid because of the terror of the Lord, and the power of his might. Even so. Amen."

immortality engrave their names. It is not the statues in bronze and marble where because of vanity they enshrine their images. They will all pass away.

But an idea, a truth, a testimony from heaven—those will endure despite all hell raging. Send the moths, the rust and thieves against truth, and the truth will prevail despite this fallen world's conspiracy against it.

Where is your heart? What do you meditate on day and night? Do you dream of wealth and power, of fame and recognition? Do you ponder how you might acquire more and receive more? Do you meditate on the lusts of the body? What occupies the spare moments of your life?

Do you let virtue garnish your thoughts so that your confidence may be strong in the presence of the Lord?[895] Do you meditate constantly on the things God has shown to you?[896]

Have you prayed and pondered so you may understand a great mystery?[897] Have you prayed and fasted so as to be filled with the spirit of revelation?[898]

Where your heart is, there is your treasure. Where your treasure is, there is your heart. They are linked. You can tell what is treasured and where the heart is by what things you meditate upon night and day with idle moments.

I've deliberately had a morning and afternoon post on this blog to assist in giving something to ponder twice during the day, at widely separated times. It is my view that there is nothing better to meditate on than the scriptures.

Here's a recent random reflection I had on one matter answered by scripture:

---

[895] D&C 121: 45: "Let thy bowels also be full of charity towards all men, and to the household of faith, and let virtue garnish thy thoughts unceasingly; then shall thy confidence wax strong in the presence of God; and the doctrine of the priesthood shall distil upon thy soul as the dews from heaven."

[896] 2 Ne. 4: 16: "Behold, my soul delighteth in the things of the Lord; and my heart pondereth continually upon the things which I have seen and heard."

[897] D&C 138: 11: "As I pondered over these things which are written, the eyes of my understanding were opened, and the Spirit of the Lord rested upon me, and I saw the hosts of the dead, both small and great."

[898] Alma 17: 3: "But this is not all; they had given themselves to much prayer, and fasting; therefore they had the spirit of prophecy, and the spirit of revelation, and when they taught, they taught with power and authority of God."

In a recent Gospel Doctrine discussion I was told about a teacher who was reluctant to admit David was a prophet, because David fell.[899] The notion that a prophet could fall undermines the current false notion that a President of the LDS Church cannot fail. That is rubbish, of course. But it is well circulated and ardently defended rubbish.

- The need to preserve the idea means that the teacher needed to disqualify David from ever being accepted as a prophet. The reasoning goes that if David isn't a prophet then his fall proves nothing.

- When Peter was preaching after Pentecost, he freely acknowledged David's status as a prophet.[900] So even if the Gospel Doctrine teacher won't admit David's status, the scriptures do.

- I wonder how it is plausible to some folks to believe prophets cannot fall today, when they fell anciently? It seems to me just a lazy way to shift responsibility for salvation away from each individual and onto an institution. Clearly the institution wants this idea to be accepted. No doubt someone will be damned for that notion.

- Anyone can fall. Seems to me that it is more important for me to worry about my own fall than it is to foolishly trust in some other person's success or failure. We are all accountable for our own sins.[901]

- In the Topical Guide I read every entry under "Accountability" and could find nothing to support the notion that there is accountability shifting from individual onto church president.

- Why do the gentiles always wind up having someone whom they regard as their benefactor boss them around?[902]

---

899 D&C 132: 39: "David's wives and concubines were given unto him of me, by the hand of Nathan, my servant, and others of the prophets who had the keys of this power; and in none of these things did he sin against me save in the case of Uriah and his wife; and, therefore he hath fallen from his exaltation, and received his portion; and he shall not inherit them out of the world, for I gave them unto another, saith the Lord."

900 Acts 2: 29-30: "Men *and* brethren, let me freely speak unto you of the patriarch David, that he is both dead and buried, and his sepulchre is with us unto this day. Therefore being a prophet, and knowing that God had sworn with an oath to him, that of the fruit of his loins, according to the flesh, he would raise up Christ to sit on his throne;"

901 Article of Faith 2: "We believe that men will be punished for their own sins, and not for Adam's transgression."

902 Luke 22: 25: "And he said unto them, The kings of the Gentiles exercise lordship over them; and they that exercise authority upon them are called benefactors."

- When you make one mistake (prophet can't fall or lead astray), then you compound it by needing another (David wasn't a prophet). Little wonder doctrine is not studied as much. Our foolishness would become exposed. Who was it that removed from a prophet his right to choose? When did moral agency to choose get taken away from a church president?

3 Nephi 13: 22-23

> **"The light of the body is the eye; if, therefore, thine eye be single, thy whole body shall be full of light. But if thine eye be evil, thy whole body shall be full ofd arkness. If, therefore, the light that is in thee be darkness, how great is that darkness!"**

The "eye" is better put "your mind's eye." It is what you meditate on, what fills you. You choose what you fill yourself with by what you give attention. What you notice is what you care to notice.

Christ's admonition is troubling because the cares of this world distract us all. They impose upon us all. But Christ advises us to search endlessly for light.

The difference between filling yourself with light and filling yourself with darkness is what thoughts you entertain.

Everything begins in the mind. Words and works flow from thoughts.[903] While all three will be judged, it is in the mind where all else begins.

It is not enough to attempt to avoid evil by memorizing hymns. You can spend as many wasted hours humming hymns as singing rock songs. Neither one will particularly elevate you. Meditating on doctrine, pressing understanding, pondering deeply and engaging the mysteries of God are what will fill the mind with light.

There is so much in our faith that distracts and substitutes for light and truth. Think about these verses and filling your mind with light and truth: "And that which doth not edify is not of God, and is darkness. That which is of God is light; and he that receiveth light, and continueth in God, receiveth more light; and that light groweth brighter and brighter until the perfect day. And again, verily I say unto you, and I say it that you may know the truth, that you may chase darkness from among you;"[904]

---

[903] Alma 12: 14: "For our words will condemn us, yea, all our works will condemn us; we shall not be found spotless; and our thoughts will also condemn us; and in this awful state we shall not dare to look up to our God; and we would fain be glad if we could command the rocks and the mountains to fall upon us to hide us from his presence."

[904] D&C 50: 23-25: "And that which doth not edify is not of God, and is darkness. That which is of God is light; and he that receiveth light, and continueth in God, receiveth more light; and that light groweth brighter and brighter until the perfect day. And again, verily I say unto you, and I say it that you may know the truth, that you may chase darkness from among you;"

The Psalms were quoted by Christ more than any other scripture. They are filled with truths worth meditation.

Having darkness within you does not require an effort to be deliberately vile. The cares of this world, and coping with Babylon is all that is needed to keep you from acquiring light. Finding light requires a deliberate effort to notice it and take it in.

When we are filled with light the heavens notice. In fact, it is the light within us that heaven notices even from afar.

3 Nephi 13: 24

> **"No man can serve two masters; for either he will hate the one and love the other, or else he will hold to the one and despise the other. Ye cannot serve God and Mammon."**

This is Christ's great division. We all have but one Master. Choose carefully.

This is another way to describe the "jealous God" of the Old Covenant.[905] Since He requires everything of you, any holding back is infidelity to Him.

Christ is reaffirming God's primacy. Your affection for Him cannot be shared. It simply can't be done. When attempted, it shows you "hate" or "despise" Him, because when you share your fidelity, you reject His direction.

It is this principle that justified the earlier prophets in likening Israel to a "harlot" or a "whore" when she worshiped other gods.[906] It is not possible to be converted to the Lord and not be devoted to Him.

All of what is "Mammon" is subordinate to God. The Lord's ways require the things you have in this life to be used for His purposes and according to His desire. His commandments cover all things, and you cannot divorce your temporal concerns from His teachings.[907]

Devotion to Him requires that what you do, say, and think be aligned with Him. Conversion is a progressive process where you develop to be

---

[905] Ex. 34: 14: "For thou shalt worship no other god: for the Lord, whose name *is* Jealous, *is* a jealous God:"

[906] Jer. 3: 6: "The Lord said also unto me in the days of Josiah the king, Hast thou seen *that* which backsliding Israel hath done? she is gone up upon every high mountain and under every green tree, and there hath played the harlot."
Hosea 9: 1: "Rejoice not, O Israel, for joy, as *other* people: for thou hast gone a whoring from thy God, thou hast loved a reward upon every cornfloor."
Judges 8: 33: "And it came to pass, as soon as Gideon was dead, that the children of Israel turned again, and went a whoring after Baalim, and made Baal-berith their god."

[907] D&C 29: 35: "Behold, I gave unto him that he should be an agent unto himself; and I gave unto him commandment, but no temporal commandment gave I unto him, for my commandments are spiritual; they are not natural nor temporal, neither carnal nor sensual."

more like Him throughout life. You can't just "get a testimony" and then not be completely converted to Him. He expects to completely remake you. This sermon is the blueprint for the new creation you are to become.

This statement deals in absolutes because the Lord's way is the way of absolutes. He can accept nothing less than all. The adversary knows this and is content with getting even a little from you. The adversary knows that a little compromise is everything when compromising your faithfulness to the Lord.

The world will accept anything half-hearted. The world knows you love it, if you will just give in a little to its persuasion. Contamination is contamination and will eventually poison you. So any degree of unrighteousness is enough to please the world. For the Lord, however, it is all or nothing. It is complete fidelity to Him which alone will satisfy. Keeping one foot in the world, while giving lip service to Him will never meet the requirements for loving Him.[908]

Those who think the Lord is announcing a new, easier system to replace the earlier, more demanding Law of Moses do not understand His teachings. This is far more exact and moves the battleground into your heart. He is asking you to transform the soul. He is asking you to become like Him. This is not outward observances. However troubling and wearisome those may have been, they were at least something that could be done without battling in your heart with motive, intent and desires. Here Christ wants you to conform everything, even your desires, to be instruments of your salvation.

This is a call to a much higher way of life. It is a much deeper and more meaningful way to approach God. It is inside you.

3 Nephi 13: 25

> **"And now it came to pass that when Jesus had spoken these words he looked upon the twelve whom he had chosen, and said unto them: Remember the words which I have spoken. For behold, ye are they whom I have chosen to minister unto this people. Therefore I say unto you, take no thought for your life, what ye shall eat, or what ye shall drink; nor yet for your body, what ye shall put on. Is not the life more than meat, and the body than raiment?"**

The preceding teachings were given to all who were there. Christ changes the audience at this point, and addresses the twelve whom He had given power to baptize. To them He addresses the admonition: "Remember the words which I have spoken." These are two things: First, a Divine admonition to follow. Second, an empowerment to make it possible to do as He asks. Without both, they would have been unable

---

908 D&C 1: 31: "For I the Lord cannot look upon sin with the least degree of allowance;"

to preserve the record of the teachings. As will become apparent from the text, they will later meet following His ascension and reduce the words taught to a transcript that all twelve will be able to present to the audience that assembles the next day.

The reason these same twelve who had power to baptize were given power to "remember the words [Christ] had spoken" was because they were "chosen to minister unto this people." When Christ chooses a minister to speak for Him, He enables them to accomplish the mission or ministry assigned to them.[909] They receive His support. That makes them more than equal to the assignment given them.

It is the chosen twelve, and not the the multitude, who are told to "take no thought for your life, what ye shall eat, or what he shall drink." It is those who are to minister who are freed from the earthly cares of providing for their needs. Their lives are to be given over to ministering to others, and not to work for their support. The Lord intends to provide for them.

This is a very narrow group to whom this promise is made. It does not include others in the audience. For the rest, we are required to provide for our families. If we fail to provide for them by laboring for their support, we have denied the faith.[910] Wives are to be supported by their husband's labor.[911] Children are to be supported by their parents.[912] This requires all to labor.[913] But as to these twelve, their labor is the ministry and their support will come from the Lord.

It is a small thing for the Lord to provide for His ministers. To Him property is nothing.[914] He can provide for His ministers even if there is

---

909 D&C 132: 59: "Verily, if a man be called of my Father, as was Aaron, by mine own voice, and by the voice of him that sent me, and I have endowed him with the keys of the power of this priesthood, if he do anything in my name, and according to my law and by my word, he will not commit sin, and I will justify him."

910 1 Tim. 5: 8: "But if any provide not for his own, and specially for those of his own house, he hath denied the faith, and is worse than an infidel."

911 D&C 83: 2: "Women have claim on their husbands for their maintenance, until their husbands are taken; and if they are not found transgressors they shall have fellowship in the church."

912 D&C 83: 4: "All children have claim upon their parents for their maintenance until they are of age."

913 D&C 42: 42: "Thou shalt not be idle; for he that is idle shall not eat the bread nor wear the garments of the laborer."

914 D&C 117: 4: "Let them repent of all their sins, and of all their covetous desires, before me, saith the Lord; for what is property unto me? saith the Lord."

no apparent means to accomplish it.[915] The Lord has provided food for thousands when necessary.[916] Providing food for His people when

[915] 1 Kgs. 17: 8-16: "And the word of the Lord came unto him, saying, Arise, get thee to Zarephath, which *belongeth* to Zidon, and dwell there: behold, I have commanded a widow woman there to sustain thee. So he arose and went to Zarephath. And when he came to the gate of the city, behold, the widow woman *was* there gathering of sticks: and he called to her, and said, Fetch me, I pray thee, a little water in a vessel, that I may drink. And as she was going to fetch *it,* he called to her, and said, Bring me, I pray thee, a morsel of bread in thine hand. And she said, *As* the Lord thy God liveth, I have not a cake, but an handful of meal in a barrel, and a little oil in a cruse: and, behold, I *am* gathering two sticks, that I may go in and dress it for me and my son, that we may eat it, and die. And Elijah said unto her, Fear not; go *and* do as thou hast said: but make me thereof a little cake first, and bring *it* unto me, and after make for thee and for thy son. For thus saith the Lord God of Israel, The barrel of meal shall not waste, neither shall the cruse of oil fail, until the day *that* the Lord sendeth rain upon the earth. And she went and did according to the saying of Elijah: and she, and he, and her house, did eat *many* days. *And* the barrel of meal wasted not, neither did the cruse of oil fail, according to the word of the Lord, which he spake by Elijah."

[916] Luke 9: 13-17: "But he said unto them, Give ye them to eat. And they said, We have no more but five loaves and two fishes; except we should go and buy meat for all this people. For they were about five thousand men. And he said to his disciples, Make them sit down by fifties in a company. And they did so, and made them all sit down. Then he took the five loaves and the two fishes, and looking up to heaven, he blessed them, and brake, and gave to the disciples to set before the multitude. And they did eat, and were all filled: and there was taken up of fragments that remained to them twelve baskets."

needed is within His Divine power.[917]

Why would the Lord give this commandment to the twelve? Why would He do it publicly? What responsibility does that impose upon the twelve? What responsibility does it impose upon the audience? If the twelve today were to be supported by only food given them by believers, clothes provided by followers, material given through donations from those to whom they ministered, would it be different than the system we have in place today? Would that be different from tithing money used for salaries paid them today? Would the supplemental income from book sales, service on boards of directors (which has been greatly reduced and was planned to be entirely eliminated) fit into the system Christ describes here? [President Monson's General Conference talk about his wife's surgery a while back included a reference to paying taxes. She was emerging from an eighteen day coma and her first words to him were about failing to pay

---

[917] Ex. 16: 11-31: "And the Lord spake unto Moses, saying, I have heard the murmurings of the children of Israel: speak unto them, saying, At even ye shall eat flesh, and in the morning ye shall be filled with bread; and ye shall know that I *am* the Lord your God. And it came to pass, that at even the quails came up, and covered the camp: and in the morning the dew lay round about the host. And when the dew that lay was gone up, behold, upon the face of the wilderness *there lay* a small round thing, *as* small as the hoar frost on the ground. And when the children of Israel saw *it,* they said one to another, It *is* manna: for they wist not what it *was.* And Moses said unto them, This *is* the bread which the Lord hath given you to eat. This *is* the thing which the Lord hath commanded, Gather of it every man according to his eating, an omer for every man, *according to* the number of your persons; take ye every man for *them* which *are* in his tents. And the children of Israel did so, and gathered, some more, some less. And when they did mete *it* with an omer, he that gathered much had nothing over, and he that gathered little had no lack; they gathered every man according to his eating. And Moses said, Let no man leave of it till the morning. Notwithstanding they hearkened not unto Moses; but some of them left of it until the morning, and it bred worms, and stank: and Moses was wroth with them. And they gathered it every morning, every man according to his eating: and when the sun waxed hot, it melted. And it came to pass, *that* on the sixth day they gathered twice as much bread, two omers for one *man:* and all the rulers of the congregation came and told Moses. And he said unto them, This *is that* which the Lord hath said, To morrow *is* the rest of the holy sabbath unto the Lord: bake *that* which ye will bake *to day,* and seethe that ye will seethe; and that which remaineth over lay up for you to be kept until the morning. And they laid it up till the morning, as Moses bade: and it did not stink, neither was there any worm therein. And Moses said, Eat that to day; for to day *is* a sabbath unto the Lord: to day ye shall not find it in the field. Six days ye shall gather it; but on the seventh day, *which is* the sabbath, in it there shall be none. And it came to pass, *that* there went out *some* of the people on the seventh day for to gather, and they found none. And the Lord said unto Moses, How long refuse ye to keep my commandments and my laws? See, for that the Lord hath given you the sabbath, therefore he giveth you on the sixth day the bread of two days; abide ye every man in his place, let no man go out of his place on the seventh day. So the people rested on the seventh day. And the house of Israel called the name thereof Manna: and it *was* like coriander seed, white; and the taste of it *was* like wafers *made* with honey."

the "fourth quarter income tax payment." (Abundantly Blessed, Ensign, May 2008.) These kinds of "quarterly income taxes" are self-employment taxes and would arise either from book royalties or service on boards of directors. His paycheck from the Church would have withholding and would not require quarterly deposits.]

Is the different, more simple and very direct connection between the disciples and those to whom they ministered of value today? Is our modern sophisticated society unable to provide similar support today? Is Christ's teaching on this point outdated? If it is, then can we disregard other portions also as outdated? How do we decide what to discard and what to keep?

3 Nephi 13: 26-32

> **"Behold the fowls of the air, for they sow not, neither do they reap nor gather into barns; yet your heavenly Father feedeth them. Are ye not much better than they? Which of you by taking thought can add one cubit unto his stature? And why take ye thought for raiment? Consider the lilies of the field how they grow; they toil not, neither do they spin; And yet I say unto you, that even Solomon, in all his glory, was not arrayed like one of these. Wherefore, if God so clothe the grass of the field, which today is, and tomorrow is cast into the oven, even so will he clothe you, if ye are not of little faith. Therefore take no thought, saying, What shall we eat? or, What shall we drink? or, Wherewithal shall we be clothed? For your heavenly Father knoweth that ye have need of all these things."**

Christ illustrates His teaching of how His disciples are to be supported by analogy after analogy. He likens the principle of how His disciple-ministers are to be supported to:

- Fowls of the air, provided for by God.

- Lilies of the field, whose glorious appearance comes from God.

- Grass of the field, which are adorned by natural beauty from God.

Inherent in these analogies is the message that so long as fowls shall fly, this principle ought to be followed. So long as lilies remain on the earth growing wild, this manner of supporting His disciples ought to be followed. So long as grass shall be here, this principle should be followed.

The hopelessness of man's presumed independence from God is stressed in His statement that by taking thought none of us "can add one cubit unto his stature." Our lives are not ours. They belong to Him. We have no independence from Him. We are NOT self-existent beings. We borrow all we are and have from Him. Even, as it turns out, the dust from which we are made belongs to Him.[918]

If God gives us air to breathe, power to exist, the capacity to move, and sustains all of us from moment to moment, then how little faith is required to rely on Him to provide His disciples with food and raiment?

The analogy to Solomon is also telling. "Solomon, in all his glory" is a useful way to think of the greatest man can hope for himself. The glory of Solomon was legendary. The Queen of Sheba came and

[918] Mosiah 2: 20-25: "I say unto you, my brethren, that if you should render all the thanks and praise which your whole soul has power to possess, to that God who has created you, and has kept and preserved you, and has caused that ye should rejoice, and has granted that ye should live in peace one with another—I say unto you that if ye should serve him who has created you from the beginning, and is preserving you from day to day, by lending you breath, that ye may live and move and do according to your own will, and even supporting you from one moment to another—I say, if ye should serve him with all your whole souls yet ye would be unprofitable servants. And behold, all that he requires of you is to keep his commandments; and he has promised you that if ye would keep his commandments ye should prosper in the land; and he never doth vary from that which he hath said; therefore, if ye do keep his commandments he doth bless you and prosper you. And now, in the first place, he hath created you, and granted unto you your lives, for which ye are indebted unto him. And secondly, he doth require that ye should do as he hath commanded you; for which if ye do, he doth immediately bless you; and therefore he hath paid you. And ye are still indebted unto him, and are, and will be, forever and ever; therefore, of what have ye to boast? And now I ask, can ye say aught of yourselves? I answer you, Nay. Ye cannot say that ye are even as much as the dust of the earth; yet ye were created of the dust of the earth; but behold, it belongeth to him who created you."

marveled at what she saw in his court.[919] This was splendor, wealth and power indeed! However, Christ reminds us that these man-made marvels are nothing compared with the beauty He can supply those who are "not of little faith." He can cover a man in glory indeed. Not as the world defines glory, but the real glory.[920]

The purpose of putting a man in such a dependent state before God is not to find out whether God can take care of him. God already knows what a man needs before he should even ask. But the man will, by becoming so dependent upon God, acquire a broken heart and a contrite spirit, always quick to ask, quick to listen, quick to do. Vulnerability makes a man strong in spirit. Security and wealth make a man incorrectly believe in his independence from God.

He wants His disciples to be dependent upon Him. He wants them praying, and then grateful to Him for what He provides. He wants them, in a word, to become holy.

Such a system would be impractical in a post-industrial society like ours, wouldn't it?

---

[919] 1 Kgs. 10: 1-13: "And when the queen of Sheba heard of the fame of Solomon concerning the name of the Lord, she came to prove him with hard questions. And she came to Jerusalem with a very great train, with camels that bare spices, and very much gold, and precious stones: and when she was come to Solomon, she communed with him of all that was in her heart. And Solomon told her all her questions: there was not *any* thing hid from the king, which he told her not. And when the queen of Sheba had seen all Solomon's wisdom, and the house that he had built, And the meat of his table, and the sitting of his servants, and the attendance of his ministers, and their apparel, and his cupbearers, and his ascent by which he went up unto the house of the Lord; there was no more spirit in her. And she said to the king, It was a true report that I heard in mine own land of thy acts and of thy wisdom. Howbeit I believed not the words, until I came, and mine eyes had seen *it*: and, behold, the half was not told me: thy wisdom and prosperity exceedeth the fame which I heard. Happy *are* thy men, happy *are* these thy servants, which stand continually before thee, *and* that hear thy wisdom. Blessed be the Lord thy God, which delighted in thee, to set thee on the throne of Israel: because the Lord loved Israel for ever, therefore made he thee king, to do judgment and justice. And she gave the king an hundred and twenty talents of gold, and of spices very great store, and precious stones: there came no more such abundance of spices as these which the queen of Sheba gave to king Solomon. And the navy also of Hiram, that brought gold from Ophir, brought in from Ophir great plenty of almug trees, and precious stones. And the king made of the almug trees pillars for the house of the Lord, and for the king's house, harps also and psalteries for singers: there came no such almug trees, nor were seen unto this day. And king Solomon gave unto the queen of Sheba all her desire, whatsoever she asked, beside *that* which Solomon gave her of his royal bounty. So she turned and went to her own country, she and her servants."

[920] D&C 93: 28, 36: "He that keepeth his commandments receiveth truth and light, until he is glorified in truth and knoweth all things. …The glory of God is intelligence, or, in other words, light and truth."

3 Nephi 13: 33

"But seek ye first the kingdom of God and his righteousness, and all these things shall be added unto you."

What comes first? Why?

How can "all these things" then "be added unto you?" What are "these things?" Is it the food, raiment, etc.?

Why would the Lord want the disciples to first seek the kingdom of God before promising that the things would be "added unto" them?

If they don't first seek the kingdom, then will things not be added to them?

What is "the kingdom of God?" Is there a difference between

- The Church of Jesus Christ

- The Kingdom of God

- Zion?

What is the "kingdom of God" if it is not the church? When is the "kingdom" to be found? What is necessary for it to exist? Joseph Smith taught: "What constitutes the Kingdom of God? an administrator who has the power of calling down the oracles of God, and subjects to receive those oracles no matter if there is but 3, 4, or 6 there is the kingdom of God." (William Clayton Journal entry January 22, 1843, capitalization as in original.) If we accept Joseph's definition, why would the disciples be encouraged to "seek the kingdom of God?"

What does the clarification that the "kingdom of God" should be sought first tell us about everything else?

Has the "kingdom of God" been here before now? Is it here now? What does it mean to call down the oracles of God?

Does man control this or does God?

What is man's role in establishing the "kingdom of God?" Is man's role confined to "seeking first" for it to come? How would man seek it?

If you want to "seek the kingdom of God" how would you go about doing so?

What does your "seeking" have to do with the return of the "kingdom of God?"

The Lord will not bring again Zion without there being a people who are prepared to receive what He intends to bring. How can you do that?

3 Nephi 13: 34

"Take therefore no thought for the morrow, for the morrow shall take thought for the things of itself. Sufficient is the day unto the evil thereof."

This is the child's view of life. A child is perpetually in the "now" and does not regret yesterdays or plan tomorrows. It is all about what happens to you at the moment.

Each day's challenge is the end goal. In addition to severing the disciples from regular income, regular work for support, dependence on those to whom they minister for bread, drink, shelter and clothing, the Lord adds to their burden the heavy responsibility to "take no thought for the morrow." For them their ministry is to be moment to moment. No planning and rehearsals. No staging and frantic preparation. No three-year budgets. Only now. Forever only now.

It is an interesting position Christ wants to put His chief disciples into. It forces us to carefully consider why He would do so?

Is it to keep them humble?

Is it to prevent pride and arrogance?

Is it to require they remain in constant direct touch with at least some of those over whom they minister?

Is it to keep them keenly aware of the necessity of relying on Him?

If they cannot plan for more than the day's events, how can they plan a busy travel schedule to take them all over the world? Is that somehow built in already to the "sufficient is the day unto the evil thereof?"

What kind of life would this create for His disciples chosen to minister to others? Would they ever be able to minister to more than just a few at a time under this system? If they are limited to serving only a few at a time, then how would an entire church receive benefit from this kind of spontaneous ministry? What kind of changes would that make in how a church is run and organized?

Just how impractical do we think this manner of organizing would be in a multi-national, multi-lingual, 13 million member church? If it is impractical, should the Lord's teachings be revised or should we change our way of thinking about His church and system?

If this were to be implemented, how would you go about organizing it? Would you divide the world into twelfths? Within that division, would you expect the disciple assigned to "drop in" to stake conferences and ward meetings unannounced? Would that prevent central planning and budgeting by the chief disciples? Would it force the Presiding Bishop's office to take concerns for all temporal concerns and budgets? Why would letting an Aaronic Priesthood office be concerned with temporal affairs and freeing up Melchizedek Priesthood for spiritual concerns be an unwelcome change?

Would this fundamentally transform the role of leadership? How? Would it be chaos, or would it be an improvement? Why?

Just how dumb an idea is this that Christ is teaching to the chosen twelve? If not dumb, then it is at least of limited practicality when growth in numbers and locations makes it burdensome? Was Christ's teaching here short-sighted? Did He fail to make provisions for the modern church, with its global spread and cross-language needs and budgets?

When the Book of Mormon was restored, this sermon was restored to us. When restored, it clarified how this portion of the sermon was addressed to the presiding twelve disciples. Was there a Divine purpose or message behind it? Should it be considered as meaningful to us today? Christ lived an interesting life. He more or less followed this counsel, though in truth He understood and fulfilled the prophecies concerning Himself. Yet, throughout it all, He also seemed to surrender control to the Father in everything.[921] He commented on how spontaneous a life He lived, and how unpredictable things were when following the Spirit.[922]

[921] Mark 13: 32: "But of that day and *that* hour knoweth no man, no, not the angels which are in heaven, neither the Son, but the Father."

[922] John 3: 6-8: "That which is born of the flesh is flesh; and that which is born of the Spirit is spirit. Marvel not that I said unto thee, Ye must be born again. The wind bloweth where it listeth, and thou hearest the sound thereof, but canst not tell whence it cometh, and whither it goeth: so is every one that is born of the Spirit."

3 Nephi 14

3 Nephi 14: 1-2

> **"And now it came to pass that when Jesus had spoken these words he turned again to the multitude, and did open his mouth unto them again, saying: Verily, verily, I say unto you, Judge not, that ye be not judged. For with what judgment ye judge, ye shall be judged; and with what measure ye mete, it shall be measured to you again."**

This reiterates the doctrine in the Lord's instruction on prayer. Your judgment of others will become the basis for your own judgment by the Father. Apply mercy to receive mercy. Apply forgiveness to merit forgiveness. Act harshly to receive harsh treatment. Show strict judgment, and receive it in return. It is the perfect balance. What you send out returns to you. It is karma. The words are right out of Christ's own mouth.

More importantly, notice how He transitions from speaking to His twelve about their new, spontaneous ministry into the public judgment of what was to follow? In other words, if these thoughts are related, (and I think they are) then He is saying His twelve disciples may take a while to get to the needs of those assembled. Therefore, be patient. This new lifestyle for the disciples will be difficult on them. In order to receive a reward, those who are being ministered to need to bear patiently with the ensuing efforts of the twelve.

This was to be a new community formed among these people. In it, there will be servants called to minister (the twelve), who will be limited in what they are able to do. They will be needy, dependent, and vulnerable. They will have needs. Supply the needs without being put off by what they are not able to do. View them with compassion as they seek to do as they have been told. Don't withhold substance, food, raiment, or housing from them because you are unhappy with what little they have been able to do. Show them kindness.

The statement is broader than that, of course. It implies similar patience with everyone. But the point that this practice should begin with these twelve ministers ought not be lost.

The context of "judge not that ye be not judged" is framed by the statement that "with what judgment ye judge, ye shall be judged; and with what measure ye mete, it shall be measured to you again." We do "judge" one another because we must. But the judgment should err on the side of forgiving. It should err in favor of trusting motives to be pure, and intent to be good. We should be generous with our gratitude, evaluations and suppositions. When we know someone is misbehaving, we should make allowances for their shortcomings, forgive them before they ask, and impute no retribution because of their offensive conduct.

This does not make us better than another, it makes us whole. It allows the Lord to forgive us for our own, much greater offenses against Him. For when we are generous, we merit His Divine generosity. It is how we are healed. It is the means for our own salvation. Instead of thinking ourselves better than an offender, we should look upon them with gratitude for they provide the means to obtain salvation—provided we give them forgiveness from all their offenses. This is why we should rejoice and be exceedingly glad.[923] They enable us to obtain salvation by despitefully using us, as long as we measure them by the same standard that allows God to forgive us.

What perfect symmetry: You measure to others using instrument that will be used by God to measure back to you. So your ready forgiveness is how God will treat you. All those grudges can be replaced with petitions to God to forgive those who abused you. As you lay aside all those sins against you, committed by others, it will purge from you all your own sins.

Straight and narrow indeed… But oddly appropriate and altogether within your control.

3 Nephi 14: 3-5

> **"And why beholdest thou the mote that is in thy brother's eye, but considerest not the beam that is in thine own eye? Or how wilt thou say to thy brother: Let me pull the mote out of thine eye—and behold, a beam is in thine own eye? Thou hypocrite, first cast the beam out of thine own eye; and then shalt thou see clearly to cast the mote out of thy brother's eye."**

The defect in judging is the position from which we proceed. We are blind. We have too many subjective problems in our background. Our training, education, culture, presumptions, prejudices, "things we just know to be true", ignorance, preoccupations and impatience interfere with our perceptions. We act on errors and reach wrong conclusions. We

---

[923] 3 Ne. 12: 10-12: "And blessed are all they who are persecuted for my name's sake, for theirs is the kingdom of heaven. And blessed are ye when men shall revile you and persecute, and shall say all manner of evil against you falsely, for my sake; For ye shall have great joy and be exceedingly glad, for great shall be your reward in heaven; for so persecuted they the prophets who were before you."

measure with defective tools, then decide the matter from the wrong measure.

Christ is reminding us that whenever we are inclined to correct another person, more often than not, we suffer from whatever defect we see in others. This is why we notice it. We see it because it is really us. We are sensitive to the problem because we own the problem.

First, whenever we see something amiss in another, start with the realization that we are seeing ourselves. Start inside. Ask, "why does this bother me?" "Am I really seeing myself in a mirror?" Then be grateful you saw another person display your problem. You now know what is wrong with you. Forgive them, fix you.

The tendency to withhold patience is more often than not because their "mote" excites your notice through your own "beam." A "mote" is a speck, a bit of sawdust. A "beam" is a board. Yours is the greater defect. For in you is not only the defect, but the tendency to judge others harshly. Both are wrong.

When you have at last purged the defect, struggled to overcome and conquer the temptation or tendency, perhaps the price you pay to do so will make you humble enough to assist another. Not from the position as judge and condemner, but from the position of one who can help. When you "see clearly," then you may be able to "cast the mote out of thy brother's eye." For now you see him as your "brother." And in a kindly and affectionate manner you may act to reclaim him. Not as a judge, but as a brother.

This is a continuing petition to make things better. But the only way you make them better by starting inside. It is not for you to work on others, nor move outside your own range of defects, until you have first fixed what you lack. When you can proceed with charity to assist others to overcome what you have overcome yourself, then it is appropriate to approach your "brother" in kindness to help. Until then, stop judging and start removing "beams" from yourself.

Brilliant and peaceful. Revolutionary and kind. Christ is the ultimate True Teacher. He could teach such things because He was such things. His disciples will, in turn, take His teachings and His example and do likewise.

3 Nephi 14: 6

> **"Give not that which is holy unto the dogs, neither cast ye your pearls before swine, lest they trample them under their feet, and turn again and rend you."**

This is a preamble to what immediately follows. It is a caution about how to weigh what can be said, and what is to be kept private between a person and the Lord.

Almost without exception, people who are unable to keep sacred things which are most sacred will never receive exposure to the most sacred. The Temple ordinances are an elaborate test of ones trustworthiness. There are a variety of things designated as "most sacred" which are then "guarded by covenants and obligations" that require they not be revealed "except in a certain place" which will always be limited. The material then revealed is to be kept as "most sacred," though in truth, it is a test where symbolic information is imparted to allow the spiritually mature to learn by symbol some hidden meaning and mystery about God. To the immature, the material is worthless and meaningless. Nothing of value is gained. It is a symbol without an interpretation. It can only be an idol to them as they mistake the symbol for underlying meaning.

When a person treats the information in an appropriate way, they "prove" themselves[924] worthy of weightier information to be given them.[925] Then they are laid under a strict command that they shall not impart, only according to the heed and diligence which another should give to the word.[926]

What is holy belongs to those who make themselves holy through their repentance. It does not belong to the unclean, who are "dogs" and unrepentant.

When the price is paid, the person trusted, and the mysteries shown them, they possess pearls of great price. Such things do not belong to "swine" who are unclean and unrepentant, unwilling to do what is needed to qualify for the Lord's presence, unthankful and unholy.

Entrusting the things that are in truth "most sacred" to those who are not qualified will arouse their anger. They will "turn and rend you" because you have shown them something which excites their envy, jealousy, hatred and fear. They know you have something they lack. They resent you because of what they cannot easily obtain. Therefore, you must measure carefully what you give to others. The final arbiter of the decision to impart is not made by you, it is made by the Lord.

Those who are eager to share with others any tidbit of information they learn about the sacred are not helping anyone, and may forfeit things themselves. Why would they do such a thing? Is it to make themselves look good; therefore vanity? Is it to try to help others? If it is to help, then the information should not be shared; the manner in which

---

[924] Abr. 3: 25: "And we will prove them herewith, to see if they will do all things whatsoever the Lord their God shall command them;"

[925] D&C 132: 20-21: "Then shall they be gods, because they have no end; therefore shall they be from everlasting to everlasting, because they continue; then shall they be above all, because all things are subject unto them. Then shall they be gods, because they have all power, and the angels are subject unto them. Verily, verily, I say unto you, except ye abide my law ye cannot attain to this glory."

[926] Alma 12: 9: "And now Alma began to expound these things unto him, saying: It is given unto many to know the mysteries of God; nevertheless they are laid under a strict command that they shall not impart only according to the portion of his word which he doth grant unto the children of men, according to the heed and diligence which they give unto him."

the information is gained should be shared. Teaching another the way to receive sacred information for themselves is charitable. Showing off sacred information is worse than foolish, it will bless no one, and destroy both the unprepared audience and the unwise speaker.

I have tried to be an example of this principle. First I learned something, then I began to teach it. When teaching, I have carefully measured anything I have taught against the Lord's cautions and limitations. I have affirmed in the fewest words that the promises made by the Lord are true, and that I am a witness of their truth. But I have not shared anything beyond the process, which I have taught so others may learn how to proceed. It has not been about me, or about anything I may know. It has been about the Lord and the process to know Him. It is clear that some people are completely uninterested in anything other than some new disclosure, some new mystery unfolded. They are not interested in anything other than to be titillated. I cannot help them. I have nothing to offer. But if someone wants to approach God, then I may be able to teach something of value in what I've written. But not if they are unwilling to start at the first and proceed through everything I've written in the order they were written. Jumping to the end of the process is worthless. Gathering tidbits is unwise as it gives you only enough information to be dangerous. It is the path to follow Christ that matters.

Getting to know the Lord is the definition of salvation.[927] Getting to know me will save no one. It is foolish to consider anything or anyone more important than learning the means to come back to the Lord.

3 Nephi 14: 7-8

> **"Ask, and it shall be given unto you; seek, and ye shall find; knock, and it shall be opened unto you. For every one that asketh, receiveth; and he that seeketh, findeth; and to him that knocketh, it shall be opened."**

Just after the caution to not give holy things to the unworthy, Christ reminds all of their obligation to ask, seek and knock. If you will ask it will be given to you. If you seek, you will find it. If you knock, things will be opened to you. But be careful not to give what is holy to the unworthy.

These ideas are related in two ways:

First, if you want what is holy, then stop being a "dog" or a "swine." Ask, seek and knock.

Second, if you are one who is qualified and will receive holy things by your willingness to be repentant, then press forward by asking, seeking and knocking. If you do, the things which are most holy will be given.

---

927 John 17: 3: "And this is life eternal, that they might know thee the only true God, and Jesus Christ, whom thou hast sent."

"For every one that asketh, receiveth." Really? Everyone? Even you? That is what Christ is saying. However, the manner in which you will receive is illustrated by "The Missing Virtue" in *Ten Parables*. Meaning that the effort to receive what you have asked the Lord could take nearly two decades, and a great deal of internal changing before you acquire what you lack. Receiving may include not only what you've asked to receive, but also everything you do not have in order to finally qualify to receive what you seek.

What do you associate with "findeth?" Does it suggest to you active effort, or passive receipt? To "find" something you are missing (even a small thing) what must you do? If searching is required to locate, then what do you suppose the Lord is implying by the word "findeth?"

What does it mean that "it shall be opened?" Does "opening" imply merely a view? Does it suggest also 'entering in?' If it opens to view, and you then fail to 'enter in' has "opening" been worthwhile? Has anything been accomplished? Does it suggest that there is activity required of someone who has something "opened" unto them?

It is my view that the words chosen all imply a burden upon the one who asks, seeks and knocks. They are not entitled to anything just by speaking the words. They must make the effort to search into and contemplate the things they seek. Then they must change and repent of everything amiss in their lives that is revealed to them. This is to be done before they can see what is to be shown to them. If, for example, a person wants to see the other side of the mountain, they can ask daily for a view to be opened to them without ever seeing the other side. But if the Lord prompts them to take the path to the top, the Lord has given them the means to "find" and "have opened" to them the very thing they seek. Provided, of course, they are willing to walk in the path to the top of the mountain. When they remain on the valley floor, asking or demanding more, they are not really asking, seeking and knocking. They are irritating and ungrateful. The Lord's small means are capable of taking the one who seeks to the very thing they desire.[928] But without cooperation with Him they can receive nothing.

The Lord's small means are how great things are brought to pass.[929] But for some people the Lord's answers are never enough. However, when the humble who ask, seek and knock follow Him in these small means, they will eventually stand in His presence and partake of eternal life. But not until they have done as all others have done before them.

[928] Alma 37: 7: "And the Lord God doth work by means to bring about his great and eternal purposes; and by very small means the Lord doth confound the wise and bringeth about the salvation of many souls."

[929] 1 Ne. 16: 29: "And there was also written upon them a new writing, which was plain to be read, which did give us understanding concerning the ways of the Lord; and it was written and changed from time to time, according to the faith and diligence which we gave unto it. And thus we see that by small means the Lord can bring about great things."

Faith is only replaced by knowledge when the faith is strong enough to rend the veil. At that point, there is no great advantage to the person who has already attained to this understanding by their faith. I've written about this in *The Second Comforter*. It is a true principle and remains true even today.

3 Nephi 14: 9-11

> **"Or what man is there of you, who, if his son ask bread, will give him a stone? Or if he ask a fish, will he give him a serpent? If ye then, being evil, know how to give good gifts unto your children, how much more shall your Father who is in heaven give good things to them that ask him?"**

This is not self-evident. If it were, then there would be more people with faith. The truth revealed here is that God is always going to bestow a worthy gift upon the person requesting it.

He will not give you a "stone" if you request "bread." He will give you "bread." He knows the difference. He will not disappoint you.

He knows better than any kind and caring earthly father what the needs of His children are. He intends to meet them.

However, when His children ask for something ("bread") and they do not yet qualify to receive, He sets about preparing them to receive it. He is willing to give. We are not always prepared to receive. Therefore, when He intends to bestow the gift upon the person requesting it, He first prepares the vessel.

We are impatient. We want quickly what can sometimes only be obtained in patience. We are in a rush, but our development requires patience. Some things require time and persistence to prepare us for the blessing we seek. Joseph remarked: "The things of God are of deep import, and time, experience, and careful and ponderous, and solemn thoughts, can only find them out." This is the way of God. It is adapted to give us what we lack, even if we are unaware of what we lack.

The Father always intends to give to those who ask, seek and knock just as Christ has explained. However, the Father knows "much more" than do we as to how to "give good things to them that ask." He will not merely give the thing requested. He will add to it such things as are needed to prepare you to receive them.

This, then, is the process: We ask. Without a request, the laws governing things prevent bestowal. We can't be given until first we ask.

When we have asked, the Father will give. He will give "every good gift" needed, and not just what has been asked. If there is, (as is almost always the case) a gulf between what you have asked of Him, and your capacity to receive it, then He will set about giving you every needful thing to enable you to receive.

If you ask for strength, He will provide you with that experience necessary to develop the strength you seek. If you seek for patience you will be given Divinely ordained experiences by Him that are calculated to develop in you what you have sought. He knows you and knows what you need. Whatever is asked of Him, He will set about to ordain.

It will come in a perfectly natural progression. It will occur in accordance with both natural and eternal law. If you fight against it, you prolong the time when you will receive what you have asked of Him. If you cooperate, it will flow unto you without compulsory means in a natural progression.[930]

If you do not ask, it will not be given. If you do not seek, you cannot possibly find. If you are unwilling to knock, the door will remain shut to you. But if you do these things, then you must cooperate with Him as He prepares you to receive what He will bestow.

After asking, seeking and knocking, then a process is invoked in which the Father prepares you to receive. You will receive as soon as He can prepare you by experience, by careful, thoughtful, ponderous thought through time and experiences adapted to give you what is asked. When, at last, you have been adequately prepared, you will have gone through exactly what every other soul before you has experienced to prepare them. There are no shortcuts. There are no exceptions. It is in accordance with laws ordained before the foundation of the world. Everyone who has obtained what you seek will have done so in conformity with the very same laws. The Father will work with you to prepare you to receive what you seek.

This is a reaffirmation by Christ of the process and the Father's role in bringing it to pass. If you trust Him, trust also His Father's deliverance of you. You will be delivered. You will receive from Him who knows how to bestow every good gift what you have asked of Him.

3 Nephi 14: 12

> **"Therefore, all things whatsoever ye would that men should do to you, do ye even so to them, for this is the law and the prophets."**

This thought has been taken from the talk and made a law unto itself. Perhaps it belongs there. But it also integrates into the sermon as well.

Remember what preceded this comment. The Father is the giver of "good gifts" and will give you "bread" when you ask it. He will never give you a "stone" when you ask of Him bread.

This follows. You must also become the giver of good gifts. You must also provide to others what they need from you. How you give, unlocks the Father's ability to give to you. Every principle is eternal. Every life requires the balance.

---

930 D&C 121: 46: "The Holy Ghost shall be thy constant companion, and thy scepter an unchanging scepter of righteousness and truth; and thy dominion shall be an everlasting dominion, and without compulsory means it shall flow unto thee forever and ever."

When you seek, you must free the Father's hand to give to you by what you give to others. Without equitable treatment of others, the Father cannot give you.

Your relationship with your fellow man defines your relationship with the Father. Your kindness towards others establishes the conditions of His ability to give kindness to you.

Be careful how you treat others. It affects how the Father is permitted to treat you. It is an eternal principle.[931]

The law and all the prophets were attempting to teach us to deal equitably with one another. What Christ is summarizing is the intent of all that has been given to us in the law and prophets.

Give what you want. Be fair, even generous. It will return to you. No matter how this life disappoints, discourages or frustrates you, keep pressing forward with good cheer. It will be for your good and, as it all concludes, will return to you glory.

This is how the world can be redeemed. This is how Zion will be brought again. It will be the Lord's doing, because it will be through following His commandments that people can be prepared. Those who will participate will necessarily need to heed His commandments. If they do, there will be no poor among them. They will be of one mind and one heart, because they will share the same vision of how to live. They will give one another what they would like to receive, and the result will be the return of a society that has rarely existed on this earth. Heaven can guide and teach us how it is to be done. But we must do it.

Even if no one else will live this principle, you can. If you do, the Lord is able to "take up His abode with you" and even bring you to the Father.[932] Not in some distant time, nor merely "in your heart." It is literal.[933]

The way to prove these teachings is to live them. If you do, you will know the doctrine's truth.[934]

In this brief statement Christ has captured the underlying message of all the prophets from Moses to Christ. It is the reason for God working with Israel. It is the way for any person to find their way back to God.

This message is succinct, profound, and able to transform life. Christ was the Master Teacher. In this brief statement He has proven His

---

931 Alma 41: 15: "For that which ye do send out shall return unto you again, and be restored; therefore, the word restoration more fully condemneth the sinner, and justifieth him not at all."

932 John 14: 23: "Jesus answered and said unto him, If a man love me, he will keep my words: and my Father will love him, and we will come unto him, and make our abode with him."

933 D&C 130: 3: "John 14:23—The appearing of the Father and the Son, in that verse, is a personal appearance; and the idea that the Father and the Son dwell in a man's heart is an old sectarian notion, and is false."

934 John 7: 17: "If any man will do his will, he shall know of the doctrine, whether it be of God, or *whether* I speak of myself."

standing as the greatest source of truth of all those who have instructed others. It is because of this ringing truth that Christ's message has endured through millennia of apostasy and darkness. Words such as these will outlast empires, shine in darkness and subdue critics. He was and is indeed the way, the truth and the life.[935]

3 Nephi 14: 13-14

> **"Enter ye in at the strait gate; for wide is the gate, and broad is the way, which leadeth to destruction, and many there be who go in thereat; Because strait is the gate, and narrow is the way, which leadeth unto life, and few there be that find it."**

This is re-affirmation of man's tendency to reject the right way. The narrowness of it requires surrender of the selfish, parting with pride and sacrifice of self-will.

Many prefer their ignorance to light. Therefore, they will not draw toward the light when it is revealed to them. Without drawing closer to the light they cannot comprehend what the Lord is teaching. It makes no sense to them. For it requires light to comprehend light. Therefore unless a person is willing to increase in light they are left in darkness and unable to apprehend any of what saves them. It remains a mystery to them.

The way to darkness is broad and easy. It requires no effort. It welcomes you. It tempts you with its ease. Because there are "many who go in thereat" it is also popular. When, therefore, you take opinion polling and focus group testing as the measure of a proposition you are only joining to the wide, broad way which will be popular.

Truth challenges. It requires change. It informs you of your faults and mistakes. It is difficult because you are called to rise above what the world is doing, what the world is saying and what the world accepts as good and true. This tendency to want to be popular can twist you away from truth quicker than any other corrupting influence here. This is why Nephi cautioned about the latter-day churches which crave popularity and acceptance.[936]

There will only be a "few who find it." Even in the day in which we live, the measure will always be "few." Not in a relative sense, but in an absolute sense. Few. Period. Only a small number.

---

[935] John 14: 6: "Jesus saith unto him, I am the way, the truth, and the life: no man cometh unto the Father, but by me."

[936] 1 Ne. 22: 23: "For the time speedily shall come that all churches which are built up to get gain, and all those who are built up to get power over the flesh, and those who are built up to become popular in the eyes of the world, and those who seek the lusts of the flesh and the things of the world, and to do all manner of iniquity; yea, in fine, all those who belong to the kingdom of the devil are they who need fear, and tremble, and quake; they are those who must be brought low in the dust; they are those who must be consumed as stubble; and this is according to the words of the prophet."

Looking down through the ages, speaking with the vision of a prophet, the number of those who, living in the last days would have the Father's name upon their forehead, were only 144,000.[937] Though from all ages the number would be in the millions.[938] Still, we live in the time when a living number who are prepared for the return of Christ will be but few in an absolute sense.[939] Even if they have wives and children, yet the number will remain but few.

It is foolish to believe the conditions for salvation are any different for you than they were for Enoch, Moses, Abraham, Isaiah, Elijah, Peter or Joseph. This Gospel is the same. Always and in every generation it is the same. The odds are that but few of those who are living will go in thereat. All the opinion polling to test for popular acceptance of a message cannot deliver a message from God to mankind. It can only entice you to the broad, wide gate "which leadeth to destruction."

The Lord could not be more plain. The teachings which preceded this statement are His invitation. Here He gives His prophetic description of the audience's response. From all those who will read or hear His words, every soul will be accountable. From among those, like you, who are accountable, there will be but "few who find it."

Why is that so? What is so important about the world's acceptance that a fool will treasure it before their own salvation? What can the world offer in exchange that you tempt you to give your soul?[940] How

---

[937] Rev. 7: 3-4: "Saying, Hurt not the earth, neither the sea, nor the trees, till we have sealed the servants of our God in their foreheads. And I heard the number of them which were sealed: *and there were* sealed an hundred *and* forty *and* four thousand of all the tribes of the children of Israel."

[938] Rev. 7: 9, 13-14: "After this I beheld, and, lo, a great multitude, which no man could number, of all nations, and kindreds, and people, and tongues, stood before the throne, and before the Lamb, clothed with white robes, and palms in their hands; … And one of the elders answered, saying unto me, What are these which are arrayed in white robes? and whence came they? And I said unto him, Sir, thou knowest. And he said to me, These are they which came out of great tribulation, and have washed their robes, and made them white in the blood of the Lamb."

[939] D&C 77: 11: "Q. What are we to understand by sealing the one hundred and forty-four thousand, out of all the tribes of Israel—twelve thousand out of every tribe?
A. We are to understand that those who are sealed are high priests, ordained unto the holy order of God, to administer the everlasting gospel; for they are they who are ordained out of every nation, kindred, tongue, and people, by the angels to whom is given power over the nations of the earth, to bring as many as will come to the church of the Firstborn."

[940] Matt. 16: 26: "For what is a man profited, if he shall gain the whole world, and lose his own soul? or what shall a man give in exchange for his soul?"

many will lament when the summer is passed, the harvest has come, that their soul has not been saved.[941]

This is a sobering remark by the forgiving Lord. He invites all to come to Him. But He is realistic about how few will respond. It requires repentance, baptism, receiving the Holy Ghost and living by every word which comes from Him. It is strait and therefore narrow. But it lies in a straight path before you. You can know you are on it when you encounter the gate-keeper, for He has no servant there. He alone maintains that gate through which entry to salvation is gained.[942]

Study, therefore, to show yourself approved.[943]

3 Nephi 14: 15-20

> **"Beware of false prophets, who come to you in sheep's clothing, but inwardly they are ravening wolves. Ye shall know them by their fruits. Do men gather grapes of thorns, or figs of thistles? Even so every good tree bringeth forth good fruit; but a corrupt tree bringeth forth evil fruit. A good tree cannot bring forth evil fruit, neither a corrupt tree bring forth good fruit. Every tree that bringeth not forth good fruit is hewn down, and cast into the fire. Wherefore, by their fruits ye shall know them."**

This test is only necessary if He intends to send prophets. The test is given so you may identify both true and false prophets. Implicit in this, is the obligation to personally account for your response to those He sends, and those who claim to be sent by Him. You must choose. Your choice will count for and against you. You must grow to apply the test correctly.

The concept of "sheep's clothing" is worth pondering. Why is it even possible for such a thing as "sheep's clothing?" Think about it. The attire or mantle they pretend to possess is necessarily "sheep-like" to the casual observer. That is, the "office" or the position or conduct or credentials of the false prophet must be misleading. They should appear bona fide. They need to seem authentic.

Now, lest you be confused about the "wolves" who occupy these positions, it does not mean an utterly corrupt, completely perverse man. It only requires the "wolves" to be unable to deliver a true message from

---

941 D&C 45: 2: "And again I say, hearken unto my voice, lest death shall overtake you; in an hour when ye think not the summer shall be past, and the harvest ended, and your souls not saved."

942 2 Ne. 9: 41: "O then, my beloved brethren, come unto the Lord, the Holy One. Remember that his paths are righteous. Behold, the way for man is narrow, but it lieth in a straight course before him, and the keeper of the gate is the Holy One of Israel; and he employeth no servant there; and there is none other way save it be by the gate; for he cannot be deceived, for the Lord God is his name."

943 2 Tim. 2: 15: "Study to shew thyself approved unto God, a workman that needeth not to be ashamed, rightly dividing the word of truth."

the Lord. It only requires that they not be sent with an authentic message from Him. They must pretend to be His, but He has nothing to do with their message.

So, how are we to distinguish between the "sheep" and the "wolves" who come as "prophets" from the Lord? In a word, it is the "fruit." What does the message produce?

A false prophet's message will produce as its fruit vanity, corruption, evil, foolishness, arrogance, self-assuredness, error, distance from the Lord, poor understanding, popularity, wealth, success, ease, false hopes, ingratitude, pride, displays of popularity, worldliness, hard hearts and ten thousand other meaningless or deceptive fruits.

A true prophet's message will produce repentance.

The only good fruit which can be offered in this world is repentance. When mankind lays down their sins because of a message, that message comes from Him. All others are distractions and invite you to err. The fruit which gives eternal life is repentance and a return to Christ.

When the message comes from a false prophet, you can know the messengers, along with those who listen to it, and the message itself will be "hewn down, and cast into the fire." It will be purged.

When the message comes from a true prophet, you can know the message, along with those who heed it, and the messenger will survive the burning which is to come, because they are purged by repentance and can abide the day of wrath.

Few there be that find it, indeed… It needn't be so. But as Joseph Smith commented: "The world always mistook false prophets for true ones, and those that were sent of God, they considered to be false prophets, and hence they killed, stoned, punished and imprisoned the true prophets, and these had to hide themselves 'in deserts and dens, and caves of the earth'[944], and though the most honorable men of the earth, they banished them from their society as vagabonds, whilst they cherished, honored and supported knaves, vagabonds, hypocrites, impostors, and the basest of men." (DHC 4: 574.)

I suppose that will always be the case. However, we have a guarantee the President of The Church of Jesus Christ of Latter-day Saints is unable (and will always be unable) to lead us astray. It is little wonder we cherish, honor and support that office as we do; preferring it even above scripture. (See Fourteen Fundamentals for Following the Prophet, Ezra Taft Benson, BYU Address February 26, 1980; the second fundamental; recently spoken of in our last General Conference.)

---

944 Heb. 11: 38: "(Of whom the world was not worthy:) they wandered in deserts, and *in* mountains, and *in* dens and caves of the earth."

3 Nephi 14: 21

> **"Not every one that saith unto me, Lord, Lord, shall enter into the kingdom of heaven; but he that doeth the will of my Father who is in heaven."**

This was a favorite quote from President Kimball. It really puts Christ's followers on notice that confessing with the lips with no accompanying action to obey Him will not allow anyone into the kingdom of heaven.

Christ could not be more clear in this statement. The evangelical crowd quotes Paul's statement, "For with the heart man believeth unto righteousness; and with the mouth confession is made unto salvation," as proof to contradict the Lord.[945] Paul does not explain salvation in that brief aside. Confession requires the confessor to go forward and present their entire life as a living sacrifice, continually obedient unto God (as he explains later in the very same letter).[946] This foolish error is creeping into Mormonism with each passing day. From Professor Steven Robinson's rapprochement in How Wide the Divide? to Alonzo Gaskill's awful mistake called Odds Are You're Going To Be Exalted, the erosion of doctrine to conform to the evangelical "market" continues apace.

They teach for doctrines the commandments of men. Their creeds are an abomination. The professors of these creeds are all corrupt. (I'm only quoting Christ.)[947] We would be better informed to draw the starkest, widest and clearest distinctions between ourselves and them, rather than seeking to be regarded as another brand of mainstream Christianity.

Calling Christ "Lord, Lord" will accomplish nothing. There will be those who claim they are "of Christ" but who are no better than the liars,

---

[945] Rom. 10: 10: "For with the heart man believeth unto righteousness; and with the mouth confession is made unto salvation."

[946] Rom. 12: 1-2: "I beseech you therefore, brethren, by the mercies of God, that ye present your bodies a living sacrifice, holy, acceptable unto God, *which is* your reasonable service. And be not conformed to this world: but be ye transformed by the renewing of your mind, that ye may prove what *is* that good, and acceptable, and perfect, will of God."

[947] JS-H 1: 19: "I was answered that I must join none of them, for they were all wrong; and the Personage who addressed me said that all their creeds were an abomination in his sight; that those professors were all corrupt; that: 'they draw near to me with their lips, but their hearts are far from me, they teach for doctrines the commandments of men, having a form of godliness, but they deny the power thereof'."

thieves and whoremongers.[948] It is not a "brand name" to associate with. It is a Teacher to follow.

Christ teaches the will of the Father. Conforming to the will of the Father is required to "enter into the kingdom of heaven." Confession without conformity to His will is worse than meaningless. It is evidence that you are superstitious and foolish. You want Christ as a magic talisman, to be invoked to control the outcome of your life. But you do not want to honor Him by doing as He teaches. You do not want to live as He would want you to live. You do not want to surrender your sins and seek after truth and light.

The simple life which Christ describes in this sermon is how we are to conform to His will. We have taken it bit by bit to examine how living that life should be accomplished. This is the blueprint for understanding the Lord and meeting Him. It is not intended to cause pride, but to provoke repentance. It is the means by which we can know Him.

As the sermon is ending, He reminds those present that calling out to Him and honoring Him with the title of "Lord" will never be enough. You must do as He taught.

There is no other way.

The path is identical for everyone.

You are as capable of doing this as any person who ever lived here. The difference between you and those who have succeeded only exists so long as you refuse to repent. Repentance will cure your lack of faith. Your confidence will increase in the Lord as you lay aside the sins which beset you.

The symmetry of Christ's sermon is astonishing. The closing call to follow Him is unmistakably sobering. It is not enough to sit in an audience honoring Him by showing brief attention to His talk. The talk must become alive in you.

3 Nephi 14: 22-23

> **"Many will say to me in that day: Lord, Lord, have we not prophesied in thy name, and in thy name have cast out devils, and in thy name done many wonderful works? And then will I profess unto them: I never knew you; depart from me, ye that work iniquity."**

---

948 D&C 76: 99-104: "For these are they who are of Paul, and of Apollos, and of Cephas. These are they who say they are some of one and some of another—some of Christ and some of John, and some of Moses, and some of Elias, and some of Esaias, and some of Isaiah, and some of Enoch; But received not the gospel, neither the testimony of Jesus, neither the prophets, neither the everlasting covenant. Last of all, these all are they who will not be gathered with the saints, to be caught up unto the church of the Firstborn, and received into the cloud. These are they who are liars, and sorcerers, and adulterers, and whoremongers, and whosoever loves and makes a lie. These are they who suffer the wrath of God on earth."

Another group will call out to Him in the Day of Judgment saying, "Lord, Lord" showing respect and honor by their lips. It is not the lips which honor Him. The heart must follow His path.[949]

Who will claim to have "prophesied in [His] name?"

Who will claim to have "cast out devils in [His] name?"

Who will claim to have done "many wonderful works" in His name?

What will their conduct in mortality have been in order to justify this claim in the Day of Judgment?

Despite claims to have "prophesied," and to have "cast out devils," and to have performed "many wonderful works," these people are unknown to Him. He will respond: "I never knew you; depart from me, ye that work iniquity."

How can "prophesying in Christ's name" be a work of "iniquity?"

How can "casting out devils" in Christ's name be a work of "iniquity?"

How can a person do "many wonderful works" in Christ's name yet still be doing "iniquity?"

How can people use the Lord's name with apparent success in claiming to have "prophesied," and to have "cast out devils," and done "many wonderful works" yet still be someone He does not know.

How would you determine if you were known to Him?

What would He (not you) need to do in order for you to be known to Him? How would you come to know Him and He to know you?

Do you now see why I have written what I've written? The message is an invitation to come to have Him know you. To have Him take up His abode with you. To affirm to you what your true standing is before Him. Joseph Smith could not know what his standing was before God until he asked the Lord, and received a manifestation from Him.[950] How can you know if you do not similarly ask.

This teaching by Christ does not challenge the reasons men claim to be justified. He does not say they "falsely claim" to have prophesied in His name. He merely accepts the claim without criticism. These people will genuinely believe they were prophesying, casting out devils, and

---

[949] JS-H 1: 19: "I was answered that I must join none of them, for they were all wrong; and the Personage who addressed me said that all their creeds were an abomination in his sight; that those professors were all corrupt; that: 'they draw near to me with their lips, but their hearts are far from me, they teach for doctrines the commandments of men, having a form of godliness, but they deny the power thereof'."

[950] JS-H 1: 29: "In consequence of these things, I often felt condemned for my weakness and imperfections; when, on the evening of the above-mentioned twenty-first of September, after I had retired to my bed for the night, I betook myself to prayer and supplication to Almighty God for forgiveness of all my sins and follies, and also for a manifestation to me, that I might know of my state and standing before him; for I had full confidence in obtaining a divine manifestation, as I previously had one."

doing what they believe to be many marvelous works in His name. Yet their hearts are far from Him.

Therefore, take care that you do not mislead yourself by presuming the things which are done by you in His name are accepted by Him. It is a terrible thing to take His name in vain. To claim He has sent you when He has not, is not only wrong, it is inviting the Lord to say to you in the last day: "Depart from me, ye that work iniquity."

The commandment at the front end is to not take the Lord's name in vain.[951] The result at the back end is revealed here. Take care in how you presume your acts are in harmony with Him. Until He speaks to you, and affirms that you have a work to do for Him, you may only be working iniquity.

3 Nephi 14: 24-25

> **"Therefore, whoso heareth these sayings of mine and doeth them, I will liken him unto a wise man, who built his house upon a rock—And the rain descended, and the floods came, and the winds blew, and beat upon that house; and it fell not, for it was founded upon a rock."**

The "wise man" is the one who is saved.

The "house" is an eternal family, continuation of seed, or eternal life.

The "rock" is Christ.

The descending storm represents the waters of chaos that destroyed the lives of the rebellious at the time of Noah. The rain, winds, floods are descriptive of God's judgment of mankind at that moment. Any soul must build their character, the light they possess, and their choices on Christ to withstand the day of judgment. If they do not, they construct their life on the unstable sand of this broken world, and nothing will endure.

Stability into eternity is built upon Christ's teachings. He came to us to show by example and to teach by word the things which all who are saved must become.

Few are interested in becoming what He was.

This summation is brief, cutting to the heart of the matter. But it is powerful in its plain language.

Christ was the Master Teacher. He said, with great clarity, in a few direct words what He wanted us to understand.

If we fail to heed this warning, then our eternal weakness is because of our choice. If we heed it, then He has provided both the teaching and the example to let us follow.

It is interesting how history has been affected by Christ's teachings. Wars and empires have claimed Christ as their sponsor. He has been a shield for every excess and wickedness imagined by man.

---

[951] Ex. 20: 7: "Thou shalt not take the name of the Lord thy God in vain; for the Lord will not hold him guiltless that taketh his name in vain."

These comments are not about how to build a country, empire or corporation. It is about how to build your life. You cannot control anything other than your choices. But you can choose to follow Him, build your life on the teachings we have been looking at in this sermon. If you do, you build upon the Rock of Heaven.[952]

[952] Moses 7: 53: "And the Lord said: Blessed is he through whose seed Messiah shall come; for he saith—I am Messiah, the King of Zion, the Rock of Heaven, which is broad as eternity; whoso cometh in at the gate and climbeth up by me shall never fall; wherefore, blessed are they of whom I have spoken, for they shall come forth with songs of everlasting joy."

3 NEPHI 15

3 Nephi 15: 1

"And now it came to pass that when Jesus had ended these sayings he cast his eyes round about on the multitude, and said unto them: Behold, ye have heard the things which I taught before I ascended to my Father; therefore, whoso remembereth these sayings of mine and doeth them, him will I raise up at the last day."

Christ affirms that the sermon He just delivered was His sermon and teachings "before [He] ascended to [His] Father." This sermon was likely delivered at many gatherings by Him during His mortal life. For example, when, Mark mentions Him teaching without any discussion of the content (Mark 2: 13), this sermon was likely being repeated by Him. There are other occasions when His message was not preserved, but where He was clearly teaching. The remark here suggests the sermon was not a one-time event. Rather it constituted His mortal ministry's primary message.

Why do you suppose He "cast His eyes round about on the multitude?" Was that mentioned because it was important to your understanding? What should you understand by this act?

Why does He mention "ascending to the Father?" Why is it important for these people to know of that event? What does that event tell you about Him?

What is the difference between "remembering these sayings," and "remembering and doing these sayings?" Do you both remember and do them?

What does the promise to be "raised up at the last day" mean? Unto what would the Lord raise one up? Can you rise from the dead and be "raised up at the last day?" Would there be more to His "raising up at the last day" for someone who had done as He taught?

The way Christ lived His life gives Him the right to teach us all what we need to do in order to be saved. He understood because He lived these principles.

He "looks upon" each of us because we can all live these teachings. Adding a little at a time, bit by bit, precept by precept, we can all live them. Not in a rush, but deliberately and with appropriately measuring each of life's events against His teachings as they come to us.

We are capable of much more than we think.

In fact, we are capable doing and being everything He has been teaching us. He hasn't given this talk to govern the lives of some special, small group of distant icons. They were meant to be the means for healthy living. They are how we are supposed to deal with one another.

Remember them. Then live them. He will "raise you up" not only in the last day, but each day as you have His Spirit to be with you.

3 Nephi 15: 2

> **"And it came to pass that when Jesus had said these words he perceived that there were some among them who marveled, and wondered what he would concerning the law of Moses; for they understood not the saying that old things had passed away, and that all things had become new."**

In the preceding verse I asked why Christ was looking at the group. Now we see the answer. He looked about at those who listened to Him because He was taking in their presence. He was listening to them. Not with the ears, but with His eyes and His heart. He "perceived" what concerned them.

These people derived their security from the Law of Moses. It was the tradition they were raised with; it was what they understood. The Lord's declaration that it had "passed away" was disorienting.

It is troubling to find your religious tradition has run its course, and will be replaced. People crave certainty and order. This desire is so strong in people that they will endure almost anything in order to keep what is familiar to them.

Once the Lord declared that the law of Moses was fulfilled it raised concerns about how, if at all, the Sabbath was to be kept. How were disputes to be managed? What were the laws respecting interest or usury? Servitude for debt? Punishment for certain crimes? What were the rules to govern society as life went forward?

What does it mean that "all things had become new?" Were the things He just said to take effect now? What of animal sacrifice? What of the other offerings? How were religious festivities to be kept, if they were to be kept at all? Which? When?

The Lord recognized these people did not understand what the old things passing away meant. He realized there was fear and confusion because of the statement. They needed more teaching. They needed further explanation.

Moments of transition in religious epochs are troubling. Most people simply do not want to accept the new acts performed by the Lord, and those He sends. They want to wait. They want to see if the new change prospers; let others decide first, and then join after there is proof of success. They want the security of following along with others. When there are 20 million followers of a new movement, then they can accept the new movement. Not before. The problem is that by the time a movement has acquired 20 million followers, the world has required such compromises to have been made that the original movement has been diluted, altered, compromised and weakened. It may be moving forward claiming to have authority, but it will likely have lost much of its power along the way.

Followers of the Lord who were there on the day of this sermon were being told how the new movement was to proceed. He perceives the insecurities of those who are listening. He will take time to explain what is coming next.

The Lord is patient. He will instruct those who follow Him sufficiently that they can go forward with His new dispensation. However, He will expect them to perform exactly as He has taught before they can receive exactly what He has promised.

It is perfect. It is ever the way of the Lord. When He makes an offer, anyone can accept it. But it must be accepted on the terms He established. If you cannot understand, it is not because He did not make it clear enough. Rather, it is because you will not obey in order to gain the light necessary to comprehend what He is teaching. It is your choice to draw away rather than toward Him. As a result, you cannot understand.

3 Nephi 15: 3-5

> **"And he said unto them: Marvel not that I said unto you that old things had passed away, and that all things had become new. Behold, I say unto you that the law is fulfilled that was given unto Moses. Behold, I am he that gave the law, and I am he who covenanted with my people Israel; therefore, the law in me is fulfilled, for I have come to fulfil the law; therefore it hath an end."**

Here is the Lord's announcement that He who gave the law to Moses. He was on the mount. He was the great I AM of the earlier covenant. He is Jehovah. He covenanted with "[His] people Israel." Indeed, it was He who both made the covenant, and then fulfilled it. He is the one who went before and the one who came after. He was the beginning and the end of the law of Moses. In Him it was fulfilled.

All the sacrifices offered in the Mosaic system of worship were designed to point to, and testify of Christ's ministry. He established the system beforehand to point to His mortal life. They testified of Him as the great and final sacrifice. From the Passover sacrifice of an unblemished lamb, to the altar of incense before the Holy of Holies, the entire Mosaic covenant was made to symbolize His life.

This was the reason He spent most of the day of His resurrection on a seven mile walk explaining to two of His followers that the entire system of worship they followed pointed to Him. His sacrifice was necessary because Moses and the prophets all pointed to Him.[953] I've explained this further in the Appendix to *Eighteen Verses* and won't repeat it here. He is affirming to the Nephites what He had earlier affirmed to Luke and Cleopas the day He was resurrected. (I've explained why I believe Luke to be one of these two in *Come, Let Us Adore Him*, and won't repeat it.)

When the original revelation was given to Moses, it pointed to His great mortal ministry. This is His way. He will tell us beforehand so that when the events occur we can recognize His hand.[954]

These Nephites are not unlike us. They wondered at the transition from one era or dispensation to another. So also in our day there is to be a transition from the original message and promise into the fulfillment of the revelation and promise. The revelation given to us in 1830 when the Book of Mormon was published to the world was intended to inform us about the coming changes we will see through the Lord's hand. We have yet to see the larger fulfillment of the promised events contained in the Book of Mormon. Gentiles are in the spotlight. But as they fade economically, militarily, socially and politically from center stage, they will fade in significance from the Lord's final great work, as well. We spent months covering those promises and prophecies. They will all certainly come to pass. As they do, false traditions will not be able to

---

[953] Luke 24: 13-27: "And, behold, two of them went that same day to a village called Emmaus, which was from Jerusalem *about* threescore furlongs. And they talked together of all these things which had happened. And it came to pass, that, while they communed *together* and reasoned, Jesus himself drew near, and went with them. But their eyes were holden that they should not know him. And he said unto them, What manner of communications *are* these that ye have one to another, as ye walk, and are sad? And the one of them, whose name was Cleopas, answering said unto him, Art thou only a stranger in Jerusalem, and hast not known the things which are come to pass there in these days? And he said unto them, What things? And they said unto him, Concerning Jesus of Nazareth, which was a prophet mighty in deed and word before God and all the people: And how the chief priests and our rulers delivered him to be condemned to death, and have crucified him. But we trusted that it had been he which should have redeemed Israel: and beside all this, to day is the third day since these things were done. Yea, and certain women also of our company made us astonished, which were early at the sepulchre; And when they found not his body, they came, saying, that they had also seen a vision of angels, which said that he was alive. And certain of them which were with us went to the sepulchre, and found *it* even so as the women had said: but him they saw not. Then he said unto them, O fools, and slow of heart to believe all that the prophets have spoken: Ought not Christ to have suffered these things, and to enter into his glory? And beginning at Moses and all the prophets, he expounded unto them in all the scriptures the things concerning himself."

[954] Amos 3: 7: "Surely the Lord God will do nothing, but he revealeth his secret unto his servants the prophets."

keep pace with the rapid changes to come. The law given to Moses served to point to a greater work. The Book of Mormon prepares and points to another greater work soon to come, as well.

Do not think the Lord changes. He is ever the same. As a result, the tests, trials and experiences of believers in any generation will mirror one another. Some wondered at the Lord's fulfillment of the earlier law. There will also be those who are struck with wonder as the Book of Mormon prophecies unfold. If there was ever a time when the caution to be careful about false prophets pretending to be sheep, it is certainly in our generation. Keeping your eye on the Lord, and His promises is more important now than ever before. He is reliable, even if governments, others and institutions fail you.

The fulfillment of the Lord's covenants is a wonderful thing. When it happens it proves He cares[955], He keeps covenants[956], and He is in control.[957] It is not something to fear, but instead to welcome. As things change, and the pace of change itself accelerates, take heart. Though there will be perplexities of nations with distress[958], there is still the promise Abinadi reminded us of that the Lord will bring again Zion.[959]

We ought to identify with the message Christ gave these Nephites. We are going to see similar fulfillment of covenant promises made by Him in the not so distant future.

---

955 D&C 133: 52: "And now the year of my redeemed is come; and they shall mention the loving kindness of their Lord, and all that he has bestowed upon them according to his goodness, and according to his loving kindness, forever and ever."

956 Deut. 7: 9: "Know therefore that the Lord thy God, he *is* God, the faithful God, which keepeth covenant and mercy with them that love him and keep his commandments to a thousand generations;"

957 Ps. 93: 1-5: "The Lord reigneth, he is clothed with majesty; the Lord is clothed with strength, *wherewith* he hath girded himself: the world also is stablished, that it cannot be moved. Thy throne *is* established of old: thou *art* from everlasting. The floods have lifted up, O Lord, the floods have lifted up their voice; the floods lift up their waves. The Lord on high *is* mightier than the noise of many waters, *yea, than* the mighty waves of the sea. Thy testimonies are very sure: holiness becometh thine house, O Lord, for ever."

958 Luke 21: 25: "And there shall be signs in the sun, and in the moon, and in the stars; and upon the earth distress of nations, with perplexity; the sea and the waves roaring;"

959 Mosiah 15: 29-31: "Yea, Lord, thy watchmen shall lift up their voice; with the voice together shall they sing; for they shall see eye to eye, when the Lord shall bring again Zion. Break forth into joy, sing together, ye waste places of Jerusalem; for the Lord hath comforted his people, he hath redeemed Jerusalem. The Lord hath made bare his holy arm in the eyes of all the nations; and all the ends of the earth shall see the salvation of our God."

3 Nephi 15: 6-8

> **"Behold, I do not destroy the prophets, for as many as have not been fulfilled in me, verily I say unto you, shall all be fulfilled. And because I said unto you that old things have passed away, I do not destroy that which hath been spoken concerning things which are to come. For behold, the covenant which I have made with my people is not all fulfilled; but the law which was given unto Moses hath an end in me."**

The Lord does not make a promise and fail to fulfill it.[960] Therefore, when a promise has been made by Him, it will come to pass. But the promise must be His. No agent or spokesman can speak in His name and obligate Him to perform unless the words spoken are His. Even if a man should qualify to hold sealing power, that power will only bind what is in conformity with His word.[961] There is no obligation on Him to perform what is not sealed by the Holy Spirit of Promise.[962] So it is not every person who speaks, even if in a position of leading others, claiming "Lord, Lord" as they do, whose words obligate the Lord to fulfill. But the opposite is also true. If the person is clothed with nothing other than the Lord's private commission to speak, if he speaks the Lord's words they will "all be fulfilled." Abinadi was so obscure a character that we don't know if he was Lamanite or Nephite. He is the only person in the entire Book of Mormon record with the name Abinadi. He came from nowhere, was imprisoned by the leading authorities of the church, and was killed by those who presumed to exercise judgment over him. Yet it was he who bore the Lord's words.

---

[960] D&C 1: 38: "What I the Lord have spoken, I have spoken, and I excuse not myself; and though the heavens and the earth pass away, my word shall not pass away, but shall all be fulfilled, whether by mine own voice or by the voice of my servants, it is the same."

[961] Hel. 10: 5: "And now, because thou hast done this with such unwearyingness, behold, I will bless thee forever; and I will make thee mighty in word and in deed, in faith and in works; yea, even that all things shall be done unto thee according to thy word, for thou shalt not ask that which is contrary to my will."

[962] D&C 132: 18: "And again, verily I say unto you, if a man marry a wife, and make a covenant with her for time and for all eternity, if that covenant is not by me or by my word, which is my law, and is not sealed by the Holy Spirit of promise, through him whom I have anointed and appointed unto this power, then it is not valid neither of force when they are out of the world, because they are not joined by me, saith the Lord, neither by my word; when they are out of the world it cannot be received there, because the angels and the gods are appointed there, by whom they cannot pass; they cannot, therefore, inherit my glory; for my house is a house of order, saith the Lord God."
D&C 88: 3: "Wherefore, I now send upon you another Comforter, even upon you my friends, that it may abide in your hearts, even the Holy Spirit of promise; which other Comforter is the same that I promised unto my disciples, as is recorded in the testimony of John."

The entire society he preached to were held to account for both his words and how they reacted to them (and him).

When the Lord speaks of fulfilling the things to come, He is both ratifying the past prophets whose words have not come to pass, and He is establishing an eternal principal. It is as true today as it was anciently. When a message comes from Him, it is binding. The message is His. The power to make His message binding upon mankind is His. The right to govern all mankind is His.

The first clarification the Lord wants the people to understand is that His words are, and will remain sovereign. They will not be rescinded. It is not the prophets, nor the promises of His great unfolding work foretold by prophetic messages that will end. It is only the law of observances given through Moses that has now been fulfilled. It is not abandoned, but rather it is fulfilled. It pointed to Him. He lived it. He fulfilled every foreshadow, every type, every promise under that law. It was His to give, and it was His life that fulfilled it.

The intergenerational work of saving mankind is always the same. The promise to save through the chosen lineage all of mankind is still in effect. It existed before Moses, and will continue after the fulfillment of the law of Moses. The great prophecies and promises pointing to His second coming remain in effect. His first coming only fulfilled Moses' law. His second will fulfill the rest of the promises concerning Him as the great Deliverer, the world's judge, and the one whose right it is to rule as "King of kings and Lord of lords."

The crowd entertained apprehensions that the prophets were now "destroyed" by Him. He made it clear that was not the case. This is why Isaiah and Zenock remain relevant to our day. This is why He will even quote from Isaiah and add Malachi to the Nephite scriptures. This is why the Lord continues to entrust men with messages which bind Him to do His final, strange work. He intends to both fulfill and inform us so we may prepare against the day of judgment. His mission is to redeem, not to surprise or confuse the worthy. If a person will but listen to Him and those He sends, they will be prepared for the coming calamities.

The consistency of this message is so profound that it reconfirms that Joseph Smith is not the source of the Book of Mormon. This is a record of the Lord's doings among an ancient and fallen people. It is not an invention of a New England farm boy. The idea Joseph Smith wrote this account is beyond incredible. It simply isn't true. This is from the Lord, not a man. A person can get closer to God by abiding its precepts than from any other book. It is the lifeline given to us for our day. We ignore it and dismiss it at our peril.

3 Nephi 15: 9-10

> **"Behold, I am the law, and the light. Look unto me, and endure to the end, and ye shall live; for unto him that endureth to the end will I give eternal life. Behold, I have given unto you the**

commandments; therefore keep my commandments. And this is the law and the prophets, for they truly testified of me."

It is Christ who is "the law." Not a man or men. Nor even those sent by Him. They are relevant only to the extent they point to Him. When they attract notice for themselves, they interfere with His great work. He alone is the "law." He alone is the "light."

He answers the concerns these listeners have about the source they are now to look to for life and salvation. "Look unto me" He proclaims. He, not the law, is their future. They are to seek for and establish a more direct line of communication between themselves and Him.

He is the "law"—meaning that His words (both in the preceding sermon and in the revelations He will grant them) is to govern. Not a prior set of performances and ordinances.

He is the "light"—meaning, understanding will increase as they choose to follow Him. They will understand with increasing clarity as they move closer to Him. He will illuminate their understanding, because some things can only be apprehended when you draw close enough to Him for them to emerge from darkness and confusion.

"Look unto [Him]"—meaning, it is not a rule-book, ordinances or traditions which are to guide them. He will. Personally. By His involvement in their lives, through revelation, and with the comforter or Holy Ghost which He has promised to send.

"Endure to the end"—meaning, both here and in the hereafter. It will be a great while beyond this life before you have reached the "end" He desires you to attain. Therefore, enduring requires you to fight against all that opposes truth for so long as you are allowed to participate in the battle. Not passively, taking in what is wrong and showing tolerance for it, but instead actively standing for truth as long as you exist, here and hereafter.

"Ye shall live"—meaning, the kind of life which Christ gives. That life is not mortal, though you will begin it as a mortal. That is life eternal, which is to know Him and His Father. It was designed to begin here.

"To him that endureth to the end I will give eternal life"—meaning, such people will come to live as Christ and His Father live. Or, in other words, to know truth and be filled with light.[963]

"Keep my commandments"—meaning, listen and respond to what He directs. Take what He offers. Do not decline to go and do as He bids you to do; not what you presume will please Him, but what He has counseled you to do. If you do not know what that is, then you do not read the scriptures and ask. You are deliberately without knowledge of what He would ask of you.

---

[963] D&C 93: 28, 36: "He that keepeth his commandments receiveth truth and light, until he is glorified in truth and knoweth all things. ...The glory of God is intelligence, or, in other words, light and truth."

"This is the law and the prophets"—meaning, the culmination of all that has been given by Him is for man to come to know Him. This was the purpose behind all the symbols, all the rites, all the ordinances. It is still the purpose underlying it all. Come to Him. Not to a building and think yourself redeemed because you are part of a select group welcomed there. Come to Him. Not to a man who will promise you heaven itself, but to Him who will open to you the heavens.

"For they truly testify of [Him]"—meaning they have and do testify of Him. Not of themselves. Not of a program. Not of an organization. Not of men. They testify of Him. Continually. Not intermittently, occasionally and without knowledge of Him. They do not borrow light from others, but they testify of the things which they know from Him. They will always do so. This is one of the ways you can detect "wolves" from "sheep" as they come professing religion. The true sheep will testify of Him whom they know. The wolves will ask you to follow men, and they interfere with knowing Him. Though you do all the wolves bid you to do, yet you will grow more distant from Him.

Our Lord is indeed a consuming fire, and is unwilling to share adoration with mere men claiming themselves to be worthy of adoration.[964]

3 Nephi 15: 11-14

> **"And now it came to pass that when Jesus had spoken these words, he said unto those twelve whom he had chosen: Ye are my disciples; and ye are a light unto this people, who are a remnant of the house of Joseph. And behold, this is the land of your inheritance; and the Father hath given it unto you. And not at any time hath the Father given me commandment that I should tell it unto your brethren at Jerusalem."**

Christ has identified Himself as the "light. " Now refers to His chosen twelve disciples as His "disciples," and a "light unto this people." Why? How can He be the "light" and also make disciples who follow Him a "light" to others as well? What would a disciple need to be in order for them to also reflect His light to others? How would that be accomplished? What happens if the disciples no longer reflect His light, but instead seek to be a light unto themselves?[965]

Notice He identifies them as a "remnant of the house of Joseph." This would be Joseph of Egypt. Why is "this…the land of your inheritance" if it is the tribe of Joseph? How was Joseph given the Americas as his promised land? Was that foreseen? If so, how long has

---

964 Deut. 4: 24: "For the Lord thy God *is* a consuming fire, *even* a jealous God."

965 2 Ne. 26: 29: "He commandeth that there shall be no priestcrafts; for, behold, priestcrafts are that men preach and set themselves up for a light unto the world, that they may get gain and praise of the world; but they seek not the welfare of Zion."

the Lord had in mind the establishment of Joseph in the promised land of the Americas?

Why is the "Father" the one who has given the land of inheritance to Joseph? Why not Jesus Christ? Why does the Father keep in His authority to divide the land for inheritance?

What does it mean that the Father did not give Christ "commandment that I should tell it unto your brethren at Jerusalem?" If Christ knew it, why wouldn't He tell it to the "brethren at Jerusalem?" Why would Christ know something of this significance and keep it to Himself?

I've explained in *The Second Comforter* the subject of the failure of the Nephites to ask about the "other sheep" which will occupy some of this phase of the sermon. I'm not going to repeat it here, but would refer you to that discussion on the topic.

Why do you suppose the Lord would point out this monumental failure of the disciples at Jerusalem to ask about the "other sheep?"[966] What is it about the failure to seek knowledge from the Lord that makes people both stiffnecked and filled with unbelief?[967]

When the Lord will tell those who ask of Him, why is it offensive to Him that people fail to ask?

Is the admonition to "ask, seek, knock" more than an admonition? Is it in fact a commandment? Are you required to search into the mysteries of God, and know more day by day as a result of inquiring of Him? Can you substitute for that by asking others about mysteries? Why not? Why is it essential to gain your knowledge from Him?

Does the Lord's phrasing tell you something important? ("not at any time hath the Father given me commandment that I should tell it unto your brethren at Jerusalem")? Is Christ constrained to not disclose until

---

[966] 3 Ne. 16: 4: "And I command you that ye shall write these sayings after I am gone, that if it so be that my people at Jerusalem, they who have seen me and been with me in my ministry, do not ask the Father in my name, that they may receive a knowledge of you by the Holy Ghost, and also of the other tribes whom they know not of, that these sayings which ye shall write shall be kept and shall be manifested unto the Gentiles, that through the fulness of the Gentiles, the remnant of their seed, who shall be scattered forth upon the face of the earth because of their unbelief, may be brought in, or may be brought to a knowledge of me, their Redeemer."

[967] 3 Ne. 15: 18: "And now, because of stiffneckedness and unbelief they understood not my word; therefore I was commanded to say no more of the Father concerning this thing unto them."

those at Jerusalem ask of Him?[968] What does that say about how this area of revelation is governed? Must the inquiry precede the revelation? What does it mean about the duty to inquire? Again, I've explained this in *The Second Comforter*, and would refer you to that discussion.

There must be a "living relationship" between you and the Living God. If it is not alive, then God must be dead to you. And you dead to Him. Ask, for He has promised to answer. Seek, for He has just promised you will find. Knock, for He has just assured you it will open to you. Now He is walking through a subject where much could have been revealed had the inquiry been made. It will be followed in turn by the Nephite failure to ask about the "other sheep" just as those at Jerusalem failed to ask. Again, see the discussion in *The Second Comforter* for more on this.

The next portion of this sermon is dealt with in *The Second Comforter,* or in an earlier series of posts on this blog. I'm going to skip forward at this point to cover portions I have not discussed before.

---

968 3 Ne. 16: 4: "And I command you that ye shall write these sayings after I am gone, that if it so be that my people at Jerusalem, they who have seen me and been with me in my ministry, do not ask the Father in my name, that they may receive a knowledge of you by the Holy Ghost, and also of the other tribes whom they know not of, that these sayings which ye shall write shall be kept and shall be manifested unto the Gentiles, that through the fulness of the Gentiles, the remnant of their seed, who shall be scattered forth upon the face of the earth because of their unbelief, may be brought in, or may be brought to a knowledge of me, their Redeemer."

3 NEPHI 18

3 Nephi 18: 1-2

"And it came to pass that Jesus commanded his Disciples that they should bring forth some bread and wine unto him. And while they were gone for bread and wine, he commanded the multitude that they should sit themselves down upon the earth."

The Lord requires His disciples to bring some bread and wine to Him. It suggests that all 12 of these disciples were asked to retrieve the items. "While they were gone for bread and wine" suggests that all 12 were involved. Perhaps there were others, as well. What is to take place next would likely require the effort of more than 12, for it will involve all 2,500 of those present.[969]

We know what is coming. But taking this from the perspective of the Nephite audience, what would gathering "bread" foreshadow? Would they associate it with the Table of Shewbread? Would they expect a wave offering? What might their anticipation be as they awaited the arrival of the bread? How might their expectations have prepared them to receive a new ordinance? Would what follows have reaffirmed Christ fulfilled the law of Moses?

Why did the Lord ask for "wine?" What is there in the symbol of "wine" that testifies of Him? We know that in exigencies we can substitute water for wine.[970] But the Lord requested "wine" to be brought for the ordinance He was about to introduce.

Section 27:2 was given because the Prophet Joseph was on his way to procure wine from an enemy who wished him harm. The possibility

---

969 3 Ne. 17: 25: "And the multitude did see and hear and bear record; and they know that their record is true for they all of them did see and hear, every man for himself; and they were in number about two thousand and five hundred souls; and they did consist of men, women, and children."

970 D&C 27: 2: "For, behold, I say unto you, that it mattereth not what ye shall eat or what ye shall drink when ye partake of the sacrament, if it so be that ye do it with an eye single to my glory—remembering unto the Father my body which was laid down for you, and my blood which was shed for the remission of your sins."

of the wine being adulterated was significant. Since an angel met Joseph on his way and revealed that a substitute could be used, it is likely if wine had been procured it would have been poisoned. The revelation gives precautions to be taken in preparing wine for the sacrament.[971] The Saints were to prepare their own wine, and know it is safe for use in the sacrament.

To conform to this revelation, when the Saints moved west there was a "Wine Mission" established in Southern Utah. The Mormon Wine Mission did not have a formal separate existence, but was within the boundaries of the Cotton Mission of 1861. The Saints made their own wine because of D&C 27: 3-4. If the Saints did not make the wine themselves, they were to use water. Therefore, to conform to the pattern of the Lord, and the revelation to guard against the mischief of enemies, the wine mission was established to produce wine for the sacrament.

Master vintner John C. Naegle was called by Brigham Young to establish and operate a winery in Toquerville and to instruct people in the wine making process. The operation that Naegle presided over built a rock house for production which included a wine cellar underneath large enough to accommodate a wagon and a team of horses and allow them to turn around. In the production house were located the vats, presses, and other production equipment to produce and ferment the wine. They produced 500-gallon casks. The wine was shipped in smaller 40-gallon casks. It was distributed through ZCMI. Wine making became an important Southern Utah industry.

As President Grant elevated the Word of Wisdom from wise advice to a strict commandment, the practice of using wine in the sacrament came to an end. Since that time Latter-day Saints have taken a dim view of using wine in the sacrament.

Ask yourself, however, which is a more appropriate symbol of the Lord's supper: water or wine? If water were more so, then why did the Lord not institute use of water among the Nephites in the ceremony He is about to introduce in the verses which follow? Why is the sacrament prayer in both Moroni 5 and D&C 20: 78-79 spoken for "wine" rather than water?

Are we morally superior because we use water instead of wine? Have we replaced a powerful symbol with a fanatical rule? Is there such a risk of adulterated or poisoned wine by anti-Mormon suppliers that we are justified in not using wine in the sacrament?

Well, the stage is being set by the Lord for the Nephites in this verse. He is gathering attention for an ordinance to be instituted. For His purposes, our Lord asks for bread and wine. We should not impose a false cultural assessment on these words. We should not rewrite them

---

[971] D&C 27: 3-4: "Wherefore, a commandment I give unto you, that you shall not purchase wine neither strong drink of your enemies; Wherefore, you shall partake of none except it is made new among you; yea, in this my Father's kingdom which shall be built up on the earth."

because of our prejudice and bigotry into something other than what they say.

From the symbol of the crushed grape, its blood spilled and then allowed to ferment, comes a symbol of the great work of the Lord. The grape juice changes through fermentation from something which affects the senses. As the Psalmist puts it wine gladdens the heart.[972] His blood was spilled and then grew into a new power intended to gladden the heart of all those who will receive it.

The Prophet was overshadowed with foreboding on the day of his death. The reason Stephen Markham was not with them in the jail at the time the final assault took place was because he had been sent to purchase wine by the Prophet. The jailer allowed the wine to return to Joseph, Hyrum, John and Willard, but Steven Markham was excluded. There were only four in the jail when the killings occurred. The reason they sent for wine was to gladden their hearts and lift their spirits from the oppression which hung over them. It was a day of triumph for evil and the spirit of that day was heavy. The wine and John Taylor's singing were to console them in the terrible moments preceding the attack by 200 conspirators intent on killing Joseph and his brother.

We have become so fanatical about being teetotalers that the story of Joseph's use of wine on the day of his martyrdom is largely unknown today. Instead the tale of him refusing to drink whiskey as a sedative for the bone operation in his youth is retold. This is used to reinforce President Grant's harsh view of the Word of Wisdom.

Now, I am advocating nothing. I abstain from all forms of alcohol, possess a temple recommend, and accept the current view of absolute abstinence from any form of alcoholic consumption. But I do not believe it is a virtue. Nor do I believe substitution of water for wine increases the sanctity of the sacrament. It may do just the opposite.

It is often the case that when men attempt to "improve" on the Lord's teachings they go backward.

3 Nephi 18: 3-4

> **"And when the Disciples had come with bread and wine, he took of the bread and brake and blessed it; and he gave unto the Disciples and commanded that they should eat. And when they had eaten and were filled, he commanded that they should give unto the multitude."**

It is interesting these 12 are consistently referred to as "disciples" and not as "Apostles." There isn't a single "Apostle" in the Book of Mormon record. Only "disciples." There are 12 of them, and they are treated exactly as were the Apostles in Jerusalem. This was a distinction

[972] Ps. 104: 15: "And wine *that* maketh glad the heart of man, *and* oil to make *his* face to shine, and bread *which* strengtheneth man's heart."

David Whitmer believed to be significant. He disliked the claim to restore Apostles.

Well, the disciples are described as "twelve" or "the twelve" in the first references. Then they are called "disciples." In the printing we have the "D" capitalized. This is an attempt by typesetting to distinguish and make more important these "big-D" disciples from other run-of-the-mill "small-d" disciples. But printers should not trick your mind into accepting the distinction. The Lord leveled these twelve. He made them merely disciples, which is a term applied with equal meaning to any of those who were present on that day.

The twelve are taught, then asked to teach. The twelve overhear the Lord break and then bless the bread. The record at this point does not include the words Christ used to bless the bread. Moroni corrects that by adding it in at a later time in the account. Here is what Christ taught when He blessed the bread:

"The manner of their elders and priests administering the flesh and blood of Christ unto the church; and they administered it according to the commandments of Christ; wherefore we know the manner to be true; and the elder or priest did minister it—And they did kneel down with the church, and pray to the Father in the name of Christ, saying: O God, the Eternal Father, we ask thee in the name of thy Son, Jesus Christ, to bless and sanctify this bread to the souls of all those who partake of it; that they may eat in remembrance of the body of thy Son, and witness unto thee, O God, the Eternal Father, that they are willing to take upon them the name of thy Son, and always remember him, and keep his commandments which he hath given them, that they may always have his Spirit to be with them. Amen." (Moroni 4: 1-3.)

Notice in the narrative the Lord "commanded that they should eat." This is an interesting phrasing. It is more than an invitation. It is more than an offering. It is a commandment. Why? What is it about partaking of His sacrament, eating in remembrance of the body of Christ, that **must** be done? Why is it a commandment?

Notice, also, the disciples ate until they were "filled?" Does this mean their stomachs were sated? Does it mean their souls were affected? Does it mean both? How were they "filled" by partaking of the bread?

Did they need to be "filled" themselves before they would be permitted to minister to others? Was that why the Lord required them to first partake then be filled before they were commanded to minister to the others?

When they ministered to the multitude, what was it they "gave" to the multitude? Was it the bread alone? Was it also something that had "filled" them? What was going on in this ceremony?

Why would people who had seen, touched, knelt at the feet of the risen Lord, need to partake of the bread as a "witness" and "remembrance" of Him? How can this add to what they had already received? Why is the sacrament sacred enough to be celebrated by the Lord with people who are in His very presence?

Does this change in any respect how you view the sacrament? If so, how?

3 Nephi 18: 5

> **"And when the multitude had eaten and were filled, he said unto the Disciples: Behold there shall one be ordained among you, and to him will I give power that he shall break bread and bless it and give it unto the people of my church, unto all those who shall believe and be baptized in my name."**

Notice now the "multitude" takes part in eating the bread and "were filled." This raises the question of how they were filled. Were their stomachs filled because of the amount they ate? Did they eat until they were filled, or did they get filled on just a small amount of bread? Or was this a spiritual filling where each heart was touched and each person's countenance before the Lord filled with light?

This is a group which has just a few hours before engaged in a "hosanna shout" before the Lord.[973] Now, however, they are "filled." It is a profound moment with deep significance.

The Lord then tells the disciples that "there shall be one ordained among you" to break the bread. Notice it is "one." All twelve have been asked to pass the sacrament to the multitude, but from among them "shall one be ordained" to receive "power that he shall break bread and bless it." Why would only "one" be chosen to do this? All twelve had been given the power to baptize.[974] Only one of them is to bless the sacrament. What does that suggest about the sanctity of the sacrament, if it is performed in the correct manner? Should it be viewed as a "higher ordinance" because of the more exclusive reservation of the "power" conferred by the Lord? What does that tell us about the manner we ought to proceed? Have we missed something in our reading of these verses?

---

[973] 3 Ne. 11: 17: "Hosanna! Blessed be the name of the Most High God! And they did fall down at the feet of Jesus, and did worship him."

[974] 3 Ne. 11: 21-22: "And the Lord said unto him: I give unto you power that ye shall baptize this people when I am again ascended into heaven. And again the Lord called others, and said unto them likewise; and he gave unto them power to baptize. And he said unto them: On this wise shall ye baptize; and there shall be no disputations among you."

Now the record is written by Nephi.[975] He is the first one called by the Lord.[976] He is the first one given power to baptize by the Lord.[977] But the identity of the person given "power that he shall break bread and bless it" is not recorded. We can know it is Nephi because he was always the one given the other power first. More to the point, however, we can know it was him because he kept the record. Had it been another, he would have told us. But since it was him, he declined to draw further attention to himself. Identifying himself previously was necessary for the narrative to be complete. Here, however, identifying himself would call undue attention. As a humble follower of Christ, it was not appropriate for him to do so, therefore the disciple is unnamed in our account.

Why is "power [to] break bread and bless it" conferred separately from the power to baptize? In our Section 20, the authority is coextensive.[978] Why does the Lord separate it among the Nephites? Since we have this account, does it add any instruction for us about the significance of the sacrament?

Sometimes we neglect things because of our familiarity with them. We presume wrongly that we understand them because of their frequent repetition. Here, however, the sacrament seems to take on greater significance. It achieves a pinnacle that exceeds even touching the risen Lord.

When we share food with one another, we become part of the same material. We share substance. When a meal is shared, life is shared. We become one of the same substance.

The substance which binds us is the "body of Christ" in symbol. Christ "broke" the bread before it was blessed. What does breaking the bread symbolize about Christ? How is His broken body intended to unite us with one another, and with Him?

---

975 3 Ne. 1: 2: "And Nephi, the son of Helaman, had departed out of the land of Zarahemla, giving charge unto his son Nephi, who was his eldest son, concerning the plates of brass, and all the records which had been kept, and all those things which had been kept sacred from the departure of Lehi out of Jerusalem."

976 3 Ne. 11: 18: "And it came to pass that he spake unto Nephi (for Nephi was among the multitude) and he commanded him that he should come forth."

977 3 Ne. 11: 18-21: "And it came to pass that he spake unto Nephi (for Nephi was among the multitude) and he commanded him that he should come forth. And Nephi arose and went forth, and bowed himself before the Lord and did kiss his feet. And the Lord commanded him that he should arise. And he arose and stood before him. And the Lord said unto him: I give unto you power that ye shall baptize this people when I am again ascended into heaven."

978 D&C 20: 38-39, 46: "38 *The duty of the elders, priests, teachers, deacons, and members of the church of Christ*—An apostle is an elder, and it is his calling to baptize; And to ordain other elders, priests, teachers, and deacons; ...The priest's duty is to preach, teach, expound, exhort, and baptize, and administer the sacrament,"

Why is the broken bread distributed to those who "shall believe and be baptized in my name?" Does the order matter? Can a person be baptized before they believe, later come to believe, and then receive the sacrament correctly? Or must they come to believe first, then receive baptism second, before it is proper to partake of the sacrament? We've been working our way through the Lord's commandments deliberately trying to unlock their specific requirements. They are simple. They can be done by anyone. But they are specific and should be followed in the same manner the Lord instituted them. This is the "straight path" which He says is narrow and few will find. Perhaps it is not found because we proceed with inexactitude to do what He has laid out before us with exactness.

The Lord occupies the role as Master and as Example. He bids us to follow Him. And He tells us His way is plain. If we confuse it, muddle it, and fail to do it as He has asked us to do, then it is not His failure, but ours. He has made it clear that He respects no one, but is open to all. But it is open on the exact terms. And some times the terms are exacting.

3 Nephi 18: 6-7

> **"And this shall ye always observe to do, even as I have done, even as I have broken bread and blessed it and given it unto you. And this shall ye do in remembrance of my body, which I have shown unto you. And it shall be a testimony unto the Father that ye do always remember me. And if ye do always remember me ye shall have my Spirit to be with you."**

If the last post did not make the matter clear enough, the Lord emphasizes here the formula He has provided in this ordinance:

- "Always observe to do." It is to be done, and when it is done it is to be done in an "observant" way.
- "Even as I have done." His example is intended to clarify and define the manner the ordinance is to be observed. He regulates it by what He has done.
- "Even as I have broken bread and blessed it." The manner, the process, the gestures of breaking it first and then blessing it second, are to be followed exactly.
- "And given it unto you." When it is broken, then blessed, those who qualify by having repented and been baptized receive it as a gift or token from Christ. It is His body.

Now the Lord clarifies in explanation what He has earlier clarified in the blessing: This is to be done "in remembrance of [His] body." It is through His body that He, the living sacrifice, shows us the way. A loving God has died for us. His body is a testimony of life, obedience, sacrifice, cruelty, forgiveness, death, resurrection, immortality, power and glory. When you remember His life you should remember all that is associated with it.

Here the Lord reminds the Nephites they are to remember the body "which [He] has shown unto [them]." The sacred embrace and ceremony of recognition (a term I coined in *The Second Comforter*), should return to the mind of those present whenever they received the bread again. The Lord could give no greater testimony of what He had done, who He was, and how He served them than by showing to them His risen body still bearing the marks of crucifixion.

The act is intended to be a "testimony unto the Father that ye do always remember [Him]." The act of testifying is not composed merely of the act of eating the bread. To actually testify to the Father you must

1. Repent

2. Be baptized

3. Receive the bread after it has been properly blessed with power

4. Remember His body and the ten things symbolized through it

This is the acceptable sacrifice the Father will receive as a "testimony" of Christ.

Should you perform this, then you will receive power to "have [His] Spirit to be with you."

These are simple steps. They are possible to be performed. When they are, the Father receives the act as a testimony before Him of the truth that you do always remember His Son. It will be recorded in heaven, and will be a witness for your salvation in the Day of Judgment.

These are solemn things. It is clear enough that we accomplish these things. But it is not clear how often they are performed, even in a church, which at one time, conducted a ceremony twice each Sunday, and today conducts it once each Sunday.

It is interesting the Lord should give us language that makes "observing to do" and "as He has done" a required part of the process. Those words are probably best when viewed in their clearest meaning, and accomplished with exactitude. Though He measures our hearts, when instructions are given in simplicity, one fair measure of the heart is how closely we follow the instruction.

Since the result is to have His Spirit to be with you, it should be a simple matter to determine by reflection if you have His Spirit as your companion. If you can feel that He is always with you, then you have an acceptable testimony to the Father. If you do not, then perhaps you should revisit the steps He has provided to see what you might improve. There is a law irrevocably decreed before the foundation of the world upon which all blessings are predicated. And when we receive any blessing from the Lord, it is by obedience to the law upon which the blessing is provided. Therefore, it makes sense that you can determine the extent to which you have followed the formula by the result promised. Having Christ's Spirit to be with you is significant enough proof that you should know the truth of the matter. Since you know the means by which to judge, see that you judge the matter correctly.[979]

3 Nephi 18: 8

> **"And it came to pass that when he said these words, he commanded his Disciples that they should take of the wine of the cup and drink of it, and that they should also give unto the multitude that they might drink of it."**

In this description we do not have mention of the blessing pronounced upon the wine. Moroni will later clarify that it was blessed and provide us the words of His blessing: "The manner of administering the wine—Behold, they took the cup, and said: O God, the Eternal Father, we ask thee, in the name of thy Son, Jesus Christ, to bless and sanctify this wine to the souls of all those who drink of it, that they may do it in remembrance of the blood of thy Son, which was shed for them; that they may witness unto thee, O God, the Eternal Father, that they do always remember him, that they may have his Spirit to be with them. Amen." (Moroni 5: 1-2.)

Once again it is a "command" to partake. The Lord, knowing how critical this act is for salvation and a testimony before the Father, makes it a command that the disciples drink of it.

Wine was generally either purple or red. Our blood is purple when deprived of oxygen in our veins, and red when filled with oxygen in our arteries. These two colors of blood inside our bodies are akin to the predominate colors of wine.

Once again it is the disciples who partake first. Then, after having partaken, they pass it to the multitude. This illustrates the practice of receiving it before being able to pass it to others. It is not possible to pass along what has not first been received. This is true of all the Lord's ordinances. It is one of the reasons Alma rebaptized himself the instant he first began to baptize others.[980] Those who bless are to be sanctified by partaking, then they pass the sacrament as sanctified ministers. Those who are passing are not more important, but rather they are first purified. Then those to whom they minister may receive the ordinance from those who are already clean.

Our modern practice is to pass the sacrament first to the "presiding authority" who is present. The presiding authority (who is always mentioned at the beginning of the meeting) is identified, and then the priests who pass the sacrament bring it to that person first. After he

---

[979] Moroni 7: 18: "And now, my brethren, seeing that ye know the light by which ye may judge, which light is the light of Christ, see that ye do not judge wrongfully; for with that same judgment which ye judge ye shall also be judged."

[980] Mosiah 18: 14: "And after Alma had said these words, both Alma and Helam were buried in the water; and they arose and came forth out of the water rejoicing, being filled with the Spirit."

partakes, the sacrament is passed to others. We show great deference to authority in our system. In the 3 Nephi events presided over by the Lord, He shows great deference to purity.

The Lord's commandment to the disciples is followed by the instruction to provide the wine to the multitude "that they might drink." The ones officiating are "commanded," whereas the multitude is provided the opportunity to follow by example. Instead of a "commandment" to the multitude, there is an invitation. Clearly the Lord understands the importance of example and respects free will. Those who want to follow Him closest will be told what they must do. Then others are invited to follow of their own free will, and not by compulsion.

This systematic progression begins with knowledge of the Lord. They met Him. They felt the prints in His side, hands and feet. They had no veil separating them from Him. Yet, despite this knowledge, He walks them through ordinances where they qualify to return permanently to His presence. The ordinances are important enough for the Risen Lord to personally conduct and instruct on how to perform them. It is not merely what we believe, nor what we understand, but it is also what we do that matters. We must follow Him and His Divinely ordained ordinances. But to do so we need to perform them as He has instructed.

We require a priest to repeat the entire sacrament prayer if he gets a word wrong or adds a word while pronouncing the blessing. In this we show how exact we believe the ordinance is to be followed. That is a proposition with which I wholly agree. We should perform it in every particular as the Lord has instructed. When we do, then the promise of having His Spirit to always be with us is realized.

3 Nephi 18: 9

> **"And it came to pass that they did so, and did drink of it and were filled; and they gave unto the multitude, and they did drink, and they were filled."**

Partaking of the broken bread filled the disciples, and then the multitude, so again drinking the wine filled both.

What were they filled with?

Since this is an ordinance where the promised result is to "have His Spirit to be with them,"[981] is any meaning of "filled" adequate apart from being filled with His Spirit? Clearly this ceremony is not performed to merely fill the belly. It hearkens back to His promise to those who hunger and thirst for righteousness, that they are to be filled.

---

[981] 3 Ne. 18: 7: "And this shall ye do in remembrance of my body, which I have shown unto you. And it shall be a testimony unto the Father that ye do always remember me. And if ye do always remember me ye shall have my Spirit to be with you."

What the Lord presents in ceremony is the fulfillment of the earlier promise in His sermon. There is a beautiful symmetry to His sermon, His promise, the catalyst ordinance, and the reality of being "filled" which is missing from the New Testament record. In this respect, as in so many others, the Book of Mormon is the preferred, and more revealing account of the Lord's ministry.

The Lord's work is to bring about redemption for mankind. He redeems. In ceremony, and now in reality, He is working with a multitude to bring about their preparation and redemption. It is a Master Teacher, proving by His words and deeds, that He knows how to lead souls to salvation.

It is of interest that the record prepared by Mormon in such a painstaking effort takes the time to include these details for our instruction. They are intended not merely as history, but also as a guide. The plan of salvation is to be shared, so that others may follow it and themselves be "filled" with His Spirit.

Now note the prayers all refer to Christ's Spirit. This is something apart from the Holy Ghost. It is Christ's Spirit which is to "always be with them."

What does it mean to have Christ's Spirit to be with you? To guide you?

This is an important point, and worthy of some discussion by Joseph in The Lectures on Faith. If you haven't revisited that little book and that discussion for a while, you may want to do that. I've recommended that it be read once a year. The Lectures on Faith was added to the scriptures as part of the Doctrine and Covenants. It was subsequently removed without a Church vote to agree to its removal. However, the new publications adding sections were sustained, and the tradition we have is that by sustaining the new versions with additions, it implies we also sustained the deletions. Therefore, they stand removed. Despite that, it is worth another read through, much like reading any scripture, it should happen at least annually.

The Spirit of Christ is also referred to in Section 84: 45-47[982]. It is also described using the word "light" instead of His Spirit, in Section

[982] D&C 84: 45-47: "For the word of the Lord is truth, and whatsoever is truth is light, and whatsoever is light is Spirit, even the Spirit of Jesus Christ. And the Spirit giveth light to every man that cometh into the world; and the Spirit enlighteneth every man through the world, that hearkeneth to the voice of the Spirit. And every one that hearkeneth to the voice of the Spirit cometh unto God, even the Father."

88: 5-13[983]. If you read those carefully you realize that connecting with His Spirit or His light will also put you in contact with everything else governed by Him. He is the light which "enlighteneth your eyes, which is the same light that quickeneth your understandings;"

This is why Joseph commented that the closer a man draws to God the clearer his understanding will be on all subjects. Greater light means clearer perception. It involves discerning between truth and error. It allows you to see what is dark, and who is dark, and what is light and who is filled with light. The light of a person's countenance is upon them, and if the Lord's Spirit fills you then you can see others just as He sees them.

It was His Spirit that enabled the Nephites to become one. With it, Zion becomes possible. Without it, Zion is only a theory to be abused and misunderstood. Without it, Zion is a vain ambition of conspiring men. It will not come to pass. With His Spirit, Zion is inevitable, because He will bring again Zion. If you would like to see the course of this doomed people changed at least as to your part, then these teachings and following these ordinances are the means by which the Lord's Spirit becomes available to you.

3 Nephi 18: 10

> **"And when the Disciples had done this, Jesus said unto them: Blessed are ye for this thing which ye have done, for this is fulfilling my commandments, and this doth witness unto the Father that ye are willing to do that which I have commanded you."**

The phrasing is ambiguous but becomes clear from context. The reference to "big-D" disciples actually introduces the ambiguity. If the printer had left it "little-d" disciples then the meaning would be clear. The "thing which ye have done" is a reference to partaking of the wine. By introducing the "big-D" disciple term it can change the entire thing

---

[983] D&C 88: 5-13: "Which glory is that of the church of the Firstborn, even of God, the holiest of all, through Jesus Christ his Son— He that ascended up on high, as also he descended below all things, in that he comprehended all things, that he might be in all and through all things, the light of truth; Which truth shineth. This is the light of Christ. As also he is in the sun, and the light of the sun, and the power thereof by which it was made. As also he is in the moon, and is the light of the moon, and the power thereof by which it was made; As also the light of the stars, and the power thereof by which they were made; And the earth also, and the power thereof, even the earth upon which you stand. And the light which shineth, which giveth you light, is through him who enlighteneth your eyes, which is the same light that quickeneth your understandings; Which light proceedeth forth from the presence of God to fill the immensity of space— The light which is in all things, which giveth life to all things, which is the law by which all things are governed, even the power of God who sitteth upon his throne, who is in the bosom of eternity, who is in the midst of all things."

to be "the thing which ye have done" is to pass the sacrament, rather than to partake of it.

Well, the "thing which ye have done" that prompts the Lord to proclaim "Blessed are ye" is to have symbolically partaken of His blood. They have a part of Him by having eaten of His flesh and drank of His blood. They are now among those who demonstrate they hunger and thirst after righteousness. They are disciples indeed. Followers of the Master. Obedient to Him and willing to take His name upon them.

This is again identified as a "witness unto the Father" rather than a witness unto anyone else. It is not even a witness unto Christ. Nor is it a witness unto one another. It is a witness unto the Father.

This sacred event marks the testimony of faith by those who follow the Lord as a witness to the Father. These people prove they have faith in, and will obey His Son. The Father provided the Son as the Redeemer of all mankind. The only way back into the exalted state of the Father is through the saving sacrifice of the Son. It was the Son who opened the door for that return by the burdens He assumed while in His mortal body. He came under the same circumstances we did. He was separated from the Father by the veil. He suffered weaknesses of the body. He suffered the temptations of mankind, and He gave them no heed.[984] This made it possible for Him to bring many others to glory.[985]

To have part in His glory, we must partake of His flesh and blood. Both symbolically by our own bodies being made a living sacrifice,[986] and through ordinance by partaking of the symbols of His life, death, resurrection. Fort he body of Christ rose from the dead, and we have that same hope. If we are to follow Him, we must be like Him. Taking upon ourselves His flesh and blood is not optional. It must be done to testify to the Father, who alone accepts us into His family. If we think to take upon us the name of Christ, but fail to have this witness before the Father, then we have failed to secure the required testimony before the Father.

This is a required process for those who are His.

3 Nephi 18: 11

> **"And this shall ye always do to those who repent and are baptized in my name; and ye shall do it in remembrance of my blood, which I have shed for you, that ye may witness unto the**

[984] D&C 20: 22: "He suffered temptations but gave no heed unto them."

[985] Heb. 2: 10: "For it became him, for whom *are* all things, and by whom *are* all things, in bringing many sons unto glory, to make the captain of their salvation perfect through sufferings."

[986] Rom. 12: 1: "I beseech you therefore, brethren, by the mercies of God, that ye present your bodies a living sacrifice, holy, acceptable unto God, *which is* your reasonable service."

Father that ye do always remember me. And if ye do always remember me ye shall have my Spirit to be with you."

The prayer pronounced upon the sacrament reflects these same aspirations. However, this is not a petition in prayer, but a promise from the Lord. He affirms that for those who have "repented" of their sins, and "are baptized" in His name, He promises a result.

When, having done as He has asked, a person remembers His blood through this ordinance, bearing in mind that it was shed "for you" then you can properly "witness unto the Father." The witness you make to the Father by this remembrance is that "ye do always remember Christ."

This memorial before the Father, when done right, results in the promise of Christ that "ye shall always have His spirit to be with you."

This is a covenant. This is the Lord promising. His word cannot fail. He is establishing for you the means by which you can have as your guide and companion His Spirit. His light. His presence in your life.

This is more intimate than touching His side, hands and feet. This is to have His Spirit within your touch at all times. You become an extension of Him, properly taking His name upon you. For you are then, indeed, a Christian.

He will christen or anoint you, not with the symbol of oil, but with the reality of His Spirit. This anointing is the real thing, of which the oil was meant only to testify.

The Holy Ghost was intended to become a companion at the time of baptism. The Spirit of Christ is intended to become a companion in your very person as well. When there are two members of the Godhead represented in your living person, then it is the Father who receives this testimony of you, about you, by you and for you. You become His, for these three are one.

There is more going on here than an ordinance and a testimony. This is the means by which a link is formed that can and will result in the Father taking that which is corruptible and changing it into that which is incorruptible. Though, like Christ, a man or woman may be required to lay down their life, they shall have power given them to take it up again. For that which has been touched by the incorruptible power of His Spirit cannot be left without hope in the grave. All such people die firm in the knowledge they are promised a glorious resurrection.[987]

This, then, is eternal life.

3 Nephi 18: 12-13

"And I give unto you a commandment that ye shall do these things. And if ye shall always do these things blessed are ye, for ye are built upon my rock. But whoso among you shall do more

---

[987] D&C 138: 14: "All these had departed the mortal life, firm in the hope of a glorious resurrection, through the grace of God the Father and his Only Begotten Son, Jesus Christ."

or less than these are not built upon my rock, but are built upon a sandy foundation; and when the rain descends, and the floods come, and the winds blow, and beat upon them, they shall fall, and the gates of hell are ready open to receive them."

The Lord again returns to the earlier sermon's language and meaning. He reiterates how building upon the rock belonging to Him is done by observing the ordinances established by Him.

You should not do "more" than He has commanded.

You must not do "less" than He has instructed.

You must do as He has commanded, instructed, and shown. He does it to provide by His example, the way it is to be done.

If we err it is not because He failed to teach. He has made it plain to us that we may know the way to follow.

When we do more or less, we find ourselves in the sand, and no longer standing upon Him, the Rock of Heaven.[988]

Those finding themselves in the tempest of this life, tossed about by the turbulence of the sins and errors found at every turn, will fall if they are not built upon Him, the Rock of Heaven. They cannot withstand the storm because they are not anchored in Him who has the power to endure, to preserve and to save. They may cry out "Lord, Lord" but they did not do what He said. He will respond He never knew them. To be known by Him in that day will require the testimony before the Father to have been made. For the means by which He can recognize and protect them from the gates of hell is found in that testimony before the Father, given as a result of this ordinance.

The way is plain, simple, even easy. It is marked by Him at every turn. There is no great elusive mountain to climb. If we fail, it is because we are unwilling to look to Him and be saved. It is because we despise the simplicity of it all, and look for something more. We refuse to look upon Him who alone can save.[989]

It is always amusing to see those who wrongly conclude that the Lord has abandoned His people because they fail to experience any power from Him. They do not do what the Lord commands, then they fail to receive the blessing He promised. When it is not received, they

---

[988] Moses 7: 53: "And the Lord said: Blessed is he through whose seed Messiah shall come; for he saith—I am Messiah, the King of Zion, the Rock of Heaven, which is broad as eternity; whoso cometh in at the gate and climbeth up by me shall never fall; wherefore, blessed are they of whom I have spoken, for they shall come forth with songs of everlasting joy."

[989] 1 Ne. 17: 41: "And he did straiten them in the wilderness with his rod; for they hardened their hearts, even as ye have; and the Lord straitened them because of their iniquity. He sent fiery flying serpents among them; and after they were bitten he prepared a way that they might be healed; and the labor which they had to perform was to look; and because of the simpleness of the way, or the easiness of it, there were many who perished."

blame Him. When all along it was their own failure to do as He commanded that caused their problems.[990]

Those who claim to be His, calling out "Lord, Lord," but who do not do what He has instructed cannot blame the Lord. They have only themselves to blame.

3 Nephi 18: 14

> **"Therefore blessed are ye if ye shall keep my commandments, which the Father hath commanded me that I should give unto you."**

The Lord's whole purpose is to bless us. He offers blessings freely. But we will not accept them. We refuse to offer an acceptable sacrifice before the Lord. It will be a long time yet before the sons of Levi offer an offering in righteousness to the Lord.[991] The sacramental offering is a type of the earlier Levitical offerings.

However, when an acceptable offering has been made, the Lord will always bless those who keep the commandments respecting His ordinances.

Changing these things in the least robs the ordinances of the very power they were intended to confer.[992]

If you keep His commandments, the inevitable result is a blessing from Him. The greatest of these blessings is, of course, to be remembered by Him in the day of judgment. The next greatest is to always have His Spirit to be with you.

It is of note that Christ points to the Father in all things, and therefore points to the Father in this teaching, as well. The commandments He teaches are those "which the Father hath commanded [Him] that [He] should give unto you." In every respect the

---

[990] D&C 58: 31-33: "Who am I, saith the Lord, that have promised and have not fulfilled? I command and men obey not; I revoke and they receive not the blessing. Then they say in their hearts: This is not the work of the Lord, for his promises are not fulfilled. But wo unto such, for their reward lurketh beneath, and not from above."

[991] D&C 13: 1: "Upon you my fellow servants, in the name of Messiah I confer the Priesthood of Aaron, which holds the keys of the ministering of angels, and of the gospel of repentance, and of baptism by immersion for the remission of sins; and this shall never be taken again from the earth, until the sons of Levi do offer again an offering unto the Lord in righteousness."
JS-H 1: 69: "*Upon you my fellow servants, in the name of Messiah, I confer the Priesthood of Aaron, which holds the keys of the ministering of angels, and of the gospel of repentance, and of baptism by immersion for the remission of sins; and this shall never be taken again from the earth until the sons of Levi do offer again an offering unto the Lord in righteousness.*"

[992] Isa. 24: 5: "The earth also is defiled under the inhabitants thereof; because they have transgressed the laws, changed the ordinance, broken the everlasting covenant."

Son points to the Father. It is always the Father's will and the Father's glory Christ seeks to uphold.[993]

The Son seeks our glory and exaltation, while giving credit to the Father for all He does. Though the Savior occupies the central role in the process, He serves others. Selflessly He instructs us on how we may be blessed and glorified. Selflessly He points to the Father as the one to receive your testimony by obedience. Selflessly He explains the Father is the one who has commanded these things. But through it all, it is Christ who has been the messenger of salvation. He is the one whose sacrifice made possible our redemption. It is Christ whose body and blood we must partake for redemption. It is Christ of whom the Father testifies.[994] Christ bears testimony of the Father. The Father bears record of the Son. In one eternal round, they form a circle. It is Christ's work and the Father's commandment which invites us to join in that circle and become one with Them.

How simple the ways provided for us in this condescension of God. How plain the way has been given. Yet we find reasons to do "more or less" than what is asked. For that we forfeit blessings which might otherwise have been ours.

This is powerful material. Assuming we decide to "do" rather than to "say."

3 Nephi 18: 15

> **"Verily, verily, I say unto you, ye must watch and pray always, lest ye be tempted by the devil, and ye be led away captive by him."**

The caution is always added to "watch and pray always." It is not enough to fall into the correct way. You must prevent, at every turn, a misstep taking you off that path.

The devil always tempts to "do more or less" than we are instructed. To accomplish his desired results, the devil only needs to persuade you to do a little more, or do a little less, and he will have succeeded. He does not need to cut you off by a great big sin when a small one will work just as well.

---

[993] Moses 4: 2: "But, behold, my Beloved Son, which was my Beloved and Chosen from the beginning, said unto me—Father, thy will be done, and the glory be thine forever."

[994] 3 Ne. 11: 7: "Behold my Beloved Son, in whom I am well pleased, in whom I have glorified my name—hear ye him."
Matt. 17: 5: "While he yet spake, behold, a bright cloud overshadowed them: and behold a voice out of the cloud, which said, This is my beloved Son, in whom I am well pleased; hear ye him."
Luke 9: 35: "And there came a voice out of the cloud, saying, This is my beloved Son: hear him."

Lately, we've been looking carefully at the details of the account of the sacrament among the Nephites. As with anything, varying this by "more or less" is a temptation. That temptation comes from the devil. He knows better than any of us that changing ordinances is intended to rob them of their efficacy.

When good intentions lead to the conclusion that you can or ought to change an ordinance in any particular, it does not matter how well intended the underlying reason is for the change. The purpose is to defile. As Isaiah put it: "The earth also is defiled under the inhabitants thereof; because they have transgressed the laws, changed the ordinance, broken the everlasting covenant."[995] For what reason would you change the Lord's ordinances:

-People are not interested in them?

-People are offended by them?

-They seem to include unimportant details?

-They seem to conflict with your understanding of another scripture?

-The performance is uninspiring to the skeptical mind?

-The performance can be improved by a change?

-They seem to hold no real meaning?

-They can have better acceptance if altered?

-People no longer know or understand them?

-People just don't care enough to observe the details?

Perhaps there are ten-thousand reasons for making a change. Maybe you are not tempted by all, but just one of those reasons. But so long as there is one reason which persuades you, that is enough. The devil knows he must only persuade you on one point, one time to get you to change the ordinance. Once he has managed that, he has robbed the ordinance of power, defiled the earth because of its inhabitants, persuaded you to transgress the law, and destroyed the everlasting covenant.

This is a wonderful teaching from Christ. He would like us to be ever watchful precisely because the devil intends to interrupt the Gospel every time it appears on the earth. In general, it takes less than 200 years for an apostasy to set in among the people chosen by God to receive a dispensation of the Gospel. Only in a few isolated instances, among a few people, have there been occasions where the ordinances remained unchanged. Those people successfully resisted every argument

---

[995] Isa. 24: 5: "The earth also is defiled under the inhabitants thereof; because they have transgressed the laws, changed the ordinance, broken the everlasting covenant."

presented in favor of changing the ordinances and breaking the covenant with God.

The goal of our adversary is to lead us into captivity. When we lose the key to knowledge because we forfeit the light given by ordinance to us, then we struggle about in the dark. Left to your own reasoning, it is possible to establish all kinds of aberrations, calling bad good, and the light darkness. Then only isolated voices remain to challenge the overwhelming majority who believe they have improved things by their tampering.

This pattern is warned against by the Lord. He lays bare the source of such things. It is all of the devil. He is the architect of that ruin.

So it is with the entire sermon the Lord has delivered, along with the new ordinance He has just introduced. The whole is meant to be understood and followed. It is the path back to truth and light. It was meant to become our guide, our way of life. For the most part, we have very good reasons why we do not follow it.

3 Nephi 18: 16

> **"And as I have prayed among you even so shall ye pray in my church, among my people who do repent and are baptized in my name. Behold I am the light; I have set an example for you."**

The "prayer" referred to here is the sacrament prayer. There is one among the twelve disciples who is given power to dedicate the emblems of the sacrament. But all of them are to do likewise in the Church in the future.

He has provided the example for them to follow. He has taught them how, and then demonstrated how. He has explained why. Now He tells them to do "even so" in His church.

But notice once again the Lord defines His church. It is those who "do repent and are baptized in [His] name." This ordinance is not for those who are casual investigators of His doctrine. It is not for those who, though baptized, have not repented. It is reserved for those having the proper qualifications. Without having done these things first, the sacrament of the Lord's body and blood are eaten and drank to their condemnation. Instead of it being a testimony before the Father of their faithfulness, it becomes a testimony of their unfaithfulness.

Notice the Lord explains His role as "light." He "set an example for you" and therefore is "the light." The "light" is the guide. It is the pattern. It shows you the way to go. He has done that in word and in action, so that He can claim to be the "light" for those to follow.

In turn, He has told these disciples they must also become "a light unto the people."[996] To accomplish that it is essential they must "set an example for" them; meaning that they follow as the Lord has led them.

---

996 3 Ne. 15: 12: "Ye are my disciples; and ye are a light unto this people, who are a remnant of the house of Joseph."

Not an example of vainglory or superiority. Instead to meekly do as He has bidden them to do. Adding nothing, leaving nothing undone. Honing in on the things He would have done, and going about to do them.

The "light" must reflect the Lord's teachings and the Father's will. Otherwise it is darkness. A light cannot shine as His if it is distorted to reflect credit upon the man rather than the True Light, our Lord. When an erring soul entertains mistaken admiration for a man, they are damned.[997] Therefore, if a person is called upon to be a light, they cannot seek to attract notice for themselves.

The Lord saves. Messengers sent by Him point to Him. They mirror His acts, teachings and practices. They do not seek their own will, but only the will of Him who sends them.

Throughout this visit between the Lord and the Nephites, we are given an extended view of how the Lord establishes His church and doctrine. So long as it is followed, it has the power to allow mankind to always have His Spirit to be with the followers. However, when they depart from the practices and keep merely a form of godliness, they lose the power He sends to us.

These teachings are important enough for the Lord to dwell on, and Mormon to etch them into metal plates. They should be carefully studied, explicitly followed, and greatly appreciated.

3 Nephi 18: 17-18

> **"And it came to pass that when Jesus had spoken these words unto his Disciples, he turned again unto the multitude and said unto them: Behold, verily, verily, I say unto you, ye must watch and pray always lest ye enter into temptation; for Satan desireth to have you, that he may sift you as wheat."**

The image of Satan "sifting as wheat" is interesting for several reasons. One involves the early claim, now discredited, that the ancient Nephite civilization did not cultivate wheat. Under that argument they would not have understood the analogy. However, once stores of ancient wheat and barley were discovered, the criticism was debunked. There's a BYU article on this by Robert R. Bennett titled "Barley and Wheat in the Book of Mormon."

Satan "desires to have you." You are wanted. Not because he has your best interest in mind, but because he wants control. He wants to gain power over others, limit their choices, and make them his slaves.

The manner wheat was sifted was to use a sieve to separate grain from husks, tares, stones and other chaff. The wheat would be kept, the

---

[997] D&C 76: 99-101: "For these are they who are of Paul, and of Apollos, and of Cephas. These are they who say they are some of one and some of another—some of Christ and some of John, and some of Moses, and some of Elias, and some of Esaias, and some of Isaiah, and some of Enoch; But received not the gospel, neither the testimony of Jesus, neither the prophets, neither the everlasting covenant."

refuse tossed into a pile to be discarded. Sifting was vigorous and tossed the grain about to separate it. This suggests being completely under Satan's control, being tossed about, and being discarded. It is a horrifying image, because the result would be domination by the adversary of your soul.

Satan's great desire has always been to separate men from their agency. He seeks to enslave those who fall under his power. Using wickedness, appetites of the flesh, drug dependence or other addictions, the end goal is always the same. He seeks control. He craves the god-like power to have dominion over others. Since he forfeited any right to gain power in a godly way, he seeks now ungodly power through coercion and compulsion.

Whenever you find compulsion, dominion, control, or force being employed, you have found Satan.[998] He wants to cut you off from heaven, and uses control to limit access to the heavens. When people voluntarily surrender their responsibility to follow the Lord, Satan has acquired by persuasion what he craves to acquire through force.

The antidote for falling under Satan's control is to "watch and pray always." Why watch? Why "pray always?"

To watch is to be observant and detect elements of control, dominion and compulsion. It is to become vigilant in separating the will of men from the will of God. It is to keep the Lord's teachings in mind, and to measure any person's teachings, actions and persuasions against the standard the Lord has explained.

To "pray always" is to retain a personal connection with heaven. Particularly, to retain that connection through the Holy Ghost, and through Christ's Spirit, you seek to always have with you. If this is a lively connection, you are able to avoid being "sifted." If it lapses into darkness, you are vulnerable to being taken captive.

These are simple expressions anyone can understand. It is not the difficulty of the teaching, but the difficulty of the implementation which keeps people bound in darkness. Traditions, widespread acceptance of false ideas, excuses for failure, and rationalizations for why things are as they are, all prevent us from reading these teachings with the eyes of a child. The Lord's teachings are distorted even as they are being read by

---

[998] D&C 121: 37-41: "That they may be conferred upon us, it is true; but when we undertake to cover our sins, or to gratify our pride, our vain ambition, or to exercise control or dominion or compulsion upon the souls of the children of men, in any degree of unrighteousness, behold, the heavens withdraw themselves; the Spirit of the Lord is grieved; and when it is withdrawn, Amen to the priesthood or the authority of that man. Behold, ere he is aware, he is left unto himself, to kick against the pricks, to persecute the saints, and to fight against God. We have learned by sad experience that it is the nature and disposition of almost all men, as soon as they get a little authority, as they suppose, they will immediately begin to exercise unrighteous dominion. Hence many are called, but few are chosen. No power or influence can or ought to be maintained by virtue of the priesthood, only by persuasion, by long-suffering, by gentleness and meekness, and by love unfeigned;"

the blinders we wear. When the eye is filled with darkness, how great is the darkness within. Christ spoke about that in the previous sermon.

3 Nephi 18: 19-20

> **"Therefore ye must always pray unto the Father in my name; And whatsoever ye shall ask the Father in my name, which is right, b elieving that ye shall receive, behold it shall be given unto you."**

When you "always pray unto the Father" in Christ's name, there will be an inevitable closeness between you and Him. You draw closer to those with whom you associate. Praying always triggers that association. As with everything else, it is dynamic, not static. You move closer or you move farther apart, but you do not remain static.

What does "whatsoever ye shall ask" include? If you think Christ is inviting you to turn the Father into a short-order cook, jumping to your will, you do not understand this process. However, this is how some people view prayer. It is a list of wants, desires and aspirations to be imposed on the Father.

What does the limitation "which is right" do to modify "whatsoever ye shall ask?"

What does the phrase "whatsoever ye shall ask, which is right" mean?

Who determines whether a request you make "is right?" What about those occasions when the Lord invites someone to "ask anything of Him"?[999] Is there any limit to what might be asked at that moment? What does that suggest about those persons this offer is extended?

The purpose of this teaching by the Lord is to invite harmony between those who ask, and the Father, who gives. Inspired requests to Him are intended to come to you by revelation, so you may understand what you should ask. Then, when you have conformed your will to His, what you receive is according to His will, and not your own.

Throughout, the Lord is leading those who will follow into a condition of unity with the Father and the Son. The goal has always been the same. The teachings have always been the same. The Lord's

---

[999] 1 Kgs. 3: 5: "In Gibeon the Lord appeared to Solomon in a dream by night: and God said, Ask what I shall give thee."
3 Ne. 28: 1: "And it came to pass when Jesus had said these words, he spake unto his disciples, one by one, saying unto them: What is it that ye desire of me, after that I am gone to the Father?" (If you do not understand this concept it is explained in *Beloved Enos*. It occurs in a very specific setting.)

great Intercessory Prayer taught the same concept.[1000] The ability to be "one" with them is not accomplished by men persuading God to follow man's will. It is accomplished in the same manner as Christ

[1000] John 17: 1-26: "These words spake Jesus, and lifted up his eyes to heaven, and said, Father, the hour is come; glorify thy Son, that thy Son also may glorify thee: As thou hast given him power over all flesh, that he should give eternal life to as many as thou hast given him. And this is life eternal, that they might know thee the only true God, and Jesus Christ, whom thou hast sent. I have glorified thee on the earth: I have finished the work which thou gavest me to do. And now, O Father, glorify thou me with thine own self with the glory which I had with thee before the world was. I have manifested thy name unto the men which thou gavest me out of the world: thine they were, and thou gavest them me; and they have kept thy word. Now they have known that all things whatsoever thou hast given me are of thee. For I have given unto them the words which thou gavest me; and they have received *them,* and have known surely that I came out from thee, and they have believed that thou didst send me. I pray for them: I pray not for the world, but for them which thou hast given me; for they are thine. And all mine are thine, and thine are mine; and I am glorified in them. And now I am no more in the world, but these are in the world, and I come to thee. Holy Father, keep through thine own name those whom thou hast given me, that they may be one, as we *are.* While I was with them in the world, I kept them in thy name: those that thou gavest me I have kept, and none of them is lost, but the son of perdition; that the scripture might be fulfilled. And now come I to thee; and these things I speak in the world, that they might have my joy fulfilled in themselves. I have given them thy word; and the world hath hated them, because they are not of the world, even as I am not of the world. I pray not that thou shouldest take them out of the world, but that thou shouldest keep them from the evil. They are not of the world, even as I am not of the world. Sanctify them through thy truth: thy word is truth. As thou hast sent me into the world, even so have I also sent them into the world. And for their sakes I sanctify myself, that they also might be sanctified through the truth. Neither pray I for these alone, but for them also which shall believe on me through their word; That they all may be one; as thou, Father, *art* in me, and I in thee, that they also may be one in us: that the world may believe that thou hast sent me. And the glory which thou gavest me I have given them; that they may be one, even as we are one: I in them, and thou in me, that they may be made perfect in one; and that the world may know that thou hast sent me, and hast loved them, as thou hast loved me. Father, I will that they also, whom thou hast given me, be with me where I am; that they may behold my glory, which thou hast given me: for thou lovedst me before the foundation of the world. O righteous Father, the world hath not known thee: but I have known thee, and these have known that thou hast sent me. And I have declared unto them thy name, and will declare *it:* that the love wherewith thou hast loved me may be in them, and I in them."

accomplished it. That is, by conforming to the will of the Father even when it is painful, or terribly burdensome.[1001]

The whole meaning of this promise is captured in the qualification that it must be that "which is right." If you acquire an understanding of what "is right" then by asking for it, you submit to the Father's will. Even if you would shrink from it, beg that it may pass from you, and cower at the thing required of you. When you "ask of the Father in Christ's name" for whatsoever "is right" despite your desire for things to be otherwise, you are going to become one with Them. Then you will be like Them. At this time you will learn the great truth that the will of the Father IS indeed "whatsoever is right."

Joseph Smith explained it: "When the Lord has thoroughly proved him, and finds that the man is determined to serve Him at all hazards, then the man will find his calling and his election made sure, then it will be his privilege to receive the other Comforter, which the Lord hath promised the Saints." The way heaven knows a man has arrived at that point is by the offered prayers. When they seek to do the will of the Father, and the requests are "what is right," then the heavens cannot withhold anything from that man. Indeed, the Lord will prompt the right

---

[1001] D&C 19: 18-19: "Which suffering caused myself, even God, the greatest of all, to tremble because of pain, and to bleed at every pore, and to suffer both body and spirit—and would that I might not drink the bitter cup, and shrink— Nevertheless, glory be to the Father, and I partook and finished my preparations unto the children of men."

3 Ne. 11: 11: "And behold, I am the light and the life of the world; and I have drunk out of that bitter cup which the Father hath given me, and have glorified the Father in taking upon me the sins of the world, in the which I have suffered the will of the Father in all things from the beginning."

questions by what the Lord says to that man, so that the knowledge of that man will reach into the heavens.[1002]

Therefore, you must not only "pray always unto the Father in Christ's name," but you must also grow in understanding, humility and meekness so you may "ask the Father" for that "which is right." This is a process. Christ is explaining it in His sermon.

3 Nephi 18: 24-25

> **"Therefore, hold up your light that it may shine unto the world. Behold I am the light which ye shall hold up—that which ye have seen me do. Behold ye see that I have prayed unto the Father, and ye all have witnessed. And ye see that I have commanded that none of you should go away, but rather have commanded that ye should come unto me, that ye might feel and see; even so shall ye do unto the world; and whosoever breaketh this commandment suffereth himself to be led into temptation."**

Here is another clarification for the earlier sermon. When admonished to "let your light so shine before this people that they may

---

[1002] Ether 3: 9-20: "And the Lord said unto him: Because of thy faith thou hast seen that I shall take upon me flesh and blood; and never has man come before me with such exceeding faith as thou hast; for were it not so ye could not have seen my finger. Sawest thou more than this? And he answered: Nay; Lord, show thyself unto me. And the Lord said unto him: Believest thou the words which I shall speak? And he answered: Yea, Lord, I know that thou speakest the truth, for thou art a God of truth, and canst not lie. And when he had said these words, behold, the Lord showed himself unto him, and said: Because thou knowest these things ye are redeemed from the fall; therefore ye are brought back into my presence; therefore I show myself unto you. Behold, I am he who was prepared from the foundation of the world to redeem my people. Behold, I am Jesus Christ. I am the Father and the Son. In me shall all mankind have life, and that eternally, even they who shall believe on my name; and they shall become my sons and my daughters. And never have I showed myself unto man whom I have created, for never has man believed in me as thou hast. Seest thou that ye are created after mine own image? Yea, even all men were created in the beginning after mine own image. Behold, this body, which ye now behold, is the body of my spirit; and man have I created after the body of my spirit; and even as I appear unto thee to be in the spirit will I appear unto my people in the flesh. And now, as I, Moroni, said I could not make a full account of these things which are written, therefore it sufficeth me to say that Jesus showed himself unto this man in the spirit, even after the manner and in the likeness of the same body even as he showed himself unto the Nephites. And he ministered unto him even as he ministered unto the Nephites; and all this, that this man might know that he was God, because of the many great works which the Lord had showed unto him. And because of the knowledge of this man he could not be kept from beholding within the veil; and he saw the finger of Jesus, which, when he saw, he fell with fear; for he knew that it was the finger of the Lord; and he had faith no longer, for he knew, nothing doubting. Wherefore, having this perfect knowledge of God, he could not be kept from within the veil; therefore he saw Jesus; and he did minister unto him."

see your good works and glorify your Father which is in heaven"[1003] what the Lord meant is that it is He who should be held up. He alone. Not you, or your good intentions, your conspicuous acts or philanthropy. Not you at all. Him.

The obligation to hold up a light is circumscribed by His direction that He "is the light which ye shall hold up." Nothing and no one else. He is the lifeline. Therefore, when you offer, preach, teach, exhort and expound, He must be at the center of this prophesying, or you are engaging in priestcraft.[1004]

The Lord has "prayed unto the Father" in their presence. Therefore, His example points to how prayer is to occur, and to whom it is addressed. They "all have witnessed" this, and know for themselves how it is to be done.

He has not told any of those who were present to go away. He has brought the same message to all. He gives them His example of liberality: "Ye see that I have commanded that none of you should go away, but rather have commanded that ye should come unto me." No one is refused. All are welcomed. Whether those in the multitude thought someone was unworthy, or whether there were some with conflicts, it did not matter. All were invited. None were refused. They are all "commanded that they should come unto Him."

What is the reason we are commanded to come to Him? It is so "ye might feel and see." So that you might know Him. So that you can also be a witness of His physical evidence of suffering, crucifixion and death. The wounds He bears could not be received without death. His body testifies that He died. His body also testifies of His resurrection. Despite the wounds which memorialize His suffering and death, He lives! He stands before you in life! He has risen!

As you testify of Him, you must invite others to likewise come "that they might feel and see" Him. This is how witnesses of Him are commanded to "do unto the world." This is their ministry, their burden, their witness, and their command from Him. When they fail to testify, teach and proclaim, they "break this commandment and suffer themselves to be led into temptation." This is why the Lord required at my hands the book *The Second Comforter*. That is how He directs all those who are "commanded to come unto Him, that they might feel and see." It will not be in vague innuendo or veiled language. It may not be in a published book, and may well be in private. But they will all be required to invite others to likewise "come unto Him" that everyone "might feel and see" our Risen Lord.

1003 3 Ne. 12: 16: "Therefore let your light so shine before this people, that they may see your good works and glorify your Father who is in heaven."

1004 2 Ne. 26: 29: "He commandeth that there shall be no priestcrafts; for, behold, priestcrafts are that men preach and set themselves up for a light unto the world, that they may get gain and praise of the world; but they seek not the welfare of Zion."

He is accessible. He invites. More than that, He commands. All are commanded and "none of you should go away." We think it a great thing when someone testifies of Him. Yet He wants all to "come" so that everyone "might feel and see" Him.

If we have the same Gospel, we have the same commandments.

The Book of Mormon is, as I have testified in everything I have written, not merely a book of scripture. It is the preeminent volume of scripture for our day. All other volumes of scripture are not just inferior to it, but vastly so. It is the covenant we are condemned for neglecting. It is the reason I have found Him. For above all else, I have used the Book of Mormon to direct my thoughts, actions, teachings and understanding. Here in these verses we see again—He is inviting us, using the text of the Book of Mormon to find Him, individually, for ourselves.

This Book is the restoration of the Gospel. Unfortunately, most people have missed that. Nevertheless, it is true.

3 Nephi 18: 26-27

> **"And now it came to pass that when Jesus had spoken these words, he turned his eyes again upon the Disciples whom he had chosen, and said unto them: Behold verily, verily, I say unto you, I give unto you another commandment, and then I must go unto my Father that I may fulfil other commandments which he hath given me."**

Christ first introduced Himself by reference to the Father in 3 Nephi 11:11.[1005] He reiterates the connection between Him and the Father again in this scripture. He does not only testify of the Father. He makes it clear that everything done is by the will or command of the Father.

If Christ is the example in all things (and He is). Then in this He serves once again to clarify things for us.

Christ did not come to do His own will, but submitted to the will of the Father. Just like Christ submitted to the will of the Father, we too are invited to submit to the example and teachings of Christ. We ought to put away our own agendas. We ought to give credit to Him. We follow Him, we trust Him, we seek His will.

This is not just a passing point. It is the central point. Studying to know, and then working to do the will of Christ is our responsibility.

As Christ served the Father, we are to serve Him.

Christ becomes our Father when we are born again. He is the one who liberates us from sin, and will liberate us from death. Our resurrected bodies come to us as a gift from Him. Therefore, He is

---

[1005] 3 Ne. 11: 11: "And behold, I am the light and the life of the world; and I have drunk out of that bitter cup which the Father hath given me, and have glorified the Father in taking upon me the sins of the world, in the which I have suffered the will of the Father in all things from the beginning."

literally the Father of our bodies, because they return to us as a gift from Him.

As Christ has set an example in following the Father, He has thereby become our Father. We follow Him if we are hoping to go where He is.

Notice also the Lord has "other commandments" which He knows He is obligated to fulfill. The Lord has a continuing ministry under the direction of the Father. His ministry is not confined to the appearances we have in current scripture, but comprehends visits to those who have faith in Him throughout the world. He continues that ministry today, as promised in John 14: 18.[1006]

Part of the "commandments which [the Father] hath given" to Christ include the ministry to save, redeem and teach those who abide the conditions to be taught. Today as in times past.

3 Nephi 18: 28-29

> **"And now behold, this is the commandment which I give unto you, that ye shall not suffer any one knowingly to partake of my flesh and blood unworthily, when ye shall minister it; For whoso eateth and drinketh my flesh and blood unworthily eateth and drinketh damnation to his soul; therefore if ye know that a man is unworthy to eat and drink of my flesh and blood ye shall forbid him."**

This commandment about partaking of the bread and wine is the one He needed them to understand. They should take precautions to prevent those who they know to be unworthy from partaking. The reason is merciful. When they partake of His flesh and blood unworthily, they establish a testimony before the Father of their unworthiness.

Remember the bread and wine become a testimony to the Father.[1007] The observance comes to the attention of the Father. It is a witness before Him. Therefore, when the flesh and blood are taken by those who are unworthy, the witness which comes to the Father is of their unworthiness. The Father cannot look upon sin with the least degree of allowance.[1008] When a person comes before the Father in a witness of their unworthiness, such a person "eateth and drinketh damnation to his soul." This person has asked the Father to take notice of their unworthiness.

It is the responsibility of those who minister these things to "forbid him" in such circumstances. They are their brother's keeper. Though it

---

[1006] John 14: 18: "I will not leave you comfortless: I will come to you."

[1007] 3 Ne. 18: 10: "And when the Disciples had done this, Jesus said unto them: Blessed are ye for this thing which ye have done, for this is fulfilling my commandments, and this doth witness unto the Father that ye are willing to do that which I have commanded you."

[1008] D&C 1: 31: "For I the Lord cannot look upon sin with the least degree of allowance;"

may be difficult for the person to be warned, it is merciful to do so. The sacrament is to be offered to the worthy, never offered to the unworthy. The worthy should "forbid" the unworthy from taking.

This is not an unkind teaching. It is not exclusionary or discriminatory. It is based on the doctrine Christ teaches, and the import of the act which witnesses to the Father. That witness occurs whenever the sacrament is properly administered, with appropriate power to bless, in a setting the Lord has authorized, by those who have repented and are properly baptized. Among such people the bread and wine should be given only to those who are worthy.

Now, the responsibility is on the ones administering the bread and wine. But the duty only extends to those who are "knowingly… unworthy." That is, the ones who administer are not obligated to police others. They are not required to interview and determine worthiness. They are only to take note of such things as come to their attention and require the conclusion that the recipient is "unworthy." Obvious misdeeds are important, private matters and individual failings are not consequential to the ones administering the rite.

"Therefore, if ye know that a man is unworthy to eat and drink [Christ's] flesh and blood ye shall forbid him." But only if you "know" such is the case. Then, you should "forbid" him from doing so. Not by force, but by refusing to minister the sacrament to him. This becomes impractical, however, when it is a tray passed down a row of people, who cannot be forbidden to partake. In that kind of ceremony, the individual cannot be forbidden except through general teaching and warning. Then the individual is free to choose for themselves whether to heed the caution or to ignore it. The question remains, however, if that relieves the persons ministering the sacrament from their obligation to "forbid him" if he is known to be unworthy.

These are interesting points. All the more so because the Lord has taken the time to teach us these principles. And for Him to teach them, and provide them to us as part of restoring the Gospel to our day, I presume that informs us these points are to be followed.

Whether we choose to follow His teachings or not becomes, for most of us, a matter of convention and acceptance of popular behavior. If these teachings are found in the Book of Mormon, but not observed by us in how we proceed each Sabbath, then we tend to feel comfortable that what we do is right and the text has been corrected by modern practice. It is an interesting conclusion to draw. One which, upon careful examination, does not always leave us with the same feeling of comfort.

Well, the Lord had this to say about us in 1832: "your minds in times past have been darkened because of unbelief, and because you have treated lightly the things you have received—Which vanity and unbelief have brought the whole church under condemnation. And this condemnation resteth upon the children of Zion, even all. And they shall remain under this condemnation until they repent and remember the new covenant, even the Book of Mormon and the former commandments which I have given them, not only to say, but to do according to that which I have written—".[1009]

I am glad others are responsible for enacting the Church Handbook of Instructions, and not me. I was glad to attend the leadership meeting and be again informed about this newly revised handbook for use today. It was just a few short years ago President Hinckley's administration reduced it by a third. Now it has been further reduced by 12%. That is, in my view, a very healthy trend. If this keeps up we may eventually wind up with nothing but the scriptures to guide us.

3 Nephi 18: 31-32

> **"Nevertheless, ye shall not cast him out from among you, but ye shall minister unto him and shall pray for him unto the Father, in my name; and if it so be that he repenteth and is baptized in my name, then shall ye receive him, and shall minister unto him of my flesh and blood. But if he repent not he shall not be numbered among my people, that he may not destroy my people, for behold I know my sheep, and they are numbered. Nevertheless, ye shall not cast him out of your synagogues, or your places of worship, for unto such shall ye continue to minister; for ye know not but what they will return and repent, and come unto me with full purpose of heart, and I shall heal them; and ye shall be the means of bringing salvation unto them."**

Even if you know someone has violated the commandment, has partaken unworthily after you have forbidden them to do so, **even then** you are "not to cast him out from among you." Instead the Lord puts on His disciples the burden of making intercession for him, praying "unto the Father, in [Christ's] name" for such a man. For the Lord reminds us that, "if it so be that he repenteth and is baptized in [His] name" then the man's repentance will take care of his failure.

Notice the burden on His disciples. What does it mean to "minister unto him" who has transgressed? What does it mean to "pray for him unto the Father" when you know he has eaten and drank "damnation unto his soul?" Why would the Lord have His followers first forbid, then, when the forbidding fails, to follow it up with patience and prayer for the offender? Is this another extension of the teachings the Lord gave in the sermon previously? Does this again testify to you of how serious the Lord is about how kind and patient we are with others?

1009 D&C 84: 54-57: "And your minds in times past have been darkened because of unbelief, and because you have treated lightly the things you have received— Which vanity and unbelief have brought the whole church under condemnation. And this condemnation resteth upon the children of Zion, even all. And they shall remain under this condemnation until they repent and remember the new covenant, even the Book of Mormon and the former commandments which I have given them, not only to say, but to do according to that which I have written—"

How long are you to bear with the offender, hoping for his repentance? When do you decide that he is determined to "repent not?" What does it mean, after you have determined the man will not repent that "he shall not be numbered among my people?" What does that suggest about further fellowship with that man? Why would that be coupled with "that he may not destroy my people?" What would such an unrepentant man need to do before you could decide he was attempting to "destroy my people?" How would you decide that?

Now, even if you think you have a basis for deciding all this against the man, "nevertheless, ye shall not cast him out of your synagogues, or your places of worship." Did you see that? We are not to forbid even the man who is intent upon destroying the Lord's people from our places of worship. What selfless behavior is this? Enduring persecution! It is as if the Lord expects His followers to bless those who curse them, to do good to them who despitefully use them.

Why such patience? Because "ye know not but what they will return and repent, and come unto me with full purpose of heart, and I shall heal them; and ye shall be the means of bringing salvation unto them." If there is a chance for repentance, the Lord wants us to bear with, succor and uplift the non-repentant soul who drinks damnation. How often we would do otherwise. Christ instructs us to be more like Him in all we do. It is only by this patience, kindness, gentleness and meekness that He has been able to save my soul. Can a grateful person do anything less for another? Can we expect to forebear any less with the unrepentant than the Lord has with us?

How godlike the Master is in all His teachings. How much higher are His ways than are ours.

The Lord affirms that He knows His sheep. Not only knows them, but "they are numbered" to Him. He cares for each of them.

If we can add another to His fold by our own patient ministrations, then we ought to readily do so. If we do, then He will give us the credit for what we have done: "ye shall be the means of bringing salvation unto them." Did you catch that? He gives us the credit for the success! We merely follow what He instructs us to do, and if there is any benefit realized He gives us the credit for doing so. Our Savior is more than a good example. He is perfect in all His doings. It is little wonder that in the end every knee will bow before Him. Gratitude will bring some to their knees. Shame will bring the rest. No one will expect to stand or sit in His presence. For in Him we find a soul of such greatness that kneeling alone can give vent to the feelings He inspires.

I have finished what I needed to cover.

CONCLUSION

The foregoing was taken from a blog on which I posted thoughts daily, once early in the morning and once mid-afternoon, over the better part of 2010. The purpose was to give those who came to the blog an opportunity to be reminded twice a day of teachings from the Book of Mormon. This is the primary text of scripture for our day. It, above all other volumes of scripture, was intended to become the basis for the last day covenant between God and man. It has been neglected, and as a result we have fallen under condemnation. The only way to remove that condemnation is to repent, and remember this book, not merely to say but to do what it teaches. A revelation given in 1832 told the Latter-day Saints the following: "And your minds in times past have been darkened because of unbelief, and because you have treated lightly the things you have received—Which vanity and unbelief have brought the whole church under condemnation. And this condemnation resteth upon the children of Zion, even all. And they shall remain under this condemnation until they repent and remember the new covenant, even the Book of Mormon and the former commandments, which I have given them, not only to say, but to do according to that which I have written." (D&C 84: 54-57.)

I have written previous books, and now added the blog which is preserved in this book, intending to do what little I am able to remove the condemnation under which we have labored since 1832. I have tried to provide a twice-daily reminder to keep the Book of Mormon on top of our thoughts. This book is not merely a collection of expressed ideas, but also has the unexpressed idea that the approach given here may give you a system of thought through which you can approach the Book of Mormon in your individual study.

My thoughts are far less important that learning to meditate upon the Book of Mormon yourself. It is a deep well, from which we have failed as yet to draw except in the most shallow of takes. We need to do more. We need fewer superficial expositions, fewer scholarly attempts to show its antiquity, and far more done to understand its doctrine. More importantly, we need to do more to live its teachings. It was designed to be a covenant. The revelation condemning us speaks of it as the "new covenant, even the Book of Mormon." A covenant is more than merely a collection of stories about an ancient people. It is intended to animate how we act. It is intended to control how we approach God.

God is approachable. He is accessible. It was always intended for man to live in a covenant relationship with Him. He was supposed to be a familiar personage to mankind. When I wrote my first book, *The Second Comforter: Conversing With the Lord Through the Veil,* it was the Book of Mormon which became the primary source for scriptural teachings about returning to God's presence. That book demonstrates the Book of Mormon contains the most holy, most lofty, most edifying doctrines of the restored Gospel of Jesus Christ. It was intended to be a covenant. Until we recognize it as that, we will remain under condemnation.

I have avoided giving details of my own return to God's presence. I have instead taught the process by which you may do so. My own experiences are not important, other than to me. I cannot save you, nor can my experiences benefit you. You must have your own. You also must return to His presence. He was always intended to be your Teacher. Any other teacher can only benefit you by pointing to Him.

In account after account, the Book of Mormon is filled with Second Comforter experiences. It is the great manual on the return to God. Witness after witness testifies to God's accessibility. I add my voice to that chorus. I also believe to my core the only reason I have been able to find Him is because I took the Book of Mormon seriously; not only to say but to do what it teaches.

Come remove your own condemnation. Take this volume of scripture as a guide. Not merely as a series of stories with some virtue to teach, but as a manual for returning to God's presence. Follow its teachings and you will find it is the most correct book. You will discover that you are able to draw closer to God by abiding its precepts than you can from any other book. It is the primary scripture for our day.

The End.

Made in the USA
Lexington, KY
29 August 2011